Lecture Notes in Computer Science   14781

Founding Editors

Gerhard Goos
Juris Hartmanis

The series Lecture Notes in Computer Science (LNCS), including its subseries Lecture Notes in Artificial Intelligence (LNAI) and Lecture Notes in Bioinformatics (LNBI), has established itself as a medium for the publication of new developments in computer science and information technology research, teaching, and education.

LNCS enjoys close cooperation with the computer science R & D community, the series counts many renowned academics among its volume editors and paper authors, and collaborates with prestigious societies. Its mission is to serve this international community by providing an invaluable service, mainly focused on the publication of conference and workshop proceedings and postproceedings. LNCS commenced publication in 1973.

Ana Cavalcanti · James Baxter
Editors

The Practice of Formal Methods

Essays in Honour of Cliff Jones
Part II

 Springer

Editors
Ana Cavalcanti Ⓘ
University of York
York, UK

James Baxter Ⓘ
University of York
York, UK

ISSN 0302-9743 ISSN 1611-3349 (electronic)
Lecture Notes in Computer Science
ISBN 978-3-031-66672-8 ISBN 978-3-031-66673-5 (eBook)
https://doi.org/10.1007/978-3-031-66673-5

Cover illustration: The cover figure is based on a picture contributed by Eric Hehner (one of the testimonial authors) with some colour adjustment and a filter applied for a more stylised picture.

This Springer imprint is published by the registered company Springer Nature Switzerland AG
The registered company address is: Gewerbestrasse 11, 6330 Cham, Switzerland

If disposing of this product, please recycle the paper.

Preface

Cliff Jones is one of the foremost computer scientists globally. He has an exceptional international standing for his groundbreaking research and leadership within the practice of formal methods. His distinguished career encompasses significant contributions to academia, industry, policy, and service.

The absence of a Festschrift for such a distinguished scientist was noticeable, and something had to be done about that. Cliff has had a key role in creating the RoboStar Centre of Excellence on Software Engineering for Robotics.[1] Cliff has shown continued support for early-career researchers and women in science. So, we decided we were in as good a position as any to edit such a book. We contacted the rather extensive community of Cliff's collaborators to organise this Festschrift, and found that colleagues were absolutely keen and thrilled to contribute. Springer could not have been more supportive.

We have here the work of 90 scientists, spread over 14 countries, who all want to say "thank you" to Cliff. It just so happens that this is the year of Cliff's 80th birthday. This book, however, is not "just" a celebration of this special birthday. It is a celebration of a lifetime of achievements, and of commitment to a field, to his fellow scientists, and to his students. Some close collaborators are no longer able to contribute a paper. Six of these have chosen to contribute with a testimonial, providing heartfelt accounts of their collegial interactions.

The 30 papers included here provide a snapshot of the many current scientific developments inspired by or built upon Cliff's contributions. At least three colleagues reviewed each paper, but most had four reviews.

Cliff was an early advocate for the practical application of formal methods. He spearheaded pioneering research that spurred investments from industry giants like ARM, IBM, Intel, Microsoft, and QinetiQ. His visionary initiatives include founding the esteemed international ACM journal, Formal Aspects of Computing, and establishing the renowned Formal Methods Symposium in 1989.

Within IFIP, he has played a pivotal role as a longstanding member and chair of WG 2.3 on Programming Methodology, and as a founding member of WG 1.9/2.7 on Verified Software. His policy advocacy, notably for institutions like the UK Royal Academy of Engineering, has been instrumental in fostering public discourse on the reliability of computing systems.

Throughout his career, Cliff has championed the essential role of formalism in design processes. Notably, his collaboration at IBM in the 1970s led to the creation of the Vienna Development Method (VDM), a seminal contribution that has influenced both practical industry applications and theoretical advancements. His pioneering work on rely-guarantee thinking has been foundational for reasoning about shared-variable concurrency, with enduring impact across various domains, including the influential

---

[1] robostar.cs.york.ac.uk.

Separation Logic. Moreover, Cliff's pioneering efforts in logic, such as the Logic of Partial Functions, have provided invaluable support for reasoning about complex program development.

Cliff's unwavering dedication to advancing formal methods has helped shape the research community worldwide. In recognition of his outstanding contributions, the Royal Academy of Engineering Awarded him a Fellowship in 2003. Later, in 2015, the Formal Methods Europe Association awarded Cliff Jones a Fellowship, expressing gratitude for his transformative impact on the field.

We are honoured to have been able to put together this Festschrift. We are grateful for the professionalism and enthusiasm of all scientists who contributed, as authors, as reviewers, or by offering a testimonial.

September 2024   Ana Cavalcanti
                                                                     James Baxter

Organization

Additional Reviewers

Bargmann, Lara
Carbone, Marco
Chaudhuri, Kaustuv
Giunti, Marco
Heiner, Scott
Marshall, Lynn
Mazzara, Manuel
Murray, Toby

Rutenkolk, Kristin
Smith, Eric
Steggles, Jason
Su, Roger
Vassor, Martin
Xu, Xiong
Zhang, Wei

Contents – Part II

Contents – Part I

Reasoning About Distributive Laws
in a Concurrent Refinement Algebra

Larissa A. Meinicke⊙ and Ian J. Hayes$^{(\boxtimes)}$⊙

School of Electrical Engineering and Computer Science, The University of Queensland,
Brisbane, QLD 4072, Australia
Ian.Hayes@uq.edu.au

Abstract. Distributive laws are important for algebraic reasoning in arithmetic
and logic. They are equally important for algebraic reasoning about concurrent
programs. In existing theories such as Concurrent Kleene Algebra, only partial
correctness is handled, and many of its distributive laws are weak, in the sense
that they are only refinements in one direction, rather than equalities. The focus of
this paper is on strengthening our theory to support the proof of strong distributive
laws that are equalities, and in doing so come up with laws that are quite general.
Our concurrent refinement algebra supports total correctness by allowing both
finite and infinite behaviours. It supports the rely/guarantee approach of Jones
by encoding rely and guarantee conditions as rely and guarantee commands. The
strong distributive laws may then be used to distribute rely and guarantee commands over sequential compositions and into (and out of) finite iterations. They
may also be used to distribute other commands, such as commands that specify
a termination requirement, a fairness requirement, an evolution invariant, and a
generalised invariant, in exactly the same way. Strong (equality) distributive laws
are essential for handling data refinement of concurrent programs.

1 Introduction

The fundamental insights of Cliff Jones provided a compositional approach to shared-
memory concurrency [16–18]. In collaboration with Cliff over the last decade or so,
we have developed a rely/guarantee program algebra. The research presented in this
paper further supports Cliff's rely/guarantee approach by developing distributive laws
that facilitate the manipulation of rely and guarantee conditions. We also formalise
evolution invariants, as introduced by Cliff and Pierre Collette [3]. The distributive laws
are essential to support data reification, another area where Cliff has made significant
contributions.

1.1 Rely/Guarantee Concurrency

The concurrent refinement algebra is intended to support the rely/guarantee style of
reasoning of Jones [16–18]. To provide a compositional approach to reasoning about
concurrent programs, Jones makes use of a rely condition, r, a binary relation between
states, that corresponds to an assumption that any interference on a thread from its environment, satisfies r. Complementing this, each thread has a guarantee condition g, also

ⓒ The Author(s), under exclusive license to Springer Nature Switzerland AG 2024
A. Cavalcanti and J. Baxter (Eds.): *The Practice of Formal Methods*, LNCS 14781, pp. 1–22, 2024.
https://doi.org/10.1007/978-3-031-66673-5_1

a binary relation between states, and the thread must ensure every program transition it makes satisfies g. Figure 1 gives an execution trace that satisfies a rely/guarantee specification. For a set of parallel threads, the guarantee of each thread must imply the rely condition of every other thread.

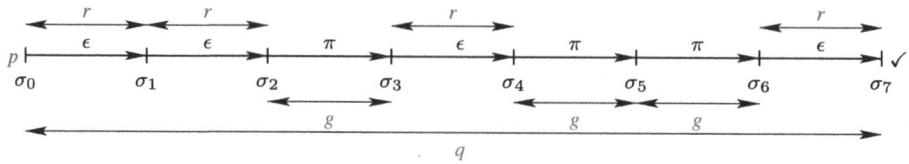

Fig. 1. An execution trace (of a program in an environment) consisting of states σ_0 through σ_7. Transitions of the program are labelled π and transitions of its environment are labelled ϵ. A trace satisfies a specification with pre-condition p, post-condition q, rely condition r and guarantee condition g, if whenever the initial state satisfies p and all environment transitions satisfy r, the post-condition q (a binary relation between states) holds between the initial and final states, and every program transition satisfies g. Importantly, a trace of a thread includes transitions of both itself (π) and its environment (ϵ) [1].

1.2 Refinement

The sequential refinement calculus [2, 22] encodes Floyd/Hoare preconditions and post-conditions [8, 13] via an assertion command, $\{p\}$, and a specification command, $[q]$, respectively. It uses a refinement relation,[1] $c_1 \succeq c_2$, meaning c_1 is refined (or implemented by) c_2. The Hoare triple,[2] $p\{c\}q$, is encoded as the refinement, $\{p\} \,;\, [q] \succeq c$.

For rely and guarantee conditions we follow the same approach as for preconditions and postconditions, and encode them as the commands, rely r and $\text{guar}_\pi\, g$, respectively. A guarantee command, $\text{guar}_\pi\, g$, ensures every program (π) transition from state σ to state σ' satisfies the binary relation between states g, that is, $(\sigma, \sigma') \in g$. It puts no constraints on environment (ϵ) transitions. A rely command, rely r, represents an assumption that every environment (ϵ) transition from σ to σ' satisfies the binary relation r, that is $(\sigma, \sigma') \in r$. In the sequential refinement calculus, an assertion command, $\{p\}$, either acts as a no-operation if p holds or irrecoverably aborts if p does not hold, where aborting behaviour corresponds to Dijkstra's abort command [5, 6]. The same approach is used for a rely command: it allows any transitions unless the environment makes a transition not satisfying r, in which case the rely command then aborts.

Naming Conventions and Syntactic Precedence of Operators. Commands are represented by c and d, sets of commands by C, test commands by t, atomic commands by

---

[1] In the program algebra literature [15] refinement is written, $c_1 \succeq c_2$, but in the refinement calculus literature it is written, $c_1 \sqsubseteq c_2$. We follow the former convention in this paper.

[2] Note that the use of braces in a Hoare triple differs from their use for an assertion command. This is the only place where we use a Hoare triple.

a and b (Sect. 1.8), pseudo-atomic commands by z (Sect. 1.9), sets of states by p, and binary relations between states by g, r and q. The above naming conventions also apply to subscripted forms of the above names. We assume the binary operator $\vee$ has the lowest precedence and sequential composition (;) has the highest precedence but otherwise make no assumptions about operator precedence and use parentheses to disambiguate.

1.3 Weak Conjunction

A rely/guarantee specification combines rely and guarantee commands with a pre/post specification using the weak conjunction operator, $\Cap$, where each transition of the weak conjunction of two commands, $c_1 \Cap c_2$, must be a transition of both c_1 and c_2, unless either c_1 or c_2 aborts, in which case $c_1 \Cap c_2$ aborts. For example, rely $r \Cap c$, behaves as c unless the environment makes a transition not satisfying r, in which case the rely command aborts, and hence the whole command, rely $r \Cap c$, irrecoverably aborts, so that any behaviour whatsoever is possible from that point on. As a more concrete example, an operation to remove an element v from a set w, of type $\mathbb{P}S$ for some set S, (i.e. $w \subseteq S$), in a context where other threads may also be removing elements from w, has a rely condition that w is non-increasing, $w_0 \supseteq w$, where w_0 stands for the before value of w and w (undecorated) stands for its after value, a guarantee condition that it only removes v and does not add any elements, $w_0 - w \subseteq \{v\} \wedge w_0 \supseteq w$, a precondition that v is in S, and a postcondition that v has been removed from w, $v \notin w$.

$$\mathsf{rely}(w_0 \supseteq w) \Cap \mathsf{guar}_\pi (w_0 - w \subseteq \{v\} \wedge w_0 \supseteq w) \Cap \{v \in S\} \, ; \, [v \notin w] \succeq \mathit{remove}(v)$$

Note that the usual sequential postcondition, $w = w_0 - \{v\}$, cannot be attained in a context where other threads are also modifying w. For the concurrent specification, the sequential postcondition is effectively split into a guarantee that only v is removed and a postcondition that on termination v is not in w. That postcondition is stable under a rely that only removes elements from w.

Commands form a lattice for which the lattice join, $c_1 \vee c_2$, is non-deterministic choice, that can behave as either c_1 or c_2, and the lattice meet, $c_1 \wedge c_2$, is a strong form of conjunction that has the common behaviours of c_1 and c_2. Dijkstra's abort command, written $\frac{1}{2}$ here, allows any behaviour whatsoever and hence it is the top command in the lattice, and hence $\frac{1}{2} \wedge c = c$ for any command c, so that $c_1 \wedge c_2$ can only abort if both c_1 and c_2 agree to abort. When combining a rely command, which may abort, with the remainder of a specification, one needs to ensure that if the rely command aborts the whole specification aborts (i.e. when an assumption is not met, the remaining commitments are no longer obliged to be fulfilled). This is achieved by using the weak conjunction operator, $c_1 \Cap c_2$. In particular, $\frac{1}{2} \Cap c = \frac{1}{2}$, as compared with strong conjunction where $\frac{1}{2} \wedge c = c$. If neither c_1 nor c_2 aborts, every behaviour of $c_1 \Cap c_2$ is both a behaviour of c_1 and a behaviour of c_2, that is, weak and strong conjunction coincide for commands that never abort. Weak conjunction is associative, commutative and idempotent. To illustrate the difference between weak ($\Cap$) and strong ($\wedge$) conjunction of commands, consider combining two specifications in the sequential refinement calculus [9,27].

$$\{p_1\} ; [q_1] \Cap \{p_2\} ; [q_2] = \{p_1 \cap p_2\} ; [q_1 \cap q_2] \tag{1}$$

$$\{p_1\} ; [q_1] \wedge \{p_2\} ; [q_2] = \{p_1 \cup p_2\} ; [(p_1 \rightarrow q_1) \cap (p_2 \rightarrow q_2)] \tag{2}$$

For weak conjunction, if both preconditions p_1 and p_2 hold initially, both postconditions must hold at termination, whereas for strong conjunction, if either precondition holds initially, then if p_1 holds initially, q_1 must hold on termination, and if p_2 holds initially, q_2 must hold on termination. The property for strong conjunction follows from the fact that it is the lattice meet, and hence it must refine both specification commands.

1.4   Distributive Laws for Rely/Guarantee Concurrency

In mathematics, distributive laws are important in algebraic reasoning, for example, in arithmetic, $x*(y+z) = x*y+x*z$, and in logic, $p \wedge (q \vee r) = (p \wedge q) \vee (p \wedge r)$. Distributive laws hold an equally important place in algebraic reasoning about programs [14], for example,

$$d \parallel (c_1 \vee c_2) = d \parallel c_1 \vee d \parallel c_2, \tag{3}$$

where $\parallel$ is parallel composition and $\vee$ is non-deterministic choice.

Both parallel composition and weak conjunction of a guarantee command distribute over sequential composition (4–5), as does a rely command (6–7).

$$\mathsf{guar}_\pi\, g \parallel c_1 ; c_2 = (\mathsf{guar}_\pi\, g \parallel c_1) ; (\mathsf{guar}_\pi\, g \parallel c_2) \tag{4}$$

$$\mathsf{guar}_\pi\, g \Cap c_1 ; c_2 = (\mathsf{guar}_\pi\, g \Cap c_1) ; (\mathsf{guar}_\pi\, g \Cap c_2) \tag{5}$$

$$\mathsf{rely}\, r \parallel c_1 ; c_2 = (\mathsf{rely}\, r \parallel c_1) ; (\mathsf{rely}\, r \parallel c_2) \tag{6}$$

$$\mathsf{rely}\, r \Cap c_1 ; c_2 = (\mathsf{rely}\, r \Cap c_1) ; (\mathsf{rely}\, r \Cap c_2) \tag{7}$$

1.5   The Abstract Synchronisation Operator

In our theory, parallel composition and weak conjunction are both synchronous operators [11, 12, 21], meaning they synchronise by combining the first transitions of each operand to give a transition of their composition before synchronising the continuations of the two operand commands. Parallel and weak conjunction share many axioms, so in our theory, we introduce an abstract synchronisation operator, $\otimes$, that has just their shared axioms. For example, $\otimes$ is associative and commutative and, abstracting (3), the abstract synchronisation operator distributes over choice,

$$d \otimes (c_1 \vee c_2) = d \otimes c_1 \vee d \otimes c_2 \tag{8}$$

and hence $\otimes$ is monotone in both arguments. Any laws that are proven for $\otimes$ can be applied to either parallel or weak conjunction. For example, (4) and (5) are both instances of (9), and (6) and (7) are both instances of (10).

$$\mathsf{guar}_\pi\, g \otimes c_1 ; c_2 = (\mathsf{guar}_\pi\, g \otimes c_1) ; (\mathsf{guar}_\pi\, g \otimes c_2) \tag{9}$$

$$\mathsf{rely}\, r \otimes c_1 ; c_2 = (\mathsf{rely}\, r \otimes c_1) ; (\mathsf{rely}\, r \otimes c_2) \tag{10}$$

The main challenge addressed in this paper is to devise suitable restrictions on a command d to ensure,

$$d \otimes c_1 \,; c_2 = (d \otimes c_1) \,; (d \otimes c_2) \tag{11}$$

so that (9) and (10) are instances of (11).

1.6 Weak Distributive Laws

It is straightforward to show the weak distributive law,

$$d \otimes c_1 \,; c_2 \succeq (d \otimes c_1) \,; (d \otimes c_2) \qquad\qquad \text{if } d \succeq d \,; d \tag{12}$$

because synchronisation satisfies a weak interchange axiom with sequential composition,[3] similar to that in Concurrent Kleene Algebra [15]:

$$d_1 \,; d_2 \otimes c_1 \,; c_2 \succeq (d_1 \otimes c_1) \,; (d_2 \otimes c_2). \tag{13}$$

Law (12) follows from the assumption $(d \succeq d \,; d)$, monotonicity of $\otimes$, and (13):

$$d \otimes c_1 \,; c_2 \succeq d \,; d \otimes c_1 \,; c_2 \succeq (d \otimes c_1) \,; (d \otimes c_2).$$

Fixed iteration, c^i, of a command c, i times for $i \in \mathbb{N}$, is defined inductively by,

$$c^0 = \tau \tag{14} \qquad\qquad c^{i+1} = c \,; c^i \tag{15}$$

where τ is the command that terminates immediately from any state; it is the identity of sequential composition, that is, $\tau \,; c = c = c \,; \tau$ for any command c. Weakly distributing d into a fixed iteration holds for all $i \in \mathbb{N}$ as follows.

$$d \otimes c^i \succeq (d \otimes c)^i \qquad\qquad \text{if } d \otimes \tau \succeq \tau \text{ and } d \succeq d \,; d \tag{16}$$

The proof is by induction on i: the base case for i zero is handled by (14) and the first assumption, $d \otimes \tau \succeq \tau$, and the inductive case uses (15), (12) using the second assumption, the inductive hypothesis and finally (15):

$$d \otimes c^{i+1} = d \otimes c \,; c^i \succeq (d \otimes c) \,; (d \otimes c^i) \succeq (d \otimes c) \,; (d \otimes c)^i = (d \otimes c)^{i+1}.$$

Finite iteration of a command c, zero or more times, corresponds to the choice over all the fixed iterations, c^i, for $i \in \mathbb{N}$,

$$c^\star = \bigvee_{i \in \mathbb{N}} c^i. \tag{17}$$

Weakly distributing d into a finite iteration holds under the same assumptions as for fixed iteration.

$$d \otimes c^\star \succeq (d \otimes c)^\star \qquad\qquad \text{if } d \otimes \tau \succeq \tau \text{ and } d \succeq d \,; d. \tag{18}$$

The proof decomposes $c^\star$ using (17), distributes the synchronisation into the choice, applies (16) for each $i \in \mathbb{N}$, and then combines the results using (17).

$$d \otimes c^\star = d \otimes \bigvee_{i \in \mathbb{N}} c^i = \bigvee_{i \in \mathbb{N}} (d \otimes c^i) \succeq \bigvee_{i \in \mathbb{N}} (d \otimes c)^i = (d \otimes c)^\star. \tag{19}$$

---

[3] Both $\|$ and $\Cap$ satisfy this weak interchange axiom with sequential composition.

1.7   Strong Distributive Laws for Finite Sequential Compositions

While (12), (16) and (18) are refinements, there are situations where one needs the
following stronger distributive laws that are equalities rather than refinements.

$$d \otimes c_1 \,;\, c_2 = (d \otimes c_1) \,;\, (d \otimes c_2) \tag{20}$$

$$d \otimes \tau = \{p\} \qquad \text{for some set of states } p \tag{21}$$

$$d \otimes c^{i+1} = (d \otimes c)^{i+1} \qquad \text{for all } i \in \mathbb{N} \tag{22}$$

$$d \otimes c^\star = (d \otimes c)^\star \tag{23}$$

Note that for the special case when p is the complete state space Σ, (21) reduces to
$d \otimes \tau = \tau$, i.e. $d \otimes c^0 = (d \otimes c)^0$. The main contribution of this paper is to investigate
the restrictions on d that allow these laws to be strengthened to equalities.

If (20) holds for any c_1 and c_2 it is straightforward to show that (21) holds, and
then that (22) and (23) hold using proofs similar in structure to the proofs of (16) and
(18)—see Sect. 3.

For (20) to hold for any c_1 and c_2, traces of c_1 and c_2 may be of any length and
hence traces of d need to be able to be split at any point to give two traces of d. The
following subsections outline suitable forms for d so that it satisfies (20), and hence
(21), (22) and (23). Section 4 investigates restrictions on d (see (27)) so that (20) holds
for any c_1 and c_2 (Theorem 11).

1.8   Atomic Commands

The concurrent refinement algebra [11,12] includes a subset of commands, known as
atomic commands, that can only perform a single transition and then terminate. The
possibly infinite iteration of a command c, zero or more times, is denoted c^ω; it includes
both finite and infinite iterations of c, where c^∞ gives the infinite iteration of c.

$$c^\omega = c^\star \vee c^\infty \tag{24}$$

It turns out that if d is either a finite iteration, $\mathsf{a}^\star$, or a possibly infinite iteration, a^ω, of
an atomic command a, then (20) and (21) (with $p = \Sigma$) both hold, for example,

$$\mathsf{a}^\omega \otimes c_1 \,;\, c_2 = (\mathsf{a}^\omega \otimes c_1) \,;\, (\mathsf{a}^\omega \otimes c_2) \qquad \text{for any commands } c_1 \text{ and } c_2. \tag{25}$$

$$\mathsf{a}^\omega \otimes \tau = \tau \tag{26}$$

Hence (22) and (23) also hold for d as either $\mathsf{a}^\star$ or a^ω. Note that $(\mathsf{a} \,;\, \mathsf{a})^\star$ is not a suitable
candidate for d because, for example, if $c_1 = c_2 = \mathsf{b}$, for an atomic command b,
$(\mathsf{a} \,;\, \mathsf{a})^\star \otimes \mathsf{b} \,;\, \mathsf{b} = (\mathsf{a} \otimes \mathsf{b}) \,;\, (\mathsf{a} \otimes \mathsf{b})$ but $(\mathsf{a} \,;\, \mathsf{a})^\star \otimes \mathsf{b}$ cannot fully synchronise because
$(\mathsf{a} \,;\, \mathsf{a})^\star$ only has even length terminating traces, while b has only terminating traces
of length one. This counter example demonstrates that assumptions $d \otimes \tau = \tau$ and
$d = d \,;\, d$ are not sufficiently strong to show (20).

A program guarantee command, $\mathrm{guar}_\pi \, g$, can be defined as a possibly infinite iteration of an atomic command that can perform a program transition from state σ to state
σ' provided it satisfies g, (i.e. $(\sigma, \sigma') \in g$), or any environment transition. Therefore
laws (20)-(23) hold for d a guarantee command, $\mathrm{guar}_\pi \, g$—see Sect. 5.

1.9   Pseudo-atomic Commands

A pseudo-atomic command, z, can be written in the form $z = \{p\} ; (a \vee b ; \not{z})$, for some set of states p and atomic commands a and b. While an atomic command can make a single transition and terminate, a *pseudo-atomic command* can either abort immediately from states not satisfying p, make a single transition of the atomic command a and then terminate or make a single transition of the atomic command b and then abort. Pseudo-atomic commands share many properties with atomic commands.

It turns out that if d is either a finite iteration, $z^\star$, or a possibly infinite iteration, z^ω, of a pseudo-atomic command z, (20) holds and hence (21)–(23) and also hold. A rely command, rely r, is defined as a possibly infinite iteration of a pseudo-atomic command that cannot immediately abort but can make any program transition or an environment transition satisfying r and terminate, or an environment transition not satisfying r and abort. Therefore laws (20)–(23) hold for d a rely command, rely r. Evolution and generalised invariants can also be represented as possibly infinite iterations of pseudo-atomic commands, and so the distribution laws also apply to these commands—see Sect. 5.

The everywhere infeasible (and least) command, magic, is considered to be a (degenerate) atomic command; magic is a left annihilator for sequential composition, that is, magic ; c = magic, for any command c, and hence any atomic command a is a special case of a pseudo-atomic command because $\{\Sigma\} ; (a \vee magic ; \not{z})$ = $\tau ; (a \vee magic)$ = a, as $\{\Sigma\} = \tau$ and magic is the identity of non-deterministic choice. That is, atomic commands are a subset of pseudo-atomic commands.

1.10   Pseudo-atomic Fixed Points

Finite iteration, $c^\star$, of a command c is the least fixed point of the function, $(\lambda y . \tau \vee c; y)$, and possibly infinite iteration, c^ω, is the greatest fixed point of the same function. As a further generalisation, it turns out that if d is any fixed point of the function, $(\lambda y . \tau \vee z; y)$, where z is a pseudo-atomic command, that is,

$$d = \tau \vee z ; d, \tag{27}$$

then (20) holds and hence (21)–(23) also hold—see Sect. 4. We refer to commands, d, satisfying (27) as *pseudo-atomic fixed points*. Clearly, $z^\star$ and z^ω are both pseudo-atomic fixed points if z is a pseudo-atomic command, and hence so are the special case forms $a^\star$ and a^ω, for an atomic command a. The command term represents the most general command that can perform only a finite number of program transitions but does not constrain its environment, and the command fair represents the most general command that disallows preemption by the environment forever. Both term and fair are pseudo-atomic fixed points and hence both satisfy (20)–(23)—see Sect. 5.

Overview. Section 2 gives details of the synchronous algebra. Section 3 gives general laws for distributing into a finite iteration. Section 4 tackles proving the (strong) distributive laws (20)–(23) for d a pseudo-atomic fixed point, with the obvious corollaries that these laws also hold for d of the form $z^\star$ or z^ω for z a pseudo-atomic command, and hence for d of the form $a^\star$ or a^ω for an atomic command a. Section 5 applies these theorems to the rely/guarantee approach of Jones [16–18] as encoded in our concurrent refinement algebra.

2   Synchronous Algebra

Our approach is based on a synchronous algebra [11,12,25], which has been formalised in Isabelle/HOL [24]. A trace model of the algebra [4] has been developed
in Isabelle/HOL and the axioms of our theory have been shown to be consistent with it.
It includes the following primitive commands:

- instantaneous test commands, of the form $\tau\,p$, that terminate immediately if the initial state is in the set of states p but are infeasible otherwise; these are similar to tests
  in Kozen's Kleene Algebra with Tests (KAT) [19],
- atomic commands, denoted by a and b, that may take a single transition and terminate; transitions are labelled as either program (π) or environment (ϵ), and
- Dijkstra's abort command [5,6], denoted $\lightning$ here, that represents immediate catas-
  trophic failure.

The everywhere infeasible command, magic, that has no behaviours at all, corresponds to both the (least) test, $\tau\,\emptyset$, which fails in every state, and the (least) atomic
command, which can make no transitions whatsoever. The (greatest) test that succeeds
terminating immediately in every state is $\tau\,\Sigma$, where Σ is the set of all states. We abbreviate $\tau\,\Sigma$ as $\boldsymbol{\tau}$; it is the identity of sequential composition.

After aborting no further assumptions can be made about the behaviour of the
program—any behaviour is possible. Abort is a left annihilator for sequential com-
position, i.e. $\lightning\,;\,c = \lightning$, for any command c, in particular, $\lightning\,;\,\text{magic} = \lightning$, unlike some
other theories [15], in which, $c\,;\,\text{magic} = \text{magic}$, for any command c. Abort is also an
annihilator for $\otimes$, thats is, $c\otimes\lightning = \lightning$, and hence for $\|$ and $\Cap$, unlike some other theories.

An assertion, $\{p\}$, acts as a no-operation unless its initial state does not satisfy p, in
which case it aborts (28), where $\overline{p}$ denotes the set of states not in p. An assertion at the
start of either branch of a non-deterministic choice distributes (29).

$$\{p\} \mathrel{\widehat{=}} \boldsymbol{\tau} \vee \tau\,\overline{p}\,;\,\lightning \tag{28}$$

$$c \vee \{p\}\,;\,d = \{p\}\,;\,(c \vee d) \tag{29}$$

The abstract synchronisation operator, $\otimes$, is assumed to be associative and commutative, with atomic identity ι (30), and (command) identity ι^{ω} (31). Atomic steps
are closed under synchronisation, as are tests, where the synchronisation of two tests
corresponds to their conjunction (32). A test, t, distributes into a synchronisation (33).
If synchronising c_1 with $\boldsymbol{\tau}$ is infeasible, so is synchronising any extension of c_1 (34).
An atomic command cannot synchronise with $\boldsymbol{\tau}$ and hence their synchronisation corresponds to the everywhere infeasible command magic (35). The synchronisation of
two commands that both start with atomic commands first synchronises their respective
atomic commands and then synchronises their continuations (36).[4]

---

[4] Axiom (36) is the main axiom that signifies that $\otimes$ is synchronous, for example, $c \parallel d$ synchronises a program transition of c with a matching environment transition of d, or vice versa,
to give a program transition of $c \parallel d$, and matching environment transitions of both c and d to
give an environment transition of $c \parallel d$. For a non-synchronous parallel operator there are no
environment transitions and program transitions are interleaved.

$$\iota \otimes a = a \qquad\qquad \text{if a is an atomic command} \qquad (30)$$

$$\iota^\omega \otimes c = c \qquad\qquad (31)$$

$$\tau\, p_1 \otimes \tau\, p_2 = \tau(p_1 \cap p_2) \qquad\qquad (32)$$

$$t\,;(c_1 \otimes c_2) = t\,; c_1 \otimes t\,; c_2 \qquad\qquad (33)$$

$$\tau \otimes c_1\,; c_2 = \mathsf{magic} \qquad\qquad \text{if } \tau \otimes c_1 = \mathsf{magic} \qquad (34)$$

$$\tau \otimes a = \mathsf{magic} \qquad\qquad (35)$$

$$a_1\,; c_1 \otimes a_2\,; c_2 = (a_1 \otimes a_2)\,;(c_1 \otimes c_2) \qquad\qquad (36)$$

Synchronisation distributes over a non-deterministic choice over a non-empty set of commands (37). Sequential composition distributes over a non-deterministic choice from the right (38) and from the left provided the set of commands is non-empty (39). Synchronisation is abort strict (40).

$$\left(\bigvee_{c \in C} c\right) \otimes d = \bigvee_{c \in C} (c \otimes d) \qquad\qquad \text{if } C \neq \{\} \qquad (37)$$

$$\left(\bigvee_{c \in C} c\right); d = \bigvee_{c \in C} (c\,; d) \qquad\qquad (38)$$

$$d\,;\left(\bigvee_{c \in C} c\right) = \bigvee_{c \in C} (d\,; c) \qquad\qquad \text{if } C \neq \{\} \qquad (39)$$

$$\lightning \otimes c = \lightning \qquad\qquad (40)$$

From (35) one can deduce (41) because $\tau \succeq t$, for any test t. From (37) with C as $\{c_1, c_2\}$ one can deduce (8), and similarly (42) from (38). A test on a branch of a synchronisation may be pulled out as a test on the whole, if the other branch is not immediately aborting (43), i.e. if $\mathsf{magic} \otimes c_1 = \mathsf{magic}$ [12]. A test at the end of either branch of a synchronisation can be pulled out as a final test (44). An assertion at the start of either branch of a synchronisation can be pulled out of the synchronisation (45).

$$t \otimes a = \mathsf{magic} \qquad\qquad (41)$$

$$(c_1 \vee c_2)\,; c = (c_1\,; c) \vee (c_2\,; c) \qquad\qquad (42)$$

$$c_1 \otimes t\,; c_2 = t\,;(c_1 \otimes c_2) \qquad\qquad \text{if } \mathsf{magic} \otimes c_1 = \mathsf{magic} \qquad (43)$$

$$c_1\,; t \otimes c_2 = (c_1 \otimes c_2)\,; t \qquad\qquad (44)$$

$$c_1 \otimes \{p\}\,; c_2 = \{p\}\,;(c_1 \otimes c_2) \qquad\qquad (45)$$

A pseudo-atomic command, z, has laws similar to (30), (34) and (36).

Lemma 1 (pseudo-atomic-properties). *For* z *a pseudo-atomic command of the form* $\{p\}\,;(\mathsf{a} \vee \mathsf{b}\,; \lightning)$ *for some* p, a *and* b, *and* z_1 *and* z_2 *pseudo-atomic commands of similar forms (but with subscripts), and a test* t,

$$\iota \otimes z = z \qquad\qquad (46)$$

$$t \otimes z\,; c = \{p\}\,; \mathsf{magic} \qquad\qquad (47)$$

$$z_1\,; c_1 \otimes z_2\,; c_2 = (z_1 \otimes z_2)\,;(c_1 \otimes c_2) \qquad\qquad (48)$$

Proof. For (46), using the form of z, (45), (8), (30), (36), (30), (40), and the form of z:
$\iota \otimes z = \iota \otimes \{p\} ; (a \vee b ; \frac{1}{2}) = \{p\} ; (\iota \otimes (a \vee b ; \frac{1}{2})) = \{p\} ; ((\iota \otimes a) \vee (\iota ; \tau \otimes b ; \frac{1}{2})) = \{p\} ; (a \vee (\iota \otimes b) ; (\tau \otimes \frac{1}{2})) = \{p\} ; (a \vee b ; \frac{1}{2}) = z.$

For (47), using the form of z, (45), (42) and $\frac{1}{2}$ annihilates and (8), then (34) and (35)
twice: $\iota \otimes z;c = \iota \otimes \{p\};(a \vee b; \frac{1}{2});c = \{p\};(\iota \otimes (a \vee b; \frac{1}{2});c) = \{p\};((\iota \otimes a;c) \vee (\iota \otimes b; \frac{1}{2})) = \{p\} ; (\text{magic} \vee \text{magic}) = \{p\} ; \text{magic}.$

For (48), using the forms of z_1 and z_2, (45) twice and (42) twice and $\frac{1}{2}$ annihilates,
(8) thrice and (36) four times plus (40) and (42), abort annihilates and (42), then (8),
(36) and (40), then (45) twice, and the forms of z_1 and z_2, as follows.

$$z_1 ; c_1 \otimes z_2 ; c_2$$
$$= \{p_1\} ; (a_1 \vee b_1 ; \frac{1}{2}) ; c_1 \otimes \{p_2\} ; (a_2 \vee b_2 ; \frac{1}{2}) ; c_2$$
$$= \{p_1\} ; \{p_2\} ; ((a_1 ; c_1 \vee b_1 ; \frac{1}{2}) \otimes (a_2 ; c_2 \vee b_2 ; \frac{1}{2}))$$
$$= \{p_1\} ; \{p_2\} ; ((a_1 \otimes a_2) ; (c_1 \otimes c_2) \vee (a_1 \otimes b_2 \vee b_1 \otimes a_2 \vee b_1 \otimes b_2) ; \frac{1}{2})$$
$$= \{p_1\} ; \{p_2\} ; ((a_1 \otimes a_2) \vee (a_1 \otimes b_2 \vee b_1 \otimes a_2 \vee b_1 \otimes b_2) ; \frac{1}{2}) ; (c_1 \otimes c_2)$$
$$= \{p_1\} ; \{p_2\} ; ((a_1 \vee b_1 ; \frac{1}{2}) \otimes (a_2 \vee b_2 ; \frac{1}{2})) ; (c_1 \otimes c_2)$$
$$= (\{p_1\} ; (a_1 \vee b_1 ; \frac{1}{2}) \otimes \{p_2\} ; (a_2 \vee b_2 ; \frac{1}{2})) ; (c_1 \otimes c_2)$$
$$= (z_1 \otimes z_2) ; (c_1 \otimes c_2)$$

$\square$

Expanded form. An important axiom is that the behaviour of any command, c, can be decomposed into,

- an immediately aborting behaviour from initial states not in some set p_n,
- an immediately terminating behaviour from initial states in some set p_t, or
- c performs a transition of some atomic command, a', and then behaves as some continuation command, c'.

In the final case above, the continuation behaviour, c', depends on which atomic command, a', is taken, and hence a choice over a set, C, of pairs of a' and c' is required. In summary, for any command c, there exist sets of states p_n and p_t and a set, C, of pairs of atomic command and command, such that,[5]

$$c = \{p_n\} ; (\tau \, p_t \vee \bigvee_{(a',c') \in C} (a' ; c')) \tag{49}$$

The set p_t can be $\emptyset$, if no immediately terminating behaviours are possible for c, p_n can be the set of all states, Σ, if no immediately aborting behaviours are possible for c, and the set of pairs C can be empty if c cannot make any transitions.

---

[5] For readers familiar with labelled transition systems, $\overline{p_n}$ represents the set of states in which c aborts, p_t the set of (final) states in which c can terminate, and for an pair of commands (a',c') in C, c can do a transition of a' and then behave as c'. The main difference is that a pair (a',c') groups together transitions (of a') that have the same continuation, c'. We also include aborting behaviour, which is not usually available in labelled transition systems but is necessary to represent failure of assertions and rely commands.

Straightforward calculations give that, if c corresponds to the expanded form in (49), the following laws hold.

$$\tau \otimes c = \{p_n\} \,;\, \tau\, p_t \tag{50}$$

$$\mathsf{a}^{k+1} \otimes c = \{p_n\} \,;\, \bigvee_{(\mathsf{a}',c') \in C} ((\mathsf{a} \otimes \mathsf{a}') \,;\, (\mathsf{a}^k \otimes c')) \qquad \text{for } k \in \mathbb{N} \tag{51}$$

3 Distributing into Finite Iteration

In this section we show that if a command d satisfies

$$d \otimes c_1 \,;\, c_2 = (d \otimes c_1) \,;\, (d \otimes c_2) \tag{52}$$

for all commands c_1 and c_2, then one can show that d distributes over any finite sequence of commands, in particular, it distributes into fixed and finite iterations of a command.[6] First, we make the following observations.

Lemma 2 (d-sync-nil). *If* $d \otimes c_1 \,;\, c_2 = (d \otimes c_1) \,;\, (d \otimes c_2)$ *for all commands* c_1 *and* c_2, *then we have that* $d \otimes \tau = \{p\}$ *for some set of states* p.

Proof. Using the fact that τ is the sequential identity and (40), applying the assumption, applying (50) for some p_n and p_t and (40) again, simplifying we get: $\not\downarrow = d \otimes \tau \,;\, \not\downarrow = (d \otimes \tau) \,;\, (d \otimes \not\downarrow) = \{p_n\} \,;\, \tau\, p_t \,;\, \not\downarrow = \tau(\overline{p_n} \cup p_t) \,;\, \not\downarrow$, from which we can infer that $\overline{p_n} \cup p_t = \Sigma$, (i.e. $p_t \supseteq p_n$), and so $d \otimes \tau = \{p_n\} \,;\, \tau\, p_t = \{p_n\}$. □

Lemma 3 (d-pre). *If* $d \otimes \tau = \{p\}$ *for some set of states* p, *then* $\{p\} \,;\, d = d$.

Proof. From (31), and the assumption we have $d = d \otimes \iota^\omega \succeq d \otimes \tau = \{p\}$, and $d \succeq \{p\}$ is equivalent to $\{p\} \vee d = d$, which from $\{p\} = \{p\} \,;\, \{p\}$ and (29) is then equivalent to $\{p\} \,;\, (\{p\} \vee d) = d$ and hence $\{p\} \,;\, d = d$. □

We now show that any d satisfying (52) distributes into fixed and finite iterations.

Theorem 4 (distrib-fixed-iter). *If* $d \otimes c_1 \,;\, c_2 = (d \otimes c_1) \,;\, (d \otimes c_2)$ *for all commands* c_1 *and* c_2, *then*

$$d \otimes c^0 = \{p\} \qquad\qquad \text{for some set of states } p \tag{53}$$

$$d \otimes c^{i+1} = (d \otimes c)^{i+1} \qquad\qquad \text{for all } i \in \mathbb{N} \tag{54}$$

Proof. For (53), using (14), the assumption and Lemma 2 (d-sync-nil) we have $d \otimes c^0 = d \otimes \tau = \{p\}$, for some set of states p. Property (54) is shown by induction on i. It holds trivially for $i = 0$. Assuming the property for i, we show it holds for $i + 1$ using (15), the assumption, the induction hypothesis and finally (15): $d \otimes c^{i+2} = d \otimes c \,;\, c^{i+1} = (d \otimes c) \,;\, (d \otimes c^{i+1}) = (d \otimes c) \,;\, (d \otimes c)^{i+1} = (d \otimes c)^{i+2}$. □

---

[6] This has parallels with predicates over time intervals, where an interval predicate *splits* if whenever it holds for an interval I, it holds for any subinterval of I [7].

Theorem 5 (distrib-finite-iter). *If $d \otimes c_1 \,;\, c_2 = (d \otimes c_1) \,;\, (d \otimes c_2)$ for all commands c_1 and c_2, then $d \otimes c^* = (d \otimes c)^*$.*

Proof. The proof decomposes c^* using (17), splits off the zero iterations alternative and distributes over the choice using (37), applies Theorem 4 for each i using the assumption, applies (29), (39), and (15), applies (45) and the assumption with Lemma 2 (d-sync-nil) and Lemma 3 (d-pre) to get $\{p\} \,;\, d = d$, and composes the results using (15) and (17):

$$
d \otimes c^* = d \otimes \bigvee_{i \in \mathbb{N}} c^i
$$

$$
= d \otimes c^0 \vee \bigvee_{i \in \mathbb{N}} (d \otimes c^{i+1})
$$

$$
= \{p\} \vee \bigvee_{i \in \mathbb{N}} (d \otimes c)^{i+1}
$$

$$
= \tau \vee \bigvee_{i \in \mathbb{N}} \{p\} \,;\, (d \otimes c) \,;\, (d \otimes c)^i
$$

$$
= \tau \vee \bigvee_{i \in \mathbb{N}} (\{p\} \,;\, d \otimes c) \,;\, (d \otimes c)^i
$$

$$
= (d \otimes c)^0 \vee \bigvee_{i \in \mathbb{N}} (d \otimes c) \,;\, (d \otimes c)^i
$$

$$
= (d \otimes c)^0 \vee \bigvee_{i \in \mathbb{N}} (d \otimes c)^{i+1}
$$

$$
= (d \otimes c)^*
$$

$\square$

4 Pseudo-atomic Fixed Point Distributive Laws

Theorem 4 (distrib-fixed-iter) and Theorem 5 (distrib-finite-iter) assume d satisfies (52). This section focuses on properties of d that ensure it satisfies (52). A general property of d that implies (52) is that d is a *pseudo-atomic-fixed point*, that is,

$$
d = \tau \vee z \,;\, d \tag{55}
$$

for some pseudo-atomic command z. Pseudo-atomic fixed points satisfy the following basic properties.

Lemma 6 (pafp-basic-properties). *Given p is a set of states, t is a test command, a, a_1 and b are atomic commands, let $z = \{p\} \,;\, (a \vee b \,;\, \frac{1}{4})$ be a pseudo-atomic command and let d be a pseudo-atomic fixed point such that, $d = \tau \vee z \,;\, d$, then*

$$
d \otimes t = \{p\} \,;\, t \tag{56}
$$

$$
\{p\} \,;\, d = d \tag{57}
$$

$$
d \otimes a_1 \,;\, c = (z \otimes a_1) \,;\, (d \otimes c) \tag{58}
$$

$$
d \otimes a_1 = (z \otimes a_1) \,;\, \{p\} \tag{59}
$$

$$
d \otimes a_1 \,;\, c = (d \otimes a_1) \,;\, (d \otimes c) \tag{60}
$$

Proof. For (56), the proof follows by expanding d using (55), and then simplifying using (8), (32), (47), (29), and the fact that magic is the identity of non-deterministic choice: $d \otimes t = (\tau \vee z\,;d) \otimes t = (\tau \otimes t) \vee (z\,;d \otimes t) = t \vee \{p\}\,;t$. magic $= \{p\}\,;t$.

Property (57) follows from Lemma 3 (d-pre) and (56).

To verify (58) we reason as follows.

$$d \otimes \mathsf{a}_1\,;c$$

$=$ expanding d using (55) and distributing using (8)

$$(\tau \otimes \mathsf{a}_1\,;c) \vee (z\,;d \otimes \mathsf{a}_1\,;c)$$

$=$ applying (35) and (34) to show $\tau \otimes \mathsf{a}_1\,;c =$ magic

$$z\,;d \otimes \mathsf{a}_1\,;c$$

$=$ using (48) noting that a_1 is atomic and hence also pseudo-atomic

$$(z \otimes \mathsf{a}_1)\,;(d \otimes c)$$

Property (59) follows by using the fact that τ the unit of sequential composition, applying (58), and then (56): $d \otimes \mathsf{a}_1 = d \otimes \mathsf{a}_1\,;\tau = (z \otimes \mathsf{a}_1)\,;(d \otimes \tau) = (z \otimes \mathsf{a}_1)\,;\{p\}$.

Property (60) then follows by applying (59), (45), (57) and (58): $(d \otimes \mathsf{a}_1)\,;(d \otimes c) = (z \otimes \mathsf{a}_1)\,;\{p\}\,;(d \otimes c) = (z \otimes \mathsf{a}_1)\,;(\{p\}\,;d \otimes c) = (z \otimes \mathsf{a}_1)\,;(d \otimes c) = d \otimes \mathsf{a}_1\,;c$. $\square$

The proof that a pseudo-atomic fixed point distributes over a sequential composition (52), that is, $d \otimes c_1\,;c_2 = (d \otimes c_1)\,;(d \otimes c_2)$, makes use of the fact that the command c_1 can be decomposed into its finite behaviours of length k for all $k \in \mathbb{N}$, plus its infinite behaviours. The finite behaviours of length k are given by, $\iota^k \otimes c_1$, recalling that ι is the atomic identity of $\otimes$ and hence ι^k allows exactly k transitions. The infinite behaviours of c_1 correspond to $\iota^\infty \otimes c_1$. We first show the distributive law holds if c_1 is restricted to its finite traces of length k.

Lemma 7 (pseudo-atomic-distrib-length). *For pseudo-atomic fixed point d and all $k \in \mathbb{N}$,*

$$(d \otimes \iota^k \otimes c_1)\,;(d \otimes c_2) = d \otimes (\iota^k \otimes c_1)\,;c_2. \tag{61}$$

Proof. The proof is by induction on k using the properties of pseudo-atomic fixed points. We use the expanded form for c_1, that is, $c_1 = \{p_n\}\,;(\tau\,p_t \vee \bigvee_{(\mathsf{a}',c') \in C}(\mathsf{a}'\,;c'))$, for some sets of states p_n and p_t, and set of pairs of atomic command and commands C (49). Because d is a pseudo-atomic fixed point, we can assume it is of a form such that $d = \tau \vee z\,;d$, where $z = \{p\}\,;(\mathsf{a} \vee \mathsf{b}\,;\lightning)$, for some p, a and b. For $k = 0$.

$$(d \otimes \iota^0 \otimes c_1)\,;(d \otimes c_2)$$

$=$ as $\iota^0 = \tau$ by (14) and $d \otimes \tau = \{p\}$ by (56)

$$\{p\}\,;(\tau \otimes c_1)\,;(d \otimes c_2)$$

$=$ by (50) using the expanded form of c_1

$$\{p\}\,;\{p_n\}\,;\tau\,p_t\,;(d \otimes c_2)$$

$=$ expanding the form of d and the definition of z

$$\{p\}\,;\{p_n\}\,;\tau\,p_t\,;((\tau \vee \{p\}\,;(\mathsf{a} \vee \mathsf{b}\,;\lightning)\,;d) \otimes c_2)$$

$=$ pulling $\{p\}$ out by (29) and (45) and eliminate duplicate $\{p\}$

$\{p\} ; \{p_n\} ; \tau \, p_t ; ((\tau \vee (a \vee b ; \mbox{\Large\textonehalf}) ; d) \otimes c_2)$

$=$ push in $\tau \, p_t$ by (43) as $\tau \vee (a \vee b ; \mbox{\Large\textonehalf})$ is not immediately aborting

$\{p\} ; \{p_n\} ; ((\tau \vee (a \vee b ; \mbox{\Large\textonehalf}) ; d) \otimes \tau \, p_t ; c_2)$

$=$ by (45) push in $\{p_n\}$ to the right of $\otimes$ and $\{p\}$ to the left, then (29)

$(\tau \vee \{p\} ; (a \vee b ; \mbox{\Large\textonehalf}) ; d) \otimes \{p_n\} ; \tau \, p_t ; c_2$

$=$ contracting to pseudo-atomic fixed-point d (55) and (50)

$d \otimes (\iota^0 \otimes c_1) ; c_2$

For the inductive case, we assume (61) for k and show it holds for $k + 1$. For the main proof, we assume the set C in the expanded form is non-empty (so that we can apply (37)); the case when C is empty is treated below the main proof.

$(d \otimes \iota^{k+1} \otimes c_1) ; (d \otimes c_2)$

$=$ by (51) using the expanded form for c_1 and $\iota \otimes a' = a'$ by (30)

$$\left(d \otimes \left(\{p_n\} ; \bigvee_{(a',c') \in C} (a' ; (\iota^k \otimes c')) \right) \right) ; (d \otimes c_2)$$

$=$ distributing assertion by (45), then distributing by (37) and (38)

$$\{p_n\} ; \left(\bigvee_{(a',c') \in C} (d \otimes (a' ; (\iota^k \otimes c'))) ; (d \otimes c_2) \right)$$

$=$ distributing d by (60)

$$\{p_n\} ; \left(\bigvee_{(a',c') \in C} (d \otimes a') ; (d \otimes (\iota^k \otimes c')) ; (d \otimes c_2) \right)$$

$=$ using the induction hypothesis

$$\{p_n\} ; \left(\bigvee_{(a',c') \in C} (d \otimes a') ; (d \otimes ((\iota^k \otimes c') ; c_2)) \right)$$

$=$ distributing d by (60)

$$\{p_n\} ; \left(\bigvee_{(a',c') \in C} d \otimes (a' ; (\iota^k \otimes c') ; c_2) \right)$$

$=$ distributing by (38) and then (37), and then (45)

$$d \otimes \left(\left(\{p_n\} ; \bigvee_{(a',c') \in C} a' ; (\iota^k \otimes c') \right) ; c_2 \right)$$

$=$ by (51) using the expanded form for c_1 and $\iota \otimes a' = a'$ by (30)

$d \otimes (\iota^{k+1} \otimes c_1) ; c_2$

If C is empty, after the first step in the above proof we get $(d \otimes \{p_n\} \,;\, \mathsf{magic}) \,;\, (d \otimes c_2)$, which equals $\{p_n\} \,;\, \{p\} \,;\, \mathsf{magic}$, and the second last step equals $d \otimes (\{p_n\} \,;\, \mathsf{magic} \,;\, c_2) = d \otimes (\{p_n\} \,;\, \mathsf{magic}) = \{p_n\} \,;\, (d \otimes \mathsf{magic}) = \{p_n\} \,;\, \{p\} \,;\, \mathsf{magic}$, and hence the equality also holds for the case when C is empty.   □

Lemma 7 (pseudo-atomic-distrib-length) can then be generalised to the case where c is restricted any finite number of steps.

Lemma 8 (pseudo-atomic-distrib-fin). *For pseudo-atomic fixed point d,*

$$(d \otimes \iota^\star \otimes c_1) \,;\, (d \otimes c_2) = d \otimes ((\iota^\star \otimes c_1) \,;\, c_2). \tag{62}$$

Proof. The proof makes use of (17) to decompose $\iota^\star$ into $\bigvee_{k \in \mathbb{N}} \iota^k$.

$$(d \otimes \iota^\star \otimes c_1) \,;\, (d \otimes c_2)$$

$=$ using (17) and distributing using (37) and (38)

$$\bigvee_{k \in \mathbb{N}} (d \otimes \iota^k \otimes c_1) \,;\, (d \otimes c_2)$$

$=$ by Lemma 7 (pseudo-atomic-distrib-length)

$$\bigvee_{k \in \mathbb{N}} d \otimes ((\iota^k \otimes c_1) \,;\, c_2)$$

$=$ distributing using (37) and (38) and then (37) a second time

$$d \otimes ((\bigvee_{k \in \mathbb{N}} \iota^k) \otimes c_1) \,;\, c_2$$

$=$ using (17)

$$d \otimes (\iota^\star \otimes c_1) \,;\, c_2$$

    □

For the case where c is restricted to take an infinite number of steps, our distribution property holds trivially because ι^∞ left annihilates.

Lemma 9 (inf-annihilates). $(c_0^\infty \otimes c_1) \,;\, c_2 = c_0^\infty \otimes c_1$

Proof. From the fact that c_0^∞ left annihilates, $c_0^\infty = c_0^\infty \,;\, \mathsf{magic}$, and as magic equals the degenerate test, $\tau \emptyset$, we can apply (44), and the fact that magic is a left annihilator, and then reverse the steps: $(c_0^\infty \otimes c_1) \,;\, c_2 = (c_0^\infty \,;\, \mathsf{magic} \otimes c_1) \,;\, c_2 = (c_0^\infty \otimes c_1) \,;\, \mathsf{magic} = c_0^\infty \,;\, \mathsf{magic} \otimes c_1 = c_0^\infty \otimes c_1$.   □

Lemma 10 (pseudo-atomic-distrib-inf). *For pseudo-atomic fixed point d,*

$$(d \otimes \iota^\infty \otimes c_1) \,;\, (d \otimes c_2) = d \otimes ((\iota^\infty \otimes c_1) \,;\, c_2). \tag{63}$$

Proof. Applying Lemma 9 (inf-annihilates) twice, we get: $(d \otimes \iota^\infty \otimes c_1) \,;\, (d \otimes c_2) = d \otimes (\iota^\infty \otimes c_1) = d \otimes ((\iota^\infty \otimes c_1) \,;\, c_2)$.   □

The command ι^ω is the identity of $\otimes$ (31), and so from laws (24) and (8) we have for any command c,

$$c = \iota^\omega \otimes c = (\iota^\star \vee \iota^\infty) \otimes c = (\iota^\star \otimes c) \vee (\iota^\infty \otimes c).\tag{64}$$

and so distribution of pseudo-atomic-fixed points over sequential composition follow from Lemma 8 (pseudo-atomic-distrib-fin) and Lemma 10 (pseudo-atomic-distrib-inf).

Theorem 11 (pseudo-atomic-distrib-seq). *If d is a pseudo-atomic fixed point, for any commands c_1 and c_2, $d \otimes c_1 ; c_2 = (d \otimes c_1) ; (d \otimes c_2)$.*

Proof.

$$(d \otimes c_1) ; (d \otimes c_2)$$
$=$ using decomposition (64) and distributing using (8) and (42)
$$(d \otimes \iota^\star \otimes c_1) ; (d \otimes c_2) \vee (d \otimes \iota^\infty \otimes c_1) ; (d \otimes c_2)$$
$=$ by Lemma 8 (pseudo-atomic-distrib-fin) and Lemma 10
$$d \otimes ((\iota^\star \otimes c_1) ; c_2) \vee d \otimes ((\iota^\infty \otimes c_1) ; c_2)$$
$=$ distributing using (8) and (42)
$$d \otimes ((\iota^\star \otimes c_1 \vee \iota^\infty \otimes c_1) ; c_2)$$
$=$ using decomposition (64)
$$d \otimes (c_1 ; c_2)$$

$\square$

Corollaries of Theorem 11 (pseudo-atomic-distrib-seq) using Theorem 4 (distrib-fixed- iter) and Theorem 5 (distrib-finite-iter) are the following.

Corollary 12 (pseudo-atomic-distrib-fixed-iter). *If d is a pseudo-atomic fixed point then, for all $i \in \mathbb{N}$, $d \otimes c^{i+1} = (d \otimes c)^{i+1}$.*

Corollary 13 (pseudo-atomic-distrib-finite-iter). *If d is a pseudo-atomic fixed point then, $d \otimes c^\star = (d \otimes c)^\star$.*

Two pseudo-atomic fixed points synchronise to give a pseudo-atomic fixed point.

Lemma 14 (pseudo-atomic-conjunction). *If both d_1 and d_2 are pseudo-atomic fixed points, so is $d_1 \otimes d_2$.*

Proof. Because d_1 and d_2 are pseudo-atomic fixed points, for some pseudo-atomic commands z_1 and z_2, $d_1 = \tau \vee z_1 ; d_1$ and $d_2 = \tau \vee z_2 ; d_2$. Further, assuming $z_1 = \{p_1\} ; (a_1 \vee b_1 ; \frac{\prime}{\prime})$ and $z_2 = \{p_2\} ; (a_2 \vee b_2 ; \frac{\prime}{\prime})$, for some sets of states p_1 and p_2, and some atomic commands a_1, b_1, a_2 and b_2, both $z_1 ; d_1 \otimes \tau = \{p_1\} ;$ magic and $\tau \otimes z_2 ; d_2 = \{p_2\} ;$ magic by (47). Hence using (32), then (29) twice, then (45) twice, and finally (48), as follows: $d_1 \otimes d_2 = (\tau \vee z_1 ; d_1) \otimes (\tau \vee z_2 ; d_2) = \tau \vee \{p_1\} ;$ magic $\vee \{p_2\} ;$ magic $\vee (z_1 ; d_1 \otimes z_2 ; d_2) = \tau \vee \{p_1\} ; \{p_2\} ; (z_1 ; d_1 \otimes z_2 ; d_2) = \tau \vee (\{p_1\} ; z_1 \otimes \{p_2\} ; z_2) ; (d_1 \otimes d_2) = \tau \vee (z_1 \otimes z_2) ; (d_1 \otimes d_2)$. Finally, we show $z_1 \otimes z_2$ is a pseudo-atomic command because $z_1 \otimes z_2 = \{p_1\} ; (a_1 \vee b_1 ; \frac{\prime}{\prime}) \otimes \{p_2\} ; (a_2 \vee b_2 ; \frac{\prime}{\prime}) = \{p_1 \cap p_2\} ; ((a_1 \otimes a_2) \vee (a_1 \otimes b_2 \vee b_1 \otimes a_2 \vee b_1 \otimes b_2) ; \frac{\prime}{\prime})$, which is a pseudo-atomic command because atomic commands are closed under $\otimes$ and $\vee$. $\square$

5   Application to Rely/Guarantee Concurrency

To support rely/guarantee concurrency we follow the approach of Aczel [1] and record both the transitions made by a thread T (called program or π transitions) and transitions made by the environment of T (called environment or ϵ transitions) in the traces of T. The environment transitions record transitions made by any thread running in parallel with T. We make use of two atomic commands that represent program transitions by the thread, πr, and transitions by the environment of T, ϵr, for r a relation between program states. More precisely,

πr is an atomic command that can perform a single program (π) transition from state σ
   to state σ', if $(\sigma, \sigma') \in r$, and then terminate, and
ϵr is an atomic command that can perform a single environment (ϵ) transition from σ
   to σ', if $(\sigma, \sigma') \in r$, and then terminate.

The universal relation between states is denoted univ. The atomic command π can perform any single program transition (65), the atomic command ϵ can perform any single environment transition (66), the atomic command αr can perform any single transition (program or environment) satisfying r, and the atomic command α can perform any single transition (68). Note the bold fonts on the left for π, ϵ and α.

$$\pi \mathrel{\widehat{=}} \pi \, \mathsf{univ} \qquad (65) \qquad\qquad \alpha r \mathrel{\widehat{=}} \pi r \vee \epsilon r \qquad (67)$$

$$\epsilon \mathrel{\widehat{=}} \epsilon \, \mathsf{univ} \qquad (66) \qquad\qquad \alpha \mathrel{\widehat{=}} \alpha \, \mathsf{univ} \qquad (68)$$

Distributing Guarantees and Relies. A program guarantee condition g, where g is a relation between states, requires that all program transitions from σ to σ' are in g, i.e. $(\sigma, \sigma') \in g$. It places no constrains on environment transitions. A program guarantee can be encoded as a command, $\mathsf{guar}_\pi \, g$, that is defined as an iteration of the atomic command $\pi g \vee \epsilon$ (69).

$$\mathsf{guar}_\pi \, g \mathrel{\widehat{=}} (\pi g \vee \epsilon)^\omega \qquad\qquad (69)$$

A rely condition r corresponds to an assumption that all environment transitions satisfy r. It is encoded as the command, $\mathsf{rely}\, r$, that allows any transitions but aborts if the environment makes a transition not satisfying r. It is defined as an iteration of the pseudo-atomic command $\alpha \vee \epsilon \bar{r} \,;\, \lightning$, where $\bar{r}$ is the complement of the relation r (70). The rely command has an alternative equivalent form (71) because $\alpha = \pi \vee \epsilon r \vee \epsilon \bar{r}$ and $\epsilon \bar{r} \,;\, \lightning \succeq \epsilon \bar{r}$, so that $\epsilon \bar{r} \vee \epsilon \bar{r} \,;\, \lightning = \epsilon \bar{r} \,;\, \lightning$.

$$\mathsf{rely}\, r \mathrel{\widehat{=}} (\alpha \vee \epsilon \bar{r} \,;\, \lightning)^\omega \quad (70) \qquad \mathsf{rely}\, r = (\pi \vee \epsilon r \vee \epsilon \bar{r} \,;\, \lightning)^\omega \quad (71)$$

The use of abort to represent failure of a rely command is similar to the use of abort in the sequential refinement calculus to represent failure of an assertion command, $\{p\}$. Both commands encode *assumptions*: the assertion command encodes the assumption that p holds initially, and the rely command encodes the assumption that environment transitions satisfy r.

Both $\mathsf{guar}_\pi \, g$ and $\mathsf{rely}\, r$ are possibly infinite iterations of pseudo-atomic commands and hence the distributive laws detailed in the previous sections apply for distributing them with a synchronisation operator over a sequential composition by Theorem 11 (pseudo-atomic-distrib-seq) (giving (9) and (10)) and hence for parallel (giving (4) and (6)) and for weak conjunction (giving (5) and (7)), and hence they distribute via synchronisation (and hence parallel or weak conjunction) into a fixed or finite iteration by Corollary 12 (pseudo-atomic-distrib-fixed-iter) and Corollary 13 (pseudo-atomicdistrib-finite-iter), respectively.

Other Pseudo-atomic Fixed Points. The command term is the most general command that performs only a finite number of program transitions but does not constrain environment transitions (72), and the command fair is the most general command that disallows an infinite contiguous sequence of environment transitions (73).

$$\text{term} \mathrel{\widehat{=}} \alpha^* \, ; \epsilon^\omega \qquad (72) \qquad\qquad \text{fair} \mathrel{\widehat{=}} \epsilon^* \, ; (\pi \, ; \epsilon^*)^\omega \qquad (73)$$

While neither of these commands is expressed as an iteration of a (single) pseudo-atomic command, both term and fair are pseudo-atomic fixed points because they satisfy the following fixed-point equations.

$$\text{term} = \tau \lor \alpha \, ; \text{term} \qquad (74) \qquad\qquad \text{fair} = \tau \lor \alpha \, ; \text{fair} \qquad (75)$$

Hence both term and fair distribute over sequential composition and into fixed and finite iterations.

The command idle allows a finite number of program transitions that do not change the program state (i.e. they satisfy the identity relation on states, id) but does not constrain environment transitions.

$$\text{idle} \mathrel{\widehat{=}} \text{guar}_\pi \, \text{id} \Cap \text{term} \qquad (76)$$

Because both guar_π id and term are pseudo-atomic fixed points, by Lemma 14 (pseudo-atomic-conjunction) so is idle, and hence it distributes over sequential compositions and into fixed and finite iterations.

Evolution Invariants. The command, evolve r, represents an evolution invariant [3], which is useful when every transition of a command, both program and environment, is expected to satisfy a relation r. It guarantees program transitions satisfy r and relies on environment transitions satisfying r (77). Because evolve r is the conjunction of two pseudo-atomic fixed points, by Lemma 14 (pseudo-atomic-conjunction) it is a pseudo-atomic fixed point, in fact, it may be written in the form of an iteration of the pseudo-atomic command, $\pi \, r \lor \epsilon \, r \lor \epsilon \bar{r} \, ; \, \frac{1}{2}$ (78).

$$\text{evolve} \, r \mathrel{\widehat{=}} \text{guar}_\pi \, r \Cap \text{rely} \, r \qquad (77) \qquad\qquad \text{evolve} \, r = (\pi \, r \lor \epsilon \, r \lor \epsilon \bar{r} \, ; \, \tfrac{1}{2})^\omega \qquad (78)$$

Because evolution invariants are pseudo-atomic fixed points, they distribute over sequential composition and into fixed and finite iterations.

Generalised Invariants. A generalised invariant is a property that, if it holds initially, holds in every state of an execution trace [26]. The invariant command, inv p, is defined in terms of an iteration of a pseudo-atomic command (81). The pseudo-atomic command assumes p holds initially ($\{p\}$) and re-establishes p, where $\alpha \, p'$ that ensures p

holds in the final state (80). The relation $`p$ is the set of pairs of states where the first state is in p (79).

$$`p \mathrel{\widehat{=}} \{(\sigma, \sigma') . \sigma \in p\} \qquad (79) \qquad\qquad \mathsf{inv}\, p \mathrel{\widehat{=}} (\{p\} \mathbin{;} \alpha p')^{\omega} \qquad (81)$$

$$p' \mathrel{\widehat{=}} \{(\sigma, \sigma') . \sigma' \in p\} \qquad (80)$$

Because $\mathsf{inv}\, p$ is an iteration of a pseudo-atomic command and hence a pseudo-atomic fixed point, it distributes over sequential composition by Theorem 11 (pseudo-atomic-distrib-seq), and hence fixed iterations by Corollary 12 (pseudo-atomic-distrib-fixed-iter) and finite iterations by Corollary 13 (pseudo-atomic-distrib-finite-iter).

From the definition of c^{ω} as the greatest fixed point of the function $(\lambda y . \tau \vee c \mathbin{;} y)$, c^{ω} satisfies the unfolding law (82), ω-induction (83), and the leapfrog law (84) [28].

$$c^{\omega} = \tau \vee c \mathbin{;} c^{\omega} \qquad (82) \qquad\qquad (c \mathbin{;} d)^{\omega} \mathbin{;} c = c \mathbin{;} (d \mathbin{;} c)^{\omega} \qquad (84)$$

$$c^{\omega} \succeq x \ \text{ if } \ \tau \vee c \mathbin{;} x \succeq x \qquad (83)$$

Below we give two lemmas that give alternative forms for an invariant command but first we give a lemma that is needed in their proofs.

Lemma 15 (establishes-p). $(\{p\} \mathbin{;} c)^{\omega} = (\{p\} \mathbin{;} c)^{\omega} \mathbin{;} \{p\}$

Proof. The refinement from right to left holds as $\tau = \{\Sigma\} \preceq \{p\}$. The refinement from left to right holds by ω-induction (83) if, $\tau \vee \{p\} \mathbin{;} c \mathbin{;} (\{p\} \mathbin{;} c)^{\omega} \mathbin{;} \{p\} \succeq (\{p\} \mathbin{;} c)^{\omega} \mathbin{;} \{p\}$. Starting from the right side, we unfold the iteration (82), distribute using (42) and (29) twice: $(\{p\} \mathbin{;} c)^{\omega} \mathbin{;} \{p\} = (\tau \vee \{p\} \mathbin{;} c \mathbin{;} (\{p\} \mathbin{;} c)^{\omega}) \mathbin{;} \{p\} = \{p\} \vee \{p\} \mathbin{;} c \mathbin{;} (\{p\} \mathbin{;} c)^{\omega} \mathbin{;} \{p\} = \{p\} \mathbin{;} (\tau \vee c \mathbin{;} (\{p\} \mathbin{;} c)^{\omega} \mathbin{;} \{p\}) = \tau \vee \{p\} \mathbin{;} c \mathbin{;} (\{p\} \mathbin{;} c)^{\omega} \mathbin{;} \{p\}$, which equals the left side. $\square$

Lemma 16 (inv-alt). $\mathsf{inv}\, p = \{p\} \mathbin{;} (\alpha p')^{\omega}$

Proof. The proof expands the invariant definition (81), uses Lemma 15 (establishes-p), leapfrog (84), and the fact that $\alpha p'$ establishes p, i.e. $\alpha p' = \alpha p' \mathbin{;} \{p\}$, as follows: $\mathsf{inv}\, p = (\{p\} \mathbin{;} \alpha p')^{\omega} = (\{p\} \mathbin{;} \alpha p')^{\omega} \mathbin{;} \{p\} = \{p\} \mathbin{;} (\alpha p' \mathbin{;} \{p\})^{\omega} = \{p\} \mathbin{;} (\alpha p')^{\omega}$. $\square$

The relation $\overline{`p} \cup p'$ can be read: if p holds in the initial state it also holds in the final state.

Lemma 17 (inv-maintains). $\mathsf{inv}\, p = \{p\} \mathbin{;} (\alpha(\overline{`p} \cup p'))^{\omega}$

Proof. Refinement from left to right holds using the definition of an invariant (81), the fact that $\{p\} \mathbin{;} \alpha p' = \{p\} \mathbin{;} \alpha(\overline{`p} \cup p')$, applies Lemma 15 (establishes-p), then leapfrog (84), and finally removes the assertion: $\mathsf{inv}\, p = (\{p\} \mathbin{;} \alpha p')^{\omega} = (\{p\} \mathbin{;} \alpha(\overline{`p} \cup p'))^{\omega} = (\{p\} \mathbin{;} \alpha(\overline{`p} \cup p'))^{\omega} \mathbin{;} \{p\} = \{p\} \mathbin{;} (\alpha(\overline{`p} \cup p') \mathbin{;} \{p\})^{\omega} \succeq \{p\} \mathbin{;} (\alpha(\overline{`p} \cup p'))^{\omega}$.

The refinement from right to left holds by monotonicity (as $\overline{`p} \cup p' \supseteq p'$) and Lemma 16 (inv-alt): $\{p\} \mathbin{;} (\alpha(\overline{`p} \cup p'))^{\omega} \succeq \{p\} \mathbin{;} (\alpha(p'))^{\omega} = \mathsf{inv}\, p$. $\square$

An invariant can be introduced if it holds initially.

Lemma 18 (inv-introduce). $\{p\} \mathbin{;} c \succeq \mathsf{inv}\, p \mathbin{\Cap} c$

Proof. Because $(\alpha p')^{\omega}$ refines the α^{ω}, which is the identity of weak conjunction ($\Cap$), $c = \alpha^{\omega} \mathbin{\Cap} c \succeq (\alpha p')^{\omega} \mathbin{\Cap} c$. That is applied in the first step of the proof, then we apply (45), and finally Lemma 16 (inv-alt): $\{p\} \mathbin{;} c \succeq \{p\} \mathbin{;} ((\alpha p')^{\omega} \mathbin{\Cap} c) = \{p\} \mathbin{;} (\alpha p')^{\omega} \mathbin{\Cap} c = \mathsf{inv}\, p \mathbin{\Cap} c$. $\square$

6   Conclusions

Distributive laws are important in algebraic reasoning in arithmetic and logic, and they are equally important for reasoning about programs [14]. In Concurrent Kleene Algebra [15] and our earlier theory [10–12], laws for distributing over sequential composition and into iterations were only refinements in a single direction. The current paper strengthens the distributive laws to be equalities. Such strengthening requires the ability to decompose a command into an expanded form (49) in terms of its immediately terminating behaviours, its immediately aborting behaviours, and its behaviours consisting of an atomic transition followed by a continuation command. In addition, the ability to partition the reasoning about a command into its behaviours of a given length is crucial. The proofs of the strengthened distributive laws are somewhat more complex than the corresponding weak versions; they require the full power of the synchronous algebra.

The current paper focuses on distributing the abstract synchronisation operator, $\otimes$, over sequential compositions and into fixed and finite iterations. As $\otimes$ is an abstraction of both parallel composition ($\|$) and weak conjunction ($\Cap$), we immediately gain the distributive laws for both these operators. The strong distributive laws are shown to hold provided the command, d, being distributed is a pseudo-atomic fixed point. Additionally, we believe that the strong distributive laws *require* command d to be a pseudo-atomic fixed point. Examples of pseudo-atomic fixed points include rely and guarantee commands, evolution and generalised invariants, as well as the commands term and fair, all of which support reasoning in the rely/guarantee approach.

While CKA [15] and Synchronous Kleene Algebra [25] only consider partial correctness, our concurrent refinement algebra handles total correctness and hence includes infinite iteration as well as finite iteration. Further those approaches only provide weak (i.e. refinement) distributive laws, whereas our approach provides strong (i.e. equality) laws.

Our generalised invariant command was inspired by that of Morgan and Vickers [23], who introduced an invariant command in the sequential refinement calculus, with essentially the same semantics as here, that is, the invariant p is assumed initially and is maintained within the scope of the command. The main difference is that our generalised invariant command needs to deal with fine-grained concurrency. Their command has the syntax $[\![\mathsf{inv}\, p \,.\, c]\!]$, and is defined in terms of an extended weakest precondition semantics that takes an invariant (a predicate) as an additional parameter, whereas our invariant command is defined in terms of our language primitives and combined with a command using weak conjunction, an operator that is not available in their theory.

An important application of the strengthened distributive laws is for performing data refinements, where an abstract representation of a data structure is replaced by a lower-level, more efficient implementation state [20]. The invariant command (81) can be used to encode a coupling invariant for a data refinement: it relates the abstract state of a data type to the concrete implementation state. As part of proving a data refinement a (coupling) invariant is distributed into the construct being data refined, then the construct refined in that context, and finally distributing the invariant is reversed; this requires the distributive laws to be applicable in both directions.

Future Work. The iteration z^ω, in which z is a pseudo-atomic command, is a pseudo-atomic fixed point, in fact, the greatest fixed point. We believe that z^ω also satisfies both the following laws.

$$z^\omega \otimes c^\infty = (z^\omega \otimes c)^\infty \tag{85}$$
$$z^\omega \otimes c^\omega = (z^\omega \otimes c)^\omega \tag{86}$$

Note that these do not hold in general with z^ω replaced by $z^\star$ because with $z^\star$, the left sides only allow a finite number of transitions because $z^\star$ does, whereas the right sides allow an infinite number of transitions because $(z^\star \otimes c)^\omega$ allows an infinite number of iterations of $z^\star \otimes c$. Rely, guarantee and both evolution and generalised invariant commands are all defined in the form z^ω for z a pseudo-atomic command and hence laws (85) and (86) can be used for these commands.

Similar laws can be developed for distributing $\Cap$ over $\parallel$,

$$d \Cap (c_1 \parallel c_2) = (d \Cap c_1) \parallel (d \Cap c_2). \tag{87}$$

We believe this distributive law holds if d is restricted to an iteration of a pseudo-atomic command, z, for which $z = z \parallel z$. Suitable commands for d are thus $\text{guar}_\pi\, g$, evolve r, and inv p but not rely r.

Acknowledgements. Thanks are due to Joakim von Wright for introducing us to program algebra, and Callum Bannister and Dan Nathan, for feedback on ideas presented in this paper and/or contributions to the supporting Isabelle/HOL theories. Special thanks go to Cliff Jones for his continual feedback and encouragement. This work is supported by the Australian Research Council under their Discovery Program Grant No. DP190102142.

References

1. Aczel, P.H.G.: On an inference rule for parallel composition. Private communication to Cliff Jones (1983). http://homepages.cs.ncl.ac.uk/cliff.jones/publications/MSs/PHGA-traces.pdf
2. Back, R.J.R., von Wright, J.: Refinement Calculus: A Systematic Introduction. Springer, New York (1998)
3. Collette, P., Jones, C.B.: Enhancing the tractability of rely/guarantee specifications in the development of interfering operations. In: Plotkin, G., Stirling, C., Tofte, M. (eds.) Proof, Language and Interaction, chap. 10, pp. 277–307. MIT Press (2000)
4. Colvin, R.J., Hayes, I.J., Meinicke, L.A.: Designing a semantic model for a wide-spectrum language with concurrency. Formal Aspects Comput. **29**, 853–875 (2016). https://doi.org/10.1007/s00165-017-0416-4
5. Dijkstra, E.W.: Guarded commands, nondeterminacy, and a formal derivation of programs. CACM **18**, 453–458 (1975)
6. Dijkstra, E.W.: A Discipline of Programming. Prentice-Hall, Hoboken (1976)
7. Dongol, B., Hayes, I.J., Robinson, P.J.: Reasoning about goal-directed real-time teleo-reactive programs. Formal Aspects Comput. **26**(3), 563–589 (2014). https://doi.org/10.1007/s00165-012-0272-1
8. Floyd, R.W.: Assigning meanings to programs. In: Proceedings of Symposia in Applied Mathematics: Mathematical Aspects of Computer Science, vol. 19, pp. 19–32 (1967). https://doi.org/10.1090/psapm/019/0235771

9. Groves, L.: Refinement and the Z schema calculus. Electron. Notes Theor. Comput. Sci. **70**(3), 70–93 (2002)

10. Hayes, I.J.: Generalised rely-guarantee concurrency: an algebraic foundation. Formal Aspects Comput. **28**(6), 1057–1078 (2016). https://doi.org/10.1007/s00165-016-0384-0

11. Hayes, I.J., Colvin, R.J., Meinicke, L.A., Winter, K., Velykis, A.: An algebra of synchronous atomic steps. In: Fitzgerald, J., Heitmeyer, C., Gnesi, S., Philippou, A. (eds.) FM 2016. LNCS, vol. 9995, pp. 352–369. Springer, Cham (2016). https://doi.org/10.1007/978-3-319-48989-6_22

12. Hayes, I.J., Meinicke, L.A., Winter, K., Colvin, R.J.: A synchronous program algebra: a basis for reasoning about shared-memory and event-based concurrency. Formal Aspects Comput. **31**(2), 133–163 (2019). https://doi.org/10.1007/s00165-018-0464-4

13. Hoare, C.A.R.: An axiomatic basis for computer programming. Commun. ACM **12**(10), 576–580, 583 (1969). https://doi.org/10.1145/363235.363259

14. Hoare, C.A.R., et al.: Laws of programming. Commun. ACM **30**(8), 672–686 (1987). Corrigenda: CACM 30(9):770

15. Hoare, C.A.R., Möller, B., Struth, G., Wehrman, I.: Concurrent Kleene algebra and its foundations. J. Log. Algebr. Program. **80**(6), 266–296 (2011)

16. Jones, C.B.: Development methods for computer programs including a notion of interference. Ph.D. thesis, Oxford University (1981). Available as: Oxford University Computing Laboratory (now Computer Science) Technical Monograph PRG-25

17. Jones, C.B.: Specification and design of (parallel) programs. In: Proceedings of IFIP 1983, pp. 321–332. North-Holland (1983)

18. Jones, C.B.: Tentative steps toward a development method for interfering programs. ACM ToPLaS **5**(4), 596–619 (1983). https://doi.org/10.1145/69575.69577

19. Kozen, D.: Kleene algebra with tests. ACM Trans. Prog. Lang. Syst. **19**(3), 427–443 (1997)

20. Meinicke, L.A., Hayes, I.J., Jones, C.B.: Data reification in a concurrent rely-guarantee algebra (2024). arXiv:2405.05546

21. Milner, R.: Calculi for synchrony and asynchrony. Theoret. Comput. Sci. **25**(3), 267–310 (1983). https://doi.org/10.1016/0304-3975(83)90114-7

22. Morgan, C.C.: Programming from Specifications, 2nd edn. Prentice Hall, Hoboken (1994)

23. Morgan, C.C., Vickers, T.N.: Types and invariants in the refinement calculus. Sci. Comput. Program. **14**, 281–304 (1990)

24. Nipkow, T., Paulson, L.C., Wenzel, M.: Isabelle/HOL: A Proof Assistant for Higher-Order Logic. LNCS, vol. 2283. Springer, Heidelberg (2002). https://doi.org/10.1007/3-540-45949-9

25. Prisacariu, C.: Synchronous Kleene algebra. J. Logic Algebraic Program. **79**(7), 608–635 (2010)

26. Reynolds, J.C.: The Craft of Programming. Prentice/Hall International (1981)

27. Ward, N.: Adding specification constructors to the refinement calculus. In: Woodcock, J.C.P., Larsen, P.G. (eds.) FME 1993. LNCS, vol. 670, pp. 652–670. Springer, Heidelberg (1993). https://doi.org/10.1007/BFb0024672

28. Wright, J.: From Kleene algebra to refinement algebra. In: Boiten, E.A., Möller, B. (eds.) MPC 2002. LNCS, vol. 2386, pp. 233–262. Springer, Heidelberg (2002). https://doi.org/10.1007/3-540-45442-X_14

On the Formalization of the Notion of an Algorithm

Cornelis A. Middelburg$^{(\boxtimes)}$ (iD)

Informatics Institute, Faculty of Science, University of Amsterdam,
Science Park 900, 1098 XH Amsterdam, The Netherlands
C.A.Middelburg@uva.nl

Abstract. The starting point of this paper is a collection of properties of an algorithm that have been distilled from the informal descriptions of what an algorithm is that are given in standard works from the mathematical and computer science literature. Based on that, the notion of a proto-algorithm is introduced. The thought is that algorithms are equivalence classes of proto-algorithms under some equivalence relation. Three equivalence relations are defined. Two of them give bounds between which an appropriate equivalence relation must lie. The third lies in between these two and is likely an appropriate equivalence relation. A sound method is presented to prove, using an imperative process algebra based on ACP, that this equivalence relation holds between two proto-algorithms.

Keywords: Proto-algorithm · Algorithmic equivalence ·
Computational equivalence · Imperative process algebra · Algorithm
process

1 Introduction

Cliff Jones' Vienna Development Method (VDM) [14] is one of the most impactful program development methods based on formal specification and verified design. In several of his illuminating explanations of data reification and operation decomposition in VDM, Cliff uses the term algorithm for what is expressed by the result of the data reification and operation decomposition steps of a verified design. In those explanations, he can rightly rely on an intuitive understanding of what an algorithm is. However, I find it unsatisfactory that there is still no proper formalization of this central notion of computer science. This paper concerns a quest for a formalization of the notion of an algorithm.

In many works from the mathematical and computer science literature, including standard works such as [15,16,19,24], the notion of an algorithm is informally characterized by properties that are considered the most important ones of an algorithm. Most of those characterizations agree with each other and indicate that an algorithm is considered to express a pattern of behaviour by which all instances of a computational problem can be solved. A remark like "Formally, an algorithm is a Turing machine" is often made in the works concerned if additionally Turing machines are rigorously defined.

© The Author(s), under exclusive license to Springer Nature Switzerland AG 2024
A. Cavalcanti and J. Baxter (Eds.): *The Practice of Formal Methods*, LNCS 14781, pp. 23–44, 2024.
https://doi.org/10.1007/978-3-031-66673-5_2

However, the viewpoint that the formal notion of a Turing machine is a formalization of the intuitive notion of an algorithm is unsatisfactory in at least two ways: (a) a Turing machine expresses primarily a way in which a computational problem-solving pattern of behaviour can be generated and (b) a Turing machine restricts the data involved in such a pattern of behaviour to strings over some finite set of symbols. There are not many alternative formalizations of the notion of an algorithm that are regularly cited. To the best of my knowledge, the main exceptions are the ones that can be found in [12,21]. In both papers, a notion of an algorithm is formally defined that does not depend on a particular machine model such as the Turing machine model.

In [21], an algorithm is defined as a fairly complex set-theoretic object. The definition has its origins in the idea that, if a partial function is defined recursively by a system of equations, that system of equations induces an algorithm. An algorithm according to this definition fails to have many properties that are generally considered to belong to the most important ones of an algorithm.

In [12], an algorithm is defined as an object that satisfies certain postulates. The postulates concerned appear to be devised with the purpose that Gurevich's abstract state machines would satisfy them. However, this definition covers objects that have almost all properties that are generally considered to belong to the most important ones of an algorithm as well as more abstract objects that have almost none of those properties.

What is mentioned above about the formalizations of the notion of an algorithm in [12,21] makes them unsatisfactory as well. This state of affairs motivated me to start a quest for a formalization of the notion of an algorithm that is more satisfactory than the existing ones. One possibility is to investigate whether this can be done by adapting the postulates from [12] or adding postulates to them. Another possibility is to investigate whether a constructive definition can be given. This is what will be done in this paper. In addition, the connection between the resulting objects and the processes considered in the imperative process algebra presented in [20] will be investigated.

In [3], I made a first attempt to give a constructive definition. A main drawback of the approach followed there is that the data involved in an algorithm is restricted to bit strings. The idea was that this restriction could be discarded without much effort. This turned out not to be the case. Therefore, I follow a rather different approach in this paper.

2   The Informal Notion of an Algorithm

What is an algorithm? A brief answer to this question usually goes something like this: an algorithm is a procedure for solving a computational problem in a finite number of steps. This is a reasonable answer. A difficulty is that it is common to describe a computational problem informally as a problem that can be solved using an algorithm. For this reason, first a description of a computational problem that does not refer to the notion of an algorithm must be given:

A computational problem is a problem where, given an input value that belongs to a certain set, an output value that is in a certain relation to the given input value must be found if it exists. The input values that belong to the certain set are also called the instances of the problem and an output value that is in the certain relation to the given input value is also called a solution for the instance concerned.

The existing viewpoints on what an algorithm is indicate that something like the following properties are essential for an algorithm:

- an algorithm is a finite expression of a pattern of behaviour by which all instances of a computational problem can be solved;
- the pattern of behaviour expressed by an algorithm is made up of discrete steps, each of which consists of performing an elementary operation or inspecting an elementary condition unless it is the initial step or a final step;
- the pattern of behaviour expressed by an algorithm is such that there is one possible step immediately following a step that consists of performing an operation;
- the pattern of behaviour expressed by an algorithm is such that there is one possible step immediately following a step that consists of inspecting a condition for each outcome of the inspection;
- the pattern of behaviour expressed by an algorithm is such that the initial step consists of inputting an input value of the problem concerned;
- the pattern of behaviour expressed by an algorithm is such that, for each input value of the problem concerned for which a correct output value exists, a final step is reached after a finite number of steps and that final step consists of outputting a correct output value for that input value;
- the steps involved in the pattern of behaviour expressed by an algorithm are precisely and unambiguously defined and can be performed exactly in a finite amount of time.

These properties give an intuitive characterization of the notion of an algorithm and form the starting point for the formalization of this notion in upcoming sections. They have been distilled from the descriptions of what an algorithm is that are given in standard works from the mathematical and computer science literature such as [15,16,19,24]. They can also be found elsewhere in the mathematical and computer science literature and even in the philosophical literature on algorithms, see e.g. [13,22].

Usually it is also mentioned in some detail how an algorithm is generally expressed. However, usually it is mentioned at most in passing that an algorithm expresses a pattern of behaviour. Following [6], this point is central here. The reason for this is that, in order to formalize the notion of an algorithm well, it is more important to know what an algorithm expresses than how an algorithm is expressed.

Recently, discussions about the notion of an algorithm take also place in the social sciences. This leads to viewpoints on algorithms that are useless in mathematics and computer science. For example, in [26] is proposed to view algorithms as 'heterogeneous and diffuse sociotechnical systems'. Such viewpoints preclude formalization and are therefore disregarded.

It should be noted that the characterization of the notion of an algorithm given by the above-mentioned properties of an algorithm reflects a rather operational view of what an algorithm is. In a more abstract view of what an algorithm is, an algorithm expresses a collection of patterns of behaviour that are equivalent in some well-defined way. We will come back to this at the end of Sect. 3.

3   Proto-Algorithms

In this section, the notion of an proto-algorithm is introduced. The thought is that algorithms are equivalence classes of proto-algorithms under an appropriate equivalence relation. An equivalence relation that is likely an appropriate one is introduced in Sect. 4.

The notion of a proto-algorithm will be defined in terms of three auxiliary notions. The definition of one of these auxiliary notions is based on the well-known notion of a rooted labeled directed graph. However, the definitions of this notion given in the mathematical and computer science literature vary. Therefore, the definition that is used in this paper is given first.

Definition. *A rooted labeled directed graph G is a sextuple (V, E, L_v, L_e, l, r), where:*

- *V is a non-empty finite set, whose members are called the* vertices *of G;*
- *E is a subset of $V \times V$, whose members are called the* edges *of G;*
- *L_v is a countable set, whose members are called the* vertex labels *of G;*
- *L_e is a countable set, whose members are called the* edge labels *of G;*
- *l is a partial function from $V \cup E$ to $L_v \cup L_e$ such that*
    for all $v \in V$ for which $l(v)$ is defined, $l(v) \in L_v$ and
    for all $e \in E$ for which $l(e)$ is defined, $l(e) \in L_e$,
  called the labeling function *of G;*
- *$r \in V$, called the* root *of G.*

The additional graph theoretical notions defined below are also used in this paper.

Definition. *Let $G = (V, E, L_v, L_e, l, r)$ be a rooted labeled directed graph. Then a* cycle *in G is a sequence $v_1 \ldots v_{n+1} \in V^*$ such that, for all $i \in \{1, \ldots, n\}$, $(v_i, v_{i+1}) \in E$, $\mathrm{card}(\{v_1, \ldots, v_n\}) = n$, and $v_1 = v_{n+1}$. Let, moreover, $v \in V$. Then the* indegree *of v, written $\mathrm{indegree}(v)$, is $\mathrm{card}(\{v' \mid (v', v) \in E\})$ and the* outdegree *of v, written $\mathrm{outdegree}(v)$, is $\mathrm{card}(\{v' \mid (v, v') \in E\})$.*

We proceed with defining the three auxiliary notions, starting with the notion of an alphabet. This notion concerns the symbols used to refer to the operations and conditions involved in the steps of which the pattern of behaviour expressed by an algorithm is made up.

Definition. *An* alphabet Σ *is a couple* (F, P), *where:*

- *F is a countable set, whose members are called the* function symbols *of Σ;*
- *P is a countable set, whose members are called the* predicate symbols *of Σ;*
- *F and P are disjoint sets and* ini, fin $\in F$.

We write $\widetilde{F}$, where F is the set of function symbols of an alphabet, for the set $F \setminus \{\text{ini}, \text{fin}\}$.

The function symbols and predicate symbols of an alphabet refer to the operations and conditions, respectively, involved in the steps of which the pattern of behaviour expressed by an algorithm is made up. The function symbols ini and fin refer to inputting an input value and outputting an output value, respectively.

We are now ready to define the notions of a Σ-algorithm graph and a Σ-interpretation. They concern the pattern of behaviour expressed by an algorithm.

Definition. *Let $\Sigma = (F, P)$ be an alphabet. Then a Σ-algorithm graph G is a rooted labeled directed graph $(V, E, L_\mathrm{v}, L_\mathrm{e}, l, r)$ such that*

- $L_\mathrm{v} = F \cup P$;
- $L_\mathrm{e} = \{0, 1\}$;
- *for all $v \in V$:*
  - $l(v) = \text{ini}$ *iff $v = r$;*
  - *if $l(v) = \text{ini}$, then* indegree$(v) = 0$, outdegree$(v) = 1$, *and, for the unique $v' \in V$ for which $(v, v') \in E$, $l((v, v'))$ is undefined;*
  - *if $l(v) = \text{fin}$, then* indegree$(v) > 0$ *and* outdegree$(v) = 0$;
  - *if $l(v) \in \widetilde{F}$, then* indegree$(v) > 0$, outdegree$(v) = 1$, *and, for the unique $v' \in V$ for which $(v, v') \in E$, $l((v, v'))$ is undefined;*
  - *if $l(v) \in P$, then* indegree$(v) > 0$, outdegree$(v) = 2$, *and, for the unique $v' \in V$ and $v'' \in V$ with $v' \neq v''$ for which $(v, v') \in E$ and $(v, v'') \in E$, $l((v, v'))$ is defined, $l((v, v''))$ is defined, and $l((v, v')) \neq l((v, v''))$);*
- *if $v_1 \ldots v_{n+1}$ is a cycle in G, then, for some $v \in \{v_1, \ldots, v_n\}$, $l(v) \in F$.*

Σ-algorithm graphs are somewhat reminiscent of program schemes as defined, for example, in [27].

In the above definition, the condition on cycles in a Σ algorithm graph excludes infinitely many consecutive steps, each of which consists of inspecting a condition.

In the above definition, the conditions regarding the vertices of a Σ-algorithm graph correspond to the essential properties of an algorithm mentioned in Sect. 2 that concern its structure. Adding an interpretation of the symbols of the alphabet Σ to a Σ-algorithm graph yields something that has all of the mentioned essential properties of an algorithm.

Definition. *Let $\Sigma = (F, P)$ be an alphabet. Then a Σ-interpretation $\mathcal{I}$ is a quadruple $(D, D_\mathrm{in}, D_\mathrm{out}, I)$, where:*

- *D is a set, called the* main domain *of $\mathcal{I}$;*
- *D_in is a set, called the* input domain *of $\mathcal{I}$;*
- *D_out is a set, called the* output domain *of $\mathcal{I}$;*

– *I is a total function from $F \cup P$ to the set of all total computable functions from D_{in} to D, D to D_{out}, D to D or D to $\{0, 1\}$ such that:*
  • *$I(\text{ini})$ is a function from D_{in} to D;*
  • *$I(\text{fin})$ is a function from D to D_{out};*
  • *for all $f \in \widetilde{F}$, $I(f)$ is a function from D to D;*
  • *for all $p \in P$, $I(p)$ is a function from D to $\{0, 1\}$;*
– *there does not exist a $D' \subset D$ such that:*
  • *for all $d \in D_{\text{in}}$, $I(\text{ini})(d) \in D'$;*
  • *for all $f \in \widetilde{F}$, for all $d \in D'$, $I(f)(d) \in D'$.*

In the above definition, the minimality condition on D is not essential, but this condition facilitates establishing a connection between proto-algorithms and the processes considered in the imperative process algebra BPA$_{\delta\epsilon}$-I (see Sect. 6).

The pattern of behavior expressed by an algorithm can completely be represented by the combination of an alphabet Σ, a Σ-algorithm graph G, and a Σ-interpretation $\mathcal{I}$. This brings us to defining the notion of a proto-algorithm.

Definition. *A proto-algorithm A is a triple $(\Sigma, G, \mathcal{I})$, where:*

– *Σ is an alphabet, called the* alphabet *of A;*
– *G is a Σ-algorithm graph, called the* algorithm graph *of A;*
– *$\mathcal{I}$ is a Σ-interpretation, called the* interpretation *of A.*

Let $A = (\Sigma, G, \mathcal{I})$ be a proto-algorithm, where $\Sigma = (F, P)$, $G = (V, E, L_{\text{v}}, L_{\text{e}}, l, r)$, and $\mathcal{I} = (D, D_{\text{in}}, D_{\text{out}}, I)$. Then the intuition is that A is something that goes through states, where states are elements of the set $D_{\text{in}} \cup (V \times D) \cup D_{\text{out}}$. The elements of D_{in}, $V \times D$, and D_{out} are called input states, internal states, and output states, respectively. A goes from one state to the next state by making a step, it starts in an input state, and it stops in an output state. The state that A is in determines what the step to the next state consists of and what the next state is as follows:

– if A is in input state d, then the step to the next state consists of applying function $I(\text{ini})$ to d and the next state is the unique internal state (v', d') such that $(r, v') \in E$, and $I(\text{ini})(d) = d'$;
– if A is in internal state (v, d) and $l(v) \in \widetilde{F}$, then the step to the next state consists of applying function $I(l(v))$ to d and the next state is the unique internal state (v', d') such that $(v, v') \in E$, and $I(l(v))(d) = d'$;
– if A is in internal state (v, d) and $l(v) \in P$, then the step to the next state consists of applying function $I(l(v))$ to d and the next state is the unique internal state (v', d) such that $(v, v') \in E$, and $I(l(v))(d) = l((v, v'))$;
– if A is in internal state (v, d) and $l(v) = \text{fin}$, then the step to the next state consists of applying function $I(\text{fin})$ to d and the next state is the unique output state d' such that $I(\text{fin})(d) = d'$.

This informal explanation of how the state that A is in determines what the next state is, is formalized by the algorithmic step function δ_A^{a} defined in Sect. 4.

The term proto-algorithm has been chosen instead of the term algorithm because proto-algorithms are considered too concrete to be called algorithms. For example, from a mathematical point of view, it is natural to consider the behavioral patterns expressed by isomorphic proto-algorithms to be the same. Isomorphism of proto-algorithms is defined as expected.

Definition. *Let $A = (\Sigma, G, \mathcal{I})$ and $A' = (\Sigma', G', \mathcal{I}')$ be proto-algorithms, where $\Sigma = (F, P)$, $\Sigma' = (F', P')$, $G = (V, E, L_v, L_e, l, r)$, $G' = (V', E', L'_v, L'_e, l', r')$, $\mathcal{I} = (D, D_{in}, D_{out}, I)$, and $\mathcal{I}' = (D', D'_{in}, D'_{out}, I')$. Then A and A' are isomorphic, written $A \cong A'$, if there exist bijections $\beta_f : F \to F'$, $\beta_p : P \to P'$, $\beta_v : V \to V'$, $\beta_d : D \to D'$, $\beta_i : D_{in} \to D'_{in}$, $\beta_o : D_{out} \to D'_{out}$, and $\beta_b : \{0,1\} \to \{0,1\}$ such that:*

- *$\beta_f(\mathsf{ini}) = \mathsf{ini}$ and $\beta_f(\mathsf{fin}) = \mathsf{fin}$;*
- *for all $v, v' \in V$, $(v, v') \in E$ iff $(\beta_v(v), \beta_v(v')) \in E'$;*
- *for all $v \in V$ with $l(v) \in F$, $\beta_f(l(v)) = l'(\beta_v(v))$;*
- *for all $v \in V$ with $l(v) \in P$, $\beta_p(l(v)) = l'(\beta_v(v))$;*
- *for all $(v, v') \in E$ with $l((v, v'))$ is defined, $\beta_b(l((v, v'))) = l'((\beta_v(v), \beta_v(v')))$;*
- *for all $d \in D_{in}$, $\beta_d(I(\mathsf{ini})(d)) = I'(\mathsf{ini})(\beta_i(d))$;*
- *for all $d \in D$, $\beta_o(I(\mathsf{fin})(d)) = I'(\mathsf{fin})(\beta_d(d))$;*
- *for all $d \in D$ and $f \in \widetilde{F}$, $\beta_d(I(f)(d)) = I'(\beta_f(f))(\beta_d(d))$;*
- *for all $d \in D$ and $p \in P$, $\beta_b(I(p)(d)) = I'(\beta_p(p))(\beta_d(d))$.*

Proto-algorithms may also be considered too concrete in a way not covered by isomorphism of proto-algorithms. This issue is addressed in Sect. 4 and leads there to the introduction of two other equivalence relations. Although it is intuitive clear what isomorphism of proto-algorithms is, its precise definition is not easy to memorize. The equivalence relations that are given in Sect. 4 may be easier to memorize.

A proto-algorithm could also be defined as a quadruple $(D, D_{in}, D_{out}, \overline{G})$ where $\overline{G}$ is a graph that differs from a Σ-algorithm graph in that its vertex labels are computable functions from D_{in} to D, D to D_{out}, D to D or D to $\{0,1\}$ instead of function and predicate symbols from Σ. I consider the definition of a proto-algorithm given earlier more insightful because it isolates as much as possible the operations to be performed and the conditions to be inspected from its structure.

4   Algorithmic and Computational Equivalence

In Sect. 3, the intuition was given that a proto-algorithm A is something that goes through states. It was informally explained how the state that it is in determines what the next state is. The algorithmic step function δ_A^a that is defined below formalizes this. The computational step function δ_A^c that is also defined below is like the algorithmic step function δ_A^a, but conceals the steps that consist of inspecting conditions.

Definition. Let $A = (\Sigma, G, \mathcal{I})$ be a proto-algorithm, where $\Sigma = (F, P)$, $G = (V, E, L_v, L_e, l, r)$, and $\mathcal{I} = (D, D_{in}, D_{out}, I)$. Then the algorithmic step function δ_A^a induced by A is the unary total function on the set $D_{in} \cup (V \times D) \cup D_{out}$ defined by:

$$\begin{aligned}
\delta_A^a(d) &= (v', d') \text{ if } d \in D_{in}, \ (r, v') \in E, \text{ and } I(\text{ini})(d) = d'; \\
\delta_A^a((v, d)) &= (v', d') \text{ if } l(v) = o, \ o \in \widetilde{F}, \ (v, v') \in E, \text{ and } I(o)(d) = d'; \\
\delta_A^a((v, d)) &= (v', d) \text{ if } l(v) = p, \ p \in P, \ (v, v') \in E, \text{ and } I(p)(d) = l((v, v')); \\
\delta_A^a((v, d)) &= d' \quad\quad \text{ if } l(v) = \text{fin} \text{ and } I(\text{fin})(d) = d'; \\
\delta_A^a(d) &= d \quad\quad\ \text{ if } d \in D_{out};
\end{aligned}$$

and the computational step function δ_A^c induced by A is the unary total function on the set $D_{in} \cup (V \times D) \cup D_{out}$ defined by:

$$\begin{aligned}
\delta_A^c(d) &= (v', d') \quad\ \text{ if } d \in D_{in}, \ (r, v') \in E, \text{ and } I(\text{ini})(d) = d'; \\
\delta_A^c((v, d)) &= (v', d') \quad\ \text{ if } l(v) = o, \ o \in \widetilde{F}, \ (v, v') \in E, \text{ and } I(o)(d) = d'; \\
\delta_A^c((v, d)) &= \delta_A^c((v', d)) \text{ if } l(v) = p, \ p \in P, \ (v, v') \in E, \text{ and } I(p)(d) = l((v, v')); \\
\delta_A^c((v, d)) &= d' \quad\quad\quad \text{ if } l(v) = \text{fin} \text{ and } I(\text{fin})(d) = d'; \\
\delta_A^c(d) &= d \quad\quad\quad\ \ \text{ if } d \in D_{out}.
\end{aligned}$$

If a proto-algorithm A' can mimic a proto-algorithm A step-by-step, then we say that A is algorithmically simulated by A'. If the steps that consist of inspecting conditions are ignored, then we say that A is computationally simulated by A'. Algorithmic and computational simulation can be formally defined using the step functions defined above.

Definition. Let $A = (\Sigma, G, \mathcal{I})$ and $A' = (\Sigma', G', \mathcal{I}')$ be two proto-algorithms, where $G = (V, E, L_v, L_e, l, r)$, $G' = (V', E', L_v', L_e', l', r')$, $\mathcal{I} = (D, D_{in}, D_{out}, I)$, and $\mathcal{I}' = (D', D_{in}', D_{out}', I')$. Then an algorithmic simulation of A by A' is a set $R \subseteq (D_{in} \times D_{in}') \cup ((V \times D) \times (V' \times D')) \cup (D_{out} \times D_{out}')$ such that:

if $d \in D_{in}$,   then there exists a unique $d' \in D_{in}'$ such that $(d, d') \in R$;

if $d' \in D_{out}'$,   then there exists a unique $d \in D_{out}$ such that $(d, d') \in R$;

if $(d, d') \in R$, then $(\delta_A^a(d), \delta_{A'}^a(d')) \in R$;

and a computational simulation of A by A' is a set $R \subseteq (D_{in} \times D_{in}') \cup ((V \times D) \times (V' \times D')) \cup (D_{out} \times D_{out}')$ such that:

if $d \in D_{in}$,   then there exists a unique $d' \in D_{in}'$ such that $(d, d') \in R$;

if $d' \in D_{out}'$,   then there exists a unique $d \in D_{out}$ such that $(d, d') \in R$;

if $(d, d') \in R$, then $(\delta_A^c(d), \delta_{A'}^c(d')) \in R$.

A is algorithmically simulated by A', written $A \sqsubseteq_a A'$, if there exists an algorithmic simulation of A by A'.

A is computationally simulated by A', written $A \sqsubseteq_c A'$, if there exists a computational simulation of A by A'.

A is algorithmically equivalent to A', written $A \equiv_a A'$, if $A \sqsubseteq_a A'$ and $A' \sqsubseteq_a A$.

A is computationally equivalent to A', written $A \equiv_c A'$, if $A \sqsubseteq_c A'$ and $A' \sqsubseteq_c A$.

The following theorem tells us how isomorphism, algorithmic equivalence, and computational equivalence are related.

Theorem 1. *Let A and A' be proto-algorithms. Then:*

(1) $A \cong A'$ only if $A \equiv_a A'$ *(2) $A \equiv_a A'$ only if $A \equiv_c A'$.*

Proof. Let $A = (\Sigma, G, \mathcal{I})$ and $A' = (\Sigma', G', \mathcal{I}')$ be proto-algorithms, where $\Sigma = (F, P)$, $\Sigma' = (F', P')$, $G = (V, E, L_v, L_e, l, r)$, $G' = (V', E', L'_v, L'_e, l', r')$, $\mathcal{I} = (D, D_{in}, D_{out}, I)$, and $\mathcal{I}' = (D', D'_{in}, D'_{out}, I')$.

Part 1. Let β_v, β_d, β_i, and β_o be as in the definition of $\cong$, and let β be the bijection from $D_{in} \cup (V \times D) \cup D_{out}$ to $D'_{in} \cup (V' \times D') \cup D'_{out}$ defined by: $\beta(d) = \beta_i(d)$ if $d \in D_{in}$, $\beta((v, d)) = (\beta_v(v), \beta_d(d))$, and $\beta(d) = \beta_o(d)$ if $d \in D_{out}$. It is easy to show that, for all $d \in D_{in} \cup (V \times D) \cup D_{out}$, $\beta(\delta_A^a(d)) = \delta_{A'}^a(\beta(d))$. It immediately follows that the set $\{(\delta_A^{a\,n}(d), \beta(\delta_A^{a\,n}(d))) \mid d \in D_{in} \wedge n \in \mathbb{N}\}$ is an algorithmic simulation of A by A'.[1] Hence, $A \sqsubseteq_a A'$. The proof of $A' \sqsubseteq_a A$ is done in the same way.

Part 2. Because $A \equiv_a A'$, there exists an algorithmic simulation of A by A'. Let R be an algorithmic simulation of A by A'. Then it is easy to show that, for all $(d, d') \in R$, $(\delta_A^c(d), \delta_{A'}^c(d')) \in R$. It immediately follows that R is also a computational simulation of A by A'. Hence, $A \sqsubseteq_c A'$. The proof of $A' \sqsubseteq_c A$ is done in the same way.   □

We do not have that $A \cong A'$ if $A \equiv_a A'$. The following example illustrates this. Take proto-algorithms $A = (\Sigma, G, \mathcal{I})$ and $A' = (\Sigma, G', \mathcal{I})$ where:

- G contains edges (v_1, v'_1), (v'_1, v''), (v_2, v'_2), and (v'_2, v'') where the vertices v'_1 and v'_2 are labeled by the same function symbol;
- G' is obtained from G by replacing the edge (v_2, v'_2) by (v_2, v'_1) and removing the edge (v'_2, v'').

Clearly, A and A' are algorithmically equivalent, but not isomorphic.

We also do not have $A \equiv_a A'$ if $A \equiv_c A'$. The following example illustrates this. Take proto-algorithms $A = (\Sigma, G, \mathcal{I})$ and $A' = (\Sigma, G', \mathcal{I})$ where:

- G contains a cycle in which only one vertex occurs that is labeled by a predicate symbol p and the outgoing edge of this vertex that is not part of the cycle is labeled by 1;
- G' is obtained from G by adding immediately before the cycle a copy of the cycle in which the predicate symbol p is replaced by a predicate symbol p' whose interpretation yields 1 whenever the interpretation of p yields 1.

It is easy to see that A and A' are computationally equivalent, but not algorithmically equivalent.

---

[1] The notation $\delta_A^{a\,n}(d)$, where $n \in \mathbb{N}$, is used for the n-fold application of δ_A^a to d, i.e. $\delta_A^{a\,0}(d) = d$ and $\delta_A^{a\,n+1}(d) = \delta^a(\delta_A^{a\,n}(d))$.

The definition of algorithmic equivalence suggests that the patterns of behaviour expressed by algorithmically equivalent proto-algorithms must be considered the same. This suggests in turn that algorithms are equivalence classes of proto-algorithms under algorithmic equivalence.

If two proto-algorithms are computationally equivalent, then, for each input value, they lead to the same sequence of operations being performed. The point of view should not be taken that the patterns of behaviour expressed by computationally equivalent proto-algorithms are the same: the steps that consist of inspecting a condition are treated as if they do not belong to the patterns of behaviour.

The relevance of the computational equivalence relation is that any equivalence relation that captures the sameness of the patterns of behaviour expressed by proto-algorithms to a higher degree than the algorithmic equivalence relation must be finer than the computational equivalence relation.

Definition. *Let $A = (\Sigma, G, \mathcal{I})$ be a proto-algorithm, where $\Sigma = (F, P)$, $G = (V, E, L_{\mathrm{v}}, L_{\mathrm{e}}, l, r)$, and $\mathcal{I} = (D, D_{\mathrm{in}}, D_{\mathrm{out}}, I)$. Then the function $\widehat{A}$ computed by A is the partial function from D_{in} to D_{out} defined by $\widehat{A}(d) = \delta_A^{\mathrm{a}*}(d)$, where $\delta_A^{\mathrm{a}*}$ is the least-defined unary partial function on $D_{\mathrm{in}} \cup (V \times D) \cup D_{\mathrm{out}}$ satisfying*

$$\delta_A^{\mathrm{a}*}(d) = \delta_A^{\mathrm{a}*}(\delta_A^{\mathrm{a}}(d)) \ \ \textit{if } \delta_A^{\mathrm{a}}(d) \in V \times D;$$
$$\delta_A^{\mathrm{a}*}(d) = \delta_A^{\mathrm{a}}(d) \qquad \textit{if } \delta_A^{\mathrm{a}}(d) \in D_{\mathrm{out}}.$$

Let, moreover, $d \in D_{\mathrm{in}}$ be such that $\widehat{A}(d)$ is defined. Then the number of algorithmic steps to compute $\widehat{A}(d)$ by A, written $\#_{\mathrm{astep}}(A, d)$, is the smallest $n \in \mathbb{N}$ such that $\delta_A^{\mathrm{a}\,n}(d) = \widehat{A}(d)$.

The following theorem tells us that, if a proto-algorithm A is simulated by a proto-algorithm A', then (a) the function computed by A' models the function computed by A (in the sense of e.g. [14]) and (b) for each input value for which A eventually outputs an output value, A' does so in the same number of algorithmic steps.

Theorem 2. *Let $A = (\Sigma, G, \mathcal{I})$ and $A' = (\Sigma', G', \mathcal{I}')$ be proto-algorithms, where $\mathcal{I} = (D, D_{\mathrm{in}}, D_{\mathrm{out}}, I)$ and $\mathcal{I}' = (D', D'_{\mathrm{in}}, D'_{\mathrm{out}}, I')$. Then $A \sqsubseteq_{\mathrm{a}} A'$ only if there exist total functions $\gamma_{\mathrm{i}} : D_{\mathrm{in}} \to D'_{\mathrm{in}}$ and $\gamma_{\mathrm{o}} : D'_{\mathrm{out}} \to D_{\mathrm{out}}$ such that:*

(1) for all $d \in D_{\mathrm{in}}$, $\widehat{A}(d)$ is defined only if $\widehat{A'}(\gamma_{\mathrm{i}}(d))$ is defined;
(2) for all $d \in D_{\mathrm{in}}$ and $d' \in D_{\mathrm{out}}$, $\widehat{A}(d) = d'$ only if $\gamma_{\mathrm{o}}(\widehat{A'}(\gamma_{\mathrm{i}}(d))) = d'$;
(3) for all $d \in D_{\mathrm{in}}$ such that $\widehat{A}(d)$ is defined, $\#_{\mathrm{astep}}(A, d) = \#_{\mathrm{astep}}(A', \gamma_{\mathrm{i}}(d))$.

Proof. Because $A \sqsubseteq_{\mathrm{a}} A'$, there exists an algorithmic simulation of A by A'. Let R be an algorithmic simulation of A by A', let γ_{i} be the unique function from D_{in} to D'_{in} such that, for all $d \in D_{\mathrm{in}}$, $(d, \gamma_{\mathrm{i}}(d)) \in R$, and let γ_{o} be the unique function from D'_{out} to D_{out} such that, for all $d' \in D'_{\mathrm{out}}$, $(\gamma_{\mathrm{o}}(d'), d') \in R$. From the definition of an algorithmic simulation, it follows immediately that, for all $d \in D_{\mathrm{in}}$, for all $n \in \mathbb{N}$, $(\delta_A^{\mathrm{a}\,n}(d), \delta_{A'}^{\mathrm{a}\,n}(\gamma_{\mathrm{i}}(d))) \in R$. From this result and the definition of an algorithmic simulation, it follows immediately that, for all $d \in D_{\mathrm{in}}$, for all $n \in \mathbb{N}$:

(a) $\delta_A^{\mathrm{a}\,n}(d) \in D_{\mathrm{out}}$ iff $\delta_{A'}^{\mathrm{a}\,n}(\gamma_{\mathrm{i}}(d)) \in D'_{\mathrm{out}}$;

(b) for all $d' \in D_{\mathrm{out}}$, $\delta_A^{\mathrm{a}\,n}(d) = d'$ iff there exists a $d'' \in D'_{\mathrm{out}}$ such that $\delta_{A'}^{\mathrm{a}\,n}(\gamma_{\mathrm{i}}(d)) = d''$ and $\gamma_{\mathrm{o}}(d'') = d'$.

By the definition of the function computed by a proto-algorithm, we have that $\widehat{A}(d)$ is defined iff there exists an $n \in \mathbb{N}$ such that $\delta_A^{\mathrm{a}\,n}(d) \in D_{\mathrm{out}}$ and that $\widehat{A'}(\gamma_{\mathrm{i}}(d))$ is defined iff there exists an $n \in \mathbb{N}$ such that $\delta_{A'}^{\mathrm{a}\,n}(\gamma_{\mathrm{i}}(d)) \in D'_{\mathrm{out}}$. From this and (a), (1) follows immediately.

By the definition of the function computed by a proto-algorithm, we have that $\widehat{A}(d) = d'$ iff there exists an $n \in \mathbb{N}$ such that $\delta_A^{\mathrm{a}\,n}(d) = d'$ and that $\widehat{A'}(\gamma_{\mathrm{i}}(d)) = d''$ iff there exists an $n \in \mathbb{N}$ such that $\delta_{A'}^{\mathrm{a}\,n}(\gamma_{\mathrm{i}}(d)) = d''$. From this and (b), (2) follows immediately.

By the definition of $\#_{\mathrm{astep}}$ and (a), (3) also follows immediately.   □

It is easy to see that, for all $d \in D_{\mathrm{in}}$, $\widehat{A}(d) = \delta_A^{\mathrm{c}\,*}(d)$, where $\delta_A^{\mathrm{c}\,*}$ is the least-defined unary partial function on $D_{\mathrm{in}} \cup (V \times D) \cup D_{\mathrm{out}}$ satisfying

$$\delta_A^{\mathrm{c}\,*}(d) = \delta_A^{\mathrm{c}\,*}(\delta_A^{\mathrm{c}}(d)) \text{ if } \delta_A^{\mathrm{c}}(d) \in V \times D;$$
$$\delta_A^{\mathrm{c}\,*}(d) = \delta_A^{\mathrm{c}}(d) \qquad \text{ if } \delta_A^{\mathrm{c}}(d) \in D_{\mathrm{out}}.$$

This means that Theorem 2 goes through as far as (1) and (2) are concerned if algorithmic simulation is replaced by computational simulation. It follows immediately from the example of computationally equivalent proto-algorithms given earlier that (3) does not go through if algorithmic simulation is replaced by computational simulation.

5   The Imperative Process Algebra BPA$_{\delta\epsilon}$-I

In Sect. 6, a connection is made between proto-algorithms and the processes that are considered in the imperative process algebra BPA$_{\delta\epsilon}$-I. In this section, a short survey of BPA$_{\delta\epsilon}$-I and recursion in the setting of BPA$_{\delta\epsilon}$-I is given. The constants and operators of the algebraic theory BPA$_{\delta\epsilon}$-I and the additional constants of its extension with recursion are discussed. The axioms of BPA$_{\delta\epsilon}$-I are given in the Appendix. BPA$_{\delta\epsilon}$-I is a subtheory of ACP$_\epsilon^\tau$-I. In [20], a comprehensive treatment of ACP$_\epsilon^\tau$-I can be found. The axioms of BPA$_{\delta\epsilon}$-I are the axioms of ACP$_\epsilon^\tau$-I in which only constants and operators of BPA$_{\delta\epsilon}$-I occur. The additional axioms of the extension of BPA$_{\delta\epsilon}$-I with recursion are simply the additional axioms of the extension of ACP$_\epsilon^\tau$-I with recursion.

5.1   BPA with Inaction and Empty Process

First, a short survey of BPA$_{\delta\epsilon}$ is given. BPA$_{\delta\epsilon}$ is the version of BPA with inaction and empty process constants that was first presented in [1, Section 2.2]. In Sect. 5.2, BPA$_{\delta\epsilon}$-I will be introduced as an extension of BPA$_{\delta\epsilon}$.

In BPA$_{\delta\epsilon}$, it is assumed that a fixed but arbitrary finite set A of *basic actions*, with $\delta, \epsilon \notin \mathsf{A}$, has been given. Basic actions are taken as atomic processes.

The algebraic theory $\mathrm{BPA}_{\delta\epsilon}$ has one sort: the sort $\mathbf{P}$ of *processes*. This sort is made explicit to anticipate the need for many-sortedness later on. The algebraic theory $\mathrm{BPA}_{\delta\epsilon}$ has the following constants and operators to build terms of sort $\mathbf{P}$:

- a *basic action* constant $a : \mathbf{P}$ for each $a \in \mathsf{A}$;
- an *inaction* constant $\delta : \mathbf{P}$;
- an *empty process* constant $\epsilon : \mathbf{P}$;
- a binary *alternative composition* or *choice* operator $+ : \mathbf{P} \times \mathbf{P} \to \mathbf{P}$;
- a binary *sequential composition* operator $\cdot : \mathbf{P} \times \mathbf{P} \to \mathbf{P}$.

It is assumed that there is a countably infinite set $\mathcal{X}$ of variables of sort $\mathbf{P}$, which contains x, y and z. Terms are built as usual. Infix notation is used for the operators $+$ and $\cdot$. The following precedence convention are used to reduce the need for parentheses: the operator $\cdot$ binds stronger than the operator $+$.

The constants a ($a \in \mathsf{A}$), ϵ, and δ can be explained as follows: (a) a denotes the process that first performs the action a and then terminates successfully, (b) ϵ denotes the process that terminates successfully without performing any action, and (c) δ denotes the process that cannot do anything, it cannot even terminate successfully.

Let t and t' be closed $\mathrm{BPA}_{\delta\epsilon}$ terms. Then the operators $+$ and $\cdot$ can be explained as follows: (a) $t + t'$ denotes the process that behaves as the process denoted by t or as the process denoted by t', where the choice between the two is resolved at the instant that one of them does something, and (b) $t \cdot t'$ denotes the process that first behaves as the process denoted by t and following successful termination of that process behaves as the process denoted by t'.

5.2   Imperative $\mathrm{BPA}_{\delta\epsilon}$

$\mathrm{BPA}_{\delta\epsilon}$-I, imperative $\mathrm{BPA}_{\delta\epsilon}$, extends $\mathrm{BPA}_{\delta\epsilon}$ with features to change data involved in a process in the course of the process and to proceed at certain stages of a process in a way that depends on the changing data.

In $\mathrm{BPA}_{\delta\epsilon}$-I, it is assumed that the following has been given with respect to data:

- a many-sorted signature $\Sigma_{\mathfrak{D}}$ that includes:
  - a sort $\mathbf{D}$ of *data* and a sort $\mathbf{B}$ of *bits*;
  - constants of sort $\mathbf{D}$ and/or operators with result sort $\mathbf{D}$;
  - constants 0 and 1 of sort $\mathbf{B}$ and operators with result sort $\mathbf{B}$;
- a minimal algebra $\mathfrak{D}$ of signature $\Sigma_{\mathfrak{D}}$ in which the carrier of sort $\mathbf{B}$ has cardinality 2 and the equation $0 = 1$ does not hold.

We write $\mathbb{D}$ for the set of all closed terms over the signature $\Sigma_{\mathfrak{D}}$ of sort $\mathbf{D}$.

In $\mathrm{BPA}_{\delta\epsilon}$-I, it is moreover assumed that a finite or countably infinite set $\mathcal{V}$ of *flexible variables* has been given. A flexible variable is a variable whose value may change in the course of a process.[2]

---

[2] The term flexible variable is used for this kind of variables in e.g. [17,25].

A *flexible variable valuation* is a total function from $\mathcal{V}$ to $\mathbb{D}$. We write $\mathcal{VVal}$ for the set of all flexible variable valuations.

Flexible variable valuations provide closed terms from $\mathbb{D}$ that denote the members of $\mathfrak{D}$'s carrier of sort $\mathbf{D}$ assigned to flexible variables when a $\mathrm{BPA}_{\delta\epsilon}$-I term of sort $\mathbf{D}$ is evaluated. Because $\mathfrak{D}$ is a minimal algebra, each member of $\mathfrak{D}$'s carrier of sort $\mathbf{D}$ can be represented by a term from $\mathbb{D}$. We write d, where d is a member of $\mathfrak{D}$'s carrier of sort $\mathbf{D}$, for a fixed but arbitrary term from $\mathbb{D}$ representing d when it is clear from the context that a term from $\mathbb{D}$ is expected.

$\mathrm{BPA}_{\delta\epsilon}$-I has the following sorts: the sorts included in $\Sigma_{\mathfrak{D}}$, the sort $\mathbf{C}$ of *conditions*, and the sort $\mathbf{P}$ of *processes*.

For each sort s included in $\Sigma_{\mathfrak{D}}$ other than $\mathbf{D}$, $\mathrm{BPA}_{\delta\epsilon}$-I has only the constants and operators included in $\Sigma_{\mathfrak{D}}$ to build terms of sort s.

$\mathrm{BPA}_{\delta\epsilon}$-I has, in addition to the constants and operators included in $\Sigma_{\mathfrak{D}}$ to build terms of sorts $\mathbf{D}$, the following constants to build terms of sort $\mathbf{D}$:

– for each $v \in \mathcal{V}$, the *flexible variable* constant $v : \mathbf{D}$.

We write $\mathcal{D}$ for the set of all closed $\mathrm{BPA}_{\delta\epsilon}$-I terms of sort $\mathbf{D}$.

$\mathrm{BPA}_{\delta\epsilon}$-I has the following constants and operators to build terms of sort $\mathbf{C}$:

– a binary *equality* operator $= : \mathbf{B} \times \mathbf{B} \rightarrow \mathbf{C}$;
– a binary *equality* operator $= : \mathbf{D} \times \mathbf{D} \rightarrow \mathbf{C}$;[3]
– a *truth* constant $\mathsf{t} : \mathbf{C}$;
– a *falsity* constant $\mathsf{f} : \mathbf{C}$;
– a unary *negation* operator $\neg : \mathbf{C} \rightarrow \mathbf{C}$;
– a binary *conjunction* operator $\wedge : \mathbf{C} \times \mathbf{C} \rightarrow \mathbf{C}$;
– a binary *disjunction* operator $\vee : \mathbf{C} \times \mathbf{C} \rightarrow \mathbf{C}$;
– a binary *implication* operator $\Rightarrow : \mathbf{C} \times \mathbf{C} \rightarrow \mathbf{C}$;

We write $\mathcal{C}$ for the set of all closed $\mathrm{BPA}_{\delta\epsilon}$-I terms of sort $\mathbf{C}$.

$\mathrm{BPA}_{\delta\epsilon}$-I has, in addition to the constants and operators of $\mathrm{BPA}_{\delta\epsilon}$, the following operators to build terms of sort $\mathbf{P}$:

– a unary *assignment action* operator $:=_v : \mathbf{D} \rightarrow \mathbf{P}$ for each $v \in \mathcal{V}$;
– a binary *guarded command* operator $:\rightarrow\, : \mathbf{C} \times \mathbf{P} \rightarrow \mathbf{P}$;
– a unary *evaluation* operator $\mathsf{V}_\rho : \mathbf{P} \rightarrow \mathbf{P}$ for each $\rho \in \mathcal{VVal}$.

We write $\mathcal{P}$ for the set of all closed $\mathrm{BPA}_{\delta\epsilon}$-I terms of sort $\mathbf{P}$.

It is assumed that there are countably infinite sets of variables of sort $\mathbf{D}$ and $\mathbf{C}$ and that the sets of variables of sort $\mathbf{D}$, $\mathbf{C}$, and $\mathbf{P}$ are mutually disjoint and disjoint from $\mathcal{V}$.

The same notational conventions are used as before. Infix notation is also used for the additional binary operators. Moreover, the notation $[v := e]$, where $v \in \mathcal{V}$ and e is a $\mathrm{BPA}_{\delta\epsilon}$-I term of sort $\mathbf{D}$, is used for the term $:=_v(e)$.

Each term from $\mathcal{C}$ can be taken as a formula of a first-order language with equality of $\mathfrak{D}$ by taking the flexible variable constants as variables of sort $\mathbf{D}$. The

---

[3] The overloading of $=$ can be trivially resolved if $\Sigma_{\mathfrak{D}}$ is without overloaded symbols.

flexible variable constants are implicitly taken as variables of sort **D** wherever the context asks for a formula. In this way, each term from $\mathcal{C}$ can be interpreted in $\mathfrak{D}$ as a formula.

The notation $\phi \Leftrightarrow \psi$, where ϕ and ψ are $\mathrm{BPA}_{\delta\epsilon}$-I terms of sort **C**, is used for the term $(\phi \Rightarrow \psi) \wedge (\psi \Rightarrow \phi)$. The axioms of $\mathrm{BPA}_{\delta\epsilon}$-I include an equation $\phi = \psi$ for each two terms ϕ and ψ from $\mathcal{C}$ for which the formula $\phi \Leftrightarrow \psi$ holds in $\mathfrak{D}$.

Let e be a term from $\mathcal{D}$, ϕ be a term from $\mathcal{C}$, and t be a term from $\mathcal{P}$. Then the additional operators to build terms of sort **P** can be explained as follows:

- the term $[v := e]$ denotes the process that first performs the assignment action $[v := e]$, whose intended effect is the assignment of the result of evaluating e to flexible variable v, and then terminates successfully;
- the term $\phi :\rightarrow t$ denotes the process that behaves as the process denoted by t if condition ϕ holds and as δ otherwise;
- the term $\mathsf{V}_\rho(t)$ denotes the process that behaves as the process denoted by t, except that each subterm of t that belongs to $\mathcal{D}$ is evaluated using flexible variable valuation ρ updated according to the assignment actions that have taken place at the point where the subterm is encountered.

Below will be referred to the subset $\mathcal{A}$ of $\mathcal{P}$ that consists of the terms from $\mathcal{P}$ that denote the processes that are considered to be atomic.

$\mathcal{A}$ is defined as follows: $\mathcal{A} = \mathsf{A} \cup \{[v := e] \mid v \in \mathcal{V} \wedge e \in \mathcal{D}\}$.

5.3 $\mathrm{BPA}_{\delta\epsilon}$-I with Recursion

In this section, recursion in the setting of $\mathrm{BPA}_{\delta\epsilon}$-I is treated. A closed $\mathrm{BPA}_{\delta\epsilon}$-I term of sort **P** denotes a process with a finite upper bound to the number of actions that it can perform. Recursion allows the description of processes without a finite upper bound to the number of actions that it can perform.

A *recursive specification* over $\mathrm{BPA}_{\delta\epsilon}$-I is a set $\{X = t_X \mid X \in V\}$ of *recursion equations*, where V is a subset of $\mathcal{X}$ and each t_X is a $\mathrm{BPA}_{\delta\epsilon}$-I term of sort **P** in which only variables from V occur. We write $\mathrm{vars}(S)$, where S is a recursive specification over $\mathrm{BPA}_{\delta\epsilon}$-I, for the set of all variables that occur in S.

A *solution* of a recursive specification S over $\mathrm{BPA}_{\delta\epsilon}$-I in some model of $\mathrm{BPA}_{\delta\epsilon}$-I is a set $\{p_X \mid X \in \mathrm{vars}(S)\}$ of elements of the carrier of sort **P** in that model such that each equation in S holds if, for all $X \in \mathrm{vars}(S)$, X is assigned p_X. If $\{p_X \mid X \in \mathrm{vars}(S)\}$ is a solution of a recursive specification S, then, for each $X \in \mathrm{vars}(S)$, p_X is called the X-*component* of that solution of S. Each recursive specification over $\mathrm{BPA}_{\delta\epsilon}$-I that has a unique solution in the model of $\mathrm{BPA}_{\delta\epsilon}$-I given in [20] can be rewritten to a recursive specification in which the right-hand sides of equations are linear $\mathrm{BPA}_{\delta\epsilon}$-I terms.

The set $\mathcal{L}$ of *linear* $\mathrm{BPA}_{\delta\epsilon}$-I *terms* is inductively defined by the following rules:

- $\delta \in \mathcal{L}$;
- if $\phi \in \mathcal{C}$, then $\phi :\rightarrow \epsilon \in \mathcal{L}$;
- if $\phi \in \mathcal{C}$, $\alpha \in \mathcal{A}$, and $X \in \mathcal{X}$, then $\phi :\rightarrow \alpha \cdot X \in \mathcal{L}$;
- if $t, t' \in \mathcal{L} \setminus \{\delta\}$, then $t + t' \in \mathcal{L}$.

A *linear recursive specification* over $\text{BPA}_{\delta\epsilon}$-I is a recursive specification $\{X = t_X \mid X \in V\}$ over $\text{BPA}_{\delta\epsilon}$-I where each $t_X \in \mathcal{L}$.

$\text{BPA}_{\delta\epsilon}$-I is extended with recursion by adding constants for solutions of linear recursive specifications over $\text{BPA}_{\delta\epsilon}$-I and axioms concerning these additional constants. For each linear recursive specification S over $\text{BPA}_{\delta\epsilon}$-I and each $X \in \text{vars}(S)$, a constant $\langle X|S \rangle$ of sort $\mathbf{P}$ is added to the constants of $\text{BPA}_{\delta\epsilon}$-I and axioms postulating that $\langle X|S \rangle$ stands for the X-component of the unique solution of S are added to the axioms of $\text{BPA}_{\delta\epsilon}$-I. We write $\text{BPA}_{\delta\epsilon}$-I+REC for the resulting theory.

We write $\mathcal{P}_{\text{rec}}$ for the set of all closed $\text{BPA}_{\delta\epsilon}$-I+REC terms of sort $\mathbf{P}$. We write $\vdash t = t'$, where t and t' are $\text{BPA}_{\delta\epsilon}$-I+REC terms of sort $\mathbf{P}$, to indicate that the equation $t = t'$ is derivable from the axioms of $\text{BPA}_{\delta\epsilon}$-I+REC.

6   Algorithm Processes

In this section, a connection is made between proto-algorithms and the processes considered in the imperative process algebra $\text{BPA}_{\delta\epsilon}$-I. It is assumed that $\mathsf{m} \in \mathcal{V}$.

Definition. *Let $\Sigma = (F, P)$ be an alphabet. Then a Σ-algorithm process is a constant $\langle X|S \rangle$ of $\text{BPA}_{\delta\epsilon}$-I, where S is finite, $X_\epsilon \in \text{vars}(S)$, and for each $Y \in \text{vars}(S)$:*

- *the recursion equation for Y in S has one of the following forms:*

   (1) $Y = \mathsf{t} :\rightarrow [\mathsf{m} := \text{ini}(\mathsf{m})] \cdot Z,$

   (2) $Y = \mathsf{t} :\rightarrow [\mathsf{m} := o(\mathsf{m})] \cdot Z,$

   (3) $Y = (p(\mathsf{m}) = 1) :\rightarrow [\mathsf{m} := \mathsf{m}] \cdot Z + (p(\mathsf{m}) = 0) :\rightarrow [\mathsf{m} := \mathsf{m}] \cdot Z',$

   (4) $Y = \mathsf{t} :\rightarrow [\mathsf{m} := \text{fin}(\mathsf{m})] \cdot X_\epsilon,$

   (5) $Y = \mathsf{t} :\rightarrow \epsilon,$

   where $o \in \widetilde{F}$, $p \in P$, and $Z, Z' \in \text{vars}(S) \setminus \{X_\epsilon\}$;
- *the recursion equation for Y in S is of the form (1) iff $Y \equiv X$;*
- *the recursion equation for Y in S is of the form (5) iff $Y \equiv X_\epsilon$.*

We write AlgoGraph_Σ and $\text{AlgoProcess}_\Sigma$, where Σ is an alphabet, for the set of all Σ-algorithm graphs and the set of all Σ-algorithm processes, respectively.

Definition. *Let $\Sigma = (F, P)$ be an alphabet. Then the* graph-to-process *function g2p_Σ is a total function from AlgoGraph_Σ to $\text{AlgoProcess}_\Sigma$ such that, for each Σ-algorithm graph $G = (V, E, L_\mathsf{v}, L_\mathsf{e}, l, r)$, $\text{g2p}_\Sigma(G) = \langle X|S \rangle$, where $\langle X|S \rangle$ is a Σ-algorithm process such that:*

$X = \mathsf{t} :\rightarrow [\mathsf{m} := \text{ini}(\mathsf{m})] \cdot X_{v'} \in S \text{ iff } (r, v') \in E;$

$X_v = \mathsf{t} :\rightarrow [\mathsf{m} := o(\mathsf{m})] \cdot X_{v'} \in S \quad \text{iff } v \in V, l(v) = o, o \in \widetilde{F}, (v, v') \in E;$

$X_v = p(\mathsf{m}) = 1 :\rightarrow [\mathsf{m} := \mathsf{m}] \cdot X_{v'} + p(\mathsf{m}) = 0 :\rightarrow [\mathsf{m} := \mathsf{m}] \cdot X_{v''} \in S$

$\quad \text{iff } v \in V, l(v) = p, p \in P, (v, v'), (v, v'') \in E, l((v, v')) = 1, l((v, v'')) = 0;$

$X_v = \mathsf{t} :\rightarrow [\mathsf{m} := \text{fin}(\mathsf{m})] \cdot X_\epsilon \in S \quad \text{iff } v \in V, l(v) = \text{fin};$

$X_\epsilon = \mathsf{t} :\rightarrow \epsilon;$

where, for all $v \in V$, $X_v \in \mathcal{X}$ and, for all $v' \in V$, $X_v = X_{v'}$ only if $v = v'$.

The function $g2p_\Sigma$ is uniquely defined up to renaming of variables.

The following theorem tells us that the function $g2p_\Sigma$ is a bijection from $\mathrm{AlgoGraph}_\Sigma$ to $\mathrm{AlgoProcess}_\Sigma$ up to isomorphism of algorithm graphs and renaming of variables in algorithm processes.

Theorem 3. *Let Σ be an alphabet. Then, for all $\langle X|S \rangle \in \mathrm{AlgoProcess}_\Sigma$, there exists a unique $G \in \mathrm{AlgoGraph}_\Sigma$ up to $\cong$ such that $\langle X|S \rangle$ and $g2p_\Sigma(G)$ are identical up to consistent renaming of variables.*

Proof. Let $\Sigma = (F, P)$ be an alphabet, and let $\langle X|S \rangle \in \mathrm{AlgoProcess}_\Sigma$. Then we construct a $G = (V, E, L_\mathrm{v}, L_\mathrm{e}, l, r) \in \mathrm{AlgoGraph}_\Sigma$ from $\langle X|S \rangle$ as follows:

- $V = vars(S) \setminus \{X_\epsilon\}$;
- E is the set of all $(Y, Z) \in V \times V$ for which there exists an equation in S such that Y is its left-hand side and Z occurs in its right-hand side;
- $L_\mathrm{v} = F \cup P$;
- $L_\mathrm{e} = \{0, 1\}$;
- l is defined as follows:
  - $l(X) = \mathsf{ini}$;
  - $l(Y) = o$ if $Y = \mathsf{t} :\to [\mathsf{m} := o(\mathsf{m})] \cdot Z \in S$ for some $Z \in vars(S)$;
  - $l(Y) = p$ if $Y = (p(\mathsf{m}) = 1) :\to [\mathsf{m}:=\mathsf{m}] \cdot Z + (p(\mathsf{m}) = 0) :\to [\mathsf{m}:=\mathsf{m}] \cdot Z' \in S$ for some $Z, Z' \in vars(S)$;
  - $l(Y) = \mathsf{fin}$ if $Y = \mathsf{t} :\to [\mathsf{m} := \mathsf{fin}(\mathsf{m})] \cdot X_\epsilon \in S$;
  - $l((Y, Z))$ is undefined if $Y = \mathsf{t} :\to [\mathsf{m} := o(\mathsf{m})] \cdot Z \in S$ for some $o \in F$;
  - $l((Y, Z)) = 1$ if $Y = (p(\mathsf{m}) = 1) :\to [\mathsf{m}:=\mathsf{m}] \cdot Z + (p(\mathsf{m}) = 0) :\to [\mathsf{m}:=\mathsf{m}] \cdot Z' \in S$ for some $p \in P$ and $Z' \in vars(S)$;
  - $l((Y, Z)) = 0$ if $Y = (p(\mathsf{m}) = 1) :\to [\mathsf{m}:=\mathsf{m}] \cdot Z' + (p(\mathsf{m}) = 0) :\to [\mathsf{m}:=\mathsf{m}] \cdot Z \in S$ for some $p \in P$ and $Z' \in vars(S)$;
- $r = X$.

It is easy to see that $g2p_\Sigma(G)$ and $\langle X|S \rangle$ are identical up to consistent renaming of variables and that, for all $G' \in \mathrm{AlgoGraph}_\Sigma$, $g2p_\Sigma(G')$ and $\langle X|S \rangle$ are identical up to consistent renaming of variables only if $G' \cong G$. □

It is easy to obtain the signature $\Sigma_\mathfrak{D}$ and the minimal algebra $\mathfrak{D}$ of signature $\Sigma_\mathfrak{D}$ for a given alphabet Σ and a given Σ-interpretation $(D, D_\mathrm{in}, D_\mathrm{out}, I)$ after the following issues have been addressed: (a) $D \cup D_\mathrm{in} \cup D_\mathrm{out}$ must be taken as $\mathfrak{D}$'s carrier of sort $\mathbf{D}$ and consequently the interpretation of each symbol from Σ must be extended to $D \cup D_\mathrm{in} \cup D_\mathrm{out}$ and (b) each member of D_in must be representable by a closed term of sort $\mathbf{D}$. Any extension of the functions concerned may be chosen here because we comply with the convention to use each of them only if it is known that the value to which it is applied belongs to its original domain. For simplicity, we take all members of D_in as constants of sort $\mathbf{D}$.

Below, we write $[\mathsf{m} \mapsto d]$, where d is a member of $\mathfrak{D}$'s carrier of sort $\mathbf{D}$, for a fixed but arbitrary $\rho \in \mathcal{VVal}$ such that $\rho(\mathsf{m}) = d$.

The graph-to-process function $g2p_\Sigma$ allows to characterize the algorithmic step function of a proto-algorithm $A = (\Sigma, G, \mathcal{I})$ in $\mathrm{BPA}_{\delta\epsilon}$-I+REC.

Lemma 1. *Let $A = (\Sigma, G, \mathcal{I})$ be a proto-algorithm, where $\mathcal{I} = (D, D_{\text{in}}, D_{\text{out}}, I)$ and $G = (V, E, L_{\text{v}}, L_{\text{e}}, l, r) \in \text{AlgoGraph}_\Sigma$, let $\langle X|S\rangle \in \text{AlgoProcess}_\Sigma$ be such that $\langle X|S\rangle = \text{g2p}_\Sigma(G)$. Then, for all $v, v_1, v_2 \in V$, $d, d_1, d_2 \in D$, $d_{\text{in}} \in D_{\text{in}}$, and $d_{\text{out}} \in D_{\text{out}}$:*

$$\delta_A^{\text{a}}(d_{\text{in}}) \quad\ = (v, d) \quad \text{iff} \ \vdash \mathsf{V}_{[\mathsf{m}\mapsto d_{\text{in}}]}(\langle X|S\rangle) \ = [\mathsf{m} := d] \cdot \mathsf{V}_{[\mathsf{m}\mapsto d]}(\langle X_v|S\rangle),$$
$$\delta_A^{\text{a}}((v_1, d_1)) = (v_2, d_2) \ \text{iff} \ \vdash \mathsf{V}_{[\mathsf{m}\mapsto d_1]}(\langle X_{v_1}|S\rangle) \ = [\mathsf{m} := d_2] \cdot \mathsf{V}_{[\mathsf{m}\mapsto d_2]}(\langle X_{v_2}|S\rangle),$$
$$\delta_A^{\text{a}}((v, d)) \quad = d_{\text{out}} \quad \text{iff} \ \vdash \mathsf{V}_{[\mathsf{m}\mapsto d]}(\langle X_v|S\rangle) \ = [\mathsf{m} := d_{\text{out}}] \cdot \mathsf{V}_{[\mathsf{m}\mapsto d_{\text{out}}]}(\langle X_\epsilon|S\rangle).$$

Proof. This follows easily from the definition of the algorithmic step function δ_A^{a}, the definition of the graph-to-process function g2p_Σ, and the axioms of $\text{BPA}_{\delta\epsilon}\text{-I+REC}$. $\qquad\square$

There exists a sound method for proving algorithmic equivalence of two proto-algorithms $A = (\Sigma, G, \mathcal{I})$ and $A' = (\Sigma, G', \mathcal{I})$ based on the graph-to-process function g2p_Σ.

Theorem 4. *Let $A = (\Sigma, G, \mathcal{I})$ and $A' = (\Sigma, G', \mathcal{I})$ be proto-algorithms, where $\mathcal{I} = (D, D_{\text{in}}, D_{\text{out}}, I)$. Then $A \equiv_{\text{a}} A'$ if, for all $d \in D_{\text{in}}$, $\vdash \mathsf{V}_{[\mathsf{m}\mapsto d]}(\text{g2p}_\Sigma(G)) = \mathsf{V}_{[\mathsf{m}\mapsto d]}(\text{g2p}_\Sigma(G'))$.*

Proof. Suppose that $G = (V, E, L_{\text{v}}, L_{\text{e}}, l, r)$ and $G' = (V', E', L_{\text{v}}, L_{\text{e}}, l', r')$. Let $\langle X|S\rangle, \langle X|S'\rangle \in \text{AlgoProcess}_\Sigma$ and let $d_{\text{in}} \in D_{\text{in}}$.

Starting from $\mathsf{V}_{[\mathsf{m}\mapsto d_{\text{in}}]}(\langle X|S\rangle)$, either there exists an $n \in \mathbb{N}$, such that, for some $v_1, \dots, v_{n+1} \in V$, $d_1, \dots, d_{n+1} \in D$, and $d_{\text{out}} \in D_{\text{out}}$:

$$\vdash \mathsf{V}_{[\mathsf{m}\mapsto d_{\text{in}}]}(\langle X|S\rangle) \qquad = [\mathsf{m} := d_1] \cdot \mathsf{V}_{[\mathsf{m}\mapsto d_1]}(\langle X_{v_1}|S\rangle),$$
$$\vdash \mathsf{V}_{[\mathsf{m}\mapsto d_i]}(\langle X_{v_i}|S\rangle) \qquad = [\mathsf{m} := d_{i+1}] \cdot \mathsf{V}_{[\mathsf{m}\mapsto d_{i+1}]}(\langle X_{v_{i+1}}|S\rangle)$$
$$\text{for each } i \in \{1, \dots, n\},$$
$$\vdash \mathsf{V}_{[\mathsf{m}\mapsto d_{n+1}]}(\langle X_{v_{n+1}}|S\rangle) = [\mathsf{m} := d_{\text{out}}] \cdot \mathsf{V}_{[\mathsf{m}\mapsto d_{\text{out}}]}(\langle X_\epsilon|S\rangle)$$

or, for some $v_1, v_2, \dots \in V$ and $d_1, d_2, \dots \in D$:

$$\vdash \mathsf{V}_{[\mathsf{m}\mapsto d_{\text{in}}]}(\langle X|S\rangle) \ = [\mathsf{m} := d_1] \cdot \mathsf{V}_{[\mathsf{m}\mapsto d_1]}(\langle X_{v_1}|S\rangle),$$
$$\vdash \mathsf{V}_{[\mathsf{m}\mapsto d_i]}(\langle X_{v_i}|S\rangle) = [\mathsf{m} := d_{i+1}] \cdot \mathsf{V}_{[\mathsf{m}\mapsto d_{i+1}]}(\langle X_{v_{i+1}}|S\rangle)$$
$$\text{for each } i \in \mathbb{N}.$$

From this, using $\vdash \mathsf{V}_{[\mathsf{m}\mapsto d_{\text{in}}]}(\text{g2p}_\Sigma(G)) = \mathsf{V}_{[\mathsf{m}\mapsto d_{\text{in}}]}(\text{g2p}_\Sigma(G'))$ and the fact that $\vdash \alpha \cdot t = \alpha' \cdot t'$ (where $\alpha, \alpha' \in \mathcal{A}$ and $t, t' \in \mathcal{P}_{\text{rec}}$) only if $\vdash \alpha = \alpha'$ and $\vdash t = t'$, it follows by an inductive argument that (for $i \in \{1, \dots, n\}$ or $i \in \mathbb{N}$):

$$\vdash \mathsf{V}_{[\mathsf{m}\mapsto d_{\text{in}}]}(\langle X|S\rangle) = [\mathsf{m} := d_1] \cdot \mathsf{V}_{[\mathsf{m}\mapsto d_1]}(\langle X_{v_1}|S\rangle) \text{ only if}$$
$$\vdash \mathsf{V}_{[\mathsf{m}\mapsto d_{\text{in}}]}(\langle X|S'\rangle) = [\mathsf{m} := d_1] \cdot \mathsf{V}_{[\mathsf{m}\mapsto d_1]}(\langle X_{v_1'}|S'\rangle) \text{ for some } v_1' \in V',$$

$$\vdash \mathsf{V}_{[\mathsf{m}\mapsto d_i]}(\langle X_{v_i}|S\rangle) = [\mathsf{m} := d_{i+1}] \cdot \mathsf{V}_{[\mathsf{m}\mapsto d_{i+1}]}(\langle X_{v_{i+1}}|S\rangle) \text{ only if}$$
$$\vdash \mathsf{V}_{[\mathsf{m}\mapsto d_i]}(\langle X_{v_i'}|S'\rangle) = [\mathsf{m} := d_{i+1}] \cdot \mathsf{V}_{[\mathsf{m}\mapsto d_{i+1}]}(\langle X_{v_{i+1}'}|S'\rangle) \text{ for some } v_i', v_{i+1}' \in V',$$

$$\vdash \mathsf{V}_{[\mathsf{m}\mapsto d_{n+1}]}(\langle X_{v_{n+1}}|S\rangle) = [\mathsf{m} := d_{\text{out}}] \cdot \mathsf{V}_{[\mathsf{m}\mapsto d_{\text{out}}]}(\langle X_\epsilon|S\rangle) \text{ only if}$$
$$\vdash \mathsf{V}_{[\mathsf{m}\mapsto d_{n+1}]}(\langle X_{v_{n+1}'}|S'\rangle) = [\mathsf{m} := d_{\text{out}}] \cdot \mathsf{V}_{[\mathsf{m}\mapsto d_{\text{out}}]}(\langle X_\epsilon|S'\rangle) \text{ for some } v_{n+1}' \in V'.$$

From this, using Lemma 1, it directly follows that (for $i \in \{1, \dots, n\}$ or $i \in \mathbb{N}$):

$\delta_A^a(d_{in}) = (v_1, d_1)$ only if $\delta_{A'}^a(d_{in}) = (v_1', d_1)$ for some $v_1' \in V'$,

$\delta_A^a((v_i, d_i)) = (v_{i+1}, d_{i+1})$ only if

$$\delta_{A'}^a((v_i', d_i)) = (v_{i+1}', d_{i+1}) \text{ for some } v_i', v_{i+1}' \in V',$$

$\delta_A^a((v_{n+1}, d_{n+1})) = d_{out}$ only if

$$\delta_A^a((v_{n+1}', d_{n+1})) = d_{out} \text{ for some } v_{n+1}' \in V'.$$

This means that there exists an algorithmic simulation of A by A'. In the same way, we can show that there exists an algorithmic simulation of A' by A. Hence, $A \equiv_a A'$.   □

We do not have that $A \equiv_a A'$ only if, for all $d \in D_{in}$, $\vdash \mathsf{V}_{[m \mapsto d]}(\mathsf{g2p}_\Sigma(G)) = \mathsf{V}_{[m \mapsto d]}(\mathsf{g2p}_\Sigma(G'))$. The following example illustrates this. Take proto-algorithms $A = (\Sigma, G, \mathcal{I})$ and $A' = (\Sigma, G', \mathcal{I})$, where $\Sigma = (F, P)$, $G = (V, E, L_v, L_e, l, r)$, $\mathcal{I} = (D, D_{in}, D_{out}, I)$, and G' is obtained from G by interchanging the labels of two vertices $v, v' \in V$ for which $(v, v') \in E$, indegree$(v') = 1$, $l(v), l(v') \in F$ and, for all $d \in D$, $I(l(v))(I(l(v'))(d)) = I(l(v'))(I(l(v))(d))$. This means that two steps, the latter of which is always immediately preceded by the first, and that consist of performing an operation, where the operations in question are independent, are interchanged. It is easy to see that A and A' are algorithmically equivalent. However, because of a different order of certain assignment actions in $\mathsf{g2p}_\Sigma(G)$ and $\mathsf{g2p}_\Sigma(G')$, we do not have that $\vdash \mathsf{V}_{[m \mapsto d]}(\mathsf{g2p}_\Sigma(G)) = \mathsf{V}_{[m \mapsto d]}(\mathsf{g2p}_\Sigma(G'))$.

We also do not have that $A \cong A'$ if, for all $d \in D_{in}$, $\vdash \mathsf{V}_{[m \mapsto d]}(\mathsf{g2p}_\Sigma(G)) = \mathsf{V}_{[m \mapsto d]}(\mathsf{g2p}_\Sigma(G'))$. This is illustrated by the same example as the one used to illustrate that we do not have that $A \cong A'$ if $A \equiv_a A'$.

7   Discussion of Generalizations

The notion of a proto-algorithm introduced in this paper is based on the classical informal notion of an algorithm. Several generalizations of that notion have been proposed, e.g. the notion of a non-deterministic algorithm, the notion of a parallel algorithm, and the notion of an interactive algorithm.

The generalization of the notion of a proto-algorithm to a notion of a non-deterministic proto-algorithm is easy: weaken, in the definition of a Σ-algorithm graph, the outdegree of vertices labeled with a function symbol other than fin to greater than zero. In the case of a non-deterministic proto-algorithm, most definitions involving one or more proto-algorithms and the definition of a Σ-algorithm process need an obvious adaptation. However, the definition of algorithmic equivalence needs an adaptation that is not obvious at first sight: two non-deterministic proto-algorithms A and A' are algorithmically equivalent if there exist an algorithmic simulation R of A by A' and an algorithmic simulation R' of A' by A such that $R' = R^{-1}$. The condition $R' = R^{-1}$ is necessary to guarantee that A and A' have the same choice structure. With this adaptation, Theorem 4 goes through for non-deterministic proto-algorithms.

The generalization of the notion of a proto-algorithm to a notion of a parallel proto-algorithm is not so easy. The main reason for this is that there is no consensus about what properties are essential for a parallel algorithm. A parallel algorithm is usually informally described by a sentence like "A parallel algorithm is an algorithm in which more than one step can take place simultaneously". The term parallel algorithm was introduced after the first studies on parallelization of 'classical' algorithms (see e.g. [7]). One of the earliest uses of the term in the computer science literature was in [23]. In that paper, a formalization of the notion of a parallel algorithm is given that does not depend on a particular machine model. However, the formalization is far from covering everything that is currently considered a parallel algorithm.

Since the introduction of the first models of parallel computation, it is common practice to identify parallel algorithms with the abstract machines considered in a particular model of parallel computation. Many adjustments of early models based on random access machines have been proposed, in particular of those introduced in [5,8,9,11]. The resulting wide variety of proposed models of parallel computation does not make it easier to come up with a formal notion of a parallel algorithm that encompasses everything considered a parallel algorithm. It therefore seems useful to start with distinguishing different types of parallel algorithms and generalizing the notion of a proto-algorithm to a notion of a parallel algorithm per type of parallel algorithms.

The generalization of the notion of a proto-algorithm to a notion of an interactive proto-algorithm is not so easy too. As with parallel proto-algorithms, the main reason for this is that there is no consensus on which properties are essential for an interactive algorithm. An interactive algorithm is usually informally described by a sentence like "An interactive algorithm is an algorithm that can interact with the environment in which it takes place". In [4], a specific view on the nature of interactive algorithms is discussed in detail, culminating in a characterization of interactive algorithms by a number of postulates. This view is the only one found in the computer science literature so far. Some of its details are based on choices whose impact on the generality of the characterization is not clear.

Recently, several models of interactive computation have been proposed. They are based on variants of Turing machines, to wit interactive Turing machines [18], persistent Turing machines [10], and reactive Turing machines [2]. These models are closely related. In [2], it is established that reactive Turing machines are at least as expressive as persistent Turing machines. Moreover, it is established in that paper that the behaviour of a reactive Turing machine can be defined by a recursive specification in a process algebra closely related to ACP_ϵ^τ [1, Section 5.3], an extension of $BPA_{\delta\epsilon}$ that includes parallel composition.

8   Concluding Remarks

I have reported on a quest for a satisfactory formalization of the notion of an algorithm. I have introduced the notion of a proto-algorithm. Algorithms are expected to be equivalence classes of proto-algorithms under an appropriate equivalence relation. I have defined three equivalence relations on proto-algorithms. Two of them give bounds between which an appropriate equivalence relation must lie. The third one, called algorithmic equivalence, lies in between these two and is likely an appropriate one. I have also presented a sound method for proving algorithmic equivalence of two proto-algorithms using the imperative process algebra $\text{BPA}_{\delta\epsilon}$-I+REC.

The notion of a proto-algorithm defined in this paper does not depend on any particular machine model or algorithmic language, and also has most properties that are generally considered to belong to the important ones of an algorithm. This makes it neither too concrete nor too abstract to be a appropriate basis for investigating what exactly an algorithm is in the setting of emerging types of computation, such as interactive computation.

Due to the connection between proto-algorithms and processes that is expressed by Theorem 4, ACP_ϵ^τ-I+REC [20], an extension of $\text{BPA}_{\delta\epsilon}$-I+REC that includes among other things parallel composition, is potentially a suitable tool to find out how to generalize the notion of a proto-algorithm to the different types of parallel algorithms.

Early in my career I did research, development and consultancy. Later, the emphasis increasingly shifted to what suits me best, namely research. I cannot formally prove it, but I am convinced that the conversations I had with Cliff Jones in the 1980s and early 1990s about the work we were doing are largely responsible for that. They made me realize that research suits me better than development and consultancy. This paper shows that it suits me so well that I am still doing research long after my retirement.

Disclosure of Interests. The author has no competing interests to declare that are relevant to the content of this article.

Appendix

The axioms of $\text{BPA}_{\delta\epsilon}$-I+REC are presented in Table 1. In this table, t stands for an arbitrary term from $\mathcal{P}$, ϕ and ψ stand for arbitrary terms from $\mathcal{C}$, e stands for an arbitrary term from $\mathcal{D}$, a stands for an arbitrary basic action from A, v stands for an arbitrary flexible variable from $\mathcal{V}$, ρ stands for an arbitrary flexible variable valuation from $\mathcal{VVal}$, X stands for an arbitrary variable from $\mathcal{X}$, S stands for an arbitrary linear recursive specification over $\text{BPA}_{\delta\epsilon}$-I. The notation $\langle t|S\rangle$ is used in axiom RDP for t with, for all $X \in \text{vars}(S)$, all occurrences of X in t replaced by $\langle X|S\rangle$. The homomorphic extensions of a flexible variable valuation ρ from $\mathcal{V}$ to $\mathcal{D}$ and $\mathcal{C}$ are denoted in axioms V3 and V5 by ρ as well. The notation $\rho\{e/v\}$ is used in axiom V3 for the flexible variable valuation ρ' defined by $\rho'(v') = \rho(v')$ if $v' \neq v$ and $\rho'(v) = e$.

Table 1. Axioms of $BPA_{\delta\epsilon}$-I+REC

$x + y = y + x$	A1	$\delta \cdot x = \delta$	A7
$(x + y) + z = x + (y + z)$	A2	$x \cdot \epsilon = x$	A8
$x + x = x$	A3	$\epsilon \cdot x = x$	A9
$(x + y) \cdot z = x \cdot z + y \cdot z$	A4		
$(x \cdot y) \cdot z = x \cdot (y \cdot z)$	A5	$\langle X|S\rangle = \langle t|S\rangle$ if $X = t \in S$	RDP
$x + \delta = x$	A6	$S \Rightarrow X = \langle X|S\rangle$ if $X \in \mathrm{vars}(S)$	RSP
$\mathsf{t} :\to x = x$	GC1	$\mathsf{V}_\rho(\epsilon) = \epsilon$	V1
$\mathsf{f} :\to x = \delta$	GC2	$\mathsf{V}_\rho(a \cdot x) = a \cdot \mathsf{V}_\rho(x)$	V2
$\phi :\to \delta = \delta$	GC3	$\mathsf{V}_\rho([v := e] \cdot x) = [v := \rho(e)] \cdot \mathsf{V}_{\rho\{\rho(e)/v\}}(x)$	V3
$\phi :\to (x + y) = \phi :\to x + \phi :\to y$	GC4	$\mathsf{V}_\rho(x + y) = \mathsf{V}_\rho(x) + \mathsf{V}_\rho(y)$	V4
$\phi :\to x \cdot y = (\phi :\to x) \cdot y$	GC5	$\mathsf{V}_\rho(\phi :\to y) = \rho(\phi) :\to \mathsf{V}_\rho(x)$	V5
$\phi :\to (\psi :\to x) = (\phi \wedge \psi) :\to x$	GC6	$e = e'$ if $\mathfrak{D} \models e = e'$	IMP1
$(\phi \vee \psi) :\to x = \phi :\to x + \psi :\to x$	GC7	$\phi = \psi$ if $\mathfrak{D} \models \phi \Leftrightarrow \psi$	IMP2

References

1. Baeten, J.C.M., Weijland, W.P.: Process Algebra, Cambridge Tracts in Theoretical Computer Science, vol. 18. Cambridge University Press, Cambridge (1990). https://doi.org/10.1017/CBO9780511624193
2. Baeten, J.C., Luttik, B., van Tilburg, P.: Reactive Turing machines. Inf. Comput. **231**, 143–166 (2013). https://doi.org/10.1016/j.ic.2013.08.010
3. Bergstra, J.A., Middelburg, C.A.: On algorithmic equivalence of instruction sequences for computing bit string functions. Fund. Inform. **138**(4), 411–434 (2015). https://doi.org/10.3233/FI-2015-1219
4. Blass, A., Gurevich, Y.: Ordinary interactive small-step algorithms, I. ACM Trans. Comput. Log. **7**(2), 363–419 (2006). https://doi.org/10.1145/1131313.1131320
5. Cole, R., Zajicek, O.: The APRAM: incorporating asynchrony into the PRAM model. In: SPAA 1989, pp. 169–178. ACM Press (1989). https://doi.org/10.1145/72935.72954
6. Dijkstra, E.W.: A Short Introduction to the Art of Programming, EWD, vol. 316. Technische Hogeschool Eindhoven (1971)
7. Estrin, G., Turn, R.: Automatic assignment of computations in a variable structure computer system. IEEE Trans. Electron. Comput. **EC-12**(6), 755–773 (1963). https://doi.org/10.1109/PGEC.1963.263559
8. Fortune, S., Wyllie, J.: Parallelism in random access machines. In: STOC 1978, pp. 114–118. ACM Press (1978). https://doi.org/10.1145/800133.804339
9. Gibbons, P.B.: A more practical PRAM model. In: SPAA 1989, pp. 158–168. ACM Press (1989). https://doi.org/10.1145/72935.72953
10. Goldin, D.Q., Smolka, S.A., Attie, P.C., Sonderegger, E.L.: Turing machines, transition systems, and interaction. Inf. Comput. **194**(2), 101–128 (2004). https://doi.org/10.1016/j.ic.2004.07.002
11. Goldschlager, L.M.: A unified approach to models of synchronous parallel machines. In: STOC 1978, pp. 89–94. ACM Press (1978). https://doi.org/10.1145/800133.804336
12. Gurevich, Y.: Sequential abstract-state machines capture sequential algorithms. ACM Trans. Comput. Log. **1**(1), 77–111 (2000). https://doi.org/10.1145/343369.343384

13. Hill, R.K.: What an algorithm is. Philos. Technol. **29**(1), 35–59 (2016). https://doi.org/10.1007/s13347-014-0184-5
14. Jones, C.B.: Systematic Software Development Using VDM, 2nd edn. Prentice-Hall, Hoboken (1990)
15. Kleene, S.C.: Mathematical Logic. Wiley, New York (1967)
16. Knuth, D.E.: The Art of Computer Programming: The Fundamental Algorithms, 3rd edn. Addison Wesley Longman, Redwood City (1997)
17. Lamport, L.: The temporal logic of actions. ACM Trans. Program. Lang. Syst. **16**(3), 872–923 (1994). https://doi.org/10.1145/177492.177726
18. van Leeuwen, J., Wiedermann, J.: Beyond the turing limit: evolving interactive systems. In: Pacholski, L., Ružička, P. (eds.) SOFSEM 2001. LNCS, vol. 2234, pp. 90–109. Springer, Heidelberg (2001). https://doi.org/10.1007/3-540-45627-9_8
19. Mal'cev, A.I.: Algorithm and Recursive Functions. Wolters-Noordhoff, Groningen (1970)
20. Middelburg, C.A.: Imperative process algebra with abstraction. Sci. Ann. Comput. Sci. **32**(1), 137–179 (2022). https://doi.org/10.7561/SACS.2022.1.137
21. Moschovakis, Y.N., Paschalis, V.: Elementary algorithms and their implementations. In: Cooper, S.B., Löwe, B., Sorbi, A. (eds.) New Computational Paradigms, pp. 87–118. Springer, New York (2008). https://doi.org/10.1007/978-0-387-68546-5_5
22. Papayannopoulos, P.: On algorithms, effective procedures, and their definitions. Philos. Math. **31**(3), 291–329 (2023). https://doi.org/10.1093/philmat/nkad011
23. Reiter, R.: Scheduling parallel computations. J. ACM **15**(4), 590–599 (1968). https://doi.org/10.1145/321479.321485
24. Rogers, H.: Theory of Recursive Functions and Effective Computability. McGraw-Hill, New York (1967)
25. Schneider, F.B.: On Concurrent Programming. Graduate Texts in Computer Science. Springer, New York (1997). https://doi.org/10.1007/978-1-4612-1830-2
26. Seaver, N.: Algorithms as culture: some tactics for the ethnography of algorithmic systems. Big Data Soc. **4**(2), 1–12 (2017). https://doi.org/10.1177/2053951717738104
27. Weyuker, E.J.: Modifications of the program scheme model. J. Comput. Syst. Sci. **18**(3), 281–293 (1979). https://doi.org/10.1016/0022-0000(79)90036-9

A Note on Proofs of Earley's Recognizer

Tobias Nipkow[(✉)] [ID] and Martin Rau [ID]

Technische Universität München, Munich, Germany
https://www.proof.cit.tum.de/~nipkow

Abstract. This paper presents the formalization and verification (in the proof assistant Isabelle) of an abstract inductive version of Earley's recognizer, relates it to the standard definition and derives an efficient one-pass algorithm for ε-free grammars. In particular it compares Jones development of Earley's recognizer to our own and to the literature.

1 Introduction

Earley's algorithm [3] is a parsing algorithm for all context-free grammars. Earley's *recognizer* is the part of Earley's algorithm that merely returns a yes/no decision but does not build a parse tree. We are aware of only one machine-checked verification of Earley's algorithm, the one we released recently [11,12]. However, that formalization and verification is very complex and a paper describing it only scratches the surface [13]. Now we focus on the recognizer and in particular its initial definition and correctness proofs. Rau's starting point (based on the work of Obua *et al.* [8,9]) is a simple inductive definition that differs from the standard definition. The latter comes in two flavours: an imperative program [1,3] and two nested inductive definitions, first described precisely by Jones [4,5]. Below we call the latter definition the *standard* one.

Our paper starts with the inductive definition of Earley's recognizer given by Rau [11,12], proves that it recognizes exactly the words in the formal language generated by the grammar, defines a second recognizer in the standard manner (noticing that Jones' version only works for ε-free grammars), and proves equivalence of the two definitions. The proofs are significant simplifications of the ones presented earlier [11–13]. We also derive an efficient one-pass algorithm for ε-free grammars. We concentrate on the work by Jones, Rau and Nipkow, Earley and Aho & Ullman. For a survey of the wider related literature see [13].

Our work has been formalized completely in the proof assistant Isabelle [6,7]. All definitions and theorems in the paper are taken directly from the formalization. Sometimes they are pretty-printed, e.g. using inference rule notation instead of implication. In a few cases we provide an informal counterpart to the formal notation, e.g. the so-called *dotted* productions $A \rightarrow \alpha \bullet \beta$. Readers of this paper should be familiar with functional programming notation, context-free grammars and parsing.

Dedicated to Cliff Jones on the occasion of his 80th birthday.

© The Author(s), under exclusive license to Springer Nature Switzerland AG 2024
A. Cavalcanti and J. Baxter (Eds.): *The Practice of Formal Methods*, LNCS 14781, pp. 45–55, 2024.
https://doi.org/10.1007/978-3-031-66673-5_3

2   Isabelle Notation

Isabelle is based on a fragment of higher-order logic. It supports core concepts commonly found in functional programming languages.

The notation $t :: \tau$ indicates that term t has type τ. Basic types include *bool* and *nat*, while type variables are written $'a$, $'b$ etc. Pairs are expressed as (a, b), and triples as (a, b, c), and so forth. Most type constructors are written postfix, such as $'a$ *set* and $'a$ *list*, and the function space arrow is $\Rightarrow$. Function *set* converts a list to a set.

Lists are constructed from the empty list [] using the infix cons-operator (#). The operator (@) appends two lists, $|xs|$ denotes the length of xs, $xs ! n$ returns the n-th element of the list xs (starting with $n = 0$) and *take* n xs is the prefix of length n of xs.

Algebraic data types are defined using the **datatype** keyword. A predefined data type:

datatype $'a$ *option* $=$ *None* $\mid$ *Some* $'a$

The notation $[\![A_1, \ldots, A_n]\!] \Longrightarrow B$ denotes an implication with premises $A_1, \ldots, A_n$ and conclusion B. Equality on type *bool* denotes logical equivalence.

3   Context-Free Grammars and Derivations

Our formalization is parameterized by the type of symbols $'a$ which includes both terminals and non-terminals. We use a, b, c for terminals and A, B, C for nonterminals; s represents an arbitrary symbol. Sequences (i.e. lists) of symbols (or *words*) are denoted by α, β, γ or u, v, w. The empty word is often written ε.

A *production* is a pair of type $'a \times 'a$ *list*, i.e. a nonterminal left-hand side (*lhs*) and a list of symbols on the right-hand side (*rhs*). We will also use the standard notation $A \to \gamma$ for a production (A, γ). A *context-free grammar* is a list of productions together with a start symbol:

datatype $'a$ *cfg* $=$ *CFG* $(('a \times 'a$ *list*$)$ *list*$)$ $'a$

$prods\ (CFG\ R\ \_) = R$ $\qquad$ $start\ (CFG\ \_\ S) = S$

A CFG implicitly defines the set of nonterminals as all symbols on the lhs of a production, plus the start symbol:

$nonterminals\ G = set\ (map\ lhs\ (prods\ G)) \cup \{start\ G\}$

A single-step derivation w.r.t. a CFG G is defined as follows:

$(A, \alpha) \in set\ (prods\ G) \Longrightarrow G \vdash u\ @\ [A]\ @\ v \Rightarrow u\ @\ \alpha\ @\ v$

The reflexive transitive closure and the n-fold iteration of $\Rightarrow$ are denoted by $\Rightarrow*$ and $\Rightarrow^n$.

4   Inductive Definition of Earley's State Sets

An Earley recognizer decides if some word is in the language described by a grammar by generating a set of so-called *states* and checking if it contains a *final* state. In the sequel, we fix a grammar G :: $'a\ cfg$ and an input w :: $'a\ list$. The starting point of our development of Earley's recognizer [11,13] is an abstract and compact inductive definition. In the next section we will show that this inductive definition coincides with the standard definition of Earley's recognizer.

A state is a triple $(r,\ d,\ i)$ which consists of a production $r = (A,\ \gamma)$ from the grammar G, a natural number $d \le |\gamma|$, marking how far the algorithm has recognized γ, and a natural number i representing the start index of the subword of w recognized by this state. The three projection functions are *prod*, *dot* and *from*. We use the letters x and y for states.

A production $A \to \gamma$ together with a *dot* d is shown as $A \to \alpha{\bullet}\beta$, where α is the prefix of the first d symbols of γ and β is the suffix. Consequently we will informally show states as pairs $(A \to \alpha{\bullet}\beta,\ i)$.

Below we need the following auxiliary *state* functions that query or modify the dotted production but not the *from* component of the state.

mv_dot :: $'a\ state \Rightarrow 'a\ state$ moves the dot in a state one position to the right:
$mv\_dot\ (A \to \alpha{\bullet}s\beta,\ i) = (A \to \alpha s{\bullet}\beta,\ i)$

$is\_complete$ :: $'a\ state \Rightarrow bool$ checks if the dotted production is of the form $A \to \alpha{\bullet}$.

$next\_symbol$ :: $'a\ state \Rightarrow 'a\ option$ is *None* if the state is complete, and *Some s* if the dotted production of the form $A \to \alpha{\bullet}s\beta$.

Now we come to the actual inductive definition. Technically, we define a single set *Earley* of pairs $(x,\ j)$ of states and an index. However, it is more intuitive to present it as an inductive definition of indexed state sets: we write $x \in \mathcal{S}\ j$ instead of $(x,\ j) \in Earley$. In the indexed presentation, we define state sets $\mathcal{S}\ j$, $j \le |w|$, that depend on each other. However, the dependence is in one direction only: later sets depend on earlier ones, not the other way around. Thus the $\mathcal{S}\ j$ can be generated in ascending order. This is the subject of the next section but plays no role now.

The intuitive meaning of $(r,\ d,\ i) \in \mathcal{S}\ j$ is that the subword *slice i j w* (which stands for *drop i (take j w)*) has been recognized—for the precise definition see the soundness proof below. For this reason we also call i the *start index* and j the *end index* (which is excluded).

The four defining rules are: the initial set of states, and one rule for each of the core operations that expand the set of states: scanning, prediction, and completion.

$$\frac{x \in Init}{x \in \mathcal{S}\ 0}\ \text{INIT}$$

$Init = \{(r,\ 0,\ 0)\ |\ r \in set\ (prods\ G) \wedge lhs\ r = start\ G\}$

INIT adds all initial states $(S \rightarrow \bullet\gamma, 0)$ to $\mathcal{S}\ 0$, where $S = start\ G$ and $(S, \gamma) \in set\ (prods\ G)$.

$$\frac{x \in \mathcal{S}\ j \qquad j < |w| \qquad next\_symbol\ x = Some\ (w\ !\ j)}{mv\_dot\ x \in \mathcal{S}\ (j+1)} \text{ SCAN}$$

SCAN applies when there is a terminal symbol to the right of the dot and it is the "current" symbol in the input w. In that case we move the dot and add the new state into the next state set.

$$\frac{x \in \mathcal{S}\ k \qquad x' \in Predict\ x\ k}{x' \in \mathcal{S}\ k} \text{ PREDICT}$$

$Predict\ x\ k =$
$\{(r, 0, k) \mid r \in set\ (prods\ G) \land next\_symbol\ x = Some\ (lhs\ r)\}$

PREDICT is applicable to a state in $\mathcal{S}\ k$ when there is a non-terminal symbol to the right of the dot: $A \rightarrow \alpha\bullet B\beta, i$. Then a new state $(B \rightarrow \bullet\gamma, k)$ can be added to $\mathcal{S}\ k$ for each production (B, γ) of the grammar.

$$\frac{x \in \mathcal{S}\ (from\ y) \qquad \begin{array}{c} y \in \mathcal{S}\ k \qquad is\_complete\ y \\ next\_symbol\ x = Some\ (lhs\ (prod\ y)) \end{array}}{mv\_dot\ x \in \mathcal{S}\ k} \text{ COMPLETE}$$

COMPLETE can be applied to all complete states $(B \rightarrow \gamma\bullet, j) \in \mathcal{S}\ k$. These states indicate successful recognition of *slice j k w* starting from B. Hence we can move the dot over B in any production in $\mathcal{S}\ j$: if $(B \rightarrow \alpha\bullet B\beta, i) \in \mathcal{S}\ j$ then we can add $(B \rightarrow \alpha B\bullet\beta, i)$ to $\mathcal{S}\ k$.

This concludes the inductive definition of the $\mathcal{S}\ j$.

4.1   Correctness

Input w is accepted if $\mathcal{S}\ |w|$ contains a final state $(start\ G \rightarrow \gamma\bullet, 0)$, i.e. the entire input has been recognized:

$is\_final :: {'}a\ state \Rightarrow bool$
$is\_final\ x = (lhs\ (prod\ x) = start\ G \land from\ x = 0 \land is\_complete\ x)$

$accepted = (\exists x \in \mathcal{S}\ |w|.\ is\_final\ x)$

We now need to prove $accepted = (G \vdash [start\ G] \Rightarrow^* w)$. The $\Longrightarrow$ direction is called *soundness*, the $\Longleftarrow$ direction *completeness* of the state-based acceptance w.r.t. the grammar.

But first a few auxiliary notions. A state is *well-formed* if the state's production belongs to the grammar, the dot is within the length of the rhs of the rule and the start index must not exceed the end index which must not exceed $|w|$.

$wf\_state\ x\ k =$
$(prod\ x \in set\ (prods\ G) \land dot\ x \leq |rhs\ (prod\ x)| \land from\ x \leq k \land k \leq |w|)$

It is easily proved by induction that all generated states are well-formed:

$$x \in \mathcal{S} \ k \implies wf\_state \ x \ k$$

This property comes in handy repeatedly but is swept under the carpet below.

In order to split the rhs of a dotted production into the prefix up to the dot and the suffix after the dot we introduce two functions α and β:

$$\alpha \ x \ = \ take \ (dot \ x) \ (rhs \ (prod \ x)) \qquad \beta \ x \ = \ drop \ (dot \ x) \ (rhs \ (prod \ x))$$

Soundness. Soundness is generalized to a property of states. Soundness of a state $(A \rightarrow u \bullet v, \ i)$ in $\mathcal{S} \ k$ means $G \vdash u \Rightarrow_* slice \ i \ k \ w$:

$$sound\_state \ x \ k \ = \ (G \vdash \alpha \ x \Rightarrow_* slice \ (from \ x) \ k \ w)$$

Now it is straightforward to prove soundness for all generated states by induction on $x \in \mathcal{S} \ k$

$$x \in \mathcal{S} \ k \implies sound\_state \ x \ k$$

and obtain as a corollary the soundness of *accepted*:

$$accepted \implies G \vdash [start \ G] \Rightarrow_* w$$

Completeness. We need to prove that if $G \vdash [start \ G] \Rightarrow_* w$, then there exists a final state in $\mathcal{S} \ |w|$. We generalize this to a statement that in a dotted production, the dot can be moved to the right end of the production:

$$[\![j \leq k; \ k \leq |w|; \ x = ((A, \gamma), d, i); \ x \in \mathcal{S} \ j; \ G \vdash \beta \ x \Rightarrow^n slice \ j \ k \ w]\!]$$
$$\implies ((A, \gamma), |\gamma|, i) \in \mathcal{S} \ k \tag{1}$$

The proof is by a nested induction. The outer induction is a proof by strong induction on n, the inner induction is a proof by induction on $\beta \ x$ where we need to generalize the assumption $G \vdash \beta \ x \Rightarrow^n slice \ j \ k \ w$ to $\exists m{\leq}n. \ G \vdash \beta \ x \Rightarrow^m slice \ j \ k \ w$ The base case $\beta \ x = []$ is easy. In the induction step, $\beta \ x = s \ \# \ ss$, we have $G \vdash [s] \Rightarrow^{n_1} slice \ j \ j' \ w$ and $G \vdash ss \Rightarrow^{n_2} slice \ j' \ k \ w$ for some $n_1, n_2 \leq m$ and some $j \leq j' \leq k$. Thus $next\_symbol \ x = Some \ s$. First we prove $x' \in \mathcal{S} \ j'$ where $x' = ((A, \gamma), d + 1, i)$. by a case analysis. If $n_1 = 0$ then $s = w \ ! \ j$ and SCAN moves the dot. If $n_1 = n_0 + 1$ then $G \vdash [s] \Rightarrow u$ and $G \vdash u \Rightarrow^{n_0} slice \ j \ j' \ w$ for some u. PREDICT yields $((s, u), 0, j) \in \mathcal{S} \ j$, the outer IH yields $((s, u), |u|, j) \in \mathcal{S} \ j'$ (because $n_0 < n_1 \leq m \leq n$) and COMPLETE yields the desired $x' \in \mathcal{S} \ j'$. Because $ss = \beta \ x'$ the final $((A, \gamma), |\gamma|, i) \in \mathcal{S} \ k$ follows by means of the inner IH.

Completeness follows easily. Let $S = start \ G$ and assume that $G \vdash [S] \Rightarrow_* w$ and that w is a list of terminal symbols. Thus there is some production (S, u) and some n such that $G \vdash u \Rightarrow^n w$. Let x be the state $((S, u), 0, 0)$. Thus $x \in \mathcal{S} \ 0$ and $G \vdash \beta \ x \Rightarrow^n slice \ 0 \ |w| \ w$. With the help of the inductive lemma (1) it follows that $((S, u), |u|, 0) \in \mathcal{S} \ |w|$ and thus *accepted*.

Our completeness proof is similar to the ones by Earley [2] and Jones [4]: an outer induction on the length of a derivation $\Rightarrow^n$ and an inner induction on the length of a word (which is left implicit in the earlier proofs by utilizing ellipses). This is different from Aho and Ullman's more complicated proof and is a simplification of the one by Rau [11] (which in turn is based on the work of Obua [8])) because we could obviate the additional data type of derivations (using the length of $\Rightarrow^n$ instead) and untangled the inductions.

5   The Standard Definition

The initial specification *Earley* defines a set of (state, index) pairs. It is non-deterministic in two dimensions: the $\mathcal{S}\ j$ are not generated in a fixed order and neither are the elements of each $\mathcal{S}\ j$.

For example, consider a concrete grammar with start symbol S and only two productions $S \to a$ and $S \to aa$, where a is a terminal symbol. Let $w = a$. Then we have $(S \to \bullet a, 0) \in \mathcal{S}\ 0$ by INIT and $(S \to a\bullet, 0) \in \mathcal{S}\ 1$ by SCAN and thus w is *accepted*. Note that we chose not to generate $(S \to \bullet aa, 0) \in \mathcal{S}\ 0$: it is a dead end, but there is no way of knowing that in advance—it is an angelic choice to ignore it.

The standard definition of Earley's algorithm simply generates each $\mathcal{S}\ j$ completely before moving on to $\mathcal{S}\ (j+1)$. This sequential strategy works because elements of $\mathcal{S}\ j$ do not depend on $\mathcal{S}\ k$ where $j < k$. Therefore both Earley and Jones start with a more algorithmic formulation that we first explain informally. The sets $\mathcal{S}\ 0, \mathcal{S}\ 1, \ldots, \mathcal{S}\ |w|$ are generated in that order. We follow Jones relatively closely and define a sequence of *bins* (= state sets) $B_0, \ldots, B_{|w|}$ where *closure* means closure under prediction and completion:

$B_0 = $ closure of *Init*
$B_{i+1} = $ closure of Scan of B_i, where Scan is defined below.

The aim is $B_i = \mathcal{S}\ i$, which remains to be shown.

Now we start formalizing the B_i. The obvious representation would be as a function just like $\mathcal{S}$. Instead we follow the traditional representation as a list (array) of state sets. That way each B_i is computed only once and stored in the list for future lookups. Function *bins k* recursively computes the list of bins B_0, $\ldots, B_k$:

> *bins* :: *nat* $\Rightarrow$ *'a state set list*
>
> *bins* 0 = [*Close* [] *Init*]
> *bins* (*k* + 1) = (*let Bs* = *bins k in Bs* @ [*Close Bs* (*Scan* (*last Bs*) *k*)])

In each step, it takes the (currently) last bin, generates a set of new states by scanning

> *Scan B k* = {*mv_dot x* | *x* $\in$ *B* $\wedge$ *next_symbol x* = *Some* (*w* ! *k*)}

and closes this set under prediction and completion. This can be formalized as a least fixpoint (as Jones does) or as an inductive definition. We have chosen the latter alternative simply because Isabelle provides good support for inductions involving inductive definitions. The closure operator *Close* takes two arguments: the current list of bins and the result of scanning. It is defined in the obvious way:

$$\frac{x \in B}{x \in Close\ Bs\ B} \qquad \frac{x \in Close\ Bs\ B \qquad x' \in Predict\ x\ |Bs|}{x' \in Close\ Bs\ B}$$

$$\frac{y \in Close\ Bs\ B \qquad is\_complete\ y}{x \in (Bs\ @\ [Close\ Bs\ B])\ !\ from\ y \qquad next\_symbol\ x = Some\ (lhs\ (prod\ y))}{mv\_dot\ x \in Close\ Bs\ B}$$

The only noteworthy aspect is the assumption

$$x \in (Bs\ @\ [Close\ Bs\ B])\ !\ from\ y$$

in the completion rule. This is where it differs from the abstract COMPLETE rule which simply says $x \in S$ (*from y*). Now we implicitly rely on the well-formedness property *from* $y \leq k$ but we also need to append the currently defined bin *Close Bs B* to *Bs* when we locate x because x might be in the same bin as y. This is a subtlety that Jones seems to have missed. Note that x and y can only be in the same bin if the grammar contains productions with empty rhs. For example, if $x = (A \rightarrow \alpha \bullet B\beta,\ i) \in$ bin k, the bin under construction, and there is a production $B \rightarrow \varepsilon$, then prediction implies $y = (B \rightarrow \bullet \varepsilon,\ k) \in$ bin k and thus completion applies and combines two states in the same bin.

There is another small difference of our *bins* and the definition by Jones: *bins* $0 = [Close\ []\ Init]$. We apply *Close*, and thus both prediction and completion, to *Init*. Jones only uses prediction. Again, this is not enough if there are ε-productions. For example, given a grammar with two productions $S \rightarrow \varepsilon$ and $S \rightarrow Sa]$ and an input $w = a$, then $Init = \{(S \rightarrow \bullet\varepsilon,\ 0),\ (S \rightarrow \bullet Sa,\ 0)\}$ and completion adds $(S \rightarrow S\bullet a,\ 0)$. Thus bin 1 contains the result of *Scan*, namely $(S \rightarrow Sa\bullet,\ 0)$, and thus $w = a$ is accepted. Without completion, no acceptance.

Note that in his next development step, Jones rules out ε-productions anyway, to simplify matters. See Sect. 5.2 below.

5.1   Equivalence of *bins* and S

We need to show that *bins* $|w| = [S\ 0, \ldots, S\ |w|]$. Because completion may refer to arbitrary earlier bins we prove this generalized proposition by induction on n:

$$n \leq |w| \implies \forall\, i \leq n.\ bins\ n\ !\ i = S\ i \tag{2}$$

In the base case we need $S\ 0 = Close\ []\ Init$: in one direction this is proved by induction on the definition of *Earley* (see Sect. 4), in the other direction by induction on the definition of *Close*. In the induction step in the proof of (2), the IH is $\forall\, i \leq n.\ bins\ n\ !\ i = S\ i$. It implies

$$\forall\, i {\leq} n.\ bins\ (n+1)\ !\ i = \mathcal{S}\ i$$

using $[\![i \leq m;\ m \leq n]\!] \implies bins\ m\ !\ i = bins\ n\ !\ i$, which is a corollary of $m \leq n \implies take\ (m+1)\ (bins\ n) = bins\ m$, which in turn is proved by induction on n.

As a direct corollary of (2) we obtain the desired equality:

$$i \leq |w| \implies bins\ |w|\ !\ i = \mathcal{S}\ i$$

5.2   Towards Simple Closure

Like all inductive definitions in this paper, *Close* is executable. In an iterative computation of the closure, prediction is easy: as soon as a new element x is added to *Close Bs B*, we can also add *Predict x* $|Bs|$ and x never needs to partake in prediction again. Completion, however, can combine two elements y and x, both from the currently defined set *Close Bs B*. Thus, it is not enough to use some state once for completion: as soon as new elements are added to *Close Bs B*, new combinations can arise.

To simplify the computation of the closure, Jones [4,5, Chapter 6] restricts to ε-*free* grammars, i.e. grammars without productions of the form $A \to \varepsilon$. We follow Jones throughout the rest of this section. As a result, *from y* $< |Bs|$ for all $y \in Close\ Bs\ B$ and thus $x \in (Bs\ @\ [Close\ Bs\ B])\ !\ from\ y$ in the completion rule of *Close* can be simplified to $x \in Bs\ !\ from\ y$. Formally, we define a variant *Close*1 of *Close* that is obtained from *Close* by replacing $x \in (Bs\ @\ [Close\ Bs\ B])\ !\ from\ y$ by $x \in Bs\ !\ from\ y$. For *Close*1 we obtain a strong wellformedness property

$$wf\_state1\ x\ k = (wf\_state\ x\ k \land (is\_complete\ x \longrightarrow from\ x < k))$$

that extends easily to (list of) state sets

$$wf\_bins1\ Bs = (\forall\, k{<}|Bs|.\ wf\_bin1\ (Bs\ !\ k)\ k)$$
$$wf\_bin1\ B\ k = (\forall\, x{\in}B.\ wf\_state1\ x\ k)$$

and which is preserved by *Close*1

$$[\![wf\_bins1\ Bs;\ wf\_bin1\ B\ |Bs|;\ y \in Close1\ Bs\ B]\!] \implies wf\_state1\ y\ |Bs|$$

It is straightforward to prove the equivalence of the two closures:

$$[\![wf\_bins1\ Bs;\ wf\_bin1\ B\ |Bs|]\!] \implies Close1\ Bs\ B = Close\ Bs\ B$$

5.3   One-Pass Closure

We conclude the development with an efficient one-pass formulation of *Close*1. It is still on the level of sets and intentionally nondeterministic. It would be simple to derive a specific list-based algorithm from it (e.g. the one given by Jones with only a short proof sketch). Rau [11] has already verified a version of Jones' algorithm but our starting point is different.

We formulate the one-pass closure as a transition system $Bs \vdash (B,\ C) \rightarrow (B',\ C')$ where $B,\ C,\ B',\ C'$ are sets of states: B is the current set whose closure is to be computed (the "worklist"), C is the accumulator for the closure, and $(B',\ C')$ is the result of a) moving some state $x \in B$ to the accumulator (i.e. $C' = C \cup \{x\}$) and b) extending the worklist with all results of prediction or completion (depending on x). The definition is again inductive:

$$\frac{x \in B \qquad next\_symbol\ x \neq None}{Bs \vdash (B,\ C) \rightarrow (B \cup Predict\ x\ |Bs| - (C \cup \{x\}),\ \{x\} \cup C)}$$

$$\frac{x \in B \qquad next\_symbol\ x = None}{Bs \vdash (B,\ C) \rightarrow (B \cup Complete\ Bs\ x - (C \cup \{x\}),\ C \cup \{x\})}$$

Complete Bs y =
mv_dot ' $\{x \in Bs\ !\ from\ y \mid next\_symbol\ x = Some\ (lhs\ (prod\ y))\}$

where $f\ '\ A = \{b \mid \exists\, a \in A.\ f\ a = b\}$. The full closure algorithm consists of the stepwise reduction of B to the empty set:

close2 Bs B = (SOME C. Bs $\vdash$ (B, $\emptyset$) $\rightarrow$ ($\emptyset$, C))*

where *SOME* is Hilbert's epsilon operator: *SOME x. P* denotes an arbitrary (but fixed!) x that satisfies P (if such an x exists). In our case it does exist, as witnessed by the following lemma:

⟦*wf_bins1 Bs; wf_bin1 B |Bs|; wf_bin1 C |Bs|*⟧
$\implies \exists\, C'.\ Bs \vdash (B,\ C) \rightarrow* (\emptyset,\ C')$

The proof is by induction on a suitable wellfounded relation (that is based on the fact that there are only finitely many wellformed states). Although it is not obvious, there is a unique C' such that $Bs \vdash (B,\ C) \rightarrow* (\emptyset,\ C')$, i.e. the result of *close2* is independent of which result *SOME* chooses.

As for *Close* and *Close1*, we can also prove the equivalence of *Close1* and *close2*:

⟦*wf_bins1 Bs; wf_bin1 B |Bs|*⟧ $\implies$ *close2 Bs B = Close1 Bs B*

This proof is quite involved and we cannot detail it here.

Finally we can replace *Close* by *close2* in the definition of *bins* and obtain (by proof)

bins 0 = [close2 [] Init]
bins (k + 1) = (let Bs = bins k in Bs @ [close2 Bs (Scan (last Bs) k)])

where we need to assume ε_free and $k < |w|$. The latter assumption does no harm because by definition of *accepted*, we only need to compute the bins up to $|w|$.

6   Comparison

The work of Jones is remarkable for a number of reasons in addition to mathematical rigour:

State-free algorithm At a time when algorithms were typically described in an imperative fashion, Jones standard specification is completely state-free, i.e. purely functional description of the algorithm based on standard mathematics. This is in contrast to contemporary work: both Earley and Aho & Ullman describe the initial version of Earley's recognizer/parser as an imperative program. As a result the proofs have an imperative flavour as well. Earley [2, p. 19] describes the soundness proof like this: "by induction on the number of states added to any state set before $<p, j, f, \alpha>$ is added to S_i." This is just fixpoint induction in disguise.

Fixpoint definitions The saturation loop ("perform steps (5) and (6) until no new items can be added" [1, p. 321]) is described as a least fixpoint and the corresponding proofs proceed by fixpoint reasoning (influenced by Park [10]). As a consequence, our inductive and recursive Isabelle definitions in Sect. 5 are very direct transcription of Jones' definitions.

Modularity Jones does not prove a specific algorithm correct. Instead he sets up an interface in the form of requirements that the generated state sets must satisfy and shows that the state sets generated by a particular algorithm satisfy the requirements.

7   Conclusions

We have presented an abstract inductive definition of Earley state sets, have shown its correctness w.r.t. the language generated by the grammar, and have proved equivalence with the standard definition from the literature given by Jones, the latter being particularly well-suited for a machine-checked formalization. In a final step we have derived an efficient one-pass algorithm for ε-free grammars.

Obvious future work is the derivation of a list-based implementation from our final one-pass set-based algorithm, including a verified running-time analysis.

References

1. Aho, A.V., Ullman, J.D.: The Theory of Parsing, Translation, and Compiling. Prentice-Hall, Hoboken (1972)
2. Earley, J.: An efficient context-free parsing algorithm. Ph.D. thesis, Carnegie-Mellon University, Computer Science Department (1968)
3. Earley, J.: An efficient context-free parsing algorithm. Commun. ACM **13**(2), 94–102 (1970). https://doi.org/10.1145/362007.362035
4. Jones, C.: Formal development of correct algorithms: an example based on Earley's recogniser. Technical report, T.R.12.095, IBM United Kingdom Laboratories, Hursley Park (1971). http://homepages.cs.ncl.ac.uk/cliff.jones/publications/Other-TRs/TR12.095.pdf

5. Jones, C.B.: Formal development of correct algorithms: An example based on Earley's recogniser. In: Proceedings of ACM Conference on Proving Assertions About Programs, pp. 150–169. ACM (1972). https://doi.org/10.1145/800235.807083
6. Nipkow, T., Klein, G.: Concrete Semantics with Isabelle/HOL. Springer, Cham (2014). http://concrete-semantics.org
7. Nipkow, T., Paulson, L.C., Wenzel, M.: Isabelle/HOL – A Proof Assistant for Higher-Order Logic. LNCS, vol. 2283. Springer, Heidelberg (2002). https://doi.org/10.1007/3-540-45949-9
8. Obua, S.: Local lexing. Archive of Formal Proofs (2017). https://isa-afp.org/entries/LocalLexing.html. Formal proof development
9. Obua, S., Scott, P., Fleuriot, J.D.: Local lexing. CoRR abs/1702.03277 (2017). http://arxiv.org/abs/1702.03277
10. Park, D.: Fixpoint induction and proofs of program properties. In: Michie, D., Meltzer, B. (eds.) Machine Intelligence, vol. 5. Edinburgh University Press (1971)
11. Rau, M.: Earley parser. Archive of Formal Proofs (2023). https://isa-afp.org/entries/Earley_Parser.html. Formal proof development
12. Rau, M.: Formal verification of an earley parser. Master's thesis, Department of Informatics, Technische Universität München (2023)
13. Rau, M., Nipkow, T.: A verified Earley parser. In: Bertot, Y., Kutsia, T., Norrish, M. (eds.) 14th International Conference on Interactive Theorem Proving (ITP 2023). Leibniz International Proceedings in Informatics (LIPIcs), Schloss Dagstuhl – Leibniz-Zentrum für Informatik (2024, to appear)

On the Relational Basis of Early R/G Work

José N. Oliveira$^{(\boxtimes)}$ (iD)

High Assurance Software Laboratory, INESC TEC and University of Minho,
Braga, Portugal
jno@di.uminho.pt

Abstract. The R/G approach to the development of interfering programs was initiated by the pioneering work of Cliff Jones (1981) on a *relational basis*. R/G has been the subject of much research since then, most of it deviating from the original relational set-up. This paper looks at such early work from a historical perspective and shows how it can be approached and extended using state-of-the-art relational algebra.

1 Introduction

Cliff Jones doctoral thesis, available as OUCL technical monograph PRG-25 [22] and defended in Oxford four decades ago (June 1981), is a milestone in the research on the formal semantics of parallel programs that interfere with each other over a shared state (shared variable concurrency).

Four decades is long enough for one to look at this monograph from both a historical and a technical perspective. As often happens in science history, the historical eye sharpens one's appreciation of the technical achievements.

Right at the start, the abstract is clear about *goals* and the *method* to achieve them:

> "*A relational basis is used for the systematic development of programs. Abstract data types are defined by models and a proof method of data refinement is given. (...) Interference from parallel tasks which can change shared variables is also covered in the development process.*"

By emphasizing the use of a *relational basis*, Jones is clear about his intended approach to the *systematic development of programs*. This had been a hot topic in the 1970s, a *vintage* decade which saw landmark textbooks such as [7,21,40] appear, and in which concepts such as abstract data type, data refinement and Hoare logic [18] consolidated.

It must be stressed that the use of relational methods in formal semantics was not widespread at the time. Jones cites the work of Abrial and Schuman [2] (1979), but this was essentially set-theoretic. What was already showing use of a similar *relational basis* is another of his references: the technical report "*Calculus for Recursive Program Schemes*" by J.W. de Bakker and W.P. de Roever [6], which had appeared several years earlier (1972) explicitly relying on Tarski's

© The Author(s), under exclusive license to Springer Nature Switzerland AG 2024
A. Cavalcanti and J. Baxter (Eds.): *The Practice of Formal Methods*, LNCS 14781, pp. 56–76, 2024.
https://doi.org/10.1007/978-3-031-66673-5_4

relation algebra.[1] This, together with a relational semantics for nondeterminism defined by David Park in *"On the semantics of fair parallelism"* [34] (1980), might have been Jones' main inspiration.

Jones' thesis addresses the decomposition of isolated programs first (Sect. 3) and then the development of interfering programs (Sect. 4). The approach is novel in the sense that it faces interference *throughout the development process*, rather than establishing non-interference after all sub-programs have been shown correct in isolation. This is not a minor detail: it marks the start of an *interference-first* view of programming, meaning that interference becomes an asset, not an onus. That is, the parallel $P \parallel Q$ of two programs P and Q is intended as their mutual *collaboration*, of no less importance that the sequential collaboration of P ; Q. In a metaphor with music, P ; Q is melody, $P \parallel Q$ is harmony. And what is music other than the *"harmonious interference"* of a number of players?

For this to work, the $\{pre\}P\{post\}$ development axis of sequential programming that had emerged in the 1960s from the pioneering works of Floyd and Hoare [10, 18][2], had to be complemented by an orthogonal axis capturing interfer-

$$rely \xrightarrow{\;pre\;} guarantee$$
$$post$$

ence by *relying* and *guaranteeing* mutual behavioural, thus giving birth to the *rely-guarantee* (R/G) method proposed in [22]. The news was that, while *pre* and *post* are predicates, *rely* and *guarantee* have to be state-relations, in order to express state changes made by the other parties. This might have been a strong motivation for the *relation basis* of [22]. Ten years later (1991), Jones would write, in his report *Interference Resumed* [23]:[3]

> *"The rely/guarantee work initially attracted little attention but there have recently been critiques and attempts to extend the work (...)"*

In fact, the decades to follow would witness an explosion of interest in the R/G approach (cf. [15, 16, 26, 38, 41] among much other literature) because of its upfront addressing a very relevant and difficult problem in computer science. Quoting [41] (1997):

> *"It is now well realised that parallel computer programs are among the most complicated systems that human beings have ever constructed in terms of the number of interacting components and the degree of interaction. Constructing such systems has proven to be much harder than expected."*

A challenge that, honestly speaking, remains far from fully mastered.

This paper will address the R/G approach by building upon the *relational basis* of [22] in a generic way, trying to capture the *essence* rather than the

---

[1] On the other side of the Atlantic, Alfred Tarski and his student Steven Givant were on a crusade to express *set-theory without variables* [39]. This style of doing mathematics is currently named the *pointfree* style.

[2] Among others, Alan Turing included, as Jones takes the care to remind us in [25].

[3] The research described in this report was presented at the 1991 Australian Software Engineering Conference [24].

details and variants of the method. This relational view will lead to a kind of the *"everything is a relation"* approach that, already scented in the early 1970s [6], has become the *motto* of quite successful approaches to software design [19,20]. Such an approach regards relations as *first class citizens*, thus dispensing with variables in the sense of [39]—the so-called *pointfree* approach. It will also explain why, rather than *predicate-transformers* [7], the focus goes to the *program-transformers* that emerge from the four components of the orthogonal axes shown in the scheme above.

Relational methods evolved significantly since the 1980s [1,4,5,11,12,37][4], including the search for new foundations, notation improvements and new results. In the early 1990s, the Groningen-Eindhoven group led by Backhouse [1,3] contributed decisively to the field by structuring relation algebra in terms of Galois connections. This elegant approach, which has been influential in the way (typed) relation algebra was perceived henceforth, will be followed in this paper.

2   The "Vertical Axis"

J. de Bakker and W. de Roever [6] were among the first to express Hoare triples $p \{ Q \} r$ using relation algebraic operators only, by writing

$$p \,;\, Q \subseteq Q \,;\, r \tag{1}$$

where Q is a program (regarded as a binary relation on a set of states), and p (the pre-condition) and r (the post-condition) are predicates on states. The meaning they assign to (1) is the logic statement:

$$\langle \forall\, x, y \,::\, p\,(x) \wedge x\; Q\; y \Rightarrow r\,(y) \rangle \tag{2}$$

The first thing to be noted in (2) is the use of the infix notation $x\; Q\; y$, instead of the often used $(x, y) \in Q$ that immediately freezes one's view of relations as sets of pairs. Readers will ask: since $p \,;\, Q$ means $p\,(x) \wedge x\; Q\; y$, what kind of relational operator is ";" involving a predicate and a relation? And how did the second Q of (1) disappear from (2)?

Relational Diagrams. To answer these questions we commute to the graphical expression of (1) shown in the diagram aside, where E is a given set of states. This squared diagram brings with it some changes in notation convention, cf. $Q \cdot p \subseteq r \cdot Q$. Basically, what we are doing is to use the notation $Q \cdot p$ (resp. $r \cdot Q$) that "flips" the order of the arguments in $p \,;\, Q$ (resp. $Q \,;\, r$). The reason for this "flipping" will be explained later on. Before this, how do predicates p and r fit in the square shown?

$$\begin{array}{ccc} E & \xleftarrow{\;\;p\;\;} & E \\ {\scriptstyle Q}\downarrow & \subseteq & \downarrow{\scriptstyle Q} \\ E & \xleftarrow{\;\;r\;\;} & E \end{array}$$

----

[4] There is even a conference series—RAMiCS—focussed on relational methods in computer science.

Let us start by explaining squares such as the one shown above in general, see (3) below. This square has four sides R, P, S, Q, which are binary relations. The square itself is a comparison between two paths, of two relations each:

$$
\begin{array}{ccc}
A & \xleftarrow{\ R\ } & B \\
{\scriptstyle P}\downarrow & \subseteq & \downarrow{\scriptstyle Q} \\
C & \xleftarrow{\ S\ } & D
\end{array}
\qquad\qquad P \cdot R \subseteq S \cdot Q
\tag{3}
$$

In more detail, each side is an arrow, say $A \xleftarrow{\ R\ } B$, declaring a binary relation R that relates objects of types A and B. Its meaning is as usual: given objects $a \in A$ and $b \in B$, the proposition $a\, R\, b$ tells whether or not a and b are related by R. Take for instance relation $\mathbb{N}_0 \xleftarrow{(\leqslant)} \mathbb{N}_0$. Clearly, $0 \leqslant 1$ holds (it is a true proposition) while $1 \leqslant 0$ does not.

Next, we need to say what a *path* means, say $P \cdot R$ in (3): given some $c \in C$ and some $b \in B$, $c\,(P \cdot R)\,b$ holds wherever there is some mediator $a \in A$ such that both $c\, P\, a$ and $a\, R\, b$ hold. We say that relation $P \cdot R$ is the *composition* of relations P and R. Relational composition is associative. Finally, the comparison $R \subseteq S$ of two relations $B \xleftarrow{R,S} A$ means that, for all $b \in B$ and $a \in A$, if $b\, R\, a$ holds then $b\, S\, a$ holds too. In summary, relation *inclusion* "hides" a *universal* quantifier, while relation *composition* hides an *existential* quantifier. In symbols, the logic interpretation of (3) is

$$
\langle \forall\, c, b :: \langle \exists\, a :: c\, P\, a \wedge a\, R\, b \rangle \Rightarrow \langle \exists\, d :: c\, S\, d \wedge d\, Q\, b \rangle \rangle
\tag{4}
$$

Comparisons $R \subseteq S$ form a partial order, therefore reflexive, transitive and antisymmetric.

The language compression of (3) when compared to (4) is visible to the naked eye, free of quantifiers as it is. This is what Alfred Tarski, who had a life-long struggle with quantified notation [9], was seeking in e.g. [39]. In his footsteps, de Bakker, de Roever [6] and Jones [22] were looking for a similar economy of notation in tackling problems they knew were inherently complex.

Predicates Go Relational. Every type A has its own *identity* relation $A \xleftarrow{\ id\ } A$, which is such that $a'\, id\, a \Leftrightarrow a' = a$. Therefore, $R \cdot id = R = id \cdot R$ holds for any R and thus squares involving id degenerate into triangles or even "sides".

A special case of square (3) pops up wherever R and S are *partial identities*, also called *coreflexive* relations ($R \subseteq id$ and $S \subseteq id$). These relations are one-to-one correspondent to predicates: given a predicate $p : A \to \mathbb{B}$, its associated coreflexive is the relation $p? : A \to A$ defined by

$$
a'\,(p?)\,a \Leftrightarrow a' = a \wedge p\,(a)
\tag{5}
$$

Going back to de Bakker & de Roever's $p\,;\,Q \subseteq Q\,;\,r$ (i.e. our $Q \cdot p \subseteq r \cdot Q$), we can see that p and r abbreviate the coreflexives $p?$ and $q?$, respectively, in:

$$
Q \cdot p? \subseteq r? \cdot Q
\tag{6}
$$

All relations in relational type $A \to B$ form a Boolean algebra, whose bottom and top elements are the relations $A \xrightarrow{\perp} B$ and $A \xrightarrow{\top} B$ such that, for all b and a, $b \perp a = \textit{false}$ and $b \top a = \textit{true}$, respectively. By (4) and (5) it can be easily shown that (6) and $Q \cdot p? \subseteq r? \cdot \top$ both convert to (2), and this explains how the right-hand Q disappeared through the pointwise conversion.

In the literature, Hoare triples have been written in two ways, either $p \{Q\} r$ (the original notation) [18] or $\{p\} Q \{r\}$. In a relational semantics for computer programs, the latter notation $\{p\}$ can be regarded as standing for the coreflexive $p?$. Wherever arising no ambiguity, we shall follow de Bakker & de Rover and drop the question mark from "$p?$".

Jones [23] uses a similar convention for sets:

> "When a set appears in a context where a relation is required, the appropriate identity or diagonal relation is to be used."

Generalizing, for $A \xrightarrow{R} B$ a relation and S a subset of A ($S \subseteq A$), then S in $S; R$ (i.e. our $R \cdot S$) means the coreflexive $(\in S)$? (written E_S in [22]) where $(\in S)$ is S's characteristic function. This representation of sets by coreflexives is in fact a very convenient one, as Backhouse stresses in [3]:

> "The most compelling reason, however, for choosing to represent sets by coreflexives is the dominant position occupied by composition among programming primitives."

Although restricted to homogeneous relations, the relational "palette" of [22] is quite rich, capitalizing on the role of composition just mentioned above, together with relational converse R°, written R^{-1} in [22]. Given a relation $A \xrightarrow{R} B$, its converse is the relation $A \xleftarrow{R^\circ} B$ such that $a \, R^\circ \, b \Leftrightarrow b \, R \, a$. The *kernel* $R^\circ \cdot R$ and *image* $R \cdot R^\circ$ of a relation R, when compared with the identity id, yield a taxonomy of relations (injective, surjective, etc.) that is exposed in [22], including dedicated notation. For instance, R is said to be a partial function iff $R \cdot R^\circ \subseteq id$ and Jones uses a special kind of arrow to denote such (partial) functions, $R : A \xrightarrow{\sim} B$.

Although relations generalize functions, they can be regarded as functions too. Jones writes [22]:

> "Relations are used as the underpinning of the notions of specification and satisfaction but it is easier to reason about particular programs if the specifications are given by predicates."

In this *relations-as-predicates* view, the sentence $b \, R \, a$ is interpreted literally as the outcome of applying a Boolean function to the pair (b, a), validating $b \, R \, a$ if the outcome is true. While this looks back to the predicate calculus, another most common functional approach to relations has a different flavour.

Relations as Set-Valued Functions. The adjunction between binary relations and set-valued functions is well-known: every relation $B \xleftarrow{R} A$ can be converted into a function $\Lambda R : (\mathsf{P} \, B)^A$ which obeys the following universal property [5,33]:

$$k = \Lambda R \iff \in \cdot k = R \tag{7}$$

The Λ operator is called the *power-transpose* and $B \xleftarrow{\in} \mathsf{P} B$ is the membership relation that relates every object to sets it belongs to. Making $k := \Lambda R$ in (7) we get $R = \in \cdot \Lambda R$ which corresponds to the pointwise $b \, R \, a \iff b \in \Lambda R \, (a)$. We see here how writing $b \, R \, a$ (output to the left) and not $a \, R \, b$ (output to the right) shows its advantage—writing $a \, R \, b \iff \Lambda R \, (a) \ni b$ would look quite unnatural.

On the left side of (7) we live in the world of (total) functions and their properties. On the right side, composition should be read relationally and so on. Jones [22,23] uses transposition very often, and so do Bird and Moore in their textbook [5].

Adjunction (7) has a great impact on relational methods. Because the powerset functor (P) is a monad, the standard category of relations corresponds to the Kleisli category of P [27]. The powerset inclusion ordering induces relation inclusion and thus the category of relations is order-enriched. (More details in Sect. 5.)

3   On **pre** and **post**

A very important property of relational composition $R \cdot S$ is that it is a *residuated* operator, a property captured by a Galois connection [3]:

$$Z \cdot Y \subseteq X \iff Z \subseteq X/Y \tag{8}$$

This introduces the concept of *relational residual* X / Y, also called relational *quotient* or *division*. The reason for this "multiplicative" terminology is the analogy with a similar Galois connection

$$z \times y \leqslant x \iff z \leqslant x \div y \tag{9}$$

that defines integer division $x \div y$ in terms of multiplication (its "adjoint" operation $z \times y$).

Noting that $(/Y)$ can be regarded as an operator that *transforms* a relation X into another relation X / Y (a *relational transformer*), the question is—what is the meaning of the transformation? From (8) it can be observed that X / Y is the *largest* relation Z such that $Z \cdot Y \subseteq X$—just read (8) from left to right, i.e. the ($\Rightarrow$) part of ($\iff$). Moreover, it can be shown that the pointwise meaning of X / Y is:

$$c \, (X / Y) \, a \iff \langle \forall \, b :: a \, Y \, b \Rightarrow c \, X \, b \rangle \tag{10}$$

Given a predicate p and a program P (regarded as a relation, in the current context), let us consider the relational division of relation P by the coreflexive p? (abbreviated to p, as suggested above) by introducing:

$$\mathsf{pre} \, p \, P = P / p \tag{11}$$

So (pre p) is an operator that picks a program P and transforms it into another program, $P \,/\, p$—a *program transformer*. Clearly, pre $p\ P$ is larger than P:

$$P \subseteq \text{pre } p\ P$$

$\Leftrightarrow \qquad \{\ (11);\ (8)\ \}$

$$P \cdot p \subseteq P$$

$\Leftarrow \qquad \{\ P = P \cdot id\ ;\ \text{monotonicity of } (P \cdot)\ \}$

$$p \subseteq id$$

$\Leftrightarrow \qquad \{\ \text{coreflexive } p\ \}$

$\qquad true$

In fact, pre $p\ P$ is the *largest* program that behaves like P wherever its inputs satisfy p; that is, b (pre $p\ P$) a is equivalent to $p\ (a) \Rightarrow b\ P\ a$.

Relational Post-conditions. Jones [22] deviates from the original Hoare triple presentation [18] in the sense that his post-conditions are binary relations, not predicates:

> *"Operations will be specified by defining a set of states; a pre-condition which is a predicate of one state; and a post-condition which is a predicate of two states, thus:*

$St = \cdots$
$pre : St \to Bool$
$post : St \times St \to Bool"$

That is, post-conditions and programs are both relations of type $St \to St$ and to express the fact that a particular program P satisfies a post-condition S one just has to prove $P \subseteq S$. What does it mean to add a pre-condition p to post-condition S? From this instance of (8) via (11),

$$P \subseteq \text{pre } p\ S\ \Leftrightarrow\ P \cdot p \subseteq S \tag{12}$$

we see that P is freed to behave as it wishes wherever not constrained by pre-condition p. Jones laconically writes:

> *"(...) about states which do not satisfy the pre-condition, the specification has nothing to say."* [22]

The scope of the relational post-condition approach is actually broader than it first appears. First, it includes predicate post-conditions q as special case, just make $S = q \cdot \top$. Moreover, note that S in (12) can be of any relational type $A \to B$, not just a relation between states. This lets the so-called *implicit definition* of a function [21] to become part of this unifying schema, for instance.

The Specification Statement. Back to predicate-only Hoare triples, let us now introduce a program transformer capturing the post-conditioning effect:

$$\mathsf{post}\ q\ P = q \cdot P \tag{13}$$

By contrast with $\mathsf{pre}\ p\ P$, $\mathsf{post}\ q\ P$ is smaller than P by the same monotonicity argument used above. The intuition is that it cannot fire for inputs that lead to outputs not meeting the post-condition q. What kind of program transformation is obtained by chaining $\mathsf{pre}\ p \cdot \mathsf{post}\ q$? Let us apply such a transformation to some S:

$$Q \subseteq \mathsf{pre}\ p\ (\mathsf{post}\ q\ S)$$
$$\Leftrightarrow \quad \{\ \text{definitions (11) and (13)}\ \}$$
$$Q \subseteq (q \cdot S)\ /\ p$$
$$\Leftrightarrow \quad \{\ (8)\ \}$$
$$Q \cdot p \subseteq q \cdot S$$

We conclude that $\mathsf{pre}\ p\ (\mathsf{post}\ q\ S)$ is the largest program Q such that, for inputs satisfying p, behaves like S *and* ensures q on the output. (Again note that Q is not constrained to be a state-to-state relation.) For the largest possible S we get:

$$Q \subseteq \mathsf{pre}\ p\ (\mathsf{post}\ q\ \top)$$
$$\Leftrightarrow \quad \{\ \text{above}\ \}$$
$$Q \cdot p \subseteq q \cdot \top$$
$$\Leftrightarrow \quad \{\ \text{Hoare triple}\ \}$$
$$\{p\}\ Q\ \{q\}$$

Thus $\mathsf{pre}\ p\ (\mathsf{post}\ q\ \top)$ is the largest program Q that can fit in the Hoare triple $\{p\}\ Q\ \{q\}$. This corresponds to what Carroll Morgan [29] calls *the specification statement*, written $[p, q]$. Using this notation, we have:

$$Q \subseteq [p, q]\ \Leftrightarrow\ \{p\}\ Q\ \{q\} \tag{14}$$

4   The "Horizontal Axis"

Back to the scheme of Sect. 1, what we presented in the previous sections amounts to capturing the vertical development axis through the two pre and post program transformers, which were easy to define on a *relational basis*.

The agenda for the other axis, where programs are allowed to interfere with each other, is the same: find two other program transformers, say rely and guar, able to express the dynamics of program interference. However, interference is not as easy to formalize and will have dramatic implications on the simplicity of what we have done so far. In particular, programs will no longer be state-to-state relations, although their atomic steps will still be so.

In the composite program transformer pre p · post q it may be the case that $p = q$, that is, a predicate p is maintained—a so-called *invariant*. This suggests the definition:

$$\text{inv } p = \text{pre } p \cdot \text{post } p \tag{15}$$

Then inv p P behaves like P but all its transitions that do not maintain invariant p are cancelled.[5]

Although expressed in a different way (15) was proposed by Morgan and Vickers [30] (1990) and seems to have inspired Hayes, Jones and Colvin [16] in 2012 to define guar and rely in a similar fashion:

> *"(...) This paper reports on a complete reformulation of the key ideas of rely-guarantee reasoning in a refinement calculus style. (...) The approach makes use of two new commands: a guarantee (...) and a rely command (...) The idea behind this new command was motivated by the analogy with the invariant command of Morgan and Vickers."*

A shift from the relational basis of [22] towards the refinement calculus is clear from above. But, a few years later (2015), Stephan van Staden would cast their approach back to the relational setting [38]. Informally, the main ideas in [16,38] were that:

- rely R P should be the *largest* program which refines P under the interference of other programs bound by rely-condition R (a binary relation on program states); (16)
- guar G P should be the *largest* refinement of program P whose steps satisfy guarantee-condition G (another such binary relation). (17)

Let us leave "what a program P is" open for now in this new setting and only require that P should be decomposable in its atomic steps, *steps* P.[6] This enables us to put the informal definition (17) in symbols as follows:

$$\textit{steps } Q \subseteq G \wedge Q \subseteq P \ \Leftrightarrow \ Q \subseteq \text{guar } G \ P \tag{18}$$

Thus we have a semantics for guar G in the form of a Galois connection, as happens in (12). Can we infer from (18) a closed definition for guar G?

Yes, but we need to be able to reason about *steps*. As the reader will see shortly, the key ingredient will be the rich algebra of Galois connections—a device known but barely explored in computer science when Jones [22] triggered this research trend. Such a device is briefly reviewed next.

---

[5] It can be easily seen that P needs to be an endorelation in this case, i.e. its input and output types coincide.

[6] In [38] programs are sets of traces, a trace being a sequence of state pairs. (See Sect. 7 for an alternative model.) Where clear from the context, we follow [38] and overload the operator symbols that are *Boolean algebraic*, using them for both relations and programs, e.g. $Q \subseteq P$ where P and Q are programs, $R \subseteq G$ where R and G are relations, and so on.

5 Galois Connections

Things in everyday life often come "in pairs", in dichotomies such as e.g. *good/bad, action/reaction, the left/the right, lower/upper, easy/hard* and so on. In a sense, each pair defines itself: one element of the pair exists... because the other also exists, and is its *opposite* (i.e. *antithesis*). Despite the circularity, common everyday language survives over such dualities.

The perfect antithesis (opposition, inversion) is the *bijection* or *isomorphism*. For instance, *multiplication* and *division* are inverses of each other in the positive reals: $\frac{x}{y} \times y = x$ and $\frac{x \times y}{y} = x$. That is, no information is lost when dividing or multiplying. In general, f and g such that $f(g(b)) = b$ and $g(f(a)) = a$ hold are termed *isomorphisms* and regarded as *lossless* transformations.

Data transformations in practice are *lossy* because such equalities do not hold. However, it is often the case that loss of information in such imperfect inversions can be expressed in this way,

$$\begin{cases} f(g(b)) \leqslant b \\ a \sqsubseteq g(f(a)) \end{cases} \tag{19}$$

saying "how bad" each *"round trip"* is. This relies on under and over *approximations* captured by two *preorders* ($\leqslant$) and ($\sqsubseteq$), i.e. reflexive and transitive relations.

A reasonable assumption about f and g is that they should be monotone. It is a general theorem that monotone f and g that satisfy (19) form a Galois connection (GC):[7]

$$f(a) \leqslant b \quad \Leftrightarrow \quad a \sqsubseteq g(b) \tag{20}$$

Functions f and g are said to be *adjoint* to each other: f (resp. g) is the *left*, or *lower* adjoint (resp. *right*, or *upper* adjoint). When the preorders ($\leqslant$) and ($\sqsubseteq$) are implicit from the context, it is standard to abbreviate (20) by simply writing $f \dashv g$. Note that the inequalities (19) can be easily derived from (20) by cancelling each side.

If we decompose the equivalence of (20) in its $\Leftarrow$ and $\Rightarrow$ parts, we get an indirect way of *specifying* f and g, not by explicit definition but by approximation:

– $g(b)$ is the largest a such that $f(a) \leqslant b$
– $f(a)$ is the smallest b such that $a \sqsubseteq g(b)$.

This indirect, mutual *specification* of f and g may sound odd at first reading, but it is welcome wherever the explicit definitions are clumsy and hard to manipulate. Moreover, it is often the case that one of f or g is easier to define than the other, thus providing help in reasoning about the hard one. In GC (9), for instance, a few properties of ($\div$), a "difficult" operator, emerge by reasoning about easier properties of multiplication [31].

---

[7] Theorem 5.25 of [3].

GC-reasoning becomes particularly powerful wherever the preorders are partial orders, enabling the principle of *indirect equality* [8]: for a partial order, if being at most one object a is logically equivalent to being at most another object b, then $a = b$.

If, in particular, the orderings form complete lattices, then the framework gets even richer. This is what happens in GC-structured relational algebra [3]: the type[8] $A \to B$ of all relations from A to B forms a complete lattice (actually, a complete Boolean algebra), which includes a least relation $\bot$, a top relation $\top$, and the meet $(R \cap S)$ and join $(R \cup S)$ of two relations R and S of the same type. Such is the setting in (8), i.e. $(\cdot Y) \dashv (/Y)$: relational pre-composition is adjoint to the so-called *right division* operator.[9]

Galois connections can be formulated or detected in different ways and have many useful properties [3]. Rather than listing them all here, they will be mentioned as used below. In particular, we will show how a GC-based approach to R/G program transformers is advantageous, saving much proof work.

6   R/G Program Transformers

In (18) we saw the need to decompose a program Q into its step-relation $R = steps\ Q$. Dually, one may think of, from a step-relation R, generating programs P such that $steps\ P \subseteq R$. Let us conjecture the existence of some function *traces* that yields the largest possible program whose steps do not fall off R:

$$traces\ R = \bigcup \{ P \mid steps\ P \subseteq R \}$$

This definition (which is what many of us would write) is not handy enough for ourpurposes. Here is a turn around: from

$$traces\ (steps\ Q) = \bigcup \{ P \mid steps\ P \subseteq steps\ Q \}$$

we get $Q \subseteq traces\ (steps\ Q)$. Also, $steps\ (traces\ R) \subseteq R$ is to be expected from the "requirements". Since we also expect these functions to be monotone, we immediately infer[10] that they should be adjoints of a GC:

$$steps\ P \subseteq R \quad \Leftrightarrow \quad P \subseteq traces\ R \qquad (21)$$

Armed with (21) we go back to (18) and reason:

$$Q \subseteq \mathsf{guar}\ G\ P$$
$$\Leftrightarrow \quad \{ (18) \}$$
$$steps\ Q \subseteq G \wedge Q \subseteq P$$
$$\Leftrightarrow \quad \{ (21) \}$$

---

[8] Called "homset" in the terminology of category theory [27].

[9] As relational composition is not commutative, a dual GC $(Y\cdot) \dashv (Y\backslash)$ also holds, where $(Y\backslash)$ is termed *left* division.

[10] Theorem 5.25 of [3].

$Q \subseteq traces\ G \wedge Q \subseteq P$

$\Leftrightarrow$ $\{$ GC defining $(\cap)$ [3] $\}$

$Q \subseteq traces\ G \cap P$

$::$ $\{$ indirect equality [8] since $\subseteq$ is a partial order $\}$

$\text{guar}\ G\ P = traces\ G \cap P$ (22)

Thus we get program transformer $\text{guar}\ G$ defined. As it happens with transformer $\text{post}\ p$ (13), $\text{guar}\ G\ P \subseteq P$.

To put (16) in symbols we need to conjecture the existence of a program-level operator $P \parallel Q$ expressing the "running in parallel" of two programs P and Q.[11] Then interference trimmed by some rely relation R is given by $(\parallel traces\ R)$ and another program transformer emerges as another GC,

$Q \parallel (traces\ R) \subseteq P \;\Leftrightarrow\; Q \subseteq \text{rely}\ R\ P$ (23)

i.e. $(\_ \parallel traces\ R) \dashv (\text{rely}\ R\ \_)$.[12] As GCs compose, from (23, 18) we get:

$steps\ Q \subseteq G \wedge Q \parallel (traces\ R) \subseteq P \;\Leftrightarrow\; Q \subseteq \text{guar}\ G\ (\text{rely}\ R\ P)$ (24)

This composite GC will be central for defining R/G quintuples in the style of [38]. We just have to assume that (14) also holds for the semantic domain chosen for programs. (Sets of traces in the case of [38].) Then, by expanding assertion $P \subseteq \text{guar}\ G\ (\text{rely}\ R\ [p, q])$ via (24) and (14) we obtain $\{p\}\ (P \parallel traces\ R)\ \{q\}$ $\wedge\ steps\ P \subseteq G$, which is regarded as one of two possible trace semantics for RG-quintuple $p\ R\ \{P\}\ G\ q$ in [38].

This relational meaning of RG-quintuples matches the interest of this paper in analysing and extending the relational basis proposed in [22]. Below we seek to exploit the algebraic potential of "universal" properties (23) and (18) in the derivation of R/G laws and inference rules. Two of these,

$steps\ (\text{guar}\ G\ P) \subseteq G \quad \text{and} \quad \text{guar}\ G\ P \subseteq P$ (25)

are the cancellation (19) corollaries of (18).[13] Also note that GC $steps \dashv traces$ grants a number of properties for free, for instance:

– $steps$ and $traces$ are monotonic
– lower (resp. upper) adjoint distributes by suprema (resp. infima) and thus:

$steps\ (P \cup Q) = steps\ P \cup steps\ Q$ (26)

$traces\ (R \cap S) = traces\ R \cap traces\ S$ (27)

– the ranges of $steps$ and $traces$ are isomorphic posets.[14]

---

[11] For programs being sets of traces, this corresponds to iterating the well-known shuffle product of two sequences to all possible trace combinations [38].

[12] A similar GC is developed in [15]. All this is inspired by law 31 *(rely-refinement)* of [16].

[13] Note that the right conjunct of (25) is law 28 (**Intro-g**) of [26].

[14] Cf. the *unity of opposites* theorem of [3].

– composition $traces \cdot steps$ is a $closure$ operator:

$$P \subseteq traces \ (steps \ P) \qquad (28)$$

– composition $steps \cdot traces$ is an $interior$ operator:

$$steps \ (traces \ R) \ \subseteq \ R \qquad (29)$$

It turns out that this GC is $perfect$ on the $steps$ side, so (29) is actually an equality.

R/G-*Quintuples.* R/G-quintuples will be denoted in the sequel by arrows of the form $p \xrightarrow[R \to G]{P} q$, a notation which extends a similar use of arrows to express Hoare triples in [32]. Following [16,38], we define

$$p \xrightarrow[R \to G]{P} q \quad \Leftrightarrow \quad P \subseteq \textsf{guar} \ G \ (\textsf{rely} \ R \ [p, q]) \qquad (30)$$

equivalent to:

$$p \xrightarrow[R \to G]{P} q \quad \Leftrightarrow \quad \{p\} \ (P \parallel traces \ R) \ \{q\} \wedge steps \ P \ \subseteq \ G \qquad (31)$$

As example of proof in the logic of RG-quintuples that stems from the GCs defined above, we prove law (Jconc) of [38]:

$$\left\{ \begin{array}{l} p_1 \xrightarrow[R_1 \to G_1]{P_1} p_1' \\ p_2 \xrightarrow[R_2 \to G_2]{P_2} p_2' \end{array} \right. \wedge \left\{ \begin{array}{l} G_1 \subseteq R_2 \\ G_2 \subseteq R_1 \end{array} \right. \Rightarrow \quad p_1 \cap p_2 \xrightarrow[R_1 \cap R_2 \to G_1 \cup G_2]{P_1 \parallel P_2} p_1' \cap p_2' \qquad (32)$$

The following basic properties are assumed, where 1 is the program that has no steps [38]:

$$steps \ (P \parallel Q) = steps \ P \cup steps \ Q \qquad (33)$$
$$(P \parallel traces \ R) = traces \ R \ \Leftarrow \ 1 \subseteq P \subseteq traces \ R \qquad (34)$$

Proof of (32): As p_1, p_2, p_1' and p_2' abbreviate coreflexives (5), they are handled relationally. Moreover, by transitivity of $\subseteq$ we have the premises:

$$steps \ P_1 \subseteq R_2 \wedge steps \ P_2 \subseteq R_1 \qquad (35)$$

Then:

$$p_1 \cap p_2 \xrightarrow[R_1 \cap R_2 \to G_1 \cup G_2]{P_1 \parallel P_2} p_1' \cap p_2'$$

$$\Leftrightarrow \qquad \{ \ (31) \ \}$$

$$\left\{ \begin{array}{l} \{p_1 \cap p_2\} \ (P_1 \parallel P_2 \parallel traces \ (R_1 \cap R_2)) \ \{p_1' \cap p_2'\} \\ steps \ (P_1 \parallel P_2) \subseteq G_1 \cup G_2 \end{array} \right.$$

$\Leftrightarrow$ { (33) ; Hoare triples }

$$\left\{ \begin{array}{l} \left\{ \begin{array}{l} \{p_1 \cap p_2\}\,(P_1 \parallel P_2 \parallel \mathit{traces}\,(R_1 \cap R_2))\,\{p_1'\} \\ \{p_1 \cap p_2\}\,(P_1 \parallel P_2 \parallel \mathit{traces}\,(R_1 \cap R_2))\,\{p_2'\} \end{array} \right. \\ \mathit{steps}\,P_1 \subseteq G_1 \cup G_2 \wedge \mathit{steps}\,P_2 \subseteq G_1 \cup G_2 \end{array} \right.$$

$\Leftarrow$ { $\subseteq$-transitivity }

$$\left\{ \begin{array}{l} \left\{ \begin{array}{l} \{p_1\}\,(P_1 \parallel P_2 \parallel \mathit{traces}\,(R_1 \cap R_2))\,\{p_1'\} \\ \{p_2\}\,(P_1 \parallel P_2 \parallel \mathit{traces}\,(R_1 \cap R_2))\,\{p_2'\} \end{array} \right. \\ \mathit{steps}\,P_1 \subseteq G_1 \wedge \mathit{steps}\,P_2 \subseteq G_2 \end{array} \right.$$

$\Leftarrow$ { (35) ; (21); Hoare logic }

$$\left\{ \begin{array}{l} \left\{ \begin{array}{l} \{p_1\}\,(P_1 \parallel \mathit{traces}\,R_1 \parallel \mathit{traces}\,(R_1 \cap R_2))\,\{p_1'\} \\ \{p_2\}\,(\mathit{traces}\,R_2 \parallel P_2 \parallel \mathit{traces}\,(R_1 \cap R_2))\,\{p_2'\} \end{array} \right. \\ \mathit{steps}\,P_1 \subseteq G_1 \wedge \mathit{steps}\,P_2 \subseteq G_2 \end{array} \right.$$

$\Leftrightarrow$ { (34) }

$$\left\{ \begin{array}{l} \{p_1\}\,(P_1 \parallel \mathit{traces}\,R_1)\,\{p_1'\} \wedge \mathit{steps}\,P_1 \subseteq G_1 \\ \{p_2\}\,(\mathit{traces}\,R_2 \parallel P_2)\,\{p_2'\} \wedge \mathit{steps}\,P_2 \subseteq G_2 \end{array} \right.$$

$\Leftrightarrow$ { (31) twice }

$$\left\{ \begin{array}{l} p_1 \xrightarrow[R_1 \to G_1]{P_1} p_1' \\[2mm] p_2 \xrightarrow[R_2 \to G_2]{P_2} p_2' \end{array} \right.$$

7 Resumptions

In [38] programs are viewed as sets of *traces*, a trace being a sequence of state pairs. So programs are sets but not relations anymore. One may ask: is there an "extended notion" of a relation capable of expressing the *dynamics* of two or more such "relations" interfering with each other? Jones writes [22]:

> *"The conclusion accepted by some researchers in this area is that the history must be recorded in the denotation by, for example, using resumptions:*
>
> $Res = St \to \mathsf{P}\,(St \times Res)$
>
> *The parallel combination can then be built up by some form of non-deterministic merge of the steps."*

However, this construct is not directly used in the operational semantics that follows in [22], which uses a "control tree"-like concept, as Jones puts it. Interestingly, resumptions would surface again ten years later in a technical report of the U. Manchester [23]:

> *"(...) There are various forms of resumption domain; for the current purposes the most appropriate appears to be*

$$Res = \Sigma \to \mathsf{P} \ (\Sigma_\perp \times Res)"$$

By (7) one can see how this is consistent with the relational basis of [22]—*Res transposes* a binary relation, albeit an *inductive* one. Indeed, the topic of extending relations inductively in this way was under scrutiny at the time, notably by Robin Milner [28] (1975) and Gordon Plotkin [36] (1976).

Report [23] does not seem to have attracted much attention, being rarely cited in the R/G literature. That Jones is in [23] extending his *relational basis* can be found in the definition of a function *flatten* : $Res \to (\Sigma \to \mathsf{P} \ \Sigma_\perp)$ that "delivers an extension denotation" (of a resumption). In his language, a program is a statement (the grammar of which contains the expected constructs, obviously including the parallel of two statements) and the semantics of a statement is a resumption *Res*. But the semantics of programs *flattens* such resumptions back to state-to-state relations $(\Sigma \to \mathsf{P} \ \Sigma_\perp)$.[15]

Note that $Res \cong \Sigma \to \mathsf{P} \ (\Sigma_\perp \times Res)$ is not exactly the model that had appeared before in e.g. [36], $Res \cong \Sigma \to \mathsf{P} \ (\Sigma_\perp + \Sigma_\perp \times Res)$. As it turns out, the layout of Jones's functions on *Res* follows this other model implicitly, in its systematic separation of "stopping" pairs $(\sigma, \lambda\sigma.\{\})$ from the inductive ones. Below we drop $\perp$ from $\Sigma_\perp$ (because its role is orthogonal to our analysis) and consider the isomorphism given alongside.

Let us represent the *flatten* function of [23] in the form of diagrams, the first using resumptions as in the original definition (i.e. power transposed) and the second undoing

$$Res \ \underset{res}{\overset{res^\circ}{\cong}} \ \mathsf{P} \ (\Sigma + Res \times \Sigma)^\Sigma$$

the transpositions. For this it is more convenient to handle *flatten* : $Res \to (\Sigma \to \mathsf{P} \ \Sigma)$ in the uncurried format, say *uflatten* : $Res \times \Sigma \to \mathsf{P} \ \Sigma$. We also uncurry res°, named *unres* in the diagram:

$$
\begin{array}{ccccc}
 & \overset{outRes}{\overbrace{\hspace{6cm}}} & & & \\
Res \times \Sigma & \xrightarrow{\ unres\ } & \mathsf{P} \ (\Sigma + Res \times \Sigma) & \xrightarrow{\ \alpha\ } & \mathsf{P} \ \Sigma \times \mathsf{P} \ (Res \times \Sigma) \\
{\scriptstyle uflatten} \downarrow & & & & \downarrow {\scriptstyle id \times \mathsf{P} \ (uflatten)} \\
\mathsf{P} \ \Sigma & \xleftarrow{\hspace{4cm}} & & & \mathsf{P} \ \Sigma \times \mathsf{P}^2 \ \Sigma \\
 & & {\scriptstyle join} & &
\end{array}
$$

Isomorphism α establishes $\mathsf{P} \ (A + B) \cong \mathsf{P} \ A \times \mathsf{P} \ B$. The product of functions is the expected, $(f \times b) \ (a, b) = (f \ a, g \ b)$. The outcome of *outRes* (r, σ) is to unfold r at its input σ, separating the stop cases from the inductive ones. Function *join* $(x, y) = x \cup \bigcup y$ collects all output states found.

Note that the same could have been written without the α isomorphism. In such a version, all arrows are P-resultric and therefore can be turned into relations by post-composing them with set membership (7), leading to the following, fully relational version of the previous diagram,

---

[15] This is immediately useful in e.g. extending (14) to resumptions: for a given $r \in Res$, $\{p\} \ r \ \{q\} \ \Leftrightarrow \ flatten \ r \subseteq [p, q]$.

$$Res \times \Sigma \xrightarrow{\;Unres\;} \Sigma + Res \times \Sigma$$

$$\downarrow Flat \qquad\qquad\qquad \downarrow id + Flat \qquad\qquad (36)$$

$$\Sigma \xleftarrow{\quad [id,id] \quad} \Sigma + \Sigma$$

meaning

$$Flat = [id, id] \cdot (id + Flat) \cdot Unres \qquad\qquad (37)$$

Thus *Flat* can be regarded as a nondeterministic "while-loop" that either collects stop states or dives down one level to collect more of them. To retrieve the original function, just transpose *Flat* and then curry it, *flatten* = $\overline{\Lambda Flat}$. Also note that $Unres = \in \cdot unres$.

In the diagram, the *codiagonal* $[id, id]$ exhibits a relational construct that is missing from [22]—the *alternative* $[R, S]$ of two relations [5]. This is associated with the disjoint union $X + Y$, which is inhabited by data taken from either X or Y via two range-disjoint injections $i_1 : X \to X + Y$ and $i_2 : Y \to X + Y$. So the equation $i_1\, x = i_2\, y$ has no solution in $X + Y$ and thus any relation of type $X + Y \to Z$ is made of two independent components, one of type $X \to Z$ and the other of type $Y \to Z$, which "run alternatively" depending on which side of the sum the input is. Such an alternative is denoted by $[R, S]$ and defined by:

$$[R, S] = R \cdot i_1^{\circ} \cup S \cdot i_2^{\circ}.$$

Then the *direct sum* of two relations can be defined,

$$R + S = [R \cdot i_1, S \cdot i_2]$$

which is used in the recursive branch of (36). The following laws concerning these operators [5] will be useful in the sequel:

$$[R, S] \cdot [Q, U]^{\circ} = R \cdot Q^{\circ} \cup S \cdot U^{\circ} \qquad\qquad (38)$$

$$(R + S) \cdot (P + Q) = R \cdot P + S \cdot Q \qquad\qquad (39)$$

$$[R, S] \cdot (P + Q) = [R \cdot P, S \cdot Q] \qquad\qquad (40)$$

An expressive algebra is defined in [23] around *Res* which includes the expected merge operator, $r_1 \| r_2 = r_1\, before\, r_2 \mathbin{\dot{\cup}} r_2\, before\, r_1$, where $r\, before\, s$ is defined using the same pattern as *flatten* and can be handled in the same way.

8   Resumptions Resumed

What is absent from [23] is the *steps* function needed in (18), which in this context will be typed $steps : Res \to (\Sigma \to \mathsf{P}\,\Sigma)$. One may proceed in the same way as in (36) by defining $steps = \overline{\Lambda Steps}$, where *Steps* is as follows:

$$Res \times \Sigma \xrightarrow{\;Unres\;} \Sigma + Res \times \Sigma \xrightarrow{\;id + \langle id, \pi_2 \rangle\;} \Sigma + (Res \times \Sigma) \times \Sigma$$

$$\downarrow Steps \qquad\qquad\qquad\qquad\qquad \downarrow id + Steps \times id \qquad\qquad (41)$$

$$\Sigma \xleftarrow{\qquad\qquad [id, \pi_1 \cup \pi_2] \qquad\qquad} \Sigma + \Sigma \times \Sigma$$

Note how *Steps* extends *Flat* by adding an extra stage that copies the visited states, so as to collect them too. (*Steps* is thus larger than *Flat*.) The pairing combinator used in the extra step is defined by $\langle f, g \rangle\ a = (f\ a, g\ a)$[16] and functions π_1, π_2 are the usual pair-projections: $\pi_1\ (a, b) = a$ and $\pi_2\ (a, b) = b$.

Jones [23] uses *Res* as a semantic domain but does not give explicit proofs of R/G laws on top of it. Such a follow-up work is worth doing in point-free relation algebra, but the full exercise is beyond the scope of the current paper. Instead, we just give the starting steps as an illustration.

Following the figurine of Sect. 6, a GC *steps ⊣ traces* must be shown to hold for resumptions. As *Steps* and *Flat* show, the relational approach to resumptions leads to inductive relations, termed relational *hylomorphisms* in [5]. The full theory of [5] can thus be applied to this setting and a foretaste of all such work is given next.[17]

We start by looking at the "lower side" of the *steps ⊣ traces* GC (21), whereby we want to characterise all resumptions r whose steps are bound by some relation Q. That is, the lifted inclusion *steps* $r \subseteq \Lambda Q$ holds. Then:

$$steps\ r\ \dot{\subseteq}\ \Lambda Q$$

$\Leftrightarrow$ { definition of *steps*; unfold the lifted inclusion }

$$\overline{\Lambda Steps}\ r\ \sigma\ \subseteq\ \Lambda Q\ \sigma$$

$\Leftrightarrow$ { uncurrying; $\pi_2\ (x, y) = y$ }

$$\Lambda Steps\ (r, \sigma)\ \subseteq\ \Lambda Q\ (\pi_2\ (r, \sigma))$$

$\Leftrightarrow$ { drop variables; drop transposes }

$$Steps\ \subseteq\ Q \cdot \pi_2 \tag{42}$$

Relational hylomorphisms express divide and conquer strategies that are usually defined by relational equations, say $H = R \cdot \mathsf{F}\ H \cdot S$, where functor F captures the recursive pattern, S is the divide step and R is the conquer step. Notation $[\![R, S]\!]$ is often used to denote the least fixpoint of the equation. For instance, *Flat* (37) can be regarded as the hylomorphism $[\![[id, id], Unres]\!]$. The following property

$$[\![R, S]\!] \subseteq X\ \Leftarrow\ R \cdot \mathsf{F}\ X \cdot S \subseteq X \tag{43}$$

suits our needs concerning *Steps* $\subseteq\ Q \cdot \pi_2$, provided we characterise *Steps* as a hylomorphism too, which is immediate, for $\mathsf{F}\ X = id + X \times id$: *Steps* $= [\![R, S]\!]$ where $R = [id, \pi_1 \cup \pi_2]$ and $S = (id + \langle id, \pi_2 \rangle) \cdot Unres$, recall (41).

To proceed, it is useful to recall that any relation $R : A + B \to C$ can be expressed as $R = [P, Q]$, where $P : A \to C$ and $Q : B \to C$ are unique. Noting

---

[16] Pairing extends to relations in the obvious way: $(a, b)\ \langle R, S \rangle\ c\ \Leftrightarrow\ a\ R\ c \wedge b\ S\ c$.

[17] This may sound a bit too technical for those not versed in the relational algebra of programming [5], but it is still interesting to see how reasoning on such a *relational basis* unfolds.

that $Unres°$ is of type $\Sigma + Res \times \Sigma \to Res$, we establish

$$Unres° = [Stops°, Nexts°] \tag{44}$$

where $Stops : Res \to \Sigma$ is the part of $Unres$ concerned with stop states and $Nexts : Res \to Res \times \Sigma$ covers all other cases. Armed with these developments, let us finally address (42):

$$Steps \subseteq Q \cdot \pi_2$$

$\Leftarrow \qquad \{ \; Steps = [\![R, S]\!] \text{ above}; \text{ (43) } \}$

$$R \cdot (id + Q \cdot \pi_2 \times id) \cdot S \subseteq Q \cdot \pi_2$$

$\Leftrightarrow \qquad \{ \text{ in-line definitions of } R \text{ and } S \; \}$

$$[id, \pi_1 \cup \pi_2] \cdot (id + Q \cdot \pi_2 \times id) \cdot (id + \langle id, \pi_2 \rangle) \cdot Unres \subseteq Q \cdot \pi_2$$

$\Leftrightarrow \qquad \{ \text{ (39) } \}$

$$[id, \pi_1 \cup \pi_2] \cdot (id + (Q \cdot \pi_2 \times id) \cdot \langle id, \pi_2 \rangle) \cdot Unres \subseteq Q \cdot \pi_2$$

$\Leftrightarrow \qquad \{ \; (40); (R \times S) \cdot \langle P, Q \rangle = \langle R \cdot P, S \cdot Q \rangle \; [5] \; \}$

$$[id, (\pi_1 \cup \pi_2) \cdot \langle Q \cdot \pi_2, \pi_2 \rangle] \cdot Unres \subseteq Q \cdot \pi_2$$

$\Leftrightarrow \qquad \{ \; (44) \; ; (R°)° = R \; \}$

$$[id, (\pi_1 \cup \pi_2) \cdot \langle Q \cdot \pi_2, \pi_2 \rangle] \cdot [Stops°, Nexts°]° \subseteq Q \cdot \pi_2$$

$\Leftrightarrow \qquad \{ \; (38); \text{ GC that defines } (\cup); (R°)° = R \; \}$

$$\begin{cases} Stops \subseteq Q \cdot \pi_2 \\ (\pi_1 \cup \pi_2) \cdot \langle Q \cdot \pi_2, \pi_2 \rangle \cdot Nexts \subseteq Q \cdot \pi_2 \end{cases}$$

$\Leftrightarrow \qquad \{ \text{ linearity}: (R \cup S) \cdot Q = R \cdot Q \cup S \cdot Q \; \}$

$$\begin{cases} Stops \subseteq Q \cdot \pi_2 \\ Q \cdot \pi_2 \cdot Nexts \subseteq Q \cdot \pi_2 \\ (\pi_1 \cup \pi_2) \cdot \langle Q \cdot \pi_2, \pi_2 \rangle \cdot Nexts \subseteq Q \cdot \pi_2 \end{cases}$$

$\Leftarrow \qquad \{ \text{ linearity again}; \pi_2 \cdot \langle R, S \rangle \subseteq S \; \}$

$$\begin{cases} Stops \subseteq Q \cdot \pi_2 \\ Q \cdot \pi_2 \cdot Nexts \subseteq Q \cdot \pi_2 \\ \pi_2 \cdot Nexts \subseteq Q \cdot \pi_2 \end{cases}$$

Going pointwise, we obtain three clauses that were to be expected:[18]

$$\begin{cases} \sigma' \; Stops \; (r, \sigma) \Rightarrow \sigma' \; Q \; \sigma \\ (r_1, \sigma_1) \; Nexts \; (r, \sigma) \wedge \sigma_2 \; Q \; \sigma_1 \Rightarrow \sigma_2 \; Q \; \sigma \\ (r', \sigma') \; Next \; (r, \sigma) \Rightarrow \sigma' \; Q \; \sigma \end{cases}$$

The first and last clauses force stop and next states to stay within Q. The second clause calls for the *stability* of Q under $Nexts$, in the second argument. (A relation Q is said to be stable under a relation R iff $Q \cdot R \subseteq Q$ holds [17].)

---

[18] Mind that, rather than being *invented*, the three clauses were inferred by *calculation*.

Clearly, much more work is needed to complete this exercise along the principles of Sect. 6. But an extended relational basis was set-up, finding its roots and inspiration in [22,23] and following a path similar to [16,38].

9 Summary

This paper gives a brief, history-flavoured perspective on the pioneering contributions of Cliff Jones arising from his D.Phil thesis [22] and other early work. There is no intention (nor space!) to do the comprehensive review that the subject definitely deserves. The focus is on his early R/G research, which is where one can best feel his genius at work facing a difficult problem.

The main topic chosen for analysis is his early use of mathematical relations (his *relational basis*) in both the *pointwise* and *pointfree* styles. The analysis is combined with a relational approach to R/G reasoning due to [38]. The attractiveness of this approach comes from its *program transformers*, which are supported by suitable Galois connections leading to a rich, generic theory. (In spite of its elegance, it must be mentioned that very recent R/G research [17] is not enthusiastic about the nesting of rely and guarantee operators when applying the theory to practical problems.)

Relational reasoning about resumptions is given as an example of how previous work by Jones [23] could be extended. Resumptions have been in the spotlight in more recent times, see e.g. [13,14,35], where they are framed in the theories of free-monads and final-coalgebras. It will be worth studying these alternatives, in particular in what concerns infinite behaviour.

Acknowledgement. The author was a postgraduate student at Manchester University when Cliff Jones joined its Computer Science Department in 1981. His (the author's) high school interest in relations as a useful device of mathematics could only be spiced up by reading [22]. This thesis and a contemporary textbook [21] completely changed his view of software design forever and opened his mind to *formal methods*, the research area that he pursued ever since.

References

1. Aarts, C., Backhouse, R.C., Hoogendijk, P., Voermans, E., van der Woude, J.: A relational theory of datatypes, Deceber 1992. http://www.cs.nott.ac.uk/~rcb
2. Abrial, J.R., Schuman, S.A.: Non-deterministic system specification. In: Kahn, G. (ed.) Semantics of Concurrent Computation. LNCS, vol. 70, pp. 34–50. Springer, Heidelberg (1979). https://doi.org/10.1007/BFb0022462
3. Backhouse, R.C.: Mathematics of Program Construction. Unpublished book draft, 608 p. University of Nottingham (2004). http://www.cs.nott.ac.uk/~rcb
4. Berghammer, R., Neumann, F.: RelView - an OBDD-based computer algebra system for relations. In: CASC'05, pp. 40–51 (2005). https://doi.org/10.1007/11555964_4
5. Bird, R., de Moor, O.: Algebra of Programming. Prentice Hall Europe (1997). ISBN 978-0-13-507245-5

6. de Bakker, J., de Roever, W.P.: A calculus for recursive program schemes. Stichting Mathematisch Centrum Technical report 131/72, Amsterdam (1972). https://ir.cwi.nl/pub/9145

7. Dijkstra, E.W.: A Discipline of Programming. Prentice-Hall, Englewood Cliffs (1976). ISBN 0-13-215871-X

8. Dijkstra, E.W.: Indirect equality enriched (2001). Technical note EWD 1315-0

9. Feferman, S.: Tarski's influence on computer science. Log. Methods Comput. Sci. 2(1), 1–13 (2006). https://doi.org/10.2168/LMCS-2(3:6)2006

10. Floyd, R.W.: Assigning meanings to programs. In: Schwartz, J.T. (ed.) Mathematical Aspects of Computer Science, vol. 19, pp. 19–32. AMS (1967). https://doi.org/10.1090/psapm/019

11. Freyd, P.J., Scedrov, A.: Categories, Allegories. Mathematical Library, vol. 39. North-Holland (1990). ISBN 9780444703682

12. Frias, M.F., Maddux, R.D.: Completeness of a relational calculus for program schemes. Theor. Comput. Sci. 254(1–2), 543–556 (2001). https://doi.org/10.1016/S0304-3975(99)00343-6

13. Harrison, W.L.: The essence of multitasking. In: Johnson, M., Vene, V. (eds.) AMAST 2006. LNCS, vol. 4019, pp. 158–172. Springer, Heidelberg (2006). https://doi.org/10.1007/11784180_14

14. Hasuo, I., Jacobs, B.: Traces for coalgebraic components. MSCS 21, 267–320 (2011). https://doi.org/10.1017/S0960129510000551

15. Hayes, I.J.: Generalised rely-guarantee concurrency: an algebraic foundation. FAoC 28(6), 1057–1078 (2016). https://doi.org/10.1007/s00165-016-0384-0

16. Hayes, I.J., Jones, C.B., Colvin, R.J.: Refining rely-guarantee thinking. Technical report CS-TR-1334, Newcastle University (2012)

17. Hayes, I.J., Jones, C.B., Meinicke, L.A.: Specifying and reasoning about shared-variable concurrency. In: Bowen, J.P., Li, Q., Xu, Q. (eds.) Theories of Programming and Formal Methods. LNCS, vol. 14080, pp. 110–135. Springer, Cham (2023). https://doi.org/10.1007/978-3-031-40436-8_5

18. Hoare, C.A.R.: An axiomatic basis for computer programming. CACM 12(10), 576–580, 583 (1969). https://doi.org/10.1145/363235.363259

19. ISO: ISO/IEC 13568:2002. Information Technology—Z Formal Specification Notation: Syntax, Type System and Semantics, 196 p. (2002). https://www.iso.org/standard/21573.html. Accessed 1 July 2002

20. Jackson, D.: Software Abstractions: Logic, Language, and Analysis, Revised edn. The MIT Press, Cambridge (2012). ISBN 0-262-01715-2

21. Jones, C.B.: Software Development—A Rigorous Approach. Prentice-Hall, London (1980). ISBN 0138218846

22. Jones, C.B.: Development Methods for Computer Programs including a Notion of Interference. Ph.D. thesis, Oxford University, June 1981. Printed as: PRG, Tech. Monograph 25. http://www.cs.ox.ac.uk/files/9025/PRG-25.pdf

23. Jones, C.B.: Interference resumed. Technical report UMCS-91-5-1, Department of Computer Science, U. Manchester, May 1991

24. Jones, C.B.: Interference resumed. In: Bailes, P. (ed.) Engineering Safe Software, pp. 31–56. Australian Computer Society (1991). http://search.informit.com.au/documentSummary;dn=546299491532331;res=IELENG

25. Jones, C.B.: The early search for tractable ways of reasoning about programs. IEEE Ann. Hist. Comput. 25(2), 26–49 (2003). https://doi.org/10.1109/MAHC.2003.1203057

26. Jones, C.B., Hayes, I.J., Colvin, R.J.: Balancing expressiveness in formal approaches to concurrency. FAoC **27**(3), 475–497 (2015). https://doi.org/10.1007/s00165-014-0310-2
27. MacLane, S.: Categories for the Working Mathematician. Springer, New York (1971). https://doi.org/10.1007/978-1-4757-4721-8
28. Milner, R.: Processes: a mathematical model of computing agents. In: Logic Colloq.'73, pp. 157–173. North-Holland (1975). ISBN 0444106421
29. Morgan, C.: The specification statement. ACM ToPLAS **10**(3), 403–419 (1988). https://doi.org/10.1145/44501.44503
30. Morgan, C., Vickers, T.: Types and invariants in the refinement calculus. Sci. Comput. Program. **14**(2–3), 281–304 (1990). https://doi.org/10.1016/0167-6423(90)90024-8
31. Mu, S.-C., Oliveira, J.N.: Programming from Galois connections. JLAP **81**(6), 680–704 (2012). https://doi.org/10.1016/j.jlap.2012.05.003
32. Oliveira, J.N.: Extended static checking by calculation using the pointfree transform. In: Bove, A., Barbosa, L.S., Pardo, A., Pinto, J.S. (eds.) LerNet 2008. LNCS, vol. 5520, pp. 195–251. Springer, Heidelberg (2009). https://doi.org/10.1007/978-3-642-03153-3_5
33. Oliveira, J.N.: Why adjunctions matter—a functional programmer perspective. In: Madeira, A., Martins, M.A. (eds.) WADT 2022. Lecture Notes in Computer Science, vol. 13710, pp. 25–59. Springer, Cham (2023). https://doi.org/10.1007/978-3-031-43345-0_2
34. Park, D.: On the semantics of fair parallelism. In: Bjøorner, D. (ed.) Abstract Software Specifications. LNCS, vol. 86, pp. 504–526. Springer, Heidelberg (1980). https://doi.org/10.1007/3-540-10007-5_47
35. Piróg, M., Gibbons, J.: The coinductive resumption monad. ENTCS **308**, 273–288 (2014). https://doi.org/10.1016/j.entcs.2014.10.015
36. Plotkin, G.: A powerdomain construction. SIAM J. Comput. **5**(3), 452–489 (1976). https://doi.org/10.1137/0205035
37. Schmidt, G.: Relational Mathematics
38. Staden, S.: On rely-guarantee reasoning. In: MPC 2015, pp. 30–49 (2015). https://doi.org/10.1007/978-3-319-19797-5_2
39. Tarski, A., Givant, S.: A Formalization of Set Theory without Variables. AMS, vol. 41. AMS Colloquium Publications (1987). ISBN 0821810413
40. Wirth, N.: Algorithms + Data Structures = Programs. Prentice-Hall, Hoboken (1976). ISBN 978-0-13-022418-7
41. Xu, Q., de Roever, W.-P., He, J.: The rely-guarantee method for verifying shared variable concurrent programs. FAoC **9**(2), 149–174 (1997). https://doi.org/10.1007/BF01211617

Model Refinement: Generating Refinements for Algorithm and System Design

Douglas R. Smith[1](✉) and Srinivas Nedunuri[2]

[1] Kestrel Institute, Palo Alto, CA 94304, USA
smith@kestrel.edu
[2] Sandia National Laboratories, Livermore, CA 94550, USA
snedunu@sandia.gov

Abstract. Deductive model refinement (hereafter simply "model refinement") is a uniform approach to generating correct-by-construction designs for algorithms and systems from formal specifications. Given an overapproximating model $\mathcal{M}$ of system dynamics and a set Φ of required properties, model refinement is an iterative process that eliminates behaviors of $\mathcal{M}$ that do not satisfy the required properties. The result of model refinement is a refined model $\mathcal{M}'$ that satisfies by construction the required properties Φ. The calculations needed to generate refinements of $\mathcal{M}$ typically involve quantifier elimination and extensive formula/term simplification modulo the underlying domain theories. This paper focuses on the enforcement of basic safety properties in the form of state, action, and path invariants. We have run a prototype implementation of model refinement based on the Z3 SMT solver over a variety of system and algorithm design problems.

Keywords: Refinement · model-based design · formal specification · reactive synthesis · function synthesis · program synthesis

1 Introduction

Formal specifications characterize the acceptable behaviors of a desired program. Among the various means for specifying requirements on a desired program are (1) *logical specifications* in which predicates expressed in a suitable logic decide the desired behaviors, and (2) *models* whose computable behaviors are a superset or overapproximation of the desired behaviors. We view logical specifications and models as having complementary strengths and believe that their combination can lead to simpler and more natural specifications of systems and algorithms.

Formal development methods aim to systematically develop programs from their specifications often by a process of refinement. Jones [16], Back and Wright [2], and others systematized the rigorous development of programs together with proofs via refinement relations between levels of design. This line of work has tended to emphasize the creative development and verification of refinement

© The Author(s), under exclusive license to Springer Nature Switzerland AG 2024
A. Cavalcanti and J. Baxter (Eds.): *The Practice of Formal Methods*, LNCS 14781, pp. 77–96, 2024.
https://doi.org/10.1007/978-3-031-66673-5_5

steps. Our work has been motivated in part by trying to create generative versions of the kinds of proof rules pioneered by Jones, including data reification and rely-guarantee reasoning. That is, our goal is to explore automatic transformations that map a specification or intermediate design to an equivalent form or to a correct-by-construction refinement. The field of *program synthesis* focuses on automatic generation of programs from formal specifications using such transformations. Obviously, any formal development process will benefit to the extent that its refinement steps can be automatically generated. Human insight is still needed to choose appropriate transformations and to specify how to apply them.

In this paper we propose a unifying synthesis framework, called *deductive model refinement* (or simply model refinement), that starts with a formal specification comprised of models and logical properties. From a given model and logical properties, we define a constraint system that characterizes refinements of the model that satisfy the logical properties. Solving the constraint system corresponds to eliminating undesired behaviors from the model. Model refinement serves to unify and extend previous work on function/algorithm synthesis with reactive system synthesis.

Given a model $\mathcal{M}$ that overapproximates desired behaviors and a set Φ of required properties, the goal of model refinement is to generate the least refinement $\mathcal{M}'$ of model $\mathcal{M}$ such that $\mathcal{M}'$ satisfies the specified properties Φ (where the refinement relation defines a lattice of models). If the set of legal initial states in $\mathcal{M}'$ differs from the initial states of $\mathcal{M}$, then the difference characterizes the set of initial states from which the system does not have any acceptable behaviors.

Overapproximating models can arise in a variety of ways. For control system problems, the model captures the dynamics of a physical asset (a.k.a. the "plant") to be controlled. In software system design, the model captures the APIs and possible operations of a component and perhaps a restricted grammar for expressing programs [1]. In general system design, a model can express a system design pattern [5, 11, 25]. In algorithm design, a model can reflect the imposition of a parametric solution pattern, such as an algorithm theory [29] or a sketch [34].

Model refinement techniques are common in science and engineering. Our approach is called *deductive model refinement* due to the use of deductive techniques to enforce logical requirement properties on a model. Examples of data-driven or inductive model refinement can be found in (1) statistical model estimation techniques that fit, say, a Bayesian Network model to given data, and (2) machine learning techniques for refining an artificial neural network model with training data. In these examples the model provides the abstract computational pattern and the data provides the requirements on the refined model.

This paper focuses on enforcement of basic safety properties. In [30], we introduce a wider fragment of temporal logic that can be reduced to the basic safety fragment. Most current work on the synthesis of reactive systems focuses on circuit design and starts with specifications in propositional Linear Temporal Logic (LTL) [4, 15]. It is therefore limited to finite state models. Our approach to model refinement allows specifications that are first-order and uses a temporal logic of action (similar to TLA [18]) that is amenable to refinement, allowing possibly-infinite state spaces and allowing a broader range of applications to be tackled.

Model refinement is intended to support highly automated refinement-generating tools that produce correct-by-construction designs together with checkable proofs. One barrier to automation is the computational complexity of formula simplification in the application domain theories that support the specification. When the domain theories are decidable (e.g. by SMT solvers) and admit quantifier elimination, then model refinement can run fully automatically. We have used our Z3-based prototype to perform model refinement on a variety of examples, each solvable in a few seconds or minutes.

Our novel contributions include

1. a uniform framework for specifying algorithms and reactive systems by a combination of overapproximating behavioral models and logical specifications of required behavior,
2. a characterization of model refinement via a system of definite constraints that can be efficiently solved by fixpoint-iteration procedures,
3. a variety of examples to show the breadth of the technique,
4. a prototype implementation based on the Z3 SMT-solver.

After introducing basic concepts, the paper first focuses on reactive system synthesis as constraint-solving via iterated constraint propagation, with examples. Function specifications that arise during reactive system synthesis then provide a natural segue into a treatment of function/algorithm synthesis as generalized iterated constraint propagation over paths.

2 Preliminaries

2.1 Required Properties

We focus on safety properties formulated in a simple linear temporal logic of actions, similar to Lamport's TLA [18]. A *state* is a (type-consistent) map from variables to values. *State predicates* are boolean expressions formed over the variables of a state and the constants (including functions) relevant to an application domain. A state predicate p denotes a relation $[\![p]\!]$ over states, so $p(s)$ denotes the truth value $[\![p]\!](s)$ for state s. *Actions* are boolean expressions formed over variables, primed variables, and the constants (including functions) relevant to an application domain. An action a specifies a state transition and it denotes a predicate $[\![a]\!]$ over a pair of states, and $a(s,t)$ denotes the truth value $[\![a]\!](s,t)$ for states s and t. The expression $x' = x + 1 + y$ is a typical action where the unprimed variables refer to the first state and primed variables refer to the second state.

A *basic safety property* (or simply a safety property) has the form φ or $\Box\varphi$ where φ is a state predicate or an action. The truth of a safety property φ at position n of a trace σ (an infinite sequence of states), written $\sigma, n \models \varphi$, is defined as follows:

- $\sigma, n \vDash p$, for p a state predicate, if p holds at state $\sigma[n]$, i.e. $[\![p]\!](\sigma[n])$;
- $\sigma, n \vDash a$, for a an action, if a holds over the states $\sigma[n], \sigma[n+1]$, i.e. $[\![a]\!](\sigma[n], \sigma[n+1])$;
- $\sigma, n \vDash \Box\varphi$ if $\sigma, i \vDash \varphi$ for all $i \geq n$.

2.2 Behavioral Models

Formally, a model is a *labeled transition system* (LTS) $\mathcal{M} = \langle \mathcal{V}, N, A, \mathcal{L} \rangle$ where

- $\mathcal{V}$: a countable set of variables; implicitly each variable has a type with a finite (typically first-order) specification of the predicates and functions that provides vocabulary for expressions and constrains their meaning via axioms. The aggregation of these variable specifications is called the *application domain theory* (or simply domain theory) of the problem at hand.
- N: a finite set of nodes. Associated with each node $m \in N$, we have a finite subset of observable variables $V(m) \subseteq \mathcal{V}$. N has a distinguished node m_0 that is the initial node. An LTS is *arc-like* if it also has a designated final node m_f.
- A: a finite set of directed arcs, $A \subseteq N \times N$. Each node m has an identity self-transition $id_m = \langle m, m \rangle$, called *stutter*, that changes the values of no observable variables.
- $\mathcal{L}$: a set of labels. For each node $m \in N$, we have a label $L_m \in \mathcal{L}$ that is a state predicate over $V(m)$ representing a node invariant. For each arc $a = \langle m, n \rangle$, label $L_a \in \mathcal{L}$ is an action over $V(m)$, $V(n)$, and auxiliary variables e and u which are discussed below.

In reactive system design, it is commonly the case that the variables at all nodes are the same, so $V(m) = V(n)$ for all nodes $m, n \in N$ and all variables are global. In functional algorithm design it is typical that the variables at each node are disjoint, effectively treating all variables as local to a unique node. Most programming languages, of course, support models that have both global and local variables.

To simplify notation, we often write $L_m(st)$ to denote $st \vDash L_m(V(m))$ for state st (and similarly for arc labels). A node m denotes the set of states $[\![m]\!] = \{st \mid L_m(st)\}$. The label L_{m_0} is the *initial condition* of the model and denotes the set of initial states.

Arc label L_a generally specifies a nondeterministic action, whose nondeterminism may be reduced under refinement. In reactive systems, which have a game-like character, some of the nondeterminism is due to the uncontrollable behavior of the environment or an adversarial agent. For refinement purposes, it is necessary to specify which parts of the nondeterminism are refinable and which are unrefinable. Accordingly, the label L_a of an action has the general form:

$$L_a(st_m, e, u, st_n) \equiv e \in E_a(st_m) \wedge U_a(st_m, u) \wedge st_n = f_a(st_m, u, e)$$

where

1. e is treated as an uncontrollable Environment or adversary input that ranges over the unrefinable set $E_a(st_m)$;
2. u is treated as a controllable value that satisfies the refinable constraint $U_a(st_m, u)$;
3. function f_a gives the deterministic response of the action.

The variability of the control value specifies the refinable part of $L_a(st_m, e, u, st_n)$. This kind of formulation of actions is common in modeling discrete and continuous control systems [35]. Let

$$[\![a]\!] = \{\langle st_m, st_n \rangle \mid \exists e, u.\, L_a(st_m, e, u, st_n)\}.$$

Note that e and u are independent of each other. Alternative formulations are easily made in which one depends on the other.

Semantics. A *trace* is a possibly infinite sequence of states. An LTS $\mathcal{M} = \langle \mathcal{V}, N, A, \mathcal{L} \rangle$ generates a trace $tr = st_0, st_1, \ldots$ if

1. Initially, st_0 is a legal state of the initial node m_0, i.e. $st_0 \in [\![m_0]\!]$;
2. Inductively, if $i \geq 0$ and st_i is a legal state of node m, i.e. $st_i \in [\![m]\!]$, then there exists arc $a = \langle m, n \rangle$ where $\langle st_i, st_{i+1} \rangle \in [\![a]\!]$ and where st_{i+1} is a legal state of node n; i.e. $st_{i+1} \in [\![n]\!]$.

$[\![\mathcal{M}]\!]$ is the set of all traces that can be generated by $\mathcal{M}$.

A node m and a legal state st_m is *nonblocking* if there is an arc $a = \langle m, n \rangle$ and control choice u such that $U_a(st_m, u)$ and a transitions to a legal state of n regardless of the environment input. In game-theoretic terms, if all reachable nodes and states of the model are nonblocking, then the system has a winning strategy. A key part of model refinement is the elimination of blocking states in the model.

2.3 Specification and Refinement

Refinement of LTS model $\mathcal{M}_1$ to model $\mathcal{M}_2$ is a preorder relation, written $\mathcal{M}_1 \sqsubseteq \mathcal{M}_2$, that holds when there exists a *simulation map* $\xi : \mathcal{M}_2 \rightarrow \mathcal{M}_1$ that maps the nodes and arcs of $\mathcal{M}_2$ to the nodes and arcs of $\mathcal{M}_1$; i.e. where $\xi : N^{\mathcal{M}_2} \rightarrow N^{\mathcal{M}_1}$ and $\xi : A^{\mathcal{M}_2} \rightarrow A^{\mathcal{M}_1}$ such that

1. Initial nodes are preserved: $\xi(m_0^{\mathcal{M}_2}) = m_0^{\mathcal{M}_1}$;
2. Observable variables: $V^{\mathcal{M}_2}(m) \supseteq V^{\mathcal{M}_1}(\xi(m))$ for each node $m \in N^{\mathcal{M}_2}$;
3. Node labels: $L_m^{\mathcal{M}_2} \implies L_{\xi(m)}^{\mathcal{M}_1}$ for each node $m \in N^{\mathcal{M}_2}$;
4. Arc labels: $L_a^{\mathcal{M}_2} \implies L_{\xi(a)}^{\mathcal{M}_1}$ for each arc $a \in A^{\mathcal{M}_2}$.

There are several kinds of transformations of models that generate refinements, including (1) strengthening the invariant at a node, and (2) strengthening the action at an arc. These are used in the model refinement procedure in the next section. A third transformation, *structure refinement*, replaces an arc by an arc-like LTS. This transformation may be used when imposing a design pattern or program scheme as a constraint on how to achieve the action of the arc. An example of this is given in Sect. 5.1.

A *specification* $\mathcal{S} = \langle \mathcal{M}, \Phi \rangle$ is comprised of a model $\mathcal{M}$ and a set of properties Φ that we require to incorporate or enforce in $\mathcal{M}$. A specification denotes the set of traces generable by $\mathcal{M}$ that also satisfy all properties in Φ:

$$[\![\mathcal{S}]\!] = \{tr \mid tr \in [\![\mathcal{M}]\!] \wedge tr \models \Phi\} = [\![\mathcal{M}]\!] \cap [\![\Phi]\!].$$

Refinement of specification $\mathcal{S}$ to specification $\mathcal{T}$ is a preorder relation, written $\mathcal{S} \sqsubseteq \mathcal{T}$, that holds when there is a mapping ξ from traces of $\mathcal{T}$ to traces of $\mathcal{S}$ such that

$$\forall \sigma. \sigma \in [\![\mathcal{T}]\!] \implies \xi(\sigma) \in [\![\mathcal{S}]\!]$$

or more succinctly $\xi([\![\mathcal{T}]\!]) \subseteq [\![\mathcal{S}]\!]$.

Theorem 1. If (1) $\mathcal{S}_1 = \langle \mathcal{M}_1, \Phi_1 \rangle$ and $\mathcal{S}_2 = \langle \mathcal{M}_2, \Phi_2 \rangle$ are specifications, (2) $\xi : \mathcal{M}_2 \to \mathcal{M}_1$ is a simulation map, and (3) $\Phi_2 \implies \Phi_1$, then $\mathcal{S}_1 \sqsubseteq \mathcal{S}_2$.

The proof, given in [30], shows how ξ induces a map $\hat{\xi}$ of traces of $\mathcal{S}_2$ such that $\hat{\xi}([\![\mathcal{S}_2]\!]) \subseteq [\![\mathcal{S}_1]\!]$.

3   Model Refinement as Constraint Solving

Model refinement transforms a model $\mathcal{M}$ and required properties Φ into a model $\mathcal{M}'$ such that $\mathcal{M} \sqsubseteq \mathcal{M}' \wedge \mathcal{M}' \models \Phi$. We define now a constraint system whose solutions correspond to refinements of $\mathcal{M}$ that satisfy Φ. The intent is to find the greatest solution of the constraint system, which corresponds to the minimal refinement of $\mathcal{M}$ that satisfies Φ. In later sections we discuss several situations in which only a near-greatest solution can be found.

In formulating model refinement as a constraint satisfaction problem, we treat the node labels L_m and arc labels L_a as variables, whose assigned values are state and action predicates, respectively. We can view the constraint system as taking place in the Boolean lattice of formulas with implication as the partial order (i.e. a Tarski-Lindenbaum algebra). Each constraint provides an upper bound on feasible values of one variable. A feasible solution to the constraint system is an assignment of formulas to each variable that satisfies all the constraints of the system. We discuss below how to assure finite convergence of the constraint solving process as the lattice is typically of infinite height for nonpropositional logics.

For arc $a = \langle m, n \rangle$, arc label L_a, and node label L_n, let $wcp(L_a, L_n)$ be the *weakest controllable predecessor* predicate transformer which is defined by

$$wcp(L_a, L_n) \equiv \forall e. \, e \in E(st_m) \implies \exists st_n. \, st_n = f_a(st_m, e, u) \wedge L_n(st_n)$$

or, simply

$$wcp(L_a, L_n) \equiv \forall e. \, e \in E(st_m) \implies L_n(f_a(st_m, e, u)).$$

if φ is a state predicate
    then for all $m \in N : L_m \leftarrow L_m \wedge \varphi$
    else for all $a \in A : L_a \leftarrow L_a \wedge \varphi$
do
    for all $a \in A : U_a \leftarrow U_a \wedge wcp(L_a, L_n)$
    for all $m \in N : L_m \leftarrow L_m \wedge \bigvee_{a=\langle m,n \rangle} \exists u. U_a$
until L_m is unchanged for all nodes $m \in N$.

Fig. 1. Model Refinement Algorithm

$wcp(L_a, L_n)$ is the weakest formula over $V(m) \cup \{u\}$ such that for any environment input e the transition a is assured to reach a state st_n satisfying the post-state predicate L_n. Its effect is to define the nonblocking states of node m – those states from which there is some control value that forces the transition to a legal state at n regardless of the environment input.

The constraint system is comprised of the following four sets of constraints for each required temporal property $\Box\varphi$:

1. **Node Localization:** $L_m \implies \varphi$ for each node $m \in N$ if φ is a state predicate expressed over the variables at m;
2. **Arc Localization:** $L_a \implies \varphi$ for each arc $a = \langle m, n \rangle \in A$ if φ is an action predicate expressed over the variables at m and n;
3. **Control Constraint:** $U_a \implies wcp(L_a, L_n)$ for each arc $a = \langle m, n \rangle$
4. **Node Invariant:** $L_m \implies \bigvee_{a=\langle m,n \rangle} \exists u. U_a$ for each node $m \in N$.

The Localization constraints (1) and (2) provide upper bounds on the node labels. The Control constraints (3) are the essentially synthetic aspect of model refinement as they serve to eliminate any state transitions in which the environment can force the system to a state not satisfying the safety properties. The Node Invariant constraints (4) serve to eliminate blocking states of a node with respect to all of its outgoing arcs. Given a specification $S = \langle M, \Phi \rangle$, the model refinement transformation refines the specification by solving the constraint system. In other words, a solution to the constraints is a model that refines the input model and the solution process generates a refinement.

A straightforward algorithm for solving the constraint system over the labels on a model is presented in Fig. 1. The iteration converges to a fixpoint when the labels do not change in an iteration. Upon convergence to a refined model $\mathcal{M}'$, we have $[\![\mathcal{M}']\!] \subseteq [\![\mathcal{M}]\!] \cap [\![\Phi]\!]$, and in the case that the algorithm converges to a greatest fixpoint we have $[\![\mathcal{M}']\!] = [\![\mathcal{M}]\!] \cap [\![\Phi]\!]$. The algorithm in [24] provides a more efficient control strategy that exploits dependencies between the constraints.

The *derived initial condition* is the final refined invariant L_{m_0} which characterizes the set of nonblocking initial states from which the system can ensure that all behaviors satisfy the specified safety properties. In a model-checking scenario where the model doesn't check, the derived initial condition may provide a useful characterization of the model's failure.

The correctness of this algorithm is a consequence of Tarski's theorem. Each constraint has definite form $v \leq g(v)$ where g is monotone, so we can express solutions as fixpoints of $v = g(v)$. As we are looking for the most general (i.e. least refinement of the initial model), the algorithm aims to converge on the greatest fixpoint using a Kleene iteration. If the state space is finite, then the fixpoint iteration process will be finite too. In fact, the number of iterations is linear in the height of the lattice [24]. Techniques to improve the complexity of the algorithm and to guarantee convergence to a fixpoint are further discussed in [30].

Example: Packet Flow Control

In this example, based on [26], a buffer is used to control and smooth the flow of packets in a communication system. We model this problem as in discrete control theory with a plant (a buffer of length buf), environment input e, and control value u. The environment supplies a stream of packets that varies up to 4 packets per time unit. The plant is modeled by a single linear transition that updates the state of the plant. The goal is to assure that the system keeps no more than 20 packets in the buffer buf and keeps the outflow rate out at no more than 4 packets per time unit.

This is a classical discrete control problem with a single node and a single linear transition. It can be specified by the following TLA-like notation for an LTS, which lists (1) the global state variables, (2) their initial invariants, (3) the one node, (4) the one arc and its initial action (dependent on environment input e and control value u), (5) the required safety properties, and (6) currently known theorems, which are empty here but are extended by the model refinement process.

Specification FC0
> **Vars:** $buf, out : Integer$
> **Invariant:** $0 \leq buf \wedge 0 \leq out$
> **Node:** m_0
> **Arc:** $a = \langle m_0, m_0 \rangle : -1 \leq u \leq 1 \wedge 0 \leq e \leq 4$
> $\qquad\qquad\qquad \wedge\ buf' = buf + e - out\ \wedge\ out' = out + u$
>
> **Required Properties**
> > $buf = 0$
> > $out = 0$
> > $\square\ 0 \leq buf\ \wedge\ buf \leq 20\ \wedge\ 0 \leq out\ \wedge\ out \leq 4$
>
> **Theorems**

End Specification

The first two required properties determine the initial state values. For the last required property, the algorithm in Fig. 1 instantiates wcp to generate the following formula as an upper bound on the control condition

$U(buf, out, u) \equiv -1 \leq u \leq 1 \wedge 0 \leq out + u \leq 4$
$$\wedge \forall e. \, 0 \leq e \leq 4 \implies 0 \leq buf + e - out \leq 20.$$

This formula is in the language of integer linear arithmetic which admits quantifier elimination and our Z3-based prototype simplifies it to the equivalent of

$$1 \leq buf - out \leq 16 \wedge 0 \leq out + u \leq 4.$$

According to the algorithm in Fig. 1, the control condition $U(buf, out, u)$ strengthens to

$$-1 \leq u \leq 1 \wedge 1 \leq buf - out \leq 16 \wedge 0 \leq out + u \leq 4$$

and the state invariant strengthens to

$$0 \leq buf \wedge 0 \leq out \wedge 1 \leq out - buf \leq 16.$$

Next, our prototype simplifies the control condition with respect to the strengthened state invariant, and the control condition becomes

$$-1 \leq u \leq 1 \wedge 0 \leq out + u \leq 4.$$

Since the control condition for the sole transition has changed, the iteration continues. For this problem convergence happens after four iterations and generates the following refined model, in which the required properties are enforced by construction and so they become theorems of the model, as can be verified by a model checker.

Specification FC1
  Vars: $buf, out : Integer = 0$
  Invariant: $0 \leq out \leq 4 \wedge 0 \leq buf - out \leq 16$
         $\wedge -3 \leq buf - 3 * out \leq 11 \wedge -6 \leq buf - 4 * out \leq 10$
  Node: m_0
  Arc: $a = \langle m_0, m_0 \rangle : \; -1 \leq u \leq 1 \wedge 0 \leq out + u \leq 4 \wedge 0 \leq e \leq 4$
         $\wedge -6 \leq buf - 4 * u - 5 * out \leq 6$
         $\wedge -1 \leq buf - 2 * u - 3 * out \leq 9$
         $\wedge buf' = buf + e - out \wedge out' = out + u$
  Theorems: $buf = 0 \wedge out = 0 \wedge \square \, (0 \leq buf \leq 20 \wedge 0 \leq out \leq 4)$
End Specification

   Again, note how the Required Properties of the initial model have been transformed into Theorems of the refined model, by construction. The strengthened state invariant on node m_0 is also the derived initial condition and specifies the set of initial states from which we have assurance that the system will keep within the required bounds regardless of environment inputs.

   The refined transition now defines a somewhat complex polyhedron around the control values. If there are no more required properties to enforce, then the next step will be to synthesize a control function that selects a specific control value u in each given state. For game-like problems, this is also known as extracting a winning strategy for the system game modulo the derived initial conditions.

Our prototype model refinement system converges on the model above in a few seconds. The version of this problem in which the variables are Reals or Rationals, with an infinite state space, is also solved in a small number of iterations in a few seconds, with a different invariant polytope and derived initial condition defining the safe operating space.

Other Examples

The Cinderella-Stepmother game has been posed as a challenge problem for synthesis systems (cf. [3]). It is a turn-based game between Cinderella and her wicked stepmother. The game centers on a ring of five buckets that can each hold up to c units of water, where initially the buckets are empty. In each round of the game the stepmother adds one unit of water distributed over the buckets, and then Cinderella empties two adjacent buckets. If any of the buckets ever overflow, then the stepmother wins, otherwise Cinderella wins.

Specification Cinderella-Stepmother
    Vars: $b_0, b_1, b_2, b_3, b_4, c : NonNegativeReal$
        $e_0, e_1, e_2, e_3, e_4 : NonNegativeReal$
    Invariant: $\bigwedge_{i=0,4} b_i = 0$
    Nodes: m_C, m_S
    Arc: $Add = \langle m_S, m_C \rangle : \sum_{i=0,4} b'_i = 1 + \sum_{i=0,4} b_i$
                  $\wedge \bigwedge_{i=0,4} b'_i = b_i + e_i$
    Arc: $Empty = \langle m_C, m_S \rangle : b'_u = 0 \wedge b'_{(u+1)\%5} = 0$
    Required Properties: $\Box \bigwedge_{i=0,4} b_i \leq c$
End Specification

Our specification for this game-like problem has two nodes, one for the turn or each player. The game is parametric on a real value $c > 0$ used to define the Stepmother's (antagonist's) task. In [3], a controller for the game is found using sketches as hints to the solver. There it is conjectured that automatic solutions (i.e. without human-provided hints) are "unrealistic" for values of c in range [1.5,3] (the problem is relatively easy outside that range). Our model refinement prototype automatically generates winning strategies in that range using roughly a minute of CPU time.

Other problems for which we have synthesized code include the classic readers-writers problem, elevator control, model-repair [3], and a reactive controller for a secure enclave. The latter problem has time-bounded responsive requirements and in [30] we introduce transformations that reduce a collection of time-bounded temporal operators to basic safety properties. After that reduction then the model refinement algorithm can be applied.

4   Function Synthesis

Model refinement naturally gives rise to the specification of several functions. For example, in the final model of the Flow Control example, the action constrains the control choice u to satisfy

$$-1 \leq u \leq 1 \ \wedge \ 0 \leq out + u \leq 4 \ \wedge \ -6 \leq buf - 4 * u - 5 * out \leq 6$$
$$\wedge -1 \leq buf - 2 * u - 3 * out \leq 9. \tag{1}$$

To make that choice, we must synthesize a control function

$$FlowControl(\langle buf, out \rangle) = u \ such \ that \ (1).$$

Generally, for each arc $a = \langle m, n \rangle$ in the final model, model refinement generates a specification for a control function for a that outputs a satisfying control value. The desired control function may be specified as

$$Control_a(st \mid L_m(st)) \ = \ u \ such \ that \ U_a(st, u)$$

where $L_m(st)$ is the precondition and $U_a(st, u)$ is the postcondition. Algorithm or function synthesis is appropriate for this specification, since the behaviors are specified by a simple input-output relation which we treat as a safety property over traces of length 2 (input state followed by output state). A variety of techniques for function synthesis have been developed, many of which stem from the original work on deductive synthesis [8, 14, 20]. Later approaches to synthesis of functions exploit algorithm design patterns [29], sketches [34], and transformations from high-level function definitions [22].

Here, since the control variable u only takes on three values, a simple transformation to form a conditional function can be applied resulting in the following (see [30] for details).

$controlFun(\langle buf, out \rangle \mid 0 \leq out \leq 4 \wedge 0 \leq buf - out \leq 16$
$\qquad\qquad\qquad \wedge -3 \leq buf - 3 * out \leq 11 \wedge -6 \leq buf - 4 * out \leq 1)) =$
$\quad$ **if** $4 * out - buf > -5 \ \wedge \ 2 * out - buf > -12$
$\qquad\qquad\qquad \wedge \ out \geq 1 \ \wedge \ 5 * out - buf > -3$ **then** -1
$\quad$ **else if** $buf - 2 * out > 0 \ \wedge \ out \leq 3$ **then** 0
$\quad$ **else** 1

5   Path Properties

In the previous section we discussed how function specification naturally arises during model refinement. In this section we present a general approach to function synthesis that generalizes the model refinement approach. Reactive synthesis tends to generate control systems with relatively flat structure whereas algorithm/function design generates smaller programs with deeper structure (via a hierarchy of subfunctions). Our intent is to have model refinement as the unifying framework for synthesizing both reactive systems and functions.

Some required properties are naturally expressed over the nodes of a path in the model, rather than being localized to a node (state invarient) or arc (action invariants). They express required properties that hold between values that are not near in time or space. We define *path properties* to be predicates over the variables of nodes along some path in the model. An action property is a special case of a path property since it is expressed over a path of length one. When necessary we prefix a variable with the node at which the value is referenced. If a variable is only accessible at one node or arc (i.e. it is local), the prefix can be omitted.

We define next some refinement rules that can be used to reduce path properties to action properties. The refinement rules work by propagating the path property through the structure of the path, resulting in the strengthening of the labels on particular arcs. The resulting refined path implies the path property by construction. At that point, the constraint system of Sect. 3 can be defined and solved.

Path properties may arise by the imposition of model substructure, where an arc is replaced by an arc-like LTS (i.e. a submodel). This may happen when an action specifies a complex state change that requires, say, an iterative or recursive computation to complete. We call this process *arc refinement*. Suppose that we have a required property $\varphi_{m,p}(st_m, st_p)$ that relates the state at node m to the state at node p, where there exists a path from m to p in the model $\mathcal{M}$. Our strategy is to propagate φ through the structure of $\mathcal{M}$ until we have inferred properties that can be localized to the nodes and arcs of $\mathcal{M}$. For purposes of reasoning about path properties we proceed as if we have path labels in $\mathcal{M}$ for all pairs of nodes; e.g. $L_{m,p}$ is treated as the label expressing properties of the paths from node m to node p.

There are two propagation rules that reduce the scope of a path property, with the goal of reducing the property to action properties in the path: either propagate forward from node m toward p, or propagate backward from node p toward m. Rules for both are defined next. Each rule reduces the span of a path predicate by one, so we iterate their application until we generate a path predicate than spans a single arc, whereupon we can enforce it locally.

Forward Propagation: Let $\mathcal{S} = \langle \mathcal{M}, \Phi \rangle$ be a specification and let $\varphi_{m,p} \in \Phi$ be a path property from node m to node p. We can refine $\mathcal{S}$ to reduce the path property $\varphi_{m,p}$ as follows: (1) Delete $\varphi_{m,p}$ from Φ, and (2) for each arc $a = \langle m, n \rangle \in Arc$, add the path formula $wcPostSpec(L_a, \varphi_{m,p})$ to Φ where $wcPostSpec(L_a, \theta)$ is the *Weakest Controllable PostSpecification* of action L_a with respect to path formula θ over $V(m) \cup V(p)$ and is defined by

$$\forall st_m, u, e. \ L_m(st_m) \wedge U(st_m, u) \wedge e \in E(st_m) \implies \theta(f_a(st_m, u, e)).$$

$wcPostSpec$ is the weakest path formula over $V(n) \cup V(p)$ such that for any transition instance of a from some state st_m to state st_n, there is some st_p such that $\theta(st_m, st_p)$. We repeat Forward Propagation until all path properties have been reduced to actions (and thus can be enforced by model refinement).

Backward Propagation: Let $\mathcal{S} = \langle \mathcal{M}, \Phi \rangle$ be a system specification and let $\varphi_{m,p} \in \Phi$ be a path formula from node m to node p. We can refine $\mathcal{S}$ to reduce the path property occurrences as follows: (1) Delete $\varphi_{m,p}$ from Φ, and (2) for each arc $a = \langle n, p \rangle \in Arc$ where there exists a path from m to n, add the path formula $wcPreSpec(L_a, \varphi_{m,p})$ to Φ where $wcPreSpec(L_a, \theta)$ is the *Weakest Controllable PreSpecification* of action L_a with respect to path formula θ over $V(m) \cup V(p)$ and is defined by

$$\forall u, e.\ L_n(st_n) \ \wedge \ U(st_n, u) \ \wedge \ e \in E(st_n) \implies \theta(st_m, f_a(st_n, u, e)).$$

$wcPreSpec$ is the weakest path formula over $V(m) \cup V(n)$ such that for any transition instance of a from some state st_n to state st_p, there is some st_m such that $\theta(st_m, st_p)$. We repeat Backward Propagation until all path properties have been reduced to actions (and thus can be enforced by model refinement).

Both of these propagation rules work by propagating the path property φ through the transition a, whether forward or backwards. To get useful results, there must be some structure in L_a. These rules are often applied after one has chosen a candidate function/operation for transition a and then desires to play out the consequences. This process is analogous to SAT algorithms in which one chooses a variable and a value heuristically and then explores the consequences via boolean propagation and conflict-driven learning in the failure case. The choice of a simple operation that is natural in context, as an arc refinement, enables the propagation to go through. This is a choice and alternative choices lead to different designs, as illustrated in the next section.

5.1   Algorithm Design Example: Sorting

One feature of model refinement is that it subsumes a major part of the automated algorithm design work performed in earlier function synthesis systems such as KIDS [28]. In retrospect, the success of KIDS in algorithm design is partly due to its automated inference system which was designed to propagate output conditions through the structure of a chosen program scheme. To illustrate, consider the design of a sorting algorithm using a binary divide-and-conquer program scheme as a model. In a functional notation, the model can be expressed as

$$F(x{:}D) : (z{:}R) = \ \text{if } primitive(x) \text{ then } direct(x)$$
$$\text{else } compose \circ (F \times F) \circ decompose(x)$$

and the required property is $bag(x) = bag(z) \wedge ordered(z)$, where x and z are lists of numbers, $bag(x)$ returns the bag or multiset of elements in list x, and $ordered(z)$ holds when list z is in sorted order. The property is simply an input/output predicate since the only observable behavior of an algorithm is its (uncontrollable) input and (controllable) output value. In a functional setting, there are no global variables and hence no global state. The input to each functional component is the environment input and the control value is the output of the action.

There are several common tactics for designing divide-and-conquer algorithms. One is to select a simple *decompose* operation on the input type, and then to calculate a *compose* operator that achieves the correct output. A dual tactic is to select a simple *compose* operation on the output type, and then calculate a *decompose* operator that achieves a decomposition of the input into parts that can be solved and composed to yield a correct solution.

We might represent the key recursive part of the scheme as a dataflow path:

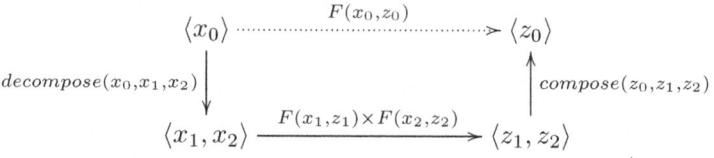

where a node represents a state by the variables that exist in it (and their properties), and each arc specifies an action by a predicate over input and output variables. This particular model derives from a functional program, so the abstract "states" actually do not represent stored values, but the value flow at intermediate points in a computation. For simplicity and clarity, we use this graphical representation rather than perform the straightforward translation to the TLA-like notation used in previous examples.

In terms of the dataflow path, the goal constraint is a predicate over x_0 and z_0: $\varphi(x_0, z_0) \equiv bag(x_0) = bag(z_0) \land ordered(z_0)$. Suppose that we follow the second tactic and refine the model by choosing list concatenation as our *compose* operator: *compose* $\mapsto z_0 = z_1 {+\!\!+} z_2$. The ultimate effect of this choice is to derive a variant of a quicksort algorithm. Note that in this case the environment input is the pair $\langle z_1, z_2 \rangle$ and the control value is the output z_0. The Backward Propagation Rule applies here since the goal property is not expressed over the input and output variables of *compose*, so we calculate:

$wcPreSpec(compose, \varphi(x_0, z_0))$
$\equiv \quad \forall z_0.\, z_0 = z_1 {+\!\!+} z_2 \implies bag(x_0) = bag(z_0) \land ordered(z_0)$
$\equiv \quad \{$ quantifier elimination on z_0 $\}$
$\quad bag(x_0) = bag(z_1 {+\!\!+} z_2) \land ordered(z_1 {+\!\!+} z_2)$
$\equiv \quad \{$ distributivity laws and simplification$\}$
$\quad bag(x_0) = bag(z_1) \cup bag(z_2) \land ordered(z_1) \land ordered(z_2) \land bag(z_1) \leq bag(z_2).$

where we have used domain-specific laws for distributing *bag* and *ordered* over list concatenation, and $b_1 \leq b_2$ holds when each element of bag b_1 is less than or equal to each element of bag b_2. As this remains a path predicate $\varphi(x_0, z_1, z_2)$ (i.e. not localizable to an arc), we continue by propagating this derived goal backward through the recursive calls:

$wcPreSpec(F \times F,\; \varphi(x_0, z_1, z_2))$
$\equiv \quad \{$ unfold $\}$

$$\forall z_1, z_2. \, bag(x_1) = bag(z_1) \wedge ordered(z_1) \wedge bag(x_2) = bag(z_2) \wedge ordered(z_2)$$
$$\implies bag(x_0) = bag(z_1) \cup bag(z_2)$$
$$\wedge \, ordered(z_1) \wedge ordered(z_1) \wedge bag(z_1) \leq bag(z_2)$$
$$\equiv \quad \{ \text{ simplification and quantifier elimination} \}$$
$$bag(x_0) = bag(x_1) \cup bag(x_2) \wedge bag(x_1) \leq bag(x_2).$$

This last predicate is expressed over the input/output variables of the *decompose* operator, so it can be localized and enforced by strengthening the *decompose* action to

$$bag(x_0) = bag(x_1) \cup bag(x_2) \wedge bag(x_1) \leq bag(x_2).$$

Note that this is a specification for (a version of) the well-known partition sub-algorithm of Quicksort. It asserts that if we decompose the input list x_0 into two lists x_1 and x_2 whose collective elements are the same as the elements in x_0, and such that each element of x_1 is less-than-or-equal-to each element of x_2, then when we recursively sort x_1 and x_2, and then concatenate them, the result will be a sorted version of x_0. If we had included a well-founded order in the decompose operator, we would infer a derived initial condition of $length(x_0) > 1$ on *decompose*. This serves as a guard on the recursive path in the algorithm.

In summary, we have used propagation rules to infer a specification on the *decompose* action that, if realized by further refinement, is sufficient to establish the correctness of the whole algorithm.

6   Related Work

Our previous work on functional algorithm design used algorithm theories as over-approximating models for various classes of algorithms. Algorithm theories and design tactics [29] were implemented in KIDS [28] and Specware [17]. These synthesis systems used a form of model refinement to instantiate algorithm models for divide-and-conquer [27], global search, dynamic programming, and other classes. Synthesized applications include schedulers [31], SAT-solvers [33], and garbage collectors [32].

Sketching [34] is a currently popular program synthesis approach that can be seen as a special case of model refinement. The model is supplied in the form of a program template with holes for missing code. In the case of SyGuS [1], a grammar is given as an over-approximation to the missing code. The property to be enforced may be expressed using the language of an SMT-solver, so that guesses as to how to fill the hole can be verified. While the problem setup is similar to model refinement, the synthesis process is based on generate-and-test rather than predicate transformer-based calculation.

Model refinement is most obviously derived from the extensive literature on controller synthesis [10, 23] and reactive system design [21]. Most current work on the synthesis of reactive systems focuses on circuit design and starts with specifications in propositional Linear Temporal Logic (LTL) or GR(1) [4, 15]. Model refinement allows specifications that are first-order and uses a temporal logic of actions that is amenable to refinement, allowing a broader range of applications to be tackled.

The algorithm derivation in Sect. 5 highlights a novel aspect of model refinement: the imposition of a design template rather than a plant or game model as it typical in reactive system design. Design templates in the systems world are often discussed as Design Patterns. The refinement mechanism is arc refinement (see Sect. 2.3) which refines a model arc by an arc-like LTS, in effect, replacing the arc with a design pattern (here, a divide-and-conquer algorithm pattern). The arc specification becomes a path property and the refinement rules in Sect. 5 are used to localize the property by strengthening arc labels along the path. It is typical of algorithm derivation that arc refinements are needed to implement arc/action specifications, resulting in the top-down synthesis of subalgorithms. Algorithms often have a deeper hierarchy of subcomputations than system control codes.

The model refinement constraints are a kind of Constrained Horn Clause (CHC) and specialized algorithms have been explored for these as a generalization of SMT solving [9,12,13]. The main application is finding inductive invariants for program verification. Our approach aims to find a maximal solution whereas CHC tools typically aim to find any solution, since any inductive invariant is sufficient to establish the specified verification condition.

Model checking [7] can be viewed as a special case of model refinement in which refinement of the model is not an option. Counter-example-driven model refinement is performed in CEGAR with the goal to prove a specific property on a model of a fixed underlying program [6]. The goal of CEGAR is not to synthesize a correct program from properties but to verify properties of a given program.

7   Concluding Remarks

The starting point of this work is the observation that logical properties and computational models have complementary strengths for purposes of formally stating requirements on desired computer behavior. The key questions then are (1) how to combine these strengths into a coherent formalism for specifying requirements, and (2) how to calculate programs that are consistent with specifications stated in the formalism.

In this paper we have presented an instance of these general ideas, using (1) a first-order temporal logic of actions to specify logical properties and (2) labelled transition systems to express concrete and abstract computational models and their refinement order. For illustration purposes we have further focused on basic safety properties.

Physical plants (as in the Flow Control problem) and game-like problems (as in the Cinderella-Stepmother problem) provide concrete models upon which model refinement can propagate logical properties over actions. The imposition of abstract designs as abstract models (as in the Sorting example and more generally in the form of design patterns, algorithm schemas, sketches, etc.) naturally transforms property specifications into path predicates over abstract models. This paper has presented model refinement as a unified treatment of reactive and functional design using iterated constraint propagation of (1) path predicates over abstract models and (2) state/action predicates over concrete model steps/arcs.

While this paper provides a fairly general and mechanizable framework for user-guided, yet highly automated design, it also admits the possibility of high computational complexity or undecidability due to the expressiveness of the first-order formulas. By suitably restricting the domain of discourse to decidable theories, we can define a more automated design process. Our prototype implementation restricts constraints to the decidable theories in Z3, which is sufficient for a range of applications including the examples presented above. Extension to handle liveness properties ($\Psi\varphi$) and reactivity properties ($\Box\Psi\varphi$) can also be handled as definite constraint systems whose fixpoints can be found by Kleene iteration combined with widening. However, for practical purposes, reactive systems typically want guarantees of bounded-time responsiveness, which is a safety property.

Model refinement is intended to be part of a library of refinement-generating transformations that are used to develop complex algorithms and systems. In our view, a practical synthesis environment generates a refinement chain from an initial specification down to compilable code. Each step of the refinement chain is generated by a transformation that is also capable of emitting proofs of the refinement relation between the pre- and post-specification [6,32]. Model refinement would tend to be used earlier in the refinement chain since it translates logical requirements into operational designs, by enforcing properties in the model. Other refinement-generating transformations are necessary to improve the performance of the evolving model including expression simplification, finite-differencing or incrementalization, and datatype refinements [19,28].

Treating a specification as a model plus required properties is a key aspect of model refinement. Models are essentially programs annotated with invariant properties. While temporal logics can be translated into automata (and vice-versa), for complex designs, the models can be much more compact than logic, especially when the nodes have rich properties and the control structure is complex. Initially, models serve to succinctly capture fixed behavioral structure in the problem domain, such as physical plant dynamics and information system APIs. During refinement, the model serves as the accumulation of the design decisions made so far. Another intended use of models is via the imposition of design patterns for algorithms and systems. Patterns from a library capture best-practice designs that might be difficult to find by search; e.g. when there is a delicate tradeoff between objectives, such as between precision of output and runtime.

We are currently working on the design of a processor (model) that asynchronously receives and processes tasks for which we want to enforce capacity and timeliness properties. To enforce fairness and timeliness the design composes in an abstract scheduler (design pattern). We hope to report on this work in a future paper.

Acknowledgments. The authors would like to thank Alessandro Coglio, Grant Jurgenson, Christoph Kreitz, and the reviewers for their comments on this paper. This work has been sponsored in part by NSF under contract CCF-0737840, ONR under contract N00014-04-1-0727, and by the Laboratory Directed Research and Development program at Sandia National Laboratories, a multimission laboratory managed and operated by National Technology & Engineering Solutions of Sandia, LLC, a wholly owned subsidiary of Honeywell International Inc., for the U.S. Department of Energy's National Nuclear Security Administration under contract DE-NA0003525. This paper describes objective technical results and analysis. Any subjective views or opinions that might be expressed in the paper do not necessarily represent the views of the U.S. Department of Energy or the United States Government.

Disclosure of Interests. The authors have no competing interests to declare that are relevant to the content of this article.

References

1. Alur, R., et al.: Syntax-guided synthesis. In: Proceedings of the IEEE International Conference on Formal Methods in Computer-Aided Design (FMCAD), pp. 1–17 (2013)
2. Back, R.J., Wright, J.V.: The Refinement Calculus: A Systematic Introduction. Springer, Berlin (1998). https://doi.org/10.1007/978-1-4612-1674-2
3. Beyene, T., Chaudhuri, S., Popeea, C., Rybalchenko, A.: A constraint-based approach to solving games on infinite graphs. In: Proceedings of the 41st ACM SIGPLAN-SIGACT Symposium on Principles of Programming Languages, pp. 221–233 (2014)
4. Bloem, R., Jobstmann, B., Piterman, N., Pnueli, A., Saar, Y.: Synthesis of reactive(1) designs. J. Comput. Syst. Sci. **78**(3), 911–938 (2012)
5. Buschmann, F., Meunier, R., Rohnert, H., Sommerlad, P., Stal, M.: Pattern-Oriented Software Architecture, Volume 1: A System of Patterns. Wiley, New York (1996)
6. Clarke, E., Grumberg, O., Jha, S., Lu, Y., Veith, H.: Counterexample-guided abstraction refinement. In: Emerson, E.A., Sistla, A.P. (eds.) CAV 2000. LNCS, vol. 1855, pp. 154–169. Springer, Heidelberg (2000). https://doi.org/10.1007/10722167_15
7. Clarke, E.M., Grumberg, O., Peled, D.A.: Model Checking. MIT Press, Cambridge (2000)
8. Constable, R.L.: Constructive mathematics and automatic program writers. In: Information Processing 71, pp. 229–233. IFIP, Ljubljana, Yugoslavia (1971)
9. Fedyukovich, G., Prabhu, S., Madhukar, K., Gupta, A.: Solving constrained horn clauses using syntax and data. In: 2018 Formal Methods in Computer Aided Design (FMCAD), pp. 1–9 (2018). https://doi.org/10.23919/FMCAD.2018.8603011
10. Filippidis, I., Dathathri, S., Livingston, S.C., Ozay, N., Murray, R.M.: Control design for hybrid systems with TuLiP: the temporal logic planning toolbox. In: 2016 IEEE Conference on Control Applications (CCA), pp. 1030–1041 (2016)
11. Gamma, E., Helm, R., Johnson, R., Vlissides, J.: Design Patterns: Elements of Reusable Object-Oriented Software. Addison-Wesley, Boston (1994)
12. Govind, V., Shoham, S., Gurfinkel, A.: Solving constrained horn clauses modulo algebraic data types and recursive functions. Proc. ACM Program. Lang. **6**(POPL) (2022)

13. Grebenshchikov, S., Lopes, N.P., Popeea, C., Rybalchenko, A.: Synthesizing software verifiers from proof rules. In: Proceedings of the 33rd ACM SIGPLAN Conference on Programming Language Design and Implementation, pp. 405—416 (2012)
14. Green, C.: Application of theorem proving to problem solving. In: Proceedings of the First International Joint Conference on Artificial Intelligence, pp. 219–239 (1969)
15. Jacobs, S., Klein, F., Schirmer, S.: A high-level LTL synthesis format: TLSF v1.1. Electron. Proc. Theor. Comput. Sci. **229**, 112–132 (2016)
16. Jones, C.B.: Systematic Software Development Using VDM. Prentice-Hall, Englewood Cliffs (1986)
17. Kestrel Institute: Specware System and documentation (2003). http://www.specware.org/
18. Lamport, L.: The temporal logic of actions. ACM Trans. Program. Lang. Syst. **16**(3), 872–923 (1994)
19. Liu, Y.: Systematic Program Design: From Clarity to Efficiency. Cambridge University Press, Cambridge (2013)
20. Manna, Z., Waldinger, R.: A deductive approach to program synthesis. ACM Trans. Program. Lang. Syst. **2**(1), 90–121 (1980)
21. Pnueli, A., Rosner, R.: On the synthesis of a reactive module. In: Proceedings of the 16th ACM SIGPLAN-SIGACT Symposium on Principles of Programming Languages, pp. 179—190 (1989)
22. Püschel, M., et al.: Spiral: a generator for platform-adapted libraries of signal processing algorithms. Int. J. High Perform. Comput. Appl. **18**(1), 21–45 (2004)
23. Ramadge, P., Wonham, W.: The control of discrete event systems. Proc. IEEE **77**(1), 81–98 (1989)
24. Rehof, J., Mogensen, T.: Tractable constraints in finite semilattices. Sci. Comput. Program. **35**, 191–221 (1999)
25. Schmidt, D.C., Stal, M., Rohnert, H., Buschmann, F.: Pattern-Oriented Software Architecture, Volume 2: Patterns for Concurrent and Networked Objects. Wiley, New York (2000)
26. Slanina, M., Sankaranarayanan, S., Sipma, H., Manna, Z.: Controller synthesis of discrete linear plants using polyhedra. Technical report, REACT-TR-2007-01, Stanford University (2007)
27. Smith, D.R.: Top-down synthesis of divide-and-conquer algorithms. Artificial Intelligence **27**(1), 43–96 (1985), (Reprinted In: Rich, C., Waters, R. (eds.) Readings in Artificial Intelligence and Software Engineering. Morgan Kaufmann, Los Altos (1986))
28. Smith, D.R.: KIDS – a semi-automatic program development system. IEEE Trans. Softw. Eng. Spec. Issue Formal Methods Softw. Eng. **16**(9), 1024–1043 (1990). citeseer.ist.psu.edu/article/smith90kids.html
29. Smith, D.R., Lowry, M.R.: Algorithm theories and design tactics. In: van de Snepscheut, J.L.A. (ed.) MPC 1989. LNCS, vol. 375, pp. 379–398. Springer, Heidelberg (1989). https://doi.org/10.1007/3-540-51305-1_23
30. Smith, D.R., Nedunuri, S.: Model refinement. TechnIcal report 21.0, Kestrel Institute (2021). https://www.kestrel.edu/people/smith/pub/MR-TR.pdf
31. Smith, D.R., Parra, E.A., Westfold, S.J.: Synthesis of planning and scheduling software. In: Tate, A. (ed.) Advanced Planning Technology, pp. 226–234. AAAI Press, Menlo Park (1996)
32. Smith, D.R., Westbrook, E., Westfold, S.J.: Deriving concurrent garbage collectors: final report. Technical report, Kestrel Institute (2015). http://www.kestrel.edu/home/people/smith/pub/Crash-FR.pdf

33. Smith, D.R., Westfold, S.: Toward the Synthesis of Constraint Solvers. Technical report, Kestrel Institute (2013). http://www.kestrel.edu/home/people/smith/pub/CW-report.pdf
34. Solar-Lezama, A.: The sketching approach to program synthesis. In: Hu, Z. (ed.) APLAS 2009. LNCS, vol. 5904, pp. 4–13. Springer, Heidelberg (2009). https://doi.org/10.1007/978-3-642-10672-9_3
35. Sontag, E.: Mathematical Control Theory. Springer, New York (1998). https://doi.org/10.1007/978-1-4612-0577-7

Analysing the Safety Implications of Security Risks in Cyber-Physical Systems

Colin Snook[1]([✉])[iD], Thai Son Hoang[1][iD], Asieh Salehi Fathabadi[1][iD], Michael Butler[1][iD], and Martin Kubisch[2]

[1] ECS, University of Southampton, Southampton, UK
{cfs,t.s.hoang,a.salehi-fathabadi,m.j.butler}@soton.ac.uk
[2] Airbus Central Research and Technology, Munich, Germany
martin.kubisch@airbus.com

Abstract. Cyber-physical systems (CPS) often use open communications to expedite interactions and hence introduce security risks which can be exploited by attackers to cause unsafe failure conditions. Interfaces within the system require security properties (e.g. confidentiality, authentication and reliability) in order to ensure that potential risks are eliminated. However, different applications may differ in their sensitivity to particular security properties. Avionics standards such as ED202A require developers to analyse potential security risks to ensure that their impact on the safe operation of an aircraft is acceptable. We show how Event-B modelling can be used to evaluate which security properties affect safety, and other properties such as liveness, in a particular CPS application.

Keywords: Formal Methods · Event-B · Security · Safety

1 Introduction and Motivation

The safety of systems has traditionally been considered from the viewpoint of unintentional failures. However, as systems increasingly use communications protocols whose specifications are available in the open domain, intentional malevolent attacks become a more significant area of concern fo1r systems designers. In the avionics domain, standards such as ED202A [3] and ED203A [4] mandate security risk assessments to be carried out at different stages of design. These standards are only concerned with security as it relates to aircraft safety and define a security threat condition as an effect on the aircraft that has been caused by an "intentional unauthorised electronic interaction". However, security attacks may be categorized into different types according to the nature of the security threat and the property of the interface that is exploited. Here we show how formal modelling in Event-B and its refinement approach can be used to analyse how particular types of security attacks affect the system and hence which properties must be guaranteed by interfaces in order to ensure safety.

A. Cavalcanti and J. Baxter (Eds.): *The Practice of Formal Methods*, LNCS 14781, pp. 97–119, 2024.
https://doi.org/10.1007/978-3-031-66673-5_6

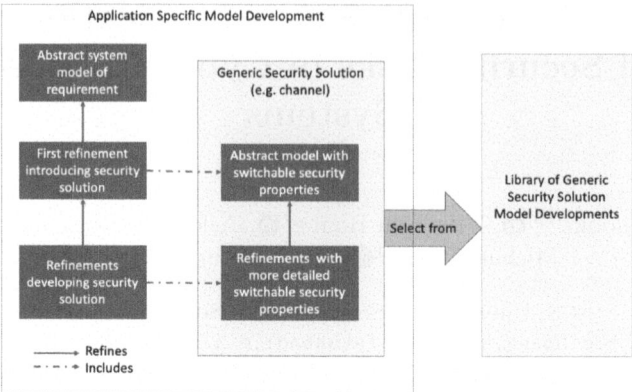

Fig. 1. A modular methodology to formal modelling of security solutions

A methodology to analyse the safety implications of security risks. The proposed
model architecture to support the methodology is shown in Fig. 1. There are two
parts to our modelling and verification methodology.

1. The first part is the development of generic models of communication channels
   with options for security properties (*authenticity, confidentiality*, and *reliability*), together with refinements that introduce mechanisms (such as cryptographic protocols) that achieve the desired security properties. We envision a
   library of model developments of generic security solutions (right-hand side
   of Fig. 1).
2. For the second part of our methodology, we start from an abstract model of
   the requirements which expresses the pure functionality (top left of Fig. 1)
   without introducing the interface mechanisms that involve security threats.
   We then use refinement to incorporate generic interfaces exploring how choices
   of security properties impact the correctness of a critical service. For example,
   in Sect. 5, we show how authenticity in a channel is required to prevent unsafe
   refuelling, whereas confidentiality is not required. A key aspect is that the
   analysis of the service correctness is achieved by working with the abstraction
   of the secure channel rather than a detailed design model.

Further refinements of the application model can include refined versions of
security solutions which have already been introduced, or can introduce new
generic interfaces for other features of the application model. In either case the
refinement is proved to satisfy the previous level. For the latter case, security
properties can be switched on and off to test which are actually needed, so that
an appropriate security solution can be selected.

A Step-by-Step Guideline for Designing Critical Applications. Given a library of
generic security solutions, based on the above methodology, we have the following
guideline for developing a critical application (e.g. aircraft servicing).

1. **Step 1**: Specify the application focusing on the functional requirements of the systems without its implementation details.
2. **Step 2**: Introduce the design of the systems using generic channels to implement some features of the system.
3. **Step 3**: Explore the choices of security properties of the generic channels to identify the required security properties.
4. **Step 4**: Choose a security solution that satisfies the identified properties from the above steps.

Steps 2, 3, 4 are repeated for further features of the system.

The rest of our paper is structured as follows. Section 2 provides background about Event-B and associated tools. Section 3 introduces a case study example with an abstract model of its requirements and main safety property as well as an overview of the design/implementation that follows. In Sect. 4, we develop a model of a generic channel with switchable security properties and its refinement using message hashing with a shared secret key to provide a channel that guarantees authenticity. In Sect. 5, we refine the case study application to use the generic channel models, showing that authenticity is needed and subsequently achieved. We then look at an alternative protocol for the same case study, which requires time-bounded reliability instead of authenticity, and develop an alternative generic channel and an alternative model of the application (Sect. 6) to show this. Section 7 discusses the influence of Rely/Guarantee thinking [8] on our work. Section 8 concludes and outlines future directions.

2   Background

Event-B. [1] is a refinement-based formal method for system development. The mathematical language of Event-B is based on set theory and first-order logic. An Event-B model consists of two parts: *contexts* for static data and *machines* for dynamic behaviour. Contexts contain carrier sets s, constants c, and axioms $A(c)$ constraining the carrier sets and constants. Machines contain variables v, invariant predicates $I(v)$ that constrain the variables, and events. In Event-B, a machine corresponds to a transition system where *variables* represent the states and *events* specify the transitions.

An event comprises a guard denoting its enabling condition and an action describing how the variables are modified when the event is executed. In general, an event e has the form **any** t **where** $G(t,v)$ **then** $v := E(t,v)$ **end**, where t is the event parameters, $G(t, v)$ is the guard of the event, and $v := E(t, v)$ is the action of the event.

An Event-B model is constructed by making progressive refinements starting from an initial abstract model which may have more general behaviours and gradually introducing more detail that constrains the behaviour towards the desired system. This is done by adding or refining the variables of the previous abstract model and by modifying the events so that they use the new variables.

Event-B is supported by the Rodin toolset [2], an extensible open-source toolkit which includes facilities for modelling and verifying the consistency of models using theorem proving. The remainder of this section describes the Rodin plug-in extensions that we use for composition modelling, model checking, and model validation via simulation-based approaches.

Machine Inclusion. [6] allows a model to be incorporated into another with instantiation by renaming. Several renamed copies of the same or different model developments can be incorporated. Events of the included model can be synchronised (i.e., fire together) with events of the including machine using parameters to link their local values. The machine inclusion extension to CamilleX [7] provides the concepts for a machine to include other machines and for an event to synchronise with one or more events from the (different) included machines. We summarise the main ideas for *machine* A *to include machine* B below:

- A inherits all variables of B.
- A inherits all invariants of B.
- B's variables can only be modified from A via synchronising with a B' event.
- Multiple instances of B can be included via *prefixing* and in that case, B's variables, events, and event parameters are renamed accordingly.

ProB. [10] is an animator and model checker for the B-Method. It also supports Event-B and can be installed within the Rodin toolset. The ProB model checking facility complements Event-B theorem proving for verifying Event-B models by finding invariant violations and deadlocks. ProB also enables the validation of the model behaviour by exploring execution traces, which can be constructed by the manual selection of enabled events.

Scenario Checker. [13] is an animation tool that we developed for validating systems by recording and replaying scenarios. It extends ProB to support two new functionalities: a 'run-to-completion' style execution of controller events, and a record/replay style user interface for running test scenarios. In Event-B we model a closed system of interacting components including the environment and any controlling device without distinguishing between the different kinds of events. However, an environment event may trigger a sequence of controller events representing the controller's response. These internal controller steps are not usually explicitly specified by scenarios. Hence, to support scenario animation, we distinguish between external environment events and internal controller events. To simplify the scenario execution, the scenario checker records and replays the external events automatically firing any enabled internal events until none are enabled. Then the scenario checker will wait for the next external event to be selected by the user or by replaying the recorded scenario.

3   Case Study: Ground Unit Servicing of Aircraft

The case study used for our running example is aircraft ground servicing. During aircraft turnaround various services such as re-fuelling and air conditioning are performed on the aircraft by ground units. In order to provide integrated management and reduce turn-around times new systems are being developed to allow wireless communication between the aircraft and the service-providing ground units so that the aircraft can tell the ground unit how much of a service it needs (Fig. 2).

Although the aircraft apron is a highly controlled area, the security implications of wireless communication needs to be considered. Clearly, incorrect provision of such services (fuel, air temperature) can constitute a safety hazard. In the example in this paper we have simplified and generalised the functionality. We consider the case where an aircraft sends a message telling the servicing ground

Fig. 2. Aircraft - Ground Unit servicing

unit what quantity of the service it needs. This strategy requires the authenticity of the communications to be safe and the reliability of the communications to be effective. That is if an attacker can spoof messages containing incorrect instructions, the safety invariant could be violated and if an attacker can consume instructions the safety invariant is not violated but the functionality may not be provided. We also consider an alternative strategy where the aircraft sends a message telling the ground unit when to stop providing the service. This strategy requires the reliability of the communications for the system to be safe because, if an attacker consumes instructions to stop fuelling, the safety invariant will be violated.

3.1   Model of Requirements for an Aircraft Re-fuelling Service

In the context (Fig. 3) we introduce the subsets AC and GU of AGENTS which represent aircraft and ground units respectively. Also the constant relationship servicing is a function from ground units to aircraft representing the relationship between the ground units and the aircraft that they are servicing. It is functional and injective because a ground unit can only service one aircraft at a time and an aircraft cannot be serviced by more than one ground unit (this is possibly not true in real life but simplifies the example here). Note that we model this as a constant because we just want to focus on the communication. In reality the servicing relationship is variable. The constant Limit, gives the fuel capacity for each aircraft. (It is under-specified since we do not give the actual values, but just that there is a limit value for each aircraft).

The abstract model (Fig. 4), representing the requirements of the system, has a variable level which gives the current fuel level for each aircraft. A safety invariant specifies that the level for every aircraft must not exceed the Limit of that aircraft. A single event servicing represents the ground unit adding an amount to the level of the aircraft that it is servicing, where the amount is chosen so that it will not break the safety invariant. This abstract model corresponds to **Step 1** of our approach (as mentioned in Sect. 1).

```
context sys_x0 extends x0
constants AC GU servicing Limit
axioms
   @axm1: AC ∈ ℙ(AGENT)   // AC (aircraft) are a set of agents
   @axm2: GU ∈ ℙ(AGENT)   // GU (ground units) are a set of agents
   @axm3: servicing ∈ GU ↣ AC  // One−to−one relationships between GU and AC
   @axm4: Limit ∈ AC → ℕ₁  // Every aircraft has a (positive) limit for refuelling.
```

Fig. 3. Abstract model of system requirements for refuelling - context

3.2   Implementation for an Aircraft Re-fueling Service

The abstract requirements introduced in Sect. 3.1 could be implemented in various designs which have different security implications. For example, the aircraft could send a message to tell the ground unit how much fuel to give it. Alternatively the aircraft could send a message to tell the ground unit when to stop delivering fuel. Depending on the protocol, different types of communications will be required.

The following sections describe an example Event-B model of the GU-AC servicing functionality illustrating how the impact of various security properties can be tested to see whether or not they affect safety. The model is constructed in such a way that security properties can be easily enabled or disabled so that the need for each property can be explored. First we develop a re-usable generic channel (Sect. 4), showing that an agent can send messages to another agent via a uni-directional and dedicated channel while attackers can spoof, peek or intercept messages depending on the security properties of the channel. The three security properties can be turned on and off easily so that their effect on safety in a particular application can be tested. In the refinements we model a generic channel solution for the authenticity property. We then model the case study application (Sect. 5), starting with an abstract model of the application requirements capturing the safety property, followed by a refinement of the abstract requirements using the generic channel, via inclusion. In our refinement we assume that an authentic ground until will provide the correct service. This refinement allows us to demonstrate that authenticity is needed in order

```
machine sys_m0 sees sys_x0
// Current fuel level for individual aircraft
variable level : AC → ℕ = AC × {0}
// Safety limit for every aircraft
invariant @safety: ∀ ac · ac ∈ AC ⇒ (level(ac) ≤ Limit(ac))
//Service an @amount of fuel for an aircraft from an individual ground unit @gu
event service
any gu amount
where
   @prm_gu:  gu ∈ GU
   @prm_amount: amount ∈ ℕ
   @grd1:   level(servicing(gu)) + amount ≤ Limit(servicing(gu))
then
   @act1:   level(servicing(gu)) := level(servicing(gu)) + amount
end
```

Fig. 4. Abstract model of system requirements for refuelling - machine

to achieve the safety critical functional behaviour that relies on messages sent via the channel. We then discuss an alternative implementation strategy that requires time-bounded reliability (TBR) using a generic channel with TBR in an alternative refinement of the abstract requirements (Sect. 6).

4   Modelling a Generic Channel with Security Properties

In this section we develop models of a generic communication channel that achieves authenticity using an HMAC. The abstract model of the channel has switchable security properties so that it can be used to test which properties are needed in a particular application by switching on/off different properties to test their effect on the proof/verification of the safety invariants. The abstract model (with those needed security properties enabled) is then refined to a solution that achieves the desired security. The refined channel models can be used as a generic security solution by inclusion within an application model.

The structure of the model is as follows:

- We first model an idealised abstract meaning of channel authenticity (as well as reliability and confidentiality). In an ideal world, attackers cannot spoof messages of an abstract channel.
- However, for accessible open communication mechanisms, it is difficult to prevent spoofing attempts and solutions must rely on detecting and rejecting them instead. We therefore refine the model to allow spoofing, but for channels that guaranteed authenticity, non-authentic messages are rejected by the receiver.
- We then introduce the mechanism by which the receiver detects which messages are authentic and which are not. In this example we use hashing to annotate the authentic messages with the assumption that the attacker cannot guess the correct hash for the message that it creates.

Notice that our model of generic communication channels only focus on certain properties, namely, *authenticity, confidentiality, reliability*. Other properties currently omitted include *integrity, availability*, etc. Having a "complete" model of communication channels is outside the scope of this paper.

Abstract Channel. The context (Fig. 5) introduces new types for CHANNEL and MESSAGE as well as constants for channel_sender and channel_receiver (the intended sender and receiver AGENT for a particular channel). The switchable security properties for authenticity, reliability and confidentiality of a channel are also included here.

The abstract model introduces the following channel properties as variables:

- actual_sender of a message (might not be the intended channel_sender if the message is a spoof),
- actual_receiver of a message (might not be the intended channel_receiver if the message is intercepted),

```
context chan_x0_abstract extends x0
sets CHANNEL MESSAGE
constants channel_sender channel_receiver authenticity confidentiality reliability
axioms
  @axm5: finite(MESSAGE)
  @axm6: channel_receiver ∈ CHANNEL → AGENT
  @axm7: channel_sender ∈ CHANNEL → AGENT
  @axm8: authenticity ∈ CHANNEL → BOOL
  @axm9: confidentiality ∈ CHANNEL → BOOL
  @axm10: reliability ∈ CHANNEL → BOOL
```

Fig. 5. Abstract model of channel - context

- channel of a message (the channel that a message is being transmitted on),
- knows - the agents that have seen the message, including the actual sender and receiver as well as any attacker that has managed to peek the message,
- messages - the set of all messages which have been sent,
- consumed_messages - the subset of messages that have been received,
- existing_messages - the subset of messages that are still in the channel (sent but not received),
- intercepted_messages - the subset of messages that have been intercepted by attackers.

As well as the variable typing invariants, there are three invariants that express the desired security properties (Fig. 6). These are

- Authenticity - if a message is on an authentic channel then the actual_sender of the message must be the intended channel_sender.
- Confidentiality - if a message is consumed from a confidential channel then the actual_receiver of the message must be the intended channel_receiver.
- Reliability - if a message is intercepted then it was not on a reliable channel.

Event send represents an authentic transmission of a message on a channel. The message is created by adding it to the set messages and its subset existing_messages, the actual_sender is set to the channel_sender and the sender is recorded as knowing the message.

Event receive represents the successful receipt of a message. The message is removed from existing_messages and added to consumed_messages. At the same time, the actual_sender is set to the intended channel_receiver and the receiver is recorded as knowing the message.

The same model includes the following behaviour of attackers as events.

```
invariants
  @authenticity:   ∀m.m∈messages ⇒ (authenticity(channel(m)) = TRUE ⇒
         actual_sender(m) = channel_sender(channel(m))
  @confidentiality:  ∀m.m∈messages ⇒ (confidentiality(channel(m)) = TRUE ⇒
         knows~[{m}]⊆{actual_sender(m), channel_receiver(channel(m))})
  @reliability:    ∀m.m:intercepted_messages ⇒ (reliability(channel(m)) = FALSE)
```

Fig. 6. Abstract model of channel - invariants

- intercept messages on channels that are not reliable, removing them from the existing_messages and adding them to the intercepted messages.
- peek at messages on channels that are not confidential, adding them to the messages they know about.
- spoof messages on channels that are not authentic, adding them to the existing_messages and the messages they know about.

4.1 Channel Authenticity by Rejection of Spoofed Messages

While the idealised abstraction prevented attackers from spoofing messages, this is not possible in an open communication medium (where attackers have access to the medium). Instead, we must achieve authenticity by detecting and rejecting the spoofed messages. In the first refinement we prepare for this class of generic solution without specifying what the detection mechanism is (representing it as a simple boolean property of a message, authentic). Hence we can develop different implementations of this class of generic solution by further refining this model. Since the set of messages has changed (because it contains new spoofed messages that were not present in the abstract set of messages) we have to perform a data refinement to introduce new variables for the sets of messages. We introduce a new set of variables (prefixed *conceptual*) representing the sets of messages (possibly including new spoofed messages on channels that ensure authenticity) to replace the abstract ones (Fig. 7). The only abstract variable that is unchanged and retained is actual_receiver. A new variable conceptual_rejected_messages represents the spoofed messages that are rejected as non-authentic by the receiver. Also, a new variable is added to indicate which messages are authentic.

We present some, but, for brevity, not all, of the important gluing invariants linking the new variables and the old abstract ones, for the understanding of the authentic messages (Fig. 8).

- Invariant inv15: any conceptual existing message on an unauthentic channel is also an abstract existing messages. (There were spoofed messages on unauthentic channels of the abstract model).
- Invariant inv16: If a conceptual message is authentic, it is also an abstract messages.

```
machine chan_m1_authenticity refines chan_m0_abstract sees chan_x1_conceptual
variables actual_receiver
//new variables that refine abstract ones
  conceptual_messages conceptual_existing_messages conceptual_consumed_messages
      conceptual_intercepted_messages conceptual_channel conceptual_actual_sender
      conceptual_knows
//new variables
  conceptual_rejected_messages authentic
```

Fig. 7. Channel refined for rejection of spoofed messages - machine variables

invariants ...
// gluing relations
...
@inv15: ∀m·m∈ conceptual_existing_messages ∧ authenticity(conceptual_channel(m))=FALSE ⇒ m
    ∈ existing_messages
@inv16: ∀m·m∈ conceptual_messages ∧ authentic(m)=TRUE ⇒ m ∈ messages
@inv17: ∀m·m∈ conceptual_messages ∧ authenticity(conceptual_channel(m))=TRUE ∧ authentic(m)
    =FALSE ⇒ m ∉ messages
@inv18: ∀m·m∈ conceptual_existing_messages ∧ authentic(m)=TRUE ⇒ m ∈ existing_messages
@inv19: ∀m·m∈ conceptual_existing_messages ∧ authenticity(conceptual_channel(m))=TRUE ∧
    authentic(m)=FALSE ⇒ m ∉ existing_messages

Fig. 8. Channel refined for rejection of spoofed messages - machine invariants

- Invariant inv17: If a conceptual message on an authentic channel is NOT authentic, then it is not an abstract message. (There were no spoofed messages on authentic channels of the abstract model).
- Invariants inv18 and inv19: Similar to Invariants inv16 and inv17, but for the set of existing messages.

The above gluing invariants are important for proving the consistency between the concrete model (using conceptual messages) and the abstract model. Figure 9 shows some important details for the refinement of send and receive events and the new event reject. The send event has an action (@act5) to flag the message that is sent as authentic. The receive event has a new guard (@grd3) so that, on channels that ensure authenticity, it only receives authentic messages. Finally, the new reject event rejects any non-authentic messages on channels that ensure authenticity (by moving them to conceptual_rejected_messages).

Figure 10 shows some important details for the refinement of existing events intercept, peek, spoof, and a new event spoof2 (for sending a spoof message on an authentic channel). Both intercept and peek events are similar to their refined abstract counterparts but we have to add a guard that they only act on authentic messages otherwise they do not refine the abstract behaviour (when non-authentic messages did not exist). We do not really care whether attackers

```
event send refines send any m s c where
    @prm_m: m ∉ conceptual_messages
    @grd1: s=channel_sender(c)
then ...
    @act5: authentic(m) := TRUE // An authentic message is sent
end
event receive refines receive any r m where
    ...
    //for authenticated channels the message is only accepted if it is authentic
    @grd3: authenticity(conceptual_channel(m))=TRUE ⇒ authentic(m)=TRUE
then ... end
//new event to reject spoofed messages for authenticated channels only
event reject any r m where
    ...
    @grd3: authenticity(conceptual_channel(m))=TRUE
    @grd4: authentic(m)=FALSE
then ... end
```

Fig. 9. Channel refined for rejection of spoofed messages - events (1/2)

```
event intercept refines intercept any m r where
    ...
    @grd4: authentic(m)=TRUE  // Intercept only on authentic messages
then ... end

event peek refines peek any m r where
    ...
    @grd2: authentic(m)=TRUE  // Peek only on authentic messages
then ... end
event spoof refines spoof any m s c where
    ...
    @grd1: authenticity(c)=FALSE // Spoof on unauthentic channel
then ...
    @act6: authentic(m) := TRUE  // Set the message as authentic
end
// New event to spoof messages on authentic channels.
event spoof2 any m s c where
    ...
    @grd2: authenticity(c)=TRUE  // Spoof on authentic channel
then ...
    @act6: authentic(m) := FALSE  // Cannot imitate the authentic flag on authentic channel
end
```

Fig. 10. Channel refined for rejection of spoofed messages - events (2/2)

```
context chan_x2 extends chan_x1
sets KEY
constants hmac channelKey
axioms
    @typ2: hmac ∈ MESSAGE×KEY → ℕ
    @typ3: channelKey ∈ CHANNEL → KEY
```

Fig. 11. Channel refined for authenticity by hash - context

intercept or peek spoofed messages, but we could add new events to cover these cases if needed. The refined event spoof sends, apparently authentic messages on unauthentic channels and hence the message is flagged as authentic. The new spoof2 event allows attackers to spoof messages on a channel that ensures authenticity, but they cannot subvert the authentication mechanism to make the spoofed message look authentic (i.e. authentic(m) is set to FALSE).

4.2   Channel Authenticity by Rejection Using HMAC

This refinement models a mechanism for detecting which messages are spoofed and should be rejected. The refinement replaces the boolean flag authentic with a hash. Only the channel sender and receiver know the key, so it is assumed that the attacker cannot guess what the hash should be.

In the context (Fig. 11) we introduce a new set KEY. The constant hmac gives the hash number for each message key pair. The constant channelKey gives the key for each channel. In the model it is assumed that only the channel_sender and channel_receiver have access to the channel_key function and hence are the only agents able to determine the key to use for the channel.

The refined model (Fig. 12) introduces a new variable hash that gives a number (the hash) for some conceptual messages. The gluing invariants explain how hash implements the authentic flag from the previous model.

```
machine chan_m2 refines chan_m1 sees chan_x2
variables
 ... //abstract variables that are not refined
 hash //new variables
invariants
@inv1:   hash ∈ conceptual_messages ⇸ ℕ
@inv_glue1: ∀m · m ∈ dom(hash) ∧ hash(m)= hmac(m↦channelKey(conceptual_channel(m))) ⇒
     authentic(m)=TRUE
@inv_glue2: ∀m · m ∈ dom(hash) ∧ hash(m) ≠ hmac(m↦channelKey(conceptual_channel(m))) ⇒
     authentic(m)=FALSE
@inv_glue3: ∀m · m ∈ conceptual_messages \ dom(hash) ⇒ authentic(m)=FALSE
```

Fig. 12. Channel refined for authenticity by hash - variables and invariants

- Invariant @inv_glue1: if the message has a hash and it is the correct one (matching that given by the hmac function for the message and the channel key for the channel that the message is on) then the message is authentic (i.e. corresponds to one of the messages with authentic = TRUE in the previous refinement).
- Invariant @inv_glue2: Vice versa, if the message has an incorrect hash then the message is not authentic.
- Invariant @inv_glue3: If the message does not have a hash, it is not authentic.

```
event send refines send any m s c where ...
    then ...
      // s (channel send) knows the key for the channel and can calculate the correct hash code
      @act5: hash(m) := hmac(m↦channelKey(c))
    end
event receive refines receive any r m where ...
      // r (channel receiver) knows the key for the channel and can check the hash code
      @grd3: authenticity(conceptual_channel(m))=TRUE ⇒
         (m ∈ dom(hash) ∧ hash(m)= hmac(m↦channelKey(conceptual_channel(m))))
    then ... end
event reject refines reject any r m where ...
      // the message does not have a hash or it is not the correct hash
      @grd4: m ∉ dom(hash) ∨ hash(m) ≠ hmac(m↦channelKey(conceptual_channel(m)))
    then ... end
event intercept refines intercept any m r where ...
      // authentic messages has correct hash
      @grd4: m ∈ dom(hash) ∧ hash(m)= hmac(m↦channelKey(conceptual_channel(m)))
    then ... end
event peek refines peek any m r where ...
      // authentic messages has correct hash
      @grd2: m ∈ dom(hash) ∧ hash(m)= hmac(m↦channelKey(conceptual_channel(m)))
    then ... end
//for non−authenticated channels the attacker can send a message with the correct hash
event spoof refines spoof any m s c where ... then ...
      @act7: hash(m) := hmac(m↦channelKey(c)) // the attacker somehow knows the correct hash
    end
// for authenticated channels the attacker can send a message but can not guess the correct hash
event spoof2 refines spoof2 any m s c h where ...
      @grd3: h ∈ ℕ
      @grd4: h ≠ hmac(m↦channelKey(c)) // the attacker does not guess the correct hash
    then ... @act6: hash(m) := h end
```

Fig. 13. Channel refined for authenticity by hash - events

Figure 13 shows some details for the refinement of existing events send, receive, reject, intercept, peak, spoof, and spoof2.

- Event send: Instead of setting authentic(m) to TRUE, the send event now sets the hash for the message it is sending to the correct value using the hmac function.
- Event receive: For authentic channels, the receive event now checks that the message has the correct hash before accepting it.
- Event reject: A message is rejected if it does not have a hash or the hash is incorrect.
- Events intercept and peek operate on messages that have a correct hash.
- Event spoof: For channels without authenticity, the attacker can somehow find the correct hash (action @act7).
- Event spoof2: If an attacker tries to spoof a message on a channel that guarantees authenticity the attacker does not guess the correct hash (@grd4).

5   Secure Aircraft Servicing Using the Generic Channel

In this section, we continue to develop the model of the aircraft servicing case study that was introduced in Sect. 3. The model uses the generic solution for channel authenticity, described in Sect. 4. The channel model is incorporated into the system model using machine inclusion. We show that we can analyse the safety of the aircraft fueling service by exploring options for the channel security properties using the generic abstract channel.

Step 2. Aircraft Re-fueling Service Using Abstract Channels. As mentioned in Sect. 1, **Step 2** of our approach is to introduce the design of the system using the abstract channels. The first refinement of the system (Fig. 14) uses the abstract channel (via inclusion of chan_m0) so that the aircraft can tell the ground unit how much fuel it needs. A new variable data is introduced which attaches a value (i.e. the amount of fuel required by the aircraft) to a message. This is needed because the generic channel abstracts away from the information that is being exchanged in the messages. The processing variable represents the mechanism of the ground unit receiving and then responding to the amount of fuel message. The handshake variable represents an acknowledgement so that the aircraft does not send more messages until the first has been processed.

```
machine sys_m1 refines sys_m0 sees sys_x1
includes chan_m0
variables level
// new variables
data processing handshake
invariants
    @inv1: data ∈ ch_messages → ℕ
    @inv2: processing ∈ GU ⇸ ch_messages
    @inv3: handshake ∈ AC → BOOL
```

Fig. 14. Refined model of system using abstract channel - variables

```
event service refines service any gu where
  @grds1:  gu ∈ dom(processing)
  @grds2:  data(processing(gu)) > 0
then
  @acts1:  level(servicing(gu)) := level(servicing(gu))+data(processing(gu))
  @acts2:  processing := {gu} ◁ processing
  @acts3:  handshake(servicing(gu)) := FALSE
with @amount:  amount = data(processing(gu)) end
event ac_send any ac synchronises send where
  @grds1:  ac = s
  @grds2:  level(ac) < Limit(ac)
  @grds3:  channel_receiver(c) ∈ GU ∧ servicing(channel_receiver(c)) = ac
  @grds4:  handshake(ac) = FALSE
then
  @acts1:  data(m) := Limit(ac) − level(ac)
  @acts2:  handshake(ac) := TRUE
end
event gu_receive any gu synchronises receive where
  @grds1:  gu = r
  @grds2:  servicing(gu) = channel_sender(channel(m))
  @grds3:  gu∉dom(processing)
then @acts1:  processing(gu) := m end
```

Fig. 15. Refined model of system using abstract channel - events

```
context sys_x1 extends sys_x0 chan_x0
axioms ...
  @authentic4AC:∀c· channel_sender(c) ∈ AC ⇒ authenticity(c)=TRUE
```

Fig. 16. Refined model of system using abstract channel - context

The existing service event (Fig. 15) is refined so that, instead of choosing an arbitrary safe amount of fuel, it uses the value in the data of the message that it is currently processing, to increase the level (see with clause). It removes itself from the processing relationship and resets the handshake flag.

In Fig. 15, two new events are introduced; one for an aircraft to send a message (ac_send) and one for a ground unit to receive a message (gu_receive). The ac_send event synchronises with the channel send event. The guard @grds1 ties the sender, s, of the channel send event to be the ac in the ac_send event. The guard @grds3 forces the channel, c, of the channel send event to be one that has as its receiver, the GU that is servicing this ac. In @acts1 the data attached to the message m that is being sent by the channel send event, is set to the remaining fuel capacity.

The gu_receive event synchronises with the channel receive event. The guard @grds1 ties the receiver, r, of the channel receive event to be the gu in the gu_receive event. The guard @grds2 forces the channel, c, of the channel send event to be one that has as its sender, the AC that this gu is servicing.

There are other events corresponding to the events from the channel model, including the attacker's events, i.e., intercept, peek, spoof (omitted here).

In order for the provers to verify the model we first assume all security properties are true. We do this in the context (Fig. 16), for example, by adding an axiom that all channels for which the channel sender is an AC have authenticity = TRUE (similarly for reliability and confidentiality).

In order to achieve the proof, several invariants must be added about the state of messages in the channel. For example the following @inv10 says that the aircraft will not send another message until the previous one has been actioned (hence the need for the handshake flag).

@inv10: ∀this_AC·this_AC∈AC ⇒ (handshake(this_AC)=FALSE ⇒ (∀m·m∈ch_existing_messages
    ⇒ channel_sender(ch_channel(m)) ≠ this_AC))

Identifying the required invariants is a challenging task and often depends on the design of the system.

Step 3. Analysis - Which Channel Security Properties are Needed in This Application?
To demonstrate which security properties are needed for safety we removed all three of the axioms that switch security properties (from Fig. 16) and replaced them one at a time. This showed that in fact the only property that is needed for safety is authenticity: Reliability and confidentiality do not affect the proof of safety. A lack of reliability can, however, deny service functionality (i.e. affect liveness).

Confidentiality. Intuitively, it is not a problem if attackers know how much fuel an aircraft needs as long as they cannot influence the refuelling service. There are no requirements in the model concerning secrecy of fuel levels or the consequences of an attacker knowing them. Hence setting confidentiality to FALSE does not affect any proofs and does not result in any liveness or other problems when the model is animated.

Authenticity. With authenticity set to false (i.e. not ensured by the channel), the method spoof is enabled and can generate messages with random data that appear to come from an AC. This breaks several of the intermediate invariants that have been added during the proof of functionality. For example @inv10 is broken because it requires there to be no existing_messages for the channel of an AC that has its handshake flag set to FALSE.

As an aside, note that the proof obligations for the safety invariant are still discharged because their proof is based on other (now unprovable) invariants. It is important to remember that none of the proofs are reliable until all of them are proved. The ProB model checker can be used to gain a better understanding of why authenticity is needed. It explores possible traces of events that could occur in the model and searches for those that cause an invariant violation. Figure 17 shows that the model checker has discovered an invariant violation. The central window shows the state of the model including (in red) the exact clause of the invariant that has been violated (amount+level exceeds Limit). The right hand window shows the trace of events that has been taken to cause this violation. In this case, an AC sent a message on Ch1 and then an attacker spoofed a message from the same AC on the same channel. This breaks two of the intermediate invariants concerning existing_messages. The intermediate invariants are broken immediately by a spoof event which prevents further exploration of the consequences. If we wish to explore how the spoof eventually leads to a violation of the

Fig. 17. Model checking to find the invariant violation when authenticity is not ensured

safety invariant, we can remove the intermediate invariants for model checking. The model checker is then used to automatically find the attack path through the internal interfaces. This technique is explored in [12].

Reliability. A lack of reliability cannot cause a safety problem (an aircraft on the ground without fuel is safe!), however it may be undesirable from a functional (liveness) point of view, since, if messages are not delivered, the aircraft could never receive its service from the GU. Event-B lacks direct support for reasoning about liveness so instead we use liveness validation by animation. We need to define an example instantiation of the constants in order to animate the model. We do this by extending the model context to introduce some instances of AC, GU and MESSAGE and defining a specific mapping for the values of the associations, channel_sender, channel_receiver and servicing. We also introduce an instance of AGENT called Attacker to represent the adversary. Figure 18 shows the model being tested with channel reliability set to false. The intercept event is always enabled (see left hand window) as an alternative to receiving a message and can therefore prevent the message from ever being received (see history in right hand window) hence preventing the GU from servicing the AC. When channel reliability is set to true, the intercept event is not enabled and the model can only progress by receiving the message.

Further Refinements. We give a summary of further refinements (but, for brevity, omit the details). These correspond to **Step 4** mentioned in Sect. 1.

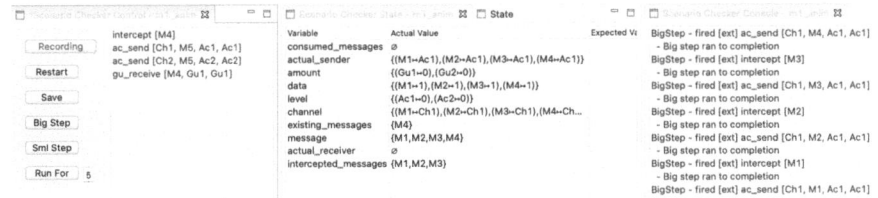

Fig. 18. Animating model to test the effect of unreliable channels

Aircraft Re-fueling Service using Refined Channel with Authenticity by Rejection.
The second refinement of the system uses the first refinement of the generic
channel model by including chan_m1. The system model is largely unchanged
except that we need to add events reject and spoof2 to reveal this new behaviour
of the generic channel in the system model.

Aircraft Re-fueling Service Using Refined Channel with HMAC Authenticity.
The final refinement uses the final refinement of the channel (via inclusion)
so that authenticity is checked using the hash. The model is exactly the same
as the previous level except for including chan_m2 instead of chan_m1 and the
service event (being unchanged) is reduced to an extends clause.

Summary. The use of inclusion allows the specific application to incorporate
a re-useable model of a generic solution for communication channels that guarantee authenticity. This improves the structure and efficiency of the model. For
example, the channel is already proved to ensure authenticity and this verification does not need to be repeated. The verification only focuses on proving that
the system is safe if authenticity is provided in this way.

6 Alternative Design with Time-Bounded Reliability

We illustrate our approach by applying it to a different design for the Secure
Aircraft Servicing example. For brevity, we only give some highlights of the
development (rather than full details as in Sect. 4 and Sect. 5). Here we consider a strategy where the aircraft sends a message telling the ground unit to
stop providing the service when appropriate. In this design, the communication
between the aircraft and the ground unit must be reliable. In particular, the
communication must have an upper bound on the delay before a message is
delivered (*time-bounded reliable*). We first discuss the model for a generic channel with time-bounded reliability (Sect. 6.1), and then discuss its application to
the aircraft servicing model (Sect. 6.2).

6.1 Modelling a Generic Channel with Time-Bounded Reliability

Generic Model of Channels - The Context. Compared to the context of
the abstract model of the channel in Fig. 5, we have an additional constant

bound $\in \mathbb{N}_1$ representing the time bound for the channel. For simplicity, we assume that all channel share this common bound. However, it is straightforward to model reliable channels with individual time bounds.

Generic Model of Channels - The Machines. First of all, in order to model the time-bounded reliability, we have a simple model of a clock with a variable time, denoting the current time, and a single event Tick that advances the time.

The generic model of the channels is similar to that described in Sect. 4.1. The model includes the Clock machine to access the time and we have an additional variable conceptual_time_bound with the following invariants.

```
variable conceptual_time_bound : conceptual_existing_messages → ℕ = ∅
invariants
  @no_past_time: ∀ m · m ∈ conceptual_existing_messages ∧
    reliability(conceptual_channel(m)) = TRUE ⇒ conceptual_time_bound(m) ≥ clock_time
  @no_far_future_time: ∀ m · m ∈ conceptual_existing_messages ∧
    reliability(conceptual_channel(m)) = TRUE ⇒ conceptual_time_bound(m) ≤ clock_time + bound
```

Here, conceptual_time_bound(m) represents the latest time that the message m has to be delivered for a time-bounded reliable channel. As a result, for a reliable channel, the conceptual time bound has to be in the future (@no_past_time invariant) and cannot be too far ahead in the future (@no_far_future_time invariant). To ensure the delivery of a message on a reliable channel, the event to advance the clock has an additional guard that ensures that there are no messages on reliable channels whose time bound would be exceeded by the advancement of time.

```
event Tick synchronises clock.Tick when
  @grd1: ∀ m · m ∈ conceptual_existing_messages ∧ reliability(conceptual_channel(m)) = TRUE
    ⇒ conceptual_time_bound(m) ≠ clock_time
end
```

6.2   Alternative Refinement of Model Using Channels with TBR

This section illustrates the use of TBR channels to providing a secure aircraft servicing system. We first model the high level of the design, then incorporate the TBR channels to implement the design.

Model of the Alternative Design. The machine sys_m1_TBR (Fig. 19) is a refinement of sys_m0 (Fig. 4). A variable active is introduced to model the active GUs that are currently fueling the aircraft. To model the servicing of aircraft as time progresses, we introduce variable gu_tocks representing the GUs that still need to service the aircraft in this "tick". When event Tick is invoked, variable gu_tocks is set to the current set of active GUs. Event service then goes through each GU in the set gu_tocks and services the corresponding aircraft accordingly. When there are no more GU to perform the service, the GUs can be activated/deactivated as specified in events activate and deactivate. Note that this model has not yet introduced the alternative design.

The alternative design is captured in a refinement (sys_m2_TBR). In particular, there are variables to represent the activation and deactivation requests

```
variable active : ℙ(GU) = ∅
variable gu_tocks : ℙ(active) = ∅
invariant @safe−fuelling: ∀gu · gu ∈ gu_tocks ⇒
       level(servicing(gu)) + fueling_rate ≤ Limit(servicing(gu))
//This servicing is now performed when the GU need to tock.
event service refines service any gu where
  @grd1: gu ∈ gu_tocks  // The GU needs to service
then
  @act1: level(servicing(gu)) := level(servicing(gu)) + fueling_rate
  @act2: gu_tocks := gu_tocks \ {gu}
with @amount: amount = fueling_rate end
event Tick when
  @grd1: gu_tocks = ∅
  @grd2: ∀gu · gu ∈ active ⇒ level(servicing(gu)) + fueling_rate ≤ Limit(servicing(gu))
then @act1: gu_tocks := active end
event activate any gu where
  @prm_gu: gu ∈ GU
  @grd1:  gu ∉ active
  @grd2:  gu_tocks = ∅  // no more GU needs to tock
then @act1:  active := active ∪ {gu} end
event deactivate any gu where
  @grd1:  gu ∈ active
  @grd2:  gu_tocks = ∅  // no more GU needs to tock
then @act1: active := active \ {gu} end
```

Fig. 19. Refined model of system using abstract TBR channel - machine

together with the timeout for deactivation requests. The two events that model
the activation and deactivation requests from an aircraft are in Fig. 20. The correctness of this refinement relies on the deactivation requests' bounded-reliability.

```
event AC_request_activation any gu where ...
  @grd1: gu ∉ active // The ground unit servicing this ac is inactive
  @grd2: gu ∉ request_activation
  // This is needed for maintenance of inv4
  @grd3: level(servicing(gu))+bound×fueling_rate≤Limit(servicing(gu))
then @act1: request_activation := request_activation ∪ {gu} end

event AC_request_deactivation any gu where ...
  @grd1: gu ∈ active // The ground unit servicing this ac is active
  @grd2: gu ∉ request_deactivation
then
  @act1: request_deactivation := request_deactivation ∪ {gu}
  @act2: request_deactivation_timeout(gu) := sys_time + bound
end
```

Fig. 20. Aircraft request activation/deactivation

Refinement Using TBR Channels. This refinement includes the generic
TBR channels for implementing the communications. For example, the event
AC_send_deactivate_request is a refinement of AC_request_deactivation. Notice
that the guard of AC_send_deactivate_request has to take into account the
potential delay (i.e., bound) and the fuelling rate (fueling_rate) to send the deactivation requests via a reliable channel as appropriate.

```
event AC_send_deactivate_request refines AC_request_deactivation any gu
synchronises ch.send
```

where ...
@grd7: level(servicing(channel_receiver(ch_c)))+bound×fueling_rate≤Limit(servicing(
        channel_receiver(ch_c)))
@grd8: reliability(ch_c) = TRUE
then
@act1: request_deactivation := request_deactivation ∪ {gu}
@act2: request_deactivation_timeout(gu) := sys_time + bound
end

Similarly, the AC_send_activate_request is also refined in a similar way, except that the channel has to be authentic. The full model is available online[1].

7   A Rely/Guarantee Thinking Approach

The Rely/Guarantee method of Jones [8] has influenced our modular reasoning approach. In particular, the idea that reasoning about the system at a high-level of abstraction, helps to identify the constraints on the components. Our approach relies on *composition* through the use of the inclusion mechanism. For a top-down development method like Event-B, *decomposition* [11] is more desirable. There is a strong link between decomposition and rely/guarantee method in [5].

Consider the aircraft servicing case study. Essentially, the aircraft and the ground units sharing information (via communications channels) and the protocols can be described using rely/guarantee concepts. The aircraft relies on the ground unit to provide the correct servicing and guarantees to send appropriate information to the ground unit. The refined model of aircraft serving in Fig. 15 describes the interaction between the aircraft and ground units.

– An aircraft provides (i.e., guarantees) the correct data for refuelling (ac_send event) and relies on the corresponding ground unit to correctly process the data (via receiving the message, i.e., event gu_receive and then service the aircraft, i.e. event service).
– A ground unit guarantees that it will supply the amount of fuel (event service) to the correct aircraft (event gu_receive), while it relies on the aircraft to provide the data correctly and to the right ground unit (event ac_send).

In fact, one could say that our model in Fig. 15 is already too detailed by including the generic channels. Ideally, the channels should be introduced as an implementation mechanism for the relies and guarantees between the aircraft and the ground units.

Our approach includes a step for analysing the model to identify the required security properties for communication. This is done by switchable properties of the channels in terms of confidentiality, authenticity, reliability, in order to identify the least constrained security properties that still guarantee the consistency of the system. In this sense, it is similar to *identify the core trusted base* as in [9]. However, our approach tends to identify these required properties at a higher-level of abstraction (a consequence of rely/guarantee thinking) and using a combination of theorem proving, model checking, and animation.

---

[1] https://doi.org/10.5258/SOTON/D3072.

8   Conclusion

We have shown how formal modelling using Event-B can be used to analyse the effect of different security properties in a specific application. Where the absence of a security property affects the system safety invariants, proofs no longer hold and this is immediately shown by the Rodin automatic proof system. Some properties may only affect liveness of the system (denial of service) and this is not shown by the proof system. Instead we can explore their effect on behaviour using animation of scenarios. Such analysis can illustrate attack paths related to threat scenarios as required by standards such as ED202A. Detailed knowledge of which security properties are crucial for a particular system allows appropriate security measures to be deployed.

In general we find that these sorts of systems (i.e. that use an open communication mechanism to send control signals between agents) rely a great deal on authenticity since it is important to prevent attackers sending erroneous control signals. They can also depend on reliability since the loss of a control signal (e.g. intercepted by an attacker) may lead to a control action not being taken when it is needed. However, we discovered that reliability is generally insufficient since, if a control action is needed, it is needed at a specific time or at least within some deadline. Hence time-bounded reliability (i.e. a message is guaranteed to be delivered within some time deadline) is a more useful security property. We did not find a direct need for confidentiality in these kinds of systems since the attributes involved are not secret. However, there is an indirect need for confidentiality to achieve authenticity if it is implemented using e.g. hashing because this relies on the attacker not being able to replicate the hash that would be used by an authentic agent, and this is implemented using secret keys. For example, we could imagine the keys being used for hash functions to have a limited duration secrecy before the attacker cracks them (e.g. using quantum computing). Hence a system might use high integrity message passing to pass a list of shorter low integrity (but highly efficient) keys which will be used for short durations before being assumed unreliable due to the possibility of having been discovered by an attacker. The hash function does not require long-term confidentiality. Hence an attacker discovering a key later, when it is no longer used, is not a problem.

Formal modelling with refinement and verification by theorem provers has brought significant benefits but also raised some challenges and revealed room for improvement in the tools used. The benefits of refinement are that we can start with a simple but mathematically rigorous expression of the requirements and progress through design and implementation decisions with absolute assurance (assuming the models are valid) that the initial safety properties are being maintained. Additionally, the process of this formal verification and the consideration of unproven (tool generated) proof obligations leads us to develop the model. For example it leads us to add new invariants needed to achieve the proof. These invariants require a mixture of domain knowledge and formal modelling experience but represent real properties of the system design that are needed for it to work. Hence we gain insight into *why* the system works.

Refinement must be done in small incremental steps without making too much of a conceptual leap in one step, otherwise proving the refinement can become difficult. For example at first we introduced in one step the notion of the aircraft giving the command to stop refuelling, with its implementation via a message passed via a channel. We found this too difficult to prove and eventually had to introduce the concept of the command (which introduces the need for time-bounded reliability) as an intermediate step before introducing the generic security solution of time-bounded reliable channels. However, in doing refinements one has to be careful not to introduce idealisations. Initially in this new intermediate refinement (Sect. 4.1) we did not allow for deactivation by any means other than the command. This means that the next refinement must implement this lack of other deactivations in the channel mechanism, which introduces a need for message authenticity. Since other deactivations are safe we had intended to allow attackers to spoof deactivations but accidentally excluded that possibility by not allowing invalid deactivations in the abstract model.

As well as proof we also have recourse to model checkers that automatically explore the possible behaviours of the model to search for ways it could violate the invariant properties. While this is useful for easily detecting problems in the model, it is usually not exhaustive and hence not as complete a verification as proof. Also the model checking process brings less insight into the system than proof does. Nonetheless, model checkers can be used in single step mode to animate the behaviour of the model for validation purposes. Although we have focused on proof we continued to use animation to illustrate the model's behaviour, including what attack paths can/cannot lead to security violations.

References

1. Abrial, J.R.: Modeling in Event-B: System and Software Engineering. Cambridge University Press, Cambridge (2010). https://doi.org/10.1017/CBO9781139195881
2. Abrial, J.R., Butler, M., Hallerstede, S., Hoang, T., Mehta, F., Voisin, L.: Rodin: an open toolset for modelling and reasoning in Event-B. STTT **12**(6), 447–466 (2010). https://doi.org/10.1007/S10009-010-0145-Y
3. Eurocae: ED-202A - airworthiness security process specification. https://eshop.eurocae.net/eurocae-documents-and-reports/ed-202a/ (2014)
4. Eurocae: ED-203A - airworthiness security methods and considerations (2018). https://eshop.eurocae.net/eurocae-documents-and-reports/ed-203a/
5. Hoang, T.S., Abrial, J.-R.: Event-B decomposition for parallel programs. In: Frappier, M., Glässer, U., Khurshid, S., Laleau, R., Reeves, S. (eds.) ABZ 2010. LNCS, vol. 5977, pp. 319–333. Springer, Heidelberg (2010). https://doi.org/10.1007/978-3-642-11811-1_24
6. Hoang, T.S., Dghaym, D., Snook, C.F., Butler, M.J.: A composition mechanism for refinement-based methods. In: ICECCS 2017, Fukuoka, Japan pp. 100–109. IEEE Computer Society (2017). https://doi.org/10.1109/ICECCS.2017.27
7. Hoang, T.S., Snook, C.F., Dghaym, D., Fathabadi, A.S., Butler, M.J.: Building an extensible textual framework for the Rodin platform. In: Masci, P., Bernardeschi, C., Graziani, P., Koddenbrock, M., Palmieri, M. (eds.) SEFM 2022. LNCS, vol. 13765, pp. 132–147. Springer, Cham (2022). https://doi.org/10.1007/978-3-031-26236-4_11

8. Jones, C.B.: Tentative steps toward a development method for interfering pro-grams. ACM Trans. Program. Lang. Syst. **5**(4), 596–619 (1983). https://doi.org/10.1145/69575.69577

9. Kang, E., Jackson, D.: Dependability arguments with trusted bases. In: RE 2010, Sydney, Australia, pp. 262–271. IEEE Computer Society (2010). https://doi.org/10.1109/RE.2010.38

10. Leuschel, M., Butler, M.: ProB: an automated analysis toolset for the B method. Softw. Tools Technol. Transf. (STTT) **10**(2), 185–203 (2008). https://doi.org/10.1007/S10009-007-0063-9

11. Silva, R., Pascal, C., Hoang, T.S., Butler, M.J.: Decomposition tool for Event-B. Softw. Pract. Exp. **41**(2), 199–208 (2011). https://doi.org/10.1002/SPE.1002

12. Snook, C., Hoang, T.S., Butler, M.: Analysing security protocols using refine-ment in iUML-B. In: Barrett, C., Davies, M., Kahsai, T. (eds.) NFM 2017. LNCS, vol. 10227, pp. 84–98. Springer, Cham (2017). https://doi.org/10.1007/978-3-319-57288-8_6

13. Snook, C., Hoang, T.S., Dghaym, D., Fathabadi, A.S., Butler, M.: Domain-specific scenarios for refinement-based methods. J. Syst. Archit. (2020). https://doi.org/10.1016/j.sysarc.2020.101833

Rely-Guarantee Interpretation of Sequence Diagrams

Ketil Stølen$^{(\boxtimes)}$ (ID)

Department of Informatics, University of Oslo, Oslo, Norway
ketils@ifi.uio.no

Abstract. The term "rely/guarantee" was coined by Cliff Jones in his influential PhD-thesis from 1981. Compositional specification of concurrent systems requires a rely/guarantee approach. This paper suggests a rely-guarantee interpretation of sequence diagrams. In the general case, sequence diagrams are represented by sets of trace sets. Each trace set corresponds to a scenario that must be reflected by the specified component. The semantics is compositional and supported by a notion of refinement. The parallel operator is shown to be monotonic with respect to refinement.

1 Introduction

Cliff Jones has made several significant contributions to the field of formal methods. One of the most important is the rely-guarantee method for shared-state concurrency resulting from his PhD research at Oxford University [6,7]. I did my PhD on the rely-guarantee method at the University of Manchester 1987–1990. My thesis [13–15] made three contributions: (1) Rules for total correctness of shared-state concurrent programs; (2) A compositional treatment of auxiliary variables; (3) Proofs of soundness and relative completeness. I was fortunate to have Cliff Jones as my supervisor. In a book to his honor it seems appropriate to demonstrate the wide applicability of his thinking. My contribution in this respect is a rely-guarantee interpretation of sequence diagrams.

The sequence diagram notation is one of the most popular specification approaches in the world. The formalism originates from the telecommunications sector and is also known as Message Sequence Charts [5] and UML [11] interactions amongst others.

2 Sequence Diagrams

A sequence diagram consists of a finite set of lifelines. Each lifeline represents an actor that may transmit and receive messages. The message exchange is asynchronous. The diagrams in Fig. 1 have two lifelines. The diagrams describe two (of many) scenarios. An external user is trying to order some goods via a front-end – one fails, one is successful. The successful ordering is confirmed by email in addition to a message from the front-end.

A. Cavalcanti and J. Baxter (Eds.): *The Practice of Formal Methods*, LNCS 14781, pp. 120–140, 2024.
https://doi.org/10.1007/978-3-031-66673-5_7

For each message m, there is a transmission event $!m$ and reception event $?m$. Events are instantaneous. For messages crossing the diagram frame, one event takes place in the environment. The crossing-point between the diagram frame and a message (out or in) is known as a gate and does not represent an event.

A trace is a sequence of events. Gates are not reflected in the traces because their ordering (on the frame) do not necessarily reflect the ordering of the corresponding environment events. A trace representing a valid execution is required to fulfill two constraints:

causality: The transmission event of a message is ordered before its reception event.

weak-sequencing: The events on each lifeline are totally ordered from the top and downwards.

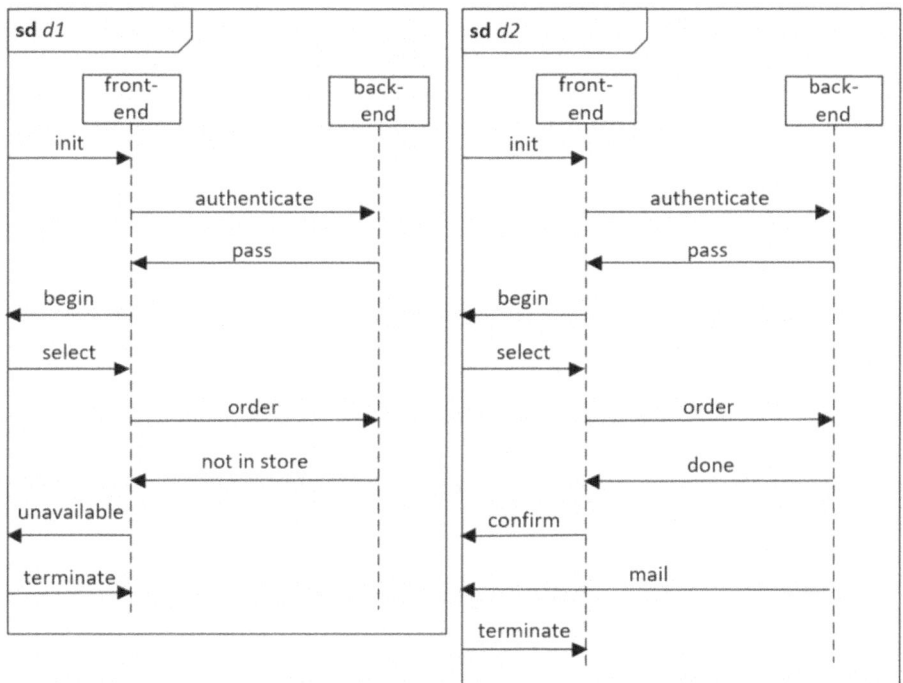

Fig. 1. Sequence diagrams

This means that $d1$ (Fig. 1) describes only one trace – for simplicity, each message name (signal) is represented by its initial letter:

$$\langle ?i, !a, ?a, !p, ?p, !b, ?s, !o, ?o, !n, ?n, !u, ?t \rangle$$

On the other hand, *d2* describes four traces:

$$\langle ?i, !a, ?a, !p, ?p, !b, ?s, !o, ?o, !d, !m, ?d, !c, ?t \rangle$$
$$\langle ?i, !a, ?a, !p, ?p, !b, ?s, !o, ?o, !d, ?d, !m, !c, ?t \rangle$$
$$\langle ?i, !a, ?a, !p, ?p, !b, ?s, !o, ?o, !d, ?d, !c, !m, ?t \rangle$$
$$\langle ?i, !a, ?a, !p, ?p, !b, ?s, !o, ?o, !d, ?d, !c, ?t, !m \rangle$$

$[\![\, d \,]\!]$ denotes the set of complete[1] traces of the diagram d in the sense described above. This means that $[\![\, d1 \,]\!]$ has one element, while $[\![\, d2 \,]\!]$ contains four.

2.1   Rely-Guarantee Interpretation

In general, rely-guarantee approaches distinguish between positive, negative and inconclusive behaviors. As illustrated by Table 1, the positive fulfill both the rely and the guarantee, the negative fulfill the rely and falsify the guarantee, while the inconclusive falsify the rely. Moreover, the rely is normally a safety property while the guarantee may also impose liveness constraints. In the following we stick to the convention that the rely is a safety property. Rely-guarantee concerns external behavior. In the case of a sequence diagram, this means the interaction between the diagram and its environment. Purely internal events are filtered away. For *d2* there are three external traces:

$$\langle ?i, !b, ?s, !m, !c, ?t \rangle$$
$$\langle ?i, !b, ?s, !c, !m, ?t \rangle$$
$$\langle ?i, !b, ?s, !c, ?t, !m \rangle$$

Rely-guarantee does not constrain the environment. This means that the specified component and its environment are unequal partners. It cannot be taken for granted that the environment will play its part of the game. With respect to the external traces above, it could be that some inputs from the environment

Table 1. Rely-guarantee classification

behavior	rely	guarantee	interpretation
positive	true	true	specified component fulfills guarantee as long as environment fulfills rely
negative	true	false	specified component breaks guarantee before environment breaks rely
inconclusive	false	NA	environment breaks rely before specified component breaks guarantee

---

[1] An incomplete trace is a prefix of a complete trace.

($?i$, $?s$ or $?t$) will never arrive in which case the "execution" of the diagram will be stuck forever. The three external traces below represent such executions:

$$\langle \rangle$$
$$\langle ?i, !b \rangle$$
$$\langle ?i, !b, ?s, !c, !m \rangle$$

They represent situations where the specified component may end up awaiting environment input forever.

A trace is negative if the wrong message is sent to the environment although the environment has behaved correctly until that point (e.g. the diagram $d1$ sends u and not b in response to i). Note that there is an implicit assumption of progress. Thus, the specified component will always eventually progress if it can.

The inconclusive traces correspond to situations where the environment sends the wrong message although the specified component has behaved correctly until that point (e.g. the environment sends a message different from i initially).

3   Formalization

3.1   Sequences

A sequence is a mapping from indices to elements. The set of indices may be finite ($[1 \ldots N]$) or infinite ($\mathbb{N} \setminus \{0\}$). Q^{ω} is the set of sequences over Q, while Q^{∞} is the subset of infinite sequences.

For a sequence v, $\mathsf{dom}(v)$, $\mathsf{rng}(v)$ and $\#v$ denote the set of indices, the set of elements and the length of v. Moreover, $v[j]$ and $v|_j$ capture the jth element and the prefix of length j.

Finally, $v \sqsubseteq v'$ if v is a prefix of or equal to v', and $v \frown v'$ represents concatenation. $v \frown v'$ equals v if v is infinite; otherwise, the sequence consisting of v followed by v'.

3.2   Chains

A chain c is an infinite sequence of sequences such that

$$\forall j \in \mathsf{dom}(c) : c[j] \sqsubseteq c[j+1]$$

$\mathbb{C}(s)$ is the set of chains over the set of sequences s. Hence:

$$c \in \mathbb{C}(s) \Rightarrow \mathsf{rng}(c) \subseteq s$$

$\sqcup c$ denotes the least upper bound of the chain c.

3.3   Messages

A message is a triple (s, tr, re) of a signal s, a transmitter tr, and a receiver re. The transmitter and receiver are lifelines. $\mathbb{L}$ and $\mathbb{M}$ denote respectively the set of lifelines and the set of messages.

3.4   Events

An event is a pair of a kind (input or output) and a message:

$$(k, m) \in \{!, ?\} \times \mathbb{M}$$

$?m$ and $!m$ are shorthands for $(?, m)$ and $(!, m)$. $\mathbb{E}$ denotes the set of events. The functions

$$k._- \in \mathbb{E} \to \{!, ?\} \qquad tr._-, re._- \in \mathbb{E} \to \mathbb{L} \qquad m._- \in \mathbb{E} \to \mathbb{M}$$

yield the kind, transmitter, receiver and message of an event, respectively. The function

$$l._- \in \mathbb{E} \to \mathbb{L}$$

returns the lifeline of an event:

$$k.e = ? \Rightarrow l.e = re.e \qquad k.e = ! \Rightarrow l.e = tr.e$$

X returns the external events with respect to a set of lifelines:

$$X(L) \stackrel{\text{def}}{=} \{e \in \mathbb{E} \mid l.e \in L \wedge (tr.e \notin L \vee re.e \notin L)\}$$

3.5   Traces

A trace is a sequence of events. The function l is lifted from events to traces t and trace sets s:

$$l.t \stackrel{\text{def}}{=} \{l.e \mid e \in \mathsf{rng}(t)\} \qquad l.s \stackrel{\text{def}}{=} \bigcup_{t \in s} l.t$$

The trace obtained from t by filtering away every event not in E is denoted by $E \textcircled{s} t$.

t/L and s/L project the trace t and the trace set s on the external events of the lifelines L:

$$t/L \stackrel{\text{def}}{=} X(L) \textcircled{s} t \qquad s/L \stackrel{\text{def}}{=} \bigcup_{t \in s} t/L$$

A trace t is causal if for any prefix $t' \sqsubseteq t$:

$$\forall e \in \mathbb{E}, m \in \mathbb{M} : m.e = m \wedge \{tr.e, re.e\} \subseteq l.t \Rightarrow \#\{!m\} \textcircled{s} t' \geq \#\{?m\} \textcircled{s} t'$$

Hence, a message is not received if it has not already been sent. $\mathbb{T}$ is the set of causal traces.

3.6   Sequence Diagrams

$[\![\, d \,]\!]$ denotes the set of complete traces of the sequence diagram d. Each trace in $[\![\, d \,]\!]$ is causal. Sequence diagrams without composition operators are known as basic. Composition operators are introduced in Sect. 6.

3.7   Rely-Guarantee

To facilitate reuse in Sect. 6, rely-guarantee is formalized at the semantic level. In the following, $s = [\![\, d \,]\!]$ for some sequence diagram d.

The set of external complete traces is the result of filtering away the internal events:

$$C(s) \stackrel{\text{def}}{=} s/l.s$$

The rely $R(s)$ is the union of the prefix closure $R_p(s)$ and the infinite closure $R_i(s)$:

$$R(s) \stackrel{\text{def}}{=} R_p(s) \cup R_i(s)$$

The prefix closure of the set of complete external traces formalizes what the environment is assumed to do as long as the specified component behaves according to the diagram:

$$R_p(s) \stackrel{\text{def}}{=} \{t \in \mathbb{T} \mid \exists t' \in C(s) : t \sqsubseteq t'\}$$

The infinite closure makes sure that any assumption about the environment at infinite time can be deduced from the assumptions about the environment at finite time[2]:

$$R_i(s) \stackrel{\text{def}}{=} \{t \in \mathbb{T} \mid \exists c \in \mathbb{C}(R_p(s)) : t = \sqcup c\}$$

As explained above, the environment may not provide the input required for the "execution" of the diagram to progress in which case the specified component ends up waiting forever. Hence, in addition to the external complete traces, there is also a set of external wait traces:

$$
\begin{aligned}
W(s) \stackrel{\text{def}}{=} \{t \in R(s) \mid \\
(\forall e \in \mathbb{E} : t \frown \langle e \rangle \in R(s) \Rightarrow k.e = ?) \land \exists e \in E : t \frown \langle e \rangle \in R(s)\}
\end{aligned}
$$

Note that t is a complete trace if there is no e such that the second conjunct holds.

---

[2] The chains become relevant when loop is introduced in Sect. 6.

If the environment does not break the rely $R(s)$ then the diagram requires the specified component to either produce a complete trace in $C(s)$ or end up waiting forever after having produced a wait trace in $W(s)$. If the environment in addition always provides input when allowed then the diagram requires the specified component to produce a complete trace in $C(s)$ (possibly at infinite time).

An external positive trace is either an external complete trace or an external wait trace:

$$P(s) \stackrel{\text{def}}{=} C(s) \cup W(s)$$

An external trace is negative if the specified component sends a wrong message although the environment has provided input as it should:

$$N(s) \stackrel{\text{def}}{=} \{t \in \mathbb{T}/l.s \mid \exists t' \in R(s), m \in \mathbb{M} : t' \frown \langle !m \rangle \sqsubseteq t \wedge t' \frown \langle !m \rangle \notin R(s)\}$$

Remember that the specified component is assumed to eventually progress if it can.

An external trace is inconclusive if the environment sends a wrong message although the specified component has provided output as it should:

$$I(s) \stackrel{\text{def}}{=} \{t \in \mathbb{T}/l.s \mid \exists t' \in R(s), m \in \mathbb{M} : t' \frown \langle ?m \rangle \sqsubseteq t \wedge t' \frown \langle ?m \rangle \notin R(s)\}$$

Lemma 1.

$$P(s) \cap (N(s) \cup I(s)) = N(s) \cap I(s) = \emptyset$$

4   Sets of Diagrams

A basic sequence diagram describes a single scenario. A nontrivial component is involved in many scenarios. For the same component there are therefore typically many basic sequence diagrams. Each sequence diagram describes a scenario that should be reflected by the component. With respect to the sequence diagrams in Fig. 1, it should be possible to respond that the selected goods is unavailable (as specified in $d1$), but also to confirm a successful ordering (as specified in $d2$). Hence, both outcomes of what at this level of abstraction appears as a non-deterministic choice, should be offered by the component.

The same is not true for the non-determinism within each diagram. A component fulfilling $d2$ may allow all four complete traces, but if due to some design decision or mechanism, only one of these may appear then this is also fine. Hence, this kind of non-determinism is just under-specification.

Semantically, the two kinds of non-determinism should be kept apart. The semantics of a set of basic sequence diagrams D is therefore a set of sets of complete traces:

$$[\![D]\!] \stackrel{\text{def}}{=} \{[\![d]\!] \mid d \in D\}$$

In general, a lifeline in one diagram may belong to the environment of another. Hence, the diagrams within a set may interact with each other in various ways. The rely-guarantee setting, however, requires a clear interface between the component and its environment. A set of diagrams with no mutual interaction is in the following referred to as a component specification. A set of diagrams D is a component specification if:

$$\forall d \in D : X(l.[\![\, d \,]\!]) \subseteq X(\bigcup_{d \in D} l.[\![\, d \,]\!])$$

An external trace that is positive in one diagram $d \in D$ may also be positive in another diagram $d' \in D$. For example, if $d2'$ is obtained from $d2$ by inserting an additional internal message as shown in Fig. 2, then $!m$ can no longer appear before $!c$ and the number of external complete traces is reduced to two. The third has become negative. Similarly, a trace that is negative in one diagram may be positive or inconclusive in another.

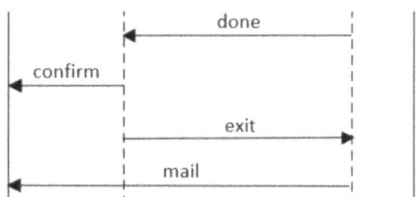

Fig. 2. Fragment of $d2'$

5 Refinement

A conventional rely-guarantee specification can be refined by weakening the rely, by strengthening the guarantee, or by doing both. The data structure (representation of variables, signals etc.) may also be refined, but this is ignored here. Component specifications, as defined above, describe the behavior of sets of scenarios. Each scenario should be reflected by the component. Weakening the rely and strengthening the guarantee of each individual diagram still makes sense. However, to support the process of requirement capture, it should also be possible to add new scenarios. Below, refinement is defined formally in two steps: First, for denotations[3] of sequence diagrams, and second for component specifications.

In the following, it is assumed that:

$$s = [\![\, d \,]\!] \quad s' = [\![\, d' \,]\!]$$

The behavior of the environment may depend on the behavior of the specified component. If d' is a refinement of d, certain environment behaviors may no

---

[3] For denotations, and not directly on sequence diagrams, to facilitate reuse in Sect. 6.

longer be possible for d' because they concern component behaviors that have been disallowed by the strengthening of the guarantee. Those behaviors must be taken into consideration to properly characterize what it means to weaken the rely, and this is the role of N below:

$$R(s) \subseteq R(s') \cup N(s')$$

This condition would be false if the refinement imposed constraints on the behavior of the environment. In that case some traces would end up in $I(s')$ which is disjoint from $N(s')$.

The strengthening of the guarantee amounts to:

$$R(s) \cap C(s') \subseteq C(s)$$

Note that this condition does not refer to wait traces. This is because the diagrams are assumed to fulfill the usual syntactic constraints that arrows representing internal messages are connected to lifelines at both ends (hence, a message sent by a lifeline in the diagram to another lifeline in the diagram is received, etc.). The arrows may cross, but only when pointing downwards. This means, a diagram can get stuck only if its waits for input from the environment:

$$C(s') \subseteq C(s) \Rightarrow W(s') \subseteq W(s)$$

Hence, the wait traces are not relevant for the definition of refinement because they are completely determined by the set of complete traces and may only result from inactivity of the environment.

Definition 1. *Let d, d' be basic sequence diagrams. Assume*

$$s = [\![\, d \,]\!], \quad s' = [\![\, d' \,]\!]$$

Then d' refines d, written $d \rightsquigarrow d'$, if

$$
\begin{array}{ll}
R(s) \subseteq R(s') \cup N(s') & \text{(weakening rely)} \\
R(s) \cap C(s') \subseteq C(s) & \text{(strengthening guarantee)}
\end{array}
$$

Lemma 2. *The refinement relation for basic sequence diagrams is transitive.*

Proof. Given

$$
\begin{array}{l}
(1)\, d_1 \rightsquigarrow d_2 \\
(2)\, d_2 \rightsquigarrow d_3
\end{array}
$$

It must be shown that

$$(3)\, d_1 \rightsquigarrow d_3$$

Let $s_1 = [\![\, d_1 \,]\!]$, $s_2 = [\![\, d_2 \,]\!]$, $s_3 = [\![\, d_3 \,]\!]$. (1), (2) correspond to

$$(4)\, R(s_1) \subseteq R(s_2) \cup N(s_2)$$
$$(5)\, R(s_1) \cap C(s_2) \subseteq C(s_1)$$
$$(6)\, R(s_2) \subseteq R(s_3) \cup N(s_3)$$
$$(7)\, R(s_2) \cap C(s_3) \subseteq C(s_2)$$

(3) follows if it can be shown that

$$(8)\, R(s_1) \subseteq R(s_3) \cup N(s_3)$$
$$(9)\, R(s_1) \cap C(s_3) \subseteq C(s_1)$$

To prove (8), assume

$$(10)\, t \in R(s_1)$$

(4), (6), (10) give

$$(11)\, t \in N(s_2) \cup R(s_3) \cup N(s_3)$$

(8) follows if it can be be shown that

$$(12)\, t \in N(s_2) \Rightarrow t \in R(s_3) \cup N(s_3)$$

Assume

$$(13)\, t \in N(s_2)$$

(13) implies there are t', m such that

$$(14)\, t' \in R(s_2) \wedge t' \frown \langle !m \rangle \sqsubseteq t \wedge t' \frown \langle !m \rangle \notin R(s_2)$$

(6), (14) imply

$$(15)\, t' \in R(s_3) \cup N(s_3) \wedge t' \frown \langle !m \rangle \sqsubseteq t \wedge t' \frown \langle !m \rangle \notin R(s_2)$$

(15) and $t' \in N(s_3)$ imply $t \in N(s_3)$ in which case (8) holds. Assume

$$(16)\, t' \in R(s_3)$$

(7), first and third conjunct of (14) give a contradiction unless

$$(17)\, t' \frown \langle !m \rangle \notin R(s_3)$$

Second conjunct of (14), (16), (17) imply $t \in N(s_3)$ in which case (8) holds.

To prove (9), assume t such that

$$(18)\, t \in R(s_1) \cap C(s_3)$$

(4), (18) imply

$$(19)\, t \in R(s_1) \cap (R(s_2) \cup N(s_2)) \cap C(s_3)$$

There are two cases:

$$(20)\, t \in R(s_1) \cap R(s_2) \cap C(s_3)$$
$$(21)\, t \in R(s_1) \cap N(s_2) \cap C(s_3)$$

case Assume (20):
(7), (20) imply

$$(22)\, t \in R(s_1) \cap C(s_2)$$

(5), (22) imply

$$(23)\, t \in C(s_1)$$

case Assume (21):
(21), Lemma 1 imply

$$(24)\, t \in R(s_1) \cap N(s_2) \cap C(s_3) \wedge t \notin C(s_2)$$

(7), (24) imply

$$(25)\, t \in R(s_1) \cap N(s_2) \cap C(s_3) \wedge t \notin R(s_2) \cap C(s_3)$$

(25) is a contradiction.

Definition 2. *A component specification D' refines a component specification D, written $D \rightsquigarrow D'$, if*

$$\forall d \in D : \exists d' \in D' : d \rightsquigarrow d'$$

The refinement relation for component specifications allows adding scenarios for not yet considered environment behaviors. It also allows introducing new scenarios for already considered or partly overlapping environment behaviors[4].

Lemma 3. *The refinement relation for component specifications is transitive.*

Proof. Straightforwardly from Lemma 2.

6   Composed Diagrams

An alternative to working with sets of basic sequence diagrams is to introduce composition operators in the style of UML.

The xalt operator allows different scenarios to be expressed in the same sequence diagram:

$$\llbracket\, \mathsf{xalt}(d_1, \ldots, d_N)\, \rrbracket \;\overset{\text{def}}{=}\; \bigcup_{j=1}^{N} \llbracket\, d_j\, \rrbracket$$

Note that the trace sets of each operand are kept unchanged. In Fig. 3 the two diagrams *d1* and *d2* from Fig. 1 are combined using xalt. The frame of the xalt

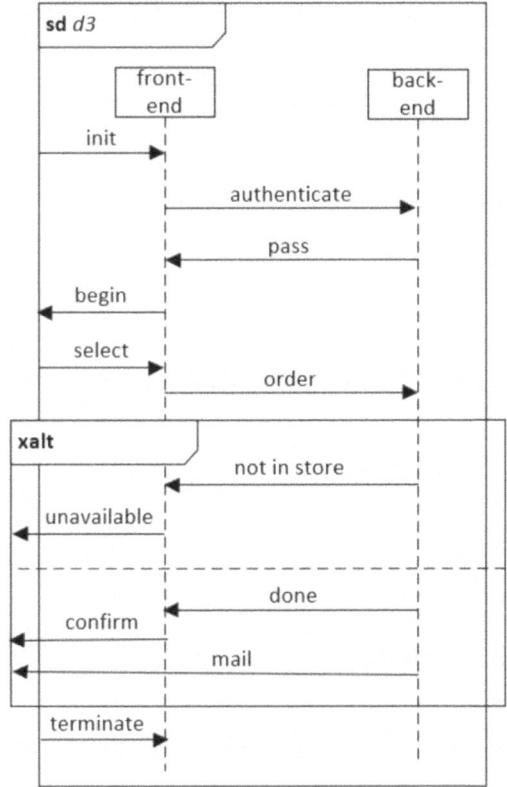

Fig. 3. Using xalt to integrate *d1* and *d2*

---

[4] If at some point additional scenarios are not desirable, the notion of refinement might be strengthened with the following constraint:

$$\forall d' \in D' : \exists d \in D : d \rightsquigarrow d'$$

is partly outside the frame of the diagram to signal that this choice is global to the diagram. This way of drawing sequence diagrams is useful when working in a white-box setting. The diagram $d3$ would then be referred to using the ref construct[5], the details of which are outside the scope of this paper. As explained in [12], xalt is used to specify alternative scenarios, each of which must be reflected by a correct implementation. This includes inherent non-determinism as in the specification of a coin toss, alternative behaviors due to different inputs that the component must be able to handle, and alternative behaviors where the conditions for these being positive are abstracted away (as in Fig. 3).

The alt operator can be used to specify choice in the meaning of underspecification. Semantically, each tuple of trace sets selected point-wise from its operands is merged into a single trace set. For trace sets S, S', let:

$$S \uplus S' \overset{\text{def}}{=} \{s \cup s' \mid s \in S \wedge s' \in S'\}$$

Then alt is defined as follows:

$$[\![\, \mathsf{alt}(d_1, \ldots, d_N) \,]\!] \overset{\text{def}}{=} \biguplus_{j=1}^{N} [\![\, d_j \,]\!]$$

The opt operator is a binary alt with skip as one of the options:

$$[\![\, \mathsf{opt}(d) \,]\!] \overset{\text{def}}{=} [\![\, d \,]\!] \uplus \{\{\langle\rangle\}\}$$

The predicate $intl$ characterizes what it means for the trace t to be an interleaving of the traces t' and t''. The sequence p (an "oracle") is used to characterize possible interleavings:

$$
\begin{aligned}
intl(t', t'', t) \overset{\text{def}}{=}\ &\exists p \in \{1,2\}^\omega : \\
&\#(\{1\} \circledS p) = \#t' \wedge \#(\{2\} \circledS p) = \#t'' \wedge \#p = \#t \wedge \\
&\forall j \in \mathsf{dom}(t) : \\
&\quad p[j] = 1 \Rightarrow t[j] = t'[\#(\{1\} \circledS (p|_j))] \wedge \\
&\quad p[j] = 2 \Rightarrow t[j] = t''[\#(\{2\} \circledS (p|_j))]
\end{aligned}
$$

The par operator can then be defined as follows:

$$
\begin{aligned}
&[\![\, \mathsf{par}(d_1, d_2) \,]\!] \overset{\text{def}}{=} \{s_1 \parallel s_2 \mid s_1 \in [\![\, d_1 \,]\!] \wedge s_2 \in [\![\, d_2 \,]\!]\} \\
&s_1 \parallel s_2 \overset{\text{def}}{=} \{t \in \mathbb{T} \mid \exists t_1 \in s_1, t_2 \in s_2 : intl(t_1, t_2, t)\}
\end{aligned}
$$

The seq operator is the implicit composition operator in a basic sequence diagram. seq is like par if the operands have disjoint sets of lifelines. If not, the

---

[5] The ref construct is used to call another sequence diagram, in the meaning of procedure call.

weak sequencing constraint requires the ordering of events on each lifeline to be maintained:

$$ord(t', t'', t) \stackrel{\text{def}}{=} \forall l \in L : \{e \in E \mid l.e = l\} \circledS t = \{e \in E \mid l.e = l\} \circledS (t' ^\frown t'')$$

The weak sequencing operator seq can then be defined as follows:

$$[\![\text{ seq}(d_1, d_2)]\!] \stackrel{\text{def}}{=} \{s_1 \succeq s_2 \mid s_1 \in [\![d_1]\!] \wedge s_2 \in [\![d_2]\!]\}$$
$$s_1 \succeq s_2 \stackrel{\text{def}}{=} \{t \in \mathbb{T} \mid \exists t_1 \in s_1, t_2 \in s_2 : intl(t_1, t_2, t) \wedge ord(t_1, t_2, t)\}$$

If the number of iterations is left open, loop is also a kind of alt:

$$[\![\text{ loop}(d)]\!] \stackrel{\text{def}}{=} \biguplus_{n \in \mathbb{N} \cup \{\infty\}} [\![\text{ loop}_n(d)]\!]$$

For finite n, loop_n is defined recursively using seq:

$$[\![\text{ loop}_j(d)]\!] \stackrel{\text{def}}{=} [\![\text{ seq}(d, \text{loop}_{j-1}(d))]\!] \quad \text{if } j > 0$$
$$[\![\text{ loop}_0(d)]\!] \stackrel{\text{def}}{=} \{\{\langle\rangle\}\}$$

In the infinite case, the traces are captured as least upper bounds of chains:

$$[\![\text{ loop}_\infty(d)]\!] \stackrel{\text{def}}{=} \{\sqcup c \mid c \in \mathbb{C}(\mathbb{T}) \wedge \forall j \in \mathbb{N} : c[j] \in [\![\text{ loop}_j(d)]\!]\}$$

The sequence diagram notation is of course much richer than the notation defined above. In particular, guards, message parameters, local variables and the already mentioned ref construct are not covered in this paper. The same holds for the UML notation used to specify negative traces explicitly.

6.1   Refinement and Transitivity

Definition 3. *A composed sequence diagram d' refines a composed sequence diagram d, written $d \rightsquigarrow d'$, if*

$$\forall s \in [\![d]\!] : \exists s' \in [\![d']\!] :$$
$$R(s) \subseteq R(s') \cup N(s') \wedge \qquad \text{(weakening rely)}$$
$$R(s) \cap C(s') \subseteq C(s) \qquad \text{(strengthening guarantee)}$$

Theorem 1 (Transitivity). *The refinement relation for composed diagrams is transitive.*

Proof. Straightforwardly from Lemma 3.

6.2   Refinement and Monotonicity

An important aspect of rely-guarantee is the monotonicity of parallel composition with respect to refinement. Formally:

$$d_1 \rightsquigarrow d_1' \wedge d_2 \rightsquigarrow d_2' \Rightarrow d_1 \parallel d_2 \rightsquigarrow d_1' \parallel d_2'$$

In the following, it is assumed that the component specifications and the overall environment influence each other only by message exchange. They do not share alt/xalt operands (remember, loop is one big alt). Hence, a non-deterministic choice made in one component specification does not impose a corresponding "choice" in the other (and likewise for the environment). This excludes, for example, the use of "global" xalt as in Fig. 3.

As already mentioned, arrows representing internal messages are connected to lifelines at both ends. The arrows may cross, but only when pointing downwards. Hence, time locks are not possible. The component specifications of the parallel compositions do not share lifelines.

Lemma 4. *Assume $d_1 \parallel d_2$ is a sequence diagram obeying the restrictions above. If t_1, t_2 are complete traces of d_1, d_2 then there is a complete trace t of $d_1 \parallel d_2$ such that $intl(t_1, t_2, t)$.*

Proof. t may be constructed in a step-wise manner by interleaving t_1, t_2 in such a way that the resulting t is causal. If at some point the next event in t_1 (t_2) is a reception event for a transmission event not yet interleaved into t then events have to be picked from t_2 (t_1) until the missing transmission event is in place. The next events in t_1 and t_2 cannot at the same time both be reception events for transmission events not yet interleaved into t because this would mean that $d_1 \parallel d_2$ has a time lock. Remember, there are no fairness constraints imposed on the sequence diagrams. This means that the argument above is sufficient also in the infinite case.

The proof of monotonicity makes use of two further lemmas. They are proved first.

Lemma 5. *Assume $l.s_1 \cap l.s_2 = \emptyset$ and $t \in \mathbb{T}/l.(s_1 \parallel s_2)$. Then*

$$t \in C(s_1 \parallel s_2) \Leftrightarrow t/l.s_1 \in C(s_1)/l.(s_1 \parallel s_2) \wedge t/l.s_2 \in C(s_2)/l.(s_1 \parallel s_2)$$

Proof. Given

$$(1)\, l.s_1 \cap l.s_2 = \emptyset \wedge t \in \mathbb{T}/l.(s_1 \parallel s_2)$$

To prove $\Rightarrow$, assume

$$(2)\, t \in C(s_1 \parallel s_2)$$

(2) implies there are t', t_1, t_2 such that

$$(3) \, t' \in s_1 \parallel s_2 \wedge t_1 \in s_1 \wedge t_2 \in s_2$$
$$(4) \, t = t'/l.(s_1 \parallel s_2)$$
$$(5) \, intl(t_1, t_2, t')$$

(3) implies

$$(6) \, t_1/l.s_1 \in C(s_1) \wedge t_2/l.s_2 \in C(s_2)$$

(6) implies

$$(7) \, t_1/l.s_1/l.(s_1 \parallel s_2) \in C(s_1)/l.(s_1 \parallel s_2) \wedge t_2/l.s_2/l.(s_1 \parallel s_2) \in C(s_2)/l.(s_1 \parallel s_2)$$

(3), (4), (5), (7) imply

$$(8) \, t/l.s_1 \in C(s_1)/l.(s_1 \parallel s_2) \wedge t/l.s_2 \in C(s_2)/l.(s_1 \parallel s_2)$$

To prove $\Leftarrow$, assume

$$(9) \, t/l.s_1 \in C(s_1)/l.(s_1 \parallel s_2) \wedge t/l.s_2 \in C(s_2)/l.(s_1 \parallel s_2)$$

(9) implies there are t_1, t_2 such that

$$(10) \, t_1 \in s_1 \wedge t_2 \in s_2$$
$$(11) \, t/l.s_1 = t_1/l.s_1/l.(s_1 \parallel s_2) \wedge t/l.s_2 = t_2/l.s_2/l.(s_1 \parallel s_2)$$

(10), Lemma 4 imply there is a t' be such that

$$(12) \, intl(t_1, t_2, t')$$
$$(13) \, t' \in s_1 \parallel s_2$$

(13) implies

$$(14) \, t'/l.(s_1 \parallel s_2) \in C(s_1 \parallel s_2)$$

(11), (12), (14) imply

$$(15) \, t \in C(s_1 \parallel s_2)$$

Lemma 6. *Assume $l.s_1 \cap l.s_2 = \emptyset$ and $t \in \mathbb{T}/l.(s_1 \parallel s_2)$. Then*

$$t \in R(s_1 \parallel s_2) \Leftrightarrow t/l.s_1 \in R(s_1)/l.(s_1 \parallel s_2) \wedge t/l.s_2 \in R(s_2)/l.(s_1 \parallel s_2)$$

Proof. Given

$$(1) \, l.s_1 \cap l.s_2 = \emptyset \wedge t \in \mathbb{T}/l.(s_1 \parallel s_2)$$

To prove $\Rightarrow$, assume

$$(2) \, t \in R(s_1 \parallel s_2)$$

(2) implies there is a t' such that

$$(3)\, t \sqsubseteq t'$$
$$(4)\, t' \in C(s_1 \parallel s_2)$$

(1), (4), Lemma 5 give

$$(5)\, t'/l.s_1 \in C(s_1)/l.(s_1 \parallel s_2) \wedge t'/l.s_2 \in C(s_2)/l.(s_1 \parallel s_2)$$

(3), (5) give

$$(6)\, t/l.s_1 \in R(s_1)/l.(s_1 \parallel s_2) \wedge t/l.s_2 \in R(s_2)/l.(s_1 \parallel s_2)$$

To prove $\Leftarrow$, assume

$$(7)\, t/l.s_1 \in R(s_1)/l.(s_1 \parallel s_2) \wedge t/l.s_2 \in R(s_2)/l.(s_1 \parallel s_2)$$

(7) implies there are t_1, t_2 such that

$$(8)\, t_1 \in s_1 \wedge t_2 \in s_2$$
$$(9)\, t/l.s_1 \sqsubseteq t_1/l.s_1/l.(s_1 \parallel s_2) \wedge t/l.s_2 \sqsubseteq t_2/l.s_2/l.(s_1 \parallel s_2)$$

(8), Lemma 4 imply there is a t' such that

$$(10)\, intl(t_1, t_2, t')$$
$$(11)\, t' \in s_1 \parallel s_2$$

(11) implies

$$(12)\, t'/l.(s_1 \parallel s_2) \in C(s_1 \parallel s_2)$$

(1), (7), (9), (10), (12) imply

$$(13)\, t \in R(s_1 \parallel s_2)$$

Theorem 2 (Monotonicity). *Let d_1, d_2 be sequence diagrams such that $l.d_1 \cap l.d_2 = \emptyset$, $l.d_1 = l.d_1'$ and $l.d_2 = l.d_2'$. Then*

$$d_1 \rightsquigarrow d_1' \wedge d_2 \rightsquigarrow d_2' \Rightarrow d_1 \parallel d_2 \rightsquigarrow d_1' \parallel d_2'$$

Proof. Given

$$(1)\, l.d_1 \cap l.d_2 = \emptyset \wedge l.d_1 = l.d_1' \wedge l.d_2 = l.d_2'$$
$$(2)\, d_1 \rightsquigarrow d_1' \wedge d_2 \rightsquigarrow d_2'$$

Let s_1, s_2 be such that

$$(3)\, s_1 \in [\![\, d_1 \,]\!] \wedge s_2 \in [\![\, d_2 \,]\!]$$

(2), (3) imply there are s_1', s_2' such that

$$(4)\, s_1' \in [\![\, d_1'\,]\!] \wedge s_2' \in [\![\, d_2'\,]\!]$$
$$(5)\, R(s_1) \subseteq R(s_1') \cup N(s_1') \wedge R(s_1) \cap C(s_1') \subseteq C(s_1)$$
$$(6)\, R(s_2) \subseteq R(s_2') \cup N(s_2') \wedge R(s_2) \cap C(s_2') \subseteq C(s_2)$$

It must be shown that

$$(7)\, R(s_1 \parallel s_2) \subseteq R(s_1' \parallel s_2') \cup N(s_1' \parallel s_2')$$
$$(8)\, R(s_1 \parallel s_2) \cap C(s_1' \parallel s_2') \subseteq C(s_1 \parallel s_2)$$

To prove (7), assume

$$(9)\, t \in R(s_1 \parallel s_2)$$

(9) and Lemma 6 imply

$$(10)\, t/l.s_1 \in R(s_1)/l.(s_1 \parallel s_2) \wedge t/l.s_2 \in R(s_2)/l.(s_1 \parallel s_2)$$

(5), (6), (10) imply

$$(11)\, t/l.s_1 \in R(s_1') \cup N(s_1')/l.(s_1 \parallel s_2) \wedge t/l.s_2 \in R(s_2') \cup N(s_2')/l.(s_1 \parallel s_2)$$

This gives two cases

$$(12)\, t/l.s_1 \in R(s_1')/l.(s_1 \parallel s_2) \wedge t/l.s_2 \in R(s_2')/l.(s_1 \parallel s_2)$$
$$(13)\, t/l.s_1 \in N(s_1')/l.(s_1 \parallel s_2) \setminus R(s_1')/l.(s_1 \parallel s_2) \vee$$
$$t/l.s_2 \in N(s_2')/l.(s_1 \parallel s_2) \setminus R(s_2')/l.(s_1 \parallel s_2)$$

case Assume (12):
(12), Lemma 6 imply

$$(14)\, t \in R(s_1' \parallel s_2')$$

case Assume (13):
(1), (3), (9), (13) imply there is a maximal j such that

$$(15)\, t|_j/l.s_1 \in R(s_1')/l.(s_1 \parallel s_2) \wedge t|_j/l.s_2 \in R(s_2')/l.(s_1 \parallel s_2)$$

(15), Lemma 6 imply

$$(16)\, t|_j \in R(s_1' \parallel s_2')$$

Without loss of generality, assume

$$(17)\, t|_{j+1}/l.s_1 \in N(s_1')/l.(s_1 \parallel s_2) \setminus R(s_1')/l.(s_1 \parallel s_2)$$

(15), (17) imply

$$(18)\, k.t[j+1] = ! \wedge l.t[j+1] \in l.s_1$$

(16), (17), (18), Lemma 6 imply

$$(19)\, t \in N(s_1' \parallel s_2')$$

To prove (8), assume

$$(20)\, t \in R(s_1 \parallel s_2) \cap C(s_1' \parallel s_2')$$

(1), (20), Lemma 5, Lemma 6 imply

$$(21)\, t/l.s_1 \in R(s_1)/l.(s_1 \parallel s_2) \wedge t/l.s_2 \in R(s_2)/l.(s_1 \parallel s_2)$$
$$(22)\, t/l.s_1 \in C(s_1')/l.(s_1 \parallel s_2) \wedge t/l.s_2 \in C(s_2')/l.(s_1 \parallel s_2)$$

(5), (6), (21), (22) imply

$$(23)\, t/l.s_1 \in C(s_1)/l.(s_1 \parallel s_2) \wedge t/l.s_2 \in C(s_2)/l.(s_1 \parallel s_2)$$

(23), Lemma 5 imply

$$(24)\, t \in C(s_1' \parallel s_2')$$

7   Conclusion

Contrary to many modeling languages, sequence diagrams describe system scenarios and not complete systems. This has profound implications for their interpretation. In particular, it is necessary to distinguish between two kinds of nondeterminism. I have previously co-authored several papers [3, 8, 12] on the semantics of sequence diagrams. Those papers aimed to represent sequence diagrams in compliance with UML. This meant the use of dedicated operators to specify negative behavior and viewing the specified component and its environment as more or less equal partners. This paper differs from those by imposing a strict rely-guarantee paradigm:

- The environment cannot be constrained.
- For each scenario there is a rely and a guarantee.
- There are tight constraints on what it means to comply with a scenario. A scenario describes both positive and negative behavior.
- The notion of refinement is conventional. The rely can only become weaker. The guarantee can only become stronger.

The rely-guarantee paradigm is inspired by Hoare-logic [4]. In Hoare-logic the pre-condition is a rely, while the post-condition is a guarantee. Cliff Jones' contribution [6] was to generalize the compositional reasoning of Hoare-logic from sequential software to shared-state parallel programs. At about the same time

Mani Chandy and Jayadev Misra did the same for hand-shake based concurrency [10]. These early ideas have been followed up in a plethora of specializations, generalizations and combinations with other software engineering approaches. They are often referred to as assumption-commitment [2] or assumption-guarantee [1].

There is also considerable literature on the semantics of sequence diagrams. See [9] for an overview. The ones most closely related to the approach put forward in this paper are the ones I co-authored on STAIRS already discussed above.

References

1. Abadi, M., Lamport, L.: Conjoining specifications. ACM Trans. Programm. Lang. Syst. **17**, 507–533 (1995). https://doi.org/10.1145/203095.201069
2. de Roever, W.-P., de Boer, F., Hannemann, U., Hooman, J., Lakhnech, Y., Poel, M., Zwiers, J.: Concurrency Verification. Cambridge University Press (2001)
3. Haugen, Ø., Husa, K.E., Runde, R.K., Stølen, K.: STAIRS towards formal design with sequence diagrams. Softw. Syst. Model. **22**(4), 349–458 (2005). https://doi.org/10.1007/s10270-005-0087-0
4. Hoare, C.A.R.: An axiomatic basis for computer programming. Commun. ACM **12**, 576–583 (1969). https://doi.org/10.1145/363235.363259
5. International Telecommunication Union. Recommendation Z.120 – Message Sequence Chart (MSC) (1996)
6. Jones, C.B.: Development methods for computer programs including a notion of interference. Ph.D. thesis, Oxford University (1981). Available as Technical Monograph PRG-25, Oxford University Computing Laboratory (now Computer Science)
7. Jones, C.B.: Specification and design of (parallel) programs. In: Information Processing, North-Holland, pp. 321–331 (1983)
8. Lund, M.S., Stølen, K.: A fully operational semantics for UML 2.0 sequence diagrams with potential and mandatory choice. In: Misra, J., Nipkow, T., Sekerinski, E. (eds.) FM 2006. LNCS, vol. 4085, pp. 380–395. Springer, Heidelberg (2006). https://doi.org/10.1007/11813040_26
9. Micskei, Z., Waeselynck, H.: The many meanings of UML 2 sequence diagrams: a survey. Softw. Syst. Model. **10**, 489–514 (2011). https://doi.org/10.1007/s10270-010-0157-9
10. Misra, J., Chandy, K.M.: Proofs of networks of processes. IEEE Trans. Softw. Eng. **7**, 417–426 (1981). https://doi.org/10.1109/TSE.1981.230844
11. Rumbaugh, J., Jacobson, I., Booch, G.: The Unified Modeling Language Reference Manual, 2nd edn. Addison-Wesley (2004)
12. Runde, R.K., Haugen, Ø., Stølen, K.: The pragmatics of STAIRS. In: de Boer, F.S., Bonsangue, M.M., Graf, S., de Roever, W.-P. (eds.) FMCO 2005. LNCS, vol. 4111, pp. 88–114. Springer, Heidelberg (2006). https://doi.org/10.1007/11804192_5
13. Stølen, K.: Development of parallel programs on shared data-structures. Ph.D. thesis, University of Manchester (1990). Also available as technical report UMCS-91-1-1, University of Manchester. See URL for revised version with all known bugs corrected. https://doi.org/10.48550/arXiv.2404.16624

14. Stølen, K.: An attempt to reason about shared-state concurrency in the style of VDM. In: Prehn, S., Toetenel, W.J. (eds.) VDM 1991. LNCS, vol. 551, pp. 324–342. Springer, Heidelberg (1991). https://doi.org/10.1007/3-540-54834-3_20

15. Stølen, K.: A method for the development of totally correct shared-state parallel programs. In: Baeten, J.C.M., Groote, J.F. (eds.) CONCUR 1991. LNCS, vol. 527, pp. 510–525. Springer, Heidelberg (1991). https://doi.org/10.1007/3-540-54430-5_110

Formal Analysis of Interactions Between Safety and Security Requirements

Elena Troubitsyna$^{(\boxtimes)}$

KTH – Royal Institute of Technology, Stockholm, Sweden
elenatro@kth.se

Abstract. Modern safety-critical control systems rely on networking to provide safety-critical functions. Network technologies not only offers a variety of benefits but also introduces cybersecurity threats. Exploiting security vulnerabilities might result in a loss of control and situation awareness as well as directly threaten safety. Therefore, the development of safety-critical systems should encompass a systematic analysis of the impact of potential cyberattacks on safety and explicit identification of security requirements early in the system development life cycle. In this paper, we propose a formal approach to modelling networked safety-critical systems within Event-B framework. We demonstrate how modelling and refinement in Event-B can systematically identify mutual interdependencies between safety and security and facilitate deriving explicit security requirements necessary for achieving system safety.

Keywords: Safety · security · control systems · formal modelling · Event-B

1 Introduction

Modern industrial control systems constitute a large class of cyber-physical systems that "encompasses several types of control systems, including supervisory control and data acquisition (SCADA) systems, distributed control systems ... often found in the ... critical infrastructures" [11]. These system usually belong to the class of safety-critical systems and provide services vital for society [11].

Extensive reliance on network technologies has made SCADA systems increasingly exposed to Internet threats [25]. The recent cyberattacks, especially on electric grids [6], demonstrated that exploit of security vulnerabilities can potentially jeopardise system safety. Therefore, to guarantee safety, it is important to uncover implicit security requirements early in the system development and systematically analyse interactions between safety and security requirements.

In this paper, we present a formal approach that allows the designers to systematically analyse interactions between safety and security requirements

---

The author would like to thank Inna Vistbakka for long-standing cooperation that contributed to this paper.

A. Cavalcanti and J. Baxter (Eds.): *The Practice of Formal Methods*, LNCS 14781, pp. 141–161, 2024.
https://doi.org/10.1007/978-3-031-66673-5_8

and uncover the implicit security requirements that are implied by the explicit system-level safety goals.

We use the rely-guarantee style [10] to reason about safety-security interdependence at the abstract level of the interaction of the physical and cyber worlds. By following the systems thinking approach [7], we identify the high-level properties of the system environment that should be fulfilled to guarantee safety of the overall system. Then, to reap the benefits of the automated tool support while deriving the detailed formal specification of the system, we proceed with the formal system development within the Event-B framework [1] automated by Rodin platform [18].

Event-B is a rigorous approach to correct-by-construction system development by refinement. Development starts from an abstract specification that models the most essential system functionality. The correct-by-construction development by refinement transforms the abstract model into a detailed specification. While refining the system model, we can explicitly represent both the nominal and failure behaviour of the system components as well as define the mechanisms for error detection and recovery. We can also explicitly represent the effect of exploiting security vulnerabilities such as tampering, spoofing and denial-of-service (DOS) attacks and analyse their impact on system safety.

We believe that the proposed approach facilitates an integration of the security consideration into the safety-driven design of control systems. It allows us to capture the dynamic nature of safety and security interplay, i.e., analyse the impact of deploying the security mechanisms on safety assurance and vice versa.

Our approach is inspired by the seminal works of Cliff Jones on rely-guarantee reasoning [10] and its application to support systems thinking in the specification of control systems [7]. I belong to the generation of researchers who have been strongly influenced by the foundational ideas of Professor Jones. I first met him in Turku in June 2000, when he was invited as an external examiner (opponent) at one of the public PhD defences. A charismatic scientist in Oxford academic gown spoke about formal methods with such great intellectual grace, his questions were so deep and intriguing that it has immediately broadened my research horizons and increased my motivation to pursue an academic carreer.

I was also privileged to cooperate with Professor Jones in European projects RODIN [2] and Deploy [19] and witnessed how a profound thinker can approach applied problems with mathematical rigour and strategic scientific foresight. This made a significant impact on my research work in the area of applied formal methods.

2   Systems View on Safety and Security Interdependence

We start by describing the reference architecture of a control system. A control system has a cyclic behaviour. The goal of the system is to control a certain physical process. The input device – a sensor – monitors the state of the physical process by measuring the value of the controlled parameter. Such a measurement is taken as an input by the controller. Upon receiving the corresponding input,

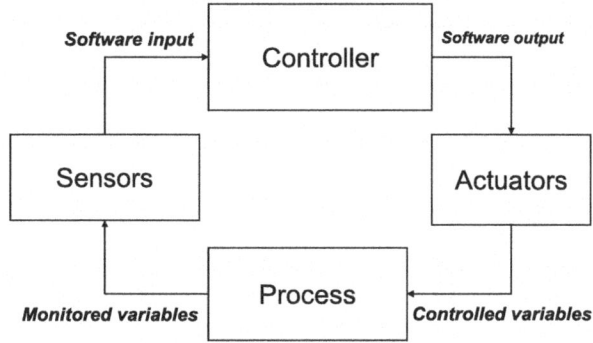

Fig. 1. The four-variable model

the controller computes the output – the state of the actuator. The actuator affects the behaviour of the controlled physical process, i.e., it changes the value of the monitored variable to achieve the desired behaviour. In Fig. 1, we present the reference architecture of a control system in the style of a four-variable model [4] introduced by Parnas.

An important requirement, which is usually imposed on the majority of control systems, is to guarantee safety, i.e., ensure that the system would not cause accidents resulting in a loss of human lives or environmental damage [14].

Let us now analyse the behaviour of the system and define safety requirements in the rely-guarantee style [10]. The goal of the system is to achieve a certain behaviour in the problem world [7], i.e., guarantee that the controlled physical parameter has the desired values that are also kept within the safe boundaries. As the input, the system receives the measurements of the values of the monitored variables and as the output it computes the values of the controlled variables.

A high-level generic specification of the controlling system can be defined as follows:

$$SafeControlSystem \triangleq$$
system
input $software\_input$
output $software\_output$
guarantee $Functional\ Requirements \wedge Safety$

Modern industrial control systems are significantly less isolated from the outside world and increasingly use wireless networking [11]. Often the sensor measurements are transmitted via network channels to the controller from remote locations. Similarly, the controller sends the commands to the actuators that might be geographically distant from it. In Fig. 2, we present our proposal to refine the reference architecture of the control system to explicitly represent the networking aspect.

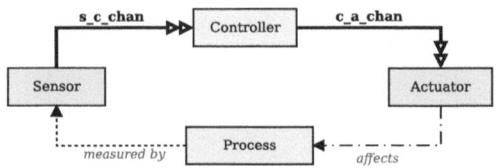

Fig. 2. Generic architecture of a control system

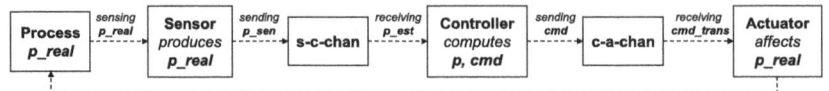

Fig. 3. Data flow within a control cycle

We assume that the state of the controlled physical process is defined by the (physical) variable *p_real*. The value of *p_real* is measured by the sensor. The sensor can be a physical device, i.e., a hardware component that converts the physical value of *p_real* into its digital representation *p_sen*. However, it can be also a logical sensor – a module of a controlling program that computes an estimate of *p_real* based on some other measurements of the controlled process. In either case, the sensor measurements provide estimates of the values of *monitored variables* in our initial abstract model.

In general, sensing is remote, i.e., the measured value *p_sen* is transmitted to the input of the controller. Hence, the transmission channel between the sensor and the controller *s-c-chan* might be untrusted, i.e., it might be a subject of security attack, the value that is received by the controller – *p_est* might be different from *p_sen*.

Since we consider a feedback control system (feedback is received via the monitored variables), we assume that at each cycle the controller can predict the interval of reasonable values of monitored variables to be received at the next cycle. In terms of the data flow within the control cycle depicted in Fig. 3, we assume that controlling software can check the reasonableness of the received *p_est*. Then it can decide to use it as the current estimate of *p_real*, i.e., *p* := *p_est* or ignore it.

The value *p* that the controller adopts as its current estimate of the process state should pass the feasibility check to be adopted as the current value of the monitored variables.

The value of *p* is used to calculate the next state of the actuator – the physical device that affects the controlled process, i.e., causes the changes in the value of *p_real*. The command from the controller to the actuator is transmitted over a network. In the similar way, the transmission channel from the controller to the actuator *c-a-chan* might be attacked. Hence, the command *cmd_trans* received by the actuator might be different from the command *cmd* computed by the controller.

The behaviour of the system is cyclic. At each cycle, the sensor measures *p_real*, produces *p_sen* and sends it over the *s-c-chan* channel to the controller. The controller receives *p_est*, checks it and computes *p* and the actuator command *cmd*. After that it sends *cmd* over the *c-a-chan*. The actuator receives the *cmd_trans* command and applies it, which should result in the desirable change of the process state, as illustrated in Fig. 3.

In this work, we focus on the failsafe systems, i.e., consider the control systems that can be put into a safe non-operational state to preclude an occurrence of a safety failure [14]. Often system safety is defined over the parameters of the controlled physical process, i.e. it is required that the controlled parameter stays within safe boundaries while the system is operational or the system is shut down. The typical examples of failsafe control systems are trains or nuclear reactors. They deliver their services – moving along the route or producing energy – while it is deemed to be safe. Once safety of operation cannot be established, the system enters safe non-operational state, i.e., the train is stopped or the reactor is shut down correspondingly. In such a state, the system cease to deliver its intended services to avoid an occurrence of safety hazards. Once the situation is rectified (usually by a human operator), the system resumes its operation.

For instance, in our generic control system, we can define safety as the following predicate

$$Safety \,\hat{=}\, p\_real \leq safe\_threshold \,\vee\, failsafe \,=\, TRUE.$$

It means that the controlled process should be kept within the safety boundaries while the system is operational; otherwise, the system should be put in an non-operational safe state. Shutting down the system is usually achieved via various combinations of programmable and non-programmable means. Nevertheless, the controller knows whether the system is operational.

We consider the system that consists of controlling software that receives inputs and computes outputs, while network channels, sensors, actuators and physical process itself belong to the system environment.

Reasoning in rely-guarantee style helps us to uncover the implicit assumptions about the system environment that influence the specification of the controller. Our aim is to construct controlling software, which is under the given assumptions and properties folded in the **rely** clause satisfies properties stated in the **guarantee** clause.

Let us discuss the considerations that should be taken into account while analysing the interactions of cyber and physical world. The control of the physical world relies on the continuous time model of the controlled process. The desired behaviour of the physical process is defined as a stability property, which also implies safety [24]. Stable and safe behaviour of the physical process is guaranteed only if the process receives periodic control commands from the cyber world. A tolerable delay can be calculated and should be not exceeded.

The physical process also has some inertia, i.e., even "imprecise" with respect to the current process state control commands can be tolerated for some bounded period of time. Under the assumption that the controlling algorithm is correct, we can identify two causes of imprecision of control commands: software is provided with distorted values of monitored variables and the controlled variables are assigned distorted values of software output.

The tolerable "imprecision" should be analysed using the continuous-time model of the physical process and formulated in terms of the properties on which the cyber world can rely.

The first property $R1$: $p\_sen = p\_real \pm \Delta_1$ states that the sensor measurements are sufficiently precise and imprecision is bounded, i.e., the software input provides a sufficiently close measurement of the physical parameter – the monitored variable. It implies a safety requirement: sensor should have high reliability. Here Δ_1 is the maximal imprecision value for the sensor.

Next property $R2$: $p = p\_sen + \Delta_2 \wedge \Delta_2 = k\Delta_3$ states that the controller always can adopts a measurement of the value of the process parameter that either coincides with p_sen, i.e., $k = 0$, or is calculated based on the physical properties of the controlled process and tolerable control command imprecision. It is based on the last good value of the received input and Δ_3 – the maximal possible increase of the value p_real per cycle ($\Delta_2 = k\Delta_3$, where k is the number of cycles).

This property implies both safety and security requirements. Namely, we either should guarantee that the channel s-c-$chan$ is tamper resistant and the sensor is spoofing resistant or the controlling software is able to check the validity of the input parameter and ignore it, if the check fails. The property $R2$ also implies that, in case of DOS attack on the channel s-c-$chan$, the system can continue to function by relying of the last good value for some bounded time, which is constraint by the inertia of the physical process.

The following property

$$R3: (failsafe = FALSE \wedge cmd\_trans = cmd) \vee failsafe = TRUE$$

implies that if a failure or an attack on the channel c-a-$chan$ can be detected and then the system can be put in a failsafe state. In some sense, this is a meta-property designating that the system should have some (possibly non-programmable) way to execute a shutdown in case the channel c-a-$chan$ becomes unreliable.

The next set of properties describes the effect that control commands are assumed to have on the physical world. They are based on the physical laws governing the behaviour of the controlled process in real world and their interdependencies.

$R4$: $cmd = incr \Rightarrow p\_real(t + 1) \geq p\_real(t)$ for any t, while the system is operational

$R5$: $cmd = decr \Rightarrow p\_real(t + 1) < p\_real(t)$ for any t, while the system is operational

$R6$: $max|(p\_real(t + 1) - p\_real(t))| = \Delta_3$

$R7$: $failsafe = TRUE \Rightarrow p\_real(t + 1) \leq p\_real(t)$ for any t, while the system is shut down

The property $R4$ states that an execution of the command *incr* results in the increase of the value *p_real*. Similarly, the property $R5$ states that an execution of the command *decr* results in the decrease of the value *p_real*.

The property $R6$ states that the maximal possible increase of *p_real* per cycle is known and bounded. This value is obtained from the continuous time modelling of the controlled process. The property $R7$ is also a meta-property that describes the actual failsafe state, i.e., it stipulates that when the system is put in the failsafe state, the value of the physical parameter does not increase.

As a result, we arrive at the following specification:

$SafeControlSystem \triangleq$
system
input $p\_est : REAL$
output $cmd : incr|decr$
output $failsafe : BOOL$
rely $R1 \wedge R2 \wedge R3 \wedge R4 \wedge R5 \wedge R6 \wedge R7$
guarantee $p\_real \leq safe\_threshold \vee failsafe = TRUE$

For brevity, we skip the discussion of a derivation of functional behaviour of the controller and focus on specifying only the safety-related aspect. Essentially, we should guarantee that if *p_real* approaches the safety margin, the controller should always issue the command resulting in the decrease of *p_real*.

$Set\_Actuator\_Decr \triangleq$
system
input $p\_est : REAL$
output $cmd : incr|decr$
output $failsafe : BOOL$
rely $p\_est + \Sigma_{i=1}^{3}\Delta_i \geq safe\_threshold \wedge failsafe = FALSE$
guarantee $cmd=decr$

We arrive at the following refined specification:

$SafeControlSystem' \triangleq SafeControlSystem \wedge Set\_Actuator\_To\_Decrease.$

Our system level analysis has demonstrated that both safety and security aspects are critical for fulfilling the system-level goal of ensuring safety. Hence, both these aspects should be explicitly addressed during the system development. It is easy to observe, that we had to define a large number of requirements even for a generic high-level system architecture. Hence, to facilitate formal development process, it would be desirable to employ automated tool support. In the next section, we briefly overview Event-B and then demonstrate how to conduct formal analysis of interactions between safety and security within the integrated modelling environment of Rodin platform.

3   Modelling and Refinement in Event-B

Event-B [1] is a state-based framework that promotes the correct-by-construction approach to system development and formal verification by theorem proving. In Event-B, a system model is specified using the notion of an *abstract state machine* (ASM). ASM encapsulates the model state, represented as a collection of variables, and defines operations on the state, i.e., it describes the dynamic behaviour of a modelled system. A machine also has an accompanying component, called *context*, which includes user-defined sets, constants and their properties given as axioms.

The dynamic behaviour of the system is defined by a set of atomic *events*. Generally, an event has the following form:

$$e \cong \textbf{any } a \textbf{ where } G_e \textbf{ then } R_e \textbf{ end},$$

where e is the event's name, a is the list of local variables, the *guard* G_e is a predicate over the local variables of the event and the state variables of the system. The body of an event is defined by a *multiple* (possibly nondeterministic) assignment over the system variables. The guard defines the conditions under which the event is *enabled*, i.e., its body can be executed. If several events are enabled at the same time, any of them can be chosen for execution nondeterministically.

Event-B employs a top-down refinement-based approach to system development. Development typically starts from an abstract specification that nondeterministically models the most essential functional requirements. In a sequence of refinement steps, we gradually reduce nondeterminism and introduce detailed design decisions. In particular, we can add new events, split events as well as replace abstract variables by their concrete counterparts, i.e., perform *data refinement*. When data refinement is performed, we should define *gluing invariants* as a part of the invariants of the refined machine. They define the relationship between the abstract and concrete variables. The proof of data refinement is often supported by supplying *witnesses* – the concrete values for the replaced abstract variables and parameters. Witnesses are specified in the event clause **with**.

The consistency of Event-B models, i.e., verification of well-formedness, invariant preservation and correctness of refinement steps, is demonstrated by discharging a number of verification conditions – proof obligations. The Rodin platform [18] provides an automated support for formal modelling and verification in Event-B. It automatically generates the required proof obligations and attempts to discharge (prove) them automatically. It also provides a support for an interactive proving.

4   Generic Development of a Control System

In this section, we present a generic methodology for the refinement-based development of control systems that facilitates identifying implicit security requirements that should be fulfilled to satisfy the safety goals.

4.1   Abstract Specification: Overall System Behaviour

In the initial Event-B model, we introduce an abstract representation of the system architecture with the explicit definition of the communication

```
Process ≙
  when   phase=PROC   then      phase:=SEN  C_A_Chan ≙
end                                            when  phase=TO_ACTUA ∧
Sensor ≙                                            failure=FALSE
  when  phase=SEN ∧ failure=FALSE             then  phase:=ACTUA end
  then   phase:=TO_CONTR end                Actuator ≙
S_C_Chan ≙ ...                                 when phase=ACTUA ∧ failure=FALSE
  when phase=TO_CONTR ∧ failure=FALSE       then  phase:=PROC end
  then   phase:=CONTR end                   FailureDetection ≙ ...
Controller ≙                                 FailSafe ≙ ...
  when  phase=CONTR ∧ failure=FALSE         end
  then   phase:=TO_ACTUA end
```

Fig. 4. Events of the machine ControlSystem_SS_m0

channels as defined in Fig. 2. The abstract model (given in Fig. 4) – the machine ControlSystem_SS_m0 – represents the overall behaviour of the system as an interleaving between the events modelling the phases of the *control cycle* defined in Sect. 2.

We define a variable $phase \in PHASES$ to designate the current stage of the control cycle. The set $PHASES$

$$PHASES = \{PROC, SEN, TO\_CONTR, CONTR, TO\_ACTUA, ACTUA\}$$

contains the constants denoting the corresponding stages of the control cycle, while *phase* is used to enforce the pre-defined cyclic execution order of events:

Process → Sensor → S_C_Chan → Controller → C_A_Chan → Actuator → Process → ...

Process event models the behaviour of the monitored physical process. Sensor event models the behaviour of the sensor, while Controller event specifies the behaviour of the controlling software. The events S_C_Chan and C_A_Chan model communication channels. Finally, Actuator event models the behaviour of the actuator.

In the initial model, we also abstractly specify an occurrence of faults. The event FailureDetection models a failure detection by non-deterministically assigning the variable *failure* the value $TRUE$ or $FALSE$. In our further refinement steps, we will distinguish between the criticality of failures, and hence, will execute shutdown (enable the event FailSafe) less often.

Let us note that in our initial specification, we have not yet formulated safety as a model invariant. Since the initial model defines only the control flow, we do not have the sufficiently detailed "knowledge" to define and prove the desired safety property. This goal will be achieved via the refinement process.

4.2   First Refinement: Introducing Model Data

Our first refinement step aims at augmenting the abstract model with the explicit specification of the variables that are updated by the components and transmitted via the communication channels within the control cycle. At this refinement step, we also elaborate on the model of the controlled process, i.e., define the behaviour of the physical process characterised by the variable *p_real*. We also model the dependencies between the actuator state and the expected range of *p_real* value.

In the dynamic part of the Event-B model – the machine ControlSystem _SS_m1 – we introduce four variables that explicitly represent the variable *p_real* and its "perception" at each stage of the controlled process:

- *p_real* – the current physical value defining the state of the process;
- *p_sen* – the value of the physical variable measured by the sensor. It can be affected by the sensor imprecision or failures;
- *p_est* – the value of the sensor measurement received by the controller as an input. It can be affected by the security attacks (tampering or spoofing);
- *p* – the value adopted by the controller as the current estimate of the process value.

Moreover, we also introduce a representation of the controller output – the command issued to the actuator – and corresponding command received by the actuator:

- *cmd* – the controller output;
- *cmd_trans* – the command received by the actuator. It can be affected by security attacks (tampering or spoofing) on the transmission channel.

The type of the variables *cmd* and *cmd_trans* is defined as the enumerated set $COMMANDS$ that contains the elements $\{INCR, DECR, ND, DOS\}$. The constants $INCR$ and $DECR$ stand for *increasing* and *decreasing* commands to the actuator, ND – for the initialisation command. The constant DOS is an abstract representation of a DOS attack or channel failure. It models the fact that the actuator does not receive any (fresh) command at the current control cycle.

Finally, we define a variable *act_state* representing the current state of the actuator. The actuator can be either switched off (consequently, $act\_state = OFF$) or switched on ($act\_state = ON$). For simplicity, we assume that when the actuator is switched on then the value of *p_real* is increasing and when it is switched off, it is decreasing correspondingly.

The event Sensor models the behaviour of the sensor by assigning the variable *p_sen* any value from the range *p_real* - *delta1* .. *p_real* + *delta1*, where *delta1* is the maximal imprecision value for the sensor introduced as a constant in the model context. Hence, we model the sensor imprecision defined in our property **P1** in Sect. 2. The event SensorFailure models the sensor failure. In case of failure, the sensor produces the reading that is out of the expected range.

The abstract event S_C_Chan models the transmission of the sensor reading (*p_sen* value) to the controller. Since the transmission channel *s-c-chan* might be a subject of a security attack, the input *p_est* received by the controller might differ from the *p_sen* value. We refine the event S_C_Chan by two concrete ones: modelling the normal and abnormal transmissions.

Process refines Process $\widehat{=}$	**Controller refines** Controller $\widehat{=}$
when $phase=PROC$	**any** $k, delta3$
then $phase:=SEN$	**where** $phase=CONTR \wedge failure=FALSE\wedge$
$\quad p\_real := p\_func(p\_real \mapsto act\_state)$	$\quad k \in \{0..3\} \wedge delta2 = delta3*k$
end	**then** $phase:=TO\_ACTUA$
Sensor refines Sensor $\widehat{=}$	$\quad p :\mid (p' \in \{p\_est, p\} \vee p' \in p - delta3 .. p + delta3)$
when $phase=SEN \wedge failure=FALSE$	$\quad cmd :\in COMMANDS$ **end**
then $phase:=TO\_CONTR$	**C_A_Chan_normal refines** C_A_Chan $\widehat{=}$
$\quad p\_sen :\in p\_real - delta1 ... p\_real + delta1$	**when** $phase=TO\_ACTUA \wedge failure=FALSE$
end	**then** $phase:=ACTUA \parallel cmd\_trans := cmd$
S_C_Chan_normal refines S_C_Chan $\widehat{=}$	**end**
when $phase=TO\_CONTR \wedge$	**C_A_Chan_failed refines** C_A_Chan $\widehat{=}$
$\quad failure=FALSE$	**when** $phase=TO\_ACTUA \wedge failure=FALSE$
then $phase:=CONTR$	**then** $phase:=ACTUA \parallel$
$\quad p\_est := p\_sen$	$\quad cmd\_trans :\in COMMANDS$ **end**
end	**Actuator_normal refines** Actuator $\widehat{=}$
S_C_Chan_failed refines S_C_Chan $\widehat{=}$	**when** $phase=ACTUA \wedge failure=FALSE$
when $phase=TO\_CONTR \wedge$	$\quad cmd\_trans \in \{INCR, DECR\}$
$\quad failure=FALSE$	**then** $phase:=PROC$
then $phase:=CONTR$	$act\_state :\mid (cms\_trans=INCR \Rightarrow act\_state' = ON)$
$\quad p\_est : \mid (p\_est' \in \mathbb{N} \wedge p\_est' \neq p\_sen)$	$\quad \vee (cms\_trans=DECR \Rightarrow act\_state' = OFF)$
end	**end**

Fig. 5. Events of the machine ControlSystem_SS_m1

The event Controller is refined to abstractly specify behaviour of the controller. We model the procedure of computing the current estimate p. The controller either accepts the current input or relies on the last good value, or calculates a new value p on the basis of the last good value and the maximal possible increase per cycle. The computed value of p is used to calculate the output – the next state of the actuator, i.e., update the variable cmd. Similar to the S_C_Chan event, we refine the abstract event C_A_Chan by two events modelling successful and failed command transmission from the controller to the actuator (Fig. 5).

Upon receiving the command from the controller, the actuator changes its state accordingly. This behaviour is modelled by the event Actuator. The actuator behaviour preserves the following invariants:

$$phase = PROC \wedge cmd\_trans = INCR \Rightarrow act\_state = ON,$$
$$phase = PROC \wedge cmd\_trans = DECR \Rightarrow act\_state = OFF.$$

They postulate that the actuator is switched on when the increasing command is received, and vice versa.

We also specify our knowledge about the environment process by introducing the abstract function p_func into the extended model context:

$$p\_func \in \mathbb{N} \times ACTUATOR\_STATES \to \mathbb{N}.$$

The function models the next predicted value for the process p_real. It takes the previous value of p_real as well as the actuator state as the input and returns a new predicted value in the next cycle. While the actuator is switched on, the value of p_real is increasing. Correspondingly, while the actuator is switched off,

```
┌─────────────────────────────────────────────────────────────────────────┐
│ Controller_normal_DECR refines Controller ≙                               │
│   where phase=CONTR ∧                    Controller_retry_DECR refines Controller ≙ │
│         failure=FALSE ∧                    any p_new, delta3               │
│         p_est = p_func(p ↦ act_state) ∧    where phase=CONTR ∧ failure=FALSE ∧ │
│         p_est > p_max                             p_est ≠ p_func(p ↦ act_state) ∧ │
│   with  k=0                                       retry ≤ 2 ∧ delta3 = (retry+1)delta2 ∧ │
│         delta3=0                                  p_new ∈ p-delta3...p+delta3 ∧ p_est > p_max │
│   then  phase:=TO_ACTUA                    with  k=retry+1                  │
│         p := p_est                         then  phase:=TO_ACTUA           │
│         cmd := DECR                              p := p_new                │
│         retry := 0                               cmd := DECR               │
│   end                                            retry := retry+1          │
│                                            end                             │
└─────────────────────────────────────────────────────────────────────────┘
```

Fig. 6. Excerpt from the machine ControlSystem_SS_m2

the value of p_real is decreasing. We formulate these properties as the following model axiom:

$$\forall n \cdot n \in \mathbb{N} \Rightarrow p\_func(n \mapsto ON) \geq n, \ \forall n \cdot n \in \mathbb{N} \Rightarrow p\_func(n \mapsto OFF) \leq n$$

These axioms formalize the properties **R4** and **R5** discussed in Sect. 2. Moreover, the following constraint in the context component

$$\forall n \cdot n \in 0 .. p\_max + delta1 \Rightarrow p\_func(n \mapsto ON) \leq safe\_threshold.$$

requires that, if the process state is currently in the safe range $[0..p\_max + delta1]$, it cannot exceed the critical range within the next cycle, i.e., the safety gap between p_max and $safe\_threshold$ is sufficiently large.

4.3   Second Refinement: Specifying Controller Logic

Our second refinement step aims at introducing a detailed specification of the behaviour of the controlling software. Namely, we refine the abstract event Controller to represent its different alternatives that depend on the received input.

The output of the controller – the next state of the actuator – depends on the value of p adopted by the controller as the current estimate of the process state. Upon receiving the input – p_est – the controller checks its reasonableness. If the check is successful then p obtains the value of p_est. Then the controller proceeds by checks whether p exceeds p_max or is in the safe range $[0..p\_max]$. These alternatives are modelled by the events Controller_normal_DECR (see Fig. 6) and Controller_normal, correspondingly.

If the input does not pass the reasonableness check, the controller calculates the value of the process parameter using the last good input value and the maximal possible increase of the value p_real per cycle $delta2$. Then, the controller checks whether p exceeds p_max and computes the output. These alternatives are covered by the events Controller_retry_DECR and Controller_retry, correspondingly. Here the variable $retry$ is introduced to model the number of retries (cycles) before the failure is considered to be a permanent and system is shut down.

The behaviour of the controller preserves the following invariant:

$$phase = TO\_ACTUA \land p > p\_max \Rightarrow cmd = DECR,$$
$$phase = TO\_ACTUA \land p \in 0..p\_max \Rightarrow cmd = INCR \lor cmd = DECR,$$

It postulates that the controller issues the command $DECR$ if the parameter p is approaching the critically high value ($safe\_threshold$). If the controlled parameter is within the safety region then the controller output might be either $DECR$ or $INCR$.

4.4 Third Refinement: Attack Modelling

In a networked control system, the communication channels are used to transmit the sensor data to the controller as well as the commands issued by the controller to the actuator. However, such channels could be possibly vulnerable to the security attacks. The goal of our third refinement step is to introduce into the Event-B model an abstract representation of the attacks and the system reaction on them.

To achieve this, we add several new events and variables into the refined system specification as shown in Fig. 7. Firstly, we introduce a new event Attack_S_C_Chan to model a possible attack on the channel s-c-$chan$. The attack can happen anytime while transmitting the sensed data to the controller. The variable $attack\_s\_c \in BOOL$ indicates whether the system is under attack. If the event Attack_S_C_Chan is triggered, the value of $attack\_s\_c$ becomes $TRUE$, otherwise it equals to $FALSE$. Let us note that the event Attack_S_C_Chan is merely an abstraction introduced to represent the results of the security monitoring. In general, a security monitoring relies on the anomaly detection including checks of well-formedness of data packets, deviations in response time or periodicity, etc. (An implementation of the security monitoring mechanisms is out of scope of this paper.) Similarly to modelling the attack on the channel s-c-$chan$, we introduce the event Attack_S_A_Chan to model a possible attack on the channel c-a-$chan$.

We define the additional guards in the events S_C_Chan_normal and C_A_Chan_normal to ensure that the events are enabled only if no attacks have been detected, i.e., $attack\_s\_c = FALSE$ or $attack\_c\_a = FALSE$, correspondingly.

According to the property $P2$, in case of an attack on the channel s-c-$chan$, the system continues to function for some time, i.e., the controller relies on the last good input received for some bounded time, as discussed in Sect. 2. If an attack on the channel c-a-$chan$ has occurred then the controller output would differ from the command received by the actuator. In case of the DOS attack (or in general a channel unavailability), the actuator would not receive any command at all. For simplicity, we model it by assigning the constant DOS to the cmd_trans variable. Safety cannot be ensured if an attack on the channel c-a-$chan$ is detected and hence the system should be shut down.

We formulate and prove the following properties as the model invariant:

$$attack\_s\_c = FALSE \wedge phase = CONTR \Rightarrow p\_est = p\_sen,$$
$$attack\_c\_a = FALSE \wedge phase = ACTUA \Rightarrow cmd = cmd\_trans.$$

They describe the effect of the attacks on the controller input and output.

As a result of this refinement step, we arrive at a sufficiently detailed specification to define and prove the following safety invariant: $p\_real \in 0 .. safe\_threshold$.

Next we will demonstrate how the proposed generic refinement process can be applied to develop a case study – a water treatment control system [17].

5   Case Study: Water Treatment Control System

In this section, we present our case study – industrial water treatment system [17] and in the next section, we will demonstrate how to develop a detailed specification of this system by refinement and uncover the mutual interdependencies between safety and security requirements through the process of formal development. In our development we will rely on the generic development presented in Sect. 4.

```
Events ...
Attack_S_C_Chan ≘                              C_A_Chan_failure ...
  when phase=TO_CONTR ∧                          when phase=TO_ACTUA ∧ ... ∧
       attack_s_c=FALSE                               attack_c_a=TRUE
  then   attack_s_c:=TRUE                        then   phase:=ACTUA
  end                                                   cmd := DOS
S_C_Chan_normal refines S_C_Chan_normal ≘      end
  when ... ∧ attack_s_c=FALSE                   C_A_Chan_AttackDetection refines FailureDetection
  ...                                             when ... ∧ failure=FALSE ∧ cmd=DOS
Attack_C_A_Chan ≘                                then   failure:=TRUE
  when phase=TO_ACTUA ∧                          end
       attack_c_a=FALSE                          ...
  then   attack_c_a:=TRUE                        end
  end
```

Fig. 7. Excerpt from the machine ControlSystem_SS_m3

5.1   Case Study Description

We consider a modern industrial water treatment system (WTS) [17] illustrated in Fig. 8. The physical process (water level) is measured by distributed sensors and manipulated by actuators. These sensors and actuators operate by receiving and sending analog signals. The analog signals are converted into digital signals by Programmable Logic Controllers (PLCs). The digital signals are then

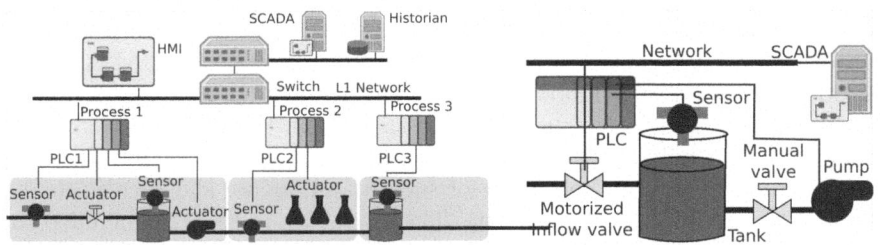

Fig. 8. WTS architecture (left). Case study scenario of water tank (right)

exchanged between PLCs and a central supervisory control system (SCADA) using industrial communication protocols.

The involved components are illustrated in Fig. 8 (right). The system performs the following global scenario. A motorized inflow valve, initially open, let water flows into a tank through a pipe. A tank is equipped with a sensor which checks the level of the water inside the tank. The sensor communicates its reading of the level of the water inside the tank to a PLC. When the level of the water reaches a certain upper threshold, the PLC communicates to the motorized inflow valve to close and to the pump to start. Symmetrically, when the water reaches a certain lower threshold, the PLC communicates to the inflow valve to open and to the pump to stop. A central SCADA control that communicates with the PLC over the network.

The main hazard associated with the system is water spillage (or burst) in the tank component. Therefore, the safety goal of the system is to keep the water level within the safety boundaries. In case the system cannot reliably assess the current water level using the programmable means, a safe shutdown should be executed. Hence, the system architecture should have a reliable mechanism for controlling the water treatment procedure and, in case of hazardous deviations, be able to stop the flow of the water, i.e., make a transition to a failsafe state.

The top-level safety goal of WTS is to keep the level of the water inside the tank within the predefined boundaries. Let wl_real correspond to the real physical value of such a parameter. The system safety property can be formulated as follows:

$$0 \leq wl\_real \leq wl\_max\_crit,$$

where 0 and wl_max_crit denote the lowest and highest boundaries correspondingly. The safety goal is achieved by changing the state of the inflow valve/pump that regulate a water flow.

WTS is an example of the networked system. Hence, it could be potentially vulnerable to security attacks. We assume that the attacker's goal is to cause a water spillage (or burst) in the tank component. The abstract messages exchanged over the network are quite simple. The valve controls the inflow of the water to the tank; the sensor of the tank reports the current fill state to the

PLC as analog signals. The PLC converts the analog signals into digital messages (monitored inflow value in Fig. 8) that it sends to the SCADA. If the water level in the tank has crossed certain high/low thresholds, the SCADA sends a close/open message to the inflow valve and on/off to the pump.

Assume that the attacker drops the messages from the PLC to the SCADA. As result, the tank will overflow and the attacker will achieve his goal. Therefore, while reasoning about the behaviour of such a system, we should also analyse the impact of security threats on safety. The discussion in Sect. 2 concluded that safety cannot be guaranteed when the controller-actuator channel is attacked. Therefore, the WTS should include an additional component – a manual valve – that should be placed in the systems architecture. The behavior of the manual valve is the same as the inflow valve. The only difference is that the manual valve can only be manually operated (e.g., to change its status from open to close), i.e., cannot be operated using network messages. Such a non-programmable component can put the system in the failsafe state to guarantee safety.

Next we discuss an Event-B specification of WTS.

5.2   Event-B Development of the Water Treatment System

In this section, we will present a formal Event-B development of WTS. Our development relies on the generic development presented in Sect. 4. Since the developed models are fairly large, we only highlight the most important modelling solutions of the development. The overall refinement structure of the WTS model is presented on Fig. 9.

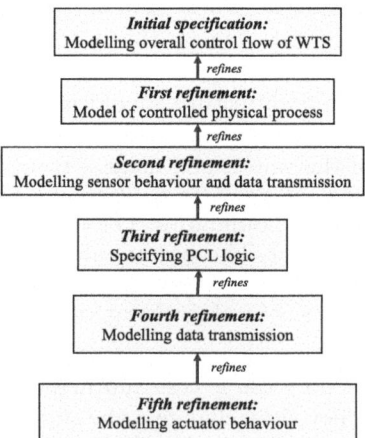

Fig. 9. Overview of the Event-B development of WTS

Initial Specification. We start with a simple Event-B model of WTS, which defines its essential behaviour. Similarly to the behaviour of a control system, WTS's behaviour is cyclic, yet with several differences. In the initial Event-B specification WaterTreatment_Abs, we model these activities by the corresponding events.

By following the guidelines defined in Sect. 4, we introduce an abstract representation of the control cycle and define the phases of the cycle.

WaterTank event models the changes of the water level parameter *wl_real* while charging. Sen_estim event models the estimation of this parameter (that is defined by *wl* variable). PLC event specifies the WTS actions (i.e., sending the command to open or close valve and to stop pump) and Transm event models transmission of the corresponding command to the inflow valve to open and to the pump to stop. Finally, Actions event models the required actions upon receiving the commands from PLC.

First Refinement. At this step we elaborate on the dynamics of the controlled process, i.e., define the changes in the water level *wl_real*.

Second Refinement. Here we model the behaviour of the sensor and unfold the value of the physical variable *wl_sen* measured by the sensor. Since this value can be affected by the sensor imprecision or failures, we address it in our model. Moreover, we model the transmission of the sensor reading to PLC.

Third Refinement. This step aims at introducing a detailed specification of the PLC logic. We define the control algorithm, i.e., model the behavior of the controller. The controller calculates the commands to be send to the valve and pump using the current estimate of the water level.

At each control cycle, the PLC controller receives the current estimate of the water level from the sensor. The controller checks whether the water level is still in safe range and sends commands to continue to open valve or close valve and stop the pump. The decision to continue water supply can be made only if the controller verifies that the water level at the end of the next cycle will still be in the safe range $[0 \dots wl\_max\_crit]$.

We refine the abstract events of the previous refinement step to represent different alternatives of PLC behaviour. At this stage we can formulate the following invariants:

$$phase = TRANSM \wedge wl \geq wl\_max \Rightarrow signal = STOP,$$
$$phase = TRANSM \wedge wl < wl\_max \Rightarrow signal = CONT.$$

They postulate that the WTS issues the signal to stop when the parameter *wl* is approaching the critically high value (*wl_max_crit*), and vice versa. To give the system a time to react, WTS sends the stopping command to the actuators whenever the value *wl* breaches the predefined value *wl_max*.

Fourth Refinement. We model signal transmission issued by PLC to the valve and the pump. Here we model different cases of the nominal and abnormal signal transmission (including DOS attack, security failure, etc.). We incorporate a mechanism that would allow the system to transmit the signal in a secure way. In particular, we add a new component – security gateway – between the WTS and the external actuators. It can control the network access according to predefined security policies as well as inspect the packet content to detect intruder attacks and anomalies.

Fifth Refinement. Finally, we elaborate on the behaviour of the actuators. Upon receiving the command from PLC, the valve closes and the pump starts or valve opens. As a result of the last refinement step, we arrive at a sufficiently detailed formal specification to define and prove the desired system level property:

$$wl\_real \in 0 \; .. \; wl\_max\_crit.$$

The specification obtained at this step is sufficiently detailed and allows us to prove the desired safety property as a model invariant: $wl\_real \in 0 \; .. \; wl\_max\_crit$.

5.3   Discussion

In the case study, we have followed the generic development process described in Sect. 4. We had to introduce some adjustments while specifying WTS to cater to the behaviour pertaining to this particular system. However, the deviations from the generic development have been minor and hence, we believe that the proposed generic development pattern have been successfully validated.

An automated support provided by Rodin platform has been indispensable for our development. The resulting specification is quite large. Reliance on refinement helped us to cope with complexity by allowing us to gradually capture the requirements in the refinement process. We relied on both automated and interactive theorem provers integrated in Rodin platform.

There are several observations, which we made as a result of the case study. In our modelling, we have adopted an implicit discrete model of time. Namely, we define the abstract function representing the change in the dynamics of the controlled process as well as the constraints relating the components behaviour in the successive iterations. Such an approach is based on our previous experience in modelling control systems, e.g., [13].

To support reasoning about safety-security interplay, we have to explicitly model the impact of accidental and malicious faults on the system behaviour, i.e., introduce in our specification an explicit representation of failure modes. As a result, the complexity of the specification increases. To address this issue, we can rely on the modularisation approach [8].

To cope with the complexity of a formal specification, which explicitly integrates the failure behaviour, we can employ such an architectural mechanism as the mode-based reasoning, as proposed, e.g., in [9]. We can distinguish between the normal operational mode, the degraded mode caused by the accidental component failures as well as the attacked and failsafe modes. By defining and verifying such a high-level mode logic, we can facilitate a structured analysis of the complex failure behaviour.

6   Related Work and Conclusions

Research investigating safety and security interaction has received significant attention. It has been recognised that there is a need for the approaches facilitating an integrated analysis of safety and security [15, 21–23, 26]. This problem has been addressed by several techniques demonstrating how to adapt conventional techniques for analysing safety risks (e.g., FMECA, fault trees) to perform a security-informed safety analysis [5, 20]. The techniques aim at providing the engineers with a structured way to discover and analyse security vulnerabilities that have safety implications. Since the use of such techniques facilitates a systematic analysis of failure modes and results in discovering important safety and security requirements, the proposed approaches can provide a valuable input for our modelling.

There are several works that address formal analysis of safety/security requirements interactions [12, 16]. Majority of these works demonstrate also how to find conflicts between them. In our approach, we treat the problem of safety-security interplay at a more detailed level, i.e., we analyse the system architecture and investigate the impact of security failures on safe implementation of system functions. Such an approach allows us to analyse the dynamic nature of safety-security interactions. The work [16] presents on-going work on a method enabling co-engineering of security and safety requirements. It illustrates how Goal-Oriented Requirements Engineering can support co-engineering to address the safety and security dimensions in cyber-physical systems.

The distributed MILS approach [3] employs a number of advanced modelling techniques to create a platform for a formal architectural analysis of safety and security. The approach supports a powerful analysis of the properties of the data flow using model checking and facilitates derivation of security contracts. Since our approach enables incremental construction of complex distributed architectures, it would be interesting to combine these techniques to support an integrated safety-security analysis throughout the entire formal model-based system development.

In this work, we have proposed a formal approach enabling derivation of implicit security requirements from system safety goals. The proposed approach allows us to derive the constraints that should be imposed on the system to guarantee its safety even in presence of cyber-attacks. The high-level reasoning about safety-security interactions was conducted in the rely-guarantee style, which proceeded with the derivation of formal system specification in Event-B. While specifying the system, we have followed the systems approach, i.e., modelled the controlling software together with its environment. Such an approach has allowed us to systematically derive the constraints that should be imposed on components, communication channels and software to guarantee safety in the presence of accidental (due to the component failures) and security failures. A distinctive feature of our approach is a support for the integrated consideration of safety and security.

The approach presented in this work generalises the results of our experience with formal refinement-based development in the Event-B conducted in the context of verification of safety-critical control system. The results have demonstrated that the formal development significantly facilitates derivation of safety and security requirements. We have also observed that the integrated safety-security modelling in Event-B could be facilitated by the use of external tools supporting constraint solving and continuous behaviour simulation. Such an integration would be interesting to investigate in our future work.

References

1. Abrial, J.R.: Modeling in Event-B. Cambridge University Press (2010)
2. Butler, M., Jones, C., Romanovsky, A., Troubitsyna, E.: Rigorous Development of Complex Fault-Tolerant Systems. LNCS, Springer, Heidelberg (2007). https://doi.org/10.1007/11916246
3. Cimatti, A., DeLong, R., Marcantonio, D., Tonetta, S.: Combining MILS with contract-based design for safety and security requirements. In: Koornneef, F., van Gulijk, C. (eds.) SAFECOMP 2015 Workshops. LNCS, vol. 9338, pp. 264–276. Springer, Cham (2015). https://doi.org/10.1007/978-3-319-24249-1_23
4. Parnas, D.L., Madey, J.: Functional documents for computer systems. Sci. Comput. Program. **25**, 41–61 (1995)
5. Fovino, I.N., Masera, M., Cian, A.D.: Integrating cyber attacks within fault trees. Rel. Eng. Sys. Saf. **94**(9), 1394–1402 (2009)
6. Ghiasi, M., Niknam, T., Wang, Z., Mehrandezh, M., Dehghani, M., Ghadimi, N.: A comprehensive review of cyber-attacks and defense mechanisms for improving security in smart grid energy systems: past, present and future. Electr. Power Syst. Res. **215**, 108975 (2023). https://www.sciencedirect.com/science/article/pii/S0378779622010240
7. Hayes, I.J., Jackson, M.A., Jones, C.B.: Determining the specification of a control system from that of its environment. In: Araki, K., Gnesi, S., Mandrioli, D. (eds.) FME 2003. LNCS, vol. 2805. Springer, Heidelberg (2003). https://doi.org/10.1007/978-3-540-45236-2_10. https://api.semanticscholar.org/CorpusID:1077875
8. Iliasov, A., et al.: Supporting reuse in event-B development: modularisation approach. In: Frappier, M., Glässer, U., Khurshid, S., Laleau, R., Reeves, S. (eds.) ABZ 2010. LNCS, vol. 5977, pp. 174–188. Springer, Heidelberg (2010). https://doi.org/10.1007/978-3-642-11811-1_14
9. Iliasov, A., et al.: Developing mode-rich satellite software by refinement in event-B. Sci. Comput. Program. **78**(7), 884–905 (2013)
10. Jones, C.B.: Software Development: A Rigorous Approach. Prentice Hall PTR, USA (1980)
11. Stouffer, K., Falco, J., Scarfone, K.: Guide to industrial control systems (ICS) security - supervisory control and data acquisition (SCADA) systems, distributed control systems (DCS), and other control system configurations such as programmable logic controllers (PLC) (2011-06-07 2011) (2013)
12. Kriaa, S., Bouissou, M., Colin, F., Halgand, Y., Piètre-Cambacédès, L.: Safety and security interactions modeling using the BDMP formalism: case study of a PipeliLeve. In: Bondavalli, A., Di Giandomenico, F. (eds). SAFECOMP 2014. LNCS, vol. 8666, pp. 326–341. Springer, Cham (2014). https://doi.org/10.1007/978-3-319-10506-2_22

13. Laibinis, L., Troubitsyna, E.: Refinement of fault tolerant control systems in B. In: Heisel, M., Liggesmeyer, P., Wittmann, S. (eds.) SAFECOMP 2004. LNCS, vol. 3219, pp. 254–268. Springer, Cham (2004). https://doi.org/10.1007/978-3-540-30138-7_22
14. Leveson, N.G.: Safeware: System Safety and Computers. Addison-Wesley (1995)
15. Paul, S., Rioux, L.: Over 20 years of research into cybersecurity and safety engineering: a short bibliography. Saf. Secur. Eng. **VI**(335) (2015)
16. Ponsard, C., Dallons, G., Massone, P.: Goal-oriented co-engineering of security and safety requirements in cyber-physical systems. In: Skavhaug, A., Guiochet, J., Schoitsch, E., Bitsch, F. (eds.) SAFECOMP 2016. LNCS, vol. 9923, pp. 334–345. Springer, Cham (2016). https://doi.org/10.1007/978-3-319-45480-1_27
17. Rocchetto, M., Tippenhauer, N.O.: CPDY: extending the Dolev-Yao attacker with physical-layer interactions. In: Ogata, K., Lawford, M., Liu, S. (eds.) ICFEM 2016. LNCS, vol. 10009, pp. 175–192. Springer, Cham (2016). https://doi.org/10.1007/978-3-319-47846-3_12
18. Rodin: Event-B platform. http://www.event-b.org/
19. Romanovsky, A., Thomas, M.: Industrial Deployment of System Engineering Methods. Springer, Heidelberg (2013). https://doi.org/10.1007/978-3-642-33170-1
20. Schmittner, C., Ma, Z., Smith, P.: FMVEA for safety and security analysis of intelligent and cooperative vehicles. In: Bondavalli, A., Ceccarelli, A., Ortmeier, F. (eds.) SAFECOMP 2014. LNCS, vol. 8696, pp. 282–288. Springer, Cham (2014). https://doi.org/10.1007/978-3-319-10557-4_31
21. Troubitsyna, E., Laibinis, L., Pereverzeva, I., Kuismin, T., Ilic, D., Latvala, T.: Towards security-explicit formal modelling of safety-critical systems. In: Skavhaug, A., Guiochet, J., Bitsch, F. (eds.) SAFECOMP 2016. LNCS, vol. 9922, pp. 213–225. Springer, Cham (2016). https://doi.org/10.1007/978-3-319-45477-1_17
22. Vistbakka, I., Troubitsyna, E.: Towards a formal approach to analysing security of safety-critical systems. In: EDCC 2018, pp. 182–189. IEEE Computer Society (2018)
23. Vistbakka, I., Troubitsyna, E., Kuismin, T., Latvala, T.: Co-engineering safety and security in industrial control systems: a formal outlook. In: Romanovsky, A., Troubitsyna, E. (eds.) SERENE 2017. LNCS, vol. 10479, pp. 96–114. Springer, Cham (2017). https://doi.org/10.1007/978-3-319-65948-0_7
24. Vreman, N., Pazzaglia, P., Magron, V., Wang, J., Maggio, M.: Stability of linear systems under extended weakly-hard constraints. IEEE Control Syst. Lett. **6**, 2900–2905 (2021)
25. Yadav, G., Paul, K.: Architecture and security of SCADA systems: a review. Int. J. Crit. Infrastruct. Prot. **34**, 100433 (2021)
26. Young, W., Leveson, N.G.: An integrated approach to safety and security based on systems theory. Commun. ACM **57**(2), 31–35 (2014)

About Trust and Proof: An Experimental Framework for Heterogeneous Verification

Farah Al Wardani[iD], Kaustuv Chaudhuri[iD], and Dale Miller[✉][iD]

Inria Saclay and LIX, Institut Polytechnique de Paris, Palaiseau, France
dale.miller@inria.fr

Abstract. Information and opinions come to us daily from a wide range of actors, including scientists, journalists, and pundits. Some actors may be biased or malicious, while others rely on physical measurements, statistics, or in-depth research. Some sources may be signed or edited, while others are anonymous and unmoderated. Trusting information from such diverse sources is a serious challenge facing society today. In this paper, we will describe another domain—the world of machine-checked logic and mathematics—in which many similar issues can appear but in which tractable solutions are possible. Many actors (people or software systems) assert that certain logical statements are theorems in this domain. We describe the Distributed Assertion Management Framework (DAMF) that explicitly manages claims by theorem provers that they have proved certain theorems from associated contexts. Provers willing to trust other provers will be able to avoid rechecking proofs.

1 Introduction

Confidence in formal methods to provide significant practical benefits in the construction of digital infrastructure goes back several decades and is illustrated by the following quote by Cliff Jones in 1987: "Of the many problems presented by the development of major computer systems, some can be ameliorated using formal methods [24]". Today's society is deeply integrated with powerful computer systems like the World Wide Web and cloud-based computing. While concerns about faulty implementations persist in the decades since 1987, novel challenges have emerged. A particularly pressing concern involves the trustworthiness of information and data that rapidly and fluidly traverses the globe. This paper considers how formal methods and trust might influence each other.

2 Trust Crisis in the Digital World

Trust in our understanding of how the world functions has been a long standing problem. An early chapter in systematically addressing such trust dates back to Sir Francis Bacon's introduction of the scientific method—with its focus on reproducible results—and the creed *Nullius in verba* (take no one's word for it): that is, before trusting something, check it for yourself. In human affairs different

© The Author(s), under exclusive license to Springer Nature Switzerland AG 2024
A. Cavalcanti and J. Baxter (Eds.): *The Practice of Formal Methods*, LNCS 14781, pp. 162–183, 2024.
https://doi.org/10.1007/978-3-031-66673-5_9

from those involving scientific experimentation and the analysis of data, other methods of gaining trust involved the inventions of such social institutions as judges, magistrates, and jury trials. In recent centuries, trust in the world of politics and foreign affairs is often offered by a limited number of media organizations acting as gatekeepers of information for which there was an economic incentive to maintain the trustworthiness of their media products.

In today's internet-dominated world, information flows freely and without gatekeepers, but trust is scarce. Our current experience of attempting to trust information in the internet era is made worse by the existence of various individuals, groups, and governments who deliberately carry out propaganda and misinformation campaigns. For example, the RAND Corporation described Russian propaganda tactics used during the 2016 USA presidential election as a "Firehose of Falsehood" [36]. This technique involves generating a large volume of false or misleading information and spreading it rapidly and repeatedly across multiple channels, such as newspapers, social media, and online forums. Often, the goal of this tactic is not to convince an audience about specific policies but rather to overwhelm the audience, sow confusion, and make it difficult to distinguish facts from fiction. There are also perverse financial incentives for media agencies to fuel misinformation campaigns by prioritizing clicks and revenue over truth.

While Internet technology has enabled the rapid composing and global distribution of information and misinformation, it has also created another shift in the media world: almost all media is now in electronic form. This shift makes it possible to consider the following approach to addressing misinformation.

Agents should cryptographically sign the information sources they produce. Consumers of information should maintain curated *allow-lists* of agents they have explicitly or provisionally chosen to trust.

Of course, the remarkable naivety of this approach will certainly stop people from considering it seriously. However, history shows that exploring "naive" solutions can lead to unexpected breakthroughs. Consider the following two seemingly naive-sounding ideas: both are problems that the digital era has forced society to consider and for which digital solutions have been proposed.

– **Problem:** Your mobile phone gives out too much information about you and your location. **Solution:** Have your phone lie for you. This approach is at the heart of *differential privacy*, which studies how the degree of lying can affect the utility of the data collected from multiple users [17].
– **Problem:** The binary file you plan to download could be a security risk on your computer. **Solution:** Require that that code is paired with a formal proof that it is not dangerous. This approach has been studied under the title *proof-carrying code* [32].

We now add the following problem and solution pair.

– **Problem:** Worried that the documents you get are forged, fake, or generated by an internet bot farm. **Solution:** Have all documents cryptographically signed by their authors. This problem and the proposed solution is the starting point for this paper.

It is worth noting that the sign-everything-by-trusted-parties approach is used in some computer systems. For example, the secure booting of computers can be accomplished with the UEFI (Unified Extensible Firmware Interface) framework, which is designed to prevent the loading of unauthorized software during the boot process of a computer. All code that is eventually loaded into a machine's firmware and memory is signed by agents whose public keys are on an allow-list [34]. Another example is Debian's SecureApt, which secures the `apt` manager in Debian Linux distributions. It uses cryptographic signatures to verify the integrity and authenticity of packages downloaded from software repositories, ensuring that what is installed is genuine and unmodified software [14].

3   A Shift in Scope to Trust Within Theorem Proving

We (the authors) have insufficient expertise to address the crisis in trust described above. This crisis is vast and multifaceted: if a comprehensive solution is possible, then expertise beyond computer science will certainly be needed. However, since our expertise is limited to computer science, we will significantly narrow the scope of our focus in this paper. In particular, some problems surrounding trust in the digital world reappear in mechanized proof-checking systems, where we have more expertise. This paper focuses on the following two goals: (1) to determine how trust within the theorem-proving community can be addressed, and (2) to explore the costs and benefits of a particular approach to managing trusting relationships.

The beginning of *proof checking* can be traced back to at least 1666, when Leibniz envisioned that there could be a universal symbolic language (*characteristica universalis*) for stating propositions and that two people who were arguing over the veracity of some particular statement could agree on *calculemus* ("Let us calculate"). The result of such a calculation would indicate which person was making the correct statement [40].

A more modern effort at proof-checking can be found in the work of Gordon, Milner, & Wadsworth in 1979, where proofs in the *logic for computational functions* (LCF) were built in a programmable system using an early version of the ML functional programming language [20]. Since those early days, a great many interactive theorem-proving systems have been built, a short list of which includes nqthm (a.k.a. Boyer-Moore theorem prover) [11], Isabelle [33,37], Coq [10], HOL [21], PVS [35], Abella [7], and Lean [28].

It is now common to hear of large and complex formal proofs being built for mathematical theorems or computer system properties. Such proofs can involve many people working over many years. Even in that setting, most of the theorem provers used in such tasks are *autarkic*: they only trust their proof-checking kernels. Conversely, some theorem provers in the domain of program verification have been designed to exploit and explicitly trust specific, special-purpose theorem provers. For example, the Why3 prover relies on external theorem provers, such as Coq, and SMT solvers, such as CVC4 and Z3, to discharge verification conditions. Also, the TLA+ Proof System (TLAPS) relies on back-end provers, such as Isabelle and Zenon, and SMT solvers, such as CVC3, Yices, and Z3. In general, however, provers are not designed to trust other provers.

The implemented logical framework Dedukti [6] is an interesting component in the space of theorem-proving systems. Dedukti provides a simple but expressive logic and proof system based on a small logical core (dependently typed λ-calculus with rewriting). Its simplicity makes it relatively easy to implement a proof checker and trust its correctness; in particular, a skeptic could reimplement it. This system can provide an independent, secondary proof checker for other provers that can output significant parts of their proof libraries (e.g., HOL, Isabelle, Coq) [15]. Such independent proof checking offers more confidence in proofs. In practice, however, once a proof is available in a rather explicit and straightforward format such as that offered by Dedukti, it is not a big step to formally print Dedukti proofs into a range of other proof formats. Thus, if prover A wants to use a proof by prover B, the latter prover outputs its proof to Dedukti, which can then print that proof in a format that prover A can check. As a result of this role of Dedukti, prover A does not need to trust either Dedukti or prover B. Thus, Dedukti can be used to maintain the autarkic environment of provers. The framework we describe in this paper is orthogonal to systems like Dedukti since we may wish to trust a theorem prover even if no formal proof certificate is made available.

4   "Trust Requires Proof" vs "Proof Requires Trust"

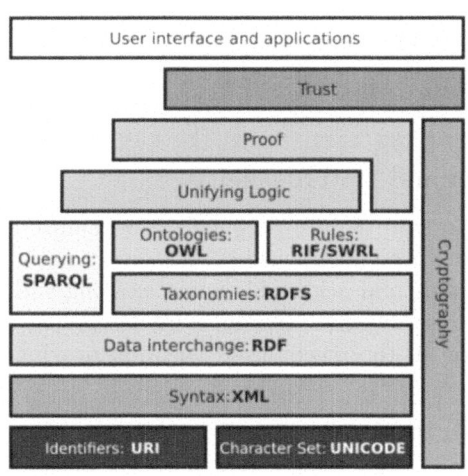

Fig. 1. The semantic web stack

We are all familiar with the implication that the existence of proofs can instill trust in the veracity of statements. This "trust requires proof" perspective has been a part of mathematics since at least the times of Euclid. This perspective has also been promulgated in the design of the *semantic web stack* [9], which is displayed in Fig. 1. In that stack, cryptography provides some notion of trust (via digital signatures, for example) while proofs of logical statements based on taxonomies and database queries provide the bulk of trust. Presumably, the proofs involved in the semantic web will be significantly more shallow than those involved in modern mathematics and program verification.

In the rest of this paper, we shall, however, explore the converse perspective, namely, that "proof requires trust". This perspective arises from the following two facts.

1. Formal proofs are generally large and detailed objects; they can only be checked by computer programs.
2. Computer programs and their executions can be wrong.

Indeed, carefully designed and constructed proof checkers have been found to have errors, usually leading to proofs of false. We must speak explicitly about trusting proof checkers.

5   Establishing a Design in a Distributed Context

In this section, we reiterate over the analogy made in Sect. 3, between problems surrounding trust in the digital world and in the world of mechanized proof-checking systems. We illustrate how they should be considered similarly in a distributed and heterogeneous setting, and then set the stepping stone for our investigation.

The following example illustrates a typical approach to using a proof assistant. Consider that one wants to build a formal and machine-checked proof that the number $\zeta(3) = \sum_{i=1}^{\infty} \frac{1}{i^3}$ is irrational. (A three-page proof outline was published in 1978 by Apéry [5] and a more complete proof was eventually developed by others; see [39] for a description of that development). The process of developing a formal proof of this result is described in [29]. As documented there, a particular prover is chosen (in this case, Coq), along with a specific set of definitions and theorems already verified within Coq (in this case, the Mathematical Components libraries). While the authors utilized additional computer tools like Maple to help organize the Coq proof; these tools were not relied upon for verification. In the end, all computation and deduction steps were achieved within Coq, and, as a result, only Coq needed to be trusted for the verification of Apéry's Theorem.

5.1   Considerations for Distribution and Heterogeneity

As exemplified by the scenario above, the traditional approach to mechanized theorem proving in mathematics is autarkic. In today's world, alternatives to centralized systems and authorities are desirable and achievable using existing and well-understood technologies. We briefly describe three reasons why heterogeneity and distribution are worth considering in the mechanized theorem-proving context.

1. Logic and proof serve diverse purposes, ranging from their uses in programming, type systems, model checking, SAT and UNSAT solving, and mechanized theorem proving. Expecting a single proof-checking kernel to handle all of these uses equally seems undesirable since the computational demands of checking proofs in these various domains can vary greatly. For example, type checking generally requires unification, while checking UNSAT proofs often requires optimizing memory storage. Expecting one checker to provide good performance on both of these dimensions while also being simple enough to inspect for a lack of errors seems unreasonable.

2. Generally, people already trust several agents in a passive sense. For instance, users within the Coq community that use the Coq standard libraries do not believe or claim that the theorems developed by the Isabelle community, curated in the Isabelle standard libraries, are wrong. We propose extending this trust paradigm to an active form, enabling users to reference and depend explicitly on externally proved theorems. Such enabling leads to distributed trust, where multiple entities, not just a single one, contribute to the trust foundation of a formal development.

3. Having advocated for enabling a common context that incorporates diverse expression forms, verification procedures, and interacting agents, it naturally leads us to consider an alternative approach for constructing libraries of formal developments. In this new paradigm, structures become emergent and interconnected rather than hierarchical and isolated. Provers, previously packaged with their own libraries, transition to the edge, acting as tools for certifying results. Consequently, curation processes no longer inherently depend on specific provers. Instead, the fact that a theorem within a curation has been formally certified, whether by a single agent or a combination of agents and tools, becomes simply another piece of information to be conveyed.

5.2 Off-the-Shelf, Enabling Technologies Used by DAMF

After establishing why we are addressing the *non-autarkic* approach to theorem proving in a *distributed* and *heterogeneous* context, we proceed by asking two simple questions: How can we allow a user of one theorem prover to be able to reuse and refer to a theorem proved in another theorem prover by another *agent*? How can such a scenario keep track of dependencies and multiple agents in a clear, verifiable, reproducible, and, thus, trustable manner?

We now describe our system, the *Distributed Assertion Management Framework* (DAMF) [4], which provides structures that track who and what is being trusted. As its name implies, DAMF centers around the concept of assertions. When an agent produces a result or makes a claim, that agent generates an assertion to allow others to do one of the following. *Reuse the information with trust*: this option involves trusting the agent and accepting the information without further verification. *Simply reference the information*: users can refer to the information without necessarily trusting the agent. An assertion acts like a stamp attached to the information, signifying the agent's statement: "You can trust me if you want to use this information without further verification." Technically, an assertion is a signed claim. DAMF employs various readily available technologies, the most important of which are described next.

Public-Key Cryptography. Assertions link two pieces of information: *who* makes a claim, and *what* is claimed. In DAMF, the *who* is called an *agent*, and an agent is identified by a public-private key pair. The private key is used to sign the content of the claim, and the public key is used to validate that signature. Public-key cryptography is used in DAMF because it is tamper-resistant and associates the signature with a globally identifiable signer. As such, assertions are independent information units that do not need to be tracked back to their source for verification. Typical examples of agents are human users or automated proof-checking services provided by a cloud computing platform. Different users using the same tool are naturally considered distinct agents. On the other hand, a single user using different tools may be associated with multiple keys, considered as multiple agents.

Content-Addressable, Distributed Storage: IPFS. Sharing information in a distributed setting traditionally relies on the internet, particularly the web, where resources are referenced by URLs pointing to their location on specific servers. However, this use of the web is problematic for at least a couple of reasons: the content of a URL can be altered, compromising the trustworthiness of any links pointing to it, and server outages can render information inaccessible. Content-addressed storage offers a solution to those shortcomings since it identifies information using a cryptographic hash, essentially a unique digital fingerprint. This use of hashes separates information from its physical location, eliminating the issues associated with location-based addressing. This decoupling also aligns well with the considerations of DAMF, as will be elaborated in subsequent sections. These sections will define specific objects, each uniquely identified by its content and equally retrievable from multiple locations. Issues arising from potential name conflicts (for instance, two different objects being given the same name by two agents unaware of each other) and with circular dependencies are naturally avoided.

The InterPlanetary File System (IPFS) [8] provides the necessary infrastructure to interact with and leverage a content-addressed protocol within our DAMF implementation. The next section showcases an example of an assertion object in IPFS, identified by its Content Identifier (`cid`) and represented as JSON:[1]

```
// cid: bafyreiek2t75whn7gi6ygrymegguescqi4iudjj56ui..
{ "format": "assertion",
  "agent": "-----BEGIN PUBLIC KEY-----\nMFIwEA...",
  "signature": "3040021e10db76a6606d7a813747849028c79e..."
  "claim": {"/": "bafyreibvtxzqhvht5rfxpw3rkgx..." } }
```

Notice the `"claim"` attribute: its value represents an *IPLD Link*[2] to another object stored in IPFS. The above *assertion* object represents a DAG with nodes that can be traversed from the root object or accessed separately by their `cid`: adding `/claim` to the mentioned link in the footnote returns the referenced *claim* object, and so on. This use of linked data proves to be an essential enabling mechanism in the implementation of DAMF. For instance, presenting the *claim* as a separate, independent object *linked* from the assertion structure instead of being included directly within it allows a clear, transparent representation of multiple agents asserting the same claim.

---

[1] Can be accessed through this link.

[2] InterPlanetary Linked Data; a way to represent linked data in IPFS.

6   Designing **DAMF**: Structures and Main Concepts

We mentioned in Sect. 5 that *assertions* are the principal concept in DAMF. The main kind of assertions addressed in our current development is meant to denote asserting whether a *formula* is a proved *theorem*, a *conjecture*, or a theorem that depends on some *lemma*, where that lemma is also a *formula*. We thus need a clear representation of a *formula* object, which we describe first.

6.1   Languages, Contexts, and Formulas

To be as general as possible, we represent the formulas used in assertions as *strings*, i.e., in a format suitable as an input to a parser of the source proof system. In order to determine that the input is well-formed, the source proof system may need further information about the *features*—symbols, predicates, functions, types, notations, hints, etc.—used in the formula. Such additional information is the *context* of the formula, which we represent as a document fragment in the language of the source proof system.

For example, take the following theorem written in Coq 8.16.1:

```
1    Definition lincomb (n j k : nat) := exists x y, n = x * j + y * k.
2    Theorem ex_coq : forall n:nat, 8 <= n -> lincomb n 3 5.
```

The formula corresponding to the theorem ex_coq is the literal string "forall n:nat, ⋯ lincomb n 3 5" . The symbols 8, <= , etc. are part of the standard prelude of this language, and the symbol lincomb is defined in line 1, so a sufficient context necessary for Coq 8.16.1 to parse and type-check the theorem statement is the text of line 1, which is also written in the Coq 8.16.1 language.

Abstractly, a *formula object* in DAMF is a triple (L, Σ, F) where L denotes a *language*, Σ denotes a *context*, and F denotes a *formula*, all of which may conceptually be thought of as strings. We will use the schematic variable N to range over such formula objects. The language L is a canonical identifier (specifically, the cid of a DAMF language object) which may optionally represent information about a suitable loader for the language that will make sense of the strings Σ and F; DAMF compares languages just by their identifiers. Moreover, L is interpreted as defining all the globally available features; for instance, the symbol nat is part of the standard prelude of this version of Coq and should therefore be understood as being defined in the language Coq 8.16.1. The context Σ introduces any user-defined features such as the definition lincomb above that is not part of Coq's standard prelude.

Note that DAMF formula objects are considered to be *closed*, i.e., every symbol used in the formula is defined in the language or the context. From the perspective of DAMF, a formula object is an atomic entity. Additionally, DAMF does not need to be aware of any reasoning principles of the language or context components. For instance, no mechanism in DAMF would allow the substitution of a declared symbol in the context with a concrete definition. The purpose of differentiating a formula object into three parts is purely pragmatic: the language part will in most cases be a well known object used by many agents, and the context part may potentially be shared between multiple assertions. DAMF consumers may be able to use this sharing of information to consolidate tasks such as context-processing.

6.2   Sequents, Productions, and Assertions

A *sequent* in DAMF is abstractly of the form $N_1, \ldots, N_k \vdash N_0$ where each of the N_i is a DAMF formula object defined in the previous subsection. We will use the schematic variable Γ to range over ordered lists of formula objects, and S to range over sequents. In a sequent $\Gamma \vdash N$, we say that N is the *conclusion* and Γ are the *dependencies*. Such sequent objects may be produced whenever a formal proof has been checked in a proof checker: the conclusion represents the statement of the theorem, and the dependencies are external lemmas that were used during that proof.

A sequent is a purely mathematical object: if a reader knows the languages the formulas in the sequent are built from, they can understand the meaning of the sequent. Most sequents will be *produced* by particular agents and using particular tools. Thus, DAMF has the concept of a *production* object that enriches an underlying DAMF sequent with the metadata necessary to reliably determine how the sequent was produced. This is known in DAMF as a *mode*, which can be one of the following:

- **null**, which denotes the *absence* of any mode information. If an agent signs such a production, then they assume direct and full responsibility for its correctness.
- a *tag* such as **"axiom"** or **"conjecture"**, which is like **null** except that the intended purpose of the sequent is made clear. For instance, a **"conjecture"** tagged production would mean that any agent who signs that assertion does not assert its truth directly.
- a *tool* link, which would generally be a link to a DAMF *tool* object that we do not elaborate further in this paper. Suffice it to say that any well known system would have a similarly well known DAMF tool object.

We write DAMF productions abstractly as $\Gamma \vdash_M B$ where $\Gamma \vdash B$ is an abstract DAMF sequent and M denotes the mode.

The mere fact that a production is tagged with a tool mode does not guarantee that the tool indeed was used to produce the sequent in the first place. In DAMF, the only entities that can make such guarantees are *agents*. Abstractly, an agent is a globally unique name; we use the schematic variable K to range over agents. Agents will be implemented as public-private key pairs.

We define a simple multi-sorted first-order logic where agents and sequents are primitive sorts and where the infix predicate *says* is the sole predicate; the atomic formula K *says* P, where K is an agent and P a production, is an *assertion*. The *says* predicate is implemented in DAMF using public-key cryptography. In a DAMF-aware proof system, the assertion K *says* $(N_1, \ldots, N_k \vdash_M N_0)$ is interpreted as follows:

- The pair (K, M) of the agent and the mode is treated as *trusted*. If the agent cannot be trusted for some reason, such as if K occurs in a deny list, then the assertion is unusable. Likewise, if M cannot be trusted in isolation, such as if M denotes a version of a tool known to be unsound, then the assertion is unusable. Separating agents and modes allows consumers of assertions to tailor their trust parameters to particular agents; for example, they can trust all modes for a reliable agent, or they can restrict a given agent to only those modes that they are reliable with. Note that the agent signs the entire production, including the mode, to prevent tampering of the assertions by third parties.
- The conclusion of the assertion, N_0, contains the formula representing the lemma to be used in the DAMF-aware proof system. Note, in particular, that the dependencies $N_1, \ldots, N_k$ are not relevant when using this assertion as an external dependency.

In the remainder of this paper, we will omit the modes unless relevant to simplify the presentation.

6.3 Adapters

Because every formula object packages the formula together with its context and language identifier, every formula object is independent of every other formula object. Thus, in a sequent $N_1 \vdash N_0$, there is no requirement that the conclusion N_0 and the dependency N_1 be in the same language or have a common context. When working within a single autarkic system (e.g., a proof checker using a single logic), the sequents that are generated for every theorem will probably place the conclusion and dependencies in the same language and context; however, in the wider non-autarkic world, we can use multilingual sequents as first class entities that are documented and tracked the same way as any other kind of sequent.

An important class of multilingual sequents comes from *adapters*. In order for a theorem written in the Coq 8.16.1 language to be used by a different system with a different language, say Abella 2.0.9, we will need to transform the formula objects in the former language to those in the latter language. This kind of translation is an example of a *language adapter*, which falls into the general class of *adapters*, and which creates a sequent by translating between languages or modifying the logical context by standard logical operations such as weakening (adding extra symbols), instantiation (replacing a symbol by a term), or unfolding (replacing a defined symbol by its definition).

As an example, the Coq 8.16.1 example above can be translated to the Abella 2.0.9 language as follows, where the function symbols + and * are replaced by relations in Abella.

```
1  Import "nats". % some natural numbers library
2  Define lincomb : nat -> nat -> nat -> prop by
3     lincomb N J K := exists X Y U V,
4        times X J U /\ times Y K V /\ plus U V N.
5  Theorem ex_ab : forall n, nat n -> le 8 n -> lincomb n 3 5.
```

Lines 1–4 determine the context $\Sigma_{\text{ex\_ab}}$ for the formula ex_ab on line 5. The sequent that represents this translation therefore has the form

$$(\text{Coq 8.16.1}, \Sigma_{\text{ex\_coq}}, \text{ex\_coq}) \vdash (\text{Abella 2.0.9}, \Sigma_{\text{ex\_ab}}, \text{ex\_ab}).$$

Suppose agent K_1 signs this translation and that agent K_2 signs the sequent $\vdash (\text{Coq 8.16.1}, \Sigma_{\text{ex\_coq}}, \text{ex\_coq})$. As long as K_1 and K_2 are trusted by the user of Abella 2.0.9, then the formula object $(\text{Abella 2.0.9}, \Sigma_{\text{ex\_ab}}, \text{ex\_ab})$ can also be treated as a theorem by that user thanks to *composition*, discussed next.

6.4   Composing Assertions, Trust

Assertions will be composed by means of a single rule of inference that implements a cut-like rule for sequents, COMPOSE.

$$\frac{K \text{ says } (\Gamma_1 \vdash M) \qquad K \text{ says } (M, \Gamma_2 \vdash N)}{K \text{ says } (\Gamma_1, \Gamma_2 \vdash N)} \text{ COMPOSE}$$

The effect of this rule means that the *says* predicate does not correspond one-to-one with cryptographic signatures. The conclusion of the COMPOSE rule may not be a sequent explicitly signed by agent K even if both premises are. Instead, the rule states that whenever K can be said to reliably claim, *either* by a cryptographic signature *or* by a COMPOSE-derivation tree, that both $\Gamma_1 \vdash M$ and $M, \Gamma_2 \vdash N$, then K must also reliably claim $\Gamma_1, \Gamma_2 \vdash N$.

There are many variations to *access control logic* in the literature. For example, some such logics use inference rules such as:

$$\frac{\Gamma \vdash N}{K \text{ says } (\Gamma \vdash N)} \quad \text{or} \quad \frac{K \text{ says } (\Gamma \vdash N)}{K \text{ says } (K \text{ says } (\Gamma \vdash N))}.$$

Such rules are neither syntactically well-formed nor desirable for our purposes. We use here a very weak access control logic (see [1] for a survey of such logics). Instead, checking the validity of a given derivation using COMPOSE is computationally trivial: each instance of it must eliminate exactly the leftmost dependency in the second premise, which is a DAMF formula object that is compared by cid.

Observe that the agent K does not participate in a meaningful way in a derivation that is built with the COMPOSE rule. Thus, for a given end sequent of the form $K \text{ says } (\vdash N)$, a COMPOSE derivation can be seen as a *proof outline* for the desired theorem N, with the leaves of the derivation being the assertions that need to be sourced from an assertion database (such as the DAMF global store). We say that an assertion $(K \text{ says } S)$ is *published* if it can be retrieved from such a database. The inference system is then enlarged with the following rule that can be used to complete the open leaves of the COMPOSE derivation using assertions made by different agents.

$$\frac{(K_1 \text{ says } S) \text{ is published}}{K_2 \text{ says } S} \text{ TRUST } [K_1 \mapsto K_2]$$

This rule is parameterized by a pair of agents, K_1 and K_2, and is understood to be applicable only when K_1 is in the user-specified *allow list* of K_2 (i.e., K_1 *speaks for* K_2, which we write as $[K_1 \mapsto K_2]$).

We do not assume that agents have any additional closure properties beyond COMPOSE and TRUST. For example, suppose N_A, $N_{A \to B}$, and N_B are the formula objects that correspond to the formulas A, $A \to B$, and B respectively in some language. We do not assume that the following rule is admissible:

$$\frac{K \text{ says } (\Gamma \vdash N_{A \to B}) \qquad K \text{ says } (\Gamma \vdash N_A)}{K \text{ says } (\Gamma \vdash N_B)} \text{ MP.}$$

That is, we do not assume that the formulas asserted by agent K are closed under modus ponens. Similarly, we do not assume that what agents assert are closed by substitution or instantiation of any symbols that are defined in the contexts of the formula objects. While a particular agent may not be closed under modus ponens, substitution, or instantiation, it is possible to employ other agents that can look for opportunities to apply such inference rules on the results of trusted agents. In particular, if we want the query engine to be able to use the MP rule, then the engine must construct an agent K_{MP} whose sole function is to generate assertions such as $K_{\text{MP}} \text{ says } (N_{A \to B}, N_A \vdash N_B)$ that correspond to applications of the MP rule. Of course, K_{MP} will need to be in the *allow list* for any agent wanting to use this agent.

7 Experiment: A Heterogeneous Verification Using Abella, Coq, and λProlog

This section presents a complete example of proving the following theorem in Abella [7] by trusting external lemmas from Coq and λProlog [30]:

For $n \in \mathbb{N}$, $\text{fib}(n) = n^2$ if and only if $n \in \{0, 1, 12\}$ where $\text{fib}(n)$ denotes the nth Fibonacci number.

The purpose of this example is to illustrate the communication with DAMF and the various edge provers, so the theorem itself is not particularly challenging. Nevertheless, a complete proof of this theorem inside Abella would currently require formalizing a sizable amount of integer arithmetic, not to mention automated tactics for reasoning about arithmetic. Since Coq has these components already, we will use Coq to prove the following theorem by making heavy use of its linear arithmetic solvers:

For $n \in \mathbb{N}$, if $n \geq 13$ then $\text{fib}(n) > n^2$.

On the other hand, we will use λProlog to find all the pairs $\langle n, m \rangle$ where $\text{fib}(n) = m$ and $n \in \{0, 1, \ldots, 12\}$. We could of course have used Coq to perform these computations as well, but it is pedagogically useful to see an example that combines both functional and relational programming.

Our DAMF implementation's architecture consists of a global layer stored in IPFS. This layer stores DAMF global objects, such as formulas and sequents, that any participating agent can create, publish, and access. Instead of requiring provers to interact directly with IPFS, we have implemented Dispatch, an optional intermediary tool. Dispatch acts as a bridge between edge provers/tools and the global layer. It provides standardized input and output formats corresponding to specific DAMF objects, simplifying system interaction. A DAMF-aware prover must only build and parse specific JSON objects into and from theory files. Dispatch is designed for human and tool use and currently implements the publishing and retrieval of DAMF objects to and from the global store. It also implements a lookup facility that can enumerate paths that yield some theorem starting from a given set of assertions and report the pairs *(agent, mode)* corresponding to assertions along each path, along with any remaining dependencies. Both DAMF global objects and the dispatch tool are designed to be adaptable and expandable.

Further details on this example can be found through the *distributed assertions website.*[3]

7.1   Setup in Abella

Abella has no built in notion of natural numbers. We therefore begin an Abella development (in a .thm file) by declaring the nat type together with its constructors z and s to obtain a unary representation for natural numbers. The Abella type system is only used for syntactic checks and yields no induction principles for logical reasoning, so we have to define an auxiliary inductively defined relation, also called nat, that is used for inductive reasoning. In Abella, the namespaces of types and predicates are separate, so the same name nat can be used both for type names and for predicate names. Finally, because Abella uses only λ-equivalence as its equational theory of simply-typed λ-terms, we will have to capture recursive computations in the form of relations; thus, operations such as addition and multiplication, and relations such as $\leq$, are defined using inductively defined relations. Even the Fibonacci function will be encoded using a binary relation. Thus, our Abella development begins as follows.

```
1   %% FibExample.thm
2   Kind nat type.
3   Type z nat.
4   Type s nat -> nat.
5   % nat X ≡ X is a natural number
6   Define nat : nat -> prop by nat z ; nat (s X) := nat X.
7   % le X Y ≡ X ≤ Y
8   Define le : nat -> nat -> prop by le z X ; le (s X) (s Y)
        := le X Y.
9   % lt X Y ≡ X < Y
10  Define lt : nat -> nat -> prop by ···
11  % plus X Y Z ≡ Z = X + Y
12  Define plus : nat -> nat -> nat -> prop by ···
```

---

[3] https://doi.org/10.5281/zenodo.11163505.

```
13  % times X Y Z ≡ Z = X × Y
14  Define times : nat -> nat -> nat -> prop by ···
```

The nth Fibonacci number is defined in Abella relationally as well:

```
15  Define fib : nat -> nat -> prop by
16  ; fib z z ; fib (s z) (s z)
17  ; fib (s (s X)) N := exists L M, fib X L /\ fib (s X) M /\
        plus L M N.
```

7.2 Using λProlog to Compute Ground Instances

While Abella has a logic programming engine, which implements a fragment of λProlog, as part of its search tactic, it is inefficient and cumbersome to use. We could improve this implementation in Abella, but we could also use a trusted external λProlog engine such as Teyjus [41] or ELPI [16]. In λProlog, we can define the nat type and the predicates plus and fib analogously to the Abella formulation above.

```
1  %% fib.sig: type, term, and predicate constants
2  sig fib.
3    kind nat type. type z nat. type s nat -> nat.
4    type plus nat -> nat -> nat -> o.
5    type fib  nat -> nat -> o.
```

```
1  %% fib.mod: program clauses for predicates
2  module fib.
3    plus z X X.
4    plus (s X) Y (s Z) :- plus X Y Z.
5    fib z z. fib (s z) (s z).
6    fib (s (s X)) N :- fib X L, fib (s X) M, plus L M N.
```

With this definition, we can ask a λProlog engine to solve fib goals where the first argument is ground. We can also, of course, check that a given ground predicate is indeed derivable. We have instrumented a variant of the Teyjus implementation of λProlog to produce a Dispatch assertion (i.e., in the input language of Dispatch) for such checks. For example, the above check will be written as the following JSON object.

```
1   { "format": "assertion", "agent": "exampleAgent",
2     "claim": {
3       "format": "annotated-production",
4       "annotation": {"name": "fib5"},
5       "production": {
6         "mode": "damf:bafyreic3...",
7         "sequent": { "conclusion": "fib5", "dependencies":
              [] } } },
8     "formulas": {
9       "fib5": {
10        "language": "damf:bafyreibv...",
11        "content": "fib (s (s (s (s (s z))))) ...",
```

```
12            "context": ["fib"] } },
13       "contexts": {
14          "fib": {
15             "language": "damf:bafyreibv...",
16             "content": [
17                – contents of fib.sig as a string – ,
18                – contents of fib.mod as a string –
19             ] } } }
```

The "language" values in lines 10 and 15 are understood to be canonical references to a DAMF object referencing the language of λProlog. Similarly, the "mode" value in line 6 is a canonical reference to a DAMF object describing the Teyjus implementation. The "agent" value in line 1 is the name of some agent profile created by running dispatch create-agent; Dispatch uses the private key of this agent profile to sign the assertion when publishing it to DAMF. This JSON object claims that a specific version of the Teyjus implementation of λProlog has computed the fifth Fibonacci number to be 5.

7.3   Proving Arithmetic Facts in Coq

The lemma we are ultimately interested in depends on fairly significant arithmetic reasoning. We will use Coq's linear integer arithmetic solver lia to write fairly straightforward proofs of the lemma. However, in Coq we will define fib not as a binary relation but as a recursively defined fixed point with one argument. The Coq v. 8.16.1 development is shown below, with proofs elided.

```
1  Fixpoint fib (n : nat) :=
2     match n with 0 => 0 | S j =>
3        match j with 0 => 1 | S k => fib j + fib k end end.
4  Theorem fib_square_lemma : forall n, 2 * n + 27 <= fib (n + 12).   ···
5  Theorem fib_square_above : forall n, 13 <= n -> n ^ 2 < fib n.   ···
```

These proofs are built using the linear integer arithmetic solver lia in the proofs that is distributed with Coq.

7.4   Adapting λProlog and Coq Sequents for Abella

Taking stock, we have ground facts built in the higher-order logic programming language λProlog using the tool Teyjus, and a lemma about the rate of growth of the Fibonacci function written in the calculus of inductive constructions using the tool Coq. Obviously, neither of these languages correspond to the language $\mathcal{G}$ that forms the basis of the Abella theorem prover. Thus, we need adapters for translating these external dependencies to Abella's language.

These adapters can, in principle, be quite sophisticated; for instance, they can be written using Dedukti. For illustration purposes in the present paper, we adapt the sequents by hand by asserting in Abella the intended translation at the point of importing the assertion. Imagine, for instance, that the fib5 assertion shown in Sect. 7.2 is given the cid: bafyreifu.... Here is how we would import it in Abella:

```
18  %% FibExample.thm continuing...
19  Import "damf:bafyreifu..." as
20  Theorem fib5: fib (s (s (s (s (s z))))) (s (s (s (s (s
        z))))).
```

From the perspective of Abella, this looks just like an ordinary `Theorem` statement, except there is no proof that follows. Instead, Abella would generate the
following adapter sequent (which it could then publish using Dispatch):

```
1  { "format": "assertion", "agent": "exampleAgent",
2    "claim": {
3      "format": "annotated-production",
4      "annotation": {"name": "fib5"},
5      "production": { "mode": null,
6        "sequent": {
7          "conclusion": "fib5",
8          "dependencies": [
9            "damf:bafyreifu.../claim/sequent/conclusion" ] } } },
10   "formulas": {
11     "fib5": {
12       "language": "damf:bafyreiga...",
13       "content": "fib (s (s (s (s (s z))))) ...",
14       "context": ["fib5!context"] } },
15   "contexts": {
16     "fib5!context": {
17       "language": "damf:bafyreiga...",
18       "content": [
19         "Kind nat type.", "Type z nat.", "Type s nat -> nat.",
20         "Define fib : nat -> nat -> prop by ...." ] } } }
```

Lines 12 and 17 above are references to a DAMF object describing the Abella
language. In line 5, the `"mode"` field is left as `null` to indicate that this assertion
was not created by any tool; in other words, the agent `"exampleAgent"` is solely
responsible for the assertion. If a tool had been used instead, this field would
refer to the DAMF description of that tool. Finally, in line 9, the dependency that
is included is the `cid` of the *conclusion* of the assertion object that was produced
by λProlog, and in turn imported by Abella in line 19 of `FibExample.thm`. The
dependencies in a sequent are *formula objects*, not assertions; the same formula
object can have several different proofs of it asserted by a variety of agents, and
the use of the formula as a lemma should not be seen as privileging any particular
assertion above others. From Abella's perspective, then, the name `fib5` denotes
just the formula on line 20 of `FibExample.thm`.

The Coq lemma `fib_square_above` is imported into Abella in a similar fashion.
The only difference is that the Abella translation of the Coq theorem needs to be
sensitive to the fact that the type `nat` of Abella is not inductively defined as in
Coq, and arithmetic operations are defined relationally. A conservative treatment
is as follows:

```
21  %% FibExample.thm continuing...
22  Import "damf:bafyreibr..." as
23  Theorem fib_square_above : forall n, nat n -> le (s¹³ z) n ->
24    forall u, times n n u -> forall v, fib n v -> lt u v.
```

The `cid damf:bafyreibr...` on line 22 is that of the assertion corresponding to the theorem `fib_square_above` in Coq. The imported assertion is rewritten as shown in lines 23–24. As before with λProlog, the assertion corresponding to this translation, with the `"mode"` of production set to `null`, can be easily generated and published by Abella.

Given these external lemmas from λProlog and Coq, the final desired theorem is fairly straightforward to assemble. The interested reader can find the full details in the online walk-through [3].

8   A DAMF-Aware Prover: Costs and Benefits

We list three potential costs of adopting DAMF within the theorem-proving community and comment on why they are relatively inexpensive.

1. *New standards and processes must be adopted.* Any exercise in communicating between different software systems must rely on some standards that define the structure of the data communicated. Here, we have focused on keeping those standards close to a minimum, keeping close to generic requirements for a range of theorem provers. The actual communicated artifacts use a standardized structure (here, JSON).
2. *New software is needed.* Adding a new feature to a theorem prover requires new code. Our implementation of DAMF factors that new software into two parts: (1) the Dispatch tool that is written in easily deployable JavaScript using off-the-shelf technology and (2) new code located in the printing and parsing subsystem of individual provers. As illustrated in Sect. 7, the logical kernel of provers does not need to be touched to employ DAMF.
3. *Agents must manage public and private keys and allow lists.* While this is a new feature for the theorem-proving community, it is standard technology used by online service providers, ranging from banking to cloud computing.

Next, we highlight the possible benefits a framework such as DAMF could have for the general proof-checking community and also for an individual prover.

8.1   Potential *Benefits* for the Community

One benefit of using a framework that explicitly addresses trust within the proof-checking community is that it helps to document the possible roles of special-purpose theorem provers within general-purpose proof-checkers. Most proof assistants, such as Coq and Isabelle, are general-purpose in the sense that they can be used in a wide array of areas in mathematics and computer verification. Many other formal method tools, such as SAT solvers, work in very restricted domains: as a result, proof checkers in those more narrow domains can be significantly optimized for modern operating systems and computer hardware to improve their usage of time and memory. If we are committed to being autarkic, the proof certificate generated by UNSAT (using, for example, the DRUP format [22]) would need to be rechecked by the one proof checker we trust.

While such rechecking can be done in practice [13], a general purpose kernel is not likely to be able to recheck successfully the large proof certificates that have been generated recently for open mathematical problems. For example, DRUP-based proof certificates that the Erdös discrepancy conjecture is true when its parameter is set to 2 has been reported as being 1.88 gigabytes in size [26], while a DRUP-based proof certificate answering the Schur Number Five problem is much larger, weighing in at 2 petabytes [23]. If these results were to be needed in conventional and general-purpose proof assistants, it is unlikely that their kernel rechecks them: the only other options would be to *explicitly trust* another, specialized proof checker or to find another, presumably smaller proof. Using DAMF, of course, we would not require this rechecking to be done; instead, that framework would track the explicit trusting of such a specialized prover.

As we have described in Sect. 6.3, adapters are used to translate theorems and their context in one language to theorems and contexts in another language. In essence, adapters are a pairing of a parser for one language and a printer for another language. Given that the correctness of both printing and parsing is a significant problem in the setting of theorem provers (see, for example, [25,38]), our use of adapters explicitly elevates this pairing to be a named tool that one can choose to trust or not. The considerable work that has gone into representing logics and proof systems in generic ways, such as Dedukti [6] and MMT [42], can be used to construct high-quality and broadly applicable adapters.

In contrast, many modern theorem provers come with a central repository containing a structured library of theories: see, for example, libraries associated to Lean [43] and Coq [31]. Given that the underlying file structure of DAMF is based on IPFS, there is no *a priori* hierarchy imposed on the structure of theories (i.e., collections of definitions, lemmas, and theorems). As a result, the theorems that appear in the DAMF *global store* or *information layer* can be curated into any number of collections to suit different needs. For example, a textbook in one area of mathematics might organize its collection of theorems differently than those used by software developers attempting to prove correct some safety-critical computer components.

A final benefit for the proof checking community is the "let a thousand flowers bloom" principle: efforts to prove theorems in many different domains with many different methods should be encouraged. If these efforts yield results that can be trusted, their results should be available directly to any other prover willing to, at least, tentatively trust them. Specialized proof languages for specialized settings could then be incorporated into the community activity of establishing proofs: examples of such systems are the geometrically-based prover GeoGebra [18] and a graphic presentation of commuting diagrams [27].

8.2   Potential *Benefits* for an Individual Theorem Prover

While the structure of DAMF has been motivated around issues involved with a community of different theorem provers, there are several reasons that an individual theorem prover might adopt elements of DAMF for internal reasons.

Version control tracking yields an immediate and natural use of DAMF. If a theorem has been checked by version n of a prover, can we trust that theorem in version $n + 1$ or insist that it be rechecked by version $n + 1$? Certain features of the newer proof checker may have stayed the same, and, as a result, one might be willing to accept certain theorems checked by the earlier version of the prover.

Since deploying a framework like DAMF removes the emphasis on rechecking proofs, it removes the need for kernel implementations to chase performance by means of complicated techniques whose correctness conditions may be unclear. As a result of avoiding such optimizations, the kernel can be simpler and, hence, more accessible to inspect, maintain, and trust.

Adapters can provide features and logical expressiveness without incorporating them into the kernel's logical core. For example, the logic behind both λProlog and Abella is based on Church's Simple Theory of Types [12]. While this logic allows for quantification at all simple types, it does not allow for *type variables* and type instantiation, i.e., polymorphism. Some form of polymorphism is however immensely useful and it is therefore demanded by users of these two systems. One approach to providing polymorphism can be to extend the foundations of Church's logic to include type variables (for example, by moving to a much more expressive logic like System F [19]). Enriching the logic in this way can make the kernels of these systems much more involved (especially since the kernels of both λProlog and Abella involve unification of λ-terms). Another approach that does not involve any changes to the kernel would be to write an adapter that takes as input definitions and theorems that mention a generic type constant, say a, and then outputs versions of those definitions and theorems in which a is instantiated with different types. For example, the Abella file in Fig. 2 defines the append relation on lists of simple type `list a`. As far as Abella's kernel is concerned, the type a is basic type, and this file checks in the (unmodified) kernel. A rather simple adapter can be written that specializes the type a to arbitrary types, such as `nat` or `bool`, and then create specialized versions of the `append` predicate and associated theorems. The adapter must of course be trusted to perform this specialization correctly, but the kernel does not need to be touched.

Finally, web browsers are emerging as possible interfaces for theorem provers; for example, a version of Abella is available as a client-side JavaScript program [2]. Because web browsers in a browser context usually run in a sandbox, there is the problem of having a persistent store (such as a file system). IPFS and DAMF readily solve this problem by persisting developments to the global cloud. Note that because of its content-addressed nature, unless some other node in the network accesses these files by their `cids`, they will not propagate; thus, private developments will remain private as long as the `cids` are not published.

```
 1  Kind  list   type -> type.
 2  Kind  a      type.
 3  Type  empty  list a.
 4  Type  cons   a -> list a -> list a.
 5
 6  Define append : list a -> list a -> list a -> prop by
 7    append empty L L ;
 8    append (cons X L) K (cons X M) := append L K M.
 9
10  Theorem append_associative : forall A B C AB ABC,
11     append A B AB -> append AB C ABC ->
12       exists BC, append B C BC /\ append A BC ABC.
13  induction on 1. intros. case H1.
14     search.
15     case H2. apply IH to H3 H4. search.
```

Fig. 2. An example of accommodating type instantiation.

9 Conclusion

We have focused on describing a framework that explicitly tracks the trust that one must have when using multiple proof checkers. The Distributed Assertion Management Framework (DAMF) uses the InterPlanetary FileSystem to distribute proof-checking assertions using public key cryptography. DAMF provides for declaring and managing the kinds of dependencies that occur within theorem provers without an explicit reference to a centralized library structure. This approach can be implemented in provers with minimal modifications using the Dispatch tool. We have illustrated how the Abella theorem prover benefits from including DAMF features, and we have argued that other provers might expect similar benefits. Lifting the DAMF framework to handle other domains, such as journalism and experimental science, will require the treatment of new dimensions of trust and mistrust, such as observational data and computations based on such data. Whether or not such a lifting is possible is still open.

References

1. Abadi, M.: Variations in access control logic. In: van der Meyden, R., van der Torre, L.W.N. (eds.) DEON 2008. LNCS, vol. 5076, pp. 96–109. Springer, Cham (2008). https://doi.org/10.1007/978-3-540-70525-3_9
2. Abella in your browser (2015). https://abella-prover.org/tutorial/try
3. Al Wardani, F., Chaudhuri, K., Miller, D.: The distributed assertions website, May 2024. Archived version. https://doi.org/10.5281/zenodo.11163505
4. Al Wardani, F., Chaudhuri, K., Miller, D.: Formal reasoning using distributed assertions. In: Sattler, U., Suda, M. (eds.) FroCoS 2023. LNAI, vol. 14279, pp. 176–194. Springer, Cham (2023). https://doi.org/10.1007/978-3-031-43369-6_10
5. Apéry, R.: Irrationalité de $\zeta 2$ et $\zeta 3$. Journées Arithmétiques de Luminy, Astérisque **61**, 11–13 (1979)

6. Assaf, A., et al.: Dedukti: a logical framework based on the λΠ-calculus modulo theory (2016). https://theses.hal.science/INRIA-SACLAY-2015/hal-04281492v1

7. Baelde, D., et al.: Abella: a system for reasoning about relational specifications. J. Formalized Reason. **7**(2), 1–89 (2014). https://doi.org/10.6092/issn.1972-5787/4650

8. Benet, J.: IPFS-content addressed, versioned, P2P file system (2014). https://doi.org/10.48550/arxiv.1407.3561

9. Berners-Lee, T., Hendler, J., Lassila, O.: The semantic web. In: Linking the World's Information, pp. 91–103. ACM (2023). https://doi.org/10.1145/3591366.3591376

10. Bertot, Y., Castéran, P.: Interactive Theorem Proving and Program Development. Coq'Art: The Calculus of Inductive Constructions. Texts in Theoretical Computer Science. Springer, Heidelberg (2004).https://doi.org/10.1007/978-3-662-07964-5

11. Boyer, R.S., Moore, J.S.: A Computational Logic. Academic Press (1979)

12. Church, A.: A formulation of the simple theory of types. J. Symbolic Logic **5**, 56–68 (1940). https://doi.org/10.2307/2266170

13. Cruz-Filipe, L., Marques-Silva, J., Schneider-Kamp, P.: Efficient certified resolution proof checking. In: Legay, A., Margaria, T. (eds.) TACAS 2017. LNCS, vol. 10205, pp. 118–135. Springer, Heidelberg (2017). https://doi.org/10.1007/978-3-662-54577-5_7

14. Debian's SecureApt. https://wiki.debian.org/SecureApt

15. Dowek, G., Thiré, F.: Logipedia: a multi-system encyclopedia of formal proofs. Technical report. abs/2305.00064, ArXiV (2023). https://doi.org/10.48550/ARXIV.2305.00064

16. Dunchev, C., Guidi, F., Coen, C.S., Tassi, E.: ELPI: fast, embeddable, λProlog interpreter. In: Davis, M., Fehnker, A., McIver, A., Voronkov, A. (eds.) LPAR 2020. LNCS, vol. 9450, pp. 460–468. Springer, Cham (2015). https://doi.org/10.1007/978-3-662-48899-7_32

17. Dwork, C., Roth, A.: The algorithmic foundations of differential privacy. Found. Trends Theor. Comput. Sci. **9**(3-4), 211–407 (2014). https://doi.org/10.1561/0400000042

18. GeoGebra for teaching and learning math. https://www.geogebra.org/

19. Girard, J.Y.: The system F of variable types: fifteen years later. Theoret. Comput. Sci. **45**, 159–192 (1986). https://doi.org/10.1016/0304-3975(86)90044-7

20. Gordon, M.J., Milner, A.J., Wadsworth, C.P.: Edinburgh LCF: A Mechanised Logic of Computation. LNCS, vol. 78. Springer, Heidelberg (1979). https://doi.org/10.1007/3-540-09724-4

21. Gordon, M.: HOL: A machine oriented formulation of higher-order logic. Technical report, 68, University of Cambridge, July 1985. https://www.cl.cam.ac.uk/techreports/UCAM-CL-TR-68.pdf

22. Heule, Jr. M., Hunt, W.A., Wetzler, N.: Trimming while checking clausal proofs. In: Formal Methods in Computer-Aided Design, FMCAD 2013, pp. 181–188. IEEE (2013). https://doi.org/10.1109/FMCAD.2013.6679408

23. Heule, M.J.H.: Schur number five. In: McIlraith, S.A., Weinberger, K.Q. (eds.) Proceedings of the Thirty-Second Conference on Artificial Intelligence (AAAI 2018), pp. 6598–6606. AAAI Press (2018). https://doi.org/10.1609/AAAI.V32I1.12209

24. Jones, C.B.: VDM proof obligations and their justification. In: Bjørner, D., Jones, C.B., Mac an Airchinnigh, M., Neuhold, E.J. (eds.) VDM 1987. LNCS, vol. 252, pp. 260–286. Springer, Cham (1987). https://doi.org/10.1007/3-540-17654-3_15

25. Jourdan, J.H., Pottier, F., Leroy, X.: Validating LR(1) parsers. In: Seidl, H. (ed.) ESOP 2012, vol. 7211, pp. 397–416. Springer, Heidelberg (2012). https://doi.org/10.1007/978-3-642-28869-2_20

26. Konev, B., Lisitsa, A.: Computer-aided proof of Erdös discrepancy properties. Artif. Intell. **224**, 103–118 (2015). https://doi.org/10.1016/j.artint.2015.03.004
27. Lafont, A.: A diagram editor to mechanise categorical proofs. In: JFLA 2024: Journées Francophones des Langages Applicatifs. Saint-Jacut-de-la-Mer, France, January 2024. https://hal.science/hal-04407118
28. The Lean Reference Manual. https://leanprover.github.io/reference/
29. Mahboubi, A., Sibut-Pinote, T.: A formal proof of the irrationality of $\zeta(3)$. Log. Methods Comput. Sci. **17**(1), 1–25 (2021). https://doi.org/10.23638/LMCS-17(1:16)2021
30. Miller, D., Nadathur, G.: Programming with Higher-Order Logic. Cambridge University Press (2012). https://doi.org/10.1017/CBO9781139021326
31. Müller, D., Rabe, F., Coen, C.S.: The Coq library as a theory graph. In: Kaliszyk, C., Brady, E., Kohlhase, A., Sacerdoti Coen, C. (eds.) CICM 2019. LNCS, vol. 11617, pp. 171–186. Springer, Cham (2019). https://doi.org/10.1007/978-3-030-23250-4_12
32. Necula, G.C.: Proof-carrying code. In: 24th Symposium on Principles of Programming Languages, vol. 97, pp. 106–119. ACM, Paris, France (1997). https://doi.org/10.1145/263699.263712
33. Nipkow, T., Paulson, L.C., Wenzel, M.: Isabelle/HOL—A Proof Assistant for Higher-Order Logic. LNCS, vol. 2283. Springer, Heidelberg (2002). https://doi.org/10.1007/3-540-45949-9
34. Nystrom, et al.: UEFI networking and pre-OS security. Intel Technol. J. UEFI Today Boostrapping Continuum **15**(1), 80–101 (2011)
35. Owre, S., Rushby, J.M., , Shankar, N.: PVS: a prototype verification system. In: Kapur, D. (ed.) CADE 1992. LNCS, vol. 607, pp. 748–752. Springer, Heidelberg (1992). https://doi.org/10.1007/3-540-55602-8_217
36. Paul, C., Matthews, M.: The Russian "Firehose of Falsehood" propaganda model. Rand Corporation **2**(7), 1–10 (2016). https://www.rand.org/pubs/perspectives/PE198.html
37. Paulson, L.C.: Isabelle: A Generic Theorem Prover. LNCS, vol. 828. Springer, Cham (1994). https://doi.org/10.1007/BFb0030541
38. Pollack, R.: How to believe a machine-checked proof. In: Sambin, G., Smith, J. (eds.) Twenty Five Years of Constructive Type Theory. Oxford University Press (1998)
39. van der Poorten, A.: A proof that Euler missed .... In: Berggren, L., Borwein, J., Borwein, P. (eds.) Pi: A Source Book, pp. 439–447. Springer, New York (2000). https://doi.org/10.1007/978-1-4757-3240-5_49
40. Portoraro, F.: Automated reasoning. In: Zalta, E.N., Nodelman, U. (eds.) The Stanford Encyclopedia of Philosophy. Spring (2024). https://plato.stanford.edu/archives/spr2024/entries/reasoning-automated/
41. Qi, X., Gacek, A., Holte, S., Nadathur, G., Snow, Z.: The Teyjus system – version 2 (2015). https://teyjus.cs.umn.edu/
42. Rabe, F.: The future of logic: foundation-independence. Logica Universalis **10**(1), 1–20 (2016). https://doi.org/10.1007/s11787-015-0132-x
43. The mathlib Community: The Lean mathematical library. In: CPP 2020: International Conference on Certified Programs and Proofs, pp. 367–381. ACM, January 2020. https://doi.org/10.1145/3372885.3373824

Uncertainty and Probabilistic UTP

Jim Woodcock[1,2,3]

[1] Southwest University, Chongqing, China
`jim.woodcock@york.ac.uk`
[2] Aarhus University, Aarhus, Denmark
[3] University of York, York, England
`https://www.cs.york.ac.uk/people/jim`

Abstract. This paper is dedicated to Cliff Jones, whom I have known for nearly 45 years. I describe my personal and professional friendship with him, including our interests in logic, semantics, and formal program development. The second part of the paper describes the relational semantics in UTP for probabilistic programming, inspired by the elegant work of Hehner. With Ye and Foster, we have mechanised this theory elsewhere using the Isabelle/UTP theorem prover. Here, we focus on motivating definitions and giving careful hand-written proofs of critical results. We start by describing Iverson brackets, a correspondence between predicates and arithmetic, which provides a link between conventional and probabilistic programming. We describe our semantic domain in UTP: a relational calculus of mappings from states to discrete state distributions. We give semantics to a simple probabilistic programming language. Following Hehner, we show how to extend the domain to provide the programming language with Bayesian semantics, transforming a priori distributions to a posteriori ones. This Bayesian semantics captures how we learn new facts in an uncertain world. We apply this to a simple robot localisation. Our treatment is characteristic of Hoare and He's Unifying UTP. We take Hehner's work and formalise it to unify it with other notations and tools. We conclude by discussing the advantages of doing this.

Keywords: Clifford B. Jones · Uncertainty · Predicative semantics · UTP (Unifying Theories of Programming) · Probabilistic semantics

1 Dedication

I left the University of Liverpool in 1980 when I completed my PhD. My supervisor, Mike Hennell, impulsively gave me a book as a leaving present.[1] A Prentice-Hall representative had left the book behind after visiting the department. Maybe the book was too heavy to take back to Hemel Hempstead? The red and white book was *Software Development: A Rigorous Approach* (SDRA) by Cliff Jones [42]. I had already been to my first formal methods conference, so I

---

[1] Mike Hennell was a Professor of Mathematical Sciences at the University of Liverpool, the founder of the software testing tools company Liverpool Data Research Associates, and academic great[6]-grandson of Thomas Huxley, Darwin's bulldog.

A. Cavalcanti and J. Baxter (Eds.): *The Practice of Formal Methods*, LNCS 14781, pp. 184–205, 2024.
https://doi.org/10.1007/978-3-031-66673-5_10

was pleased with the gift, perhaps more pleased than Mike had expected! My new employer, GEC's Hirst Research Centre near the football stadium in Wembley, sent me to Cliff's BCS FACS Christmas lectures at Imperial College that winter.[2] Cliff's lectures were on VDM, based on his book. Although I was too shy to introduce myself to him, I worked hard at the lectures. I returned to work in the new year and verified aspects of a distributed telephone exchange, including the routing algorithm, in VDM using rely and guarantee thinking.[3] I collaborated with my colleague at GEC Telecoms, Brian Dickinson. To explain our work, I wrote a VDM specification for a public automated branch exchange (PABX), what Pamela Zave might call a plain old telephone system [80].[4] The PABX has a clear state machine expressed in VDM and proved accessible to readers. I toured System X development teams at GEC, Plessey, STL, and BT, using the PABX as a familiar application for engineers. Some started to use VDM in their routine work. I helped develop System X's call processing subsystem and the production exchange version of the storage manager.

GEC then drafted me into Systems X's Joint Curriculum Development Team.[5] We created a professional development programme for System X engineers with three VDM courses: discrete mathematics, modelling, and reification to code. Our work on using VDM with rely and guarantee conditions [65,74] revealed a problem with VDM's operation decomposition and data reification rules. Although our design was intuitively correct, we could not prove this in VDM. We concluded that the rules are incomplete. We looked at the decomposition of atomic operations. We wanted to specify operations as atomic at an abstract level: nothing interferes with them. We wanted to decompose each abstract atomic operation into concrete operations with the obvious property that nothing interferes with their combined effect. We showed that VDM with rely and guarantee conditions does not allow such a development. I would return later to both these issues [62]. Our work was the first evaluation of rely and guarantee conditions, apart from Jones [44] and a description in Barringer [6].

---

[2] The British Computer Society's Formal Aspects of Computing Science specialist group is one of the oldest practitioner groups worldwide, founded in 1978. Members included Dan Simpson, John Cooke, and Cliff Jones, who founded *Formal Aspects of Computing* in 1989 [14]. Springer was the original publisher; since 2022, the Association of Computing Machinery has published it. Cliff was the founding editor-in-chief and still plays a significant role in its management.

[3] Cliff sent me an Oxford monograph containing a copy of his "late" PhD: *Development methods for computer programs including a notion of interference* [43]. The monograph is his seminal work on rely and guarantee thinking and one of the 12 computer science books (including SDRA) that changed my professional life.

[4] I translated the VDM specification into a Z specification and published it [75]. Jean-Raymond Abrial translated my Z specification (with acknowledgement) into the B notation and published it in the B-book [1]. Bernhard Aichernig translated Abrial's B specification into VDM [2], completing the cycle. (Bernhard may have been unaware of the previous VDM and Z specifications.).

[5] The team included Roger Shaw (who later worked for Lloyds Register and was a notable industrial supporter of Cliff's formal approaches).

Cliff invited me to lecture on Z [47,61,64,73,75] as part of his industrial VDM courses. I recall lecturing at the Winfrith Nuclear Power Station in Dorset and ICL Bracknell (with Cliff and Ian Cottam). On one happy occasion, I went to St Hughes College, Cambridge, in a heavy snow blizzard, greeted by a roaring log fire, a cheerful Christmas tree, and Cliff and Roger Shaw. I lectured on many occasions with Cliff, and I was always impressed by his ability to connect theory and practice and relate to students' experiences. I was developing my industrial courses with Oxford's Programming Research Group. I later moved from GEC to Oxford and made my career in continuing professional development in formal methods. The Oxford Software Engineering Programme started in 1993 with Cliff's encouragement. It continues to this day.

When you get to know someone, you notice what others say about them. Over the years, I've heard people describe Cliff's characteristics: modest,[6] gentle, open, vegetarian (like me), a conversationalist, and good company, though not a fan of large groups. Cliff has good taste, moderation, and generosity. He has a huge capacity for friendship, especially with young people. He is clever, sound, open-minded,[7] kind, warm, loyal, and committed. Cliff is thoughtful, well-read, and enjoys writing. He likes good food and wine. He uses the word "super" when feeling enthusiastic.[8] He doesn't have blanket dislikes; pop music is an exception. Cliff's gifts of Champagne marked several stages of my career. Since Cliff knows a lot about wine, it was always the good stuff. Recently, he gave me a CD set of *Winterreise*, Franz Schubert's terrifying song cycle for voice and piano. Of course, this came with a scholarly book explaining the song cycle because, as Cliff once said to me, *everything worthwhile can be studied*.

2   Probabilistic Programming

We use the probabilistic programming paradigm to specify models and infer results automatically [22]. In 2013, the US Defense Advanced Research Projects Agency initiated a machine learning (ML) research programme [12]. DARPA described probabilistic programming as *a new paradigm for managing uncertain information*. The managers wanted to incorporate probabilistic programming

---

[6] Cliff will hate this section of the article. When he reached 65, I suggested we organise a Festschrift symposium to celebrate because many people would like to express their admiration. Cliff firmly said no: "That would be *toe-curlingly awful!*" .

[7] Cliff has been closely associated with VDM throughout his career but has always been open-minded. He immediately agreed when I suggested changing the *VDM Europe Symposium* to become the *Formal Methods Europe Symposium*. Later, I organised comparative specifications of common systems as part of Tony Hoare's Grand Challenge on Software Verification [45,66], including verifying the Mondex smart card [5,20,76]. Cliff strongly supported this work, highlighting that many formal notations and tools have the same capabilities. What matters is *methodology*, such as state-based modelling, the use of state invariants, and the connection between specifications, designs, and implementations through refinement.

[8] I've noticed many of Cliff's younger colleagues use this word too. I'm certain Cliff has inspired them, which is just super.

into ML to significantly increase the number of people who can build ML applications and make machine-learning experts more effective.

Probabilistic programming is an emerging research area, attracting interest from artificial intelligence, machine learning, statistics, and theoretical computer science. It uses programming to structure complex statistical models. It has applications in many settings, recently including pandemic modelling. In October 2023, the UK's Alan Turing Institute opened a call for research proposals [35], emphasising the development, adoption, and awareness of probabilistic programming. It proposed the following themes: compositionality, parallelisation, programmable inference, semantics, verification, probabilistic programs and neural nets, flagship applications, and community projects.

We present a unified semantics for probabilistic programming as a foundation for probabilistic program logic. As Hoare says [30], a unifying theory is *complementary* to the theories it links and does not replace them. Program logics associate a modality $[P]$ with each program P in a particular language [63]. The formula $[P]A$ asserts that A holds after executing P, as in Hoare logic [29]. Pratt developed this idea in dynamic logic (DL) [59] and Fischer and Ladner, in turn, developed *propositional* DL (PDL) [16]. Kozen introduced *probabilistic* propositional DL (PPDL) in 1985 [49]. Morgan et al. [54] and McIver and Morgan [51] introduced a predicative logic for imperative probabilistic programs using expectations. The following researchers extended this work on expectations: Hurd et al. [34], Audebaud and Paulin-Mohring [4], Katoen et al. [46], and Gretz et al. [24]. Den Hartog [13] and others have developed program logic with probabilistic input and output distributions. Hölzl [32] has mechanised discrete-time Markov chains and Markov decision processes. Hölzl and Heller [33] have mechanised probabilistic semantics in Isabelle/HOL. Our starting point is Hehner's probabilistic predictive programming theory [26]. Our contribution is to present Hehner's semantics in UTP. We use this unified semantics to mechanise Hehner's work [79] in Isabelle/UTP [17,72].

Section 3 links standard and probabilistic programming, introducing Iverson's brackets, mapping boolean values into probabilities, and its algebra. Section 4 formalises Hehner's probabilistic semantics in Hoare and He's UTP, where operations are functions from states to discrete state distributions. Section 5 extends this to Bayesian semantics, where operations are transformations of discrete state distributions. Section 6 illustrates the semantics using robot localisation starting from an uncertain position. We discuss related and future work in Sect. 7.

3   Iverson Brackets

Iverson brackets establish a correspondence between predicates and arithmetic.[9] In particular, we use Iverson brackets to express the bounds for summations.

---

[9]   Iverson brackets are a notation for the characteristic function on predicates. Kenneth Iverson invented the convention in 1962 [36]. Knuth [48] and Graham et al. [23] advocate using brackets to avoid ambiguity in parenthesised logical expressions.

Definition 1 (Iverson bracket). *For any predicate P, the Iverson expression* $[P]$ *is 1 if P is true and 0 otherwise* [10] [11] $[P] \,\hat{=}\, (1 \lhd P \rhd 0)$

Iverson brackets map any predicate into a function of its free variables to the set $\{0,1\}$. In UTP, $[P]$ has free variables up to αP and value in $\{0,1\}$. Iverson brackets are monotone in terms of the ordering of integers.

Proposition 1 (Iverson monotone). $P \sqsupseteq Q \Rightarrow [P] \leq [Q]$

The logical operators distribute Iverson brackets in various ways.

Proposition 2 (Properties of Iverson brackets).

$$
\begin{aligned}
[P \wedge Q] &= [P] * [Q] \\
[P \vee Q] &= [P] + [Q] - [P] * [Q] \\
[\neg P] &= 1 - [P] \\
[k \in A] + [k \in B] &= [k \in A \cup B] + [k \in A \cap B] \\
[x \in A \cap B] &= [x \in A] * [x \in B] \\
[\forall m \bullet P(k,m)] &= \prod m \bullet [P(k,m)] \\
[\exists m \bullet P(k,m)] &= min\{1, \sum m \bullet [P(k,m)]\} \\
\#\{m \mid P(k,m)\} &= \sum m \bullet [P(k,m)]
\end{aligned}
$$

Iverson notation simplifies reasoning about sums over a domain: here, all integers. We transfer sub- and superscripts to Iverson expressions within the quantifier scope. The laws for combining summations do not specify how these bounds interact; the laws for Iverson expressions take care of that. We define Iverson summation using the usual mathematical operator.

Definition 2 (Iverson summation). $\sum k \bullet f(k) * [P(k)] \,\hat{=}\, \sum_{P(k)} f(k)$

4   Probabilistic UTP

Unifying Theories of Programming (UTP) is a long-term research agenda to articulate common principles and conceptual frameworks that underlie the variety of programming paradigms and languages. The goal is to find common ground and unify our understanding of different programming methods. Programming languages vary significantly, from imperative languages like C to declarative languages like Haskell. UTP identifies fundamental principles that explain the commonalities and differences among these diverse approaches. The definitive reference is Hoare and He's book [31]. Woodcock and Cavalcanti have introductions to UTP [11,67,70]. Key aspects explored in unifying theories of programming include: (1) Understanding how different languages facilitate abstraction and encapsulation of code. (2) Examining the underlying computational models. (3) Analysing the role and characteristics of type systems. (4)

---

[10]   We sometimes write $[P]_{\mathcal{I}}$ to avoid confusion with UTP's universal closure $[P]$.

[11]   The notation $(m \lhd P \rhd n)$ is taken from UTP. It is a conditional expression that takes the m value if P is true and n otherwise.

Investigating the semantics of programming constructs and their different presentations: denotational, operational, algebraic, and axiomatic. (5) Exploring how different languages handle concurrent execution. (6) Evaluating the expressive power of paradigms and languages using Galois connections.

We propose theories that capture the essence of programming across various paradigms. By identifying common principles, these unifying theories provide insights that can be valuable for designing new languages, understanding existing ones, and fostering cross-paradigm collaboration.

Our theory of probabilistic programs is similar to the relational theory of Hoare and He [31, Chap. 2]. Following Hehner [26,27] and using Iverson notation, we generalise our domain from boolean to probabilistic. The boolean values 0 (*false*) and 1 (*true*) are extreme probabilities, real numbers in the closed interval $[0, 1]$. As in Prism [50], we do not need the additional expressive power of UTP's designs [31, Chap. 3]: we want our programs to be total.

4.1 Discrete Distributions

Definition 3 (Discrete distribution). *Suppose that e is an expression with free variables v. The expression e is a discrete distribution if it satisfies two criteria: its value (for all assignments of values to v) is a probability, and its sum (over all assignments of values to v) is 1: (i) $[0 \leq e \leq 1]$ and (ii) $\sum v \bullet e = 1$.*

Example 1 (Hehner). Suppose that n and m are strictly positive integers. Then the expression $(1/2)^{n+m}$ is a distribution because it satisfies our two criteria:

Lemma 1. $\forall\, n, m : 1 .. \infty \bullet 0 \leq (1/2)^{n+m} \leq 1$

Recall the identity $\left(\sum k : 1 .. \infty \bullet z^k\right) = z/(1 - z)$. Specialising z to $1/2$: $\left(\sum k : 1 .. \infty \bullet (1/2)^k\right) = 1$ (identity †).

Lemma 2. $\left(\sum n, m : 1 .. \infty \bullet (1/2)^{n+m}\right) = 1$

Example 2 (Hehner). Suppose that n and m are *nonnegative* integers (in contrast to the last example). Then the expression $(1/2)^{n+m}$ is not a distribution because it fails our second criterion:

$$\left(\sum n, m : 1 .. \infty \bullet (1/2)^{n+m}\right) = 1$$

To see this, we first prove a result in summation algebra, where we detach the minimum term in a range with two bound variables.

Lemma 3 (Summation detach double variables)

$$\sum n, m \bullet [\, n \in 0 .. \infty\,] * [\, m \in 0 .. \infty\,] * A$$
$$= A[0, 0/n, m]$$
$$+ \left(\sum m \bullet [\, m \in 1 .. \infty\,] * A[0/n]\right) + \left(\sum n \bullet [\, n \in 1 .. \infty\,] * A[0/m]\right)$$
$$+ \left(\sum n, m \bullet [\, n \in 1 .. \infty\,] * [\, m \in 1 .. \infty\,] * A\right)$$

With this detachment lemma, we now prove our result.

Lemma 4

$$\sum n, m : 0 .. \infty \bullet (1/2)^{n+m} = 4$$

Proof

$$\sum n, m : 0 .. \infty \bullet (1/2)^{n+m}$$

=   { lemma: sum algebra detach double variables }

$$(1/2)^0 + (\sum n : 1 .. \infty \bullet (1/2)^n) + (\sum m : 1 .. \infty \bullet (1/2)^m)$$
$$+ (\sum n, m : 1 .. \infty \bullet (1/2)^{n+m})$$

=   { arithmetic }

$$1 + (\sum n : 1 .. \infty \bullet (1/2)^n) + (\sum m : 1 .. \infty \bullet (1/2)^m)$$
$$+ (\sum n, m : 1 .. \infty \bullet (1/2)^{n+m})$$

=   { identity †, twice }

$$1 + 1 + 1 + (\sum n, m : 1 .. \infty \bullet (1/2)^{n+m})$$

=   { lemma: previous }

$$1 + 1 + 1 + 1$$

=   { arithmetic }

$$4$$

4.2   Normalisation

If E is an expression whose value (for all assignments) is nonnegative and whose sum is strictly between 0 and ∞, then E normalised, written $\mathbf{N}(E)$, is the distribution whose values are in the same proportion as those of E.

Definition 4 (Normalisation). *If the variables are n and m (as before), then*

$$\mathbf{N}(E) \;\hat{=}\; E / (\sum n, m \bullet E)$$

Example 3. Consider the uniform distribution over an interval $a .. b$. We can specify this as a function on a natural number variable x:

$$\begin{array}{|l}
\mathcal{U} : \mathbb{N} \to [0, 1] \\
\hline
\forall x : \mathbb{N} \bullet \mathcal{U}(x) = [x \in a .. b]
\end{array}$$

But this is not a distribution. Suppose we take $a = 0$ and $b = 2$, then we have

$$\mathcal{U} = \{0 \mapsto 1, 1 \mapsto 1, 2 \mapsto 1\} \cup \{x : \mathbb{N} \mid x \notin \{0, 1, 2\} \bullet x \mapsto 0\}$$

Clearly, $\forall x : \mathbb{N} \bullet 0 \leq \mathcal{U}(x) \leq 1$ but $\sum x \bullet \mathcal{U}(x) = 3$. But if we normalise $\mathcal{U}$, then we can guarantee it is indeed a distribution:

$$\mathbf{N}(\mathcal{U}(x)) = \mathcal{U} = \{0 \mapsto \tfrac{1}{3}, 1 \mapsto \tfrac{1}{3}, 2 \mapsto \tfrac{1}{3}\} \cup \{x : \mathbb{N} \mid x \notin \{0, 1, 2\} \bullet x \mapsto 0\}$$

Lemma 5 (Normalisation is probabilistic). $\forall n \bullet 0 \leq \mathbf{N}(E) \leq 1$

Lemma 6 (Normalisation sums to 1). $(\sum n \bullet \mathbf{N}(E)) = 1$

Theorem 1 (Normalisation is a distribution). $\mathbf{N}(E) \in \mathcal{D}$

Proof. Directly from Lemmas 5 and 6.

Example 4 (Hehner). We normalise the expression from Example 2.

$$\mathbf{N}\left((\tfrac{1}{2})^{n+m}\right)$$
$$= \quad \{ \text{ definition: normalisation } \}$$
$$(\tfrac{1}{2})^{n+m} / \left(\sum n, m \bullet (\tfrac{1}{2})^{n+m}\right)$$
$$= \quad \{ \text{ previous example } \}$$
$$(\tfrac{1}{2})^{n+m} / 4$$
$$= \quad \{ \text{ arithmetic } \}$$
$$(\tfrac{1}{2})^{n+m-2}$$

From Theorem 1, this is a distribution.

Proposition 3 (Normalisation distributes through multiplication).
Suppose E is an expression with free variable x and F is an expression with free variable y, where x and y are distinct variables. Then $\mathbf{N}(E * F) = \mathbf{N}(E) * \mathbf{N}(F)$

Example 5 (Normalisation). Consider normalising $[\, x' = x + 1 \vee x' = x + 2\,]$. By definition, we have

$$\mathbf{N}([\, x' = x + 1 \vee x' = x + 2\,])$$

$$= \frac{[\, x' = x + 1 \vee x' = x + 2\,]}{(\sum x, x' \bullet [\, x \in 1 .. n \wedge x' \in 1 .. n\,] * ([\, x' = x + 1\,] + [\, x' = x + 2\,]))}$$

The divisor tells us how many values of the pair (x, x') satisfy the expression. Suppose that x and x' are in the $1 .. n$. Then, there are $2 * n - 3$ ways of satisfying the expression. We can prove this using Iverson summation. Now we have:

$$\mathbf{N}([\, x' = x + 1 \vee x' = x + 2\,]) = [\, x' = x + 1 \vee x' = x + 2\,] / (2 * n - 3)$$

which is a discrete probability distribution for the variable pair (x, x').

In this example, we found the distribution of the initial and final variables in the expression. Often, we want the distribution of just the final variables, given values for the initial variables. We define an alphabetised normalisation:

Definition 5 (Alphabetised normalisation). *If the free variables of the expression E are x, y, then*

$$\mathbf{N}_x(E) \mathrel{\widehat{=}} E / \left(\sum x \bullet E\right)$$

Example 6 (Alphabetised normalisation). Normalise $[\, x' = x + 1 \vee x' = x + 2\,]$ with respect to the final variable x'. By definition, we have

$$\mathbf{N}_{x'}([\,x' = x + 1 \vee x' = x + 2\,])$$

$$= \frac{[\,x' = x + 1 \vee x' = x + 2\,]}{(\sum x' \bullet [\,x \in 1 \mathinner{\ldotp\ldotp} n \wedge x' \in 1 \mathinner{\ldotp\ldotp} n\,] * ([\,x' = x + 1\,] + [\,x' = x + 2\,]))}$$

The divisor tells us how many values of the variable x' satisfy the expression. Again, suppose that x' is in $1 \mathinner{\ldotp\ldotp} n$. Then, there are just two ways of satisfying the expression. Assume that $x \in 1 \mathinner{\ldotp\ldotp} n - 2$, so the target expression is well-defined.

$$\sum x' \bullet [\,x' \in 1 \mathinner{\ldotp\ldotp} n\,] * ([\,x' = x + 1\,] + [\,x' = x + 2\,]) = 2$$

Now we have our result:

$$\mathbf{N}_{x'}([\,x' = x + 1 \vee x' = x + 2\,]) \;=\; [\,x' = x + 1 \vee x' = x + 2\,]/2$$

which is a discrete probability distribution for the variable x'.

The predicate $x' = e$ corresponds to a one-point distribution that takes the value 1 at the point $x = e$ and 0 elsewhere.

Proposition 4 (One-point distribution). *Assume $e \in 1 \mathinner{\ldotp\ldotp} n$. Then,*

$$\mathbf{N}_{x'}([\,x' = e\,]) \;=\; [\,x' = e\,]$$

Proposition 5 (Normalisation one-point).

$$\mathbf{N}_{x,y}([\,E\,] * [\,y = e\,]) \;=\; \mathbf{N}_x(E[e/y]) * [\,y = e\,]$$

4.3   A Probabilistic Programming Language

We introduce a simple programming language.[12] [13] Suppose our programs use only the variables x and y for simplicity.

Null. The command *skip* has no effect on the variables and terminates immediately. Its semantics is the one-point distribution: $(x' = x) * (y' = y)$. On termination, the after-state equals the before-state with probability 1; all other assignments to the after-state have probability 0.

Assignment. The command $x := e$ is a one-point distribution of the final state. If, before execution of $x := 1$, the variables x and y have values x_0 and y_0, then after execution, the final values of x and y will certainly be 1 and y_0.

Conditional. The command **if** c **then** A **else** B composes the weighted distributions of A and B. The conditional **if** $\frac{1}{3}$ **then** $x := 0$ **else** $x := 1$ means that with probability $\frac{1}{3}$, we assign the value 0 to x and with the remaining probability $\frac{2}{3}$ we assign 1 to x.[14]

---

[12] We use the probabilistic programming language considered by Hehner [26].

[13] We omit nondeterministic choice. Following Hehner, we define nondeterministic choice as an unnormalised random choice. See the discussion in Hehner [26, Sect. 10].

[14] Hehner's notation for probabilistic choice nicely generalises the usual conditional.

Sequence. The command A ; B is the serial composition of the distribution A with the distribution B. It is the conditional probability of B, given A.

Parallel. The command $A \parallel B$ is the parallel composition of the distribution A with the distribution B. It is the joint probability of A and B. In its most general form, neither A nor B need to be proper distributions, but the result will be guaranteed by the parallel operator's underlying normalisation.[15]

This simple language has the following semantics in probabilistic UTP.

Definition 6 (Probabilistic programming language)

$$skip \mathrel{\widehat{=}} (x' = x) * (y' = y)$$
$$x := e \mathrel{\widehat{=}} (x' = e) * (y' = y)$$
$$\textbf{if } c \textbf{ then } A \textbf{ else } B \mathrel{\widehat{=}} c * A + (1 - c) * B$$
$$A \mathbin{;} B \mathrel{\widehat{=}} \sum x_0, y_0 \bullet A[x_0, y_0/x', y'] * B[x_0, y_0/x, y]$$
$$A \parallel B \mathrel{\widehat{=}} \mathbf{N}(A * B)$$

The semantics is closed under these operators. For example, the sequential composition of two distributions is itself a distribution.

Proposition 6 (Normalised sequence)

$$\mathbf{N}_{x'}(A) \mathbin{;} \mathbf{N}_{x'}(B) = \sum x_0 \bullet \mathbf{N}_{x_0}(A[x_0/x']) * \mathbf{N}_{x'}(B[x_0/x])$$

Proof

$$\mathbf{N}_{x'}(A) \mathbin{;} \mathbf{N}_{x'}(B)$$
$=$ { sequential composition definition }
$$\sum x_0 \bullet (\mathbf{N}_{x'}(A))[x_0/x'] * (\mathbf{N}_{x'}(B))[x_0/x]$$
$=$ { alphabetised normalisation definition }
$$\sum x_0 \bullet (A/(\sum x' \bullet A))[x_0/x'] * (B/(\sum x' \bullet B))[x_0/x]$$
$=$ { substitution }
$$\sum x_0 \bullet (A[x_0/x']/(\sum x' \bullet A)) * (B[x_0/x]/(\sum x' \bullet B[x_0/x]))$$
$=$ { summation: change of variable }
$$\sum x_0 \bullet (A[x_0/x']/(\sum x_0 \bullet A[x_0/x'])) * (B[x_0/x]/(\sum x' \bullet B[x_0/x]))$$
$=$ { alphabetised normalisation definition }
$$\sum x_0 \bullet \mathbf{N}_{x_0}(A[x_0/x']) * \mathbf{N}_{x'}(B[x_0/x]))$$

Many familiar laws of programming carry over into the probabilistic setting. The following example demonstrates the *following assignment* law.

Example 7. We prove that

$$(\textbf{if } \tfrac{1}{2} \textbf{ then } x := 1 \textbf{ else } x := 2) \mathbin{;} x := x + 1 = \textbf{if } \tfrac{1}{2} \textbf{ then } x := 2 \textbf{ else } x := 3$$

First, we prove a small lemma about a two-point distribution:

---

[15] This is not parallel-by-merge from UTP [31]. Here, we combine two state distributions. Parallel-by-merge combines two update sequences merged for consistency.

Lemma 7 (Two-point distribution)

$$\mathbf{N}_{x'}([\, x' = 1 \vee x' = 2\,]) \;=\; [\, x' = 1 \vee x' = 2\,]/2$$

Next, we derive the semantics of the conditional expression in our program:

Lemma 8

$$\textbf{if } \tfrac{1}{2} \textbf{ then } x := 1 \textbf{ else } x := 2 \;=\; \mathbf{N}_{x'}([\, x' = 1 \vee x' = 2\,])$$

Finally, we prove our result:

Lemma 9

$$(\textbf{if } \tfrac{1}{2} \textbf{ then } x := 1 \textbf{ else } x := 2)\; ;\; x := x + 1 \;=\; \textbf{if } \tfrac{1}{2} \textbf{ then } x := 2 \textbf{ else } x := 3$$

Proof

$$(\textbf{if } \tfrac{1}{2} \textbf{ then } x := 1 \textbf{ else } x := 2)\; ;\; x := x + 1$$

$=$ { previous result }

$$\mathbf{N}_{x'}([\, x' = 1 \vee x' = 2\,])\; ;\; [\, x' = x + 1\,]$$

$=$ { Proposition 6: normalised sequence }

$$\sum x_0 \bullet \mathbf{N}_{x_0}([\, x' = 1 \vee x' = 2\,][x_0/x']) \ast [\, x' = x + 1\,][x_0/x]$$

$=$ { substitution }

$$\sum x_0 \bullet \mathbf{N}_{x_0}([\, x_0 = 1 \vee x_0 = 2\,]) \ast [\, x' = x_0 + 1\,]$$

$=$ { arithmetic }

$$\sum x_0 \bullet \mathbf{N}_{x_0}([\, x_0 = 1 \vee x_0 = 2\,]) \ast [\, x_0 = x' - 1\,]$$

$=$ { summation one-point }

$$\mathbf{N}_{x_0}([\, x_0 = 1 \vee x_0 = 2\,])[x' - 1/x_0]$$

$=$ { alphabetised normalisation }

$$([\, x_0 = 1 \vee x_0 = 2\,]/(\sum x_0 \bullet [\, x_0 = 1 \vee x_0 = 2\,]))\, [x' - 1/x_0]$$

$=$ { substitution }

$$[\, x' - 1 = 1 \vee x' - 1 = 2\,]/(\sum x_0 \bullet [\, x_0 = 1 \vee x_0 = 2\,])$$

$=$ { arithmetic }

$$[\, x' = 2 \vee x' = 3\,]/(\sum x_0 \bullet [\, x_0 = 1 \vee x_0 = 2\,])$$

$=$ { summation distributes through sum }

$$[\, x' = 2 \vee x' = 3\,]/((\sum x_0 \bullet [\, x_0 = 1\,]) + (\sum x_0 \bullet [\, x_0 = 2\,]))$$

$=$ { summation one-point, twice }

$$[\, x' = 2 \vee x' = 3\,]/(1 + 1)$$

$=$ { arithmetic }

$$[\, x' = 2 \vee x' = 3\,]/2$$

$$= \quad \{ \text{ alphabetised normalisation } \}$$
$$\mathbf{N}_{x'}([\, x' = 2 \vee x' = 3\,])$$
$$= \quad \{ \text{ previous result } \}$$
$$\textbf{if } \tfrac{1}{2} \textbf{ then } x := 2 \textbf{ else } x := 3$$

5 Learning New Facts

Suppose our program is the $2^{-n'}$ distribution, where $n' \geq 0$, and we learn a new fact about the computation; maybe n' is an even number. Hehner shows how to add this fact using parallel composition [27]. The new distribution is

$$2^{-n'} \parallel even(n')$$
$$= \quad \mathbf{N}\left(2^{-n'} * even(n')\right)$$
$$= \quad (2^{-n'} * even(n'))/\left(\sum n'' \bullet 2^{-n''} * even(n'')\right)$$
$$= \quad (2^{-n'} * even(n'))/(1/3)$$
$$= \quad 2^{-n'} * even(n') * 3$$

When we learn that the result is even, we drop the probability for each odd number to 0 and triple the likelihood for each even number.

Lemma 10

$$\sum n' \bullet ([\, n' = n + 1\,]/3 + [\, n' = n + 2\,] * 2/3) * [\, even(n')\,]$$
$$= \quad ([\, odd(n)\,] + 2 * [\, even(n)\,]) \,/\, 3$$

Proof

$$\sum n' \bullet ([\, n' = n + 1\,]/3 + [\, n' = n + 2\,] * 2/3) * [\, even(n')\,]$$
$$= \quad \{ \text{ summation algebra: } \sum x \bullet A \,/\, b = \left(\sum x \bullet A\right) / b \}$$
$$\left(\sum n' \bullet ([\, n' = n + 1\,] + 2 * [\, n' = n + 2\,]) * [\, even(n')\,]\right) / 3$$
$$= \quad \{ \text{ arithmetic } \}$$
$$\left(\sum n' \bullet [\, n' = n + 1\,] * [\, even(n')\,] + 2 * [\, n' = n + 2\,] * [\, even(n')\,]\right) / 3$$
$$= \quad \{ \text{ summation distributes through sum } \}$$
$$\left(\left(\sum n' \bullet [\, n' = n + 1\,] * [\, even(n')\,]\right)\right.$$
$$\left. + \left(\sum n' \bullet 2 * [\, n' = n + 2\,] * [\, even(n')\,]\right)\right) / 3$$
$$= \quad \{ \text{ one-point rule (twice) } \}$$
$$([\, even(n + 1)\,] + 2 * [\, even(n + 2)\,]) \,/\, 3$$
$$= \quad \{ \text{ properties of } even: (even(n + 1) = odd(n)) \text{ and } (even(n + 2) = even(n)) \}$$
$$([\, odd(n)\,] + 2 * [\, even(n)\,]) \,/\, 3$$

$$= \left\{ \begin{array}{l} \text{case analysis and arithmetic:} \\[2pt] \text{case: } odd(n) \ \Rightarrow \ \left[\begin{array}{l} [\,odd(n)\,] + 2 * [\,even(n)\,] \\ = 1 \\ = [\,even(n)\,] + 1 \end{array} \right] \\[20pt] \text{case: } even(n) \Rightarrow \ \left[\begin{array}{l} [\,odd(n)\,] + 2 * [\,even(n)\,] \\ = 2 \\ = [\,even(n)\,] + 1 \end{array} \right] \end{array} \right\}$$

$$([\,even(n)\,] + 1) \,/\, 3$$

6   Localisation

We illustrate the semantics using robot *localisation*, a *state estimation* problem. A robot operates in a circular room with only three positions around the wall, labelled $0..2$. There are doors at 0 and 2. Position 1 is a blank wall. A robot has a door sensor mapping the position to door or wall: $door(p) = (p = 0) \vee (p = 2)$. The robot models the room as a distribution of the probability of positions. It records its belief in the variable $bel \in 0..2$. Initially, the robot does not know where it is: the belief is simply the uniform distribution.

$bel := $ **if** $\frac{1}{3}$ **then** 0 **else if** $\frac{1}{2}$ **then** 1 **else** 2

$= \quad$ { conditional-assignment }
  if $\frac{1}{3}$ **then** $bel := 0$ **else if** $\frac{1}{2}$ **then** $bel := 1$ **else** $bel := 2$

$= \quad$ { conditional semantics $\times$ 2 }
  $\frac{1}{3} * (bel := 0) + \frac{2}{3} * (\frac{1}{2} * (bel := 1) + \frac{1}{2} * (bel := 2))$

$= \quad$ { arithmetic }
  $\frac{1}{3} * (bel := 0) + \frac{1}{3} * (bel := 1) + \frac{1}{3} * (bel := 2)$

After initialisation, the robot interacts with its environment through sensors and actions. The robot learns something about its environment from its initial position. Suppose it senses a door. It must update its current belief with this new fact. It can be sure of its reading if the sensor operates perfectly. But in most robotic systems, noise is inevitable, corrupting the reading. We model a noisy door sensor reading with some uncertainty. Suppose the sensor reading is four times more likely to be correct than wrong.

if $[\,door(bel)\,]$ **then** 4 **else** 1 $\ = \ 3 * [\,door(bel)\,] + 1$

Now, we can use parallel composition to update the current belief:

$\left(bel := \textbf{if } \frac{1}{3} \textbf{ then } 0 \textbf{ else if } \frac{1}{2} \textbf{ then } 1 \textbf{ else } 2\right) \ \| \ \left(3 * [\,door(bel')\,] + 1\right)$

This update transforms the robot's prior belief into a posterior belief. The prior is the initial assumption that the robot is equally likely to be in any position:

$\frac{1}{3} * (bel := 0) + \frac{1}{3} * (bel := 1) + \frac{1}{3} * (bel := 2)$

We calculate the posterior distribution from the a priori now and the new fact:

$$\left(bel := \mathbf{if}\ \tfrac{1}{3}\ \mathbf{then}\ 0\ \mathbf{else\ if}\ \tfrac{1}{2}\ \mathbf{then}\ 1\ \mathbf{else}\ 2\right) * \left(3 * [\,door(bel')\,] + 1\right)$$
$$= \tfrac{4}{3} * (bel := 0) + \tfrac{1}{3} * (bel := 1) + \tfrac{4}{3} * (bel := 2)$$

This product is not a distribution (it sums to 3). We must normalise it:

$$\sum bel' \bullet \left(\begin{array}{c} (bel := \mathbf{if}\ \tfrac{1}{3}\ \mathbf{then}\ 0\ \mathbf{else\ if}\ \tfrac{1}{2}\ \mathbf{then}\ 1\ \mathbf{else}\ 2) \\ * \left(3 * [\,door(bel')\,] + 1\right) \end{array} \right) = 3$$

The normalised product is then the new (posterior) belief:

$$\left(bel := \mathbf{if}\ \tfrac{1}{3}\ \mathbf{then}\ 0\ \mathbf{else\ if}\ \tfrac{1}{2}\ \mathbf{then}\ 1\ \mathbf{else}\ 2\right) \parallel \left(3 * [\,door(bel')\,] + 1\right)$$
$$= \tfrac{4}{9} * (bel := 0) + \tfrac{1}{9} * (bel := 1) + \tfrac{4}{9} * (bel := 2)$$

The robot acquired new knowledge and updated its beliefs accordingly. Our computation for sensing the environment uses *parallel computation*:

$$\left(bel := \mathbf{if}\ \tfrac{1}{3}\ \mathbf{then}\ 0\ \mathbf{else\ if}\ \tfrac{1}{2}\ \mathbf{then}\ 1\ \mathbf{else}\ 2\right) \parallel \left(3 * [\,door(bel')\,] + 1\right)$$

We calculate the new belief as

$$Posterior = \left(\,Prior \parallel Likelihood\,\right) = \mathbf{N}\left(\,Prior * Likelihood\,\right)$$

Action, on the other hand, is *sequential composition*:

$$Posterior = Prior\ ;\ Action$$

The robot moves one space to the right to improve its knowledge. How do we update its beliefs? We need to shift the probabilities in the distribution to record the movement. The robot believed previously there was a probability p of being at position i. After moving, the robot now believes there is a probability p of being at position $i \oplus_3 1$ (addition, modulo 3). What does the robot know now?

$$\left(\tfrac{4}{9} * (bel := 0) + \tfrac{1}{9} * (bel := 1) + \tfrac{4}{9} * (bel := 2)\right)\ ;\ bel := bel \oplus_3 1$$

The new belief is

$$\tfrac{4}{9} * (bel := 0) + \tfrac{4}{9} * (bel := 1) + \tfrac{1}{9} * (bel := 2)$$

The robot reads the sensor in this new position. Suppose it reads **door**. We need to update the belief again. The current belief is the prior distribution

$$\tfrac{4}{9} * (bel := 0) + \tfrac{4}{9} * (bel := 1) + \tfrac{1}{9} * (bel := 2)$$

The product is

$$\left(\tfrac{4}{9} * (bel := 0) + \tfrac{4}{9} * (bel := 1) + \tfrac{1}{9} * (bel := 2)\right) * \left(3 * [\,door(bel')\,] + 1\right)$$
$$= \tfrac{16}{9} * (bel := 0) + \tfrac{4}{9} * (bel := 1) + \tfrac{4}{9} * (bel := 2)$$

The normalising sum is

$$\sum bel' \bullet \tfrac{16}{9} * (bel := 0) + \tfrac{4}{9} * (bel := 1) + \tfrac{4}{9} * (bel := 2) \;=\; \tfrac{24}{9}$$

So, the posterior distribution is

$$\left(\tfrac{4}{9} * (bel := 0) + \tfrac{4}{9} * (bel := 1) + \tfrac{1}{9} * (bel := 2)\right) \parallel \left(3 * [\, door(bel')\,] + 1\right)$$
$$= \tfrac{2}{3} * (bel := 0) + \tfrac{1}{6} * (bel := 1) + \tfrac{1}{6} * (bel := 2)$$

The robot moves another step to the right. What do we know now?

$$\left(\tfrac{2}{3} * (bel := 0) + \tfrac{1}{6} * (bel := 1) + \tfrac{1}{6} * (bel := 2)\right) \,;\, bel := bel \oplus_3 1$$
$$= \tfrac{1}{6} * (bel := 0) + \tfrac{2}{3} * (bel := 1) + \tfrac{1}{6} * (bel := 2)$$

The robot can take another sensor reading. Suppose this reading is wall. We update the belief again. The product is

$$\left(\tfrac{1}{6} * (bel := 0) + \tfrac{2}{3} * (bel := 1) + \tfrac{1}{6} * (bel := 2)\right) \parallel \left(3 * [\, \neg\, door(bel')\,] + 1\right)$$
$$= \tfrac{1}{6} * (bel := 0) + \tfrac{8}{3} * (bel := 1) + \tfrac{1}{6} * (bel := 2)$$

The sum is

$$\sum bel' \bullet \left(\tfrac{1}{6} * (bel{:=}0) + \tfrac{2}{3} * (bel{:=}1) + \tfrac{1}{6} * (bel{:=}2)\right) * \left(3 * [\, \neg\, door(bel')\,] + 1\right) = 3$$

The posterior is:

$$\left(\tfrac{1}{6} * (bel := 0) + \tfrac{2}{3} * (bel := 1) + \tfrac{1}{6} * (bel := 2)\right) \parallel \left(3 * [\, \neg\, door(bel')\,] + 1\right)$$
$$= \tfrac{1}{18} * (bel := 0) + \tfrac{8}{9} * (bel := 1) + \tfrac{1}{18} * (bel := 2)$$

The robot now has good reason to believe it is at position 2. The robot started in an unknown position and then had the behaviour:

$$\langle\, sense(\mathsf{door}),\, move(\mathsf{right}),\, sense(\mathsf{door}),\, move(\mathsf{right}),\, sense(\mathsf{wall})\,\rangle$$

We model this as the probabilistic program

$$((bel := rand(0..2)) \parallel scale(bel', \mathsf{door})) \,;$$
$$(move(\mathsf{right}) \parallel scale(bel', \mathsf{door})) \,;$$
$$(move(\mathsf{right}) \parallel scale(bel', \mathsf{wall}))$$

This is a distribution of final states. Starting from an arbitrary initial state, it ends up in position 1 with probability $\tfrac{8}{9}$. Formally, its meaning is:

$$\tfrac{1}{18} * (bel := 0) + \tfrac{8}{9} * (bel := 1) + \tfrac{1}{18} * (bel := 2)$$

We are 88.8% certain the robot started at position 2 and finished at 1. (We know the most likely finishing position and how many steps it took, so we also know with equal probability where it started.)

7   Related and Further Work

We are interested in probabilistic semantics as a foundation for modelling and reasoning about *cyber-physical systems*, including robotics. There are many challenges to the satisfactory operation of cyber-physical systems. They include architectural issues, real-time properties, human interaction, autonomy, privacy, safety, security, and *uncertainty*. Researchers who have analysed CPSs cite problems linked to security and uncertainty as the most common causes of failure [3]. The semantics we present in this paper focuses on programming uncertainty: a lack of knowledge about a system's state.

Computer scientists have proposed formalisms for dealing with uncertainty. Probabilistic and statistical model checkers, such as Prism [50] and Storm [28], analyse a range of semantic models for these formalisms. These include discrete and continuous-time Markov chains and their nondeterministic extensions. These tools are good at interoperability. Verification-oriented formalisms include the following: Hehner's probabilistic predicative programming [26], probabilistic Hoare logic [13], the conditional probabilistic guarded command language [58], and partially observable Markov decision processes [53].

We restrict ourselves to summarising the related work in UTP. He et al. [39] present two different UTP semantics for an extension of Dijkstra's guarded command language extended with probabilistic choice. They recommend their second model, which extends (Claire) Jones's probabilistic semantics [41] to a cpo with nondeterminism. He and Hoare [37] propose a theory of probabilistic programming based on UTP's relational calculus. Their semantics maps a probabilistic distribution over initial states to a set of probabilistic distributions over final states. They present a series of semantic models. Each model defines a different and progressively smaller class of program. Healthiness conditions that increase in strength characterise these classes. He and Hoare prove that the healthiness conditions are closed under the program operators and that every theory conserves the definition of recursion.

He et al. [38] propose a novel methodology for constructing probabilistic semantics in UTP: the *weakest completion semantics*. (1) Select a standard semantics for a nondeterministic programming language. (2) Propose a new probabilistic semantic domain.(3) Construct a forgetful function from the probabilistic semantic domain to the standard semantic domain. (4) Use the inverse of the forgetful function to embed the standard semantic domain in the probabilistic semantic domain. (5) Demonstrate that this embedding preserves program structure. (5) Define probabilistic choice in the probabilistic domain. Woodcock et al. [71] give probabilistic semantics to RoboChart [52] using He et al.'s weakest completion method [38]. Woodcock et al.'s contribution is an explication of the technique with meticulous proofs suitable for mechanisation in Isabelle/UTP [17]. In [78], Ye et al. mechanise this work in the Isabelle/UTP theorem prover [17,72]. Ye et al. [77] present an automatic technique implemented in RoboTool to transform a RoboChart model into Prism [50] for verification. Filho et al. [15] further develop the probabilistic semantics of RoboChart. They show how to analyse RoboChart with probabilities using a version of the

FDR refinement-based model checker supporting probabilistic choice; see Gold-smith [21]. Instead of modifying FDR to perform probabilistic analysis, Gold-smith adds a new algorithm that creates a Prism specification [50] from a prob-abilistic CSP specification.

Future work includes combining our probabilistic semantics with UTP the-ories, especially those related to the *Circus* language [7,9,10,55–57,60,69]. This includes integration into the semantics of *Circus* [56] and its refinement the-ory [8,18]. It includes exploring the combination with specialist *Circus* theo-ries [19,25]. Research describing and analysing uncertainty raises many ques-tions (Woodcock [68]). What does a unifying theory for uncertainty look like? What connects the semantics and tools supporting different approaches? Can we establish more connections? Can we support probabilistic and statistical model checking with theorem proving? Can we support theorem proving with proba-bilistic and statistical model checking? Can we establish uncertainty properties using correctness by construction? What about probabilistic refinement-based model checking? Can we qualify one analysis tool (like DO-178C [40]) and then map soundly into that tool for high assurance? What is the formal testing theory for a CPS with unknown MDP semantics? What are the testability hypotheses (in Gaudel's sense)? How do we exploit the interplay between testing, proof, and model checking? What about uncertainty modelling and runtime verification? What role can unifying uncertainty play in developing, applying, and evaluating CPSs? Our future work will address these questions.

Acknowledgements. In 2016, I completed my term as Head of Computer Science at the University of York. I spent 2017 in Brazil, visiting Augusto Sampaio at the Federal University of Pernambuco. I wanted a new research direction, so I immersed myself in probabilistic semantics. I learnt Prism and taught a course on probabilistic model checking with Alexandre Mota. I verified mobile autonomous robotics after discussions with Ana Cavalcanti, Alvaro Miyazawa, Pedro Ribeiro, and Jon Timmis. I was influ-enced by the work of Eric Hehner, He Jifeng, Annabelle McIver, and Carroll Morgan. Students and colleagues patiently listened to seminars on my developing ideas. Back in York, I collaborated with Simon Foster and Kangfeng Ye to present the concepts in UTP and mechanism them in Isabelle/UTP. I thank all these colleagues. I gratefully acknowledge the support of the UK EPSRC for the following grants: EP/M025756/1: A Calculus for Software Engineering of Mobile and Autonomous Robots; EP/R025479/1: RoboTest: Systematic Model-Based Testing and Simulation of Mobile Autonomous Robots; EP/V026801/1, UKRI Trustworthy Autonomous Systems Node in Verifiabil-ity. Finally, I thank the four reviewers for their helpful comments.

References

1. Abrial, J.-R.: The B-Book–Assigning Programs to Meanings. Cambridge University Press, New York (1996)
2. Aichernig, B.K.: Overture tool: formal modelling in VDM. Download. Examples repository. A telephone exchange in VDM-SL. www.overturetool.org/download/examples/VDMSL/telephoneSL/index.html, November 1998

3. Asmat, M., Khan, S.U.R., Hussain, S.: Uncertainty handling in cyber-physical systems: state-of-the-art approaches, tools, causes, and future directions. J. Softw. Evol. Process **35**, e2428 (2022)
4. Audebaud, P., Paulin-Mohring, C.: Proofs of randomized algorithms in Coq. Sci. Comput. Program. **74**(8), 568–589 (2009)
5. Aydal, E.G., Paige, R.F., Woodcock, J.: Evaluation of OCL for large-scale modelling: a different view of the Mondex purse. Electron. Commun. Eur. Assoc. Softw. Sci. Technol. **9** (2008)
6. Barringer, H.: A Survey of Verification Techniques for Parallel Programs. LNCS, vol. 191. Springer, Heidelberg (1985). https://doi.org/10.1007/3-540-15239-3
7. Butterfield, A., Sherif, A., Woodcock, J.: Slotted-circus. In: Davies, J., Gibbons, J. (eds.) IFM 2007. LNCS, vol. 4591, pp. 75–97. Springer, Heidelberg (2007). https://doi.org/10.1007/978-3-540-73210-5_5
8. Cavalcanti, A., Sampaio, A., Woodcock, J.: Refinement of actions in circus. In: Derrick, J., Boiten, E.A., Woodcock, J., von Wright, J.: (eds.) BCS FACS Refinement Workshop 2002, Refine 2002, Satellite Event of FLoC 2002, Copenhagen, Denmark, 20–21 July 2002. Electronic Notes in Theoretical Computer Science, vol. 70, pp. 132–162. Elsevier (2002)
9. Cavalcanti, A., Sampaio, A., Woodcock, J.: A refinement strategy for Circus. Formal Aspects Comput. **15**(2–3), 146–181 (2003)
10. Cavalcanti, A., Woodcock, J.: Predicate transformers in the semantics of Circus. IEE Proc. Softw. **150**(2), 85–94 (2003)
11. Cavalcanti, A., Woodcock, J.: A tutorial introduction to CSP in *unifying theories of programming*. In: Cavalcanti, A., Sampaio, A., Woodcock, J. (eds.) PSSE 2004. LNCS, vol. 3167, pp. 220–268. Springer, Heidelberg (2006). https://doi.org/10.1007/11889229_6
12. DARPA: Probabilistic programming for advancing machine learning (PPAML). www.darpa.mil/program/probabilistic-programming-for-advancing-machine-Learning. Accessed 03 Mar 2024
13. den Hartog, J., de Vink, E.P.: Verifying probabilistic programs using a Hoare like logic. Int. J. Found. Comput. Sci. **13**(3), 315–340 (2002)
14. Formal Aspects of Computing. Springer and Association for Computing Machinery, 1989–present. dl.acm.org/journal/fac
15. Conserva Filho, M.S., Marinho, R., Mota, A., Woodcock, J.: Analysing RoboChart with probabilities. In: Massoni, T., Mousavi, M.R. (eds.) SBMF 2018. LNCS, vol. 11254, pp. 198–214. Springer, Cham (2018). https://doi.org/10.1007/978-3-030-03044-5_13
16. Fischer, M.J., Ladner, R.E.: Propositional dynamic logic of regular programs. J. Comput. Syst. Sci. **18**(2), 194–211 (1979)
17. Foster, S., Baxter, J., Cavalcanti, A., Woodcock, J., Zeyda, F.: Unifying semantic foundations for automated verification tools in Isabelle/UTP. Sci. Comput. Program. **197**, 102510 (2020)
18. Foster, S., Cavalcanti, A., Canham, S., Woodcock, J., Zeyda, F.: Unifying theories of reactive design contracts. Theor. Comput. Sci. **802**, 105–140 (2020)
19. Foster, S., Zeyda, F., Woodcock, J.: Unifying heterogeneous state-spaces with lenses. In: Sampaio, A., Wang, F. (eds.) ICTAC 2016. LNCS, vol. 9965, pp. 295–314. Springer, Cham (2016). https://doi.org/10.1007/978-3-319-46750-4_17
20. Freitas, L., Woodcock, J.: Mechanising Mondex with Z/Eves. Formal Aspects Comput. **20**(1), 117–139 (2008)

21. Goldsmith, M.: CSP: the best concurrent-system description language in the world—Probably! In: Communicating Process Architectures, pp. 227–232 (2004) he best concurrent-system description language in the world—Probably! In: Communicating Process Architectures, pp. 227–232 (2004)

22. Gordon, A.D., Henzinger, T.A., Nori, A.V., Rajamani, S.K.: Probabilistic programming. In: Herbsleb, J.D., Dwyer, M.B. (eds.) Proceedings of the on Future of Software Engineering, FOSE 2014, Hyderabad, India, May 31–June 7 2014, pp. 167–181. ACM (2014)

23. Graham, R.L., Knuth, D.E., Patashnik, O.: Concrete Mathematics: A Foundation for Computer Science, 2nd edn. Addison-Wesley, Reading (1994)

24. Gretz, F., Katoen, J.-P., McIver, A.: PRINSYS—on a quest for probabilistic loop invariants. In: Joshi, K., Siegle, M., Stoelinga, M., D'Argenio, P.R. (eds.) QEST 2013. LNCS, vol. 8054, pp. 193–208. Springer, Heidelberg (2013). https://doi.org/10.1007/978-3-642-40196-1_17

25. Harwood, W., Cavalcanti, A., Woodcock, J.: A theory of pointers for the UTP. In: Fitzgerald, J.S., Haxthausen, A.E., Yenigun, H. (eds.) ICTAC 2008. LNCS, vol. 5160, pp. 141–155. Springer, Heidelberg (2008). https://doi.org/10.1007/978-3-540-85762-4_10

26. Hehner, E.C.R.: Probabilistic predicative programming. In: Kozen, D. (ed.) MPC 2004. LNCS, vol. 3125, pp. 169–185. Springer, Heidelberg (2004). https://doi.org/10.1007/978-3-540-27764-4_10

27. Hehner, E.C.R.: A probability perspective. Formal Aspects Comput. **23**(4), 391–419 (2011)

28. Hensel, C., Junges, S., Katoen, J.-P., Quatmann, T., Volk, M.: The probabilistic model checker Storm. Int. J. Softw. Tools Technol. Transf. **24**(4), 589–610 (2022)

29. Hoare, C.A.R.: An axiomatic basis for computer programming. Commun. ACM **12**(10), 576–580 (1969)

30. Hoare, T.: Unification of theories: a challenge for computing science. In: Haveraaen, M., Owe, O., Dahl, O.-J. (eds.) ADT/COMPASS -1995. LNCS, vol. 1130, pp. 49–57. Springer, Heidelberg (1996). https://doi.org/10.1007/3-540-61629-2_35

31. Hoare, C.A.R., He, J.: Unifying Theories of Programming. Prentice Hall, London (1998)

32. Hölzl, J.: Formalising semantics for expected running time of probabilistic programs. In: Blanchette, J.C., Merz, S. (eds.) ITP 2016. LNCS, vol. 9807, pp. 475–482. Springer, Cham (2016). https://doi.org/10.1007/978-3-319-43144-4_30

33. Hölzl, J., Heller, A.: Three chapters of measure theory in Isabelle/HOL. In: van Eekelen, M., Geuvers, H., Schmaltz, J., Wiedijk, F. (eds.) ITP 2011. LNCS, vol. 6898, pp. 135–151. Springer, Heidelberg (2011). https://doi.org/10.1007/978-3-642-22863-6_12

34. Hurd, J., McIver, A., Morgan, C.: Probabilistic guarded commands mechanized in HOL. Theor. Comput. Sci. **346**(1), 96–112 (2005)

35. Alan Turing Institute: Probabilistic programming open call. Closing date Tue, 10/10/2023 - 13:00. www.turing.ac.uk/work-turing/probabilistic-programming-open-call

36. Iverson, K.E.: A programming language. In: Barnard III, G.A. (ed.) Proceedings of the 1962 Spring Joint Computer Conference, AFIPS 1962 (Spring), San Francisco, California, USA, 1–3 May 1962, pp. 345–351. ACM (1962)

37. He, J., Hoare, C.A.R.: Linking theories in probabilistic programming. Inf. Sci. **119**(3–4), 205–218 (1999)

38. Jifeng, H., Morgan, C., McIver, A.: Deriving probabilistic semantics via the 'weakest completion'. In: Davies, J., Schulte, W., Barnett, M. (eds.) ICFEM 2004. LNCS, vol. 3308, pp. 131–145. Springer, Heidelberg (2004). https://doi.org/10.1007/978-3-540-30482-1_17

39. Jifeng, H., Seidel, K., McIver, A.: Probabilistic models for the guarded command language. Sci. Comput. Program. **28**(2–3), 171–192 (1997)

40. Johnson, L.A.: DO-178B: software considerations in airborne systems and equipment certification. Crosstalk **199**, 11–20 (1998)

41. Jones, C.: Probabilistic non-determinism. Ph.D. thesis, University of Edinburgh, UK (1990)

42. Jones, C.B.: Software Development–a Rigorous Approach. International Series in Computer Science. Prentice Hall, Upper Saddle River (1980)

43. Jones, C.B.: Development methods for computer programs including a notion of interference. DPhil thesis, Technical Monograph 25, University of Oxford, Programming Research Group, June 1981

44. Jones, C.B.: Tentative steps toward a development method for interfering programs. ACM Trans. Program. Lang. Syst. **5**(4), 596–619 (1983)

45. Jones, C.B., O'Hearn, P.W., Woodcock, J.: Verified software: a grand challenge. Computer **39**(4), 93–95 (2006)

46. Katoen, J.-P., McIver, A.K., Meinicke, L.A., Morgan, C.C.: Linear-invariant generation for probabilistic programs. In: Cousot, R., Martel, M. (eds.) SAS 2010. LNCS, vol. 6337, pp. 390–406. Springer, Heidelberg (2010). https://doi.org/10.1007/978-3-642-15769-1_24

47. King, S., Holm Sørensen, I., Woodcock, J.: Z: grammar and concrete and abstract syntaxes. Technical Monograph PRG-68, Oxford University Computing Laboratory, Programming Research Group, 8–11 Keble Road, Oxford OX1 3QD UK, July 1988. Version 2.0

48. Knuth, D.E.: Two notes on notation. Am. Math. Mon. **99**(5), 403–422 (1992)

49. Kozen, D.: A probabilistic PDL. J. Comput. Syst. Sci. **30**(2), 162–178 (1985)

50. Kwiatkowska, M., Norman, G., Parker, D.: PRISM 4.0: verification of probabilistic real-time systems. In: Gopalakrishnan, G., Qadeer, S. (eds.) CAV 2011. LNCS, vol. 6806, pp. 585–591. Springer, Heidelberg (2011). https://doi.org/10.1007/978-3-642-22110-1_47

51. McIver, A., Morgan, C.: Abstraction, Refinement and Proof for Probabilistic Systems. Monographs in Computer Science. Springer, New York (2005). https://doi.org/10.1007/b138392

52. Miyazawa, A., Ribeiro, P., Li, W., Cavalcanti, A., Timmis, J., Woodcock, J.: RoboChart: modelling and verification of the functional behaviour of robotic applications. Softw. Syst. Model. **18**(5), 3097–3149 (2019)

53. Monahan, G.E.: A survey of partially observable Markov decision processes: theory, models, and algorithms. Manage. Sci. **28**(1), 1–16 (1982)

54. Morgan, C., McIver, A., Seidel, K.: Probabilistic predicate transformers. ACM Trans. Program. Lang. Syst. **18**(3), 325–353 (1996)

55. Oliveira, M., Cavalcanti, A., Woodcock, J.: Formal development of industrial-scale systems in Circus. Innov. Syst. Softw. Eng. **1**(2), 125–146 (2005)

56. Oliveira, M., Cavalcanti, A., Woodcock, J.: A denotational semantics for Circus. In: Aichernig, B.K., Boiten, E.A., Derrick, J., Groves, L. (eds.) Proceedings of the 11th Refinement Workshop, Refine@ICFEM 2006, Macao, 31 October 2006. Electronic Notes in Theoretical Computer Science, vol. 187, pp. 107–123. Elsevier (2006)

57. Oliveira, M., Cavalcanti, A., Woodcock, J.: A UTP semantics for Circus. Formal Aspects Comput. **21**(1–2), 3–32 (2009)
58. Olmedo, F., Gretz, F., Jansen, N., Kaminski, B.L., Katoen, J.-P., McIver, A.: Conditioning in probabilistic programming. ACM Trans. Program. Lang. Syst. **40**(1), 4:1-4:50 (2018)
59. Pratt, V.R.: Semantical considerations on Floyd-Hoare logic. In: 17th Annual Symposium on Foundations of Computer Science, Houston, Texas, USA, 25–27 October 1976, pp. 109–121. IEEE Computer Society (1976)
60. Sampaio, A., Woodcock, J., Cavalcanti, A.: Refinement in *Circus*. In: Eriksson, L.-H., Lindsay, P.A. (eds.) FME 2002. LNCS, vol. 2391, pp. 451–470. Springer, Heidelberg (2002). https://doi.org/10.1007/3-540-45614-7_26
61. Michael Spivey, J.: Z Notation–A reference manual. International Series in Computer Science, 2nd edn. Prentice Hall, Upper Saddle River (1992)
62. Stepney, S., Cooper, D., Woodcock, J.: More powerful Z data refinement: pushing the state of the art in industrial refinement. In: Bowen, J.P., Fett, A., Hinchey, M.G. (eds.) ZUM 1998. LNCS, vol. 1493, pp. 284–307. Springer, Heidelberg (1998). https://doi.org/10.1007/978-3-540-49676-2_20
63. Troquard, N., Balbiani, P.: Propositional dynamic logic. In: Zalta, E.N., Nodelman, U. (eds.) The Stanford Encyclopedia of Philosophy. Metaphysics Research Lab, Stanford University, fall 2023 edition (2023)
64. Woodcock, J.C.P.: Properties of Z specifications. ACM SIGSOFT Softw. Eng. Notes **14**(5), 43–54 (1989)
65. Woodcock, J.C.P., Dickinson, B.: Using VDM with rely and guarantee-conditions: Experiences from a real project. Technical report, Programming Research Group, Oxford University (1988). Full version
66. Woodcock, J.: First steps in the verified software grand challenge. Computer **39**(10), 57–64 (2006)
67. Woodcock, J.: Hoare and He's unifying theories of programming. In: Jones, C.B., Misra, J. (eds.) Theories of Programming: The Life and Works of Tony Hoare, volume 39 of *ACM Books*, pp. 285–316. ACM/Morgan & Claypool (2021)
68. Woodcock, J.: Towards a unifying framework for uncertainty in cyber-physical systems. In: Haxthausen, A.E., Huang, W.l., Roggenbach, M. (eds.) Applicable Formal Methods for Safe Industrial Products. LNCS, vol. 14165, pp. 237–253. Springer, Cham (2023). https://doi.org/10.1007/978-3-031-40132-9_15
69. Woodcock, J., Cavalcanti, A.: The semantics of *Circus*. In: Bert, D., Bowen, J.P., Henson, M.C., Robinson, K. (eds.) ZB 2002. LNCS, vol. 2272, pp. 184–203. Springer, Heidelberg (2002). https://doi.org/10.1007/3-540-45648-1_10
70. Woodcock, J., Cavalcanti, A.: A tutorial introduction to designs in unifying theories of programming. In: Boiten, E.A., Derrick, J., Smith, G. (eds.) IFM 2004. LNCS, vol. 2999, pp. 40–66. Springer, Heidelberg (2004). https://doi.org/10.1007/978-3-540-24756-2_4
71. Woodcock, J., Cavalcanti, A., Foster, S., Mota, A., Ye, K.: Probabilistic semantics for RoboChart. In: Ribeiro, P., Sampaio, A. (eds.) UTP 2019. LNCS, vol. 11885, pp. 80–105. Springer, Cham (2019). https://doi.org/10.1007/978-3-030-31038-7_5
72. Woodcock, J., Cavalcanti, A., Foster, S., Oliveira, M., Sampaio, A., Zeyda, F.: UTP, circus, and Isabelle. In: Bowen, J.P., Li, Q., Xu, Q. (eds.) Theories of programming and formal methods. LNCS, vol. 14080, pp. 19–51. Springer, Cham (2023). https://doi.org/10.1007/978-3-031-40436-8_2
73. Woodcock, J., Davies, J.: Using Z-Specification, Refinement, and Proof. International Series in Computer Science. Prentice Hall, Upper Saddle River (1996)

74. Woodcock, J.C.P., Dickinson, B.: Using VDM with rely and guarantee-conditions. In: Bloomfield, R.E., Marshall, L.S., Jones, R.B. (eds.) VDM 1988. LNCS, vol. 328, pp. 434–458. Springer, Heidelberg (1988). https://doi.org/10.1007/3-540-50214-9_27

75. Woodcock, J., Loomes, M.: Software Engineering Mathematics. Addison-Wesley, Boston (1989)

76. Woodcock, J., Stepney, S., Cooper, D., Clark, J.A., Jacob, J.: The certification of the Mondex electronic purse to ITSEC Level E6. Formal Aspects Comput. **20**(1), 5–19 (2008)

77. Ye, K., Cavalcanti, A., Foster, S., Miyazawa, A., Woodcock, J.: Probabilistic modelling and verification using RoboChart and PRISM. Softw. Syst. Model. **21**(2), 667–716 (2022)

78. Ye, K., Foster, S., Woodcock, J.: Automated reasoning for probabilistic sequential programs with theorem proving. In: Fahrenberg, U., Gehrke, M., Santocanale, L., Winter, M. (eds.) RAMiCS 2021. LNCS, vol. 13027, pp. 465–482. Springer, Cham (2021). https://doi.org/10.1007/978-3-030-88701-8_28

79. Ye, K., Woodcock, J., Foster, S.: Probabilistic relations for modelling epistemic and aleatoric uncertainty: its semantics and automated reasoning with theorem proving. *CoRR*, abs/2303.09692 (2023)

80. Zave, P.: Calls considered harmful' and other observations: a tutorial on telephony. In: Margaria, T., Steffen, B., Rückert, R., Posegga, J. (eds.) Services and Visualization Towards User-Friendly Design. LNCS, vol. 1385, pp. 8–27. Springer, Heidelberg (1998). https://doi.org/10.1007/BFb0053493

Modelling and Verifying Programs Under the Total Store Order Memory Model in an Algebraic Semantics Style

Lili Xiao[1], Huibiao Zhu[2]([✉]), Jonathan P. Bowen[3,4], and Sini Chen[2]

[1] Donghua University, Shanghai, China
[2] East China Normal University, Shanghai, China
hbzhu@sei.ecnu.edu.cn
[3] London South Bank University, London, UK
[4] Southwest University, Chongqing, China

Abstract. Modelling and verification of multi-threaded programs are difficult since one must consider all the ways that instructions in different threads can be interleaved. Modern hardware architectures and mainstream programming languages employ relaxed memory models for efficiency purposes, and the additional interleavings from them make the modelling and verification more complex. Total Store Order (TSO) is a widely used relaxed memory model in SPARC implementations and x86 architecture. In this paper, we are committed to proposing a lightweight method for formally modelling and verifying programs under the TSO memory model. Above all, we apply *Unifying Theories of Programming* (UTP) to investigate a set of algebraic laws, which can dynamically generate configuration sequences of programs under TSO. At the meantime, the information of each configuration is recorded. During this process, we define three properties (including *Write-Read Reordering*, *Read-after-Write Elimination* and *Barrier*) related to the unique features of TSO, and check whether the properties are satisfied. The algebraic laws are implemented in the rewriting engine Maude, and the verification is also conducted in Maude. The verification results show that the properties are all in line with our expectations.

Keywords: Relaxed Memory Models · Total Store Order (TSO) · Algebraic Laws · Unifying Theories of Programming (UTP) · Verification

1 Background

This paper is written in tribute to Cliff Jones on the occasion of his 80th birthday. Cliff has dedicated his professional live to research into formal methods [18]. Initially, he worked on an extension to Hoare logic, working under Tony Hoare in the Programming Research Group at the Oxford University Computing Laboratory, and completing his doctoral thesis in 1981 [5]. Cliff also worked

© The Author(s), under exclusive license to Springer Nature Switzerland AG 2024
A. Cavalcanti and J. Baxter (Eds.): *The Practice of Formal Methods*, LNCS 14781, pp. 206–225, 2024.
https://doi.org/10.1007/978-3-031-66673-5_11

at IBM in the company's laboratories at Hursley (UK) and Vienna (Austria). Working with Dines Bjørner, Peter Lucas, and others, he developed the Vienna Development Method (VDM) for specifying and verifying programs [6]. Later he became a professor at the University of Manchester and then Newcastle University. He has always had an interest in the history of computing, especially formal methods, including the work of the computing pioneer Alan Turing [7,16], with a wonderful ability to compare his own research interests with other approaches in a very even-handed way.

In parallel, Jifeng He and Tony Hoare developed their *Unifying Theories of Programming* (UTP) approach to program semantics, which demonstrates how to relate algebraic semantics, denotational semantics, and operational semantics in an elegant manner [4]. Cliff Jones has compared this approach with others when surveying the various ways of specifying and abstracting the semantics of programs [8,9]. He has continued his interest in formal methods research well past "normal" retirement age, including work influenced by UTP, for example concerning shared-variable concurrency [3]. In this paper, we also follow a UTP approach for shared-memory systems, related to shared-variable programming languages [21,22]. We thank Cliff for his stalwart dedication to the field of formal methods and friendly support for fellow researchers over the years.

2   Introduction

It remains a great challenge to model and verify multi-threaded programs, because all the ways, that instructions in different threads can be interleaved, need to be taken into consideration [1]. Modern hardware architectures like x86 and ARM, and mainstream programming languages like Java and C/C++ provide relaxed memory models for efficiency purposes [10], which bring in additional interleavings, which makes matters worse.

Among these relaxed memory models, Total Store Order (TSO) is a widely implemented model [19]. The TSO memory model is supported by the x86 architecture and SPARC implementations [17]. It omits store-load (write-read) constraints by allowing each thread to employ a write buffer.

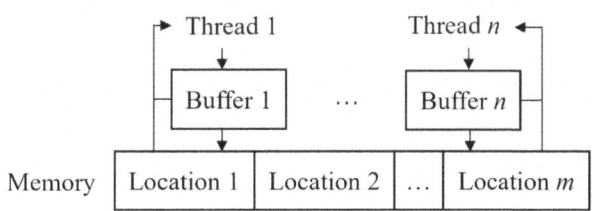

Fig. 1. The TSO Architecture.

As exhibited in Fig. 1, every memory write works on its thread's private buffer first, and then the information in the write buffer will be propagated into the shared memory sequentially at some point in the future. A read from location x always demands to check whether the thread's buffer contains such a write to the same location. If yes, the latest value is returned and the read operation terminates successfully. Otherwise, the main memory will be explored. In addition, a full "fence" is introduced to prevent reordering between two instructions.

Unifying Theories of Programming (UTP) [4] was developed by Hoare and He in 1998. It targets proposing a convincing unified framework to combine and link operational semantics, denotational semantics and algebraic semantics. Each of the semantics has distinctive advantages for theories of programming. In particular, "*Algebra is well-suited for direct use by engineers in symbolic calculation of parameters and the structure of an optimal design. Algebraic proof by term rewriting is a promising approach*" [4].

Runtime verification (RV) is a lightweight mathematical formal verification method, which is mainly used to monitor whether the running track of the target system satisfies the expected specifications. Inspired by RV, in this paper, we investigate a set of algebraic laws for the TSO memory model, where our approach is based on UTP. With the application of the proposed laws, the configuration sequences of programs under TSO can be dynamically generated. During the process, we define three properties related to the characteristic features of TSO, namely *Write-Read Reordering*, *Read-after-Write Elimination* and *Barrier*, and check whether the produced sequences conform to these properties. The algebraic laws are implemented and the verification is conducted in the Maude system [2]. Our framework is illustrated in Fig. 2.

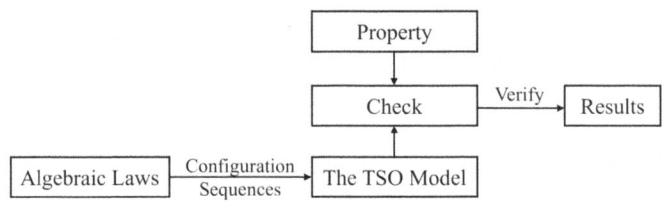

Fig. 2. The Framework of Our Work.

The rest of this paper is organized as follows. Section 3 gives a brief introduction to the syntax of TSO and the Maude system. We propose the algebraic semantics for TSO in Sect. 4. Section 5 presents the implementation. We describe the properties and conduct the verification in Sect. 6. Section 7 concludes the paper and discusses possible future work.

3 Syntax and Maude

This section introduces the syntax of the TSO memory model and the rewriting engine Maude [2] briefly.

3.1 Syntax of TSO

In this section, we give the description of programs under TSO with a simple imperative language, which is adapted and extended from [11]. In the following syntax, e ranges over arithmetic expressions on real numbers, h over boolean expressions and p over programs.

$$v ::= ..., -2, -1, 0, 1, 2, ...$$
$$e ::= v \mid x \mid e_1 + e_2 \mid e_1 * e_2 \mid ...$$
$$h ::= \text{true} \mid \text{false} \mid e_1 = e_2 \mid \neg h \mid h_1 \vee h_2 \mid h_1 \wedge h_2 \mid ...$$
$$p ::= x := e \mid \text{fence} \mid \text{if } h \text{ then } p_1 \text{ else } p_2 \mid \text{while } h \text{ do } p \mid p_1; p_2 \mid p_1 \| p_2$$

Here, variable x can be global or local. Fence instructions force the writes in private buffers to be propagated. Therefore, the absolute order in a process can be guaranteed.

3.2 Rewriting Engine Maude

Rewriting logic is a general semantic and logical framework [13–15], and the rewriting engine Maude [2] is an implementation for rewriting logic. We give the syntax of a subset of Maude which will be used in the following sections.

- **sort**: In algebraic specification, the types of data are usually called *sorts*. A sort is declared using the **sort** keyword followed by the sort name, as follows: **sort** $\langle Sort \rangle$. Multiple sorts can be declared using the **sorts** keyword, i.e., **sorts** $\langle Sort\_1 \rangle$ ... $\langle Sort\_k \rangle$. Sorts can be partially ordered through a **subsort** relation.
- **op**: In the Maude system, an operator is declared with the keyword **op** followed by its name, a colon, the list of sorts for its arguments, "->" and the sort of its result. Generally, it has the form of **op** $\langle OpName \rangle$: $\langle Sort\_1 \rangle$ ... $\langle Sort\_k \rangle$ -> $\langle Sort \rangle$ [$\langle OperatorAttributes \rangle$]. The attribute declaration is optional.
- **var**: A variable is always constrained to range over a particular sort. Multiple variables of the same sort are declared using the keyword **vars**.
- **eq** and **ceq**: Unconditional equations and conditional equations are declared using the keywords **eq** and **ceq**. A condition can be either a single equation or a conjunction of equations. Furthermore, the syntax of equations in conditions has a variant called *Boolean equations*, which are constructed using equality "_==_", inequality "_=/=_", "not_", "_and_" and "_or_".
- **rl** and **crl**: Unconditional rules and conditional rules are declared using keywords **rl** and **crl**, respectively.

4 Algebraic Semantics

In [20], the sequential and parallel expansion laws for the TSO memory model were proposed. The discussion of parallel laws is always based on the configuration sequences of each component achieved from sequential laws. Instead, in this section, we aim to investigate a set of algebraic laws, which can generate configuration sequences of programs under TSO dynamically. It is useful for the conduction of lightweight verification in the following section.

4.1   Guarded Choice

Now we introduce the concept of guarded choice, whose target is to support the algebraic laws. A guarded choice is composed of a set of guarded components expressed as $h\&(act, tid, idx) \leftrightsquigarrow P[q]$, and $h\&(act, tid, idx)$ is a configuration, where,

- h is a Boolean condition. Except for branching conditions, h is true and can be ignored for simplicity.
- act is abstracted from a program statement. It can be $\langle x = e \rangle$ denoting writing to the write buffer (under this situation, q is in the form of $h\&(act', tid, idx')$, where act' is the corresponding propagation operation), or $x = e$ representing propagating to the shared memory, or $a = e$ indicating writing to the private register, or fence.
- tid records the identity of the thread that performs the associated action. Example 1 below is used to provide an intuitive understanding of it.
- For facilitating the exploration of the associated algebraic laws, the tree structure for any sequential program needs to be constructed. On this basis, we introduce the parameter idx to mark the unique branch of each action.
    - Regarding a memory write $x := 1$, committing the write to x to the write buffer $\langle x = 1 \rangle$'s idx is $\langle 1 \rangle$, while moving the same write to the memory $x = 1$'s idx is $\langle 2 \rangle$. Also, the parameter idx of the action $a = 1$ abstracted from a register write $a := 1$ is $\langle 1 \rangle$, and the analysis of the fence is similar.
    - For the sequential program which has more than one statement, the generation of each action's idx is realized by the second sequential expansion law (seq-2) in the subsequent section.

Finally, the guarded choice is in the form of $[]_{i \in I}\{h_i\&(act_i, tid_i, idx_i) \leftrightsquigarrow P_i[q_i]\}$, where a Boolean condition is satisfied, the corresponding action can be selected to execute.

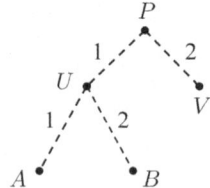

Fig. 3. The Introduction to Thread id.

Example 1. Consider the parallel process P, where $P =_{\text{df}} U||V$, and $U =_{\text{df}} A||B$. The notation "$=_{\text{df}}$" refers to definitions. Firstly, we assume that every sequential process has a thread id λ.

As shown in Fig. 3, the left edge is assigned a label whose value is 1, while the label of the right one is 2. For the parallel composition $U||V$, the thread id of U is $\langle 1 \rangle^\wedge \lambda$ and that of V is $\langle 2 \rangle^\wedge \lambda$. Then, for the parallel composition $A||B$, the thread id of A is $\langle 1 \rangle^\wedge \langle 1 \rangle^\wedge \lambda$, and that of B is $\langle 1 \rangle^\wedge \langle 2 \rangle^\wedge \lambda$.

For simplicity, we use $\langle 1, 1 \rangle$ and $\langle 1, 2 \rangle$ instead of $\langle 1 \rangle^\wedge \langle 1 \rangle$ and $\langle 1 \rangle^\wedge \langle 2 \rangle$, and we have $tid^\wedge \lambda = tid$.

$\square$

4.2   Head Normal Form

In this section, we assign every program P a normal form named as *head normal form HF(P)*.

1) For a register write $a := e$, the remaining part after the first step expansion is empty, which is denoted by the notation E.

$$HF(a := e) =_{\text{df}} [\![\{ \text{true} \& (a = e, \lambda, \langle 1 \rangle) \looparrowright E \}$$

The analysis of the fence is similar.

$$HF(\text{fence}) =_{\text{df}} [\![\{ \text{true} \& (\text{fence}, \lambda, \langle 1 \rangle) \looparrowright E \}$$

2) Different from register writes, for a memory write $x := e$, it is split into two parts. One is writing to the store buffer and the other is propagating to the main memory. The configuration of the propagation operation is put in the square brackets.

$$HF(x := e) =_{\text{df}} [\![\{ \text{true} \& (\langle x = e \rangle, \lambda, \langle 1 \rangle) \looparrowright E[(x = e, \lambda, \langle 2 \rangle)] \}$$

3) For *Condition*, configurations $h\&(\epsilon, \lambda, \langle 1 \rangle)$ and $\neg h\&(\epsilon, \lambda, \langle 1 \rangle)$ are applied to generate the head normal form of *Condition*.

$$HF(\text{if } b \text{ then } P \text{ else } Q) =_{\text{df}} [\![\{ h\&(\epsilon, \lambda, \langle 1 \rangle) \looparrowright P, \neg h\&(\epsilon, \lambda, \langle 1 \rangle) \looparrowright Q \}$$

4) With regard to *Iteration*, the analysis is similar to that of *Condition*.

$$HF(\text{while } b \text{ do } P)$$
$$=_{\text{df}} [\![\{ h\&(\epsilon, \lambda, \langle 1 \rangle) \looparrowright (P; \text{while } b \text{ do } P), \neg h\&(\epsilon, \lambda, \langle 1 \rangle) \looparrowright E \}$$

The definition of the head normal form of sequential and parallel composition is obtained with the application of the algebraic laws in the next subsection.

4.3   Algebraic Laws

The focus of this section is to present a set of algebraic laws. Law (seq-1) is responsible for transferring program statements into configurations. When the subsequent program Q involves making a sequential composition, the memory operation q (if it exists) is supposed to act on the whole program $P'; Q$.

> (seq-1)
> Let $P = \|\{h\&(act, tid, idx) \leadsto P'[q]\}$,
> Then $P; Q = \|\{h\&(act, tid, idx) \leadsto (P'; Q)[q]\}$

The transferred configurations are independent of each other. Since we want to construct a tree structure for each sequential program, the program order relation should be reflected. It is described and formalized by the law (seq-2).

> (seq-2)
> $h\&(act, tid, idx) \leadsto P'[q] = h\&(act, tid, idx) \rightarrow (\langle 1 \rangle^\wedge P')[q]$,
> where, $h\&(act, tid, idx) \leadsto E = h\&(act, tid, idx), E[q] = q$

Except for the fetched configuration $h\&(act, tid, idx)$ and the corresponding q (if it exists), the parameter idx in each configuration of the subsequent program should add a prefix $\langle 1 \rangle$, which can be achieved by the function below. Here, "$/$" represents the replacement operator.

$$\langle 1 \rangle^\wedge P =_{df} \forall h\&(act, tid, idx) \in P \cdot P[h\&(act, tid, \langle 1 \rangle^\wedge idx)/h\&(act, tid, idx)]$$

So far, we have introduced two operators. One is "$\leadsto$" which is used to connect the configurations with the original indices. If the indices can reflect the program order relation, we use the operator "$\rightarrow$" instead.

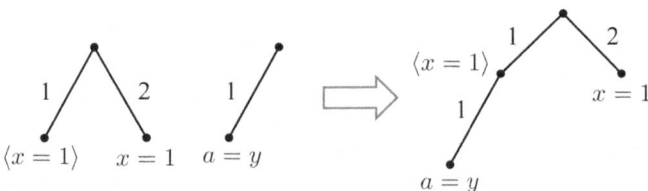

Fig. 4. The Tree Structure of $x := 1; a := y$.

Example 2. Consider the program $P; Q$, where $P =_{df} x := 1$, and $Q =_{df} a := y$, variables x and y are global, and a is a local variable. The head normal form of such a sequential program is formalized as below.

$$HF(x := 1) = (\langle x = 1 \rangle, \lambda, \langle 1 \rangle) \looparrowright E[(x = 1, \lambda, \langle 2 \rangle)]$$

$$HF(x := 1; a := y) = (\langle x = 1 \rangle, \lambda, \langle 1 \rangle) \looparrowright (E; a := y)[(x = 1, \lambda, \langle 2 \rangle)]$$

$$= (\langle x = 1 \rangle, \lambda, \langle 1 \rangle) \looparrowright ((a = y, \lambda, \langle 1 \rangle) \looparrowright E)[(x = 1, \lambda, \langle 2 \rangle)]$$

$$= (\langle x = 1 \rangle, \lambda, \langle 1 \rangle) \rightarrow (a = y, \lambda, \boxed{\langle 1, 1 \rangle})[(x = 1, \lambda, \langle 2 \rangle)]$$

The parameter idx of $a = y$ is $\langle 1, 1 \rangle$, which is the same as Fig. 4. □

Next, the investigation moves to how the configuration sequences of programs can be generated dynamically. As exhibited in Fig. 5, the operation of the first statement (except for the propagation operation of a memory write) of any thread, modelled by p_1 or q_1 in formula (3.1) as below, can be firstly scheduled. If p_1 (or q_1) is not of a buffer operation, s (or t) is ϵ.

Different from the traditional interleaving semantics, if the configuration p_1 in the left branch (i.e., P) is chosen, the prefix $\langle 1 \rangle$ should be added to the thread id tid_{i1} of p_1, shown in formula (3.2). Otherwise, the prefix $\langle 2 \rangle$ is attached to the thread id tid_{j1} of q_1, shown in formula (3.3).

(seqpar-1)

$P \| Q$

$$= (p_1 \rightarrow (p_2 \rightarrow P')[s]) \| (q_1 \rightarrow (q_2 \rightarrow Q')[t]) \tag{3.1}$$

$$= p_1[(\langle 1 \rangle^\wedge tid_{i1})/tid_{i1}] \rightarrow ((p_2 \rightarrow P')[s] \| (q_1 \rightarrow (q_2 \rightarrow Q')[t])) \tag{3.2}$$

$\parallel$

$$q_1[(\langle 2 \rangle^\wedge tid_{j1})/tid_{j1}] \rightarrow ((p_1 \rightarrow (p_2 \rightarrow P')[s]) \| (q_2 \rightarrow Q')[t]) \tag{3.3}$$

$$= p_1[(\langle 1 \rangle^\wedge tid_{i1})/tid_{i1}] \rightarrow$$

$$\begin{pmatrix} (\boxed{s[(\langle 1 \rangle^\wedge tid_{i1})/tid_{i1}]} \rightarrow (\boxed{(p_2 \rightarrow P')} \| (q_1 \rightarrow (q_2 \rightarrow Q')[t]))) \\ \parallel \\ (\boxed{p_2[(\langle 1 \rangle^\wedge tid_{i2})/tid_{i2}]} \rightarrow (\boxed{P'[s]} \| (q_1 \rightarrow (q_2 \rightarrow Q')[t]))) \text{ if } c_i \\ \parallel \\ (q_1[(\langle 2 \rangle^\wedge tid_{j1})/tid_{j1}] \rightarrow ((p_2 \rightarrow P')[s]) \| ((q_2 \rightarrow Q')[t])) \end{pmatrix} \tag{3.4}$$

$\parallel$

$$q_1[(\langle 2 \rangle^\wedge tid_{j1})/tid_{j1}] \rightarrow$$

$$\begin{pmatrix} (p_1[(\langle 1 \rangle^\wedge tid_{i1})/tid_{i1}] \rightarrow (((p_2 \rightarrow P')[s]) \| (q_2 \rightarrow Q')[t])) \\ \parallel \\ (\boxed{t[(\langle 2 \rangle^\wedge tid_{j1})/tid_{j1}]} \rightarrow ((p_1 \rightarrow (p_2 \rightarrow P')[s]) \| \boxed{(q_2 \rightarrow Q')})) \\ \parallel \\ (\boxed{q_2[(\langle 2 \rangle^\wedge tid_{j2})/tid_{j2}]} \rightarrow ((p_1 \rightarrow (p_2 \rightarrow P')[s]) \| \boxed{Q'[t]})) \text{ if } c_j \end{pmatrix}$$

where, $p_1 = h_{i1} \& (act_{i1}, tid_{i1}, idx_{i1})$, $p_2 = h_{i2} \& (act_{i2}, tid_{i2}, idx_{i2})$, $s = h_{i1} \& (act'_{i1}, tid_{i1}, idx'_{i1})$, $q_1 = h_{j1} \& (act_{j1}, tid_{j1}, idx_{j1})$, $q_2 = h_{j2} \& (act_{j2}, tid_{j2}, idx_{j2})$ and $t = h_{j1} \& (act'_{j1}, tid_{j1}, idx'_{j1})$.

After the first step expansion, we need to consider the order between the configuration s of the propagation operation (if it exists) and its subsequent program $p_2 \rightarrow P'$. s can be performed without any constraint, as shown in the formula (3.4). However, if the first configuration p_2 in the subsequent program wants to be triggered, some requirements are supposed to be satisfied, formalized as below.

$$c_i =_{\mathrm{df}} \left(\begin{array}{l} (lt(\pi_3(p_2)) \neq 2 \wedge \pi_1(p_2) \neq \mathrm{fence}) \\ \vee \; (lt(\pi_3(p_2)) = 2 \wedge len(\pi_3(p_2)) < len(\pi_3(s))) \end{array} \right)$$

The full fence instruction works as a barrier and prevents the reordering between two statements. Then, when meeting the fence, any propagation operation belonging to the statement before the full fence instruction should be already executed. It says that, if the parameter idx of p_2 does not end with 2, p_2 cannot be the configuration of the fence. Here, $lt(idx)$ denotes the last element in idx.

In addition, since the write buffer of any thread conforms to the FIFO (First-In-First-Out) principle, the memory actions should be performed sequentially. Formally, if p_2's idx ends with 2, the length of p_2's idx should be smaller than that of s's idx. The notation $len(idx)$ is used to record the length of idx. The analysis of the order between t and $q_2 \rightarrow Q'$ is similar.

For simplicity, some boundary conditions are omitted here. For example, the parallel composition of a memory write and a register write can be formalized by letting p_2, q_2 and t to be ϵ, P' and Q' to be E. Specifically, the sequential program in Example 2 can be modeled by letting q_1, q_2 and t to be ϵ, and P' and Q' to be E.

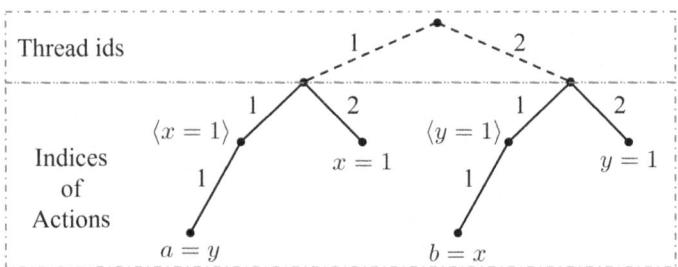

Fig. 5. The Combination of $x := 1; a := y$ and $y := 1; b := x$.

Example 2: Continuation
Consider the program $(x := 1; a := y) \| (y := 1; b := x)$, where x and y are global variables, while a and b are local variables. The incomplete head normal form of

the parallel program is formalized as below.

$$HF((x := 1; a := y)||(y := 1; b := x))$$
$$=((\langle x = 1\rangle, \lambda, \langle 1\rangle) \to (a = y, \lambda, \langle 1, 1\rangle)[(x = 1, \lambda, \langle 2\rangle)]$$
$$||(\langle y = 1\rangle, \lambda, \langle 1\rangle) \to (b = x, \lambda, \langle 1, 1\rangle)[(y = 1, \lambda, \langle 2\rangle)]$$
$$=((\langle x = 1\rangle, \boxed{\langle 1\rangle}, \langle 1\rangle) \to (x = 1, \boxed{\langle 1\rangle}, \langle 2\rangle) \to$$
$$(a = y, \lambda, \langle 1, 1\rangle)||(\langle y = 1\rangle, \lambda, \langle 1\rangle) \to (b = x, \lambda, \langle 1, 1\rangle)[(y = 1, \lambda, \langle 2\rangle)]$$
$$||(\langle x = 1\rangle, \boxed{\langle 1\rangle}, \langle 1\rangle) \to (a = y, \boxed{\langle 1\rangle}, \langle 1, 1\rangle) \to$$
$$(x = 1, \lambda, \langle 2\rangle)||(\langle y = 1\rangle, \lambda, \langle 1\rangle) \to (b = x, \lambda, \langle 1, 1\rangle)[(y = 1, \lambda, \langle 2\rangle)]$$
$$||(\langle x = 1\rangle, \boxed{\langle 1\rangle}, \langle 1\rangle) \to (\langle y = 1\rangle, \boxed{\langle 2\rangle}, \langle 1\rangle) \to$$
$$(a = y, \lambda, \langle 1, 1\rangle)[(x = 1, \lambda, \langle 2\rangle)]||(b = x, \lambda, \langle 1, 1\rangle)[(y = 1, \lambda, \langle 2\rangle)]$$
$$||(\langle y = 1\rangle, \boxed{\langle 2\rangle}, \langle 1\rangle) \to (\langle x = 1\rangle, \boxed{\langle 1\rangle}, \langle 1\rangle) \to$$
$$(a = y, \lambda, \langle 1, 1\rangle)[(x = 1, \lambda, \langle 2\rangle)]||(b = x, \lambda, \langle 1, 1\rangle)[(y = 1, \lambda, \langle 2\rangle)]$$
$$||(\langle y = 1\rangle, \boxed{\langle 2\rangle}, \langle 1\rangle) \to (y = 1, \boxed{\langle 2\rangle}, \langle 2\rangle) \to$$
$$((\langle x = 1\rangle, \lambda, \langle 1\rangle) \to (a = y, \lambda, \langle 1, 1\rangle)[(x = 1, \lambda, \langle 2\rangle)]||(b = x, \lambda, \langle 1, 1\rangle)$$
$$||(\langle y = 1\rangle, \boxed{\langle 2\rangle}, \langle 1\rangle) \to (b = x, \boxed{\langle 2\rangle}, \langle 1, 1\rangle) \to$$
$$((\langle x = 1\rangle, \lambda, \langle 1\rangle) \to (a = y, \lambda, \langle 1, 1\rangle)[(x = 1, \lambda, \langle 2\rangle)]||(y = 1, \lambda, \langle 2\rangle)$$

As exhibited in Fig. 5, the thread id *tid* of the generated configurations is $\langle 1\rangle$ or $\langle 2\rangle$ instead of λ. The shadow area represents the configurations to be generated.   □

5 Implementation

This section shows the implementation of the proposed algebraic laws in Maude. We only list some parts of them here due to space limitations.

Since the operations on global variables and local variables are different, we firstly give the basic sorts l-Variable and g-Variable. For convenience, global variables, such as x, y and z, are implemented as g(1), g(2) and g(3) in Maude. Similarly, local variables, such as a, b and c, are implemented as l(1), l(2) and l(3), respectively. Hence, we provide two operators g(_) and l(_).

```
1  sorts Variable l-Variable g-Variable Expression .
2  op g(_) : Nat -> g-Variable .
3  op l(_) : Nat -> l-Variable .
```

The functionality of the sequential expansion law (seq-1) is to transfer statements into configurations. Specifically, if the transferred statement is a memory write, encoded as g_x := e, two configurations are produced, shown in lines 4 and 5 as below. Note that, before such a transformation, the statement is guided by the notation bl, and after that, the generated configuration is guided by al.

```
1   var g_x : g-Variable .
2   var l_x : l-Variable .
3   var e : Expression .
4   rl bl(g_x := e,T1,L1 1) ; b =>
5   al(g_x := e,T1,L1 1) +> b[al(g_x := e,T1,L1 2)] .
6   rl bl(l_x := e,T1,L1 1) ; b =>
7   al(l_x := e,T1,L1 1) +> b .
```

The sequential expansion law (seq-2) is used to reflect the program order relation by updating the third parameter of each configuration from (seq-1). The updated configurations are guided by the notation cl. Since the configurations with original indices and those with updated indices are guided with different notations, we can merely use the symbol "+>" in Maude. If the updated configuration cl(s1,T1,M1 1) is of committing to the private buffer and at the head of one sequence, the next operation is on the corresponding configuration al(s1,T1,M1 2), and the only modification is to replace the notation al with cl to mark its completion, shown in lines 1 and 2 below.

```
1   rl cl(s1,T1,M1 1) +> b[al(s1,T1,M1 2)] =>
2   cl(s1,T1,M1 1) +> b[cl(s1,T1,M1 2)] .
3   rl cl(s1,T1,M1) +>
4   (al(s2,T2,M2 1) +> b[al(s2,T2,M2 2)])[c1] =>
5   cl(s1,T1,M1) +> cl(s2,T2,M1 M2 1) +>
6   b[cl(s2,T2,M1 M2 2)][c1] .
7   rl cl(s1,T1,M1) +> (al(s2,T2,M2 1) +> b)[c1] =>
8   cl(s1,T1,M1) +> cl(s2,T2,M1 M2 1) +> b[c1] .
```

We assume that both configurations of a memory write w_1 have been updated (here, we do not care about whether cl(s1,T1,M1) is of its buffer operation). If the first in the subsequent program is another memory write w_2, the modification on its configurations al(s2,T2,M2 1) and al(s2,T2,M2 2) is to add a prefix M1 in the third parameters. Upon completion, the guided notations in them are updated to cl. These operations are encoded in lines 3 to 6 as above. If not, the difference is that the prefix will be attached to the single configuration, i.e., (al(s2,T2,M2 1) in line 7.

Next, we introduce the operator par(_||_) to achieve the functionality of the law (seqpar-1). The boundary conditions are set using the operator empty and the unconditional rules in lines 3 to 7 as below.

```
1   op par(_||_) : block block -> block [ctor assoc] .
2   op empty : -> block .
3   rl par(cl(s1,T,M) || b) =>
4   cl(s1,1 T,M) +> par(empty || b) .
5   rl par(b || cl(s1,T,M)) =>
```

```
6  cl(s1,2 T,M) +> par(b || empty) .
7  rl b +> par(empty || empty) => b .
```

Now, we take the trigger of configurations in the left branch for an example, and that of the right branch is similar. Mainly, there are five cases.

1. If the first statement is a memory write, the configuration cl(s1,T1,M 1) of its buffer operation can be scheduled without any condition. In consequence, it can be encoded by using an unconditional rule. Here, before and after the update, the configurations are both guided with cl. The difference between them is inside and outside the par environment. Moreover, the second parameter of the one outside par has a prefix 1.
2. If the update in item 1 has been done, the remaining part is b[cl(s1,T1,M 2)], configuration cl(s1,T1,M 2) can also be triggered without any condition.
3. When b in item 2 is in the form of (cl(s1,T1,M1 1) +> b), the schedule of cl(s1,T1,M1 1) should satisfy the condition that s1 is not fence, encoded by the equation not-other.
4. When b in item 2 is expressed as (cl(s1,T1,M1 2) +> b), the trigger of cl(s1,T1,M1 2) should meet the requirement that the length of (M1 2) is shorter than that of (M2 2) in configuration cl(s2,T1,M2 2), encoded by larger-other in line 10.
5. The last item is to handle the configurations of register writes.

```
1   rl par(cl(s1,T1,M 1) +> (b[cl(s1,T1,M 2)]) || b1) =>
2   cl(s1,1 T1,M 1) +> par((b[cl(s1,T1,M 2)]) || b1) .
3   rl par((b[cl(s1,T1,M 2)]) || b1) =>
4   cl(s1,1 T1,M 2) +> par(b || b1) .
5   crl par((cl(s1,T1,M1 1) +> b)[cl(s2,T1,M2 2)] || b1) =>
6   cl(s1,1 T1,M1 1) +> par((b[cl(s2,T1,M2 2)]) || b1)
7   if not-other(cl(s1,T1,M1 1), cl(s2,T1,M2 2)) .
8   crl par((cl(s1,T1,M1 2) +> b)[cl(s2,T1,M2 2)] || b1) =>
9   cl(s1,1 T1,M1 2) +> par((b[cl(s2,T1,M2 2)]) || b1)
10  if larger-other(cl(s2,T1,M2 2), cl(s1,T1,M1 2)) .
11  rl par(cl(s1,T,M) +> c1 || b) =>
12  cl(s1,1 T,M) +> par(c1 || b) .
```

Example 2: Further Continuation
As exhibited in Fig. 6, we show the results when applying the algebraic laws to the parallel program $(x := 1; a := y) || (y := 1; b := x)$ in the Maude system.

1. With the application of sequential expansion law (seq-1) (arrow (1) in Fig. 6) and the search command in Maude, the initial configuration sequence of the program $x := 1; a := y$ is yielded.
2. The program order relation cannot be reflected by configurations al(g(1) := 1,nil,1) and al(1(1) := g(2),nil,1). Then we encode the sequential expansion law (seq-2) (arrow (3) in Fig. 6) in Maude and use the search command again. The length of the third parameter in configuration cl(1(1) := g(2),nil,1 1) is 2, which conforms to the fact that the statement $a := y$ is the second in $x := 1; a := y$.

$\downarrow(1)$

Maude> search bl(g(1) := 1, nil, 1) ;
bl(l(1) := g(2), nil, 1) =>! X:block .
Solution 1 (state 2)
states: 3 rewrites: 2 in 0ms cpu (0ms real) (~
rewrites/second)
X:block --> al(g(1) := 1, nil, 1) +>
(al(l(1) := g(2), nil, 1)[al(g(1) := 1, nil, 2)])
No more solutions.

$\downarrow(2)$

Maude> search bl(g(2) := 1, nil, 1) ;
bl(l(2) := g(1), nil, 1) =>! X:block .
Solution 1 (state 2)
states: 3 rewrites: 2 in 0ms cpu (0ms real) (~
rewrites/second)
X:block --> al(g(2) := 1, nil, 1) +> (al(l(2) :=
g(1), nil, 1)[al(g(2) := 1, nil, 2)])
No more solutions.

$\downarrow(3)$

Maude> search cl(g(1) := 1, nil, 1) +>
(al(l(1) := g(2), nil, 1)[al(g(1) := 1, nil, 2)])
=>! X:block .
Solution 1 (state 2)
states: 3 rewrites: 2 in 0ms cpu (0ms real) (~
rewrites/second)
X:block --> cl(g(1) := 1, nil, 1) +>
(cl(l(1) := g(2), nil, 1 1)[cl(g(1) := 1, nil, 2)])
No more solutions.

$\downarrow(4)$

Maude> search cl(g(2) := 1, nil, 1) +>
(al(l(2) := g(1), nil, 1)[al(g(2) := 1, nil, 2)])
=>! X:block .
Solution 1 (state 2)
states: 3 rewrites: 2 in 0ms cpu (0ms real) (~
rewrites/second)
X:block --> cl(g(2) := 1, nil, 1) +> (cl(l(2) :=
g(1), nil, 1 1)[cl(g(2) := 1, nil, 2)])
No more solutions.

$\downarrow(5)$ $\downarrow(6)$

Maude> search par(cl(g(1) := 1, nil, 1) +> (cl(l(1) := g(2), nil, 1 1)[cl(g(1) := 1, nil, 2)]) ||
cl(g(2) := 1, nil, 1) +> (cl(l(2) := g(1), nil, 1 1)[cl(g(2) := 1, nil, 2)])) =>! X:block .
Solution 1 (state 225)
states: 305 rewrites: 840 in 0ms cpu (4ms real) (~ rewrites/second)
X:block --> cl(g(1) := 1, 1, 1) +> cl(g(1) := 1, 1, 2) +> cl(g(2) := 1, 2, 1) +> cl(g(2) := 1, 2, 2)
+> cl(l(1) := g(2), 1, 1 1) +> cl(l(2) := g(1), 2, 1 1)
...
Solution 80 (state 304)
states: 305 rewrites: 840 in 0ms cpu (45ms real) (~ rewrites/second)
X:block --> cl(g(2) := 1, 2, 1) +> cl(l(2) := g(1), 2, 1 1) +> cl(g(2) := 1, 2, 2) +> cl(g(1) := 1, 1,
1) +> cl(l(1) := g(2), 1, 1 1) +> cl(g(1) := 1, 1, 2)
No more solutions.

Fig. 6. The Implementation of Algebraic Laws.

3. The analysis of $y := 1; b := x$ is similar, shown as arrows (2) and (4) in Fig. 6.
4. Based on the generated configuration sequences in items 2 and 3, shown as
   arrows (5) and (6) in Fig. 6, the law (seqpar-1) is implemented in Maude
   and all the possible configuration sequences (the total number is 80) of $(x :=
   1; a := y)||(y := 1; a := x)$ are provided.   □

6   Verification

From the perspective of syntax and semantics, we can conduct the lightweight
general or value-based verification of programs under the TSO memory model.

   "Lightweight" can be deduced from the random execution of par for generating configuration sequences dynamically, GV for recording the data states of

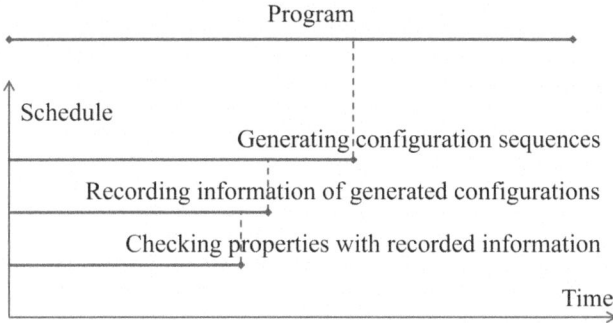

Fig. 7. The Background of Lightweight Verification.

the generated configurations and themselves, and Check for verifying properties related to the unique features of TSO with recorded information, exhibited in Fig. 7.

6.1   Preparation

Now, we pay attention to the GV part. To conduct different levels of verification, we introduce the sort Current in the form of [var_1 <- val_1, var_2 <- val_2,..., var_n <- val_n] <> d. The part before <> can be used to record the data states of any configuration. Then the configuration is guided by dl, and attached to d, which is composed of the configurations whose data states have been already recorded.

```
1  sort History .
2  sort Current .
3  subsort Current < History .
4  op _<>_ : Current d-block -> Current .
5  op _<-_ : Variable NatList -> Current .
```

In addition to the full declaration of Current, the instance of Current can also be obtained from the sub-sequence of [var_1 <- val_1, var_2 <- val_2,..., var_n <- val_n]. his from History is the sequence of instances from Current with full declaration.

For a memory write $x := e$, updating the parameter his depends on the assignment to x. Based on the most recent instance in his (i.e., last(his)), this assignment brings in new_his.

```
1  op _,_ : History History -> History [assoc] .
2  var his new_his : History .
3  crl GV(his,d +> cl(s1,T1,M1) +> b) =>
4  GV(his,new_his,d +> dl(s1,T1,M1) +> b)
5  if new_his := assign(last(his),cl(s1,T1,M1)) .
```

Now, we explain assign by taking the two parts in memory writes as an example. For committing a write to g(t,i) to the thread t's private buffer, the calculated value is attached to the tail of n1, with the application of append in line 4. For propagating to the main memory, the bottom in n2 (i.e., head(n2)) is used to replace n1, and then n2 is updated to be tail(n2). Here tail(n2) records the remaining after moving the element head(n2) from n2.

```
1   op g(_,_) : Nat Nat -> g-Variable .
2   eq assign([cr1, (g(t,i) <- n1), cr2] <> d,
3   cl(g(i) := e,t T1,M1 1)) =
4   [cr1, (g(t,i) <- append(n1,
5   cal([cr1, (g(t,i) <- n1), cr2], e, t T1))), cr2] <>
6   (d +> dl(g(i) := e,t T1,M1 1)) .
7   eq assign([cr1, (g(0,i) <- n1), cr2, (g(t,i) <- n2), cr3]
8   <> d, cl(g(i) := e,t T1,M1 2)) =
9   [cr1, (g(0,i) <- head(n2)), cr2, (g(t,i) <- tail(n2)), cr3]
10  <> (d +> dl(g(i) := e,t T1,M1 2)) .
```

In the operator g(_ , _), the first parameter indicates the identities of threads. Specifically, g(0,1)<-0 represents that the variable x in the shared memory is equal to 0.

The read operations on variables in expression e make contributions to the mentioned assignment. If the private buffer in the thread t has writes to g(i), i.e., (g(t,i) <- n1) and not size(n1) == 0, the most recent value in n1 recorded as last(n1) in line 2 is returned. Otherwise, we call cal([cr1, (g(t,i) <- n1), cr2], g(i), 0) to get the value from the shared memory.

```
1   ceq cal([cr1, (g(t,i) <- n1), cr2], g(i), t T1) =
2   last(n1) if not (size(n1) == 0) .
3   ceq cal([cr1, (g(t,i) <- n1), cr2], g(i), t T1) =
4   cal([cr1, (g(t,i) <- n1), cr2], g(i), 0) if size(n1) == 0.
5   eq cal([cr1, (g(0,i) <- n1), cr2], g(i), 0) = n1 .
```

Example 3 below is provided to help in understanding the process of GV intuitively.

Example 3. Consider the program $x := 1; a := y$, where x and y are global, while a is local. Here, we choose one execution to describe the generated configurations, whose corresponding data states have been updated. For simplicity, the data states only include the variables x and y in the memory, and x, y and a in a thread. Initially, cur from Current is ([(g(0,1) <- 0),(g(0,2) <- 0),(g(1,1) <- nil), (g(1,2) <- nil),1(1,1) <- 0] <> emptyd).

When performing the buffer operation of $x := 1$, variable cur is updated to ([(g(0,1) <- 0),(g(0,2) <- 0),(g(1,1) <- 1),(g(1,2) <-nil),1(1,1) <- 0] <> (emptyd +> dl(g(1) := 1,1,1))). Once the corresponding propagation operation is executed, the value of g(1,1) is reset to be nil. Afterwards, cur is ([(g(0,1) <- 1),(g(0,2) <- 0),(g(1,1) <- nil),(g(1,2) <- nil),1(1,1) <- 0] <> (emptyd +> dl(g(1) := 1,1,1) +> dl(g(1) := 1,1,2))).

When the read operation on y and the register write have been performed, cur is changed to ([(g(0,1) <- 1),(g(0,2) <- 0),(g(1,1) <- nil),(g(1,2) <-

```
nil),l(1,1) <- 0] <> (emptyd +> dl(g(1) := 1,1,1) +> dl(g(1) := 1,1, 2)
+> dl(l(1) := g(2),1,1 1))).
```

At the end of execution, variable his from History is the combination of cur in all moments.   □

6.2   Verification Properties and Results

In this section, we focus on the verification of three well-defined properties related to the unique features of the TSO memory model, namely *Write-Read Reordering*, *Read-after-Write Elimination* and *Barrier*.

1) **Write-Read Reordering:** It describes that a write and a read follow the program order relation, but the effect of the read may happen before that of the write [12].

In general, if a configuration dl(v2 := e2,T1,M2 2) of a propagation operation appears after such a configuration dl(v1 := e1,T1,M1) whose length of index is longer, encoded by len(M1) > len(M2 2), we claim that *Write-Read Reordering* happens. The additional requirement is that the configuration dl(v1 := e1,T1,M1) includes some read operations on memory locations formalized by checkread(e1).

```
1  crl Check(GV(his, b1), st) => true if checkst(last(his)) .
2  eq checkst([cr1] <> (d1 +> dl(v1 := e1,T1,M1) +>
3  dl(v2 := e2,T1,M2 2) +> d3)) =
4  len(M1) > len(M2 2) and checkread(e1) .
```

We conduct the verification on the simple program $(x := 1; a := y) \| (y := 1; b := x)$. If the conditions in Property *Write-Read Reordering* are achieved, the check terminates with a solution. From Fig. 8, we find that the property is valid, and the result can be returned without searching the whole sequence.

Maude> search Check(GV([(g(0,1) <- 0), (g(0,2) <- 0), (g(1,1) <- nil), (g(1,2) <- nil), (l(1,1) <- 0), (l(1,2) <- 0), (g(2,1) <- nil), (g(2,2) <- nil), (l(2,1) <- 0), (l(2,2) <- 0)] <> emptyd, par(cl(g(1) := 1, nil, 1) +> (cl(l(1) := g(2), nil, 1 1)[cl(g(1) := 1, nil, 2)]) ‖ cl(g(2) := 1, nil, 1) +> (cl(l(2) := g(1), nil, 1 1)[cl(g(2) := 1, nil, 2)]))) , st) =>! true .
Solution 1 (state 536)
states: 855 rewrites: 5555 in 0ms cpu (22ms real) (~ rewrites/second)
empty substitution
No more solutions.
states: 1888 rewrites: 25241 in 0ms cpu (82ms real) (~ rewrites/second)

Fig. 8. The General Verification of Write-Read Reordering.

In addition, we would like to provide a value-based solution to Property *Write-Read Reordering*, exploring whether a program can reach a certain data state. Then, the elements in cur and those in the state should be in one-to-one correspondence, modelled in the unconditional equation below.

```
1  crl Checkcon(GV(his, d), [cr1]) => true
2  if checkcr(last(his), [cr1]) .
3  eq checkcr([cr1, (g(0,i) <- n1), cr2] <> d1,
4  [(g(i) <- n2), cr3]) = (n1 == n2) and
5  checkcr([cr1, (g(0,i) <- n1), cr2] <> d1, [cr3]) .
```

Consider the program $(x := 1; a := y)||(y := 1; b := x)$, where $x := 1; a := y$ is performed in the thread T_1, while $y := 1; b := x$ is executed in T_2.

Maude> search Checkcon(GV([(g(0,1) <- 0), (g(0,2) <- 0), (g(1,1) <- nil), (g(1,2) <- nil), (l(1,1) <- 0), (l(1,2) <- 0), (g(2,1) <- nil), (g(2,2) <- nil), (l(2,1) <- 0), (l(2,2) <- 0)] <> emptyd, par(cl(g(1) := 1, nil, 1) +> (cl(l(1) := g(2), nil, 1 1)[cl(g(1) := 1, nil, 2)]) || cl(g(2) := 1, nil, 1) +> (cl(l(2) := g(1), nil, 1 1)[cl(g(2) := 1, nil, 2)]))) , [(g(1) <- 1), (g(2) <- 1), (l(1,1) <- 0), (l(2,2) <- 0)]) =>! true .
Solution 1 (state 1887)
states: 1888 rewrites: 15356 in 0ms cpu (52ms real) (~ rewrites/second)
empty substitution
No more solutions.
states: 1888 rewrites: 15356 in 0ms cpu (53ms real) (~ rewrites/second)

Fig. 9. The Value-based Verification of Write-Read Reordering.

What we need to check is whether a in T_1 and b in T_2 are equal to 0 when T_1 and T_2 have updated x and y in the memory. It means that the condition `[(g(1) <- 1), (g(2) <- 1), (l(1,1) <- 0), (l(2,2) <- 0)]` should be satisfied in the final state of the execution of one configuration sequence. As exhibited in Fig. 9, the value-based property is also valid.

2) **Read-after-Write Elimination:** It replaces a read from some location directly after a write to that location by the value written by the write.

```
1  crl Check(GV(his, b1), fr) => true if checkfr(last(his)) .
2  eq checkfr([cr1] <> (d1 +> dl(v1 := e1,T1,M1) +>
3  dl(g_x := e2,T1,M2 2) +> d3)) =
4  len(M1) > len(M2 2) and not (notexist(e1, g_x)) .
```

The equation is similar to that in Property 1. The difference is that `g_x` in the configuration `dl(g_x := e2,T1,M2 2)` of the write should be contained in `e1` in the configuration `dl(v1 := e1,T1,M1)` of the read. It is formalized by `not (notexist(e1, g_x))`. When carrying out the verification on the sequential program $x := 1; a := x; y := 1$, Fig. 10 shows that the property is valid when the states are not completely traversed.

3) **Barrier:** When a full fence instruction comes, it will flush all the contents in the buffer. That is, no configurations whose length of the index is smaller appear after that of the fence.

```
1   crl Check(GV(his, b1), ff) => false if checkff(last(his)).
2   eq checkff([cr1] <> (d1 +> dl(fence,T1,M2) +>
3   dl(g_x := e1,T1,M1 2) +> d2)) = len(M1 2) < len(M2) .
```

All the configuration sequences are supposed to be examined, and the result is assigned to be false once it is violated. We carry out the verification on $x :=$ 1; fence; $a := y$, Fig. 11 says that the property is valid via No solution.

Maude> search Check(GV([(g(0,1) <- 0), (g(0,2) <- 0), (g(1,1) <- nil), (g(1,2) <- nil), (l(1,1) <- 0)] <> emptyd , par(cl(g(1) := 1, nil, 1) +> ((cl(l(1) := g(1), nil, 1 1) +> (cl(g(2) := 1, nil, 1 1 1)[cl(g(2) := 1, nil, 1 1 2)]))[cl(g(1) := 1, nil, 2)]) || empty)) , fr) =>! true .
Solution 1 (state 47)
states: 59 rewrites: 604 in 0ms cpu (2ms real) (~ rewrites/second)
empty substitution
No more solutions.
states: 76 rewrites: 1161 in 0ms cpu (4ms real) (~ rewrites/second)

Fig. 10. The General Verification of Read-after-Write Elimination.

Maude> search Check(GV([(g(0,1) <- 0), (g(0,2) <- 0), (g(1,1) <- nil), (g(1,2) <- nil), (l(1,1) <- 0)] <> emptyd, par(cl(g(1) := 1, nil, 1) +> cl(fence, nil, 1 1) +> (cl(l(1) := g(2), nil, 1 1 1)[cl(g(1) := 1, nil, 2)]) || empty)) , ff) =>! false .
No solution.
states: 34 rewrites: 228 in 0ms cpu (1ms real) (~ rewrites/second)

Fig. 11. The General Verification of Barrier.

7 Conclusion

Total Store Order (TSO) is a widely implemented relaxed memory model which allows store-load reordering through each thread's write buffer. This paper presented a set of algebraic laws to dynamically produce configuration sequences of programs under the TSO memory model. During this process, a lightweight verification method was proposed and three well-defined properties related to the characteristic features of TSO were verified in a general or value-based way. The verification results show that our algebraic model conforms to the specification of TSO. In the future, we wish to provide a general framework for conducting the lightweight verification on different relaxed memory models.

Finally, we thank Cliff Jones for his generosity of support for formal methods research over the years and wish him a very happy 80th birthday.

Acknowledgments. This work was partially supported by the National Natural Science Foundation of China (No. 62032024), the "Digital Silk Road" Shanghai International Joint Lab of Trustworthy Intelligent Software (No. 22510750100), and Shanghai Trusted Industry Internet Software Collaborative Innovation Center.

References

1. Abdulla, P.A., Aronis, S., Atig, M.F., Jonsson, B., Leonardsson, C., Sagonas, K.: Stateless model checking for TSO and PSO. Acta Informatica **54**, 789–818 (2017). https://doi.org/10.1007/s00236-016-0275-0

2. Clavel, M., et al.: The Maude 2.0 system. In: Nieuwenhuis, R. (ed.) RTA 2003. LNCS, vol. 2706, pp. 76–87. Springer, Heidelberg (2003). https://doi.org/10.1007/3-540-44881-0_7

3. Hayes, I.J., Jones, C.B., Meinicke, L.A.: Specifying and reasoning about shared-variable concurrency. In: Bowen, J.P., Li, Q., Xu, Q. (eds.) Theories of Programming and Formal Methods. LNCS, vol. 14080, pp. 110–135. Springer, Cham (2023). https://doi.org/10.1007/978-3-031-40436-8_5

4. Hoare, C.A.R., He, J.: Unifying Theories of Programming. Prentice Hall International Series in Computer Science (1998). http://www.unifyingtheories.org

5. Jones, C.B.: Development Methods for Computer Programs Including a Notion of Interference. Technical Monograph **PRG-25**, Programming Research Group, Oxford University Computing Laboratory (1981). https://www.cs.ox.ac.uk/files/9025/PRG-25.pdf

6. Jones, C.B.: Systematic Software Development using VDM, 2nd edn. Prentice Hall International Series in Computer Science (1990)

7. Jones, C.B.: The Turing Guide [book review]. Formal Aspects Comput. **29**, 1121–1122 (2017). https://doi.org/10.1007/s00165-017-0446-y

8. Jones, C.B.: Other semantic approaches. In: Understanding Programming Languages, pp. 95–117. Springer, Cham (2020). https://doi.org/10.1007/978-3-030-59257-8_7

9. Jones, C.B., Misra, J.: Finding effective abstractions. In: Jones, C.B., Misra, J. (eds.) Theories of Programming: The Life and Works of Tony Hoare, chap. 2, pp. 23–40. Association for Computing Machinery (2021). https://doi.org/10.1145/3477355

10. Kang, J., Hur, C.K., Lahav, O., Vafeiadis, V., Dreyer, D.: A promising semantics for relaxed-memory concurrency. ACM SIGPLAN Not. **52**(1), 175–189 (2017). https://doi.org/10.1145/3009837.3009850

11. Kavanagh, R., Brookes, S.: A denotational semantics for SPARC TSO. Log. Meth. Comput. Sci. **15**(2) (2019). https://doi.org/10.23638/LMCS-15(2:10)2019

12. Lahav, O., Vafeiadis, V.: Explaining relaxed memory models with program transformations. In: Fitzgerald, J., Heitmeyer, C., Gnesi, S., Philippou, A. (eds.) FM 2016. LNCS, vol. 9995, pp. 479–495. Springer, Cham (2016). https://doi.org/10.1007/978-3-319-48989-6_29

13. Martí-Oliet, N., Meseguer, J.: Rewriting logic as a logical and semantic framework. Electron. Notes Theor. Comput. Sci. **4**, 190–225 (1996). https://doi.org/10.1016/S1571-0661(04)00040-4

14. Martí-Oliet, N., Meseguer, J.: Rewriting logic: roadmap and bibliography. Theoret. Comput. Sci. **285**(2), 121–154 (2002). https://doi.org/10.1016/S0304-3975(01)00357-7

15. Meseguer, J.: Twenty years of rewriting logic. J. Logic Algebraic Program. **81**(7–8), 721–781 (2012). https://doi.org/10.1016/j.jlap.2012.06.003

16. Morris, F.L., Jones, C.B.: An early proof by Alan Turing. IEEE Ann. Hist. Comput. **6**(2), 139–143 (1984). https://doi.org/10.1109/MAHC.1984.10017

17. Owens, S., Sarkar, S., Sewell, P.: A better x86 memory model: x86-TSO. In: Berghofer, S., Nipkow, T., Urban, C., Wenzel, M. (eds.) TPHOLs 2009. LNCS, vol. 5674, pp. 391–407. Springer, Heidelberg (2009). https://doi.org/10.1007/978-3-642-03359-9_27

18. Saiedian, H., et al.: An invitation to formal methods. Computer **29**(4), 16–30 (1996). https://doi.org/10.1109/MC.1996.488298

19. Sorin, D., Hill, M., Wood, D.: A Primer on Memory Consistency and Cache Coherence. Morgan & Claypool Publishers, San Rafael (2011)

20. Xiao, L., Zhu, H., Xu, Q.: Trace semantics and algebraic laws for total store order memory model. J. Comput. Sci. Technol. **36**(6), 1269–1290 (2021). https://doi.org/10.1007/s11390-021-1616-1

21. Zhu, H., Qin, S., He, J., Bowen, J.P.: PTSC: probability, time and shared-variable concurrency. Innovations Syst. Softw. Eng. **5**, 271–284 (2009). https://doi.org/10.1007/s11334-009-0100-9

22. Zhu, H., Yang, F., He, J., Bowen, J.P., Sanders, J.W., Qin, S.: Linking operational semantics and algebraic semantics for a probabilistic timed shared-variable language. J. Logic Algebraic Program. **81**(1), 2–25 (2012). https://doi.org/10.1016/j.jlap.2011.06.003

Case Study: Modeling, Simulation, Verification, and Code Generation of an Automatic Cruise Control System

Xiong Xu[1], Shuling Wang[3], Zekun Ji[1,2], Qiang Gao[1,2],
Xiangyu Jin[1,2], Bohua Zhan[1,4], and Naijun Zhan[1,5(✉)]

[1] KLSS (CAS) and SKLCS, Institute of Software, Chinese Academy of Sciences,
Beijing, China
{xux,jizk,gaoqiang,jinxy,bzhan}@ios.ac.cn
[2] University of Chinese Academy of Sciences, Beijing, China
[3] National Key Laboratory of Space Integrated Information System,
Institute of Software, Chinese Academy of Sciences, Beijing, China
wangsl@ios.ac.cn
[4] Huawei Technologies Co., Ltd., Beijing, China
[5] School of Computer Science, Peking University, Beijing, China
znj@ios.ac.cn

Abstract. Cyber-Physical Systems (CPSs) seamlessly integrate computational and physical capabilities, that expand the capabilities of physical world through communication, computation, and control. As pointed out by Jones, any failure of these systems may cause severe catastrophes, especially for safety-critical applications. The Model Based Design (MBD) approach can control complexity of systems by appropriate abstraction/refinement and composition/decomposition, and meanwhile provides techniques based on modeling, analysis, and verification in order to detect and correct errors in the early stage of design. However, the MBD for CPSs faces challenges, for it is difficult to consider all the three aspects, including physical processes, software functionality, and system architecture, uniformly in CPS design. To address this issue, we proposed a unified graphical framework combing AADL and Simulink/Stateflow, called AADL⊕S/S, for modeling all the three aspects of CPSs, and we also presented the translation from informal AADL⊕S/S to formal Hybrid Communicating Sequential Processes (HCSP) and finally to C code. In this paper, we introduce a case study of a realistically-scaled automatic cruise control system. The goal of this case study is to show the whole procedure of modeling, simulation, verification, and code generation of the MBD methodology, illustrate the combined framework of AADL and Simulink/Stateflow to cover all the three aspects of CPS design, as well as the capability of analyzing the combined model, and finally demonstrate the practicability of our MBD approach for complex CPSs.

Keywords: CPS · MBD · AADL · Simulink/Stateflow · HCSP · Simulation · Verification · Code Generation

A. Cavalcanti and J. Baxter (Eds.): *The Practice of Formal Methods*, LNCS 14781, pp. 226–246, 2024.
https://doi.org/10.1007/978-3-031-66673-5_12

1   Introduction

Cyber-physical systems (CPSs) tightly couple hardware and software to sense and actuate a physical environment. CPSs are ubiquitous in our daily life such as aerospace, high-speed train, and automotive, and are expected to achieve desired behaviors, especially for safety-critical ones. CPS can be dated back to Jones's computer-based systems [17], later his DSoS (*dependable systems of systems*) [14]. As stressed by Jones [4,17], dependability and reliability are essential for these systems. To attack these issues, model based design (MBD), has become a popular development approach in the CPS community. In the MBD approach, a system is usually modeled as different levels of abstraction for different purposes. However, the MBD of CPSs is not such easy. The key reason for the difficulty is that when modeling CPSs, it is paramount to take multiple perspectives e.g. their software functionalities, physical environment, hardware platform and system architecture into account uniformly, as shown in Fig. 1.

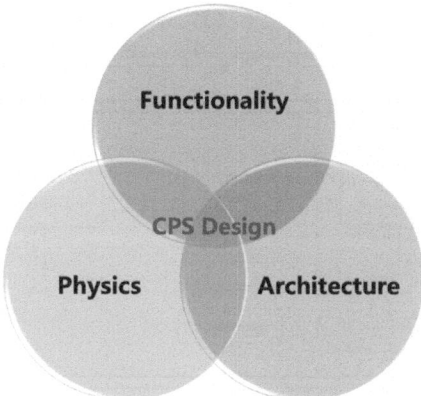

Fig. 1. The three perspectives of CPS design

Unfortunately, most of existing design methodologies and workflows do not support all these design aspects uniformly. For example, AADL [11,23] features strong capabilities for describing the architecture of a system due to the pragmatic effectiveness of combining software and hardware component models. However, the core of AADL only supports modeling of embedded system hardware and abstraction of its relevant discrete behavior, and does not support the description of the continuous physical processes to be controlled and its combination with software. By contrast, Simulink/Stateflow [19,20], the de-facto industry standard for model-based analysis and design of embedded systems, is best-suited for modeling and analyzing continuous physical processes, discrete computations and their combination, but it cannot naturally model system architectures and hardware platforms.

To address the above issue, we presented AADL⊕S/S [27,30], a combination of AADL and Simulink/Stateflow (S/S), that provides a unified graphical modeling formalism to represent all three perspectives of CPS design in Fig. 1. An overview of AADL⊕S/S is given in Fig. 2. Using AADL⊕S/S, a CPS is modeled with the following three layers:

Architecture layer. The system architecture and its hardware platform are described by AADL components that define the structure, type and characteristics of composed hardware and software components.

Software layer. The software behavior can be modelled either through AADL behavioral annexes or Simulink/Stateflow diagrams.

Physical layer. The physics of the CPS and its interaction with the hardware/software platform are modeled by Simulink/Stateflow diagrams.

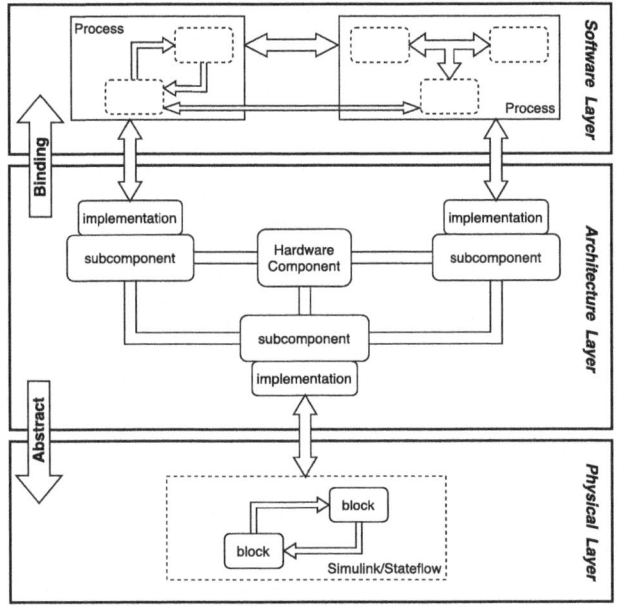

Fig. 2. An overview of AADL⊕S/S

We have developed a toolchain, called Mars [7,29], for modeling, analysis, verification, and code generation of CPSs. With the aid of the toolchain, this paper will introduce a realistically-scaled example of an automatic cruise control system to illustrate the whole procedure of the MBD approach for CPSs, including modeling, simulation, verification, and code generation. Concretely, the graphical model of the system is constructed using AADL⊕S/S and then it is translated to a formal HCSP (Hybrid Communicating Sequential Processes) model, based on which the simulation and verification can be performed. From the verified HCSP model, we can continue to generate the C code. Since the correctness of the translation is guaranteed, the generated C code is more reliable. The case study is an extension of our previous work in [27], including:

- The translation of Simulink/Stateflow is simplified and improved.
- The verification is enhanced by a more automated HHL prover.
- The C code generation from the translated HCSP model is considered.

Paper Organization. Section 2 introduces briefly the basic notions in our formalism, including the informal aspect including AADL and Simulink/Stateflow, the formal aspect HCSP, and the framework of our toolchain Mars. The automatic cruise control system as the case study is illustrated in detail in Sect. 3, followed with the simulation, verification, and code generation of this complex system in Sect. 4 and 5. After reviewing related works in Sect. 6, we conclude in Sect. 7.

2   Background

2.1   AADL

AADL is an Architecture Analysis & Design Language used to model embedded real-time systems as assembly of software components mapped onto execution platforms [10,11,23]. An AADL specification is composed of software, hardware, and composite systems. However, at present, there is no suitable AADL component describing the continuous behavior of physical environments. Thus, in our setting, we choose to represent the physical environments as system components.

Software in AADL consists of data, subprogram, threads, and processes. A data component represents a data type. A subprogram component represents executable code that can be called, with parameters provided by threads and other subprograms. A thread component represents the fundamental unit for executing a sequential flow of control behavior. A process component, which is closely affiliated to a processor component, refers to a software instance responsible for executing threads. It usually contains multiple thread components, whose execution is managed by a scheduler.

The hardware side represents computation and communication resources including processor, memory, bus and device components. A processor component represents the hardware and software responsible for scheduling and executing task threads. A memory component is used to represent storage entities for data and code. A device component models a component interacting with the environment, such as sensor or actuator. A bus component represents a physical connection among execution platform components. Finally, a system is a top-level component consisting of a hierarchy of software and hardware components.

Communication among different components is realized by connections via ports, parameters and access to shared data. Especially, port connection represents transmission of data, event, or data/event between different threads, or between threads and hardware components such as processors or devices.

2.2   Simulink/Stateflow

Simulink [19] is an environment for model-based design of dynamical systems, and has become a de-facto standard in the embedded systems industry. Generally, a Simulink diagram contains a set of blocks, subsystems, and wires, where blocks and subsystems cooperate by exchanging data flows through connected wires. Simulink provides an extensive library of pre-defined blocks for building and managing such block diagrams, and also a rich set of fixed-step and variable-step ODE solvers for simulating dynamical systems. Blocks can be grouped into subsystems, such as normal, triggered, and enabled subsystems, to establish a hierarchical structure on Simulink diagrams. A hierarchical Simulink model is thus composed of blocks, subsystems, and lines between them. After a Simulink model is built, it is ready for simulation. Each step of simulation corresponds to one sample time of the overall diagram.

Stateflow [20] is a toolbox adding facilities for modeling and simulating reactive systems by means of hierarchical statecharts. They can be defined as Simulink blocks, fed with Simulink inputs and producing Simulink outputs. It extends Simulink's scope to event-driven and hybrid forms of embedded control. A Stateflow diagram is composed of transitions, states and junctions. Each transition connects a source state to a destination state. It supports construction of *flow charts* using connective junctions and transitions, which can be used between states to specify decision logics to form transition networks. The Stateflow states can be composed to form hierarchical diagrams: *Or diagram*, for which the states are mutually exclusive and only one state becomes active at a time, and *And diagram*, for which the states are parallel and all of them become active simultaneously.

2.3   HCSP

HCSP is an extension of Hoare's Communicating Sequential Processes (CSP) for hybrid systems [15,32]. In HCSP, differential equations are introduced to model continuous evolution of the physical processes (in the physical environment) along with interrupts. A hybrid system in HCSP is a parallel composition of networked sequential processes interacting through dedicated channels, or a repetition of a sub-system. Processes in parallel can only interact through communication, and no shared variables are allowed.

Syntax. The processes of HCSP are constructed as follows:

$$P ::= \text{skip} \mid x := e \mid \text{wait}(d) \mid ch?x \mid ch!e \mid B \to P \mid \langle \dot{s} = F(s)\&B \rangle$$
$$\mid []_{i \in I}(ch_i\Box_i \longrightarrow P_i) \mid \langle \dot{s} = F(s)\&B \rangle \unrhd []_{i \in I}(ch_i\Box_i \longrightarrow P_i)$$
$$\mid X \mid \mu X.P \mid P \,\mathring{,}\, P' \mid P \sqcup P'$$
$$S ::= P \mid S\|S'$$

where P, P', and P_i represent sequential processes, whereas S and S' stand for (sub)systems, ch and ch_i are communication channels, while $ch_i\Box_i$ is a communication event which can either be an input event $ch?x$ or an output event

$ch!e$, B and e are boolean and arithmetic expressions respectively, and d is a non-negative real constant.

Process skip terminates immediately without updating variables, and process $x := e$ assigns the value of expression e to variable x and then terminates. Process wait(d) keeps idle for d time units without any change to respective variables. Interaction between processes is based on two types of communication events: $ch!e$ sends the value of e along channel ch and $ch?x$ assigns the value received along channel ch to variable x. Communication takes place when both the source, and the destination processes are ready.

HCSP supports both sequential and concurrent composition. A sequentially composed process $P \,\mathbf{;}\, P'$ behaves as P first, and if it terminates, as P' afterwards. The process $B \rightarrow P$ behaves as P only if B is true and terminates otherwise.

Internal choice between processes P and P', denoted as $P \sqcup P'$, is resolved by the process itself. Communication controlled external choice $[]_{i \in I}(ch_i \square_i \longrightarrow P_i)$ specifies that as soon as one of the communications $ch_i \square_i$ takes place, the process starts behaving as respective process P_i.

Continuous evolution is specified as $\langle \dot{s} = F(s) \& B \rangle$. Real variables s evolve continuously according to differential equations F as long as the boolean expression B is true. B defines the domain of s and we require B to be open. For example, $x > 0$ and $x \neq 0$ are open while $x \geq 0$ and $x = 0$ are not. In HCSP, continuous evolution can be preempted due to the following interrupts:

Boundary Violation. Process $\langle \dot{s} = F(s) \& B \rangle$ evolves until the boundary condition B becomes false.

Communication. Process $\langle \dot{s} = F(s) \& B \rangle \trianglerighteq []_{i \in I}(ch_i \square_i \longrightarrow P_i)$ behaves like $\langle \dot{s} = F(s) \& B \rangle$, except that the continuous evolution is preempted whenever one of the communications $ch_i \square_i$ takes place, followed by respective P_i.

The recursion $\mu X.P$ means that the execution of P can be repeated by replacing each occurrence of X with $\mu X.P$ itself during executing P, i.e., $\mu X.P$ behaves like $P[\mu X.P]$. Finally, S defines an HCSP system on the top level. A parallel composition $S \| S'$ behaves as if S and S' run independently except that they need to synchronize along the common communication channels.

2.4   From AADL⊕S/S to HCSP

The translation of AADL⊕S/S models to HCSP is introduced in [27] and we give a brief overview here. The combined model is implemented in two ways: First, the physical environment of the system can be described by a continuous Simulink diagram; Second, the behavior of threads in AADL can be modeled by discrete Simulink/Stateflow diagrams. The translation procedures for Simulink and Stateflow are described in [29]. The connections between threads can be translated into buffer and bus processes for coordinating asynchronous communication between components. Processors are translated into scheduler processes managing the execution of threads according to the specified scheduling policies. In addition, devices can be modeled directly by HCSP processes for producing simulated signals, or modeled as Simulink blocks like `signalBuilder` and then translated into HCSP processes. Finally, these separated HCSP processes can be integrated in parallel to form the whole model of the system.

2.5   The Mars Toolchain

We developed a toolchain, called Mars 2.0 [29], for modeling, analysis, verification, and code generation of CPSs. As shown in Fig. 3, Mars 2.0 (right) integrates Mars 1.0 [7] (left) with significant extensions and improvements, allowing the design of CPSs using the combination of AADL and Simulink/Stateflow (AADL$\oplus$S/S). The toolchain automatically translates AADL$\oplus$S/S models into HCSP; the translated HCSP can then be simulated using the HCSP simulator [27], and to complement incomplete simulation, it can be verified using the Hybrid Hoare Logic prover [33] in Isabelle/HOL, as well as the more automated HHLPy prover [25]. Finally, implementations in SystemC [28] or C [26] can be automatically generated from the verified HCSP processes. On the other side, the toolchain can translate AADL$\oplus$S/S models directly into C code [30], but the correctness of the translation cannot be guaranteed.

The architecture of the previous version of this tool, i.e., Mars 1.0, is mainly composed of three parts: translators Sim2HCSP and HCSP2Sim, and an HHL prover. HCSP2Sim is used to justify the correctness of Sim2HCSP, and HHL prover verifies HCSP formal models. In Mars 2.0, the correctness of the translation procedures is proved formally, thus HCSP2Sim is no longer necessary. In summary, Mars 2.0 extends Mar 1.0 mainly from the following aspects:

– The co-modeling with AADL;
– The HCSP simulator and improved HHL provers;
– The code generation from HCSP models.

In what follows, we illustrate the whole procedure of Mars 2.0 by the case study of an automatically cruise control system introduced in the next section.

3   An Automatic Cruise Control System

In this section, we introduce an automatic cruise control system (ACCS for short) as the case study to illustrate the whole procedure of modelling, simulation, verification, and code generation by our toolchain Mars introduced in Sect. 2.5. This example is adapted from the self-driving car system in [10], where it is modelled only in AADL, and then extended in [27] by adding physical environment and control components modelled in Simulink/Stateflow.

The architecture of the ACCS decomposes to three levels, shown in Fig. 4. The physical layer contains the physical vehicle. The software level defines control of the system and it contains three processes for obstacle detection, velocity control, and panel control, and each process is composed of several threads. These processes interact with the environment (the physical layer) through devices. The platform layer consists of a bus, a processor, and some devices. The connections

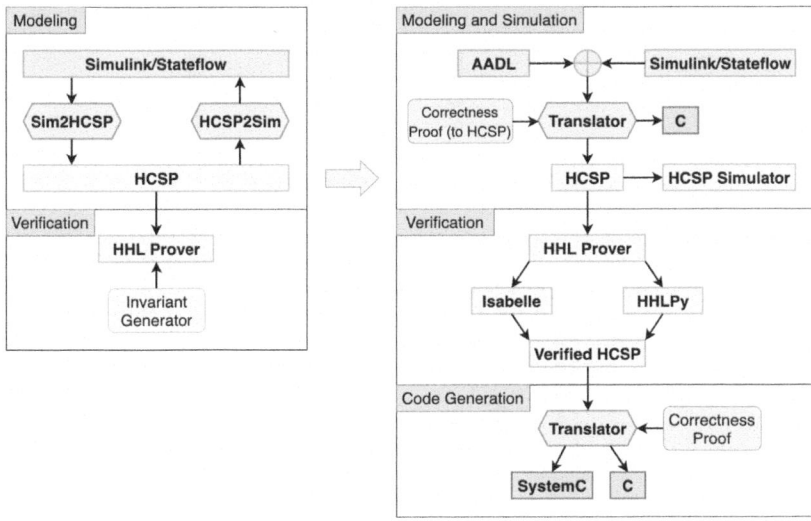

Fig. 3. Mars 1.0 (left, [7]) and 2.0 (right)

between processes and devices could be bound to the bus and all the threads are bound to the processor, with HPF (High-Priority-First) scheduling policy.

The execution of the ACCS is as follows. A vehicle is placed at the starting point initially and the driver can accelerate (inc) and decelerate (dec) the vehicle by the user_panel. Thread pan_ctr_th deals with the commands from the driver and then sends desired velocities (des_v) to the discrete PI controller (thread PI_ctr). Meanwhile, process obs_det detects the obstacles ahead by a camera and a radar and provides the velocity controller process (vel_ctr) with the real-time position of obstacle (obs_pos). Thread velo_voter in process vel_ctr monitors the velocity of the vehicle using laser and another device located on one wheel of the vehicle and produces the real-time velocity of the vehicle (veh_v) to the discrete PI controller PI_ctr and the emergency control thread (emerg). Based on the real-time velocity of vehicle and the desired velocity received, PI_ctr computes a desired acceleration (des_a) which will be sent to emerg. Finally, emerg collects the real-time position (veh_pos by GPS) and velocity of the vehicle, the desired velocity set by the driver, and the real-time position of the obstacle to work out a command, by some emergency control strategy, which will update the acceleration of the vehicle through actuator. The vehicle moves according to the new acceleration and the above procedure repeats.

3.1   Physical Level

The physical level is represented by an AADL *system component* which contains a Simulink diagram (shown in Fig. 4) describing how the vehicle moves. Specifically, it receives an ac(de)celeration a from the input port veh_a, based on which the velocity v and position s of the vehicle evolve. The evolution can easily be

234   X. Xu et al.

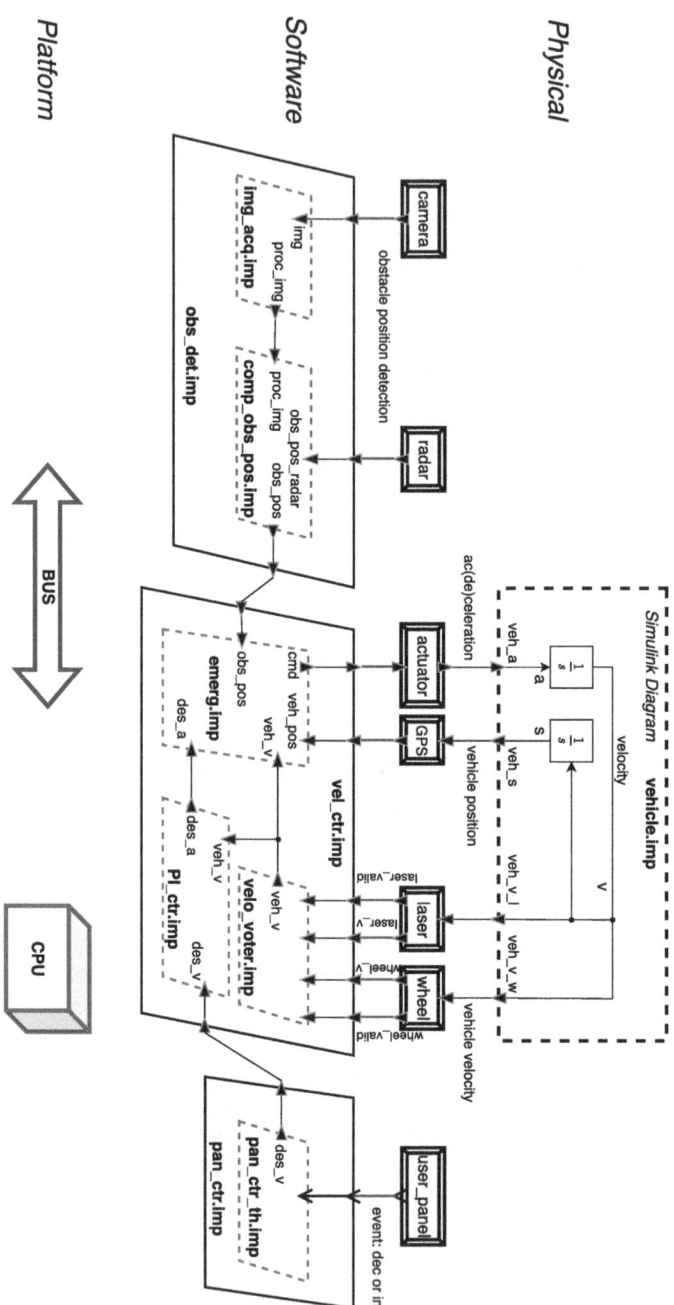

Fig. 4. Automatic Cruise Control System

described by a set of ODEs $\{\dot{s} = v, \dot{v} = a\}$. During the evolution, the vehicle can interact with its environment (composed of several devices) at any time: it can be actuated by the **actuator** and its position and velocity can be sensed by the GPS and two speedometers (**laser** and **wheel**), respectively.

3.2 Software Level

The software level is composed of three AADL processes: **obs_det** for detecting the obstacle in front of the vehicle, **vel_ctr** for controlling the vehicle, and **pan_ctr** for dealing with the commands from the user panel. These three processes are connected to make the evolution of the vehicle follow the driver's intent as much as possible, and in the meantime the vehicle should not collide into the obstacle ahead.

Obstacle Detection. The obstacle detection process **obs_det** is composed of two threads: **img_acq** for dealing with the obstacle image from the **camera** and **comp_obs_pos** for computing the position of the obstacle according to the image from the **camera** and the signal from the **radar**. Concretely, the thread **img_acq** acquires from a camera raw images (**img**) of the road ahead and then sends the processed images (**proc_img**) to the thread **comp_obs_pos** which also receives obstacle information detected by a **radar**. The thread **comp_obs_pos** then outputs the final position of the obstacle (**obs_pos**). The image processing of **img_acq** may cause some delay, so its behavior is simply abstracted as a Simulink diagram containing only a **unit delay** (Fig. 5), because the detail of the image processing is not a concern in this case study. The behavior of **comp_obs_pos** is also described by a discrete Simulink diagram (Fig. 6) which combines the two inputs in a conservative way: it takes the minimal of the *valid* (≥ 0) obstacle positions detected as the final value and then sends it out.

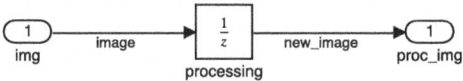

Fig. 5. The behavior of thread **img_acq**

Velocity Control. The process **vel_ctr** for velocity control consists of three threads. The thread **vel_voter** is a voter procedure combining velocity information received from the **wheel** and **laser** of the vehicle. Concretely, if the **wheel** is valid (**wheel_valid** > 0) but the **laser** is not (**laser_valid** ≤ 0), then the velocity information from the **wheel** will be sent out; if, symmetrically, the **laser** is valid but the **wheel** is not, i.e., **laser_valid** $> 0 \wedge$ **wheel_valid** ≤ 0, then the velocity sensed by the **laser** will be taken; otherwise, i.e., both are valid

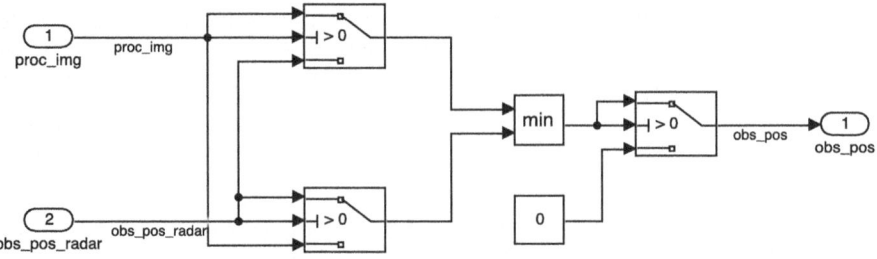

Fig. 6. The behavior of thread `comp_obs_pos`

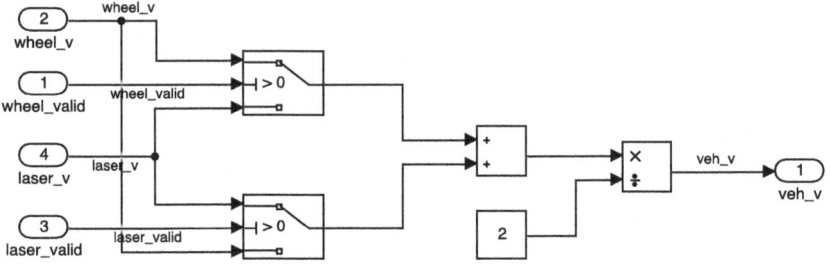

Fig. 7. The behavior of thread `velo_voter`

or invalid, the mean of the sensed velocity values will be regarded as the final velocity of the vehicle. The Simulink diagram in Fig. 7 models this behavior.

The thread `PI_ctr` receives the vehicle speed (`veh_v`) produced by `vel_voter` and a desired speed (`des_v`) from the user panel and then computes a desired acceleration (`des_a`). Concretely, it computes the difference between the desired and the real velocities of the vehicle and then sends the difference to discrete PI controller with a wind-up method (back-calculation) to calculate a desired acceleration. The Simulink diagram in Fig. 8 models this behavior.

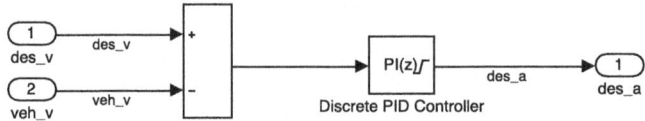

Fig. 8. The behavior of thread `PI_ctr`

The thread `emerg` receives obstacle position (`obs_pos`) from `obs_det`, vehicle position (`veh_pos`) from GPS, vehicle speed (`veh_v`) from `vel_voter` and the desired acceleration (`des_a`) from `PI_ctr`, and computes a command (`veh_a`) to the actuator based on all these inputs. It checks whether the acceleration output by `PI_ctr` is safe with respect to obstacle position. If so this is allowed as the final command. Otherwise, it overrides the command with a safe deceleration.

Concretely, the control of emerg is based on the Maximum Protection Curve [27] computed as follows:

$$V_{lim}(s) = \begin{cases} v_{max} & \text{if } s_{obs} - s \geq \frac{v_{max}^2}{(-2a_{min})} \\ \sqrt{-2a_{min} \cdot (s_{obs} - s)} & \text{if } 0 < s_{obs} - s < \frac{v_{max}^2}{(-2a_{min})} \\ 0 & \text{otherwise} \end{cases}$$

where s and s_{obs} are the respective current positions of the vehicle and the obstacle, v_{max} is the maximum velocity that the vehicle can reach and $a_{min} < 0$ is the braking deceleration of the vehicle. If the obstacle is out of the safe distance $(-v_{max}^2/2a_{min})$ of the vehicle, the upper limit velocity of the vehicle can be the maximum v_{max}; if not, the velocity should not exceed $\sqrt{-2a_{min} \cdot (s_{obs} - s)}$ in order to avoid the collision (provided $s_{obs} - s > 0$); otherwise, if $s_{obs} - s \leq 0$, then a collision has already happened, and the vehicle should stop ($V_{lim} = 0$).

At each iteration, emerg predicts the position s_{next} and velocity v_{next} of the vehicle at the next period based on the desired acceleration (a_{des}) provided by PI_ctr (see Fig. 4). Concretely, they can be computed by

$$v_{next} = v + a_{des} \cdot period$$
$$s_{next} = s + v \cdot period + \tfrac{1}{2} \cdot a_{des} \cdot period^2$$

where *period* is the period of the thread emerg.

If, at the next period, the velocity does not exceed the upper limit computed as above, i.e., $v_{next} \leq V_{lim}(s_{next})$, then the desired acceleration a_{des} is safe; if not, it continues to test if the constant velocity (no acceleration or deceleration) is safe ($v \leq V_{lim}(s + v \cdot period)$); otherwise, the emergency alerts and the thread emerg outputs the minimal deceleration ($a_{min} < 0$) to brake the vehicle. The above control strategy can be summarized as

$$a(s, v) = \begin{cases} a_{des} & \text{if } v_{next} \leq V_{lim}(s_{next}) \\ 0 & \text{if } v \leq V_{lim}(s + v \cdot period) \\ a_{min} & \text{otherwise} \end{cases}$$

and it is modeled by the Stateflow diagram shown in Fig. 9.

Panel Control. The process pan_ctr includes only one thread pan_ctr_th. It receives events from device user_panel. The driver can control user_panel by triggering events inc and dec to increase and decrease the desired speed, respectively. The behavior of the thread pan_ctr_th is modeled by a Stateflow diagram shown in Fig. 10.

3.3 Platform Level

The hardware platform is composed of a bus, a processor, and some devices such as camera, radar, and actuator, connecting the physical and software levels. The behavior of each device is described directly by HCSP using *HCSP*

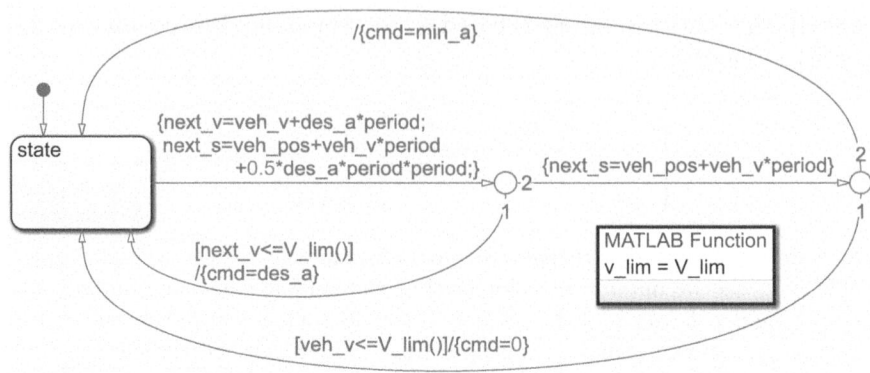

Fig. 9. The behavior of thread `emerg`

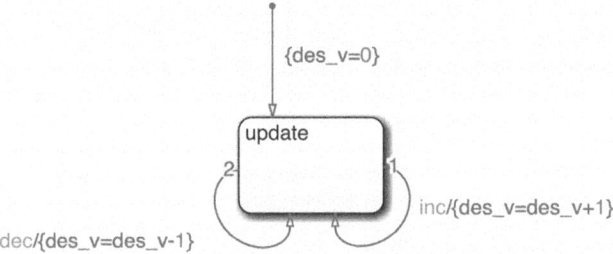

Fig. 10. The behavior of thread `pan_ctr_th`

Annex. In the ACCS architecture (Fig. 4), the connections between devices and processes are all bound to a bus, and all the threads in the processes are bound to a processor adopting HPF (High-Priority-First) scheduling policy. Each bus has the property of latency denoting the transfer delay, thus we can consider different settings of number of buses and their latency to observe the impact on the system performance caused by bus.

3.4   Restrictions on AADL

We only take part of AADL components including processes, threads, processors, buses, devices, abstract components (used to model physical environment), and the connections between components, into account. Other components have not been considered, for instance, memories and processors with more scheduling policies. The reasons for the restrictions include:

1. We concern more on the abstract and formal model of AADL. The design details of AADL will lead to complex and redundant formal models, which prevents us from verifying the key properties (like safety and latency) of AADL models;

2. The Simulink/Stateflow diagrams are used to describe the hybrid and physical behaviors of components, i.e., we focus more on behavioral components like threads. The components regarding resource (for instance, memories) are not the concern. In our future work, we will consider the effect of resource constraints on AADL models.

4   Simulation and Verification

The ACCS introduced in Sect. 3 is an (informal) graphical combined model of AADL and Simulink/Stateflow (AADL $\oplus$ S/S). In order to analyze it in a formal manner, we translate it to a formal HCSP model. The translation from AADL $\oplus$ S/S to HCSP has been presented in [27] and integrated into our Mars toolchain introduced in Sect. 2.5. The correctness of the translation has also been proved [27]. Given the translated HCSP model of the ACCS, we can perform simulation and verification using the toolchain Mars.

4.1   Simulation

We set up a scenario where there is a mobile obstacle in front of the vehicle and where the driver also sets a desired speed for the vehicle. We assume that the obstacle appears at time 10 s and position 35 m, then moves ahead with velocity 2 m/s, before finally moving away at time 20 s and position 55 m. In this scenario, we assume the **camera** fails to work and thus only **radar** can detect the obstacle. Concretely, the behavior of the failed **camera** can be simply described by the HCSP program: $\mu X.\text{out}! - 1 \, \text{\fontfamily{}\selectfont °}_9 \, \text{wait}(0.2) \, \text{°}_9 X$, i.e., it outputs -1 (invalid) through its output port every 0.2 s (the period of the **camera**), and the behavior of the **radar** can be modeled by $\mu X.x := 0 \, \text{°}_9 \, (10 \leq t < 20 \to x := 2t + 15) \, \text{°}_9 \, \text{out}!x \, \text{°}_9 \, \text{wait}(0.01) \, \text{°}_9 X$, where t denotes the local time of the **radar** and is set 0 initially, and x represents the detected position of the obstacle.

On the vehicle side, we assume that at the beginning the vehicle is at rest at the initial position 0 m and the driver pushes the **inc** button (to increase the speed) three times with time interval 0.5 s in between to set a desired speed to 3 m/s. After 29 s, the driver pushes the **dec** button (to decrease the speed) twice in 0.5 s time intervals to decrease the desired speed. In summary, the behavior of the driver (**user_panel**) can be modeled by the following HCSP program:

$$\text{out}!"\text{inc}" \, \text{°}_9 \, \text{wait}(0.5) \, \text{°}_9 \, \text{out}!"\text{inc}" \, \text{°}_9 \, \text{wait}(0.5) \, \text{out}!"\text{inc}" \, \text{°}_9$$
$$\text{wait}(29) \, \text{°}_9$$
$$\text{out}!"\text{dec}" \, \text{°}_9 \, \text{wait}(0.5) \, \text{°}_9 \, \text{out}!"\text{dec}"$$

Other devices (**actuator**, **GPS**, **laser**, and **wheel**) are treated as "routers" which transfer periodically the received messages at the input ports directly through the output ports. For example, the behavior of the **GPS** can be described as $\mu X.\text{in}?x \, \text{°}_9 \, \text{out}!x \, \text{°}_9 \, \text{wait}(0.006) \, \text{°}_9 X$, where x denotes the sensed vehicle position and the period of the **GPS** is 0.006 s.

Impact of Bus. We first set the latency of the bus in ACCS (Fig. 4) to 3 ms, and the simulation results are shown in Fig. 11, from which we can see that the vehicle nearly hits the moving obstacle ahead. The reason for this dangerous situation is the competition for bus permission. The competition is so intense that the `radar` can hardly transfer the sensed obstacle position to the process `obs_det` in time. Actually, the delay of the transferring is up to 5 s in this case, which is absolutely intolerable in the real world applications.

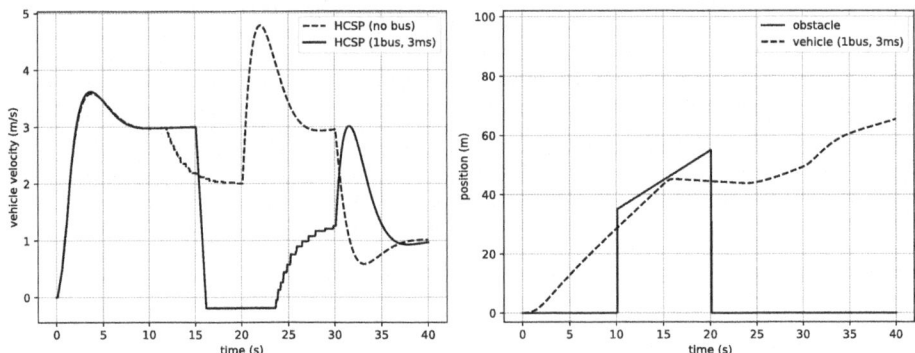

Fig. 11. One bus with the latency 3 ms

The above can be seen as a design error: the allocation of bus capacity is insufficient for the given latency. To correct this problem, we set an extra bus with the same latency (3 ms) for the `radar`. The connection between the device `radar` and the process `obs_det` is bound to this dedicated bus. The simulation result of the vehicle velocity in this case is shown in Fig. 12 (dashed line), which is similar to the case not involving buses (solid line). The minor gap between them is due to the latency of the buses.

Based on the setting of two buses, we further increase the bus latency to 5 ms to test the performance of the system. The result is that the vehicle never starts. By examining the logs of simulation, we can find that the thread `emerg` cannot obtain bus permission in order to transfer the acceleration command to actuator, causing the vehicle keeping motionless. The reason is the lack of throughput of the bus. To resolve it, we hence add another bus to the architecture and bind the connection between the thread `emerg` and the `actuator` to this bus, and the simulation result returns to normal according to Fig. 12 (dotted line).

4.2   Verification

One of the motivations of translating the AADL⊕S/S model of ACCS to HCSP is to verify the informal graphical model of ACCS. In this case study, we verify the safety property of the control strategy of the thread `emerg` (**Velocity Control** in Sect. 3.2) using trace-based Hybrid Hoare Logic.

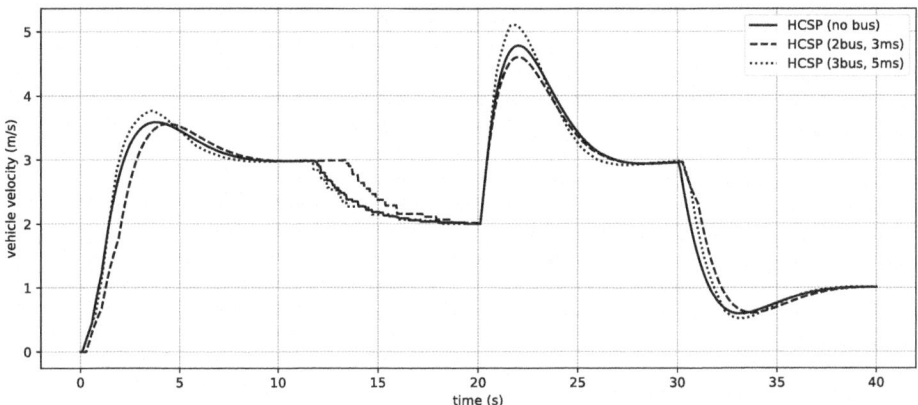

Fig. 12. Vehicle velocity under different bus settings

First, we use automated HHL prover: HHLPar to generate an assertion R on trace and state satisfying the following lemma.

Theorem 1.

$$\forall \bar{s}_0.\ p(\bar{s}_0) \longrightarrow\ \models \{\bar{s} = \bar{s}_0 \wedge tr = \epsilon\}\ \mathtt{Plant}\|\mathtt{Control}\ \{R(\bar{s}_0)\}$$

where p represents the initial condition on the starting state $\bar{s}_0$ and R maps the starting state $\bar{s}_0$ to the assertion on the state $\bar{s}$ and trace tr after the termination of the process describing the whole behaviour this parallel system.

The process $\mathtt{Plant}$ and $\mathtt{Control}$ are defined in following:

$$\mathtt{Plant} \triangleq \mathtt{ch1}!v;\ \mathtt{ch2}!s;\ (\mathtt{ch3}?a;\ \langle \dot{s} = v, \dot{v} = a \& \mathtt{true}\rangle \unrhd \,[\![\mathtt{ch1}!v \to \mathtt{ch2}!s]\!])^*$$

$$\mathtt{Control} \triangleq \mathtt{ch1}?v;\ \mathtt{ch2}?s;\ (s_{next} := s + v \cdot period + \tfrac{1}{2} \cdot a_{des} \cdot period^2;$$
$$v_{next} := v + a_{des} \cdot period;$$
$$(\mathtt{if}\ -2 \cdot a_{min} \cdot (s_{obs} - s_{next}) \geq v_{max}^2\ \mathtt{then}\ V_{lim} := v_{max}\ \mathtt{else}$$
$$\mathtt{if}\ s_{obs} - s_{next} > 0\ \mathtt{then}\ V_{lim} := \sqrt{-2 \cdot a_{min} \cdot (s_{obs} - s_{next})}$$
$$\mathtt{else}\ V_{lim} := 0);$$
$$(\mathtt{if}\ v_{next} \leq V_{lim}\ \mathtt{then}\ a := a_{des}\ \mathtt{else}$$
$$s_{next} := s + v \cdot T;$$
$$(\mathtt{if}\ -2 \cdot a_{min} \cdot (s_{obs} - s_{next}) \geq v_{max}^2\ \mathtt{then}\ V_{lim} := v_{max}\ \mathtt{else}$$
$$\mathtt{if}\ s_{obs} - s_{next} > 0\ \mathtt{then}\ V_{lim} := -2 \cdot a_{min} \cdot (s_{obs} - s_{next})$$
$$\mathtt{else}\ V_{lim} := 0);$$
$$\mathtt{if}\ v \leq V_{lim}\ \mathtt{then}\ a := 0\ \mathtt{else}\ a := a_{min});$$
$$\mathtt{ch3}!a;\ \mathtt{wait}\ period;\ \mathtt{ch1}?v;\ \mathtt{ch2}?s)^*$$

The generating procedure of R to satisfy the theorem through HHLPar includes the following three steps:

Lemma 1

$$\models \{\bar{s} = \bar{s}_1 \wedge tr = \epsilon\}\ \mathtt{Plant}\ \{R_1(\bar{s}_1)\}$$

Lemma 2

$$\models \{\bar{s} = \bar{s}_2 \wedge tr = \epsilon\} \, \texttt{Control} \, \{R_2(\bar{s}_2)\}$$

Based on the structure of a single process we automatically generate its corresponding assertions using the specification rules. For example:

$$\frac{\texttt{paramODEsol}(\overrightarrow{\dot{x}} = \overrightarrow{e}, B, \overrightarrow{p}, e) \quad \texttt{lipschitz}(\overrightarrow{\dot{x}} = \overrightarrow{e}) \quad \texttt{spec\_of}(c, Q)}{\texttt{spec\_of}(\langle \overrightarrow{\dot{x}} = \overrightarrow{e} \& B \rangle; c, \texttt{wait}(s = s0[\overrightarrow{x} \mapsto \overrightarrow{p}(s_0, t)], e, \{d \Rightarrow Q[\overrightarrow{x} := \overrightarrow{p}(s_0, d)]\}))}$$

Then we apply the synchronization rules between R_1 and R_2 to compute the R on parallel process.

Lemma 3

$$\forall \bar{s}_1 \, \bar{s}_2 , \; p(\bar{s}_1 \uplus \bar{s}_2) \longrightarrow R_1(\bar{s}_1) \| R_2(\bar{s}_2) \implies R(\bar{s}_1 \uplus \bar{s}_2)$$

The assertion R computed by HHLPar contains state changes and generated trajectories of the process and is strong enough to inference the safety property we need which can be concluded as $\texttt{Safe} \triangleq s \leq s_{obs} \wedge v \leq V_{lim}(s)$, and we have

Theorem 2

$$R(\bar{s}_0, \bar{s}, tr) \longrightarrow \texttt{Safe}(\bar{s})$$

which can be proved by Isabelle/HOL. Combining the two theorems, we can obtain complete verification of the security property of this system.

5   Code Generation

In our previous work [30], combined models of AADL $\oplus$ S/S are translated to C code directly. The translation is done by the following steps: (1) the AADL part is translated to C following the execution semantics of AADL; (2) the Simulink/Stateflow part is translated using the existing C code generation facility in Matlab; (3) the architecture part is implemented by a library in C that includes thread scheduling protocols and so on; and (4) the combined model is translated by integrating the C codes generated from the above three parts. However, the interaction (communication) between components is implemented by shared variables (without pthreads) and the correctness of the translation has not been proved.

In our latest work [26], we generate the C code of AADL $\oplus$ S/S models from their HCSP models. Since HCSP are verifiable and the correctness of the translation can be guaranteed, the generated code, especially the code for the controller, satisfies the safety requirement and therefore is reliable. The communication between processes is implemented using pthreads and the correctness of the code generation is proved based on approximate bisimulation, i.e., an HCSP model and the C code generated from it are in some approximate bisimulation relation. The generated C code is of 3500–4000 lines. The HCSP model is specified by a

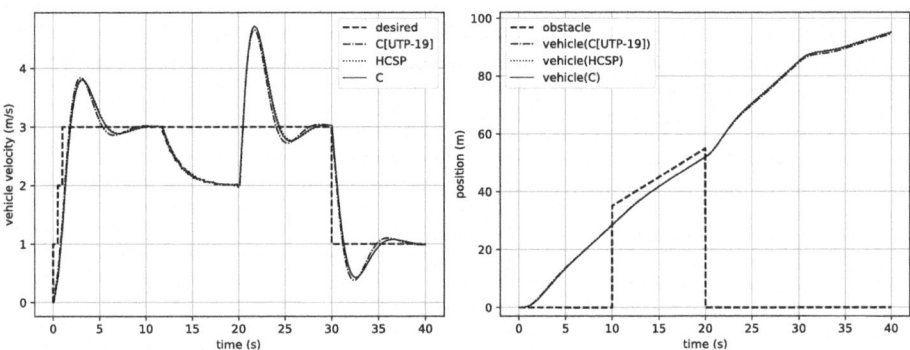

Fig. 13. Comparison of execution results where UTP-19 denotes the work of [30]

formal language and therefore verifiable. Thus, the C code generated from HCSP files is more reliable than from the graphical AADL⊕S/S model directly.

In Fig. 13, we compare our results with the simulation of the HCSP model of the ACCS and the execution of the C code generated directly from the AADL ⊕ S/S model of the ACCS ([30]). The left of Fig. 13 shows the execution results of the vehicle speed, where the black line denotes the desired velocity set by the driver. We can see that the execution result of the generated C code is almost the same as the simulation of its HCSP model. Specifically, the average relative error (ARE) between the time series of the velocity generated from the HCSP model and its C code is 0.138% with the variance 4.686×10^{-5}. Besides, we can also observe that there is a negligible difference between the results of the C code generated by [30] and the latest C code generated: the ARE is 0.182% with the variance 4.232×10^{-3}.

From both results, we can see that the vehicle accelerates to the desired speed (3 m/s) in 10 s. The fluctuation during [2s, 10s] reflects feature of PI controllers. It then decelerates to avoid the collision onto the obstacle ahead. After the obstacle moves away (at 20 s), the vehicle accelerates again to the desired speed. At 30 s, the driver pushes the `dec` button to adjust the desired velocity to 1 m/s and we can see that the vehicle decelerates to 1 m/s in about 6 s under the PI controller. The positions of the vehicle and of the obstacle with respect to time are shown on the right of Fig. 13.

6   Related Work

There exist a huge amount of work on the modeling, analysis, verification and code generation of CPSs. Several unified frameworks have been proposed for designing CPSs. The Metropolis design framework [2,9] is a platform-based design environment for heterogeneous systems, that provides simulation, verification, and code synthesis by transforming all models to a unified meta-model language. However, it lacks support for physical plant modeling. Ptolemy [22] aims to design heterogeneous systems that combine different models of computation in terms of actors and provides modeling and simulation techniques for the combined models. Functional Mock-up Interface (FMI 3.0) [18] is an industrial standard maintained by the Modelica Association that enables the exchange and co-simulation of dynamic component models. It couples different simulation tools at system level by coordinating and synchronizing their respective executions. However, Ptolemy supports very limited facilities to model continuous behaviors [8], and furthermore, both Ptolemy and FMI are not designed for hardware architecture modeling and analysis.

Other lines of work consider limited perspectives of CPSs. UML, SysML [1] and MARTE [24] are traditional model based design environments for designing discrete systems, without support for physical plants. There are some works aiming for modeling and verifying continuous and hybrid behaviors, but without considering architectures. Zélus [6] extends the synchronous language Lustre [13] with ODEs and zero-crossing events for designing and implementing hybrid systems and has also been implemented in SCADE 6. It supports analysis of hybrid models by type systems and semantics, and handles the detection of zero-crossing events [3,6]. Differential dynamic logic [21] is developed for reasoning about behaviors of hybrid dynamic models, and based on which the KeYmaera X prover [12] is implemented for safety analysis of dynamic systems. VeriPhy [5] automatically transforms verified formal models of CPSs modelled in differential dynamic logic [12,21] to controller implementations that preserve safety properties of original models.

7   Conclusion

In this paper, we introduced a realistically-scaled automatic cruise control system as the case study to illustrate the whole procedure of modeling, simulation, verification, and code generation of the MBD for CPS design. We can learn from the results in Sect. 4 that the impact on system behavior and perform can be foreseen and the defect of system design can be checked by analyzing the model of system at the very early stage, reducing the development cost significantly, reflecting the original intention of the MBD methodology.

This case study demonstrates the practicability of the MBD tool, Mars, in dealing with complex CPSs. The toolchain Mars was first proposed in [7] with limited capability, and later it is significantly improved based on our recent works including [25,27,31], and so on. Given the case study described in this paper, we will summarize the toolchain Mars into a tool paper and make it public to the MBD and CPS communities.

However, there are some limitations to our approach. First, AADL provides plenty of components and functions, while we only consider its core functionalities, which limits the practicality of our framework for more case-studying realistic CPSs. Second, at present, our verifier only scales to small HCSP models and some sequential models (no communication is involved). Thus, as future work, we will try to integrate more functionalities into our approach, such as considering more AADL components and Simulink/Stateflow blocks, modeling and verification of hybrid systems containing delay or stochastic differential equations. Correspondingly, we will improve verification efficiency and scalability by extending Jones's *rely/guarantee* [16] to CPS such that our approach can be applied to real-world case studies on a larger scale.

Acknowledgment. This work is partly funded by the National Key R&D Program of China under grants No. 2022YFA1005101 and 2022YFA1005103, the NSFC under grants No. 62192732 and 62032024, the CAS Project for Young Scientists in Basic Research under grant No. YSBR-040, and the Major Project of ISCAS (ISCAS-ZD-202302).

References

1. SysML 1.6 Beta Specification (2019). http://www.omg.org/spec/SysML
2. Balarin, F., Watanabe, Y., Hsieh, H., Lavagno, L., Passerone, C., Sangiovanni-Vincentelli, A.L.: Metropolis: an integrated electronic system design environment. Computer **36**(4), 45–52 (2003). https://doi.org/10.1109/MC.2003.1193228
3. Benveniste, A., Bourke, T., Caillaud, B., Pouzet, M.: Non-standard semantics of hybrid systems modelers. J. Comput. Syst. Sci. **78**(3), 877–910 (2012). https://doi.org/10.1016/J.JCSS.2011.08.009
4. Besnard, D., Jones, C.: Designing dependable systems needs interdisciplinarity. Saf. Crit. Syst. Club Newsl. **13**(3), 6–9 (2004). https://hal.science/hal-00724103
5. Bohrer, R., Tan, Y.K., Mitsch, S., Myreen, M.O., Platzer, A.: VeriPhy: verified controller executables from verified cyber-physical system models. In: PLDI 2018, pp. 617–630. ACM (2018). https://doi.org/10.1145/3192366.3192406
6. Bourke, T., Pouzet, M.: Zélus: a synchronous language with ODEs. In: HSCC 2013, pp. 113–118. ACM (2013). https://doi.org/10.1145/2461328.2461348
7. Chen, M., et al.: MARS: a toolchain for modelling, analysis and verification of hybrid systems. In: Hinchey, M.G., Bowen, J.P., Olderog, E.-R. (eds.) Provably Correct Systems. NMSSE, pp. 39–58. Springer, Cham (2017). https://doi.org/10.1007/978-3-319-48628-4_3
8. Cremona, F., Lohstroh, M., Broman, D., Lee, E.A., Masin, M., Tripakis, S.: Hybrid co-simulation: it's about time. Softw. Syst. Model. **18**(3), 1655–1679 (2019). https://doi.org/10.1007/S10270-017-0633-6
9. Davare, A., et al.: A next-generation design framework for platform-based design. In: DVCon 2007. Citeseer, February 2007
10. Delange, J.: AADL in Practice. Reblochon Development Company (2017)
11. Feiler, P.H., Gluch, D.P.: Model-Based Engineering with AADL: An Introduction to the SAE Architecture Analysis & Design Language. Addison-Wesley Professional, New York (2012)
12. Fulton, N., Mitsch, S., Quesel, J.-D., Völp, M., Platzer, A.: KeYmaera X: an axiomatic tactical theorem prover for hybrid systems. In: Felty, A.P., Middeldorp, A. (eds.) CADE 2015. LNCS (LNAI), vol. 9195, pp. 527–538. Springer, Cham (2015). https://doi.org/10.1007/978-3-319-21401-6_36
13. Halbwachs, N., Caspi, P., Raymond, P., Pilaud, D.: The synchronous data flow programming language LUSTRE. Proc. IEEE **79**(9), 1305–1320 (1991). https://doi.org/10.1109/5.97300
14. Hayes, I.J., Jackson, M.A., Jones, C.B.: Determining the specification of a control system from that of its environment. In: Araki, K., Gnesi, S., Mandrioli, D. (eds.) FME 2003. LNCS, vol. 2805, pp. 154–169. Springer, Heidelberg (2003). https://doi.org/10.1007/978-3-540-45236-2_10

15. He, J.: From CSP to hybrid systems, pp. 171–189. Prentice Hall International (UK) Ltd., GBR (1994)
16. Jones, C.B.: Specification and verification. IEEE Trans. Softw. Eng. **SE-10**(2), 126–127 (1984). https://doi.org/10.1109/TSE.1984.5010214
17. Jones, C.B.: Dependability of computer-based systems. In: Sampaio, A. (ed.) SBSE 2000, pp. 16–20. SBC (2000). https://doi.org/10.5753/SBES.2000.25917
18. Junghanns, A., et al.: The functional mock-up interface 3.0 - new features enabling new applications. In: Proceedings of 14th Modelica Conference 2021 (2021)
19. MathWorks Inc: Simulink User's Guide (2013). http://www.mathworks.com/help/pdf_doc/simulink/sl_using.pdf
20. MathWorks Inc.: Stateflow User's Guide (2013). http://www.mathworks.com/help/pdf_doc/stateflow/sf_ug.pdf
21. Platzer, A.: Logical Foundations of Cyber-Physical Systems (2018). https://doi.org/10.1007/978-3-319-63588-0
22. Ptolemaeus, C. (ed.): System Design, Modeling, and Simulation Using Ptolemy II. Ptolemy.org (2014). http://ptolemy.org/books/Systems
23. SAE International Standards: Architecture analysis & design language (AADL), Revision C (2017)
24. Selic, B., Gerard, S.: Modeling and Analysis for Real-time and Embedded Systems with UML and MARTE: Developing Cyber-Physical Systems. The MK/OMG Press (2013)
25. Sheng, H., Bentkamp, A., Zhan, B.: HHLPy: practical verification of hybrid systems using Hoare logic. In: Chechik, M., Katoen, JP., Leucker, M. (eds.) FM 2023. LNCS, vol. 14000, pp. 160–178. Springer, Cham (2023). https://doi.org/10.1007/978-3-031-27481-7_11
26. Wang, S., Ji, Z., Xu, X., Zhan, B., Gao, Q., Zhan, N.: Formally verified C code generation from hybrid communicating sequential processes. In: ICCPS 2024. pp. 123–134. IEEE (2024). https://doi.org/10.1109/ICCPS61052.2024.00018
27. Xu, X., Wang, S., Zhan, B., Jin, X., Talpin, J., Zhan, N.: Unified graphical co-modeling, analysis and verification of cyber-physical systems by combining AADL and Simulink/Stateflow. Theor. Comput. Sci. **903**, 1–25 (2022). https://doi.org/10.1016/J.TCS.2021.11.008
28. Yan, G., Jiao, L., Wang, S., Wang, L., Zhan, N.: Automatically generating SystemC code from HCSP formal models. ACM Trans. Softw. Eng. Methodol. **29**(1), 4:1–4:39 (2020). https://doi.org/10.1145/3360002
29. Zhan, B., et al.: Mars 2.0: a toolchain for modeling, analysis, verification and code generation of cyber-physical systems. arXiv **abs/2403.03035** (2024)
30. Zhan, H., Lin, Q., Wang, S., Talpin, J.-P., Xu, X., Zhan, N.: Unified graphical co-modelling of cyber-physical systems using AADL and simulink/stateflow. In: Ribeiro, P., Sampaio, A. (eds.) UTP 2019. LNCS, vol. 11885, pp. 109–129. Springer, Cham (2019). https://doi.org/10.1007/978-3-030-31038-7_6
31. Zhan, N., Zhan, B., Wang, S., Guelev, D.P., Jin, X.: A generalized hybrid Hoare logic. CoRR **abs/2303.15020** (2023)
32. Zhou, C., Wang, J., Ravn, A.P.: A formal description of hybrid systems. In: Alur, R., Henzinger, T.A., Sontag, E.D. (eds.) Hybrid Systems III: Verification and Control. LNCS, vol. 1066, pp. 511–530. Springer, Heidelberg (1995). https://doi.org/10.1007/BFB0020972
33. Zou, L., Zhan, N., Wang, S., Fränzle, M., Qin, S.: Verifying Simulink diagrams via a hybrid Hoare logic prover. In: EMSOFT, pp. 1–9. IEEE (2013). https://doi.org/10.1109/EMSOFT.2013.6658587

Exploring the Boundaries
of Rely/Guarantee and Links
to Linearisability

Nisansala P. Yatapanage[⊠]

School of Computing, The Australian National University, Canberra, Australia
nisansala.yatapanage@anu.edu.au

Abstract. Non-blocking concurrent algorithms are particularly challenging to verify. Linearisability is a commonly used technique for verifying such algorithms. Rely/guarantee reasoning provides a compositional approach for reasoning about concurrent systems. This paper explores the relationship between rely/guarantee and linearisability using two well-known examples: the Treiber stack and the Herlihy-Wing queue. Non-linearisable behaviour can be identified by the program making a step where the *before* and *after* states do not correspond to a valid step at the sequential level. Therefore, such invalid behaviour relates to a failure of the guarantee condition. The development of these two examples also provides useful insights into the boundaries of rely/guarantee, suggesting that these examples share common properties with another challenging problem, the Ben-Ari garbage collection algorithm studied by Jones and Yatapanage in [JY19].

Keywords: rely/guarantee · concurrency · linearisability · interference · non-blocking

1 Introduction

Concurrent algorithms are difficult to verify due to the interference between the processes. Non-blocking algorithms are notoriously difficult, as the processes are not required to wait for the other to complete a task. The rely/guarantee approach [Jon83a, Jon83b] permits compositional reasoning about concurrent processes by providing a means for describing the interference between the processes.

The rely/guarantee technique has been used to verify non-blocking algorithms such as Simpson's Four Slot [JH16]. There are, however, a class of algorithms for which it is particularly challenging to find suitable rely and guarantee conditions that capture the intended behaviour of the system. For example, in [JY19], an attempt was made to verify a concurrent garbage collecting algorithm, but it was found to require additional constructs such as ghost variables in order to achieve the desired result. This paper examines two small but challenging

© The Author(s), under exclusive license to Springer Nature Switzerland AG 2024
A. Cavalcanti and J. Baxter (Eds.): *The Practice of Formal Methods*, LNCS 14781, pp. 247–267, 2024.
https://doi.org/10.1007/978-3-031-66673-5_13

algorithms, for which it is difficult to use standard rely/guarantee conditions, but where the use of rely/guarantee still offers useful benefits and interesting insights into the behaviour of these systems.

In particular, these two examples are often used to demonstrate verification approaches that prove *linearisability*. Linearisability [HW90] ensures that a concurrent program can only exhibit behaviour that matches a sequential abstract specification, by treating each concurrent operation as if it occurs at a single point in its execution, the *linearisation point*. The trace of concurrent behaviour should match with an abstract trace, with respect to the linearisation points. This is explained further in Sect. 3.1.

The examples discussed in this paper both demonstrate an interesting feature: incorrect (non-linearisable) behaviour can be identified by considering just the single program steps of an operation. This suggests that it is possible to reason about these systems in terms of guarantee conditions that hold over program steps, rather than needing to examine the entire trace. The examples investigated are the well-known Treiber stack, a standard algorithm used for discussing linearisability, and the Herlihy-Wing queue, which is of interest due to its non-fixed linearisation points. In the Herlihy-Wing queue, the linearisation points can only be determined by considering the future actions of environment processes.

The Treiber stack and the Herlihy-Wing queue also both exhibit similar properties which make it difficult to use rely/guarantee without extra constructs. It is interesting to investigate these issues, because it helps to define the boundaries of rely/guarantee and to identify the specific properties which make such programs difficult to reason about.

The rest of the paper is structured as follows: Sect. 2 gives the required background, Sect. 3 explores the first example, the Treiber stack, along with the insights gained from specifying rely/ guarantee properties for it, Sect. 4 discusses the second example, the Herlihy-Wing Queue, Sect. 5 discusses some interesting links between these problems and another similar problem, Sect. 6 discusses related work and Sect. 7 gives the conclusions.

2   Background

2.1   Rely/Guarantee

Rely/guarantee was invented by Cliff Jones [Jon83a, Jon83b] for verifying concurrent programs. Refer to [HJ18] for a useful introduction. A rely condition is a relation describing the interference that the process can tolerate from the environment. Its counterpart, the guarantee condition, is a relation describing what the process will ensure to do. The guarantee condition must hold between the initial and final states of a program step or sequence of program steps. Similarly, the rely condition must hold between the initial and final states of an environment step or sequence of environment steps. Figure 1 illustrates rely and guarantee conditions holding over program and environment steps, respectively, on an execution trace. Note that the transitivity of the rely and guarantee conditions ensure that a rely condition must hold over any single environment step

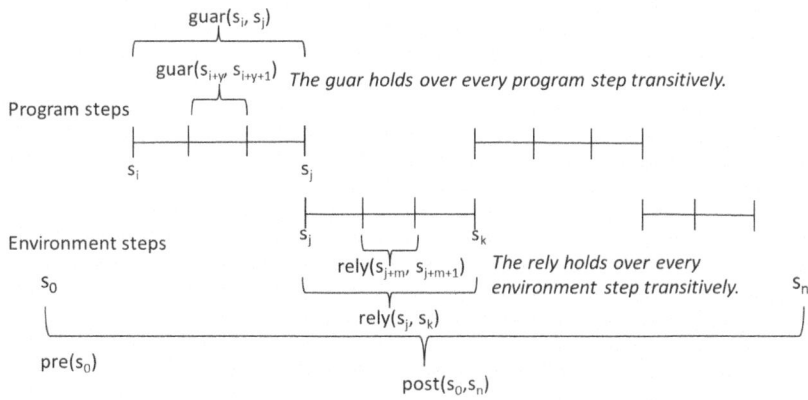

Fig. 1. Rely, Guarantee, Pre and Post Conditions

or sequence of consecutive environment steps, and similarly a guarantee condition must hold over any single program step or sequence of consecutive program states. In order for two processes to execute concurrently, the guarantee of each must satisfy the rely of the other.

2.2   Linearisability

Linearisability [HW90] is a correctness condition that requires that a set of concurrent concrete processes only exhibit behaviour that matches an abstract specification, by considering each concrete operation as effectively occurring at a specific point in its operation. This point is known as the *linearisation point* of the operation. Linearisability considers histories of events. Each event has an invocation and response point. As concurrent events may overlap, the linearisation point is the point where the event effectively takes place, i.e. where it performs the changes to the system which reflect the changes that the equivalent abstract sequential operation performs.

Example 1. Suppose a concurrent stack executed the following sequence:

            process P invokes push A
            process Q invokes push B
            process Q passes its linearisation point
            process Q response
            process R invokes pop
            process R passes its linearisation point
            process P passes its linearisation point
            process P response
            process R response

This is linearisable to an abstract sequence of:

            process Q executes push B

> process R executes pop
> process P executes push A

Although the concrete process P started its execution before Q, as it did not pass its linearisation point, the equivalent abstract sequence executes process Q before P.

Proving linearisability for a given concurrent program is usually accomplished using techniques such as simulation (see [DD15] for a comprehensive survey). As will be seen in the following sections, rely/guarantee conditions could provide an alternative formalism for verifying linearisability by specifying the linearisability requirements as part of the rely/guarantee conditions.

3   The Treiber Stack

The Treiber stack [Tre86] is a concurrent, non-blocking stack data structure. It permits the standard stack operations *push* and *pop* to run concurrently, without forcing any process to wait until the other has finished. It makes use of the *Compare-and-Swap (CAS)* operation, a low-level hardware primitive that is available on most systems, which allows an update to be atomically performed on the condition that the variable's current value is equal to a given value. For example, $CAS(x, y, z)$ will atomically check whether variable x is equal to y, and if so, x will be updated to z. The CAS returns true if it succeeds and false if it does not.

The code in Fig. 2 shows the basic idea of the *push* and *pop* operations, though this version suffers from the *ABA* problem, described in Treiber's original paper [Tre86], where a change is undetected because the original head node has been returned to the stack. This was resolved by Treiber using a *DCAS*, which atomically checks both the variable to be updated and also a count keeping track of further changes, but this paper assumes there is garbage collection, which also resolves the issue.

The *push* operation creates a new node with the given data value, records the current value of the list's head, and then sets the new node's next pointer to point to the current head. It then uses a *CAS* operation to attempt to make the new node become the new head. The *CAS* is used to ensure that no other process has changed the list in the meantime. It checks that the head still matches the value recorded earlier, and only if so, it proceeds with the change to the head. If the *CAS* fails, the operation starts again, recording the new state of the head.

The *pop* operation works in a similar manner. It notes the current value of the head. If it is null, the operation returns null. If not, the value of the head is noted and the next node after the head is also noted. The operation then uses a *CAS* to attempt to set the head to the node after the head. Again, a *CAS* is used to ensure that no other process has modified the list in the meantime. It succeeds only if the head has not been changed from the value noted earlier. If it has, the operation starts again.

```
push(v){
    Node n = new Node(v);
    do{
        x = head;
        n.next = x;
    }while(!CAS(head, x, n));
}

pop(){
    do{
        x = head;
        if (x == null) return null;
        y = x.next;
        v = x.val;
    }while(!CAS(head, x, y));
    return v;
}
```

Fig. 2. The code for the Treiber stack

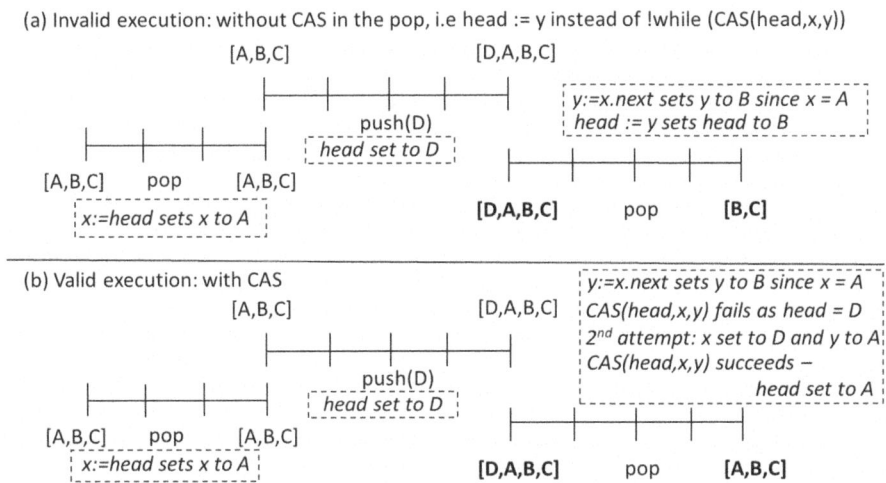

Fig. 3. Invalid and Valid Execution Traces of the Treiber stack

Example 2. Figure 3 illustrates why the *CAS* operations are necessary. Figure 3(a) shows the behaviour of the stack when the statement *head*:= *y* is used instead of the *CAS* statement in the *pop* operation. One process does a *pop*, but before it finishes, another process executes *push(D)*. The first process then continues and sets the head to *B*, which it had earlier noted was the next node after the head, effectively deleting both *A* and the new pushed node *D*. This situation is avoided using the *CAS* statements, as shown in Fig. 3(b). In this scenario, the first *CAS* attempt by the *pop* operation fails, as the head has been changed. The second *CAS* attempt then succeeds and the *pop* correctly removes only node D.

3.1 Linearisability of the Treiber Stack

The Treiber stack is a standard example used for demonstrating the concept of linearisability. In the Treiber stack, the linearisation point of the *push* operation is the CAS statement. For the *pop* there are two linearisation points: the CAS statement and the statement that returns null in the case of an empty stack. The invalid behaviour shown in Fig. 3(a) is not linearisable to an abstract specification, because if the *push* process has passed its linearisation point before the *pop* process reaches its linearisation point, then it corresponds to an abstract history where the *push* occurs before the *pop*. However, there is no such abstract history with a final list state of $[D, A, B, C]$, as the *push* would have added D and the *pop* would have then removed D.

3.2 Abstract Sequential Specification

At the abstract level, the state is defined as a sequence of values, as follows: (see [Jon90] for an introduction to the VDM notation used):

$\Sigma_0 :: list : Val^*$

At this level, the *pop* and *push* operations execute atomically. There is therefore no need of rely and guarantee conditions, as there is no interference. The effects of the operations are specified entirely in the post conditions.

The *push* operation takes a value v and inserts it as the new head of the list.

$push_0 (v: Val)$
pre true
post $list' = [v] \frown list$

The *pop* operation has no parameters and returns a value x, the original head of the list.

$pop_0 () x: Val$
pre true
post $list' = \mathbf{tl}\ list \land x' = \mathbf{hd}\ list$

3.3 Concurrent Development

At the next level of abstraction, the operations are no longer assumed to be atomic, but still operate on an abstract sequence. Rely and guarantee conditions are necessary to describe the interference at this level.

$\Sigma_1 :: list : Val^*$

A first attempt at the rely for the *push* might be to state that any environment steps either leave the list's head unchanged or set it to the second node in the list:

$rely\text{-}push_1\colon (list' = list) \lor (list' = \mathbf{tl}\ list)$

However, this would constrain the environment behaviour to be a single *pop*, whereas it is valid for several *pop* operations to be performed concurrently with this *push*, as well as for other *push* operations to execute. There is, in fact, nothing at all that can be said about the state of the list after environment steps have completed. The list may even be left completely empty, or containing a whole list of new nodes pushed by other processes.

The post conditions of both the *pop* and *push* operations are also difficult to state, because the final state of the stack is unknown. The *possible values* notation [JH16] has been used effectively to state properties of this nature, but even it is insufficient in this case. The possible values notation $\widehat{x}$ means the set of values that x held during the execution of the operation. Using possible values, it can be stated that the list contained a given node *at some state* during its operation. This would allow the post condition of *push* to state that the value to be pushed was added at least at some point:

$post\text{-}push_1\colon \exists l_1, l_2 \in \widehat{list} \cdot \mathbf{hd}\ l_2 = v \land l_1 = \mathbf{tl}\ l_2$

However, this post condition is too weak, as it does not prevent the *push* operation from making further changes to the list, which it is not supposed to do. This has to be constrained using the guarantee condition.[1]

3.4   Observations About Guarantees and Linearisability

Return to Fig. 3(a), which was one of the cases required to be prevented. Notice that before the *pop* erroneously removed both nodes D and A, there had to be a step of *push* that added node D. If there had not been such a step, then the behaviour of the *pop*, which assumed the head to still be A, would have been correct. Considered from the point of view of the *pop*, there was a sequence of environment stesp which changed the stack to $[D, A, B, C]$, followed by its own program steps which changed the stack to $[B, C]$. In other words, if the state of the stack is considered just before and after the *pop*'s program steps, its behaviour would be considered invalid, as it cannot change a stack from $[D, A, B, C]$ to $[B, C]$. This is exactly what a guarantee condition provides: the ability to reason about the state of the system before and after a sequence of program steps.

---

[1] Another issue is that since the possible values construct returns a set of states, this post condition does not specify that l_2 should occur after l_1, so it could be satisfied by an item being removed instead of inserted.

The only task remaining is to construct a suitable guarantee condition that ensures the invalid behaviour discussed above is prevented. The abstract sequential post condition of *pop* is $list' = \mathbf{tl}\ list \wedge x' = \mathbf{hd}\ list$, as the change occurs atomically in one step. With the introduction of concurrency, if the *pop* operation passes its linearisation point on a particular step, then it should match the behaviour of the abstract post condition. Otherwise, the list should be unchanged, i.e. $list' = list$. Therefore, the concrete guarantee must show that each step either matches the abstract post condition or leaves the list unchanged:

$$guar\text{-}pop_1\colon\ list' = list \vee (list' = \mathbf{tl}\ list \wedge x' = \mathbf{hd}\ list)$$

Since guarantee conditions are required to be transitive, this prevents two removals within one sequence of program steps. However, it does not prevent two removals occurring with environment steps in between.

Therefore, it is clear that the linearisation point needs to be considered. Steps that do not contain the linearisation point need to leave the shared variables unchanged, i.e. preserving $list' = list$, whereas steps containing the linearisation point should be shown to either achieve the abstract post condition or leave the list unchanged, i.e. $list' = list \vee list' = \mathbf{tl}\ list$. The option to leave the list unchanged is still required, as the guarantee must hold transitively over all program steps, and there may be steps which do not update the list.

To prevent multiple removals, a flag, *done*, is needed that indicates whether or not a removal has occurred. If the flag is true, no further removals are possible. The flag effectively models that only stuttering steps should occur before and after the linearisation point.

The full *pop* operation is:

$pop_1\ ()\ x\colon Val$
pre $\neg done$
rely $x' = x \wedge done' = done$
guar $(list' \neq list \ \Rightarrow\ list' = \mathbf{tl}\ list \wedge x' = \mathbf{hd}\ list \wedge done' \wedge \neg done) \wedge$
$\qquad (list' = list \ \Rightarrow\ done' = done)$
post $done'$

At this stage, it is assumed that when an element is removed from a list, x will be atomically set to that element.

Possible values could be used for the post condition, as follows:

$$\exists l_1, l_2 \in \widehat{list} \cdot \mathbf{hd}\ l_1 = x \wedge l_2 = \mathbf{tl}\ l_1.$$

However, this can already be deduced from the transitive closure of the rely and guarantee conditions. Furthermore, the possible values approach would not restrict the *deq* to performing only a single removal.

The question is now whether the post condition adequately covers the desired outcome. The goal of a stack is that the *pop* operations will always return the newest value. To ensure this, *push* operations must be restricted to inserting elements into the same side that the *pop* removes them from. This requires additional constraints in the rely. The problem is that there is nothing that can be stated about the behaviour of the environment, as the environment may include further *pop* or *push* operations, which could even remove all the existing elements in the list and insert new ones. For example, if a sequence of rely steps during a *pop* started in the state with a list $[A, B, C]$, even if the environment steps ended in a state with a list $[A, B, C, D]$, the *pop* cannot determine whether an incorrect insertion of D at the wrong end of the list has occurred, or whether a valid sequence of *pop* and *push* steps has occurred, in which all of the elements were removed and then reinserted after a D. What is required is to ensure that each action of the environment was a valid *push* or *pop* operation. This breaks the compositionality of the operations, since the *pop* must now know details about what occurs between each environment step, rather than only the overall effect at the end of the sequence of environment steps.

Using the possible values notation in the rely condition would achieve this, as follows:

rely-pop$_1$:
$$x' = x \land done' = done \land$$
$$\forall v \in list \cdot v \notin list' \Rightarrow \exists l_1, l_2 \in \widehat{list} \cdot \mathbf{hd}\, l_1 = v \land l_2 = \mathbf{tl}\, l_1 \land$$
$$\forall v \in list' \cdot v \notin list \Rightarrow \exists l_1, l_2 \in \widehat{list} \cdot \mathbf{hd}\, l_2 = v \land l_1 = \mathbf{tl}\, l_2$$

This states that if the environment has added an element, then it must have been added to the end of the list, and if the environment has removed an element, then it also must have been removed from the end of the list. In [JH16], the possible values notation is only defined to be used in a post condition. The semantics of using it in a rely condition here is that $\widehat{x}$ refers to the sequence of values that occur from the before state to the after state of the rely. The original definition of possible values in [JH16] returns a set; a sequence is required here to ensure that the order of the operations is correct. The main disadvantage in using possible values over rely conditions is that it potentially breaks compositionality, thereby losing the benefits of rely/guarantee[2]. Nevertheless, in examples such as this, there does not appear to be a suitable alternative. Section 5 discusses this further, and the link between the examples in this paper and the concurrent garbage collector studied in [JY19]. Cliff Jones discusses the difficulties in moving from an atomic sequential specification to a concurrent non-atomic specification in [Jon07].

push$_1$ (*v: Val*)
pre true
rely true

---

[2] A major benefit of rely/guarantee is that it provides a way of reasoning about the environment behaviour without having to know the details about each environment process. Using possible values over a rely condition could break this separation, as it allows the rely condition to refer to specific environment steps.

guar $(list' \neq list \Rightarrow list' = [v] \frown list \wedge done' = true \wedge done = false) \wedge$
$(list' = list \Rightarrow done' = done)$

post true

The *push* operation, given above, has a similar structure and the same issues are encountered when attempting to prove that it refines the atomic *push*. From here, the next level of refinement would be closer to the code level, with a structure such as a linked list to replace the sequence. In the interests of space, the further development to the code level has been omitted, as the next example provides more interesting insights.

4   The Herlihy-Wing Queue

The previous example contained *fixed* linearisation points. Some problems contain linearisation points that cannot be determined ahead of time, as they depend on the execution of the other processes. Refer to [DD15] for a comprehensive comparison of different approaches for problems with different types of linearisation points. The Herlihy-Wing queue [HW90] is an example of a problem with linearisation points that cannot be determined from the start. This makes it an interesting and challenging problem for showing that linearisability holds.

The queue is an array-based structure that allows concurrent enqueue and dequeue operations. The code for each is given in Fig. 4. Note that the *index* variables in both operations are local variables. The only shared variables are *last* and *q*.

```
enq(v){
  <index = last; last = last + 1>;
  q[index] = v;
}

deq(){
  while(true){
    range = last;
    index = 0;
    while(index < range){
      x = null;
      swap(q[index],x);
      if (x != null) return x;
      index++;
    }
  }
}
```

Fig. 4. The code for the Herlihy-Wing queue

The statements inside the angular brackets in *enq* execute atomically; the operation sets its own local *index* to *last* and increments *last* in one atomic step. It then stores a value into the slot with that index. The *deq* continuously traverses the array, searching for the first non-null node it encounters. It does this by atomically swapping the value at the current index with a null value. If the value that was read from that slot, *x*, is not null, this value is returned. Otherwise, it continues searching. This process is potentially non-terminating, if nothing is added to the queue, or if other *deq* operations running concurrently always take the items first.

The difficulty of this problem is that the linearisation point for the *enq* depends on the order of execution of the other operation. Suppose that there is an empty queue and an *enq* and a *deq* operation are about to execute. The *enq* executes its first line, setting *last* to 1, but before it completes storing the value into slot 0, the *deq* executes and checks the first slot (index = 0), finding it to be empty. The *enq* then completes its operation and a second *enq* inserts a value into the second slot (index = 1). The *deq* will therefore return the second value before the first, which appears to break the FIFO ordering of the queue.

Example 3. The following is an example execution trace that results in this situation, where a single *deq* process is interleaving with two *enq* processes, one inserting *A* and one inserting *B*:

> Initial state: *last* = 0
> *enq(A)* sets *last* to 1
> *deq* does *range* = *last*, setting *range* to 1
> *deq* enters the while loop
> *deq* checks slot 0
> *enq(A)* inserts *A* into slot 0
> *enq(B)* sets *last* to 2
> *enq(B)* inserts *B* into slot 1
> *deq* checks slot 1
> *deq* returns *B*

As explained in [DD15], this concrete execution is actually equivalent to an abstract sequence where the second value B was enqueued before the first value A. This is what creates complications for verifying linearisability.

In this case, at first it would appear that the previous section's technique of examining the state of the queue before and after a single step does not work. There is a *deq* step where the queue contains A followed by B, i.e. [A, B], before the step and [A,-] afterwards, which does not respect FIFO ordering. However, unlike for the Treiber stack, this *could* be considered acceptable behaviour, if the *deq* had already checked the first slot before A had been inserted. On the other hand, traces where the *deq* removed B first even though A had been there before the *deq* operation started should be disallowed. In other words, the transition from [A, B] to [A,-] is only valid if the current index value of the *deq* was already equal to 1 at the start of a sequence of *deq* steps. In the sequence above, before the last sequence of *deq* steps, the *index* of the *deq* was 1, so it is valid that the *deq* removed the item in slot 1.

Therefore, the pattern from the last section still holds if the states of both the queue and the local index variable are considered. Invalid behaviour is where a state with [A,B] and $index = 0$ transitions to a state with [A,-], whereas a state with [A,B] and $index = 1$ can validly transition to [A,-]. In the next section, these ideas will be used to devise an appropriate guarantee condition.

4.1 Abstract Sequential Specification

At the abstract level, the state is defined the same way as for the Treiber stack, as a sequence of values:

$\Sigma_0 :: list : Val^*$

The *enq* and *deq* operations are very similar to the *push* and *pop* of the Treiber stack, with the only difference that *enq* inserts items at the opposite end of the list than where *deq* removes them from.

enq-seq (*v*: *Val*)
pre true
post $list' = list \frown [v]$

deq-seq () *x*: *Val*
pre true
post $list' = \mathbf{tl}\ list \wedge x' = \mathbf{hd}\ list$

4.2 Concurrent Development

At this next stage of development, concurrency is introduced, but still operating on an abstract sequence.

deq_0 () *x*: [*Val*]
pre $\neg done$
rely $x' = x \wedge done' = done$
guar $(list' \neq list \Rightarrow list' = \mathbf{tl}\ list \wedge x' = \mathbf{hd}\ list \wedge done' \wedge \neg done) \wedge$
      $(list' = list \Rightarrow done' = done)$
post $done'$

However, the above specification does not adequately specify the intended behaviour of the queue. The overall intent of the queue is that the *deq* operation will always return the oldest value that was placed in the queue. Specifying this is difficult, as it requires ensuring that the environment will always only insert elements into the tail end of the queue, while the *deq* removes them from the other end.

Example 4. Consider a queue which currently contains two elements: $[A, B]$. Suppose that a deq_1 operation is running. Before the deq_1 can locate the item to be dequeued, a concurrent enqueue operation erroneously inserts C into the head end of the queue: $[C, A, B]$. The deq_1 may then select C as the first element reached, despite it being the newest element, instead of the oldest. There is no sequence of the abstract sequential operations enq_0 and deq_0 that would result in this behaviour. Recall that under the definition of linearisability, only overlapping operations may be reordered. Unlike in Example 3, where the two enq operations overlapped in execution, the incorrect enqueue C operation does not overlap with either of the other enqueue operations. Therefore, it is not linearisable to a trace $enq_0(C), enq_0(A), enq_0(B), deq(C)$.

To prevent such behaviour occurring, one solution is to strengthen the rely condition. As there is no way to determine what operations took place in the environment, the use of possible values in the rely condition is again necessary:

$rely\text{-}deq_0$:
$$x' = x \wedge done' = done \wedge$$
$$\forall v \in list' \cdot v \notin list \implies \exists l_1, l_2 \in \widehat{list} \cdot l_2 = l_1 \frown [v] \wedge$$
$$\forall v \in list \cdot v \notin list' \implies \exists l_1, l_2 \in \widehat{list} \cdot \mathbf{hd}\, l_1 = v \wedge l_2 = \mathbf{tl}\, l_1$$

This has the same problem discussed earlier regarding breaking the compositionality of the processes.

The specification of enq_0 is analogous to deq_0.

4.3 Concrete Specification

The next level is designed to model the code given in Fig. 4. This level contains a sequence of values, an index and a variable *last* representing the index of the last item inserted into the queue. Note that the concrete level could have been described at the heap level, as was done in [JY15], instead of modelling the array as a sequence. However, the points focussed on in this paper are clear from a simplified representation. The notation $[Val]^*$ refers to a sequence of values of type *Val*, including **nil**.

$$\Sigma_1 :: \qquad q : [Val]^*$$
$$index : \mathbb{N}$$
$$last : \mathbb{N}$$

The specification for *deq* is (where *done* is a local ghost variable):

deq_1 () x: *Val*
pre $\neg done$
rely $last' \geq last \wedge index' = index \wedge done' = done$
guar $(done \implies done' \wedge noChanges(\sigma, \sigma')) \wedge$
$\qquad (noChanges(\sigma, \sigma') \wedge \neg done \implies \neg done') \wedge$
$\qquad (\forall i: index \ldots (index' - 1) \cdot q(i) = \mathbf{nil}) \wedge$
$\qquad (q(index') \neq q'(index')$
$\qquad\qquad \implies (q'(index') = \mathbf{nil} \wedge x' = q(index') \wedge done')) \wedge$
$\qquad (\forall j: 0 \ldots last \cdot j \neq index' \implies q(j) = q'(j)$
post $done'$

where the function *noChange* indicates that no changes were made to either an element in the queue or the *last* and *index* variables:

$$noChange : \Sigma_1 \times \Sigma_1$$

$$noChange(s, s') \quad \triangleq$$
$$\quad (s.last = s'.last) \wedge (s.index = s'.index) \wedge$$
$$\quad (\forall i\!:\! 0 \ldots s.last) \cdot s.q(i) = s'.q(i))$$

The guarantee follows the same general structure as for the Treiber stack. The first two clauses of the guarantee involving the *done* flag and *noChanges* ensures that changes do not occur unless *done* is false and that it does not become true on stuttering steps. The third clause of the guarantee states that all the slots from the original *index* up to just before the final *index'* should have been empty slots at the time when this sequence of program steps began. This prevents the operation from ignoring slots containing elements. Using this guarantee, a state with [A,B] and *index* = 0 could not transition to a state with the index as 1. The fourth clause ensures that if the slot at *index'* has been changed, it is now **nil** (the item was dequeued), to specify the intended behaviour of the *deq*. Finally, the last clause states that the remainder of the queue is left unchanged.

As with the Treiber stack, it is impossible to specify the final state of the queue at the termination of the operation, so the post condition is simply left as *true*. An alternative is to use possible values, but this could not constrain the *deq* to only perform one removal.

The next step is to relate this concrete guarantee to the abstract specification.

Example 5. In the case where the index was 1 before the guarantee step, although the concrete queue contains [A,B], it does not actually refine an abstract queue [A,B]; in fact, the corresponding abstract queue is [B,A], where the A element was inserted after the B. This is the essence of this problem: the abstract state that corresponds to a given concrete state depends on both the index value and the queue state. The concrete queue [A,B] with *index* = 0 corresponds to an abstract queue of [A,B], whereas a concrete queue [A,B] with *index* = 1 corresponds to an abstract queue of [B,A]. This is seen when attempting to find an abstract trace that is linearisable to the concrete one. [DD15] gives an abstract trace where the second value is enqueued first, to correspond with a concrete trace that returns the second value first. The abstract trace would be: $\{enq(B), enq(A), deq()\}$.

This suggests the following retrieve function, for finding the corresponding abstract state for a given concrete state:

$$retr\text{-}deq : \Sigma_1 \to \Sigma_0$$

$$retr\text{-}deq((q, index, n)) \quad \triangleq$$
$$\quad q(index) \frown [q(first(q, 0, n)) \ldots q(index - 1)] \frown [q(index + 1) \ldots q(n))]$$

where the function *first* returns the index of the first element that is non-null in the sequence:

$$first : [\mathit{Val}]^* \times \mathbb{N} \times \mathbb{N} \to \mathbb{N}$$

$$first(q, x, n) \quad \triangleq \quad \textbf{if } x = n$$
$$\textbf{then } n$$
$$\textbf{else if } q(x) = \textbf{nil}$$
$$\textbf{then } first(q, x + 1, n)$$
$$\textbf{else } x$$

If there are any elements before the element at the *index* slot, these were effectively inserted afterwards. This is reflected in the abstract queue. The retrieve function *retr-deq* states that the corresponding abstract queue is composed of the element at the *index* slot, followed by any non-null elements from before it, followed by the remainder of the array.

Example 6. If the concrete queue is [A,B,C] and *index* is 1, then a concrete *deq* step could result in a queue of [A,-,C]. The [A,B,C] queue prior to the step corresponds to an abstract queue of [B,A,C] using *retr-deq*, while the concrete queue of [A,-,C] after the step corresponds to an abstract queue of [-,A,C]. A transition from [B,A,C] to [-,A,C] satisfies the abstract guar condition, which requires there to be a step where *list'* = **tl** *list*. Figure 5 illustrates this. Since the *deq* operation did not find an item in location 0, item *A* had not been inserted yet at the start of the *deq*. Therefore, it is valid to consider the behaviour as equivalent to a trace where item *A* was only added after *B*.

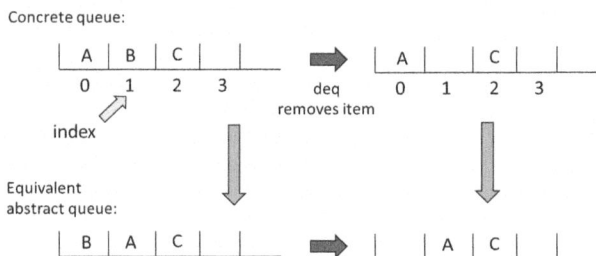

Fig. 5. Example Showing the Relationship Between Concrete and Abstract Queues

The following lemmas give the proof obligations from VDM [Jon90].

Lemma 1. *(Adequacy)*
$$\forall \sigma \in \Sigma_0 \cdot \exists \sigma_1 \in \Sigma_1 \cdot \mathit{retr\text{-}deq}(\sigma_1) = \sigma$$

Proof. For any abstract sequence in Σ_0, it is straightforward to construct a sequence in Σ_1 where each of the elements of the abstract sequence appear in the same order in the concrete sequence.[3] $\square$

Lemma 2. (Domain)
For all states $\sigma \in \Sigma_1$, $pre\text{-}deq_0(retr\text{-}deq(\sigma)) \Rightarrow pre\text{-}deq_1(\sigma)$.

Proof. The only difference between $pre\text{-}deq_0$ and $pre\text{-}deq_1$ is that $pre\text{-}deq_1$ initialises a local ghost variable, $done$. $\square$

For the following lemma, it is first necessary to replace the post condition of deq_1 with the conjunction of the post condition and the transitive closure of the rely and guarantee $((rely\text{-}deq_1 \vee guar\text{-}deq_1)^* \wedge post\text{-}deq_1)$. This is a standard rely/guarantee tactic, e.g. see the *trading law* of [HJ18].

Lemma 3. (Result)
For all states $\sigma, \sigma' \in \Sigma_1$,
$$pre\text{-}deq_0(retr\text{-}deq(\sigma)) \wedge post\text{-}deq_1(\sigma, \sigma')$$
$$\Rightarrow post\text{-}deq_0(retr\text{-}deq(\sigma), retr\text{-}deq(\sigma')).$$

Proof Outline. From $pre\text{-}deq_1(\sigma)$ (which comes from Lemma 2), $done$ is initially false and from $post\text{-}deq_1(\sigma, \sigma')$, $done$ holds at σ'. From $guar\text{-}deq_1$, there was a state where $q(index)$ was set to **nil** and x set to the previous value at that slot, and since $index$ has not changed since $done$ became true (from the 1st clause of $guar\text{-}deq_1$), this is $index'$.

From the 3rd clause of $guar\text{-}deq_1$, each program step only advances $index$ if there are empty slots, so at the initial state σ, all of the slots from 0 to $index' - 1$ were empty. Therefore, even if those slots are not empty at σ', those are all elements which were inserted after the deq had started its operation.

Thus, using $retr\text{-}deq$ on each of the states, there was a state where the queue consisted of $q(index')$ followed by any slots with indices less than $index'$ that are non-null at the state where deq removes the $q(index')$ item, (this is given by the $[q(first(q, 0, n)) \ldots q(index - 1)]$ clause in $retr\text{-}deq$), followed by the items after $index'$. Similarly, there was a state where the queue was the same as above, except with the element at $q(index')$ removed. This is equivalent to the $list' =$ **tl** $list$ requirement of $guar\text{-}deq_0$.
    $\square$

The specification of enq is:

enq_1 $(v: Val)$
pre $\neg done$
rely $last' \geq last$

---

[3] Note that there may also be many other possible concrete sequences which are equivalent to the abstract one using the retrieve function.

guar $(done \Rightarrow done' \wedge noChanges(\sigma, \sigma')) \wedge$
$(noChanges(\sigma, \sigma') \wedge \neg done \Rightarrow \neg done') \wedge$
$\forall i: 0 \ldots last' \cdot i \neq index \Rightarrow q'(i) = q(i) \wedge$
$(last' \neq last \Rightarrow last' = last + 1 \wedge index' = last \wedge setInd' \wedge \neg setInd) \wedge$
$(setInd \Rightarrow index' = index \wedge (q'(index) = v \vee noChanges(\sigma, \sigma'))) \wedge$
$(\neg setInd \Rightarrow q'(index) = q(index) \wedge$
$\qquad ((q'(last) = v \wedge done' \wedge setInd' \wedge index' = last \wedge last' = last + 1)$
$\qquad \vee (noChanges(\sigma, \sigma') \wedge index' = index)))$

post true

Note that the *index* variable here is local to the *enq* and not the same as the *index* that is local to *deq*. The first two clauses are the same as for *deq*. The third clause ensures that no slot will be updated except for the *index* slot. The fourth clause states that if *last* is updated, which occurs when the *enq* operation has chosen a slot to use, then that slot was *last* and also *last* has been incremented. The variable *setInd* is used to indicate that *index* has been set, to ensure that it will not be changed again. The fifth clause is for handling the case where *index* was already updated on a previous step, leaving the option to either make no changes on this step or add the new item to the queue. The final clause handles the case where the *index* has not been set on a previous step. On this step, both *index* is set and the new item is added, or no changes occur. (The fourth clause already covers the case where *index* is set without adding an item).

While the proofs and the rest of the development of *enq* are not shown here, the interesting feature to note is that the *enq* requires a different retrieve function than *retr-deq*. This is due to the different linearisation points. Therefore, a separate retrieve function is required per operation.

5 Boundaries of Rely/Guarantee

The issues encountered with these examples are reminiscent of the problems Jones and Yatapanage found when using rely/guarantee to verify a concurrent garbage collection algorithm [JY19]. It is not possible to verify the algorithm using standard rely/guarantee conditions alone; three possible solutions are given in [JY19], which all break compositionality in some form. The similarities to the Treiber stack and Herlihy-Wing queue are striking. Figure 6 shows the cycle of behaviour by the two components of the system: the mutator which uses and loses memory and the collector which must free the garbage. There is no way to specify the post condition of the collector (that all the lost memory has been freed) without using the notion of possible values, because after the collector locates lost memory, the mutator running concurrently can reallocate it and again lose it. This is similar to the difficulties in specifying the post conditions of the stack and queue operations, due to the extreme interference of the environment in both cases.

The aspect of the garbage collector which is the most difficult to specify, however, is the requirement that the collector imposes on the mutator: whenever the mutator redirects a pointer in the heap, it must mark the new address. This action helps the collector to achieve its goal without mistakenly deallocating

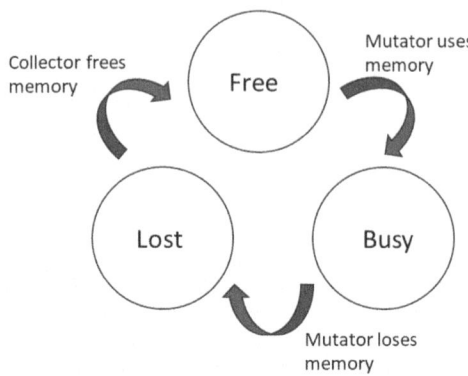

Fig. 6. Overview of the Garbage Collector Example used in [JY19]

memory that is in use. A similar problem occurs in both the Treiber stack and the Herlihy-Wing queue. Consider the difficulty in specifying the rely conditions in both cases. For example, the *deq* operation of the queue requires a rely condition which ensures that if the environment inserts a new value, it should insert it at the tail end of the queue. To specify this in Σ_1 of the queue requires being able to state the relationship between the *enq* operation's steps which identify a new slot and move the *last* variable, and the steps which actually insert the value into the chosen slot. While these two phases, which could be interrupted by other processes, can be identified using local auxiliary variables in the *enq* specification, such as the *setInd* variable, specifying it in the rely condition of the *deq* is impossible without breaking compositionality. The approach used in this paper has been to use possible values in the rely conditions, which, as discussed in previous sections, still requires a break in compositionality. A similar approach would be likely to work for the garbage collector, but would not necessarily offer a benefit over the suggested solutions given in [JY19], such as using shared ghost variables.

The conclusion appears to be that there are a class of algorithms for which standard rely and guarantee conditions are insufficient. It is useful to study these examples further, to investigate the exact properties which cause this phenomenon. It is important to be able to classify both problems and approaches, so that future problems can be handled appropriately. Another example which may be related is the Michael-Scott queue algorithm [MS96]. An interesting aspect of this algorithm is that one of the components requires the others to perform a task to help achieve the post condition. This again appears to be similar to the garbage collector's requirement by the collector for the mutator to aid in marking nodes. For future work, the author plans to investigate this algorithm to identify whether the same issues apply during verification using rely/guarantee.

6   Related Work

Many approaches exist for verifying linearisability. A comprehensive survey is given in [DD15]. Linearisability is usually associated with the relationship between concrete and abstract states. This aspect of the development of this paper is not new. However, most approaches use techniques such as simulation to relate the concrete and abstract traces. For example, [DSW08] present a mechanised proof of a concurrent stack using forward simulation conditions. Colvin and Groves [CG05] verify an array-based queue using backward simulations between I/O Automata.

Dongol and Derrick [DD13] use an interval-based logic to relate concrete operations to course-grained abstractions, to avoid the need for identifying linearisation points in the code. It would be interesting to compare whether the approach in this paper achieves the same underlying basis.

Vafeiadis presents an approach using RGSep for verifying linearisability in [Vaf07]. RGSep combines rely/guarantee and separation logic. Similarly to this paper, his approach uses the relationship between the concrete and abstract states. However, the abstract operations are embedded into the program code. The approach requires the identification of linearisation points. Auxiliary variables are used to record the location of these points. While rely and guarantee conditions are used, the approach does not consider the use of the guarantee conditions to express the linearisable behaviour.

In [SW17], the relationship between trace refinement and linearisability is investigated. They show that trace refinement implies linearisability but not the other way around. In a similar way, it would be interesting to investigate whether there is a general relationship that always allows linearisability to be expressed using rely/guarantee conditions or whether it depends on the type of problem, and perhaps the type of linearisation points.

Hayes [Hay18] investigates the Treiber stack in the context of rely/guarantee specifications, but the focus there is on specifying progress and termination conditions.

7   Conclusion

This paper has investigated the use of rely/guarantee reasoning to verify non-blocking problems, particularly ones which exhibit complex interactions where the correctness is normally ensured by proving linearisability. An interesting aspect that was identified is that the linearisability property can be re-stated in terms of a guarantee condition that must hold over single program steps (or a single sequence of program steps). The traces which are not linearisable always contain a single sequence of program steps that violate the guarantee condition. Examining the two examples shown in this paper has identified this common property, even though the two examples have different kinds of linearisation points. Future work will be to investigate whether this property holds generally, i.e. whether it is always possible to specify the linearisable behaviour as a guarantee condition of the operation.

The problems investigated have also uncovered further evidence of a class of algorithms for which standard rely/guarantee conditions do not apply. Investigating the properties of these algorithms have helped to identify the boundaries of rely/guarantee, including the reasons why standard rely/guarantee conditions are unable to solve the problems. Understanding these reasons and clearly identifying the class of algorithms which cannot be solved using standard rely/guarantee is necessary for identifying the class for which it does apply.

Acknowledgements. The connections between this work and my previous work with Cliff have been discussed. Before coming to the U.K. to work with Cliff, I had been working on model checking approaches. Cliff showed me a simple and yet elegant way of looking at concurrency. Since then, I have been finding uses of the rely/guarantee idea in many different applications, such as the work Cliff and I are currently pursuing on using rely/guarantee for security protocols [YJ23] and some ideas I have on using rely/guarantee for the safety-critical systems I worked on previously.

The most important contribution of Cliff is his nature that allows him to understand and help so many people. I would like to thank Cliff for all of his support over the years. I'm so glad that I accepted his offer to come to Newcastle to work with him over a decade ago. It was not just a postdoctoral position but a long-lasting collaboration and friendship.

The idea of using a flag to record when a change has occurred was devised during a helpful and interesting discussion with Cliff. I would also like to thank Rob Colvin, Brijesh Dongol, Graeme Smith, Roger Su and Kirsten Winter for useful discussions related to the ideas of the paper. Jimmy Gan and the anonymous reviewers provided useful suggestions for improvement.

References

[CG05] Colvin, R., Groves, L.: Formal verification of an array-based nonblocking queue. In: 10th International Conference on Engineering of Complex Computer Systems (ICECCS 2005), 16-20 June 2005, Shanghai, China, pp. 507–516. IEEE Computer Society (2005)

[DD13] Dongol, B., Derrick, J.: Simplifying proofs of linearisability using layers of abstraction. ECEASST **66** (2013)

[DD15] Dongol, B., Derrick, J.: Verifying linearisability: a comparative survey. ACM Comput. Surv. 48(2), 19:1–19:43 (2015)

[DSW08] Derrick, J., Schellhorn, G., Wehrheim, H.: Mechanizing a correctness proof for a lock-free concurrent stack. In: Barthe, G., de Boer, F.S. (eds.) Formal Methods for Open Object-Based Distributed Systems, 10th IFIP WG 6.1 Int. Conf., FMOODS 2008, Proc. LNCS, vol. 5051 pp. 78–95. Springer (2008). https://doi.org/10.1007/978-3-540-68863-1_6

[Hay18] Hayes, I.J.: Some challenges of specifying concurrent program components. In: Derrick, J., Dongol, B., Reeves, S. (eds.) Proceedings 18th Refinement Workshop, Oxford, UK, 18th July 2018, EPOTCS, vol. 282, pp. 10–22. Open Publishing Association (October 2018)

[HJ18] Hayes, I.J., Jones, C.B.: A guide to rely/guarantee thinking. In: Bowen, J.P., Liu, Z., Zhang, Z. (eds.) Engineering Trustworthy Software Systems. LNCS, vol. 11174, pp. 1–38. Springer International Publishing, Cham (2018). https://doi.org/10.1007/978-3-030-02928-9_1

[HW90]   Herlihy, M.P., Wing, J.M.: Linearizability: a correctness condition for concurrent objects. ACM Trans. Program. Lang. Syst. **12**(3), 463–492 (1990)

[JH16]   Jones, C.B., Hayes, I.J.: Possible values: exploring a concept for concurrency. J. Logical Algebraic Methods Program. **85**(5, Part 2), 972–984 (2016)

[Jon83a]   Jones, C.B.: Specification and design of (parallel) programs. In: Proceedings of IFIP 1983, pp. 321–332. North-Holland (1983)

[Jon83b]   Jones, C.B.: Tentative steps toward a development method for interfering programs. ACM ToPLaS **5**(4), 596–619 (1983)

[Jon90]   Jones, C.B.: Systematic Software Development using VDM. Prentice Hall International, second edition (1990)

[Jon07]   Jones, C.B.: Splitting atoms safely. Theoret. Comput. Sci. **375**(1–3), 109–119 (2007)

[JY15]   Jones, C.B., Yatapanage, N.: Reasoning about separation using abstraction and reification. In: Calinescu, R., Rumpe, B. (eds.) Software Engineering and Formal Methods. LNCS, vol. 9276, pp. 3–19. Springer (2015). https://doi.org/10.1007/978-3-319-22969-0_1

[JY19]   Jones, C.B., Yatapanage, N.: Investigating the limits of rely/guarantee relations based on a concurrent garbage collector example. Formal Aspects Comput. (2019) To appear

[MS96]   Michael, M.M., Scott, M.L.: Simple, fast, and practical non-blocking and blocking concurrent queue algorithms. In: Burns, J.E., Moses, Y. (eds.) Proceedings of the Fifteenth Annual ACM Symposium on Principles of Distributed Computing, Philadelphia, Pennsylvania, USA, 23-26 May 1996, pp. 267–275. ACM (1996)

[SW17]   Smith, G., Winter, K.: Relating trace refinement and linearizability. Formal Aspects Comput. Accepted 5 December 2016, Online 14 Feb 2017 (2017)

[Tre86]   Treiber, R.K.: Systems programming: Coping with parallelism. Technical Report RJ 5118, IBM Almaden Research Center (April 1986)

[Vaf07]   Vafeiadis, V.: Modular fine-grained concurrency verification. PhD thesis, University of Cambridge (2007)

[YJ23]   Yatapanage, N.P., Jones, C.B.: Using rely/guarantee to pinpoint assumptions underlying security protocols. CoRR, abs/ arXiv: 2311.15189 (2023)

Less is More Revisited
Association with Global Multiparty Session Types

Nobuko Yoshida(✉) and Ping Hou

University of Oxford, Oxford, UK
{nobuko.yoshida,ping.hou}@cs.ox.ac.uk

Abstract. Multiparty session types (MPST) [12] provide a type discipline where a programmer or architect specifies a whole view of communications as a *global protocol*, and each distributed program is locally type-checked against its *end-point projection*. After 10 years from the birth of MPST, Scalas and Yoshida [18] discovered that the *proofs* of type safety in the literature which use the end-point projection with *mergeability* are flawed. After this paper, researchers wrongly believed that the end-point projection (with mergeability) was *unsound*. We correct this misunderstanding, proposing a new general proof technique for type soundness of multiparty session π-calculus, which uses an *association* relation between a global type and its end-point projection.

1 Introduction

Today many computer science technologies are centred on *data science* and *machine learning*, which fall within the field of technology used to leverage data for creating and innovating products, services, and infrastructural systems in society. In 1996, C. B. Jones, together with J.R. Gurd, predicted this era of *data*. In their article, *the Global-yet-Personal Information System* (GyPʃIS), in *Computing Tomorrow: future research directions in computer science* edited by Wand and Milner [9], they argued that extracting meaning from data, and understanding and building methods that utilise data to inform predictions will be the central concerns in future computing, proposing the system called GyPʃIS. The thesis of GyPʃIS is that data should be *globally* consistent, *open* for everybody, and yet *personalised* (structured with respect to an individual need). They predicted that future systems would go beyond the scope of the known programming paradigm, and argued for the importance of describing and formally specifying *interactive behaviours*.

Multiparty session types (MPST) [12,13] represent a type discipline which attempts to take a step to meet the GyPʃIS challenge, by offering a programming framework to guarantee a global consistency among interactive agents or processes in the open system [10,19]. It facilitates the description, specification

Work supported by: EPSRC EP/T006544/2, EP/K011715/1, EP/K034413/1, EP/L00058X/1, EP/N027833/2, EP/N028201/1, EP/T014709/2, EP/V000462/1, EP/X015955/1, NCSS/EPSRC VeTSS, and Horizon EU TaRDIS 101093006.

A. Cavalcanti and J. Baxter (Eds.): *The Practice of Formal Methods*, LNCS 14781, pp. 268–291, 2024.
https://doi.org/10.1007/978-3-031-66673-5_14

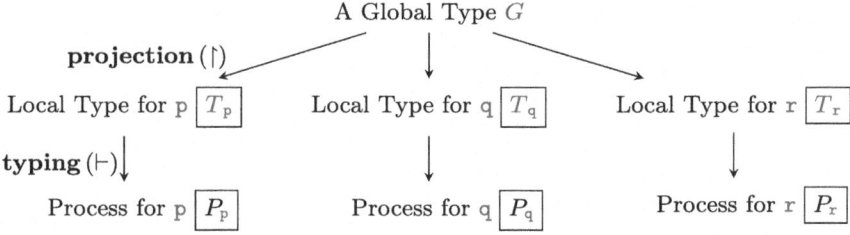

Fig. 1. Top-down methodology of multiparty session types

and verification of communications in concurrent and distributed systems based on *multiparty protocols*.

The design of multiparty protocols begins with a given *global* type (G, top in Fig. 1), and each participant's implementation (process) P_p (bottom) relies on its *local* type T_p (middle), obtained by the end-point projection of the global type. The global and local types reflect the global and local communication behaviours, respectively. Well-typed implementations (processes) that conform to a global type are guaranteed to be *correct by construction*, enjoying safety, deadlock-freedom, and liveness of interactions. In this paper, we demonstrate the rigour of the MPST *top-down* approach, revisiting the work of Scalas and Yoshida [18].

Misunderstanding on the Top-Down MPST. The work [18] has proposed a general MPST framework (called the *bottom-up* approach), which does not require global types. In the bottom-up approach, safety of processes is enforced by directly checking safety of a set of local types. This approach offers more typability, but is computationally more expensive. For worse, in the asynchronous MPST where processes communicating via infinite FIFO queues, type-checking using the bottom-up approach is undecidable, while in the top-down approach, it is decidable (as the projection is decidable).

The work [18] also pointed out that proofs of some of the top-down typing systems, which use the projection with *mergeability*, are flawed. The notion of mergeability was first introduced in [3] for modelling the end-point projection of Web Service Choreography Description Language (WS-CDL) [8]. Its aim is to broaden the typability of processes by allowing more projectable (well-formed) global types than the original limited projection [12]. Mergeability is implemented in the Scribble protocol description language [11,22,23] and other related MPST tools. Without using mergeability, most global protocols are not projectable. We define the projection and mergeability formally in Definition 3.

The statement in [18] has caused misunderstandings among researchers, leading to claims such as "the top-down approach (with mergeability) is *unsound*", and subsequently, assertions that "global types are *problematic*".

This paper proves that we can build a sound typing system using the end-point projection with mergeability, and more importantly, a utilisation of global types leads to a clear proof method for the type soundness.

Outline. Section 2 recalls the multiparty session calculus from [18]; Section 3 defines global and local types, and introduces the *association relation* $G \sqsubseteq_s \Gamma$, where global type G and a set of local types Γ of session name s are related up to *subtyping*. We then prove the sound and complete correspondence between global and local type semantics with respect to $\sqsubseteq$; Section 4 defines the typing system using $\sqsubseteq$ and proves type safety, deadlock-freedom, and liveness of typable processes; and Section 5 concludes with *Questar* by Mario T. Full proofs and auxiliary material are available in the extended version of the paper [21].

2   Multiparty Session π-Calculus

This section presents the syntax of the synchronous multiparty session π-calculus, and provides a formalisation of its operational semantics.

Syntax of Processes in Session π -Calculus. The multiparty session π-calculus models the behaviour of processes that interact using multiparty channels. For simplicity of presentation, our calculus is streamlined to focus on communication; standard extensions, such as with expressions and "if... then... else" statements, are routine and orthogonal to our formulation.

Definition 1 (Syntax of Multiparty Session π-Calculus). *The* multiparty session π-calculus *syntax is defined as follows:*

$$
\begin{array}{llll}
c & ::= & x \mid s[\mathsf{p}] & \textit{(variable or channel for session s with role } \mathsf{p}) \\
d & ::= & v \mid c & \textit{(basic value, variable, or channel with role)} \\
w & ::= & v \mid s[\mathsf{p}] & \textit{(basic value or channel with role)} \\
P, Q & ::= & \mathbf{0} \mid (\nu s)\, P & \textit{(inaction, restriction)} \\
& & c[\mathsf{q}] \oplus \mathsf{m}\langle d \rangle . P & \textit{(selection towards role } \mathsf{q}) \\
& & c[\mathsf{q}] \& \{\mathsf{m}_i(x_i).P_i\}_{i \in I} & \textit{(branching from role } \mathsf{q} \textit{ with an index set } I \neq \emptyset) \\
& & \mathbf{def}\ D\ \mathbf{in}\ P \mid X\langle \widetilde{d} \rangle & \textit{(process definition, process call)} \\
& & P \mid Q \mid \mathbf{err} & \textit{(parallel composition, error)} \\
D & ::= & X(\widetilde{x}) = P & \textit{(declaration of process variable } X)
\end{array}
$$

$\mathsf{p}, \mathsf{q}, \ldots$ *denote* roles *belonging to a set* $\mathcal{R}$; $s, s', \ldots$ *denote* sessions; $x, y, \ldots$ *denote* variables; $\mathsf{m}, \mathsf{m}', \ldots$ *denote* message labels; *and* $X, Y, \ldots$ *denote* process variables. *Restriction, branching, and process definitions and declarations act as binders, as expected;* $\mathrm{fc}(P)$ *is the set of* free channels with roles *in* P, *and* $\mathrm{fv}(P)$ *is the set of* free variables *in* P. *We adopt a form of Barendregt convention: bound sessions and process variables are assumed pairwise distinct, and different from free ones. We write* $\Pi_{i \in I} P_i$ *for the parallel composition of processes* P_i.

A *session* is a sequence of interactions, including send and receive operations, performed by a set of *roles (participants)* in a communication protocol.

The syntax of our calculus (Definition 1) is mostly standard [18]. v is a *basic value* (e.g. unit (), integers, strings). A *channel with role* (a.k.a. *session endpoint*) $s[\mathsf{p}]$ is a multiparty communication endpoint whose user plays role p in the session

$[\text{R-}\oplus\&]$ $s[\mathtt{p}][\mathtt{q}]\&\{\mathtt{m}_i(x_i).P_i\}_{i\in I} \mid s[\mathtt{q}][\mathtt{p}]\oplus\mathtt{m}_k\langle w\rangle.Q \rightarrow P_k\{w/x_k\} \mid Q$ if $k\in I$

$[\text{R-}X]$ **def** $X(x_1,\ldots,x_n) = P$ **in** $(X\langle w_1,\ldots,w_n\rangle \mid Q)$
$\rightarrow$ **def** $X(x_1,\ldots,x_n) = P$ **in** $(P\{w_1/x_1\}\cdots\{w_n/x_n\} \mid Q)$

$[\text{R-Ctx}]$ $P \rightarrow P'$ implies $\mathbb{C}[P] \rightarrow \mathbb{C}[P']$

$[\text{R-Err}]$ $s[\mathtt{p}][\mathtt{q}]\&\{\mathtt{m}_i(x_i).P_i\}_{i\in I} \mid s[\mathtt{q}][\mathtt{p}]\oplus\mathtt{m}\langle w\rangle.Q \rightarrow$ **err** if $\forall i\in I : \mathtt{m}_i\neq\mathtt{m}$

$[\text{R-}\equiv]$ $P' \equiv P \rightarrow Q \equiv Q'$ implies $P' \rightarrow Q'$

Fig. 2. Operational semantics of multiparty session π-calculus.

$$P \mid Q \equiv Q \mid P \quad (P \mid Q) \mid R \equiv P \mid (Q \mid R) \quad P \mid \mathbf{0} \equiv P \quad (\nu s)\,\mathbf{0} \equiv \mathbf{0}$$

$$(\nu s)\,(\nu s')\,P \equiv (\nu s')\,(\nu s)\,P \qquad (\nu s)\,(P \mid Q) \equiv P \mid (\nu s)\,Q \text{ if } s\notin\text{fc}(P)$$

$$\textbf{def } D \textbf{ in } \mathbf{0} \equiv \mathbf{0} \qquad \textbf{def } D \textbf{ in } (\nu s)\,P \equiv (\nu s)\,(\textbf{def } D \textbf{ in } P) \text{ if } s\notin\text{fc}(D)$$

$$\textbf{def } D \textbf{ in } (P \mid Q) \equiv (\textbf{def } D \textbf{ in } P) \mid Q \text{ if } \text{dpv}(D)\cap\text{fpv}(Q) = \emptyset$$

$$\textbf{def } D \textbf{ in } (\textbf{def } D' \textbf{ in } P) \equiv \textbf{def } D' \textbf{ in } (\textbf{def } D \textbf{ in } P)$$
$$\text{if } (\text{dpv}(D)\cup\text{fpv}(D))\cap\text{dpv}(D') = (\text{dpv}(D')\cup\text{fpv}(D'))\cap\text{dpv}(D) = \emptyset$$

Fig. 3. Standard structural congruence rules, where $\text{fpv}(D)$ is the set of *free process variables* in D, and $\text{dpv}(D)$ is the set of *declared process variables* in D.

s. Inaction $\mathbf{0}$ represents a terminated process (and is often omitted). *Session restriction* $(\nu s)\,P$ declares a new session s with its scope restricted to the process P. *Selection* (a.k.a. *internal choice*) $c[\mathtt{q}]\oplus\mathtt{m}\langle d\rangle.P$ sends a message $\mathtt{m}$ with payload d to role $\mathtt{q}$ via endpoint c, where c may be a variable or channel with role, while d may also be a basic value. *Branching* (a.k.a. *external choice*) $c[\mathtt{q}]\&\{\mathtt{m}_i(x_i).P_i\}_{i\in I}$ expects to receive a message $\mathtt{m}_i$ (for some $i \in I$) from role $\mathtt{q}$ via endpoint c, and then continues as P_i. *Process definition* **def** D **in** P and *process call* $X\langle\tilde{d}\rangle$ capture recursion: the call invokes X by expanding it into P, and replacing its formal parameters with the actual ones. *Parallel composition* $P|Q$ denotes two processes capable of concurrent execution and potential communication. Finally, **err** represents the *error* process.

Operational Semantics of Session π-Calculus. We provide the operational semantics of our multiparty session π-calculus in Definition 2, using a standard *structural congruence* $\equiv$ defined in Fig. 3.

Definition 2 (Semantics of Multiparty Session π-Calculus). *A reduction context* $\mathbb{C}$ *is defined as:* $\mathbb{C} ::= \mathbb{C} \mid P \mid (\nu s)\,\mathbb{C} \mid \textbf{def } D \textbf{ in } \mathbb{C} \mid [\,]$. *The reduction* $\rightarrow$ *is inductively defined in Fig. 2. We denote* $\rightarrow^*$ *as the reflexive and transitive closure of* $\rightarrow$. *We say that* P *has an error iff* $\exists\mathbb{C}$ *with* $P = \mathbb{C}[\textbf{err}]$.

Our operational semantics is standard [18]. The reduction context $\mathbb{C}$ defines a process with a single placeholder $[\,]$, serving as a substitute for a specific subterm P. Rule $[\text{R-}\oplus\&]$ describes a communication on session s involving receiver $\mathtt{p}$ and sender $\mathtt{q}$, provided that the transmitted message $\mathtt{m}_k$ is handled by the receiver ($k \in I$). In case of a message label mismatch, rule $[\text{R-Err}]$ is invoked to trigger an **error**. Rule $[\text{R-}X]$ initiates the expansion of process definitions when called. Additionally, rules [R-CTX] and [R-≡] facilitate the reduction of processes under reduction contexts and modulo structural congruence, respectively.

Example 1 (Syntax and Semantics of Session π-Calculus, from [1]). Processes P and Q below communicate on a session s: P uses the endpoint $s[\mathsf{p}]$ to send an endpoint $s[\mathsf{r}]$ to role q; Q uses the endpoint $s[\mathsf{q}]$ to receive an endpoint x, then sends a message to role p via x.

$$P = s[\mathsf{p}][\mathsf{q}]\oplus\mathsf{m}'\langle s[\mathsf{r}]\rangle.s[\mathsf{p}][\mathsf{r}]\&\mathsf{m}(x).\mathbf{0} \qquad Q = s[\mathsf{q}][\mathsf{p}]\&\mathsf{m}'(x).x[\mathsf{p}]\oplus\mathsf{m}\langle 42\rangle.\mathbf{0}$$

By Definition 2, successful reductions yield:

$$
\begin{aligned}
&(\nu s)\,(P \mid Q)\\
&= (\nu s)\,(s[\mathsf{p}][\mathsf{q}]\oplus\mathsf{m}'\langle s[\mathsf{r}]\rangle.s[\mathsf{p}][\mathsf{r}]\&\mathsf{m}(x).\mathbf{0} \mid s[\mathsf{q}][\mathsf{p}]\&\mathsf{m}'(x).x[\mathsf{p}]\oplus\mathsf{m}\langle 42\rangle.\mathbf{0})\\
[\text{R-}\oplus\&] \to\; &(\nu s)\,(s[\mathsf{p}][\mathsf{r}]\&\mathsf{m}(x).\mathbf{0} \mid s[\mathsf{r}][\mathsf{p}]\oplus\mathsf{m}\langle 42\rangle.\mathbf{0})\\
[\text{R-}\oplus\&] \to\; &(\nu s)\,\mathbf{0} \equiv \mathbf{0}
\end{aligned}
$$

Example 2 (OAuth Process, extended from [18]). The following process interacts on session s using channels with role $s[\mathsf{s}]$, $s[\mathsf{c}]$, $s[\mathsf{a}]$, to play resp. roles s, c, a. For brevity, we omit irrelevant message payloads.

$$(\nu s)\,(P_\mathsf{s} \mid P_\mathsf{c} \mid P_\mathsf{a}) \quad \text{where:} \begin{cases} P_\mathsf{s} = s[\mathsf{s}][\mathsf{c}]\oplus\texttt{cancel}\\ P_\mathsf{c} = s[\mathsf{c}][\mathsf{s}]\&\left\{\begin{matrix}\texttt{login}.s[\mathsf{c}][\mathsf{a}]\oplus\texttt{passwd}\langle\texttt{"XYZ"}\rangle\\ \texttt{cancel}.s[\mathsf{c}][\mathsf{a}]\oplus\texttt{quit},\texttt{fail}.s[\mathsf{c}][\mathsf{a}]\oplus\texttt{fatal}\end{matrix}\right\}\\ P_\mathsf{a} = s[\mathsf{a}][\mathsf{c}]\&\{\texttt{passwd}(y).s[\mathsf{a}][\mathsf{s}]\oplus\texttt{auth}\langle\texttt{"secret"}\rangle,\texttt{quit},\texttt{fatal}\} \end{cases}$$

Here, $(\nu s)\,(P_\mathsf{s} \mid P_\mathsf{c} \mid P_\mathsf{a})$ is the parallel composition of processes P_s, P_c, P_a in the scope of session s. In P_s, "$s[\mathsf{s}][\mathsf{c}]\oplus\texttt{cancel}$" means: use $s[\mathsf{s}]$ to send $\texttt{cancel}$ to c. Process P_c uses $s[\mathsf{c}]$ to receive $\texttt{login}$, $\texttt{cancel}$, or $\texttt{fatal}$ from s; then, in the first case, it uses $s[\mathsf{c}]$ to send $\texttt{passwd}$ to a; in the second case, it uses $s[\mathsf{c}]$ to send $\texttt{quit}$ to a; in the third case, it uses $s[\mathsf{c}]$ to send $\texttt{fatal}$ to a. By Definition 2, we have the reductions:

$$(\nu s)\,(P_\mathsf{s} \mid P_\mathsf{c} \mid P_\mathsf{a}) \to (\nu s)\,(\mathbf{0} \mid s[\mathsf{c}][\mathsf{a}]\oplus\texttt{quit} \mid P_\mathsf{a}) \to (\nu s)\,(\mathbf{0}|\mathbf{0}|\mathbf{0}) \equiv \mathbf{0}$$

3 Multiparty Session Types

This section introduces multiparty session types. We provide an extensive exploration Sect. 3.1, including syntax, projection, and subtyping. We establish a Labelled Transition System (LTS) semantics for both global types (Sect. 3.2) and typing contexts (Sect. 3.3). We explain the operational relationship between these two semantics in Sect. 3.4. Furthermore, we demonstrate that a typing context obtained via projection ensures safety, deadlock-freedom, and liveness in Sect. 3.5.

$$
\begin{array}{llll}
B & ::= & \text{int} \mid \text{bool} \mid \text{real} \mid \text{unit} \mid \ldots & \text{Basic types} \\
S & ::= & B \mid T & \text{Basic type or Session type} \\
G & ::= & \text{p} \rightarrow \text{q} \colon \{\text{m}_\text{i}(S_i).G_i\}_{i \in I} & \text{Transmission} \\
  & \mid & \mu t.G \quad \mid \quad t \quad \mid \quad \textbf{end} & \text{Recursion, Type variable, Termination} \\
T & ::= & \text{p} \& \{\text{m}_\text{i}(S_i).T_i\}_{i \in I} & \text{External choice} \\
  & \mid & \text{p} \oplus \{\text{m}_\text{i}(S_i).T_i\}_{i \in I} & \text{Internal choice} \\
  & \mid & \mu t.T \quad \mid \quad t \quad \mid \quad \textbf{end} & \text{Recursion, Type variable, Termination}
\end{array}
$$

Fig. 4. Syntax of types.

3.1 Global and Local Types

The Multiparty Session Type (MPST) theory uses *global types* to provide a comprehensive overview of communication between *roles*, such as $\text{p}, \text{q}, \text{s}, \text{t}, \ldots$, belonging to a set $\mathcal{R}$. In contrast, it employs *local types*, which are obtained via *projection* from a global type, to describe how an *individual* role communicates with other roles from a local viewpoint. The syntax of global and local types is presented in Fig. 4, where constructs are mostly standard [18].

Basic types are taken from a set $\mathcal{B}$, and describe types of values, ranging over integers, booleans, real numbers, units, *etc.*

Global types range over $G, G', G_i, \ldots$, and describe the high-level behaviour for all roles. The set of roles in a global type G is denoted by roles(G). We explain each syntactic construct of global types.

- $\text{p} \rightarrow \text{q} \colon \{\text{m}_\text{i}(S_i).G_i\}_{i \in I}$: a *transmission*, denoting a message from role p to role q, with a label m_i, a payload of type S_i (either basic or local type), and a continuation G_i, where i is taken from an index set I. We require that the index set be non-empty ($I \neq \emptyset$), labels m_i be pair-wise distinct, and self receptions be excluded (i.e. $\text{p} \neq \text{q}$).
- $\mu t.G$: a *recursive* global type, where contractive requirements apply [16, §21.8], i.e. each recursion variable t is bound within a $\mu t. \ldots$ and is guarded.
- **end**: a *terminated* global type (omitted where unambiguous).

Local types (or *session types*) range over $T, U, \ldots$, and describe the behaviour of a single role. We elucidate each syntactic construct of local types.

- $\text{p} \oplus \{\text{m}_\text{i}(S_i).T_i\}_{i \in I}$: an *internal choice* (*selection*), indicating that the *current* role is expected to *send* to role p.
- $\text{p} \& \{\text{m}_\text{i}(S_i).T_i\}_{i \in I}$: an *external choice* (*branching*), indicating that the *current* role is expected to *receive* from role p.
- $\mu t.T$: a *recursive* local type, similar to recursive global types.
- **end**: a *termination* (omitted where unambiguous).

Similar to global types, local types also need pairwise distinct, non-empty labels.

Projection is a *partial* function that provides the local type associated with a participating role in a global type. It takes a global type G and a role p, returning the corresponding local type. Our definition of projection, as given in Definition 3 below, is standard [18].

Definition 3 (Global Type Projection). *The* projection of a global type G *onto a role* $\mathbf{p}$, *written* $G \restriction \mathbf{p}$, *is:*

$$(\mathbf{q} \to \mathbf{r} \colon \{\mathtt{m}_{\mathtt{i}}(S_i).G_i\}_{i \in I}) \restriction \mathbf{p} = \begin{cases} \mathbf{r} \oplus \{\mathtt{m}_{\mathtt{i}}(S_i).(G_i \restriction \mathbf{p})\}_{i \in I} & \textit{if } \mathbf{p} = \mathbf{q} \\ \mathbf{q} \& \{\mathtt{m}_{\mathtt{i}}(S_i).(G_i \restriction \mathbf{p})\}_{i \in I} & \textit{if } \mathbf{p} = \mathbf{r} \\ \bigsqcap_{i \in I} G_i \restriction \mathbf{p} & \textit{if } \mathbf{p} \neq \mathbf{q} \textit{ and } \mathbf{p} \neq \mathbf{r} \end{cases}$$

$$(\mu\mathbf{t}.G) \restriction \mathbf{p} = \begin{cases} \mu\mathbf{t}.(G \restriction \mathbf{p}) & \textit{if } \mathbf{p} \in \mathrm{roles}(G) \textit{ or } \mathrm{fv}(\mu\mathbf{t}.G) \neq \emptyset \\ \mathbf{end} & \textit{otherwise} \end{cases} \qquad \mathbf{t} \restriction \mathbf{p} = \mathbf{t}$$
$$\mathbf{end} \restriction \mathbf{p} = \mathbf{end}$$

where $\bigsqcap$ *is the* merge operator for session types (*full merging*), *defined as:*

$$\mathbf{p} \oplus \{\mathtt{m}_{\mathtt{i}}(S_i).T_i\}_{i \in I} \sqcap \mathbf{p} \oplus \{\mathtt{m}_{\mathtt{i}}(S_i).T_i'\}_{i \in I} = \mathbf{p} \oplus \{\mathtt{m}_{\mathtt{i}}(S_i).(T_i \sqcap T_i')\}_{i \in I}$$

$$\mu\mathbf{t}.T \sqcap \mu\mathbf{t}.T' = \mu\mathbf{t}.(T \sqcap T') \quad \mathbf{t} \sqcap \mathbf{t} = \mathbf{t} \quad \mathbf{end} \sqcap \mathbf{end} = \mathbf{end}$$

$$\mathbf{p} \& \{\mathtt{m}_{\mathtt{i}}(S_i).T_i\}_{i \in I} \sqcap \mathbf{p} \& \{\mathtt{m}_{\mathtt{j}}(S_j).T_j'\}_{j \in J} = \mathbf{p} \& \{\mathtt{m}_{\mathtt{k}}(S_k).T_k''\}_{k \in I \cup J}$$

$$\textit{where} \quad T_k'' = \begin{cases} T_k \sqcap T_k' & \textit{if } k \in I \cap J \\ T_k & \textit{if } k \in I \setminus J \\ T_k' & \textit{if } k \in J \setminus I \end{cases}$$

It is noteworthy that there are global types that cannot be projected onto all of their participants. This occurs when certain global types may describe protocols that are inherently meaningless, leading to undefined merging operations, as illustrated in Example 4 following.

If a global type G starts with a transmission from role $\mathbf{p}$ to role $\mathbf{q}$, projecting it onto role $\mathbf{p}$ (resp. $\mathbf{q}$) results in an internal (resp. external) choice, provided that the continuation of each branching of G is also projectable. When projecting G onto other participants $\mathbf{r}$ ($\mathbf{r} \neq \mathbf{p}$ and $\mathbf{r} \neq \mathbf{q}$), a merge operator, as defined in Definition 3 and exemplified in Example 4 below, is used to ensure that the projections of all continuations are "compatible".

If a global type G is a termination or type variable, projecting it onto any role results in a termination or type variable, respectively. Finally, the projection of a recursive global type $\mu\mathbf{t}.G$ preserves its recursive construct when projected onto a role in G, or if there are no free type variables in $\mu\mathbf{t}.G$; otherwise, the projection yields termination.

Subtyping. We introduce a *subtyping* relation $\leqslant$ on local types, as defined in Definition 4. This subtyping relation is standard [18], and will be used later when defining local type semantics and establishing the relationship between global and local type semantics.

Definition 4 (Subtyping). *Given a standard subtyping* $<:$ *for basic types (e.g. including* int $<:$ real), *the session subtyping relation* $\leqslant$ *is coinductively defined:*

$$\frac{B <: B'}{B \leqslant B'} \ [\text{Sub-}B] \qquad \frac{\forall i \in I \quad S_i \leqslant S_i' \quad T_i \leqslant T_i'}{\text{p\&}\{\text{m}_i(S_i).T_i\}_{i \in I} \leqslant \text{p\&}\{\text{m}_i(S_i').T_i'\}_{i \in I \cup J}} \ [\text{Sub-\&}]$$

$$\frac{}{\text{end} \leqslant \text{end}} \ [\text{Sub-end}] \qquad \frac{\forall i \in I \quad S_i' \leqslant S_i \quad T_i \leqslant T_i'}{\text{p}\oplus\{\text{m}_i(S_i).T_i\}_{i \in I \cup J} \leqslant \text{p}\oplus\{\text{m}_i(S_i').T_i'\}_{i \in I}} \ [\text{Sub-}\oplus]$$

$$\frac{T[\mu t.T/t] \leqslant T'}{\mu t.T \leqslant T'} \ [\text{Sub-}\mu\text{L}] \qquad \frac{T \leqslant T'[\mu t.T'/t]}{T \leqslant \mu t.T'} \ [\text{Sub-}\mu\text{R}]$$

Rule [Sub-B] extends $\leqslant$ to basic types. The remaining rules establish that a subtype describes a more permissive session protocol w.r.t. its supertype. Rule [Sub-$\oplus$] enables the subtype of an internal choice to encompass a broader range of message labels, enabling the sending of more generic payloads. Conversely, rule [Sub-&] dictates that the subtype of an external choice supports a narrower set of input message labels, and less generic payloads. Rule [Sub-end] specifies that the type **end** is its own subtype. Finally, rules [Sub-μL] and [Sub-μR] assert the relationship between recursive types, defined up to their unfolding.

Example 3 (Types of OAuth 2.0, from [18]). Consider a protocol from OAuth 2.0 [15]: the service sends to the client *either* a request to login, *or* cancel; in the first case, c continues by sending passwd (carrying a string) to the authorisation server, who in turn sends auth to s (with a boolean, telling whether the client is authorised), and the session ends; in the second case, c sends quit to a, and the session ends. This protocol can be represented by the global type G_{auth}:

$$G_{\text{auth}} = \text{s} \to \text{c}: \left\{ \begin{array}{l} \text{login.c} \to \text{a:passwd(str).a} \to \text{s:auth(bool).end} \\ \text{cancel.c} \to \text{a:quit.end} \end{array} \right\}$$

Following the MPST top-down methodology, G_{auth} is projected onto three local types (one for each role s, c, a):

$$T_{\text{s}} = \text{c}\oplus \left\{ \begin{array}{l} \text{login.a\&auth(bool)} \\ \text{cancel} \end{array} \right\} \quad T_{\text{c}} = \text{s\&} \left\{ \begin{array}{l} \text{login.a}\oplus\text{passwd(str)} \\ \text{cancel.a}\oplus\text{quit} \end{array} \right\}$$

$$T_{\text{a}} = \text{c\&} \left\{ \begin{array}{l} \text{passwd(str).s}\oplus\text{auth(bool)} \\ \text{quit} \end{array} \right\}$$

Here, T_{s} represents the interface of s in G_{auth}: it must send ($\oplus$) to c either login or cancel; in the first case, s must then receive (&) message auth(bool) from a, and the session ends; otherwise, in the second case, the session just ends. Types T_{c} and T_{a} follow the same intuition.

Example 4 (Merge and Projection, originated from [14]). Two external choice (branching) types from the same role with disjoint labels can be merged into a type carrying both labels, e.g.

$$\text{A\&greet(str)} \sqcap \text{A\&farewell(bool)} = \text{A\&}\{\text{greet(str), farewell(bool)}\}$$

However, this does not apply to internal choices (selections), e.g. A$\oplus$greet(str)$\sqcap$ A$\oplus$farewell(bool) is undefined.

Two external choices from the same role with same labels but different payloads cannot be merged, e.g. A&greet(str) ⊓ A&greet(bool) is undefined. This also applies to internal choices.

Two external choices from different roles cannot be merged. Same for internal choices, e.g. A⊕greet(str) ⊓ B⊕greet(str) is undefined.

Additionally, two local types with same prefixes but unmergable continuations cannot be merged, e.g. A⊕greet(str) ⊓ A⊕greet(str).B&farewell(bool) is undefined as **end** ⊓ B&farewell(bool) is not mergeable.

Consider a global type:

$$G = \text{A} \rightarrow \text{B}: \begin{cases} \texttt{greet}(\text{str}).\text{C} \rightarrow \text{A}:\texttt{farewell}(\text{bool}) \\ \texttt{farewell}(\text{bool}).\text{C} \rightarrow \text{A}:\texttt{greet}(\text{str}) \end{cases}$$

G cannot be projected onto role C since:

$$G \restriction \text{C} = \text{C} \rightarrow \text{A}:\texttt{farewell}(\text{bool}) \restriction \text{C} \sqcap \text{C} \rightarrow \text{A}:\texttt{greet}(\text{str}) \restriction \text{C}$$
$$= \text{A} \oplus \texttt{farewell}(\text{bool}) \sqcap \text{A} \oplus \texttt{greet}(\text{str}) \ (\textbf{undefined})$$

$G \restriction \text{C}$ is undefined because in G, depending on whether A and B transmit greet or farewell, C is expected to send either farewell or greet to A. However, since C is not involved in the interactions between A and B, C is not aware of which message to send; that is G does not provide a valid specification for C.

3.2 Semantics of Global Types

We now present a Labelled Transition System (LTS) semantics for global types. To begin, we introduce the transition labels in Definition 5, which are also used in the LTS semantics of typing contexts (discussed later in Sect. 3.3).

Definition 5 (Transition Labels). *Let α be a transition label of the form:*

$$\alpha ::= s[\text{p}]:\text{q}\&\text{m}(S) \ \textit{(in session } s,\ \text{p} \textit{ receives } \text{m}(S) \textit{ from } \text{q)}$$
$$| \quad s[\text{p}]:\text{q}\oplus\text{m}(S) \ \textit{(in session } s,\ \text{p} \textit{ sends } \text{m}(S) \textit{ to } \text{q)}$$
$$| \quad s[\text{p}][\text{q}]\text{m} \qquad \textit{(in session } s, \textit{ message } \text{m} \textit{ is transmitted from } \text{p} \textit{ to } \text{q)}$$

The subject(s) of a transition label, written subject(α), *are defined as follows:*

$$\text{subject}(s[\text{p}]:\text{q}\&\text{m}(S)) = \text{subject}(s[\text{p}]:\text{q}\oplus\text{m}(S)) = \{\text{p}\}$$
$$\text{subject}(s[\text{p}][\text{q}]\text{m}) = \{\text{p}, \text{q}\}$$

The label $s[\text{p}][\text{q}]\text{m}$ denotes a synchronising communication between p and q via a message label m; the subject of such a label includes *both* roles. The labels $s[\text{p}]:\text{q}\oplus\text{m}(S)$ and $s[\text{p}]:\text{q}\&\text{m}(S)$ describe sending and receiving actions separately. Since we define a synchronous semantics for global types, these labels are used for the typing context semantics in Sect. 3.3.

We proceed to give a Labelled Transition System (LTS) semantics to a global type G in Definition 6.

$$\frac{G[\mu \mathbf{t}.G/\mathbf{t}] \xrightarrow{\alpha} G'}{\mu \mathbf{t}.G \xrightarrow{\alpha} G'} \text{ [GR-μ]} \qquad \frac{j \in I}{\mathbf{p} \rightarrow \mathbf{q} \colon \{\mathtt{m}_i(S_i).G'_i\}_{i \in I} \xrightarrow{s[\mathbf{p}][\mathbf{q}]\mathtt{m}_j} G'_j} \text{ [GR-$\oplus$&]}$$

$$\frac{\forall i \in I : G'_i \xrightarrow{\alpha} G''_i \quad \mathrm{subject}(\alpha) \cap \{\mathbf{p}, \mathbf{q}\} = \emptyset}{\mathbf{p} \rightarrow \mathbf{q} \colon \{\mathtt{m}_i(S_i).G'_i\}_{i \in I} \xrightarrow{\alpha} \mathbf{p} \rightarrow \mathbf{q} \colon \{\mathtt{m}_i(S_i).G''_i\}_{i \in I}} \text{ [GR-Ctx]}$$

Fig. 5. Global type reduction rules.

Definition 6 (Global Type Reductions). *The global type transition $\xrightarrow{\alpha}$ is inductively defined by the rules in Fig. 5. We use $G \rightarrow G'$ if there exists α such that $G \xrightarrow{\alpha} G'$; we write $G \rightarrow$ if there exists G' such that $G \rightarrow G'$, and $G \not\rightarrow$ for its negation (i.e. there is no G' such that $G \rightarrow G'$). Finally, $\rightarrow^*$ denotes the transitive and reflexive closure of $\rightarrow$.*

Figure 5 depicts the standard global type reduction rules [20]. Rule [GR-$\oplus$&] models the communication between two roles. Rule [GR-μ] handles recursion. Finally, rule [GR-Ctx] allows a reduction of a global type that is causally independent from its prefix, provided that all of the continuations can make the reduction of that label. This causal independence is indicated by the subjects of the label being disjoint from the prefix of the global type. For example, consider the global type $G = \mathbf{p} \rightarrow \mathbf{q} \colon \mathtt{m}_1.\mathbf{r} \rightarrow \mathbf{u} \colon \mathtt{m}_2.\mathbf{end}$. Given that the subjects of the label $s[\mathbf{r}][\mathbf{u}]\mathtt{m}_2$ are disjoint from $\mathbf{p}$ and $\mathbf{q}$, i.e. $\mathrm{subject}(s[\mathbf{r}][\mathbf{u}]\mathtt{m}_2) \cap \mathbf{p}, \mathbf{q} = \emptyset$, and $\mathbf{r} \rightarrow \mathbf{u} \colon \mathtt{m}_2.\mathbf{end} \xrightarrow{s[\mathbf{r}][\mathbf{u}]\mathtt{m}_2} \mathbf{end}$, rule [GR-Ctx] allows G to transition via $s[\mathbf{r}][\mathbf{u}]\mathtt{m}_2$: $G \xrightarrow{s[\mathbf{r}][\mathbf{u}]\mathtt{m}_2} \mathbf{p} \rightarrow \mathbf{q} \colon \mathtt{m}_1.\mathbf{end}$, which is unrelated to $\mathbf{p}$ and $\mathbf{q}$.

3.3 Semantics of Typing Context

After introducing the semantics of global types, we now present an LTS semantics for *typing contexts*, which are collections of local types. The formal definition of a typing context is provided in Definition 7, followed by its reduction rules in Definition 8.

Definition 7 (Typing Contexts). *Θ denotes a partial mapping from process variables to n-tuples of types, and Γ denotes a partial mapping from channels to types. Their syntax is defined as:*

$$\Theta \ ::= \ \emptyset \ | \ \Theta, X{:}S_1,\ldots,S_n \qquad \Gamma \ ::= \ \emptyset \ | \ \Gamma, x{:}S \ | \ \Gamma, s[\mathbf{p}]{:}T$$

The context composition Γ_1, Γ_2 is defined iff $\mathrm{dom}(\Gamma_1) \cap \mathrm{dom}(\Gamma_2) = \emptyset$. We write $s \in \Gamma$ iff $\exists \mathbf{p} : s[\mathbf{p}] \in \mathrm{dom}(\Gamma)$ (i.e. session s occurs in Γ). We write $s \notin \Gamma$ iff $\forall \mathbf{p} : s[\mathbf{p}] \notin \mathrm{dom}(\Gamma)$ (i.e. session s does not occur in Γ). We write $\mathrm{dom}(\Gamma) = \{s\}$ iff $\forall c \in \mathrm{dom}(\Gamma)$ there is $\mathbf{p}$ such that $c = s[\mathbf{p}]$ (i.e. Γ only contains session s). We write $\Gamma \leqslant \Gamma'$ iff $\mathrm{dom}(\Gamma) = \mathrm{dom}(\Gamma')$ and $\forall c \in \mathrm{dom}(\Gamma) : \Gamma(c) \leqslant \Gamma'(c)$. We

$$\frac{k \in I}{s[\mathbf{p}]:\mathbf{q}\oplus\{\mathtt{m_i}(S_i).T_i\}_{i\in I} \xrightarrow{s[\mathbf{p}]:\mathbf{q}\oplus\mathtt{m}_k(S_k)} s[\mathbf{p}]:T_k} \quad [\Gamma\text{-}\oplus]$$

$$\frac{k \in I}{s[\mathbf{p}]:\mathbf{q}\&\{\mathtt{m_i}(S_i).T_i\}_{i\in I} \xrightarrow{s[\mathbf{p}]:\mathbf{q}\&\mathtt{m}_k(S_k)} s[\mathbf{p}]:T_k} \quad [\Gamma\text{-}\&]$$

$$\frac{\Gamma_1 \xrightarrow{s[\mathbf{p}]:\mathbf{q}\oplus\mathtt{m}(S)} \Gamma_1' \quad \Gamma_2 \xrightarrow{s[\mathbf{q}]:\mathbf{p}\&\mathtt{m}(S')} \Gamma_2' \quad S \leqslant S'}{\Gamma_1,\Gamma_2 \xrightarrow{s[\mathbf{p}][\mathbf{q}]\mathtt{m}} \Gamma_1',\Gamma_2'} \quad [\Gamma\text{-}\oplus\&] \qquad \frac{s[\mathbf{p}]:T\{\mu\mathbf{t}.T/\mathbf{t}\} \xrightarrow{\alpha} \Gamma'}{s[\mathbf{p}]:\mu\mathbf{t}.T \xrightarrow{\alpha} \Gamma'} \quad [\Gamma\text{-}\mu]$$

$$\frac{\Gamma \xrightarrow{\alpha} \Gamma'}{\Gamma,x{:}B \xrightarrow{\alpha} \Gamma',x{:}B} \quad [\Gamma\text{-},B] \qquad \frac{\Gamma \xrightarrow{\alpha} \Gamma'}{\Gamma,c{:}T \xrightarrow{\alpha} \Gamma',c{:}T} \quad [\Gamma\text{-},]$$

Fig. 6. Typing context reduction rules.

write Γ_s iff $\operatorname{dom}(\Gamma_s) = \{s\}$, $\operatorname{dom}(\Gamma_s) \subseteq \operatorname{dom}(\Gamma)$, and $\forall s[\mathbf{p}] \in \operatorname{dom}(\Gamma) : \Gamma(s[\mathbf{p}]) = \Gamma_s(s[\mathbf{p}])$ (i.e. restriction of Γ to session s).

Definition 8 (Typing Context Reduction). *The* typing context transition $\xrightarrow{\alpha}$ *is inductively defined by the rules in Fig. 6. We write* $\Gamma \xrightarrow{\alpha}$ *if there exists* Γ' *such that* $\Gamma \xrightarrow{\alpha} \Gamma'$. *We define two reductions* $\Gamma \rightarrow_s \Gamma'$ *and* $\Gamma \rightarrow \Gamma'$, *as follows:*

- $\Gamma \rightarrow_s \Gamma'$ *holds iff* $\Gamma \xrightarrow{\alpha} \Gamma'$ *with* $\alpha = s[\mathbf{p}][\mathbf{q}]\mathtt{m}$ *for any* $\mathbf{p},\mathbf{q} \in \mathcal{R}$ *(recall that* $\mathcal{R}$ *is the set of all roles): this means that* Γ *can progress via message transmission on session* s*, involving any roles* $\mathbf{p}$ *and* $\mathbf{q}$*. We write* $\Gamma \rightarrow_s$ *iff* $\Gamma \rightarrow_s \Gamma'$ *for some* Γ'*, and* $\Gamma \nrightarrow_s$ *for its negation (i.e. there is no* Γ' *such that* $\Gamma \rightarrow_s \Gamma'$*), and we denote* $\rightarrow_s^*$ *as the reflexive and transitive closure of* $\rightarrow_s$*;*
- $\Gamma \rightarrow \Gamma'$ *holds iff* $\Gamma \rightarrow_s \Gamma'$ *for some* s*: this means that* Γ *can progress via message transmission on any session. We write* $\Gamma \rightarrow$ *iff* $\Gamma \rightarrow \Gamma'$ *for some* Γ'*, and* $\Gamma \nrightarrow$ *for its negation, and we denote* $\rightarrow^*$ *as the reflexive and transitive closure of* $\rightarrow$*.*

Figure 6 contains standard rules for typing context reductions [18]. Rules $[\Gamma\text{-}\oplus]$ and $[\Gamma\text{-}\&]$ specify that a typing context entry can execute an output and input transition, respectively. Rule $[\Gamma\text{-}\oplus\&]$ ensures synchronised matching input/output transitions, with payload compatibility through subtyping; consequently, the context progresses via a message transmission label $s[\mathbf{p}][\mathbf{q}]\mathtt{m}$. Rule $[\Gamma\text{-}\mu]$ pertains to recursion, while $[\Gamma\text{-},B]$ and $[\Gamma\text{-},]$ address reductions in a larger context.

3.4 Relating Semantics Between Global Types and Typing Contexts

Following the introduction of LTS semantics for global types (Definition 6) and typing contexts (definition 8), we establish a relationship between these two semantics using the projection operator $\upharpoonright$ (Definition 3) and the subtyping relation $\leqslant$ (Definition 4).

Definition 9 (Association of Global Types and Typing Contexts). *A typing context Γ is associated with a global type G for a multiparty session s, written $G \sqsubseteq_s \Gamma$, iff Γ can be split into two disjoint (possibly empty) sub-contexts $\Gamma = \Gamma_G, \Gamma_{\mathbf{end}}$ where:*

1. *Γ_G contains projections of G: $\mathrm{dom}(\Gamma_G) = \{s[\mathsf{p}] \mid \mathsf{p} \in \mathrm{roles}(G)\}$, and $\forall \mathsf{p} \in \mathrm{roles}(G) : G \upharpoonright \mathsf{p} \leqslant \Gamma(s[\mathsf{p}])$;*
2. *$\Gamma_{\mathbf{end}}$ contains only end endpoints: $\forall s[\mathsf{p}] \in \mathrm{dom}(\Gamma_{\mathbf{end}}) : \Gamma(s[\mathsf{p}]) = \mathbf{end}$.*

The association $\cdot \sqsubseteq \cdot$ is a binary relation over global types G and typing contexts Γ, parameterised by multiparty sessions s. There are two requirements for the association: (1) the typing context Γ must include an entry for each role in the multiparty session s; and (2) for each role p, the projection of the global type onto this role ($G \upharpoonright \mathsf{p}$) must be a subtype (Definition 4) of its corresponding entry in the typing context ($\Gamma(s[\mathsf{p}])$).

Example 5 (Association). Recall the global type G_{auth} and its projected local types $T_{\mathsf{s}}, T_{\mathsf{c}}, T_{\mathsf{a}}$ in Example 3. Consider the typing context $\Gamma_{\mathrm{auth}} = \Gamma_{\mathrm{auth}_{\mathsf{s}}}, \Gamma_{\mathrm{auth}_{\mathsf{c}}}, \Gamma_{\mathrm{auth}_{\mathsf{a}}}$, where:

$$\Gamma_{\mathrm{auth}_{\mathsf{s}}} = s[\mathsf{s}]{:}\mathsf{c} \oplus \mathtt{cancel} \quad \Gamma_{\mathrm{auth}_{\mathsf{c}}} = s[\mathsf{c}]{:}\mathsf{s} \& \left\{ \begin{array}{l} \mathtt{login.a} \oplus \mathtt{passwd(str)} \\ \mathtt{cancel.a} \oplus \mathtt{quit} \\ \mathtt{fail.a} \oplus \mathtt{fatal} \end{array} \right\}$$

$$\Gamma_{\mathrm{auth}_{\mathsf{a}}} = s[\mathsf{a}]{:}\mathsf{c} \& \{\mathtt{passwd(str).s} \oplus \mathtt{auth(bool)}, \mathtt{quit}, \mathtt{fatal}\}$$

Intuitively, Γ_{auth} is associated with G_{auth}, as s sends only $\mathtt{cancel}$, while c and a expect to receive additional messages $\mathtt{fail}$ and $\mathtt{fatal}$, respectively. Indeed, the entries in Γ_{auth} adhere to the communication behaviour patterns of each role of G_{auth}, though with fewer output messages and more input ones. We can formally verify the association of Γ_{auth} with G_{auth} for session s by:

- $\mathrm{roles}(G_{\mathrm{auth}}) = \{\mathsf{s}, \mathsf{c}, \mathsf{a}\}$, and $\mathrm{dom}(\Gamma_{\mathrm{auth}}) = \{s[\mathsf{s}], s[\mathsf{c}], s[\mathsf{a}]\}$
- $G_{\mathrm{auth}} \upharpoonright \mathsf{s} = T_{\mathsf{s}} = \mathsf{c} \oplus \left\{ \begin{array}{l} \mathtt{login.a} \& \mathtt{auth(bool)} \\ \mathtt{cancel} \end{array} \right\} \leqslant \Gamma_{\mathrm{auth}}(s[\mathsf{s}])$
- $G_{\mathrm{auth}} \upharpoonright \mathsf{c} = T_{\mathsf{c}} = \mathsf{s} \& \left\{ \begin{array}{l} \mathtt{login.a} \oplus \mathtt{passwd(str)} \\ \mathtt{cancel.a} \oplus \mathtt{quit} \end{array} \right\} \leqslant \Gamma_{\mathrm{auth}}(s[\mathsf{c}])$
- $G_{\mathrm{auth}} \upharpoonright \mathsf{a} = T_{\mathsf{a}} = \mathsf{c} \& \left\{ \begin{array}{l} \mathtt{passwd(str).s} \oplus \mathtt{auth(bool)} \\ \mathtt{quit} \end{array} \right\} \leqslant \Gamma_{\mathrm{auth}}(s[\mathsf{a}])$

We demonstrate the *operational correspondence* between a global type and any *associated* typing context through two main theorems: Theorem 1 shows that the reducibility of a global type aligns with that of its associated typing context; while Theorem 2 illustrates that each possible reduction of a typing context is simulated by an action in the reductions of the associated global type.

Theorem 1 (Soundness of Association). *Given associated global type G and typing context Γ for session s: $G \sqsubseteq_s \Gamma$. If $G \xrightarrow{\alpha} G'$ where $\alpha = s[\mathsf{p}][\mathsf{q}]\mathsf{m}$, then there exist α', Γ', and G'', such that $\alpha' = s[\mathsf{p}][\mathsf{q}]\mathsf{m}'$, $G \xrightarrow{\alpha'} G''$, $G'' \sqsubseteq_s \Gamma'$, and $\Gamma \xrightarrow{\alpha'} \Gamma'$.*

Theorem 2 (Completeness of Association). *Given associated global type G and typing context Γ for session s: $G \sqsubseteq_s \Gamma$. If $\Gamma \xrightarrow{\alpha} \Gamma'$ where $\alpha = s[p][q]m$, then there exists G' such that $G' \sqsubseteq_s \Gamma'$ and $G \xrightarrow{\alpha} G'$.*

Based on Theorem 1 and Theorem 2, we derive a corollary: a global type G is in operational correspondence with the typing context $\Gamma = \{s[p] : G \restriction p\}_{p \in \mathrm{roles}(G)}$, containing the projections of all roles in G.

Example 6 (Soundness and Completeness of Association). Consider the associated global type G_{auth} and typing context Γ_{auth} in Example 5.

We have $G_{\mathrm{auth}} \xrightarrow{s[s][c]\mathtt{login}}$, and by the soundness of association (Theorem 1), there exist $\alpha = s[s][c]\mathtt{cancel}$, G'_{auth}, and Γ'_{auth} such that

$$G_{\mathrm{auth}} \xrightarrow{s[s][c]\mathtt{cancel}} G'_{\mathrm{auth}} = \mathtt{c} \rightarrow \mathtt{a} : \mathtt{quit}, \Gamma_{\mathrm{auth}} \xrightarrow{s[s][c]\mathtt{cancel}} \Gamma'_{\mathrm{auth}} = \Gamma'_{\mathrm{auth}_s}, \Gamma'_{\mathrm{auth}_c}, \Gamma'_{\mathrm{auth}_a}$$

where:

$$\Gamma'_{\mathrm{auth}_s} = s[s] : \mathbf{end} \qquad \Gamma'_{\mathrm{auth}_c} = s[c] : \mathtt{a} \oplus \mathtt{quit}$$
$$\Gamma'_{\mathrm{auth}_a} = s[a] : \mathtt{c} \& \{\mathtt{passwd}(\mathtt{str}).\mathtt{s} \oplus \mathtt{auth}(\mathtt{bool}), \mathtt{quit}, \mathtt{fatal}\}$$

By Definition 9, it is easy to check $G'_{\mathrm{auth}} \sqsubseteq_s \Gamma'_{\mathrm{auth}}$. Further, we have the reduction for Γ'_{auth}:

$$\Gamma'_{\mathrm{auth}} \xrightarrow{s[c][a]\mathtt{quit}} \Gamma''_{\mathrm{auth}} = s[s] : \mathbf{end}, s[c] : \mathbf{end}, s[a] : \mathbf{end}$$

which, by the completeness of association (Theorem 2), relates to the reduction: $G'_{\mathrm{auth}} \xrightarrow{s[c][a]\mathtt{quit}} \mathbf{end}$, with $\mathbf{end} \sqsubseteq_s \Gamma''_{\mathrm{auth}}$.

Remark 1 ('Weakness' and 'Adequacy' of Soundness Theorem). Inquisitive readers might question why we opted to formulate a '*weak*' soundness theorem rather than one that mirrors the completeness theorem, as seen in existing literature [5]. This choice arises from our utilisation of the subtyping (Definition 4, notably [Sub-⊕]). A local type in the typing context might offer fewer branches for selection compared to the projected local type, leading to transmission actions in the global type that remain uninhabited.

For example, consider the global type G_{auth} and its associated typing context Γ_{auth}, as shown in Example 5. While the global type G_{auth} might transition through $s[s][c]\mathtt{login}$, the associated typing context Γ_{auth} cannot.

Nonetheless, our soundness theorem *adequately* ensures the desired properties guaranteed via association, including safety, deadlock-freedom, and liveness, as demonstrated in Sect. 3.5.

3.5 Typing Context Properties Guaranteed via Association

The design of multiparty session type theory provides a substantial advantage in guaranteeing desirable properties through its methodology. Consequently, processes adhering to the local types obtained from projections are inherently *correct by construction*. This subsection highlights three key properties: *communication safety, deadlock-freedom,* and *liveness.* We demonstrate that these properties are ensured by typing contexts associated with global types.

Communication Safety. We begin by introducing communication safety for typing contexts, a behavioural property that ensures each role can exchange compatible messages, thereby preventing label mismatches.

Definition 10 (Typing Context Safety). *Given a session s, we say that φ is an s-safety property of typing contexts iff, whenever $\varphi(\Gamma)$, we have:*

$$
\begin{array}{ll}
[\text{S-}\oplus\&] & \Gamma \xrightarrow{s[\mathsf{p}]:\mathsf{q}\oplus\mathsf{m}(S)} \text{ and } \Gamma \xrightarrow{s[\mathsf{q}]:\mathsf{p}\&\mathsf{m}'(S')} \text{ implies } \Gamma \xrightarrow{s[\mathsf{p}][\mathsf{q}]\mathsf{m}}; \\
[\text{S-}\mu] & \Gamma = \Gamma', s[\mathsf{p}]:\mu\mathsf{t}.T \text{ implies } \varphi(\Gamma', s[\mathsf{p}]:T\{\mu\mathsf{t}.T/\mathsf{t}\}); \\
[\text{S-}\to_s] & \Gamma \to_s \Gamma' \text{ implies } \varphi(\Gamma').
\end{array}
$$

We say Γ *is s-safe*, written $\mathsf{safe}(s, \Gamma)$, if $\varphi(\Gamma)$ holds for some s-safety property φ. We say Γ *is safe*, written $\mathsf{safe}(\Gamma)$, if $\varphi(\Gamma)$ holds for some property φ which is s-safe for all sessions s occurring in $\mathrm{dom}(\Gamma)$.

Our safety property is derived from a fundamental feature of generalised MPST systems [18, Def. 4.1]. As per Definition 10, safety is a *coinductive* property [17]. This means that for a given a session s, s-safe is the largest s-safety property, including the union of all s-safety properties. To demonstrate the s-safety of a typing context Γ, we must identify a property φ such that $\Gamma \in \varphi$, and subsequently prove that φ qualifies as an s-safety property. More specifically, if such a φ exists, it can be formulated as a set containing Γ and all its reductums (via transition $\to_s^*$). We then verify whether all elements of φ satisfy each clause of Definition 10.

According to clause [S-$\oplus$&], whenever two roles p and q attempt communication, the receiving role q is required to accommodate all output messages of the sending role p with compatible payload types, ensuring the feasibility of the communication. Clause [S-μ] unfolds any recursive entry, while clause [S-$\to_s$] specifies that any typing context Γ', to which Γ transitions on session s, must also belong to φ, indicating that Γ' is s-safe as well. Note that any entry $s[\mathsf{p}]:\mathbf{end}$ in Γ vacuously satisfies all clauses.

Example 7 (Typing Context Safety). Consider the typing context Γ_{auth} from Example 5. We know that Γ_{auth} is s-safe by verifying its reductions. For example, we have the reductions $\Gamma_{\mathrm{auth}} \xrightarrow{s[\mathsf{s}][\mathsf{c}]\mathsf{cancel}} \cdot \xrightarrow{s[\mathsf{c}][\mathsf{a}]\mathsf{quit}} \Gamma''_{\mathrm{auth}} = s[\mathsf{s}]:\mathbf{end}, s[\mathsf{c}]:\mathbf{end}, s[\mathsf{a}]:\mathbf{end}$, where each reductum complies with all clauses of Definition 10.

The typing context $\Gamma_A = s[\mathsf{p}]:\mathsf{q}\oplus\mathsf{m}_1.\mathsf{r}\oplus\mathsf{m}_3, s[\mathsf{q}]:\mathsf{p}\&\mathsf{m}_2, s[\mathsf{r}]:\mathsf{p}\&\mathsf{m}_4$ is *not* s-safe. Any property φ containing such a context is *not* a s-safety property, as it violates [S-$\oplus$&] of Definition 10: $\Gamma_A \xrightarrow{s[\mathsf{p}]:\mathsf{q}\oplus\mathsf{m}_1}$ and $\Gamma_A \xrightarrow{s[\mathsf{q}]:\mathsf{p}\&\mathsf{m}_2}$, but $\Gamma_A \xrightarrow{s[\mathsf{p}][\mathsf{q}]\mathsf{m}_1}$ does not hold.

Finally, let's consider the typing context $\Gamma_B = s[\mathsf{p}]:\mathsf{q}\oplus\mathsf{m}(\mathsf{real}), s[\mathsf{q}]:\mathsf{p}\&\mathsf{m}(\mathsf{int})$. Γ_B is *not* s-safe, as any property φ containing Γ_B contradicts [S-$\oplus$&]: $\Gamma_B \xrightarrow{s[\mathsf{p}]:\mathsf{q}\oplus\mathsf{m}(\mathsf{real})}$ and $\Gamma_B \xrightarrow{s[\mathsf{q}]:\mathsf{p}\&\mathsf{m}(\mathsf{int})}$, but $\Gamma_B \xrightarrow{s[\mathsf{p}][\mathsf{q}]\mathsf{m}}$ is not uphold due to $\mathsf{real} \nleq \mathsf{int}$.

Deadlock-Freedom. The property of deadlock-freedom determines whether a typing context can keep reducing without getting stuck, unless it reaches a successful terminal state.

Definition 11 (Deadlock-Free Typing Contexts). *Given a session s, a typing context Γ is s-deadlock-free, written $\mathrm{df}(s, \Gamma)$, iff $\Gamma \rightarrow_s^* \Gamma' \nrightarrow_s$ implies $\forall s[\mathrm{p}] \in \mathrm{dom}(\Gamma') : \Gamma'(s[\mathrm{p}]) = \mathbf{end}$.*

It is noteworthy that a typing context that reduces infinitely adheres to deadlock-freedom, as it consistently undergoes further reductions. Alternatively, when a terminal typing context is reached, all entries in the typing context must be terminated successfully (**end**). Consequently, a deadlock-free typing context either continues perpetual reduction or terminates.

Example 8 (Typing Context Deadlock-Freedom). The typing context Γ_{auth} in Example 5 is s-deadlock-free, as any terminal typing context Γ'_{auth}, reached from Γ_{auth} via $\Gamma_{\mathrm{auth}} \rightarrow_s^* \Gamma'_{\mathrm{auth}} \nrightarrow_s$, only contains **end** entries, which can be easily verified.

The typing context $\Gamma_C = s[\mathrm{p}]{:}\mathrm{q} \oplus \mathrm{m}_1.\mathrm{r}\&\mathrm{m}_3, s[\mathrm{q}]{:}\mathrm{r} \oplus \mathrm{m}_2.\mathrm{p}\&\mathrm{m}_1, s[\mathrm{r}]{:}\mathrm{p} \oplus \mathrm{m}_3.\mathrm{q}\&\mathrm{m}_2$ is s-safe but *not* s-deadlock-free, as its inputs and outputs, despite being dual, are arranged in the incorrect order. Specifically, there are no possible reductions for Γ_C, i.e. $\Gamma_C \nrightarrow_s$, while none of the entries in Γ_C is a termination.

Finally, the context $\Gamma_D = s[\mathrm{p}]{:}\mathrm{q} \oplus \{\mathrm{m}_1.\mathrm{r} \oplus \mathrm{m}_2, \mathrm{m}_3\}, s[\mathrm{q}]{:}\mathrm{p}\&\{\mathrm{m}_1, \mathrm{m}_2\}, s[\mathrm{r}]{:}\mathrm{p}\&\mathrm{m}_2$ is s-deadlock-free but *not* s-safe, as it consistently reaches a successful termination by transmitting m_1 between p and q; while q is unable to receive the message m_3 when p intends to send it due to the message mismatch.

Liveness. The liveness property ensures that every pending output/external choice eventually gets triggered through a message transmission. It relies on fairness, specifically based on *strong fairness of components* [7, Fact 2], to guarantee that every enabled message transmission is successfully executed. The definitions of fair and live paths for typing contexts are provided in Definition 12, and these paths are used to formalise the liveness for typing contexts in Definition 13.

Definition 12 (Fair, Live Paths). *A path is a possibly infinite sequence of typing contexts $(\Gamma_n)_{n \in N}$, where $N = \{0, 1, 2, \ldots\}$ is a set of consecutive natural numbers, and, $\forall n \in N, \Gamma_n \rightarrow \Gamma_{n+1}$. We say that a path $(\Gamma_n)_{n \in N}$ is fair for session s iff, $\forall n \in N : \Gamma_n \xrightarrow{s[\mathrm{p}][\mathrm{q}]\mathrm{m}}$ implies $\exists k, \mathrm{m}'$ such that $N \ni k \geq n$, and $\Gamma_k \xrightarrow{s[\mathrm{p}][\mathrm{q}]\mathrm{m}'} \Gamma_{k+1}$. We say that a path $(\Gamma_n)_{n \in N}$ is live for session s iff, $\forall n \in N$:*

(L1) $\Gamma_n \xrightarrow{s[\mathrm{p}]:\mathrm{q} \oplus \mathrm{m}(S)}$ *implies $\exists k, \mathrm{m}'$ such that $N \ni k \geq n$ and $\Gamma_k \xrightarrow{s[\mathrm{p}][\mathrm{q}]\mathrm{m}'} \Gamma_{k+1}$;*

(L2) $\Gamma_n \xrightarrow{s[\mathrm{q}]:\mathrm{p}\&\mathrm{m}(S)}$ *implies $\exists k, \mathrm{m}'$ such that $N \ni k \geq n$ and $\Gamma_k \xrightarrow{s[\mathrm{p}][\mathrm{q}]\mathrm{m}'} \Gamma_{k+1}$.*

A path is a (possibly infinite) sequence of reductions of a typing context. A path is fair for session s if, along the path, every enabled message transmission is eventually performed on s. Likewise, a path is live for session s if, along the path, every pending internal/external choice is eventually triggered on s.

Definition 13 (Live Typing Contexts). *Given a session s, a typing context Γ is s-live, written* live(s, Γ), *iff* $\Gamma \rightarrow_s^* \Gamma'$ *implies all paths starting with Γ' that are fair for session s are also live for s.*

A typing context Γ is s-live if any reductum of Γ (via transition $\rightarrow_s^*$) consistently generates a live path for s under fairness.

Example 9 (Fairness and Typing Context Liveness, originated from [6,18]). Consider the typing context:

$$\Gamma_E = s[\mathsf{p}]:\mathsf{p}'\oplus\mathsf{m}_1, s[\mathsf{p}']:\mathsf{p}\&\mathsf{m}_1, s[\mathsf{q}]:\mu t_{\mathsf{q}}.\mathsf{q}'\oplus\mathsf{m}_2.t_{\mathsf{q}}, s[\mathsf{q}']:\mu t_{\mathsf{q}'}.\mathsf{q}\&\mathsf{m}_2.t_{\mathsf{q}'}$$

which is s-safe and s-deadlock-free. There is an infinite path starting with Γ_E, where q and q' keep communicating in session s, while p and p' never trigger a reduction to interact, i.e. $\Gamma_E \xrightarrow{s[\mathsf{q}][\mathsf{q}']\mathsf{m}_2} \Gamma_E \xrightarrow{s[\mathsf{q}][\mathsf{q}']\mathsf{m}_2} \cdots$. Such a path is *not* fair for s because although message transmission between p and p' is enabled, it will never occur. Alternatively, along any fair path of Γ_E, all inputs and outputs can eventually be fired on s, indicating that Γ_E is s-live.

Now consider another typing context:

$$\Gamma_E' = s[\mathsf{p}]:\mu t_{\mathsf{p}}.\mathsf{q}\&\{\mathsf{m}_1.t_{\mathsf{p}}, \mathsf{m}_2.t_{\mathsf{p}}\}, s[\mathsf{q}]:\mu t_{\mathsf{q}}.\mathsf{p}\oplus\{\mathsf{m}_1.t_{\mathsf{q}}, \mathsf{m}_2.\mathsf{r}\oplus\mathsf{m}_2.t_{\mathsf{q}}\}, s[\mathsf{r}]:\mu t_{\mathsf{r}}.\mathsf{q}\&\mathsf{m}_2.t_{\mathsf{r}}$$

which is s-safe and s-deadlock-free. Γ_E' has fair and live paths, where in s, m_2 is transmitted from q to p, and then to r. However, there is also a fair path, where in s, m_1 is consistently transmitted from q to p, i.e. $\Gamma_E' \xrightarrow{s[\mathsf{q}][\mathsf{p}]\mathsf{m}_1} \Gamma_E' \xrightarrow{s[\mathsf{q}][\mathsf{p}]\mathsf{m}_1} \cdots$. In this case, r indefinitely awaits input that will never arrive. Therefore, while this path is fair for s, it is not live, and hence, Γ_E' is not s-live.

Finally, the typing context $\Gamma_E'' = s[\mathsf{p}]:\mathsf{q}\oplus\{\mathsf{m}_1, \mathsf{m}_2\}, s[\mathsf{q}]:\mathsf{p}\&\{\mathsf{m}_1, \mathsf{m}_3\}$ is s-live: there is only one path starting from Γ_E'', i.e. $\Gamma_E'' \xrightarrow{s[\mathsf{p}][\mathsf{q}]\mathsf{m}_1} s[\mathsf{p}]:\mathbf{end}, s[\mathsf{q}]:\mathbf{end}$, which is fair and live for s; while it is not s-safe.

Properties by Association. We conclude by demonstrating, as stated in Thm. 3, that a typing context associated with a global type is constructed to possess the properties of safety, deadlock-freedom, and liveness.

Theorem 3 (Safety, Deadlock-Freedom, and Liveness by Association). *Let G be a global type, Γ a typing context, and s a session. If Γ is associated with G for s: $G \sqsubseteq_s \Gamma$, then Γ is s-safe, s-deadlock-free, and s-live.*

Example 10 (Typing Context Properties Guaranteed by Association). The typing context Γ_{auth} described in Example 5 is associated with G_{auth} for session s, i.e. $G_{\mathrm{auth}} \sqsubseteq_s \Gamma_{\mathrm{auth}}$. Consequently, Γ_{auth} possesses the properties of being s-safe, s-deadlock-free (as also demonstrated in Example 7 and Example 8, respectively), and s-live.

3.6 Relationships Between Typing Context Properties

We now explore both the relationships between typing context properties, and how they relate to association, as formalised in Theorem 4 below.

Theorem 4 *For any typing context Γ and session s, the following statements are valid:*

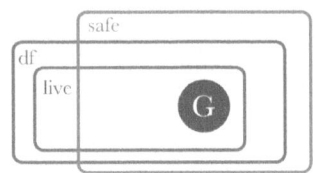

(1) $\mathrm{df}(s,\Gamma)$ $\;\not\Longleftarrow\not\Longrightarrow\;$ $\mathrm{safe}(s,\Gamma)$;

(2) $\mathrm{live}(s,\Gamma)$ $\;\not\Longleftarrow\not\Longrightarrow\;$ $\mathrm{safe}(s,\Gamma)$;

(3) $\mathrm{live}(s,\Gamma)$ $\;\not\Longleftarrow\Longrightarrow\;$ $\mathrm{df}(s,\Gamma)$;

(4) $\exists G : G \sqsubseteq_s \Gamma$ $\;\not\Longleftarrow\Longrightarrow\;$ $\mathrm{safe}(s,\Gamma)$;

(5) $\exists G : G \sqsubseteq_s \Gamma$ $\;\not\Longleftarrow\Longrightarrow\;$ $\mathrm{df}(s,\Gamma)$;

(6) $\exists G : G \sqsubseteq_s \Gamma$ $\;\not\Longleftarrow\Longrightarrow\;$ $\mathrm{live}(s,\Gamma)$.

In the diagram, the "safe" set (resp. "df" set, "live" set) contains all typing contexts that are s-safe (resp. s-deadlock-free, s-live). The red set $\mathbb{G}$ encompasses all typing contexts associated with some global type for s. The negated implications stated in Theorem 4 are showcased in Example 8, Example 9, and Example 11 (below), respectively.

Example 11 (Non-Associated Typing Context, originated from [2,18]). The typing context $\Gamma_F = s[\mathbf{p}]{:}T, s[\mathbf{q}]{:}\oplus\mathbf{m}(T).\mathbf{end}$ with $T = \mu\mathbf{t}.\mathbf{q}\oplus\mathbf{m}(\mathbf{t}).\mathbf{end}$ (from [2, Ex. 1.2]) is s-live (and hence s-deadlock-free and s-safe), but *not* associated with any global type for session s: this is because a recursion variable $\mathbf{t}$ occurs as payload in T, which is not allowed by either Definition 3 or Definition 4.

4   Multiparty Session Typing System

This section presents a type system for the multiparty session π-calculus, as explained in Sect. 2. We introduce the typing rules in Sect. 4.1, and show the main properties of typed processes: subject reduction and session fidelity, in Sect. 4.2. Finally, we demonstrate how process properties such as deadlock-freedom and liveness can be guaranteed by construction in Sect. 4.3.

4.1   Typing Rules

Two kinds of typing contexts, as introduced in Definition 7, are used in our type system: Θ, responsible for assigning an n-tuple of types to each process variable X (one type per argument), and Γ, which maps variables to payload types (basic types or session types), as well as channels with roles (endpoints) to session types. These typing contexts are jointly applied in judgments formulated as:

$$\Theta \cdot \Gamma \vdash P \quad (\text{with } \Theta \text{ omitted when empty})$$

which interprets as: "considering the process types in Θ, P uses its variables and channels *linearly* based on Γ." This *typing judgement* is defined by the rules in Fig. 7, where, for convenience, we include type annotations for channels bound by process definitions and restrictions.

The main innovation in Fig. 7 lies in rule [T-G-ν], which uses a typing context associated with a global type in some session s (Definition 9) to enforce session

$$\frac{\Theta(X) = S_1, \ldots, S_n}{\Theta \vdash X : S_1, \ldots, S_n} \text{ [T- }X\text{]} \qquad \frac{\forall i \in 1 \ldots n \quad S_i \text{ is basic or } c_i : S_i \vdash c_i : \mathbf{end}}{\mathbf{end}(c_1 : S_1, \ldots, c_n : S_n)} \text{ [T- end]}$$

$$\frac{\mathbf{end}(\Gamma)}{\Theta \cdot \Gamma \vdash \mathbf{0}} \text{ [T- 0]} \qquad \frac{v \in \mathcal{B}}{\emptyset \vdash v : B} \text{ [T- }B\text{]} \qquad \frac{\Theta \cdot \Gamma_1 \vdash P_1 \quad \Theta \cdot \Gamma_2 \vdash P_2}{\Theta \cdot \Gamma_1, \Gamma_2 \vdash P_1 \mid P_2} \text{ [T- }|\text{]}$$

$$\frac{\Theta \vdash X : S_1, \ldots, S_n \quad \mathbf{end}(\Gamma_0) \quad \forall i \in 1 \ldots n \quad \Gamma_i \vdash d_i : S_i \quad S_i \nleq \mathbf{end}}{\Theta \cdot \Gamma_0, \Gamma_1, \ldots, \Gamma_n \vdash X \langle d_1, \ldots, d_n \rangle} \text{ [T-Call]}$$

$$\frac{\Theta, X : S_1, \ldots, S_n \cdot x_1 : S_1, \ldots, x_n : S_n \vdash P \quad \Theta, X : S_1, \ldots, S_n \cdot \Gamma \vdash Q}{\Theta \cdot \Gamma \vdash \mathbf{def}\ X(x_1 : S_1, \ldots, x_n : S_n) = P\ \mathbf{in}\ Q} \text{ [T- def]}$$

$$\frac{\Gamma_1 \vdash c : \mathsf{q} \& \{\mathsf{m_i}(S_i).T_i\}_{i \in I} \quad \forall i \in I \quad \Theta \cdot \Gamma, y_i : S_i, c : T_i \vdash P_i}{\Theta \cdot \Gamma, \Gamma_1 \vdash c[\mathsf{q}] \& \{\mathsf{m_i}(y_i).P_i\}_{i \in I}} \text{ [T- \&]}$$

$$\frac{\Gamma_1 \vdash c : \mathsf{q} \oplus \{\mathsf{m}(S).T\} \quad \Gamma_2 \vdash d : S \quad S \nleq \mathbf{end} \quad \Theta \cdot \Gamma, c : T \vdash P}{\Theta \cdot \Gamma, \Gamma_1, \Gamma_2 \vdash c[\mathsf{q}] \oplus \mathsf{m} \langle d \rangle.P} \text{ [T- }\oplus\text{]}$$

$$\frac{S \leqslant S'}{c : S \vdash c : S'} \text{ [T-Sub]} \qquad \frac{G \sqsubseteq_s \Gamma' \quad s \notin \Gamma \quad \Theta \cdot \Gamma, \Gamma' \vdash P}{\Theta \cdot \Gamma \vdash (\nu s : \Gamma')\ P} \text{ [T- }G\text{-}\nu\text{]}$$

Fig. 7. Typing rules for processes.

restrictions. The rest of rules are mostly standard [18]. Rule [T-X] retrieves process variables, while rule [T-B] types a value v if it belongs to a set of basic types $\mathcal{B}$. Rule [T-Sub] applies subtyping within a singleton typing context $c : S$ when assigning type S' to a variable or channel c. Additionally, rule [T-end] introduces a predicate $\mathbf{end}(\cdot)$ for typing contexts, denoting the termination of all endpoints. This predicate is used in [T-0] to type an inactive process $\mathbf{0}$. Rules [T-$\oplus$] and [T-&] assign selection and branching types to channels used by selection and branching processes, respectively. Rules [T-**def**] and [T-Call] deal with recursive processes declarations and calls, respectively. Notably, the clauses "$S \nleq \mathbf{end}$" used in rules [T-$\oplus$] and [T-Call] prevent the sending or passing of channels typed as $\mathbf{end}$, while permitting the sending/passing of channels and data of any other type. Finally, rule [T-$|$] *linearly* divides the typing context into two parts, each used to type one sub-process.

Example 12 (Typed Process). Consider the processes P and Q from Example 1. The type context $\Gamma_H = s[\mathsf{p}] : T_{H_\mathsf{p}}, s[\mathsf{q}] : T_{H_\mathsf{q}}, s[\mathsf{r}] : T_{H_\mathsf{r}}$, with $T_{H_\mathsf{p}} = \mathsf{q} \oplus \mathsf{m}'(T_{H_\mathsf{r}})$. $\mathsf{r} \& \mathsf{m}(\mathrm{int}).\mathbf{end}, T_{H_\mathsf{q}} = \mathsf{p} \& \mathsf{m}'(T_{H_\mathsf{r}}).\mathbf{end}, T_{H_\mathsf{r}} = \mathsf{p} \oplus \mathsf{m}(\mathrm{int}).\mathbf{end}$, can type the process $P|Q$ by the following derivation:

$$\frac{\Omega \quad \dfrac{s[\mathsf{p}] : \mathsf{r} \& \mathsf{m}(\mathrm{int}).\mathbf{end} \vdash s[\mathsf{p}] : \mathsf{r} \& \mathsf{m}(\mathrm{int}).\mathbf{end} \quad \dfrac{\dfrac{x : \mathrm{int}, s[\mathsf{p}] : \mathbf{end}}{\mathbf{end}(x : \mathrm{int}, s[\mathsf{p}] : \mathbf{end})} \text{ [T-end]}}{x : \mathrm{int}, s[\mathsf{p}] : \mathbf{end} \vdash \mathbf{0}} \text{ [T-0]}}{\dfrac{s[\mathsf{p}] : \mathsf{r} \& \mathsf{m}(\mathrm{int}).\mathbf{end} \vdash s[\mathsf{p}][\mathsf{r}] \& \mathsf{m}(x).\mathbf{0}}{s[\mathsf{p}] : T_{H_\mathsf{p}}, s[\mathsf{r}] : T_{H_\mathsf{r}} \vdash P} \text{ [T-}\oplus\text{]}} \text{ [T-\&]} \qquad \dfrac{\vdots}{s[\mathsf{q}] : T_{H_\mathsf{q}} \vdash Q}}{\Gamma_H \vdash P \mid Q} \text{ [T-}|\text{]}$$

where Ω includes certain trivial conditions used as prerequisites for [T-⊕]:
$s[\mathbf{p}]:T_{H_{\mathbf{p}}} \vdash s[\mathbf{p}]:T_{H_{\mathbf{p}}}$, $s[\mathbf{r}]:T_{H_{\mathbf{r}}} \vdash s[\mathbf{r}]:T_{H_{\mathbf{r}}}$, and $T_{H_{\mathbf{r}}} \nleq$ **end**. In the omitted part
of the derivation, similar to that for $s[\mathbf{p}]:T_{H_{\mathbf{p}}}, s[\mathbf{r}]:T_{H_{\mathbf{r}}} \vdash P$, the process Q is
typed by $s[\mathbf{q}]:T_{H_{\mathbf{q}}}$, using rules [T-&], [T-⊕], [T-0], and [T-end]. Moreover, as Γ_H
is associated with a global type $G_H = \mathbf{p}{\rightarrow}\mathbf{q}:m'(\mathbf{p}{\oplus}m(\text{int})).\mathbf{r}{\rightarrow}\mathbf{p}:m(\text{int}).\mathbf{end}$ for
session s, i.e. $G_H \sqsubseteq_s \Gamma_H$, following [T-G-$\nu$], the process $P|Q$ is closed under Γ_H,
i.e. $\vdash (\nu s{:}\Gamma_H) P \mid Q$.

Take the typing contexts $\Gamma_{\text{auth}_s}, \Gamma_{\text{auth}_c}, \Gamma_{\text{auth}_a}$ from Example 5, along with
the processes P_s, P_c, P_a from Example 2. These contexts enable the typing of
the respective processes. Consequently, the context Γ_{auth} (from Example 5)
can be used to type the process $P_s \mid P_c \mid P_a$. Similar to the above example,
given Γ_{auth} is associated with the global type G_{auth} (Example 5), according to
[T-G-ν], $P_s \mid P_c \mid P_a$ is closed under Γ_{auth}. It is noteworthy that the typing context
$s[\mathbf{s}]:T_s$, using the local type T_s from Example 3, can type the process P_s, due
to $T_s \leqslant \Gamma_{\text{auth}_s}(s[\mathbf{s}])$ (as demonstrated in Example 5), and $\Gamma_{\text{auth}_s} \vdash P_s$. Similarly,
$s[\mathbf{c}]:T_c$ and $s[\mathbf{a}]:T_a$ type P_c and P_a, respectively.

4.2 Subject Reduction and Session Fidelity

We elucidate the key properties of well-typed processes, including *subject reduction* (Theorem 5), *session fidelity* (Theorem 6).

Subject reduction ensures the preservation of types during process reduction.
It states that if a well-typed process P reduces to P', then the reduction is
simulated by the typing context Γ used to type P. Note that in our subject
reduction theorem, P is *not* required to contain only one single session. Instead,
we include all restricted sessions in P, ensuring that reductions on these various
sessions maintain their respective restrictions. This is enforced by rule [T-G-ν]
in Fig. 7. Additionally, the theorem dictates that, in alignment with the MPST
top-down methodology, a process initially constructed from global types retains
this construction manner even after reductions.

Theorem 5 (Subject Reduction). *Assume* $\Theta \cdot \Gamma \vdash P$ *where* $\forall s \in \Gamma : \exists G_s :$
$G_s \sqsubseteq_s \Gamma_s$. *If* $P \rightarrow P'$, *then* $\exists \Gamma'$ *such that* $\Gamma \rightarrow^* \Gamma'$, $\Theta \cdot \Gamma' \vdash P'$, *and* $\forall s \in \Gamma' :$
$\exists G'_s : G'_s \sqsubseteq_s \Gamma'_s$.

Corollary 1 (Type Safety). *If* $\emptyset \cdot \emptyset \vdash P$ *and* $P \rightarrow^* P'$, *then* P' *has no error.*

Example 13 (Subject Reduction). Take the typed process $P|Q$ and the typing context Γ_H from Example 12. After a reduction using [R-⊕&], $P|Q$ transitions to $P \mid Q \rightarrow s[\mathbf{p}][\mathbf{r}]\&m(x).\mathbf{0} \mid s[\mathbf{r}][\mathbf{p}]\oplus m\langle 42\rangle.\mathbf{0} = P' \mid Q'$. The typing context Γ_H can reduce to $\Gamma'_H = s[\mathbf{p}]:\mathbf{r}\&m(\text{int}).\mathbf{end}, s[\mathbf{q}]:\mathbf{end}, s[\mathbf{r}]:\mathbf{p}\oplus m(\text{int}).\mathbf{end}$, via [$\Gamma$-⊕&], which can be used to type $P'|Q'$, and is associated with a global type $G'_H = \mathbf{r}{\rightarrow}\mathbf{p}:m(\text{int}).\mathbf{end}$. In fact, by applying Theorem 5, we can infer that all process reductions initiated from $P|Q$ maintain well-typedness. Furthermore, based on Corollary 1, we are ensured that they are error-free. Observe that the typing context Γ_{auth} from Examples. 5 and 12 and the process $P_s|P_c|P_a$ from Examples. 2 and 12 also follow subject reduction, ensuring type safety.

Session fidelity asserts the converse implication concerning subject reduction: if a process P is typed by Γ, and Γ can reduce along session s, then P can replicate at least one of the reductions performed by Γ (although not necessarily all such reductions, as Γ over-approximates the behaviour of P). Consequently, we can deduce P's behaviour from Γ's behaviour, as demonstrated in Theorem 7. However, this outcome does *not* hold universally for all well-typed processes: a well-typed process might loop in a recursion, such as **def** $X(\ldots){=}X$ **in** X, or it could deadlock by intricately interleaving communications across multiple sessions [4]. To address this, similarly to [18] and most session type works, we establish session fidelity specifically for processes featuring guarded recursion and implementing a single multiparty session as a parallel composition of one sub-process per role. The formalisation of session fidelity is provided in Theorem 6 below, building upon the concepts introduced in Definition 14.

Definition 14 (from [18]).   *Assume $\emptyset \cdot \Gamma \vdash P$. We say that P:*

(1) has guarded definitions *iff in each process definition in P of the form*
def $X(x_1{:}S_1, ..., x_n{:}S_n) = Q$ **in** P', *for all $i \in 1..n$, if S_i is a session type, then a call $Y\langle ..., x_i, ...\rangle$ can only occur in Q as a subterm of*
$x_i[\mathsf{q}] \,\&\, \{\mathsf{m}_j(y_j).P_j\}_{j \in J}$ *or* $x_i[\mathsf{q}] \oplus \mathsf{m}\langle d\rangle.P''$ *(i.e. after using x_i for input or output);*

(2) only plays role p *in s, by Γ* *iff:* (i) P has guarded definitions; (ii) $\mathrm{fv}(P) = \emptyset$; (iii) $\Gamma = \Gamma_0, s[\mathsf{p}]{:}T$ with $T \nleqslant \mathbf{end}$ and $\mathrm{end}(\Gamma_0)$; (iv) for all subterms $(\nu s'{:}\Gamma')\,P'$ in P, $\mathrm{end}(\Gamma')$.

We say "P only plays role p in s" iff $\exists \Gamma : \emptyset \cdot \Gamma \vdash P$, and item (2) holds.

In Definition 14, item (1) formalises guarded recursion for processes, while item (2) identifies a process that plays exactly *one* role on *one* session. It is evident that an ensemble of such processes cannot deadlock by waiting for each other on multiple sessions.

Example 14 (Playing Only Role). Consider the processes P, Q from Example 1, and the typing context Γ_H from Example 12. Observe that P does not only play either p or r in s. This arises from the fact that P can only be typed by a context of the form $s[\mathsf{p}]{:}T_\mathsf{p}, s[\mathsf{r}]{:}T_\mathsf{r}$, where neither $\mathrm{end}(s[\mathsf{p}]{:}T_\mathsf{p})$ nor $\mathrm{end}(s[\mathsf{r}]{:}T_\mathsf{r})$ holds, thus violating item (2) of Definition 14. Conversely, Q only plays role q in s, by $s[\mathsf{q}]{:}T_{H_\mathsf{q}}$, as all conditions are fulfilled. Note that the process P_s (resp. P_c, P_a) from Examples. 2 and 12 only plays role s (resp. c, a) in s, which can be easily verified.

We now formalise our session fidelity result (Theorem 6). Although the statement appears similar to Thm. 5.4 in [18], it utilises a typing context associated with a global type for a specific session s to type the process. This approach guarantees not only the fulfilment of the single-session requirements for processes (Definition 14), but also asserts that a process constructed from a global type maintains this structure even after reductions.

Theorem 6 (Session Fidelity). *Assume $\emptyset \cdot \Gamma \vdash P$, with $G \sqsubseteq_s \Gamma$, $P \equiv \Pi_{p \in I} P_p$, and $\Gamma = \bigcup_{p \in I} \Gamma_p$ such that for each P_p: (1) $\emptyset \cdot \Gamma_p \vdash P_p$, and (2) either $P_p \equiv \mathbf{0}$, or P_p only plays p in s, by Γ_p. Then, $\Gamma \to_s$ implies $\exists \Gamma', G', P'$ such that $\Gamma \to_s \Gamma'$, $P \to^* P'$, and $\emptyset \cdot \Gamma' \vdash P'$, with $G' \sqsubseteq_s \Gamma'$, $P' \equiv \Pi_{p \in I} P_p'$, and $\Gamma' = \bigcup_{p \in I} \Gamma_p'$ such that for each P_p': (1) $\emptyset \cdot \Gamma_p' \vdash P_p'$, and (2) either $P_p' \equiv \mathbf{0}$, or P_p' only plays p in s, by Γ_p'.*

Example 15 (Guarded Definitions in Session Fidelity, from [18]*).* According to rule [T-**def**] in Fig. 7, an unguarded definition $X(x{:}S) = X\langle x \rangle$ can be typed with *any* S. Therefore, for example, we have:

$$\emptyset \cdot s[p]{:}q \oplus m, s[q]{:}p \& m \vdash \mathbf{def}\ X(x{:}q \oplus m) = X\langle x \rangle\ \mathbf{in}\ X\langle s[p]\rangle \mid s[q][p] \& m$$

The above unguarded process reduces trivially by invoking X infinitely, without triggering any typing context reduction. This clarifies the necessity of guarded definitions in Theorem 6.

4.3   Properties of Typed Processes

We showcase that processes constructed from global types guarantee desirable run-time properties, including deadlock-freedom and liveness, as formalised in Definition 15. These properties are relatively straightforward: *deadlock-freedom* indicates that if a process is unable to reduce, then it consists only of inactive sub-processes ($\mathbf{0}$); *liveness* ensures that if a process attempts to perform an input or output, it will eventually succeed.

Definition 15 (Runtime Process Properties). *We say P is:*

(1) deadlock-free *iff $P \to^* P' \nrightarrow$ implies $P' \equiv \mathbf{0}$;*
(2) live *iff $P \to^* P' \equiv \mathbb{C}[Q]$ implies:*
   (a) if $Q = c[q] \oplus m\langle w \rangle.Q'$ then $\exists \mathbb{C}' : P' \to^* \mathbb{C}'[Q']$;
   (b) if $Q = c[q] \& \{m_i(x_i).Q_i'\}_{i \in I}$ then $\exists \mathbb{C}', k \in I, w : P' \to^* \mathbb{C}'[Q_k'\{w/x_k\}]$.

We conclude by illustrating how a process, typed with a typing context associated to a global type on a session, ensures both deadlock-freedom and liveness.

Theorem 7 (Process Deadlock-Freedom, Liveness). *Assume $\emptyset \cdot \Gamma \vdash P$, where $G \sqsubseteq_s \Gamma$, $P \equiv \Pi_{p \in I} P_p$, and $\Gamma = \bigcup_{p \in I} \Gamma_p$ such that for each P_p, we have $\emptyset \cdot \Gamma_p \vdash P_p$. Further, assume that each P_p is either $\mathbf{0}$ (up to $\equiv$), or only plays p in s, by Γ_p. Then, P is deadlock-free and live.*

Example 16 (Typed Process Properties). The process $P_s \mid P_c \mid P_a$ from Examples 2 and 12 is deadlock-free and live, verified by applying either Definition 15 or Theorem 7.

5 Conclusion

This paper corrects a misunderstanding in multiparty session type theory, proposing a new relation, *association* $G \sqsubseteq_s \Gamma$ between a global type G and a set of local types Γ. The top-down typing system, with the association between global types and their end-point projections given by mergeability, can guarantee *type safety*, *deadlock-freedom*, and *liveness* of session processes *by construction*.

We conclude with song lyrics written by a singer-songwriter, Mario T., who is Cliff's friend and was Nobuko Yoshida's PhD supervisor at the University of Keio. Tokoro-sensei has contributed to many fields of computer science, particularly, concurrent object-oriented languages, with which Cliff had active discussions and communications: for example, Cliff stated that the object-oriented concept proposed in [19] is an important extension from the abstract data type theme for promoting GyPʃISin [9, § 8.3.5.].

The song for Cliff's Festschrift is composed and selected by Mario T.[1]

Questar

Can't tell what is true. Can't tell what I am.
Can't tell what exists. Can't tell what's illusion.

At every moment I come to myself,
            I wonder what is true and what I am.
Decompose things into parts,
            people can know something in vain.
Consciousness is a tool to find essences,
            putting the whole out of our mind there.

And in the moment when I'm drowsing
            I see suddenly its existence,
I don't see it in pieces,
            but as a whole, the universe, and you.

Mario T.
(The lyrics were inspired by Keith Jarrett's Questar.)

References

1. Barwell, A., Scalas, A., Yoshida, N., Zhou, F.: Generalised multiparty session types with crash-stop failures. In: 33rd International Conference on Concurrency Theory. LIPIcs, vol. 243, pp. 35:1–35:25. Dagstuhl (2022). https://doi.org/10.4230/LIPIcs. CONCUR.2022.35

---

[1] Mario T.: https://www.youtube.com/@mariot.3115. Questar: https://www.youtube.com/watch?v=FM6EKa0C88Y.

2. Bernardi, G., Hennessy, M.: Using higher-order contracts to model session types. LMCS **12(2)** (2016). https://doi.org/10.2168/LMCS-12(2:10)2016
3. Carbone, M., Honda, K., Yoshida, N.: Structured Communication-Centred Programming for Web Services. In: De Nicola, R. (eds.) ESOP 2007, LNCS, vol. 4421, pp. 2–17. Springer, Cham (2007). https://doi.org/10.1007/978-3-540-71316-6_2
4. Coppo, M., Dezani-Ciancaglini, M., Yoshida, N., Padovani, L.: Global progress for dynamically interleaved multiparty sessions. MSCS **760** (2015). https://doi.org/10.1017/S0960129514000188
5. Deniélou, P.M., Yoshida, N.: Multiparty Compatibility in Communicating Automata: Characterisation and Synthesis of Global Session Types. In: 40th International Colloquium on Automata, Languages and Programming. LNCS, vol. 7966, pp. 174–186. Springer (2013). https://doi.org/10.1007/978-3-642-39212-2_18
6. Ghilezan, S., Pantović, J., Prokić, I., Scalas, A., Yoshida, N.: Precise subtyping for asynchronous multiparty sessions. ACM Trans. Comput. Logic **24** (2)(14), 1–73 (2023). https://doi.org/10.1145/3568422
7. Glabbeek, R.v., Höfner, P., Horne, R.: Assuming just enough fairness to make session types complete for lock-freedom. In: 2021 36th Annual ACM/IEEE Symposium on Logic in Computer Science (LICS), pp. 1–13 (2021).https://doi.org/10.1109/LICS52264.2021.9470531
8. Web Services Choreography Working Group (2003). http://w3.org/2002/ws/chor/
9. Gurd, J.R., Jones, C.B.: The global-yet-personal information system. In: Wand, I., Milner, R. (eds.) Computing Tomorrow, pp. 127–157. Cambridge University Press (1996). https://doi.org/10.1017/CBO9780511605611
10. Hewitt, C., de Jong, P.: Open systems. In: Brodie, M.L., Mylopoulos, J., Schmidt, J.W. (eds.) On Conceptual Modelling: Perspectives from Artificial Intelligence, Databases, and Programming Languages, pp. 147–164. Springer (1984). https://doi.org/10.1007/978-1-4612-5196-5_6
11. Honda, K., Mukhamedov, A., Brown, G., Chen, T.C., Yoshida, N.: Scribbling interactions with a formal foundation. In: Natarajan, R., Ojo, A. (eds.) ICDCIT, LNCS, vol. 6536, pp. 55–75. Springer (2011). https://doi.org/10.1007/978-3-642-19056-8_4
12. Honda, K., Yoshida, N., Carbone, M.: Multiparty asynchronous session types. In: POPL (2008). https://doi.org/10.1145/1328438.1328472, full version in [13]
13. Honda, K., Yoshida, N., Carbone, M.: Multiparty asynchronous session types. J. ACM **63**(1) (2016). https://doi.org/10.1145/2827695
14. Miu, A., Ferreira, F., Yoshida, N., Zhou, F.: Communication-safe web programming in typescript with routed multiparty session types. In: International Conference on Compiler Construction, pp. 94–106. CC (2021).https://doi.org/10.1145/3446804.3446854
15. OAuth Working Group: RFC 6749: OAuth 2.0 framework. http://tools.ietf.org/html/rfc6749 (2012)
16. Pierce, B.C.: Types and Programming Languages. The MIT Press, 1st edn. (2002). https://dl.acm.org/doi/abs/10.5555/509043
17. Sangiorgi, D.: Introduction to Bisimulation and Coinduction. Cambridge University Press (2011). https://doi.org/10.1017/CBO9780511777110
18. Scalas, A., Yoshida, N.: Less is more: multiparty session types revisited. Proc. ACM Program. Lang. **3**(POPL), 30:1–30:29 (2019).https://doi.org/10.1145/3290343
19. Tokoro, M.: The society of objects. SIGPLAN OOPS Mess. **5**(2), 3–12 (1993). https://doi.org/10.1145/260304.260305

20. Yoshida, N., Gheri, L.: A very gentle introduction to multiparty session types. In: Distributed Computing and Internet Technology - ICDCIT 2020. LNCS, vol. 11969, pp. 73–93. Springer (2020). https://doi.org/10.1007/978-3-030-36987-3_5

21. Yoshida, N., Hou, P.: Less is More Revisited. CoRR **abs/2402.16741** (2024). https://doi.org/10.48550/ARXIV.2402.16741

22. Yoshida, N., Hu, R., Neykova, R., Ng, N.: The scribble protocol language. In: Abadi, M., Lluch Lafuente, A. (eds.) Trustworthy Global Computing. LNCS, vol. 8358, pp. 22–41. Springer, Cham (2013).https://doi.org/10.1007/978-3-319-05119-2_3

23. Yoshida, N., Zhou, F., Ferreira, F.: Communicating finite state machines and an extensible toolchain for multiparty session types. In: Bampis, E., Pagourtzis, A. (eds.) Fundamentals of Computation Theory. FCT 2021. LNCS, vol. 12867, pp. 18–35. Springer, Cham (2021). https://doi.org/10.1007/978-3-030-86593-1_2

Validation of Formal Models:
A Case Study

Pamela Zave[1]($\boxtimes$) (iD) and Tim Nelson[2] (iD)

[1] Princeton University, Princeton, NJ, USA
`pamela@pamelazave.com`
[2] Brown University, Providence, RI, USA
`tbnelson@gmail.com`

Abstract. A *valid* formal model is well-defined in the portion of the real world being modeled, and relevant to the system-development project it is intended to support. This paper explains in depth what makes a formal model valid, and shows its critical importance in formal methods for system development, including program verification. The paper is based on a classroom presentation [8] of the well-known Peterson algorithm for locking in concurrent systems [23]. The paper shows how to formalize this case study in Alloy [10], and uses it to present a list of manual and automated techniques for validating formal models.

Keywords: formal methods · Alloy · Peterson lock

Dedication

This paper is dedicated to Cliff Jones, colleague, mentor, and friend. His influential invention of rely/guarantee reasoning is a well-developed and practical tool that has introduced the idea of domain modeling to many practitioners and developers of formal methods.

1 Introduction

One of the oldest sayings about computing is still one of the best: "garbage in, garbage out." This saying is equally true when the computer program is a verification tool, the input is a formal model of a computer system, and the output is verified assertions. A verified assertion is garbage if it is ill-defined or irrelevant in the real world of the computer system being modeled. Despite the excellence of today's verification tools, their output is, too often, garbage.

The process of ensuring that the input to a verification tool is not garbage, and thus will not result in garbage output, is *validation*. Validation is checking that a formal model is *valid*, meaning that it has *at least* the two properties shown in Fig. 1. *Accuracy* refers to the relationship between the real world and all modeling abstractions: the abstractions must be faithful descriptions of the

© The Author(s), under exclusive license to Springer Nature Switzerland AG 2024
A. Cavalcanti and J. Baxter (Eds.): *The Practice of Formal Methods*, LNCS 14781, pp. 292–313, 2024.
https://doi.org/10.1007/978-3-031-66673-5_15

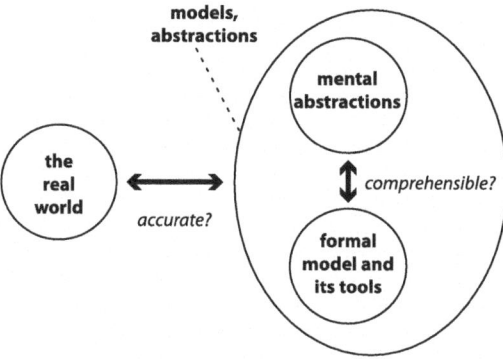

Fig. 1. The two essential questions answered by validation.

real world, whether they are intended to match the real world as it is now or as it should be. There are two kinds of abstractions, those in peoples' heads and those encoded in formal languages. *Comprehensibility* refers to the agreement between mental and formal abstractions: do the formal abstractions mean what the people working with them think they mean?

Because of the importance of mental abstractions, validation must be at least partially informal, but it can be assisted greatly by formal analysis and verification. Accuracy and comprehensibility are minimal criteria, and are often augmented with many others for an expansive definition of validity.

Informally, validation attempts to answer the questions, "Does this model mean what I think it means, and is that meaning faithful to the real world?" In considering what a formal model means, we rely on the framework summarized in Sect. 2. The crucial point of this framework is that there must be a separation between the *domain* or environment that motivates the need for a computer system, and the *system* that interacts with the domain to fulfill that need. In our experience most cases of invalid[1] formal models are due to flawed or inadequate modeling of the domain. This paper illustrates the power of good domain modeling in building good formal models.

While this seems to be a straightforward prescription for improvement, it may not be so easy to apply. Many published examples of domain/system separation are cyber-physical, where the domain is a collection of physical phenomena and the stand-alone system controls them in some way (see Jones's discussion in [16]). In contrast, most software development is concerned with adding something to an enormous base of existing code. In the latter case, the interface between domain and system lies deep in the semantics of the programming infrastructure. The domain is already formal in some sense, being constructed from digital logic, but this fact is of little use. In practice its behavior is far too complex to model completely, and much of it is unknown to the system developer.

---

[1] In the software-engineering sense of meaningless or irrelevant, not in the mathematical sense of not being a valid assertion.

The purpose of this paper is to provide an example of validating a formal model of a new software system designed to interact with an existing software system. We hope the example will serve multiple purposes. It provides a template for modeling some software domains, and also for modeling domain/system boundaries found in code. The example should serve as a tutorial on formal methods, and—most importantly—as an introduction to validation.

First, Sect. 2 summarizes the framework for associating meanings with formal models. Next, Sect. 3 introduces the the case study, and the following four sections present the case study as a sequence of models. Finally, Sect. 8 summarizes the validation steps applied, and Sect. 9 discusses the overall conclusions about validation. This paper has room to show only fragments of the formal models, but the complete set of formal models can be found online [29].

2   A Framework for Formal Modeling

The framework is drawn from three related papers on requirements engineering [12,13,28]. These papers introduce a method for deriving the specification of a computer system from its domain and requirements. Software-development processes today are more diverse, and various situations are constrained in different ways, so decisions must sometimes be made in a different order. Nevertheless, even though software development might not follow the *method* of these papers, the artifacts and relations they define are completely general and form a powerful framework for understanding the *meanings* of formal models.[2]

To be clear, it is necessary to distinguish between *meaning* and *formal semantics* as they are used here. Our favorite formal method is the combination of state-transition systems and temporal logic, as exemplified by Alloy, Event-B, TLA+, process algebras, and many others. In these related formalisms, a model is a state-transition system and its *semantics* is a set of traces.

Knowing the *semantics* of a model is not enough to know its *meaning*, which also includes how it corresponds to the real world. And without knowing its meaning, it is impossible to tell whether it is an accurate and comprehensible formal description of real or hypothetically real phenomena, i.e., whether it is valid. The simplest example of the difference concerns the primitive terms in the formal model. The meaning of the model depends on *designations*, which are natural-language descriptions of how instances of these primitive terms can be identified in the real world. In this paper, designations are spread throughout the text. Another, even more important, aspect of meaning will be discussed later in this section.

The artifacts of the Jackson/Zave framework are illustrated by Fig. 2. A *domain* or environment is the portion of the real world, digital or not, that motivates the need for a computer system. The *system* is the computer system (hardware or software) that we are interested in, and that interacts with the domain in a purposeful way. All other terms are relative to these two.

---

[2] In the literature, the framework is commonly referred to as the Jackson/Zave model.

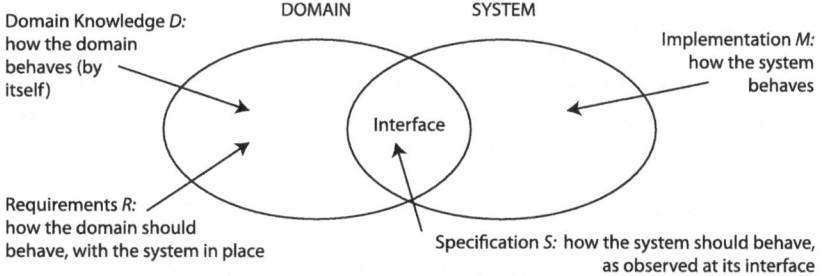

Fig. 2. The artifacts of a formal model. The Venn diagram represents sets of phenomena. Arrows indicate which phenomena are described or constrained by an artifact.

Figure 2 is a Venn diagram over the universe of all phenomena. It shows that the domain and system usually contain different phenomena, but they always have some shared phenomena, which is their *interface.*

The *specification S* is the part of the formal model that constrains the behavior of the system. Ultimately there will be an *implementation M* that produces this behavior when enacted by one or more computers. Ideally either the specification is simpler and more comprehensible than the implementation, or the specification is efficiently executable so that S and M can be the same. The diagram illustrates one important way in which the specification can be simpler than the implementation: it is confined to the phenomena of the interface, which are part of the domain as well as part of the system.

Domain knowledge D is the part of the formal model that constrains how the domain behaves all by itself, without the influence of the system. *Requirements R* are the part of the formal model that describes how the domain should behave, with the system implemented and installed.

Semantically, a formal model is nothing more than a set of constraints on its constants and variables, whose values must satisfy all the constraints at all times. *The most important way to attach meaning to a formal model is to say, for each constraint, why it is or should be true.* In other words, what enforces or will enforce the constraint? In this framework, we attach meaning to each constraint by identifying it as domain knowledge, requirement, specification property, or implementation property. The real-world domain enforces the domain knowledge, and the implementation will enforce the specification.

In software engineering, automated reasoning was first used for the purpose of program verification, which is proving that an implementation satisfies its specification. In validation, automated reasoning has other—equally important—uses. We need to know that domain knowledge D and the specification S are consistent, because if they are not, the system cannot work as specified. Most importantly, we need to know that D and S together imply (enforce) the requirements R. This tells us that if the system is developed according to its specification, it will do the job it is intended to do. The case study will also show other ways in which verification tools can help in validation.

Even for program verification, a valid domain model may be essential. For example, rely-guarantee reasoning, pioneered by Jones [14,15] and elaborated by Jones and many others [7], is a pillar of program refinement and verification. It is motivated by the fact that programs running concurrently with their environments often rely on assumptions about their environments (domains). Rely-guarantee reasoning shows how to incorporate parts of a formal domain model into proofs of program correctness.

For a much deeper and broader view of domain modeling than these brief definitions allow, you should read [11].

3   The Case Study

The subject of our case study is the well-known two-party Peterson lock used in multiprocessor programming [23]. Our presentation follows a class lecture by Herlihy [8], which presents the algorithm in a sequence of three versions, each written in Java.

In the case study, the domain consists of two user programs, each running in its own thread, and sharing a resource. The system to be developed is a lock program called by the user programs to enforce mutual exclusion with respect to accessing the resource.

The formal models in the case study are written in Alloy [10], and use the Alloy Analyzer Version 6, which incorporates linear-time temporal logic, for formal reasoning (see `alloytools.org`). Due to lack of space, this paper will explain the case study but not the Alloy language itself.

As we present the case study, we show how to address three challenges. The first challenge is converting from a program to a state-transition system, so that temporal logic can be used for specification and verification. Although there are many stylistic differences, the most important difference is that programming languages have built-in control mechanisms (e.g., method call and return, waiting by looping until a *while* condition fails) while state transitions rely exclusively on action preconditions for control.

The second challenge is to organize the model according to the Jackson/Zave framework, with a clear separation between the domain (as motivation for a software-development project) and the system (as the goal of the project). Because our example is very simple, the separation may seem grandiose and overdone, but this seems better than using an example that is more complex.

The third challenge is to validate the formal model. Herlihy's lecture tells us some things about preliminary versions of the lock. Our goal, reproducing validation in a real development project, is to discover errors without the help of an oracle. It is also important to note that the errors are realistic. Except for the known problems with preliminary versions of the lock, we committed all the modeling errors ourselves!

4   First Version: Lock 1

4.1   States

In creating a state-transition model, the first thing we think about is its state. We don't know or care what the user programs do, except that in accessing the shared resource they have three states: *Uninterested* (in using the shared resource),[3] *Waiting* to use the resource, and *InCritSec* (in a critical section accessing the resource). Figure 3 shows the state of each user program and how it changes over time in a typical scenario.

In Lock 1 there is a *Lock* object with a flag for each of the two threads. The flags are represented by a set *flagRaised* containing the identifiers of all flags now raised. Figure 3 also shows the state of the lock and how it changes over time. As seen in the figure, the basic idea of Lock 1 is that user programs call *Lock* methods *lock* and *unlock* to enter and leave their critical sections. When *lock* is called it puts the identifier of the calling thread in *flagRaised*. The call returns when and only when the caller's flag is the only one raised. After using the resource, the user program calls *unlock*, which lowers its flag and returns immediately. As shown in Fig. 3, if a thread is waiting for the lock, then the other thread's *unlock* will end the waiting.

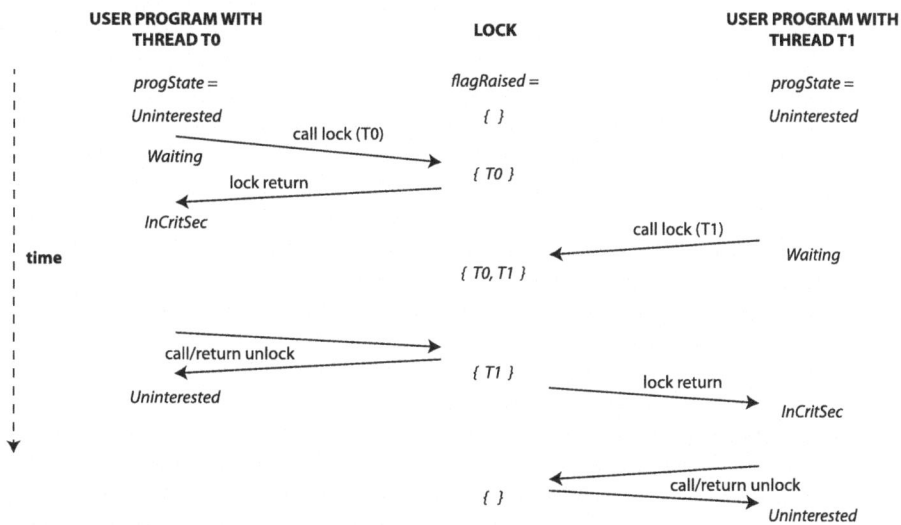

Fig. 3. A sample trace showing how Lock 1 works. Arrows show the flow of control of a thread as time passes.

On our first try, the state declarations and initial state in Alloy 6 look like this, with domain state and system state labeled:

---

[3] This state is often named *Idle*, but the program need not be idle—it can be busy doing something other than accessing the shared resource.

```
sig Thread {}

abstract sig ProgState {}
one sig Uninterested, Waiting, InCritSec extends ProgState {}

one sig Progs { var progState: Thread -> one ProgState }        -- domain

one sig Lock { var flagRaised: set Thread }                     -- system

pred initialState {
  # Thread = 2                                                  -- domain
  Progs.progState = Thread -> Uninterested                      -- domain
  no Lock.flagRaised                      }                     -- system
```

Members of the primitive set *Thread* serve as thread identifiers, as used by the operating system. The model has a *Progs* object containing a *progState* variable that is a function from threads to states of the user programs. For each thread, *progState* maps the thread to the current state of the program that the thread is running. Initially, all programs are *Uninterested*, and no flag is raised.

4.2 Actions

In a state-transition model, actions represent atomic changes to the model state. This means that all parts of an action are executed instantaneously, and cannot be interleaved with anything else. This assumption is obviously not true in the real world of this case study, and eventually we will need to check its validity—is it a safe approximation, or does it lead us into big mistakes? Fig. 3 suggests that three actions can be considered atomic: *callLock, lockReturn,* and *unlock* (call and return together).

In the model, each action has a predicate expressing its enabling condition, and a predicate expressing its state change. Busy waiting in the lock program is replaced by the enabling condition on *lockReturn*, which says that *t*'s flag is raised and the other thread's flag is *not* raised. In these actions, control of the thread as it passes between user and lock programs remains implicit.

```
pred callLockEnabled [t: Thread] {           -- action initiated by domain
  t.(Progs.progState) = Uninterested }
pred callLock [t: Thread] {
  callLockEnabled [t]
  Progs.progState' = Progs.progState ++ (t->Waiting)   --update prog state
  Lock.flagRaised' = Lock.flagRaised + t          }        -- raise flag

pred lockReturnEnabled [t: Thread] {         -- action initiated by system
  Lock.flagRaised = t            }
pred lockReturn [t: Thread] {
  lockReturnEnabled [t]
  flagRaised' = flagRaised                             -- no flag change
  Progs.progState' = Progs.progState ++ (t->InCritSec) }  --update state

pred unlockEnabled [t: Thread] {             -- action initiated by domain
  t.(Progs.progState) = InCritSec }
pred unlock [t: Thread] {
```

```
    unlockEnabled [t]
    Progs.progState' = Progs.progState ++ (t->Uninterested)   --update state
    Lock.flagRaised' = Lock.flagRaised - t                 }  -- lower flag
```

Because Alloy 6 is based on linear temporal logic, it is necessary to express which traces we want as instances of the model. A trace is an instance if its initial state satisfies *initialState*, and its subsequent states are the results of the three actions.

```
pred delta {  some t: Thread |
  (  callLock [t] || lockReturn [t] || unlock [t]   )   }

pred anyTrace {  initialState && always delta  }
run anyTrace expect 1
```

Finally, there are requirements on how the domain should behave, with the lock implemented and the user programs using it. Fortunately, the requirements on a two-party lock are well known and easily expressed in temporal logic:

```
pred mutuallyExclusive {  # (Progs.progState).InCritSec <= 1  }
assert mutualExclusion {  anyTrace => always mutuallyExclusive  }
check mutualExclusion                                     -- VERIFIED

pred nonDeadlocking {  some t: Thread |
  (callLockEnabled [t] || lockReturnEnabled [t] || unlockEnabled [t])   }
assert noDeadlocks {  anyTrace => always nonDeadlocking  }
check noDeadlocks                                         -- VERIFIED

pred nonStarvation {  all t: Thread |
  t.(Progs.progState) = Waiting =>
     eventually t.(Progs.progState) = InCritSec  }
assert noStarvation {  anyTrace => always nonStarvation  }
check noStarvation                                        -- VERIFIED
```

The *expect 1* annotation on the command *run anyTrace* says that there should be traces that satisfy *anyTrace*. We run the Alloy Analyzer, and that is true. The tool also verifies the requirements (within a bounded scope, which will be discussed later), so everything looks great! We have a working lock design!

4.3   A Little Validation

Well, maybe, just in case, we should try a little validation. In this paper validation steps fall into three categories: (i) There are general-purpose checks, that apply to many (if not all) models, especially models of concurrent systems. (ii) There are checks that the domain and system are kept properly separate. If a constraint is partly enforced by the domain and partly by the system, it will be extremely difficult to understand and work with. (iii) There are checks on the validity of the domain model, which tend to be especially powerful. Validation steps are numbered, and listed under those numbers in Table 1.

The first three validation steps are general-purpose.

(1) In this model, every action should define the variable values in the post-state completely. This we check "manually," i.e., by inspecting the model. The Alloy style updates each of the two state relations *progState* and *flagRaised* all at once, so it is unnecessary to have separate "frame conditions" to say, "the state of the other thread does not change."

(2) Whenever a model has separate state components, and we expect their values to be correlated, it is worth checking that they are correlated. This can be done in Alloy by defining a state invariant and asking the Analyzer to verify it. When explicit proofs are being constructed (which is not necessary in the Alloy context), this is often the first step of a proof.

```
assert stateInvariant {
  anyTrace => always
  (all t: Thread |
     t.(Progs.progState) = Uninterested => t ! in Lock.flagRaised
  && t.(Progs.progState) = Waiting => t in Lock.flagRaised
  && t.(Progs.progState) = InCritSec => t in Lock.flagRaised    ) }
check stateInvariant                                          -- VERIFIED
```

(3) The third validation step is a check that control in the model works as intended. In the real world, each thread executes a sequence of actions. In the model, this translates to the expectation that in each thread, at any time, only one action is enabled. This is encoded in the following assertion:

```
assert sequentialControl {
  anyTrace => always
  (all t: Thread |
     ! (callLockEnabled [t] && lockReturnEnabled [t])
  && ! (callLockEnabled [t] && unlockEnabled [t])
  && ! (lockReturnEnabled [t] && unlockEnabled [t]) )  }
check sequentialControl                                      -- NOT VERIFIED
```

As the comment shows, the model is not valid in this respect. The Analyzer provides a counterexample showing that *lockReturnEnabled* and *unlockEnabled* can both be true at the same time, for the same thread. This is an important departure from reality, and there is no telling what mischief it might cause as versions of this model evolve.

In the real world, whenever *lockReturn* is enabled, *unlock* for the same thread cannot be enabled because the lock program has control of the thread. So the real problem here is that the domain and system are not well-enough separated, making it unclear when the domain or system can initiate an action. This means that control of the thread should be modeled explicitly. To model control, we add a third state relation, which is now the interface between domain and system— both sides can observe it, and whichever side has control can give it up. A thread is in the set *runningProg* if and only if it is running the user program rather than the lock code. Here is the new state and its initialization, new actions, and a new invariant:

```
one sig Progs {  var progState: Thread -> one ProgState,      -- domain
                 var runningProg: set Thread          }     -- interface

pred initialState { . . .
   Progs.runningProg = Thread . . . }                 -- added to initialState

pred callLockEnabled [t: Thread] {           -- precondition on domain
   t.(Progs.progState) = Uninterested && t in Progs.runningProg  }
pred callLock [t: Thread] {
   callLockEnabled [t]
   Progs.progState' = Progs.progState ++ (t -> Waiting)   -- domain update
   Progs.runningProg' = Progs.runningProg - t        -- interface update
   Lock.flagRaised' = Lock.flagRaised + t         }   -- system update

pred lockReturnEnabled [t: Thread] {          -- precondition on system
   Lock.flagRaised = t && t ! in Progs.runningProg }
pred lockReturn [t: Thread] {
   lockReturnEnabled [t]
   flagRaised' = flagRaised                       -- no system change
   Progs.runningProg' = Progs.runningProg + t       -- interface update
   Progs.progState' = Progs.progState ++ (t -> InCritSec)  } --dom update

pred unlockEnabled [t: Thread] {             -- precondition on domain
   t.(Progs.progState) = InCritSec && t in Progs.runningProg  }
pred unlock [t: Thread] {
   unlockEnabled [t]
   runningProg' = runningProg            -- no apparent interface change,
   -- but interface actually changes twice, once after each state update
   Progs.progState' = Progs.progState ++ (t -> Uninterested)  --dom update
   Lock.flagRaised' = Lock.flagRaised - t             } --sys update

assert stateInvariant {
   anyTrace => always
   (all t: Thread |
      t.(Progs.progState) = Uninterested =>
         ( t in Progs.runningProg && t ! in Lock.flagRaised  )
   && t.(Progs.progState) = Waiting =>
         ( t ! in Progs.runningProg && t in Lock.flagRaised  )
   && t.(Progs.progState) = InCS =>
         ( t in Progs.runningProg && t in Lock.flagRaised  ) ) }
```

The validation check *sequentialControl* can now be verified.

(4) Having modeled thread control, we can check more thoroughly that the domain and system are kept as separate as they should be. The rules for this model are as follows: (i) Pure domain state can be read or written only when the domain has control of the thread. (ii) Pure system state can be read or written only when the system has control of the thread. (iii) Interface state can be read or written at any time. The interface variable *runningProg* is well-defined, even though it can be changed by either system or domain, because it can only be changed by one action at a time.

This validation step is a manual check, the results of which are recorded in the comments on the new action model above. For example, *callLock* is initiated by the domain, and *callLockEnabled* reads only a domain variable and an interface variable. Within the action predicate *callLock*, the domain state changes, then the method call transfers control to the lock code, then the system state changes. The comments are important because the updates within the action are sequential only in our interpretation of the model's meaning, not in the model's formal semantics.

4.4 Domain Behavior

(5, 6) The last two validation steps for Lock 1 are focused on the domain. It is always important to validate that the domain can do what it is expected to do or allowed to do, even when it is interacting with the system. We think of desired scenarios, encode them in predicates, then ask the Analyzer to instantiate the predicates. Here the first scenario is that each user program requests the lock eventually, at its own time. The second scenario is that both user programs request the lock at almost the same time, so that both *callLock* actions execute before either *lockReturn* can execute, and both users become *Waiting*.

```
pred bothProgsRequestLock [disj t0, t1: Thread]  {
   anyTrace
   eventually t0.(Progs.progState) = Waiting
   eventually t1.(Progs.progState) = Waiting       }
run bothProgsRequestLock expect 1

pred thereIsContention [disj t0, t1: Thread]  {
   anyTrace
   eventually Thread.(Progs.progState) = Waiting  }  -- both progs waiting
run thereIsContention expect 1                            -- INCONSISTENT
```

Note the way this domain knowledge and the requirements complement each other. This domain knowledge says that the programs will request the lock. The requirements say that when a program requests the lock, it will get the lock.

However, the second scenario cannot be instantiated, which is bad news—it means that, for some reason, the model is very unrealistic. But why? The actions don't look suspicious.

One part of the model that has not received much attention yet is the definition of *anyTrace*. If we look at it carefully and think about exactly what it means, it is saying that in any trace of this model, in any state, the enabling condition for one of the actions is true, and that action occurs. In other words, it is stating formally that there can be no deadlocks! The fact is that in Lock 1, contention causes a deadlock, and *thereIsContention* cannot be instantiated because an instance of this model cannot deadlock.

There is an alternative explanation having to do with the fact that Alloy 6 does not allow finite traces, but only infinite traces with finite representations ("lasso traces" terminating in loops). A deadlock stops all execution, resulting in a finite trace. Because a deadlock (in the strictest sense) results in a finite trace, no deadlock (in this strictest sense) can ever be part of the formal semantics (trace set) of an Alloy 6 model.

We think ours is a much better explanation because it is about the meaning of the model, rather than the details of some tool or temporal logic. Temporal logics with finite traces are much used in some areas of computing [5], and some model checkers allow finite traces [9].

The validation problem is fixed with the addition of a "stuttering step" *doNothing* to *delta*. This new action is enabled only when no other action is enabled. This allows a deadlocking trace to end in a loop of *doNothing* actions.

```
pred doNothingEnabled { all t: Thread | (
   ! callLockEnabled[t] && ! lockReturnEnabled[t] && ! unlockEnabled[t]) }
pred doNothing {
   doNothingEnabled && runningProg' = runningProg &&
   progState' = progState && flagRaised' = flagRaised  }

pred delta {  some t: Thread |
   ( callLock [t] || lockReturn [t] || unlock [t] || doNothing  )  }
```

Now we have a final version of Lock 1. With this version, *noDeadlocks* and *noStarvation* cannot be verified, which is the truth because Lock 1 can deadlock and starve.

5   Second Version: Lock 2

Lock 2, as presented by Herlihy, has a different mechanism with a different lock state:

```
one sig Lock { var polite: lone Thread } --polite is one or zero threads

pred initialState { . . .
   no Lock.polite  . . . } -- replaces initialization of Lock.flagRaised
```

The *callLock [t]* action sets the value of *polite*[4] to *t*. The other two actions leave it unchanged. The all-important precondition to the *lockReturn* action is

```
pred lockReturnEnabled [t: Thread] {                 -- precondition on system
   Lock.polite ! = t && t ! in Progs.runningProg  }
```

This means that when a client program calls *lock [t0]*, the call can return only when, after *t0*'s call, the other thread calls *lock [t1]*, thus setting the value of *polite* to *t1*. Because *unlock* does not change *polite*, it is an action of the user program only. Figure 4 shows the typical behavior of Lock 2.

---

[4] Presentations of this idea often call the polite thread the "victim;" we believe that "polite" more accurately conveys the intuition, while also being less alarming.

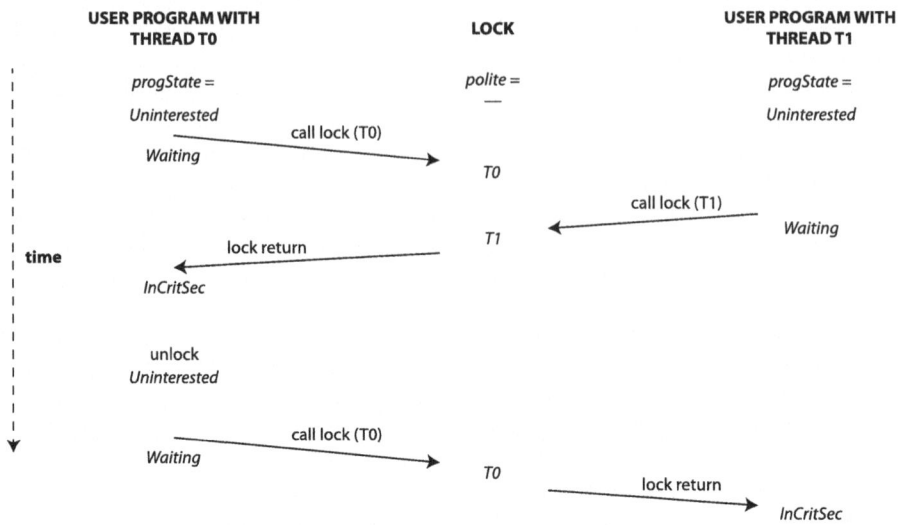

Fig. 4. A sample trace showing how Lock 2 works.

(7, 8) The model of Lock 2 satisfies all the previous validation checks. Yet it seems strange, doesn't it? This inspired us to come up with two other domain scenarios for validation. In the first scenario, one thread dies for some reason and never again requests the lock. Because there can be no contention, in a fault-tolerant system, the other thread should continue to work and access the shared resource freely. In the second scenario, there is no shared resource, so neither thread ever calls on the lock.

```
pred faultTolerantBehavior [disj t0, t1: Thread]  {
   anyTrace
   eventually always t1.(Progs.progState) = Uninterested
   always eventually t0.(Progs.progState) = InCritSec  }
run faultTolerantBehavior expect 1                    -- INCONSISTENT

pred noSharedResource [disj t0, t1: Thread]  {
   anyTrace
   always t0.(Progs.progState) = Uninterested
   always t1.(Progs.progState) = Uninterested  }
run noSharedResource expect 1                         -- INCONSISTENT
```

The Analyzer reports that *faultTolerantBehavior* is not possible with Lock 2, which pinpoints the problem with it: for a thread to continue entering a critical section, it *needs the other thread to also be interested* and take turns with it. As with the early models of Lock 1, all the requirements are verified, but because the model is not valid, verification does not mean that the requirements are actually satisfied.

The inconsistency of *noSharedResource* is different—why can't this scenario occur? The answer goes back to the discussion of stuttering steps in Sect. 4.

Because our model includes only uses of the lock, if the lock is not used, then a trace must consist of nothing but stuttering steps. Yet the current definition of *doNothingEnabled* disallows stuttering when any other action is enabled. If we go to the other extreme and allow stuttering in any state, then it will not be possible to prove progress properties. The right answer for this problem is to allow stuttering when *callLock* is enabled, so that using the lock is optional, and to disallow stuttering when the locking mechanism has something to do. So the best domain model, allowing the true freedom of the domain, has the following definition, and then *noSharedResource* can be instantiated.[5]

```
pred doNothingEnabled {  all t: Thread |
   ! lockReturnEnabled[t] && ! unlockEnabled[t]   }
```

6   Requirements in Versions 1 and 2

(9) The requirements for Lock 1 can be found in Sect. 4.2. The requirements in Lock 2 look exactly the same as for Lock 1, with the qualification that *noDeadlocks* depends on *lockReturnEnabled*, which is different in the two models. The definitions of *lockReturnEnabled* are different in the two models because each is dependent on its lock implementation, which is unfortunate because the requirements then deprive designers and developers of full engineering freedom. Requirements should constrain only domain phenomena (including the domain/system interface, which is shared between them).

Here is new version of *noDeadlocks*, without the problem of dependence on the implementation, i.e., dependence on part of the system that is not also part of the domain. *noStarvation* is also rewritten, for convenience.

```
pred nonDeadlocking [t: Thread] {
   t.(Progs.progState) = Waiting =>
      eventually t.(Progs.progState) = InCritSec  }
assert noDeadlocks {
   anyTrace => some t: Thread | always nonDeadlocking [t]  }
check noDeadlocks                                -- NOT VERIFIED

assert noStarvation {
   anyTrace => all t: Thread | always nonDeadlocking [t]  }
check noStarvation                               -- NOT VERIFIED
```

Now *noDeadlocks* and *noStarvation* have the same form, the only difference being whether there is always progress for one thread or for both. This makes a very interesting change: formerly *noDeadlocks* was a safety property, but now it is a progress property! This is not so strange if you think about viewpoint. To an omniscient observer the property is safety—the observer can see into the

---

[5] You might think that basic modeling questions such as these (What is a trace? Can it be finite? Are there stuttering steps?) should have a single standard answer, but in fact the answers are problem-dependent.

implementation state, and whenever the implementation reaches a certain state, there is a deadlock. A user program (domain) is not omniscient, however, and all it observes is that it called *lock*, which is taking a very long time to return—a progress problem.

For this particular model the two forms of the *noDeadlocks* property seem to be equivalent, in that each implies the other. This is not always the case. Consider a different domain in which *callLock* forks the thread, so that a user program can continue working on other tasks while waiting for *lockReturn*. Further, imagine that the user program can time out if it has been waiting too long, and call a lock method to withdraw its request for the lock. In this case *noDeadlocks* as defined by a bad state (the safety property) would always be satisfied by Lock 1, but *noDeadlocks* as defined by progress in at least one thread would not be.

7   Version 3: The Peterson Lock

In a very direct sense, Lock 3, known as the Peterson lock, is the sum of Locks 1 and 2. More specifically, it maintains all the state of both locks. The crucial precondition of *lockReturn*, which allows a client program to enter its critical section, is satisfied if either the precondition of *lockReturn* in Lock 1 is satisfied, *or* if the precondition of *lockReturn* in Lock 2 is satisfied. In this way, the Peterson lock combines the advantages of the previous two, and allows each one to make up for the disadvantages of the other. It passes all of the validation checks so far, and satisfies all the requirements!

7.1   A True Specification

As with any case study, we have to think about how its ideas would hold up in a much larger, more complex real development project. In this context, a limitation of the models of Locks 1 and 2 is that they lack a proper specification, visible to the system and yet independent of the lock implementation (e.g., the difference between Locks 1 and 2). To show what a true specification might look like in this simple example, in Lock 3 the interface is extended with the system's own version of *progState*, called *lockState*. Because this variable is specification only, it need not be implemented.

```
one sig Lock {  var lockState: Thread -> one ProgState,   -- interface spec
                var flagRaised: set Thread,                 -- system only
                var polite: lone Thread            }        -- system only

pred initialState { . . .
   Progs.progState = Thread -> Uninterested                 -- domain only
   Lock.lockState = Thread -> Uninterested . . . }              -- interface
```

Now the system maintains *lockState* as a copy of *progState*. The *callLock* action is a typical example:

```
pred callLockEnabled [t: Thread] {                  -- precondition on domain
   t.(Progs.progState) = Uninterested && t in Progs.runningProg  }
pred callLock [t: Thread] {
   callLockEnabled [t]
   Progs.progState' = Progs.progState ++ (t -> Waiting)   -- domain change
   Progs.runningProg' = Progs.runningProg - t            -- interface change
   Lock.lockState' = Lock.lockState ++ (t -> Waiting)
                                        -- system changes interface state
   Lock.flagRaised' = Lock.flagRaised + t               -- system change
   Lock.polite' = t                              }   -- system change
```

The requirements are unchanged. However, there is now a specification that looks very similar to the requirements, except that it refers to interface phenomena only. Notice that the specification does not constrain the lock implementation in any way.

```
pred systemMutuallyExclusive {  # (Lock.lockState).InCritSec <= 1  }
assert systemMutualExclusion { anyTrace => always systemMutuallyExclusive}
check systemMutualExclusion                               -- VERIFIED

pred systemNonDeadlocking [t: Thread] {
     t.(Lock.lockState) = Waiting
   => eventually t.(Lock.lockState) = InCritSec  }
assert systemNoDeadlocks {
   anyTrace => some t: Thread | always systemNonDeadlocking [t]  }
check systemNoDeadlocks                                   -- VERIFIED

assert systemNoStarvation {
   anyTrace => all t: Thread | always systemNonDeadlocking [t]  }
check systemNoStarvation                                  -- VERIFIED
```

In Sect. 2 we mentioned the proof obligations that are central to validation. The Lock 3 model already shows that the domain model and the specification are consistent, because the specification is verified, and the model has traces illustrating domain behaviors. The other obligation is that the specification is sufficient, meaning that if the implementation satisfies the specification and the implementation is installed in the domain, then the requirements *will* be satisfied.

(10) Because the Lock 3 model has a locking mechanism and satisfies both requirements and specification, it hides whether the specification alone is sufficient. To check this, we made another model version that stripped out the locking mechanism, leaving only the domain model, interface included. Not surprisingly, this model fails on most requirements and specification properties.[6] To check sufficiency, we then verified the following assertions:

```
assert sufficientMutexSpec {  anyTrace =>
   ((always systemMutuallyExclusive) => (always mutuallyExclusive))  }
check sufficientMutexSpec                                 -- VERIFIED

assert sufficientNostarvSpec {  anyTrace =>
   ( (all t: Thread | always systemNonDeadlocking [t])
```

---

[6] Because the no-lock lock returns immediately from all calls, it never deadlocks.

```
=> (all t: Thread | always nonDeadlocking [t])    ) }
check sufficientNostarvSpec                                -- VERIFIED
```

The assertions are saying that if any trace satisfies a specification property, it also satisfies the corresponding requirement. The assertions would not be true for any model, but they are true for this one, because the domain model ensures that *progState* and *lockState* are always equal.

7.2 Atomicity

(11) With Lock 3 comes a new general-purpose validity concern, which is whether model actions can be executed atomically by the implementation. In an implementation, *flagRaised* and *polite* might be represented by three variables: a Boolean for each thread indicating whether its flag is raised, and a thread identifier for *polite*. The *callLock* action changes two of these variables. The *lockReturn* action (in its precondition) reads two of these variables (assuming it does not also read the flag Boolean for its own thread). And all three variables can be read or written concurrently by actions of the other thread. Given that multiprocessors usually provide atomicity only at the level of accesses to individual memory cells, it does not seem that these actions are guaranteed to be atomic in the implementation.

The only way to have a truly valid model in this situation is to split up actions into smaller actions that can be guaranteed atomic. Now the expanded interface comes in handy, because the set *ProgState* can be extended with a new member *Waiting2*. The extra member will help the new lock model coordinate its extra actions. Now the former *callLock* action becomes a sequence of two actions:

```
pred callLock1Enabled [t: Thread] {             -- precondition on domain
   t.(Progs.progState) = Uninterested && t in Progs.runningProg  }
pred callLock1 [t: Thread] {
   callLock1Enabled [t]
   Progs.progState' = Progs.progState ++ (t -> Waiting)   -- domain change
   Progs.runningProg' = Progs.runningProg - t         -- interface change
   Lock.lockState' = Lock.lockState ++ (t -> Waiting)  -- interface change
   Lock.flagRaised' = Lock.flagRaised + t              -- system change
   polite' = polite                       }  -- no sys change

pred callLock2Enabled [t: Thread] {             -- precondition on system
   t.(Lock.lockState) = Waiting && t ! in Progs.runningProg  }
pred callLock2 [t: Thread] {
   callLock2Enabled [t]
   progState' = progState                     -- no domain change
   runningProg' = runningProg                 -- no interface change
   Lock.lockState' = Lock.lockState ++ (t -> Waiting2)   --interface chng
   flagRaised' = flagRaised                   -- no system change
   Lock.polite' = t                       }  -- system change
```

After *callLock1*, the *lockState* of the thread is *Waiting*. After *callLock2*, the *lockState* of the thread is *Waiting2*. In each action, only one of *flagRaised* and *polite* is modified.

The *lockReturn* action also becomes two actions, one with a precondition based on *flagRaised*, and one with a precondition based on *polite*. There is no intermediate state, however, because each action returns control to the user program, so only one is executed for each call. This is the equivalent of combining the two preconditions, shown below, with an *or* operator.

```
pred lockReturn1Enabled [t: Thread] {          -- precondition on system
     t.(Lock.lockState) = Waiting2 && t ! in Progs.runningProg
  && Lock.flagRaised = t                                              }

pred lockReturn2Enabled [t: Thread] {          -- precondition on system
     t.(Lock.lockState) = Waiting2 && t ! in Progs.runningProg
  && Lock.polite ! = t                                                }
```

With this change, the *stateInvariant* and *sequentialControl* assertions must also be rewritten, in obvious ways. Then all the previous assertions can still be verified, showing that the Peterson lock can handle the full concurrency of multiprocessor implementations. We should have expected this, knowing that the Peterson lock is being taught 43 years after its invention. But if this were a new locking algorithm, how else but with a valid model could we be sure that it works?

(12) In our final validation step, we turn our attention to the length of traces. By default, the Alloy Analyzer checks all traces up to 10 states and 10 actions. With previous model versions, in 6 actions both threads could go through a complete cycle, which makes 10 actions seem like a reasonable standard. In the new version of Lock 3, however, a thread cycles in 4 actions, and both can cycle in 8—too close to 10 for comfort. To be sure of more thorough coverage, the Lock 3 model now runs for 16 actions (steps), which may be excessive but is still efficient. Trace lengths are extended as follows.

```
check domainNoStarvation for 2 but 16 steps
```

8   Summary

Table 1 summarizes the validation steps in this paper, of which a majority are automated, and a majority found a problem of some kind. In reference to the three categories introduced in Sect. 4, steps 1, 2, 11, and 12 are general-purpose. Steps 4 and 9 ensure that the domain and system are properly separated, while steps 5, 6, 7, 8, and 10 check the validity of the domain model. Step 3 is also general-purpose, but in this model the problem it revealed was a problem of domain/system separation.

Table 1. A summary of validation steps in the case study. Early validation checks are also made on all later versions. A "problem found" can be a failure of validity, or a bug in one of the locks.

	Validation Check	Version	Manual/ Automated	Problem Found?
1	every variable is always defined		Man	No
2	expected state invariant holds		Auto	No
3	control within a thread is sequential	1	Auto	Yes
4	domain and system are separate in actions		Man	No
5	in domain, both threads can get lock		Auto	No
6	in domain, there is contention		Auto	Yes
7	in domain, there is fault-tolerance		Auto	Yes
8	in domain, shared resource can be absent	2	Auto	Yes
9	requirements constrain the domain only		Man	Yes
10	specification is sufficient to satisfy requirements		Auto	No
11	actions are atomic	3	Man	Yes
12	trace length is adequate		Man	Yes

For users of Alloy and other modeling languages, visualization of model instances is an indispensable validation tool. The Alloy Analyzer is notable for the excellence of its visualization, and has inspired a great deal of research on improving it even further (e.g., Sterling [6,26], Forge [21], et al. [1,4,18,24]).

The validation techniques presented in this paper are complementary to visualization in every way. In short, the techniques in this paper produce *focused* and *interesting* model instances to be understood, and visualization makes it easier to understand them. The techniques in this paper provide relevant questions about the model, and visualization makes it easier to answer them.

9   The Importance of Domain Models

In Sect. 2 we introduced the distinction between the *formal semantics* of a model and its *meaning*. Its meaning explains how the formal semantics apply to the real world. The meaning implies, for each explicit or implicit constraint in the model, that it should hold because the domain naturally causes it to hold, or because the system implementation will cause it to hold.

Despite its history, the idea of domain modeling still seems to be puzzling or controversial to many people. And we all know that software-engineering concepts are tricky to teach because they show their true value only in large, complex, long-lived software projects. With this in mind, we offer justifications that might appeal to students, followed by those that rely on the wisdom of experience.

For students, the main point is that the heart of the domain model is the four behavioral scenarios encoded in these predicates: *bothProgsRequestLock, thereIsContention, faultTolerantBehavior, noSharedResource*. Most directly, we know from Herlihy that there is something wrong with both Locks 1 and 2, and the exact bugs are diagnosed with these predicates alone (Steps 6 and 7). Of the four predicates, three led to the discovery of some problem, whether algorithmic bug or validation problem.

Another discussion-worthy point is the way that domain modeling converts issues of formal semantics (which can differ from language to language) to issues of meaning. There are two examples in this paper. First, there is the discussion about deadlocks in Sect. 4.4. Second, although not previously discussed, there is the technique of vacuity checking, which checks—for each implication—that the implication is not trivially true because the antecedent is unsatisfiable. In this case study, all requirements are implications with *anyTrace* as antecedent. The domain model ensures that *anyTrace* is not just satisfiable in some possibly-trivial semantic sense, but that it is satisfied by useful and common scenarios.

A colleague who teaches formal methods tells us that, "many students stop after writing and checking one or two simple predicates, believing that their model is correct." Very likely the one or two predicates were all they could think of! A final point to stress with students is that thinking about the domain gives you something real to think about—which fires the imagination and leads to much richer and more realistic models.

For more experienced audiences, we might point out that an emphasis on domain modeling is very helpful for seeing how a model might be made more general, and for encouraging generality. General models for important domains are valuable reusable artifacts [27].

More concretely, domain models are at the heart of well-known techniques such as model-based testing. A domain model can be used to enumerate sequences of operations that drive a system into a particular state or (even when state is not involved) generate tests that exercise the space of structurally-complex inputs, as in TestEra [19], Korat [20], and Whispec [25]. Domain models can even be used to aid in evaluating student testing [22]. Likewise, in property-based testing, as popularized by the QuickCheck [3] tool, the properties themselves are reliant on a (perhaps unstated) domain model. For example, properties might need to express what it means for a list of names to be sorted (by which linguistic convention?) or whether a year occurs before another (must we consider the Julian-Gregorian calendar transition?). Without the domain, we don't—and can't—know what it means for a system to be "correct."

Alloy 6 is the result of merging Alloy with Electrum [17], which adds full support for linear temporal logic to Alloy. As part of the literature on Electrum, in [2] there is a proposal for imposing more structure on actions. Do these proposed structures help support validation or force models to be more valid? In [2] there is automatic generation of frame conditions for actions, which is certainly helpful. No other aspects of their proposal would help with the validation steps in this particular case study. Nevertheless, this seems to be a promising direction for future research. Small additions to the syntax of actions might be very helpful for automating more validation checks.

From our perspective, validation is under-appreciated, and too much of what comes out of verification tools is, effectively, garbage. Some people believe that you cannot teach validation—that it is learned only in the school of hard knocks—but we do not agree. Hopefully this case study will help other teachers of formal methods think about how they would teach validation.

References

1. Bendersky, P., Galeotti, J.P., Garbervetsky, D.: The DynAlloy visualizer. In: Aguirre, N., Ribeiro, L. (eds.) Latin American Workshop on Formal Methods, vol. 139, pp. 59–64 (2013). https://doi.org/10.4204/EPTCS.139.6
2. Brunel, J., Chemouil, D., Cunha, A., Hujsa, T., Macedo, N., Tawa, J.: Proposition of an action layer for Electrum. In: Proceedings of the 6th International ABZ Conference, Southampton, United Kingdom (2018)
3. Claessen, K., Hughes, J.: QuickCheck: A lightweight tool for random testing of Haskell programs. In: International Conference on Functional Programming (2000). https://doi.org/10.1145/357766.351266
4. Couto, R., Campos, J.C., Macedo, N., Cunha, A.: Improving the visualization of Alloy instances. In: Masci, P., Monahan, R., Prevosto, V. (eds.) Proceedings 4th Workshop on Formal Integrated Development Environment, vol. 284, pp. 37–52 (2018). https://doi.org/10.4204/EPTCS.284.4
5. De Giacomo, G., Vardi, M.Y.: Synthesis for LTL and LDL on finite traces. In: Proceedings of the 24th International Joint Conference on Artificial Intelligence (2015)
6. Dyer, T., Baugh, J.: Sterling: A web-based visualizer for relational modeling languages. In: Rigorous State Based Methods (2021)
7. Hayes, I.J., Jones, C.B., Meinicke, L.M.: Specifying and reasoning about shared-variable concurrency. In: Theories of Programming and Formal Methods. LNCS, vol. 14080. Springer (2023). https://doi.org/10.1007/978-3-031-40436-8_5
8. Herlihy, M.: Multiprocessor synchronization: Mutual exclusion. https://cs.brown.edu/courses/csci1760/lectures/lecture%202%20mutual%20exclusion%20dark.pptx, Accessed 28 October 2023
9. Holzmann, G.J.: The Spin Model Checker: Primer and Reference Manual. Addison-Wesley (2004)
10. Jackson, D.: Software Abstractions: Logic, Language, and Analysis. MIT Press (2006, 2012)
11. Jackson, M.: Problem Frames. Addison-Wesley (2001)
12. Jackson, M., Zave, P.: Domain descriptions. In: Proceedings of the IEEE International Symposium on Requirements Engineering, pp. 56–64. IEEE Computer Society Press (1992)
13. Jackson, M., Zave, P.: Deriving specifications from requirements: an example. In: Proceedings of the 17th International Conference on Software Engineering, pp. 15–24. ACM Press (April 1995)
14. Jones, C.B.: Tentative steps toward a development method for interfering programs. Trans. Program. Lang. Syst. **5**(4), 596–619 (1983)
15. Jones, C.B.: Accommodating interference in the formal design of concurrent object-based programs. Formal Methods Syst. Design **8**(2), 105–122 (1996)

16. Jones, C.B.: From problem frames to HJJ and its known unknowns. In: Nuseibeh, B., Zave, P. (eds.) Software Requirements and Design: The Work of Michael Jackson, pp. 357–368. Good Friends Publishing (2010)
17. Macedo, N., Brunel, J., Chemouil, D., Cunha, A., Kuperberg, D.: Lightweight specification and analysis of dynamic systems with rich configurations. In: Proceedings of the 24th ACM SIGSOFT International Symposium on the Foundations of Software Engineering. ACM (2016)
18. Macedo, N., et al.: Experiences on teaching Alloy with an automated assessment platform. Sci. Comput. Program. **211**, 102690 (2021). https://doi.org/10.1016/j.scico.2021.102690
19. Marinov, D., Khurshid, S.: TestEra: A novel framework for automated testing of Java programs (2001). https://doi.org/10.1109/ASE.2001.989787
20. Milicevic, A., Misailovic, S., Marinov, D., Khurshid, S.: Korat: A tool for generating structurally complex test inputs (2007). https://doi.org/10.1109/ICSE.2007.48
21. Nelson, T., et al.: Forge: a tool and language for teaching formal methods. In: Object-Oriented Programming Systems, Languages, and Applications (2024), (accepted and in preparation, to appear)
22. Nelson, T., Rivera, E., Soucie, S., Del Vecchio, T., Wrenn, J., Krishnamurthi, S.: Automated, targeted testing of property-based testing predicates. In: The Art, Science, and Engineering of Programming (2022). https://doi.org/10.22152/programming-journal.org/2022/6/10
23. Peterson, G.L.: Myths about the mutual exclusion problem. Inf. Process. Lett. **12**(3), 115–116 (1981)
24. Rayside, D., Chang, F.S., Dennis, G., Seater, R., Jackson, D.: Automatic visualization of relational logic models. Electron. Commun. Eur. Assoc. Softw. Sci. Technol. **7** (2007). https://doi.org/10.14279/tuj.eceasst.7.94
25. Shao, D., Khurshid, S., Perry, D.E.: Whispec: White-box testing of libraries using declarative specifications (2007). https://doi.org/10.1145/1512762.1512764
26. Siegel, A., Santomauro, M., Dyer, T., Nelson, T., Krishnamurthi, S.: Prototyping formal methods tools: a protocol analysis case study. Protocols, Strands, and Logic, 394–413 (2021). https://doi.org/10.1007/978-3-030-91631-2_22
27. Zave, P.: Theories of everything. In: Proceedings of the 38th International Conference on Software Engineering. IEEE (2016)
28. Zave, P., Jackson, M.: Four dark corners of requirements engineering. ACM Trans. Softw. Eng. Methodol. **6**(1), 1–30 (1997)
29. Zave, P., Nelson, T.: Three versions of a two-party lock: A case study in formal modeling (2024). https://pamelazave.com/peterson.zip

Author Index

© The Editor(s) (if applicable) and The Author(s), under exclusive license
to Springer Nature Switzerland AG 2024
A. Cavalcanti and J. Baxter (Eds.): *The Practice of Formal Methods*, LNCS 14781, pp. 315–316, 2024.
https://doi.org/10.1007/978-3-031-66673-5

SPRINGER NATURE

GPSR Compliance

The European Union's (EU) General Product Safety Regulation (GPSR) is a set of rules that requires consumer products to be safe and our obligations to ensure this.

If you have any concerns about our products, you can contact us on ProductSafety@springernature.com

In case Publisher is established outside the EU, the EU authorized representative is:

Springer Nature Customer Service Center GmbH
Europaplatz 3
69115 Heidelberg, Germany

The manufacturer's authorised representative in the EU is Springer
Nature Customer Service Centre GmbH, Europaplatz 3, 69115 Heidelberg,
Germany. If you have any concerns regarding our products, please
contact ProductSafety@springernature.com

Printed and bound by CPI Group (UK) Ltd, Croydon, CR0 4YY
27/04/2026
02097586-0006